THE GRAHAM STUART THOMAS ROSE BOOK

The wonder of the world, the beauty and the power, the shapes of things,
their colours, lights and shades; these I saw. Look ye also while life lasts.

From an old Cumbrian gravestone

ALSO BY GRAHAM STUART THOMAS

THE OLD SHRUB ROSES
COLOUR IN THE WINTER GARDEN
SHRUB ROSES OF TODAY
CLIMBING ROSES OLD AND NEW
PLANTS FOR GROUND-COVER
GARDENS OF THE NATIONAL TRUST
THREE GARDENS
TREES IN THE LANDSCAPE
THE ART OF PLANTING
PERENNIAL GARDEN PLANTS
THE COMPLETE PAINTINGS AND DRAWINGS OF GRAHAM STUART THOMAS
A GARDEN OF ROSES
THE ROCK GARDEN AND ITS PLANTS
ORNAMENTAL SHRUBS CLIMBERS AND BAMBOOS
AN ENGLISH ROSE GARDEN
(U.S. title: THE ART OF GARDENING WITH ROSES)

The
Graham Stuart Thomas
Rose Book

BY

Graham Stuart Thomas, OBE, VMH, DHM, VMM
Gardens Consultant to the National Trust

Comprising his Trilogy

The Old Shrub Roses
Shrub Roses of Today
Climbing Roses Old and New

Enlarged and thoroughly revised

SAGAPRESS/TIMBER PRESS
Portland, Oregon

Composed in Monotype Centaur

The author and publishers are grateful for the use of the charming little rose sketches from *Les Roses de l'Impératrice Joséphine* by J. Gravereaux (Éditions d'Art et de Littérature, Paris 1912).

ISBN 0-88192-280-3

Printed in Hong Kong

SAGAPRESS, INC./TIMBER PRESS, INC.
The Haseltine Building
133 S.W. Second Avenue, Suite 450
Portland, Oregon 97204-3527, U.S.A.

Library of Congress Cataloging-in-Publication Data

Thomas. Graham Stuart.
    The Graham Stuart Thomas rose book / by Graham Stuart Thomas.
      p. cm.
    "Comprising The old shrub roses. Shrub roses of today, Climbing roses old and new; enlarged and thoroughly revised."
    Includes bibliographical references and index.
    ISBN 0-88192-280-3
    I Roses. 2. Roses—Varieties. 3. Rose culture.   I. Title.
II. Title: Rose book.
SB4II.T4885 1994
635.9'33372—dc20   93-33560
                                                       CIP

To all rose-lovers who are
dedicated to the re-appraisal
of historic roses

Contents

Colour Plates

Between pages 68 and 69

Pencil Drawings

Between pages 100 and 101

All drawings by the author and reproduced life size, except as indicated

Monochrome Photographs

Between pages 100 and 101

Figures in Chapter 11

The Descriptions

NAMES in **bold type** denote species and botanical varieties.

Names in **bold type** and 'single quotes' denote garden forms, varieties, and hybrids, called "cultivars."

Wherever possible the name of the raiser and the date of introduction have been given, together with synonyms and parentage.

All references are to artists' coloured illustrations, unless otherwise stated, and they are not in any particular order. There has of late years been an immense increase in the use of colour photographs in books and catalogues, and these give a good idea of the general trends in colour breeding. These illustrations, however, are for the most part concerned only with the flower, often omitting altogether the leaves, prickles, and stems. I have therefore included only a few references from these, where I consider them worthy.

For details of books consulted, see Bibliography.

The sizes given in the descriptions denote the approximate height or width to which the plants may grow in Surrey, England, but all such measurements vary with local conditions.

A "sport" ("mutation" in genetic parlance) is a shoot that is different in growth from the parent plant; these shoots usually remain constant when vegetatively propagated.

A "clone" is the vegetatively propagated progeny of a single individual.

A "perpetual" rose flowers more or less continuously during the growing season. "Remontant" or "recurrent" or "repeat-flowering" roses usually have two crops, or flower intermittently towards autumn after the main crop, but are not necessarily "perpetual."

Acknowledgements

I HAVE BEEN BLESSED with much help from kind friends, not only in the original editions but also in this much revised and enlarged edition of my trilogy on roses—*The Old Shrub Roses, Shrub Roses of Today,* and *Climbing Roses Old and New*—now amalgamated into one book for ease of reference.

My thanks go out specially to the late Rona Hurst who so kindly gave me permission all those years ago to reprint her husband's invaluable findings on the evolution of hybrid roses. These writings, now reproduced at the end of this book, gave a firm foundation on which we have built ever since. Desmond Clarke likewise benefitted us all by the immense amount of work he put into the genus *Rosa* for the eighth edition of Bean's *Trees and Shrubs Hardy in the British Isles,* to which I have referred many times. To Jack Harkness for help with the *Rosa persica* hybrids and to John Mattock for bringing me up-to-date with certain modern roses, many thanks are due, and likewise to James Russell and Anthony Lord for help in sorting out the varieties received so generously from Sangerhausen.

Hazel Le Rougetel went to great trouble over the several photographs she took for the book, as did Allen Paterson, and Michael Warren ably secured the reproductions of Redouté's paintings. It is a special pleasure to acknowledge the kindness of Siriol Sherlock, who has granted permission to include the reproduction of her beautiful painting of the Moss Rose 'James Veitch'. Then there are Professor V. M. Staicov and Michael Hayward to be thanked, who have contributed so much to the chapter on fragrance.

Permission to quote from Edmund Blunden's *Shells by a Stream* (1944) is gratefully acknowledged to Messrs Macmillan & Co. Ltd.

I am sure there are many who have given, over the years, ungrudging support to the quest, and others who in early days gave me propagating material. To all these helpers in time or material go my best thanks.

Last, I must once more record my thanks to John E. Elsley of Wayside Gardens, South Carolina, who has contributed the USDA hardiness zones to the many species and varieties, and to Margaret Neal, who has so admirably deciphered my scrawl.

NOTE ON THE NEW EDITION

This volume brings together *The Old Shrub Roses* (first published 1955), *Shrub Roses Today* (first published 1962), and *Climing Roses Old and New* (first published 1965). Fine new illustrations have been added, and new information and addenda have been incorporated.

Chapter 13, by Dr C. C. Hurst, has again been reproduced in its original form, and faithfully reflects Dr Hurst's conventions of nomenclature and style.

Introduction: The Appeal of the Rose

Ah see the Virgin Rose, how sweetly shee
Doth first peepe forth with bashfull modestee
That fairer seemes, the lesse ye see her may;
Lo see soone after, how more bold and free
Her bared bosome she doth bold display;
Lo see soone after, how she fades, and falles away.

Edmund Spenser (1552–1599), *The Faerie Queene*

IN THE PROGRESS of horticulture every plant has a place or use to which it is most suited. To maintain such a position it must be worthy in some way of the space usually given to it in cultivation. Some plants linger forever at the ground level of popularity, while others rocket quickly to the top. Again, some may disappear from general use only to be revived again when conditions or fashions alter. I think the reasons are not difficult to find.

Plants appeal to us in many ways; most of them have considerable beauty, even when they are artificially created, and they may also have the attraction that sentiment, history, botany, or association can lend them. They may be easy or temperamental to grow but, at this stage of horticultural history at least, their garden value is paramount. We all desire as much beauty, colour, fragrance, longevity, and annual goodwill as possible from our plants, and it is the purpose of this book to try to show how roses can add to the list of shrubs available for general garden use.

What is this ROSE that enslaves gardeners? Why should a society concerned solely with the rose be the strongest in members of all specialist plant societies? Why, in short, does everyone love a rose, and what has it to offer that other flowers lack? These are the questions that must have occurred to many of us in those precious times when our thoughts can muse happily on the subject of our fancy. With me, it is usually when I am weeding. We do not have to *think* when weeding; but the train of thought is sometimes punctured in a decisive way when a thorn is inadvertently grasped. . . . Certainly thorns and prickles do not endear the rose to us—but "she arayeth her thorn wyth fayr colour and good smell."

The superficial reason for the present popularity of the rose is undoubtedly because so many dozens of new varieties assail us every year. Our insatiable desire for novelty makes it worth while for the rose breeders of today to spend many hours of their time and large sums of money to produce some fresh colour or style to whet our appetites. This craving for novelty has been going on for over a hundred and fifty years, and it looks like continuing.

But this is not the whole answer. The rose has been popular for too many centuries for us to rest comfortably in the thought that the numerous varieties of modern roses constitute the whole reason for its popularity. When one discovers that it has been cultivated throughout history, one must think again. There is ample proof that the rose has been a favourite through the ages, and was grown and loved when the human race had little time for anything but the necessities of life and the battle for survival.

If we look at a wild rose analytically we do not find anything particularly flamboyant: nothing so intriguing as an Orchid, so sculptured as an Iris, nor so dazzling as a Peony or Tulip. Its shape, in those far-off days of Western civilization, was mainly single or semi-double, a circular flower, charming but not impressive. In colour it was quiet, white or pink or purplish, with brilliant exceptions in forms of *Rosa foetida* and one or two allied species. Its leaves were small, prettily divided, and patterned, but had no great effect upon art, and that it was a shrub rather than a herbaceous plant or bulb can have been no overriding factor in its favour. I have no doubt myself that it owes its perennial popularity to its scent; it was for this priceless quality that it was originally cultivated, not because it was a food. Not only could the dried petals of certain roses, notably those of the Apothecary's Rose, retain their fragrance for years when suitably stored, but "attar" or "otto" of roses could be distilled from the freshly picked blooms of the Damask Rose and some others. Throughout history we read of different ways that roses were used to please human beings, and almost always it is the scent that is the principal factor.

Had the rose been a flower of complete insignificance, this inherent yet extractable odour would have ensured its being cultivated; when we add to that odour a flower of pleasing outline and indefinable charm, produced by a plant that grows in beauty yearly, its claim on our senses is wellnigh insuperable.

I have devoted part of Chapter 12 to fragrance; while it varies greatly in strength and quality, it also varies with hybridization and in modern roses has become involved, infusing the different scents of the parents into a complex strain. Because we have much less appreciation of scent than of colour and shape, these two characters have received infinitely more attention by writers over the years. There is, moreover, no established vocabulary describing scents.

It seems contradictory that so much sweetness and beauty have to be accompanied by the inhospitable, prickly wood. But is it not just another example of how evil accompanies good throughout the walks of life, and does not the evil accentuate the good?

SINGLE ROSES

ALL ROSES were originally single, composed of five petals, or only four in the species *Rosa sericea*. Where they grew round early civilizations, perhaps chance seedlings occurred with additional petals and were treasured and propagated by cuttings or grafting. Thus we can visualize, not hundreds of new varieties occurring every year as happens today, but only a few new varieties or forms or hybrids being found and grown in each hundred years. So through its long association with Grecian and Roman civilizations, in China and in Persia and later in Western Europe, more and more colourful and more double roses appeared; some were no doubt lost, others throve and gave of their sports and hybrids over again. The first double rose recorded in literature appears to be in *Urania* by Herodotus (*c.* 470 B.C.), in which he speaks of a rose with sixty "leaves" in Macedonia. Many of our oldest varieties appeared so long ago that there is no record of them. The first Damask Rose and the first White Rose appeared possibly in the wild, and later perhaps the excellent Autumn Damask, which went on flowering until winter. And so gradually a collection of hybrids and forms was gathered together in different countries and slowly distributed, ready to be depicted and recorded by the first herbalists. So old are our oldest roses; tough, treasured heirlooms, which show no signs of the deterioration in vigour that is prophesied by certain writers of today.

I like to think of the excitement in those far-off days when the first fully double rose appeared, perhaps an Alba or a Gallica. How this new form must have set ideas running in design and decoration! And yet what an extraordinary thing it has been that the rose, of all flowers, should be so desirable when doubled. Is it perhaps its shape, a circle in one plane, that allows doubling to take place without destroying its beauty utterly as it does in a two-dimensional shape such as a daffodil or a lily? It never ceases to surprise me that a genus whose single flowers are so beautiful should be the favourite genus selected by Western civilization for elaboration in doubling. It cannot be denied that the single rose is more beautiful than the double, but a double has often more scent, longer lasting powers, and a richness of texture and shape not found in the singles. Let us examine a little more closely the various shapes of roses as they have evolved through the centuries. I feel we must say "evolved," for though during the last hundred years or more gardeners have raised millions of seedlings, it is the rose that has been the prime mover. We cannot bring forth anything that is not in the rose: all mutations and surprises are governed by natural laws that we have only recently begun to grasp through scientific research. As a sport or hybrid occurred, so was a step forward or back taken by the rose in the eyes of those who grew it, and treasured or discarded.

Originally, then, the rose was single, and in its simplicity was loved and compared with blushing cheeks and the dawn. In fact it ranked with the lily in being compared in beauty to the human face by the poets throughout the ages; they had in mind the simple beauty of the wild rose, or the rounded sweetness of *Rosa centifolia* itself, or the Moss Roses, some of which have greatest beauty when just opening. Who can deny the beauty of a wild rose as, for example, our own Dog Rose in its fresh warm pink, half open at breakfast time? There are many other single beauties: the great limp-petalled *R. gigantea*, the creamy yellow prototype of the Tea Roses; the intense colour and matt surface of *R. moyesii*, with recurved shape; *R. macrophylla* and *R. setipoda*, in both of which poise is added to perfect shape, and their smooth beauty contrasted with a hairy-glandular, purplish receptacle; or the tiny daintiness of *R. elegantula* (*farreri*) var. *persetosa* and *R. willmottiae*. In fact, all the wild species have a beauty that is never found in artificial hybrids. E. A. Bunyard, writing in the Royal Horticultural Society's *Journal* in 1916, observed that "singles are God-made, doubles are man-made; a perfect flower should have anthers and pistils." As a general rule nature cannot be improved upon, but here and there a hybrid outshines the others, and in the rose there are exceptions as successfully beautiful as two other examples that come to mind, *Rhododendron* 'Penjerrick' and *Lilium* × *testaceum*. These, with the rose 'Mermaid', with 'Frühlingsmorgen', *R.* 'Paulii Rosea' and 'Dupontii', have reached the perfection of outline and have the innate charm and poise that one associates with a wild species. These all have a species for one parent, but this is not a prerequisite for perfection in breeding single roses. Every now and again a single arises in the highly evolved modern strains of roses: early in the twentieth century we had the Irish group of single Hybrid Teas, including the exquisite 'Irish Fire-flame', 'Isobel', 'Mrs Oakley Fisher' and others, in which the rolled petal of the Hybrid Tea was revealed in a new beauty from the opening of the fluted bud to the starry flower. A particularly good coloured plate of these singles will be found in *Roses of the World in Colour* (McFarland, 1937). 'Innocence' and 'Karen Poulsen' came later; E. B. Le Grice was in the forefront of raisers of singles, with his 'Lilac Charm', 'Silver Charm' and others. Those which are not quite single, like 'News', 'White Wings', and 'Golden Wings', never reach the same standard. It is good to feel that singles and near singles are still being raised, to act as leavening to the vast numbers of doubles.

Double Roses

THE "DOUBLING" of a flower is simply due to the replacing of stamens and styles by petals. The first doubles or semi-doubles may have occurred, died out, and occurred again thousands of years before they were first *noticed*, to be lifted from the wayside and put into the first garden. But it was not until about 1820 that any considerable number of double roses had been collected together, and not until about the middle of that century that a floral style had been selected. The most nearly perfect doubles among the old roses of the flat or Gallica style were evolved as early as 1825 or thereabouts, witness such varieties as 'd'Aguesseau' (1823), 'Petite Lisette' (1817), 'Félicité Parmentier' (1836), and the incomparable 'Mme Hardy' (1832). 'Mme Hardy' set a floral style that has never been surpassed, in spite of many hundreds being raised for the next thirty years in the same style. It was a floral style that reigned until the Tea Rose upset it, with its longer petals resulting in a flower with a higher centre. So long as roses of the old style were raised the flat—"expanded"—floral style continued, and it was still paramount in many of the early Hybrid Perpetuals, as is demonstrated by 'Baronne Prévost' (1842) and 'Reine des Violettes' (1860). Meanwhile the Bourbons had come and gone, many of them with this old floral style, as found in 'Louise Odier' (1851) and 'Reine Victoria' (1872) and its sport.

It was a characteristic of this style, together with the flat fully expanded flower, that the many petals were short—all the parents had short petals—and there were so many of them in some flowers that they were folded into the otherwise empty and futile receptacle so tightly that they could not open. Often this results in a "button eye," which is one of the charms of this old style; the curved-over petals reveal their lighter undersides in contrast to the velvety upper surfaces. Good examples are 'Koenigin von Danemarck' (1826), 'Juno' (1847), and 'Capitaine John Ingram' (1856). Today this type of flower may be thought peculiar, but it is nevertheless very appealing when once recognized as a distinct floral style. There were so many petals that they grew in serried ranks often imbricated or lying directly on top of one another, forming the scalloped arrangement that we call "quartered." It was not until the China Rose was used to great effect in breeding, bringing with it a fewer-petalled, loose flower, and the Tea Rose had contributed its larger petals, that this floral style gradually disappeared, and the high-centred Tea-hybrids began, fostered by the increasing popularity of long buds forced under glass. Concurrently with the flat old roses there was also another style, deep-centred—again with short petals—found in *Rosa centifolia*, with its layers of large outer petals creating a great globular bloom. Gradually, after multitudes of Bourbons and Hybrid Perpetuals had come, been appraised and then forgotten, after the turn of the century the shape we know so well in today's Hybrid Teas was evolved, and the gracious sculptured bud appeared with its high-pointed centre and rolled-back petals.

In the old roses the bud was not of great beauty or importance, the full beauty not being attained until the flower was full blown, complete with quartering and button eye, which were all part of the fashion. "Come, and I will show you what is beautiful; it is the Rose fully blown" (Barbauld, *d.* 1825).

Today just the opposite obtains. Few Hybrid Teas are very elegant when full blown, and most varieties are depicted in bud or half open. I always think the real test of a Hybrid Tea is whether it is beautiful when fully open; not many of the older ones had sufficient petals to remain shapely, but some modern ones are better filled. Quartering or splitting of the petals into different groups is looked at disapprovingly, while a button eye could not happen with so few petals; the nearest approach to it, the "balling" of a bloom—when instead of the petals retaining the pointed-bud shape they curve over one another like a spherical cabbage—is always frowned upon. I do not like it myself. 'Mme Caroline Testout' and 'Gipsy Lass' were notable offenders.

It is interesting to look back over the pages of rose history and see how these two totally different styles developed and became perfect. For I believe the best Hybrid Teas with really shapely flowers, such as 'Ophelia', 'Congratulations', and 'Keepsake', *are* perfect in bud and half open. It remains to elongate the petals still more, so that a greater number can be accommodated in a longer bud and thus when full blown they will have a centre that remains beautiful in expansion. 'Just Joey' and 'Silver Jubilee' are two of the most satisfying of Hybrid Teas when fully opened, like well-filled peonies. The rolled-petalled, fully double shape may be recalled in some of the Hybrid Perpetuals, such as 'John Hopper' (1862) and 'Eugène Fürst' (1875), and also in 'Paul Ricault' (1845), which is not repeat-flowering, but is a close relative of them; in later times this shape occurred again in 'Dame Edith Helen' (1926), and the later 'Peer Gynt'.

This is perhaps the place to mention roses with fringed petals; they are all double, with the edges of the petals more or less cut, producing the effect of a pink or carnation. 'Fimbriata', 'F. J. Grootendorst', 'Pink Grootendorst', and 'Grootendorst Supreme' are all of Rugosa derivation, while 'Serratipetala' and the Green Rose are of fairly pure China descent.

Among the Floribundas something equally interesting is, I believe, developing. So many of the earlier varieties like 'Donald Prior' and 'Frensham' had loose, shapeless blooms, but now some varieties are showing much more form; in some, such as 'Amber Queen', 'Arthur Bell', and 'Sea Pearl', we have fairly perfect rosettes, though few-petalled, and in yet some others the old rose style, flat and packed with petals, is reappearing. I refer especially to 'Brown Velvet', 'Intrigue', 'Rosemary Rose', and 'Magenta'.

It may be that among Floribundas, though they may ape the Hybrid Teas in their colour and even approach them in shape and size, the flowers may be preferred when they are on the small side; and personally I should welcome a rather prim rosette shape. I can think of nothing so becoming on a branching stem bearing several flowers all open at one time. But with so much happening among roses today, so many new species being used for hybridizing, and so many "new" colours appearing, anything may occur, and, compared with the gentle acceleration over a decade or two in the past, we jump from one new character to another in a matter of a few years, nowadays. The leisurely progression has ceased: "progress" has arrived.

COLOURS IN ROSES

HAVING GIVEN scent a separate chapter, and having briefly sketched the alterations in shape in the single and double roses, let us now turn to colour, the character of *immediate appeal* to all who see roses, and the character which today seems to outweigh all others. I have written elsewhere how roses were mainly pink in early Western civilization; the Old Roses were predominantly pink in all groups; a few were pure white, and plum-coloured ones appeared among the Gallicas. *Rosa gallica* brought us the deepest colours, but no really true reds; the Damask Rose was only mid-pink, and yellows were practically non-existent. *Rosa gallica* varied from a deep old-rose-pink to light crimson, and it was not until 'Slater's Crimson China' in 1792 that a really true, vivid crimson was available for hybridizing.

Throughout the nineteenth century, especially towards its close, garden roses were gradually being selected for their brightness, particular landmarks in bright crimsons being the Portland Rose (prior to 1809), 'Général Jacqueminot', and 'Charles Lefèbvre' (1861). After this date bright crimson Hybrid Perpetuals were fairly common, but practically all inherited what has since been considered a failing and what was probably in those days glossed over as inevitable: the flowers developed a bluish tinge as they matured, no doubt inherited from *Rosa gallica*. We may therefore visualize all the ordinary old garden roses of the nineteenth century being white, pink, deep pink, and crimson, and all or most verging towards the bluish side of the central red of the spectrum. The Tea Rose first produced light yellows among climbers, the Tea-Noisettes, and gradually a few pale yellow and salmon-yellow bush Tea Roses were raised. The vivid yellow of *R. foetida* remained locked within itself until 1900 when Pernet-Ducher succeeded in launching 'Soleil d'Or', the ultimate result being the race of Pernetiana roses of vivid colourings, bright yellows, flames, and two-toned varieties which became gradually merged with the Hybrid Teas. And so today we have all these colours within the one hybrid race; many of the reds and flames are almost free of purplish tones when fading.

That is what happened to the popular roses of the busy raisers. Little obvious variety of colour remains to be incorporated; in fact, all species are but variations on the same theme of colour.

Colour having reached such a pitch of general brilliance, it became inevitable that a new tone would be welcomed for the sake of variety. A new colour did indeed appear in recognizable quantity in 'Gloria Mundi' (1929) and 'Paul Crampel' (1930), both Poly-poms; this new colour was pelargonidin, a vivid orange tone reminiscent of our greenhouse geraniums or Zonal Pelargoniums. Not only was this colour in the Poly-poms, but in descendants from 'Eva', a Hybrid Musk, and it has produced astonishing tones in later roses such as 'Fashion', 'Alexander', and 'Super Star'. A visit to the Royal National Rose Society's Gardens of the Rose is almost painful to the eye; the blatancy and vividness of the dazzling scarlet, orange, and flame tones predominate to an overwhelming degree. Surely the rose has become bright enough? But in these days of neon lights and fluorescent colours on posters and socks it is, I suppose, comforting to think that the rose can at least hold its own. On the other hand, Shakespeare said: "They are as sick that surfeit with too much, as they that starve with nothing."

Fortunately there is a comforting thing happening. Some of the colours that have been frowned upon for so long are being given a chance. Mauve and purple, innate in all roses and rightful to them, but suppressed and subordinate for nearly a hundred years, are once again allowed and even encouraged. Some Hybrid Teas and Floribundas such as 'Grey Pearl' (1944), 'Lavender Pinocchio' (1948), 'Magenta' (1954), 'Twilight' (1955), 'Lilac Time' (1956), 'Sterling Silver' (1957), 'Maud Cole' (1970), and 'The Prince' (1990) are restoring the balance, and perhaps before long we shall have a rose in true *bluish* lilac—although having cried "wolf" too often, with the latest so-called "blue" roses, what will the raisers do then? Up to the present I find 'Reine des Violettes' (1860) can hold its own quite comfortably with all these colours, and it is infinitely more fragrant. Very few genera of plants contain species with red, yellow, *and* blue flowers. Exceptions are *Lobelia*, *Gentiana*, and *Delphinium*. Blue is not present in any rose except in an adulterated pink, and while selection of these mauve tones may result in our getting *nearer* to blue, I understand that a genetical miracle would have to happen for a true blue rose to appear. Dr Jeffrey Harborne and Gordon Rowley explained this technical point admirably in the *National Rose Society's Annual* for 1959.

To return, 'Masquerade' (1949) and 'Cavalcade' (1950) set a new style also in their chameleon-like changes of colour. It is, however, only the strong influence of the China Rose, which always would turn darker, not lighter, on fading, that has returned. *Rosa chinensis* 'Mutabilis', known since before the turn of the twentieth century or perhaps eighty or more years previously, has been changing like this regularly every summer. Even 'Peace', 'Grand'mère Jenny', 'Perfecta', and other pale yellow roses with pink edges, and 'Pigalle'—that extraordinary mauve-pink with yellowish reverse—are not new colours. We only have to turn the pages of such a book as the *Journal des Roses* to find that these colours had already been exploited among the Hybrid Perpetuals at the end of the nineteenth century. They were of good size too; some of the greatest of these old hybrids with slight Tea admixture must have been monster blooms.

So far my remarks on colour have been mainly concerned with shrub roses and bedding, or bush, roses. Popular progress has begun to make itself felt among ramblers and climbers as well, and I do not think it will be long before 'Chaplin's Pink' and 'American Pillar' will be decked out in flame and orange, and will join hands with climbing sports of the brilliant Hybrid Teas and Floribundas. Fortunately, among the ramblers there are already some excellent varieties of purple colouring, 'Violette' (1921), 'Bleu Magenta', and the fragrant 'Veilchenblau' (1909), and some equally good whites.

I can think of nothing so desirable among Hybrid Teas as a rich murrey-purple rose, the colouring of 'Cardinal de Richelieu' with the scent, size, and texture of 'Étoile de Hollande', coupled with freedom and vigour. Here would be something worth achieving. And how useful it would be in designing a conventional rose garden with beds in a lawn, and finding one really had an alternative heavy colour to balance the dark crimson varieties. Similarly, when we have an 'Ophelia' or 'Monique' in silvery-lilac it will be a wonderful companion to the yellows and pinks. I should welcome both with open arms. Together with a really reliable white and more soft yellows like the unsurpassed—even unequalled—'Lady Hillingdon', these cool colours would have a vast and sobering effect on the vulgar blatancy that obtains today, while the changes are being rung in the tints of the spectrum between yellow and red with frightening and wearying monotony. Of course we need all these softer colours, too, in good, hearty Floribundas like 'Frensham', and with a good fragrance. Much of this envisaged perfection is with us already, particularly among David Austin's new English Roses.

No doubt in the past many unusual seedling roses were thrown away in disgust by breeders as worthless. Such would have been the fate, I think, if 'Café', 'Blue Moon', or 'Grey Pearl' had appeared in the 1930s. But today the craze for novelty and also the delight in quiet and often unusual colouring have given even these strange flowers a place in horticulture. Obviously of less conspicuous value in the garden, these greyish colourings have been appraised by the skilful flower arrangers, among whom none was more grateful for them than Constance Spry, who devoted a chapter to them in her book *Favourite Flowers* (1959).

Orange and scarlet are splendid and desirable when one is led up to them as a highlight of the border; there they can be enriched with coppery purple and golden foliage, and the whole thing becomes lighted with a Byzantine gorgeousness that can be absolutely thrilling. Gertrude Jekyll showed the way, as everyone will agree who saw her borders, and it has been followed by careful gardeners since. But it is usually done only once, even in big gardens; in small gardens it should never be repeated. Such a furnace of colour is overpowering except in occasional blasts. To have vivid colours distributed round the garden mixed up with the quieter colours is to me like having a stimulant every quarter-hour of the day. It destroys the peace and quiet which is after all what we most desire in a garden and which brings the greatest refreshment.

It is all a question of what one is used to. Those who glory in orange-red flowers of all kinds today find magentas, mauve-pinks, and crimson-purples very difficult to place in the garden. Believe me, it is far easier to cater *for* them than *without* them in a garden of all sorts of plants and shrubs. The "difficult" colours, when one has a catholic taste in plants, are not the magentas but the hard yellows, the oranges, and yellow-toned reds. These are the colours that look harsh with green—the opposite to red in the spectrum—and as the whole garden must perforce have a background of green, it stands to reason that without the flame-red tints everything blends well with its neighbours, from white and pale yellow through all greens, blues, mauves, purples, pinks, and crimsons. Plenty of the dark plum colours and crimsons must be included; without these deep bass notes, as it were, the rest are apt to sound a little thin.

SIZE OF FLOWER

SCENT, SHAPE, COLOUR, and now size. Everything today gets bigger and brighter, so I suppose we have not yet seen anything like the limit in size. As the plants are bred for vigour they will develop stronger stalks, and the stronger the stalk the bigger the bloom it can support. While a single flower can nod and still retain its charm and beauty, as in an Iceland Poppy, a Lily, or a Fritillary, a big double flower cannot be allowed this shy charm. We must be prepared for roses that are full to overflowing with colour and petals and, I hope, scent, and bigger and better than ever before. Meanwhile we can fortunately still enjoy some dainty treasures like 'Mlle Cécile Brunner', 'Perle d'Or', and 'Alister Stella Gray'; with them we can grow 'Mme Abel Chatenay' and the 'Rose d'Amour', all roses that do not owe everything to size or brilliance. They have a quintessential beauty that can bear long acquaintance and close inspection, and show the scrolled beauty of bud of the Hybrid Teas in miniature. These little roses have nearly been forgotten: they did not conform to a popular style. 'Mlle Cécile Brunner' and 'Perle d'Or' were really the first Poly-poms with a leaning towards the China Rose. It so happened that others, raised about the same time, leaned towards *Rosa multiflora* and became popular. These had little or no scent and no stylish shape, and yet they established a group, while no more China Poly-poms—exquisitely shaped, coloured, and scented and only slightly less free-flowering—appeared. This extraordinary fact has a parallel in the two groups of ramblers derived from *R. wichuraiana*. On the one hand are those several intensely fragrant large-flowered roses with glossy leaves like 'Albéric Barbier', which, except for this variety, have not been popular, while various small-flowered, scentless hybrids with poor foliage like 'Excelsa' and 'Dorothy Perkins' are found in every garden.

ROSES OF THE FUTURE

I LIKE TO THINK that this is a fair picture of the rose through the years and today. If I seem to lean towards the older types it is not because I cannot see the beauty and value of modern varieties. I was brought up on Hybrid Teas, and knew and loved them for many years before I came across other types and realized there was more in roses than at first was apparent. It seems to me that, looking at the picture broadly, and once again considering only man-made roses, we had a formalism in late Georgian and early Victorian times, followed by a fulsomeness lacking in refinement, when roses were flowers, not plants. The Tea Rose did not help matters immediately. All of these have succumbed to a dazzling display of colours, scents, and shapes—hard, sharp, clear, fitting to our modern age. The angular buds and petals of some of our modern roses are incredibly far removed from the cosy little round sweeties of a hundred and more years ago. Colours can usually be sorted and made to look well together with due care; shapes need more attention. I am sure we ought not to let roses get too far removed from a soft outline. Scent is of course paramount, otherwise the rose will lose its pride of place, and charm is an indefinable something without which the rose cannot satisfy as a flower, only as a bedding plant or a giver of colour.

At the moment the rose is on the crest of a wave of popularity. Dare we pause for a while? Nothing stands still: the Hybrid Tea, the choice favourite of today, may be a back number tomorrow, and who knows but that in twenty-five years gardeners will be witnessing a revival of the "sweet old Hybrid Teas of our forbears"? Judging by the publicity accorded them in shows, trials, catalogues, and magazines, the Floribundas—they may even be Grandifloras, of all ridiculous pretentious names!—may supplant the Hybrid Teas in a few years. The latter do not flower freely enough; they may have charm, which at the moment most of the Floribundas have not, but if in a few years the latter develop charm, will the Hybrid Teas become back numbers? I think they will, in popular esteem, provided that with charm the Floribundas develop scent. When scent, shape, floriferousness, and colour are added to charm then that rose is a paragon. If it can bring with it disease resistance and not be dependent on pruning, then it will sweep the board.

Looking back once again, we must admit that so long as the rose was thrifty and could stand on its own with a modicum of attention, all was well; it was not until the Victorian age brought a surfeit of gardeners that the new roses of the time could be grown successfully; the blooms were not very weatherproof and had to be protected. As labour in the garden dwindled through the years on account of the gradual economic squeeze, roses had to be acceptable and easily grown by amateurs, without professional gardeners, to survive. They have amply demonstrated that they are capable of doing this. That is why I think an improved type of Floribunda, perhaps with flowers somewhere between a Hybrid Tea and an Old Rose in floral style, may be the aim of the present age.

The newer, more vigorous Floribundas of today are every year becoming linked more closely with descendants from the Hybrid Musk group, and 'Heidelberg', 'Gustav Frahm', 'Erfurt', 'Golden Wings', and others are already pointers to the brighter perpetual flowering shrub roses of the future. While tall upright roses like 'Joanna Hill' and 'Queen Elizabeth' are too erect to be classed as flowering shrubs, they at least demonstrate how effective a tall modern style of rose can be. It is unfortunate when they are given beds to themselves; their stems are bare two feet from the ground, an indication that they should be surrounded by shorter-growing varieties, or should only be grown in the mixed border, among other shrubs and plants. As yet these big-growing Floribundas have scarcely become shrubs in the sense that the Hybrid Musks are shrubs, but they are a step towards the ideal of perpetual-flowering shrub roses in bright colours. Up to the present the only roses that can compare with the stature, floriferousness, and far-carrying, amazing fragrance of the Hybrid Musks are David Austin's English Roses.

The popular roses of today have become more and more givers of colour, and so their demand for use in segregated colours as bedding plants is on the increase. The lower-growing varieties are undoubtedly ideally suited for this form of culture, dull though it may be. With the stronger growers, however, their inclusion in the mixed and shrub borders becomes increasingly popular with discerning gardeners, and here the perpetual-flowering shrub roses fulfil a long-felt want. The rose has arrived first at what must be the gardener's ultimate goal—the production of new varieties of everything, in all colours, to flower throughout the season. How tiresomely bright the gardens of the future will be!

Some of the most pretentious horticultural works have been devoted to the genus *Rosa*, and a great band of artists has contributed from time to time in painting the favourites of the period; in the descriptive list of varieties later in this book I have endeavoured to indicate where reasonably accurate portraits or photographs may be found. This will, I hope, save others from hours of searching, and will also serve to show how popular certain varieties were in years gone by, when roses were still classed as flowering shrubs.

PART I

The Old Shrub Roses

I

Reappraisal

A PERSONAL APPROACH

IN MY EXAMINATION of the Old Roses in particular, I feel I am fulfilling a kind of mission, since they appeal in an increasing way to a widening circle of gardeners. I find them fascinating, and this fascination applies not only to the summer months, but also to the winter evenings spent in culling historical details from old books and catalogues, and associating the many historic figures with the period flowers whose names they bear. The only apology, therefore, with which I write these notes is that my knowledge of these roses is still incomplete; however, thanks to what has been written in the past and to the steadily increasing circle of friends whose enthusiasm and interest are continually pooled in furtherance of our quest, both in Britain and abroad, it is still growing. And so I am going to write what I hope may be considered as a gardener's rather than a botanist's approach to a few roses which we will term Old, and to extol their value in the garden—although perhaps in the course of the following pages history or botany or reminiscence may occasionally expel the horticultural aspect.

I think the rose must hold a high place in our early affection for flowers. I can distinctly remember delighting in the fragrance of the Hybrid Perpetual 'Mrs John Laing' at the age of eight; in fact 'Mrs Laing' and 'Alister Stella Gray' have been my constant companions since those early days, and never fail to give plentifully of their beauty, year by year. There was also in our Cambridge garden another very fragrant rose; it was a big bush of the plant used frequently as an understock, 'de la Grifferaie', although I was not aware of this until many years later. This is often found in old gardens, having outlived the rose budded upon it, and few roses have a more delicious scent in the fully double, almost pompon-like, magenta-pink blooms, borne in clusters along the arching sprays.

Well remembered, too, is the day on which I purchased my first rose—'Mme Caroline Testout', followed by other Hybrid Teas, now outclassed; they were recommended by an uncle who was something of a connoisseur, and in whose garden every rose bore, to my great satisfaction, a cast metal label. At the age of fourteen or fifteen I added 'General MacArthur' and 'Mrs Aaron Ward'—a new colour note to the garden—to my little collection, together with 'Mrs Herbert Stevens', 'Mme Édouard Herriot', and 'Mme Abel Chatenay'. Most of these stay in general cultivation.

At this period alpine plants claimed my full attention, Reginald Farrer's pen working upon my imagination so much that rocks and alpine plants absorbed all my spare pocket money. On leaving school I spent some years at the University Botanic Garden at Cambridge. In those days Dr H. Gilbert-Carter and F. G. Preston were there to guide my advancement in botany and horticulture, with J. Blades filling in all the details that my enthusiasm needed. I was ripe for the wider appreciation of all classes of hardy plants that may be acquired in that unique Garden—alpines, herbaceous plants, conifers, shrubs, trees, and roses. *Rosa gigantea* flowered well, and also such diverse plants as *R. banksiae lutea*, the 'Old Blush' China, *R. hardii*, *R. moyesii*, *R. rugosa*, and *R. brunonii*; Dr C. C. Hurst was busy in frames and houses with his genetical experiments; *R.* 'Cantabrigiensis' was soon to appear as a chance seedling, to be given an Award of Merit and also the Cory Cup in 1931.

It was while at the Cambridge Botanic Garden that I met Thomas Blythe, a fellow student, whose often repeated eulogies of Irish luxuriance prompted me to visit him in Ireland in 1937. I shall never forget the spectacle which his kindness unfolded for me at Rostrevor and Rowallane, while other excursions took us to his uncle's nursery at Daisy Hill, Newry, and to the Botanic Garden at Glasnevin, Dublin. At this famous Garden some most beautiful roses happened to be in flower: *Rosa* 'Paulii' and its pink form 'Rosea', *R. macrophylla*, and several other species of note, while at Newry the rather sad remnants of Tom Smith's once magnificent collection were also in full bloom. The several Old Roses grown here did not immediately appeal to me, their mauve-pinks and purples being so unexpected that, like many others newly approaching this class of rose, I was almost repelled. I could only single out the rose known as *R. gallica* 'Vivid' and the Rugosa hybrid 'Vanguard', both of which I now look upon with considerable coolness.

At the outbreak of war Brian O. Mulligan, at that time Assistant to Mr Harrow at the Royal Horticultural Society's Gardens at Wisley, Surrey, drew my attention to the great collection of Old Roses gathered together by E. A. Bunyard, which was shortly to be sold. This awakened me to the treasure stored by this enlightened man, who was so great a loss to us all in his passing. And then shortly afterwards the only other big commercial collection of shrub roses fell upon the market, that of Messrs G. Beckwith & Son of Hoddesdon, Hertfordshire. Although this collection was mainly composed of species, many of which were of doubtful horticultural value, the entire collection was acquired in the spring of 1940, and it was with much interest that we awaited flowering time the next year. There were several nuggets among the dross, such as 'Nevada', whose portrait in the *New Flora and Silva* (Vol. 8, page 245) had fired my enthusiasm, some good Provence and Moss roses, and the exquisitely fragrant Gallica, 'Belle de Crécy'. This perfectly shaped old-world rose, in its extraordinary mixture of cerise, violet, and lilac-grey, happened to be planted near to the incomparable white hybrid Damask Rose 'Mme Hardy'. I lost my heart to them during the first flowering week, and have found no better types among the Old Roses since. It was my first real appreciation of these exquisite florist's creations.

To the few enthusiasts of those days the sale of these two collections and complete disappearance of such roses from commerce seemed to be the death knell, I have been told, of the little cause that had been growing. The war dragged on, and a hayfield sprang up through our plantation of roses, but they survived, being tough and hardy and thrifty. A little later the Daisy Hill Nursery changed hands, and a few roses reached us safely; among them were 'Tuscany', 'Commandant Beaurepaire', 'Alain Blanchard', 'Coupe d'Hébé', and a striped rose that has since proved to be *R. centifolia* 'Variegata'.

Meanwhile, in 1941 I was lucky enough to find my way to Nymans, Lieutenant-Colonel L. R. C. Messel's beautiful home at Handcross, Sussex. It was my special privilege to be taken round the remarkable collection of Old Roses by Mrs Messel, whose particular hobby it had been to collect these delights before the war. Here was my first introduction to them as garden furnishings, and I recall the great beauty of 'Charles de Mills' in all its glory, four or five feet high on that rich Wealden soil, with several dozen flowers well open. At Nymans these roses were grouped in formal beds, set in grass and interspersed with apple- and mulberry-trees, in a pleasing cottage garden style. It was a great experience to see them and hear all the delightful names of these rare old varieties from so knowledgeable and enthusiastic a gardener as Mrs Messel.

There was not much time during the war to look out for roses, but an occasional visit to Nymans and Wisley, where there were several interesting varieties, to Kew and Cambridge, kept my interest alive, though suppressed and subordinate to matters of moment. Towards the end of the war my interest was greatly quickened by a visit from Constance Spry. The long French names flowed from her, enthusiasm was at bursting point; a few glances at the little lot we had collected drew forth some remarks that, while not disparaging, made me realize I had little to show. There were no half measures with Mrs Spry—a long and growing friendship proved this over and over again—and she had assiduously collected her roses from French and American nurseries, and from gardens here and there, in days before the war. It was necessary for her to move them. Could I propagate them meanwhile in order to ensure their perpetuity in case the old bushes died? This was a problem in those days, but we managed it somehow. There was nothing for it but that I must up and away to Kent and see her roses, and this I did, and was once more thoroughly convinced, not only that there was nothing like them in horticulture, but that they were good and fascinating garden material, neglected by just that generation that could make the best use of them. A few prophets of pre-war days had been crying in the wilderness, and a few keen spirits had preserved these beauties for our later enjoyment; this is a fact that will become the more apparent as the story unfolds. Messrs Pajotin-Chédane of La Maître École, Angers, France, had given up their collection when I wrote to them after the war, but Constance Spry had their most sumptuous varieties in Kent. Messrs Bobbink and Atkins of New Jersey, U.S.A., still grew a number of good varieties, but how fortunate that many of their best were already in this country, again in the Spry collection. And roses from Messrs Bunyard's had found their way through E. A. Bunyard to Nymans, and there were roses there and at Wisley from Daisy Hill Nurseries, Newry.

Another noted preserver of these plants, my old friend and mentor A.T. Johnson, of North Wales, when he found that I had become an ardent admirer of the old groups, sent me a special invitation to see his garden in June. It was indeed a joy to find 'Tuscany' suckering strongly in the poor shaley soil, the Alba roses growing to six feet high, and many a Gallica showering its blossoms over the borders. A great find was 'Félicité Parmentier', which A.T. J. had imported some years previously from the German nurseryman Peter Lambert of Trier. Not only had A.T. J. preserved numerous Old Roses from various sources, but his writings—in various journals and in his books about his enchanting small garden—did much to foster interest in these splendid garden shrubs.

With petrol again available in small quantities a few other visits became possible in 1947, one being to Sissinghurst Castle, where Sir Harold and Lady Nicolson (V. Sackville-West) grew some unique Old Roses, including the one we call 'Sissinghurst Castle', and the rare purple Hybrid Perpetual 'Souvenir du Docteur Jamain'. Another journey was to Colonel F. C. Stern's garden at Highdown, Goring-by-Sea, Sussex; good bushes of old-fashioned roses grew strongly in his chalky soil, and fine examples of Hybrid Musk Roses and many species throve amazingly well. The Oxford University Botanic Garden had one or two rare varieties with cast-metal labels, including *Rosa gallica* 'Conditorum', and on the same day I went farther, into Buckinghamshire, to Chetwode Manor. In this quiet country garden Mrs Louis Fleischmann had preserved another collection of roses; these had been mostly gathered from old gardens in England and Ireland, and 'Tour de Malakoff' was one of the great bushes, loaded with huge blooms, that greeted me. One of the rarest roses in her garden was the Autumn Damask, a precious heirloom from the days when a few late blooms were greatly treasured. I described her garden at some length in *Gardening Illustrated* for July 1951. On the way back I called on Miss Nancy Lindsay and was delighted to find several ancient roses which she had collected in Persia, together with some most beautiful French kinds, and to compare notes with her. Another garden I visited on the same trip was that belonging to Mr and Mrs Nigel Law, in Chalfont St Peter, Buckinghamshire. Some very scarce varieties were to be found carefully preserved in their garden, several of which I had not seen before, among them the Pompon variety 'Cramoisi Picoté'.

I had been in correspondence with The Hon. Robert James of St Nicholas, Richmond, Yorkshire, and was keenly interested to see his renowned collection. Accordingly, when our roses were over, with my friend James P. C. Russell of Windlesham, who had become infected with my enthusiasm, I decided to visit some northern gardens, and our first call was at St Nicholas. Mr James had preserved numerous splendid roses among other plants in his delightful garden, and I was particularly interested to find beds of the single pink *Rosa gallica*, apparently a wild type, and also the so-called 'Empress Josephine', which proved to be a form of *R. francofurtana;* both were running through the soil and thriving. We also went over the Pennines to Penrith, where magnificent bowls of purple roses and other floral decorations awaited us at Crossrigg Hall, the home of Cornish Torbock. Roses grew well in these gardens, and also at Sir William Milner's, at Appletreewick, near Skipton. One of the best things in Sir William's garden was the skilful framing of the view from his terrace, but on the more sheltered side of the house a good collection of Old Roses grew. Here we found numerous choice varieties, including a most exquisite White Rose, which has since proved to be 'Mme Legras de St Germain'. Our fourth call was at Weston Hall, Towcester, where Sacheverell Sitwell grew another splendid collection, the most striking variety being the sumptuous crimson-purple Moss, 'Maréchal Davoust'. We felt greatly elated, on completing this little northern tour, to have seen four excellent collections in such good condition, carefully preserved by these keen and discriminating gardeners.

The year 1948 was spent mostly in consolidating my own plants and getting to know the numerous varieties I had collected; comparing them with old books and sorting them into botanical groups; and writing short descriptions of each. It was therefore with some little knowledge stored that I went to Ireland again in 1949; the story of my travels from one wonderful garden to another is written elsewhere,* but I will recall here two most interesting places, Old Conna Hill, Bray, where Colonel and Mrs Riall used to tend a wide variety of plants in a beautiful setting, and Mr and Mrs Salmon's *multum in parvo* at Larchfield, Dublin. Here were a thousand or more roses closely grown in mixed borders, and Mr Salmon proudly produced a family treasure, 'Le Roi à fleur pourpre'. Also in their collection were two roses which I have, I think, traced successfully since: the pink sport or parent of 'Leda', and 'Blush Hip', the climbing pink *Rosa alba.* It was a great pleasure, too, to visit Lady Moore, at Rathfarnham, Dublin, for she specially preserved some interesting old Scots Roses, and that new rose of ancient lineage, 'Souvenir de St Anne's', a sport from the Malmaison Rose.

I was no sooner back from Ireland than Gloucestershire called me. The season is later there than in Surrey, and while our roses were going over, those at Hidcote Manor—Major

---

* *Journal of the Royal Horticultural Society,* June and August 1950.

Lawrence Johnston's garden of consummate taste and constant surprises—and Mrs J. B. Muir's garden at Kiftsgate Court, both near Chipping Campden, revealed a display of Old Roses flowering in the wildest profusion and of the greatest luxuriance. Mrs Muir's garden has received a share of its due from my pen elsewhere,* but I cannot pass on without recalling once again the satisfaction I received, and yearly regain, in going from one border to another, each of a different character and colour, and culminating in the splendour of the double 'Rosa Mundi' hedges, and the supreme touch, the white garden. These two gardens, Kiftsgate and Hidcote, display the Old Roses in much of their natural state, while at Abbotswood, Stow-on-the-Wold, Gloucestershire, there was a splendid group of old-fashioned roses carefully pruned to produce the maximum number of beautiful blooms. I need hardly say more than that a visit to Abbotswood immediately proved that the rose, old or new, had no peer for scent and colour among all the brilliant denizens even of that superb colour garden.

Meanwhile I had not been idle in regard to correspondence, and was in touch with Bobbink & Atkins of New Jersey, and the Lester Rose Gardens in California. Both firms had collected and propagated many Old Roses from all parts of that continent, and my collection was very considerably enriched by their generosity. The Morton Arboretum, Illinois, and G. D. Greene of St Louis, Missouri, also added to our collection, and Herr Wilhelm Kordes in Holstein and O. Sonderhousen of Denmark both sent me many varieties of merit. Through the great kindness and co-operation of André Leroi of the Conservation des Parcs et Jardins in Paris I was fortunate to receive a complete catalogue of all the roses grown in the renowned German National Rose Garden at Sangerhausen, in what was then East Germany. This amazingly complete list includes hundreds of Old Roses, and I managed to get the majority safely over for comparison. The Moss 'Général Kléber' and Gallica 'Cosimo Ridolfi' stand out as two most desirable varieties from this collection. It has indeed been most interesting comparing notes and descriptions, and also the living plants, side by side, from these many keen and co-operative donors. Many times does one find a name completely and utterly wrong attached to a beautiful rose, and occasionally by careful searching through old books one finds a clue to its correct name. More often than not, unfortunately, this becomes impossible, the great majority of descriptions being too vague to enable one to do more than check the colour and group.

The collecting of these roses over a number of years has not been the only aspect of the work. Together with a large range of species, a comprehensive collection of Old Shrub Roses has been established at the Gardens of the Rose of the Royal National Rose Society, Chiswell Green, St Albans, Hertfordshire. At Mottisfont Abbey, Romsey, Hampshire, the National Trust has assembled my entire original collection of Old Shrub Roses, with numerous old climbers and ramblers, in an old walled garden. There are also considerable collections in other gardens of the National Trust, particularly at Hidcote Manor, Chipping Campden, Gloucestershire; Nymans, Handcross, Sussex; Sissinghurst Castle, Cranbrook, Kent; and West Green House, Hartley Wintney, Hampshire. The Northern Horticultural Society's Garden at Harlow Carr, Harrogate, Yorkshire also has a good number, and one of the largest collections is at Castle Howard, near York. These collections can be utilized for study, to unravel the history and guess the future conduct of a glorious race.

Can I term them, also, the popular roses of the future? I do not feel it would be wise to do so. That these roses find favour with many is very true; admirers have come from America, Tasmania, New Zealand, Australia, South Africa, Tangier, Cyprus, Italy, and many other

---

* *Journal of the Royal Horticultural Society,* May 1951

countries of Europe, and those desiring to grow them in this country are increasing in numbers yearly. But they are, apart from all this, an acquired taste; at least, I have found this very true in my own approach to them. They have, as I have stated before, a colouring and form unique in the realm of horticulture, and they are easy to grow, but they do not satisfy all the modern preconceived ideas, either in colour or in their limited flowering season, and so they can never be popular within the present meaning of the word. They are "a heady subject, and like wine they go to one's head," as Selwyn Duruz says in the chapter devoted to them in his book *Flowering Shrubs*. How very true this is can be proved by the enthusiasm which they arouse in people in all walks and stations of life—including artists, fortunately, for where should we be without those capable of depicting these treasures on paper?

THE RISE OF THE OLD ROSES

> Oh, no man knows
> Through what wild centuries
> Roves back the rose.
>
>   Walter de la Mare

THE BOTANISTS enumerate between one and two hundred species of roses, according to whether they feel that small and possibly inconstant characters are sufficient to separate one species from another. It is amusing to read in Bean's *Trees and Shrubs Hardy in the British Isles* that one botanist was known to have separated the species so finely that the characters of two could be found on one bush! The genus is found throughout the temperate and sub-tropical regions of the Northern Hemisphere. Practically all, except a few from the warmer parts, are deciduous, and are bushy or trailing or climbing shrubs of varying dimensions. A number of learned works may be found in libraries dealing with them in a botanical way, but it will not be of any advantage to enter too deeply into a general botanical discussion. Suffice it to say that a mere handful of species have given us all our highly bred roses of today, and many are in what the botanists term the group Gallicanae. These form the bulk of the Old Roses which are now our concern. But there are a few other species which were also quite popular in the past in Europe, judging by the fact that they are enumerated in nearly all the old books on roses. They are the European species *Rosa glauca* (*R. rubrifolia*), whose soft plum-coloured leaves are its main attraction; *R. canina*, our native Dog Brier; *R. pulverulenta* (*R. glutinosa*), so strongly and strangely redolent of pines; the Sweet Brier, *R. eglanteria* or *rubiginosa*; and *R. pomifera*. These all belong to the Caninae section and have pink flowers, while *R. foetida* and *R. hemisphaerica*, from western Asia, the so-called Austrian Brier and the Sulphur Rose respectively, bear yellow flowers. *Rosa pendulina* (*R. alpina*), also European, and *R. moschata*, a native of North Africa, southern Europe, and western Asia, bring this little list nearly to its close.

A few of these species were grown in cultivated forms, and *Rosa foetida* has in more recent times altered the colours of our roses almost beyond recognition, but otherwise they have remained on the verge of horticulture, and have not been absorbed by it, nor have they ever entered the main ancestral popular group of roses, apart from *R. moschata* and *R. canina*.

The Gallicanae, which I have referred to as "main" and "ancestral," form a closely related group, descended, it is reasonable to suppose, from *Rosa gallica*, *R. moschata*, *R. canina*, and *R. phoenicea*. *Rosa gallica* has had predominance, and in general horticultural feeling may be considered the common ancestor of the Gallicas, the Damasks, the Provence and Moss Roses, and the White Roses. These formed the foundation of our present popular races of roses, and are examined in more detail in Chapter 3. When we read (in Dr Hurst's notes, Chapter 13) that *R. gallica* was a religious emblem of the Medes and Persians in the twelfth century B.C., it is small wonder that it has united with other wild roses in the cradle of our present civilization, and that the hybrid progeny, all fragrant presentable roses of bushy habit, should have been favourites with the southern European peoples for thousands of years. They have been preserved mainly for their beauty, because their only economic products are scent and conserves, comparatively of little importance to the survival of the human race. Nobody knows, of course, how these old races of roses developed in the first place, but one can visualize certain tribes delighting in one form or another and spreading them over limited areas where they may have become hybridized by chance with the few other species concerned.

Our roses went on in a small way, being loved and tended by the few who could devote time to such a trifling pursuit, until the general awakening of the Renaissance. In spite of the knowledge of tricky vegetative propagating—for even the grafting of fruits on various root-stocks was current in Virgil's time—roses did not profit except by limited selection of a few forms. The production of hybrids by seed was not understood. And thus one finds in very old works the same old varieties again and again—the bullate or laciniate leaf, the double or single or striped flower which in those days were sufficient spice and variety to ensure the protection of these plants.

But when the new desire for beauty, the new use or possible use of spare time, and the new awakening to the cultivation of plants arose, apart from the vegetable garden, we find a steady stream of varieties appearing. Seed began to play a part later, and, once unleashed, the rose gave forth its potentialities, stored in a complex hybrid group for these thousands of years, and became one of the most prolific of the favourite races of plants.

It is interesting to delve into some of the noted gardening books of the past to see the development of the rose. In Gerard's *Herball* (1597), 14 roses are enumerated; Parkinson, in his *Paradisi in Sole Paradisus Terrestris* (1629), mentions 24; in 1663 Mollet mentions 6 roses only for the ornamental garden, and the Rosier de Provins (*Rosa gallica* or *rubra*) is relegated to the kitchen garden. Lawrance in 1799 produced 90 coloured plates of roses; Roessig, between 1802 and 1820, depicts 121 varieties in colour. These are extremely valuable works from our point of view, many of the roses being still in cultivation, and they are accurately depicted.*

From 1817 to 1824 Redouté was producing his monumental work *Les Roses*, with text by Thory, and this really marks the beginning of our present appreciation of the rose. The three magnificent volumes are a delight to handle owing to their sumptuousness and spacious pages, and every plate shows a masterly hand delineating a fine and, in many examples, a recognizable rose. The volumes immortalize not only Redouté and Thory but also the Empress Josephine, at whose behest there was such a gathering together of roses at La Malmaison as had never before been seen; Redouté's was the task of conveying their beauties to paper.† Bunyard, in his *Old Garden Roses*, mentions that an English nurseryman, Kennedy, was employed

---

* Georg Dionysius Ehret (1708–1770), a great painter of plants, has left us some superb portraits of the roses of his time. Originals may be seen in the Victoria and Albert Museum, and they include Rosa Mundi, Common Provence, York and Lancaster, Red Provence (*R. gallica officinalis*), and Common Moss. An excellent reproduction of twelve of his pictures was published in 1953 with an introduction by Wilfrid Blunt (Traylen, Guildford).

† Among several reproductions of Redouté's rose portraits is the complete set of three great volumes reproduced facsimile by De Schutter SA of Antwerp in 1974, with a fourth volume of commentaries and botanical details by Gisèle de la Roche and Gordon D. Rowley in 1978.

by the Empress—war or no war—and between him and Dupont, the director of the Luxembourg Gardens at Paris, the world was ransacked to furnish her famous collection. "There was also a rival," Bunyard remarks, "the Countess of Bougainville, to spur to further efforts, and under such auspicious impetus the rose became the most important flower in France." Seed-raising on a grand scale had begun, and he records that Descemet, the nurseryman at St Denis, had some ten thousand seedlings when the Allies prepared to march into Paris in 1815, and that these were rescued by Vibert and taken to safety on the Marne.

Roses from then onwards were very much in the hands of nurserymen, and their erudite and comprehensive little volumes give one cause to wonder how they found the time to do their botanical and classical research and, what is almost more to the point, what sort of public it was that could regularly purchase their works. Take, for instance, Prévost, Pépiniériste à Rouen, *Catalogue descriptif, méthodique et raisonné des espèces, variétés et sous-variétés du genre rosier:* his list embraces 880 names. Our two famous English nurserymen specializing in roses at that time were Thomas Rivers and William Paul, and both made their contributions to the growing library devoted to the rose. Rivers's *Rose Amateur's Guide* (1837) is a discursive and delightful small book devoting a hundred pages to a pleasantly written enumeration of varieties, together with details of cultivation. It is a catalogue of his roses presented in a most readable fashion, and many old varieties are traced to their origin in its pages. Paul's *The Rose Garden* (1848) ("to the Rose Amateurs of Great Britain this work is most respectfully inscribed by their humble servant the Author") is a much more pretentious work, the first half being devoted to an exposition of the rose in the Arts, and its requirements in cultivation. The second half contains many chapters, each devoted to a special group of roses, all given careful descriptions, which I have found very useful and helpful; among hundreds of roses of many other groups it is wonderful to find descriptions of 87 Damask, 76 Provence, 84 Moss, and 471 French (Gallica) roses.

To these two books I must add Max Singer's *Dictionnaire des roses, ou guide général du rosieriste.* This was published in 1885, and apart from fifty pages at the beginning devoted to a few species and small groups of roses—including, rather strangely, over five dozen varieties of *Rosa alba*—this is an alphabetical enumeration of six thousand varieties, in many instances with long descriptions. His descriptions do not always tally with those of Paul, but between them there is much to be learned.

Singer's *Dictionnaire* was followed in 1906 by another French work, *Nomenclature de tous les noms de roses connus, avec indication de leur race, obtenteur, année de production, couleur et synonymes,* by Léon Simon and Pierre Cochet; their list extends to 10,953 entries, from 'Abaçon' to 'Zulmalacareguy'. What an intriguing name for a rose! It was a Provence, and is also mentioned by Paul. A most valuable German compilation, based on the collection at Sangerhausen, is August Jäger's *Rosenlexicon,* published in Leipzig in 1960. This has the advantage of giving the names of roses commemorating people, listed under their surnames; it has proved a most useful counter-check.

Many of the most shapely and sumptuous of our Old Roses were raised during the nineteenth century: 'Mme Hardy', 1832; 'Félicité Parmentier', 1836; 'Cardinal de Richelieu', 1840; 'La Ville de Bruxelles', 1849; and 'Tour de Malakoff', 1856. Their heyday of popularity was perhaps around 1810 to 1830, for the later introductions mentioned above were only isolated examples of a doomed race. Had they not been very vigorous and thrifty shrubs they would probably not have survived for a hundred and fifty years, ready to be collected together again to serve a type of garden changed beyond recognition from those which in bygone days they graced. The rose was to suffer a great revolution in common with its most ardent admirers of that time.

> Wanted: a refuge for the old roses where they may be found again when tastes change.
>
> George Paul, RHS *Journal*, 1896

That the Old Roses were in danger of being lost so early as the end of the nineteenth century may come as a surprise to many. All the more famous writers on roses during the last hundred or so years have echoed this plea for preserving the Old Roses. George Paul, who was a nephew of William Paul, the great rosarian, wanted to find some place where the roses depicted by Redouté could be assembled, together with roses of other old groups. But we had to wait until they were in danger of extinction before they were again collected. How often have I wished that I could have gone to some botanic garden and found the lot! Yet the quest would not have been so interesting, and considering how they were neglected, it is remarkable how many have survived; it can only be put down to their toughness, and their unequalled fragrance.

REVOLUTION

THE REVOLUTION that took place in the genus *Rosa* was due to the introduction in 1789 of roses from China to Europe. The Gallica, White, Damask, Provence, and Moss Roses, to which this chapter is devoted, were, with few exceptions, capable of flowering at midsummer only. The exceptions were the Autumn Damask Roses. Throughout the centuries a few forms had evolved from these hybrids (supposedly between *R. moschata* and *R. gallica*) but, as far as I am aware, until my rediscovery of the original *R. moschata*, flowering from August onwards (see Chapter 8), no satisfactory explanation had been offered as to how their autumnal flowering habit arose. Today the production of an odd bloom or two in the autumn would not be counted of much importance, but two hundred years ago this character was greatly appreciated. Although these old Quatre Saisons Roses are not of great value now, it was with considerable interest that I observed a white unnamed Moss Rose producing a pink sport without moss in 1949. Until then I had not realized that this Moss Rose was a Damask, but have since found references to it in old books, as White Perpetual Moss. It had sported back to the Autumn Damask from which it originated, and it doubled my interest to hear from Miss Murrell at Shrewsbury of a similar occurrence at about the same time, and also to find that the resultant pink Damask was identical with one at Chetwode Manor, and with one received from California.

The China Rose is almost alone among roses (*Rosa rugosa* is another notable exception) in being able to produce flowers from May to October in this climate. In warmer countries it has no resting season at all. The Chinese have records as far back as A.D. 900 of double China Roses, on their pottery, and it is a pregnant thought that this rose, preserved and evolved by their ancient civilization, should have been transported to our perhaps younger Western civilization at a time when it would most make its influence felt. It was small wonder that this rose was used for hybridizing by devoted rosarians in this country and on the continent of Europe. Whether those early raisers realized what was about to happen has not, I believe, been recorded; but the fact remains that the frail China Rose, with its smooth twigs and few translucent prickles, its smooth, delicate, pointed leaves, and loose silky blooms with little shape or variation in colour, was fused gradually with our coarser roses, resulting first in the Bourbons, Noisettes, and Boursaults, and later giving rise to the Hybrid Perpetuals.

All these newer races were selected for their capability of giving flowers from June to October, some plentifully, others only sparsely. Many gained their "remontant" habit at the expense of hardiness and scent. And so we can visualize two races of roses: the one, composed of the old summer-flowering kinds, being raised in decreasing numbers and lingering in cultivation mostly in the gardens of the poorer classes, while the new remontant roses were being produced increasingly by nurserymen, and being taken up by wealthy garden owners. It was indeed a revolution, not surpassed in rose history for a hundred years, when our modern roses began to develop flame and yellow tints due to the influence of *Rosa foetida.*

That something of this kind did happen to the rose with the infusion of the China Rose's characters is obvious from the books that appeared from about 1830 onwards. Increasing numbers of Hybrid Provence Roses, Hybrid Damasks, and the like appeared, along with numerous Bourbons and the early Hybrid Perpetuals. In fact the bulk of the names in Singer's and in Simon's books are of these classes. In 1872 Paul published his third edition—it lacks the coloured plates of the first—enumerating no fewer than 538 Hybrid Perpetuals and 142 Tea Roses, not to speak of long lists of Bourbons and similar classes. His Moss Roses have shrunk to 53; the Gallicas to 18; he lists 10 Alba varieties; 10 Damask, and 7 Provence. The corresponding collections in his first edition in 1848 I have given on page 10; this first edition also contained 106 Hybrid Perpetuals and 145 Teas. Other and smaller groups remained more static, since they were composed of roses of original and distinct types. It is only in the artificially created and all too numerous productions of man that fashions change in any genus, apart, of course, from fundamental changes in the flow of horticulture.

A contemporary picture is provided by *Les Roses,* by Hippolyte Jamain and Eugène Forney, published in 1873. This is a fine, well-illustrated work figuring almost exclusively Hybrid Perpetuals and roses of related classes. It is quite evident which way fashion was developing.

The Austrian Brier, having been mated with the popular rose of the period, eventually changed the colour of the Hybrid Teas beyond recognition. This is the third revolution we may record in the artificial evolution of our favourite flower—first, the French Revolution, which indirectly produced Josephine's great collection at Malmaison; second, the advent of the China Rose into the breeders' capable hands; and, third, the similar advent, but much more gradual and limited, of the Austrian Brier. Its first results were the Pernetiana Roses, which have since been merged into the many-hued modern roses. Just where and when the next revolution may occur remains to be seen, but I suspect and predict it is going to be some great perpetual flowering shrub rose which will produce numerous progeny. Up to the present such a rose does not seem to have been raised; 'Nevada' remains obdurate to the hybridizer, but David Austin's new English Roses and a number of separately raised hybrids from the United States and Europe are competing.

To return, we may take up another English nurseryman's book, John Cranston's *Cultural Directions for the Rose,* whose fifth edition was published in 1875; a book full of sound practical help and good points about cultivation, in which he describes many pages of Hybrid Perpetuals and numerous other groups. He says,

> The fearful havoc which was made amongst roses, especially the tender ones,
> during the severe winter of 1860 and 1861, will, I trust, be the means of
> bringing about a more hardy race . . . . This delicacy has doubtless been pro-

duced by crossing the hardier Perpetuals too freely with the Tea-scented and
other tender sorts.

The stigma of tenderness could never be applied to the old groups, but in our modern roses
can almost always be traced to Tea and sometimes to China parentage.

So far the chronicles of the rose have largely fallen to nurserymen; now begins what I like
to term the clergyman's period. Dean Hole, the Revd Shirley Hibberd, and the Revd Foster-
Melliar wrote books between 1870 and 1894; they are all charming in their way, but show
the trend of artificiality in gardening and particularly in the use of the rose, and reflect very
forcibly the ubiquity of the popular groups. By 1900 things had reached a more enlightened
peak, and from this date onwards the Hybrid Teas have marched forwards, themselves now
being by far the most numerous and popular group, thanks to the addition of the Pernetianas.

That is, however, not the end of the story. The Old Roses with iron constitutions having
been allowed to fall into obscurity, it was natural that in time their very longevity, and their
sweet scent, should bring them once more into favour, as *shrubs*—not as "roses" in the modern sense—while just those very roses which proved their undoing have, in their turn, been
neglected, and indeed have mostly vanished. The hordes of Hybrid Perpetuals have gone, except for a handful of tried favourites like 'Mrs John Laing' and 'Ulrich Brunner', 'Frau Karl
Druschki', and the Dicksons; the unique 'Reine des Violettes', 'Souvenir du Docteur Jamain',
and a few dozen other varieties which have been preserved in continental gardens such as the
Roseraie de l'Haÿ and Sangerhausen.

At this time Gertrude Jekyll, ever to the fore in sensible use of garden material, produced
a book, *Roses for English Gardens,* in collaboration with Edward Mawley; it is profusely illustrated, mostly with photographs.

> The time having come when there is a distinct need for a book that *shall not
> only show how Roses may best be grown, but how they may be most beautifully used,* and that
> will also help the amateur to acquire some idea of their nature and relation-
> ships, the present volume, with its large amount of illustration, is offered in
> the hope that it will fit usefully into a space as yet unfilled in garden literature.

The date was 1902, and the italics are mine. Such a book was certainly needed to call the
rose enthusiasts from their greenhouses and pots, their show benches and artificialities, and
to show them how the queen of flowers could grace the garden, giving colour and fragrance
and charm, in her less sophisticated forms.

Two beautifully illustrated rose books appeared in 1908 and 1913; they were Rose Kingsley's *Roses and Rose Growing* and H. H. Thomas's *The Rose Book.* Both show a wider insight into
the rose than their immediate predecessors. The former stresses the extreme beauty of old
and new types, with portraits excellently reproduced in colour; the writer is well informed,
although she confuses Rosa Mundi and York and Lancaster; she intrigues me with her mention of the Single Crimson Damask raised in 1901. This is a rose I should much like to acquire; Damasks are always the most elusive of roses. H. H. Thomas's book shows mostly
Hybrid Teas in colour, but devotes much subject-matter to old and species roses.

Meanwhile, another important work had appeared. From 1910 to 1914, Ellen Willmott
was producing *The Genus Rosa,* having secured the services of no less an artist than Alfred Parsons. This work, just falling short of the word "great" in view of its mistakes, inconsistencies,
and limitations, is packed with information mostly gathered from many earlier works, and is
superbly illustrated in colour. The plates are exquisitely drawn and show the grace of the liv-

ing plant, from an artist's point of view rather than a botanist's. Many of the portraits are of species, but several are devoted to the Old Roses. *Rosa centifolia* and its variety *alba muscosa* are depicted wrongly, and I have referred to this in my notes under these plants. The book shows the very real awakening of a great gardener to the manifold beauties of the rose, and is a landmark in horticultural history. Ellen Willmott clearly envisaged the possible turn of the tide towards garden beauty already suggested by Gertrude Jekyll, and this feeling was undoubtedly influenced by the increasing popularity of two lovely species, *R. hugonis* and *R. moyesii*, both introduced from China early in the century. These two roses have played a similar part in popularizing rose species to that played by *Lilium regale* among lilies, and *Meconopsis betonicifolia* among the blue poppies. In any select list of rose species these two are sure to be found. They epitomize the beauty and charm of the species roses, and give us colours far removed from the predominating pink.

There is no doubt that these two renowned women, Gertrude Jekyll and Ellen Willmott, each the creator of a beautiful garden, left their mark on the genus, although this mark was more in the way of a pointer to the general trend of horticulture than might at first sight be apparent. From 1914 onwards book after book has appeared, but they are nearly all concerned with the popular varieties of the day, the Hybrid Teas and Polyanthas, and they are mostly written by enthusiastic garden owners. Two other publications appeared which were, however, of much wider interest. I have an old catalogue, dated 1912, by Tom Smith of Newry, County Down, one of the fine nurserymen of that time; it contains a really amazing collection of roses of all kinds, but it is quite obvious that his first loves were the lusty shrub roses, the Rugosas, and the old groups, and he did his best to interest gardeners in trying them. And then E. A. Bunyard turned his rare ability to the Old Roses, and the result, charming, readable, and erudite, *Old Garden Roses,* appeared in 1936. This was the first book for over a hundred years which owed its inception to a deep-seated love for all the Old Roses. His life was prematurely ended, otherwise he would undoubtedly have corrected the several inaccuracies that are to be found in his book, but he gave new zest to the cause of Old Roses, and collected many varieties together. We of this generation owe much to his guidance. Since the Second World War the only publications on similar lines have been my own little booklets *Roses as Flowering Shrubs,* followed by *The Manual of Shrub Roses;* the latter ran to three editions. Many books on roses have appeared in recent years, some of them adding to our store of knowledge. The rose is at last, I believe, regaining its proper place, and when all its points are considered, it must certainly take a very high standing in our affections as a first-rate flowering shrub.

It is to my regret that a feeling of comparison between the old and the modern roses has crept repeatedly into these pages. It may be inferred that I have no use for the modern roses, but nothing could be further from the truth. To my mind the two types are not suitable for comparison. Modern roses are flowers *par excellence* for beds, providing colour throughout summer and autumn; they are also beautiful in the extreme when grown into large bushes and only lightly pruned. Their colours and scents are attractive, their shape and their poise appeal to all, and many good varieties of considerable stamina are on the market. It does, however, remain true that only in their less pruned state can they be called flowering shrubs in our present accepted sense of the word; more truly would they be described as small shrubby plants producing very finished florist's flowers. The Polyantha and Floribunda roses appeal in a different way, but have similar garden qualities.

It is encouraging to find that rose breeders of today are once again finding pleasure in fullpetalled roses of the old form, and are also producing varieties of purplish and pastel shades.

Never were comparisons more odious than between the old and the new in roses. There is room for both in our gardens, and the next section will present a considered case for the old groups.

APPRECIATION

La Tulipe est une fleur sans âme;
mais il semble que la rose et le lis en ait une.

Joubert

IT IS ONE THING to make botanical descriptions for plants, and quite another matter to convey to a gardener an image of a given plant. Let us be quite sure, therefore, that the right image is given for the contents of this section. For the dust jacket of his *The Art of Botanical Illustration* Wilfrid Blunt selected a painting by Johann Walther of Strasbourg, executed among many others for Count Johann of Nassau. It depicts the Austrian Brier, a striped Gallica, and some soft, purplish-pink Provence Roses. One shows a full, open flower with its serried ranks of imbricated petals, another the globular form of the half-open flower, and some buds show various stages of development. It is an excellent presentation of our subject, and is available for all to see in libraries catering for such books.

Considering them as a whole, I would say that the roses that are termed "Gallica" (*Rosa gallica*), "Damask" (*R. damascena*), "White" (*R. × alba*), "Provence" (*R. centifolia*), and "Moss" (*R. centifolia muscosa*) are forceful, stalwart shrubs usually from four to six feet in height, and from four to six feet in width in maturity. A few are of lax or untidy habit, or of open growth, but there is a decided shrubby similarity to be found among them. As a general rule they are prickly, the White Roses bearing a few firm, large prickles, while the Gallicas are at the other end of the scale, with the prickles absent or changed to bristles which rub off at a touch. Their leaves are of varying greens, thin and rough to the fingers, and a few bear small prickles on their leaf-stalks. The majority have glandular hairs on the stalk below the flowers and on the incipient hep, and it is these glandular hairs, often present also on the leaves, that provide one of their great attractions: a warm fragrance that stays on the hands for long after picking a bunch of flowers. This is one of the characters I should most like to see bred into our modern roses again.

The Old Roses contain all those colours found in their parent species—white through pale to dark pink and light crimson—together with a tendency to purple tones. Many of the most sumptuous of the purple-tinted varieties prove to be the most popular among the devotees of these plants. We have become so used to thinking of roses in terms of brilliant crimson, scarlet, salmon, pink, flame, orange, and yellow that we are apt to forget that these colours can be traced to the influence of three species only, while all the softer tones are natural to a far greater number of species. The exquisite colourings found in 'Charles de Mills', 'Cardinal de Richelieu', 'Belle de Crécy', and 'Tour de Malakoff'—violets, purples, mauves, magenta, and murrey, enlivened by pale and cerise pink and blush white—represent a searching of the florists after novelty. The whites and pinks had held the field for hundreds of years, but when seed-raising and other propagation came into vogue, these newer darker tones provided the perfect foil for the lighter colours while remaining all within a delightful, sympathetic range. Any of these roses blends well with the next, and all the colours are soft; some are muted, while others are radiant with life without being hard. Carnations and lilacs give us similar tones. Yet one so often reads or hears the words "a hard blue-pink"; disparagement is generally conveyed and inferred, but it seems incongruous to me that a blue-pink can be hard—at least, not among the roses. Their colours are certainly "hard" to use with our modern flaring flowers, but those in search of examples of floral colour grouping should make a pilgrimage to Kiftsgate Court and observe how the modern tones of 'Albertine' and even 'Orange Triumph' add telling point to the glorious borders devoted to pink and lavender and mauve, with the all-embracing softness of grey foliage.

Colour is, of course, only relative, and in the beholder's eye. But in studying a group such as this, or a bunch of plucked blooms, the harmonious softness of the colours, varying each with the day and the hour, is very apparent. The richly coloured varieties may display pink and magenta in cool weather, but the hot sun develops their violets and purples and gives them an incredible richness, enhanced by their velvety texture.

And their fragrance? Their fragrance is intense, intoxicating, and delicious. The scent of a sun-warmed Provence Rose, or a dew-cooled 'Maiden's Blush', is not surpassed for sweetness, although it may be equalled in its intensity, by flowers of other genera. The fragrance of typical varieties of each old group is distinct—one could not confuse the examples cited above even when blindfolded—but my senses have not yet found the means of conveying to my pen their qualities. This subtle distinction found between the groups has a relationship that was later fused by hybridization and is now misguidedly called "Damask." Poets and horticulturists alike have used "Damask" to denote richness in scent (as well as in texture), whereas a glance at the parentage of our modern roses will immediately prove that the Damask fragrance cannot really be detected in, for example, 'Crimson Glory' or 'Fragrant Cloud' at the expense of the Gallica or Provence scents. This glorious fragrance of the Old Roses comes in great part from *Rosa gallica,* but is enhanced by the infusion of the other species, notably by the heady perfume of the Musk Rose. The Musk (*R. moschata*) and its relatives and progeny, together with *R. rugosa,* are the species which in my experience float their fragrance on the air with the greatest abandon, sometimes for more than a hundred yards.

The Old Roses in their double forms are as a rule very well filled with petals, and their various modes of opening have resulted in certain terms being used in their descriptions. As with most other groups of garden hybrids and forms, such terms can be applied only to a few very distinct varieties.

During the unfolding of the petals many roses may pass from "cupped" to "globular"; they may then open with all the petals on one plane, when they are "compact." A fully open flower may reveal petals "imbricated" (piled one above the other), and then they are usually divided into "quarters." Often a number of the central petals are tucked so tightly into the receptacle that they cannot open, and thus form what I term a "button eye." Again, these button eyes may show a small green point in their centres, which is composed of abortive carpels. One rather concludes from remarks in old books that these green points were not approved; in coloured roses they may be disfiguring, but I always feel that in white roses such as 'Mme Hardy' and 'Mme Plantier' they give a delightful finish. Eventually many roses reflex, often almost into a ball, and in doing this their petals may have their edges rolled backwards. These old styles, carefully described and figured in *Les Plus Belles Roses au début du vingtième siècle,* are reproduced on page 17.

To review our findings, I think we can justly claim that in the Old Roses we find stalwart, thrifty shrubs, able to fend for themselves and bearing fairly good foliage; their flowers are borne in the utmost profusion at midsummer in colours from white through pink to violet, fragrant to an unbelievable degree, and showing a perfection of form evolved by skilled florists of the past; they thrive on a variety of soils and need little pruning.

Their faults, from a garden point of view, are that their flowers are mostly over by mid July; that some of them retain their dead petals long after they should have fallen; that some of them suffer from black spot in certain districts; and that their foliage in dry districts assumes a dusty appearance by August.

The first point we can readily forgive, considering the prodigality with which they produce their flowers at midsummer; the second is greatly obviated by pruning at the right time, namely, immediately after flowering; the third, black spot, scarcely impairs their strength or flowering capabilities, and is a common symptom of unhealthy conditions in all roses—careful attention to the plants' needs in the way of mulching and cultivation will help to rid the plants of this disfigurement; the poor late summer foliage, our last point, is unavoidable, but interplanting with suitable plants for later display will obviously help.

The shapes of Old Roses in the early years of the twentieth century. Reproduced from *Les Plus Belles Roses*.

Above left: A double flower with quartered arrangement of petals.
Above right: Semi-double cupped.
Below left: Double flower with reflexed petals, but in this drawing they are shown twisted as well.
Below right: Semi-double or double globular.

Beauty Observed

Roses, the garden's pride,
Are flowers for love and flowers for Kings,
In courts desiréd and Weddings.

Thomas Campion

OLD ROSES IN THE GARDEN

FROM EARLY SPRING onwards we watch our favourites appear; how keen we are to see the snowdrops, and to grow six or more varieties to prolong their flowering season; then the daffodils—what flower more expressly trumpets the coming of spring?—the tulips, giving off double energy when the sun's rays rebound from their richly-hued cups; and later the glistening crystalline irises; each new flower of the year more abundantly endowed than the last in colour and form. We pass, too, from the sudden awakening of *Forsythia* to the sweet fragrance of *Viburnum carlesii*, and before we are fully aware of it the great family of rhododendrons is upon us, imparting grandeur to the scene. The flowering cherries and crab-apples give way to May and *Laburnum*, and the whole horticultural world is ablaze with colour and fragrance. I await these arrivals every year with intense delight, but the coming of the rose is to me the very crown of the year. From the first delicate-flowered pale yellow species and Scots Roses that open, in company with the Cherokee and Banksian Roses on warm walls, to the last poignant autumn blooms, the rose gives unequalled beauty. There is a rose for every taste. Whether we are newly awakened to flowers and delight in the dazzling display of Floribundas, or the more exquisite blooms of the classy Hybrid Teas; or whether our senses have developed still further and embrace the perfect roses of a more refined and elegant age; or whether we go back to the exquisite grace and charm of the original species; there is, I repeat, a rose for every taste.

Roses have so much "fullness" about them; they are full of vigour if the most suitable kinds are planted and reasonably treated; they are full of contrast, their rounded flowers, sprinkled over the network of leaves, create a delightful effect; they are often full of petals, of a good texture of rich velvet or of shining silk; and they are full of scent. They are rich throughout in qualities which have been favourites with gardeners of all ages. Listen to M. Cochet-Cochet: "Le Rosier est de beaucoup le plus important de tous les arbustes cultivés pour l'ornement des jardins."

This paean of praise from a worthy French nurseryman may perhaps require a little qualification. Roses are certainly the favourite flowering shrubby plants of today, but with few

18

exceptions they cannot form the framework of a garden. Evergreens are needed for such positions. Roses are more suitable for foreground colour-work, the filling-in of bays between heavier material, the covering of stumps, hedgerows, and banks with their long trails, and for growing near to the eye and nose, that their beauties may easily reach the senses. Apart from their loss of leaves in winter the Rugosa Roses and the hybrid 'Nevada' are flowering shrubs of the heaviest calibre, and can be used in important positions governing the design of beds and borders. Most species are more airy, with a dainty refinement that I feel prompts one to place them well away from buildings. The modern and the old florist's roses are more suitable for use in conjunction with formality, whether it be of wall, path, or hedge. When the wall can be of grey Cotswold stone, or the hedge of a blend of holly and box and copper beech, the contrast is superb. A visit to Hidcote Manor, Gloucestershire will convince intending hedge-planters of the tapestry background that can be obtained from mixed hedges. For informal hedges the roses themselves present several varieties and species of great value.

It cannot be denied that a garden full of one thing can be boring to all but the ardent collector himself. While we are all entitled to do as we like with our gardens, I suggest a careful disposal of the Old Roses, so that the eye may not tire of their qualities in perspective. The Old Roses create a delightful pattern of flower and foliage at six yards' distance, but at a greater distance give a rather spotty effect, because of their small leaves and the regular dotting of flowers along the branches. I feel they very much need the foil of other foliage and the contrast of other flower shapes and styles. Particularly successful with these Old Roses are foxgloves—just the common wild type and the white, with a few of 'Sutton's Primrose' placed near the dark purple forms. Their spikes give the right contrast in form, and their colours blend happily. Also I like to use *Lilium candidum* and some of the daintier delphiniums in light colours, and the tall irises of the Orientalis section. The striking contrast of leaf and flower in these gives just the relief and uplift that is needed. Foliage of *Iris pallida* and *Sisyrinchium striatum*; *Eryngium giganteum*, the silvery-grey biennial 'Sea Holly'; sages, the ordinary culinary and the purple-leaved form; Hosta or plantain lily, of which the best is *Hosta sieboldiana*; *Stachys byzantina*, and *Santolina pinnata neapolitana* and *chamaecyparissus*—all are splendid subjects for underplanting and mixing with the old roses. The blatant yellow blooms of the *Santolina* or Cotton Lavender need never interfere with the colour scheme if the plants are clipped over in February. For bold corner-work, especially against paved paths, the Megasea saxifrages (*Bergenia*) provide the very best of materials, their big broad leathery leaves of dark green matching the stones' solidity.

These foliage plants can blend an otherwise jumbled mass of flowers and leaves into an harmonious and satisfying whole. The use of white flowers with the roses cannot be too strongly emphasized. For this purpose I have already mentioned foxgloves and *Iris orientalis*, and to them will add *Philadelphus* or Mock Orange. A great range of these is available, from small shrubs of two or three feet to giants up to fifteen feet, and the blend of their fragrance with that of the roses can be almost overwhelming on a still summer evening. A quantity of pinks—a seed-raised garden strain is the best, embracing all the tones that are found in the Highland Hybrids—'White Ladies' and others will provide the most ideal display at just the right time, and their fragrance again enters into the scheme. White flowers will intensify the purples and enrich the pink roses; pale lilac, such as may be obtained from *Campanula lactiflora*, will purify pink roses. Various contrasts, such as the clouds of greenish yellow stars and velvet leaves of *Alchemilla mollis* with 'Tuscany', will be found, and over them all a solid garden quality should reign. Flimsy annuals and ordinary daisy-flowers, so often the body of the average herbaceous border, may well be avoided.

It will be apparent that I like my Old Roses mixed with other plants, rather than arrayed in beds by themselves. They can be very pleasingly grown in this way, but the general blend of flower and foliage in a mixed border is to my mind more satisfying and appealing. In addition to creating a glorious picture at midsummer, many of the foliage plants will produce flowers earlier or later; a suitable grouping of spring bulbs, followed in late summer by galtonias (Summer Hyacinths), the hardy *Agapanthus campanulatus* and hybrids, and the free-flowering dwarf *Yucca flaccida* and *Y. filamentosa*, will provide interest through the year. Over my more stalwart roses I have just planted some of the small hardy *Clematis viticella* varieties. These can be cut to the ground every February and will provide a canopy of glorious purples, mauves, and whites to blend with fuchsias and agapanthuses in late July and August. With the Old Roses, therefore, may I suggest a blend of flowers and foliage to create a generous mixture and give colour and interest from April to October.

Rose Kingsley in *Roses and Rose-growing* (1908), sums up the matter very well:

> To my mind, the Cabbage, Moss, Gallica, and Damask Roses look most thoroughly in place in the old-fashioned mixed border along the walk in the kitchen garden, where they flower after wallflowers, daffodils, and polyanthus, with lilies and pinks, stocks and carnations, and all the delightful and fragrant odds and ends that, somehow, make it the spot in the whole garden to which all footsteps turn instinctively.

Further hints on the mixing of various plants with Old Roses will be found in my book *An English Rose Garden* (Michael Joseph, London, in association with The National Trust, 1991; issued in the United States as *The Art of Gardening with Roses*, Henry Holt and Company Inc., New York, 1991), which is lavishly illustrated.

OLD ROSES IN PICTURES

THE ROSE APPEARS in design and in pictures throughout the ages, as the principal and also as the incidental motif. In many instances the general feeling of a specific type of rose is portrayed in the old religious pictures, but otherwise it is not often that any definite species can be recognized until we come to the age when the beauty of flowers was considered individually, especially in the great upsurge of flower painting that occurred in the seventeenth and eighteenth centuries in the Low Countries.

The Dutch at this time were very much in the ascendant. With the defeat of the Armada in 1588, and the revolt of the Dutch under the Spanish yoke, the power of Spain was on the wane; England and Holland were competing for mastery of the seas. At home a strong national feeling was afoot and it is small wonder that the arts flourished under the benefit of Dutch freedom. The tulip boom is an indication of the enthusiasm of the Dutch for flowers at that time, and their paintings include many old favourite flowers. Tulips in fantastic stripes, roses, the Double Hyacinth, Double Opium Poppy, Peony, Ranunculus, Lily, Hibiscus, Crown Imperial, Hollyhock, together with fruits, insects, and birds' nests, were brought in to give variety and reality to the most magnificent pictures of their kind ever produced.

Hundreds of these old flower pieces are found all over the continent in museums, private collections, and in the hands of dealers, and there are no doubt many here and there in Great Britain. Several were in the Dutch and Flemish exhibitions at the Royal Academy in 1952, 1953, and 1954; the pictures exhibited were mainly painted in the seventeenth century, but in addition to these I was privileged to see the splendid collection (now in the Fitzwilliam Museum, Cambridge) belonging to Major The Hon. Henry R. Broughton, in which several eighteenth- and nineteenth-century works are included. It is obvious, however, that the seventeenth century saw the climax of this wonderful period of art.

In Holland Jan van Huysum (1682–1749) stands out as the creator of the most elaborate flower pieces. The transparency of the petals is exquisite to say the least, while a more extravagant statement is that trite but very true remark, "the flowers look so real that you feel as if you could pick them off the canvas." His work may be regarded as the highest achievement in a century of flower painting during which many famous names occur, among them being Jan Brueghel (1568–1625), who must be considered the earliest expert of this kind; Balthazar van der Ast (1590–1656); Ambrosius Bosschaert II (1612–45), Jan de Heem (1606–84), Jacob Marrell (1614–81), Simon Verelst (1644–1721), noted for his wonderful lighting effects and subdued colourings, Rachel Ruysch (1664–1750), Jacob van Walscapelle, who was producing pictures from 1667 to 1716, and Jan van Os (1744–1808).

In Flanders further great names are found, although national freedom was not attained until later; the widespread growth of the Renaissance, however, had obviously made itself felt. Roelandt Savery (1576–1639), Daniel Seghers (1590–1661), Jacob Jordaens (1593–1678), and Nicolaes Verendael (1640–91) are some names which are nearly as famous as the Dutch.

In his absorbing and exhaustive book, *The Art of Botanical Illustration*, Wilfrid Blunt tells us how, after van Huysum's death, Gerard van Spaendonck and others carried on the tradition, but never surpassed the great man's work, although the spark was rekindled in Spaendonck's pupil, Redouté.

No such other outpouring of floral art has recurred, although we have isolated artists producing exceptional work, such as Fantin-Latour (1836–1904). This celebrated Frenchman loved the rather squat arrangement of flowers in a bowl, the blooms closely pressed together, with a very natural softness pervading the whole. His was a soft and very sympathetic touch, and the early forms of Teas and Noisettes can be recognized in his roses, although I do not feel competent to name varieties. I am tempted to add that some of his flat, double, pale pink roses might well be 'Souvenir de la Malmaison', or even the rose we call 'Fantin-Latour' itself.

Apart from exhibitions, there are some fine examples of Dutch and Flemish art at the National Gallery, London; Fantin-Latour can be found there, and also at the Ashmolean Museum, Oxford; and for a summary or introduction the freely illustrated volume by Ralph Warner, *Dutch and Flemish Fruit and Flower Painters of the Seventeenth and Eighteenth Centuries*, may be recommended. I have also seen the illustrated volume *Flower Painting through the Centuries* by Colonel Maurice H. Grant. This is a delightful book, published in a limited edition, to record many pictures in Major Broughton's collection. The Ashmolean Museum at Oxford also has a splendid volume of illustrations of the pictures there: *A Catalogue of Dutch and Flemish Still-life Pictures in the Ashmolean Museum, Oxford*. There are without doubt other books to be seen, but during the limited time at my disposal I found the above the most helpful of those I have handled. While it is pleasant to see form and design in photogravure, one does, of course, need the original colour to enable one to appreciate the pictures to the full.

To return to the artists of the Low Countries, it seems to have been an accepted thing in those days only to paint certain types of flowers. There are, of course, many pictures with something unusual in them, but in general the same flowers occur again and again, and this applies also to roses.

Rosa centifolia is the favourite rose with them all, and there are many superlatively beautiful paintings of it; Verelst and Verendael among others have given their half-open blooms a living quality, while van Aelst alone, among the pictures I have seen, has shown the quartering of the fully open bloom. Bearing in mind the nodding grace of the half-open blooms which provides the receding centres with an added richness, it is not surprising that this was the first favourite among roses, and perhaps especially because it probably originated in Holland. In fact it is not only prominent in the old flower paintings, but is often the only flower to decorate a group of fruits, where it competes for pride of place with the amazingly transparent grapes and cherries which are depicted in an almost too lifelike freshness. Its leaves, too, are broad and broadly toothed, which gives further scope to the painter.

Van Huysum, Walscapelle, and others frequently included a large white rose, which from its similarity in shape and foliage I consider to be *Rosa centifolia* 'Unique Blanche'; but since according to all records this rose was not mentioned until 1778, this must be a wrong supposition. I have seen, however, what is undoubtedly an authentic portrait of this rose, by Arnoldus Bloemers, a celebrated Dutch painter of 1792–1844; another is a picture by J. C. Roedig (1751–1802). The flowers show very clearly the red tips of the petals, which are so often evident in sunny weather. There may have been another 'White Provence' rose earlier, but this is unlikely as it would almost certainly have been included in Redouté's portraits had it still been in cultivation. These Centifolia sports were, however, short-lived in those days when they were not widely spread in cultivation.

We have therefore to suppose that all the double white roses in these old pictures are none other than the 'Great Double White' Rose, *Rosa alba* 'Maxima'. In many instances the creamy colouring found in the centre of freshly opened blooms is carefully shown, while in others the flat, fully open flower is discarded for a shape nearer to *R. centifolia*.

I have only seen one rose in a flower group that might be *Rosa gallica*, in a painting by Marcellus, belonging to Major Broughton, and it appears to be an accurate portrayal of the form we know as *R. gallica officinalis*.

On the other hand *Rosa gallica* 'Versicolor' is obviously intended by some French artists in the same collection, namely Baptiste, Denysz, and Hardime—all, I believe, seventeenth-century painters—and also in a picture by Verelst.

An occasional *Rosa foetida* and its variety *bicolor* are found, unmistakable in their single flowers of intense colouring, but the most usual yellow rose is a fully double kind. This must inevitably be *R. hemisphaerica*, as the only other double yellow Old Rose, *R. foetida* 'Persiana' ('Persian Yellow'), was not introduced until 1837. A really good flower of this capricious variety can well have inspired the painters; it has a fine globular shape and intense sulphur yellow colouring. Here and there its shape has been made more globular still, thus representing a yellow Provence Rose of the painter's imagination. Van Huysum has some fine examples.

The double white Musk Rose (*Rosa moschata*) occurs in a few pictures; I remember pretty sprays of it by van Huysum and Verendael, and a portrait of 'de Meaux' is almost certain in a work of Jean François Bony (1760–1825).

A hundred years later, in the days of Redouté, a much wider selection of roses was portrayed; but we must remember that Redouté was deliberately figuring a collection of roses. At the same time it is remarkable that, spurred on by the beauty of the Provence Rose, artists did not search further for beauty from the Rose. The rich tones of 'Tuscany' and other purplish varieties were available, but possibly this colouring was not in fashion. Generally speaking, the flower groups painted by van Huysum and others verge towards the brilliant, red and yellow being favourites. In the rise of the arts and the success of men in those days, perhaps something more positive than the subdued tones of the Gallicas, for instance, was needed.

Looking again at a collection of these pictures, one is impressed by the rather artificial arrangement of many of the flowers. From the mixtures of spring and summer blooms in the same container it is obvious that the artist did not paint the arrangement as a whole; indeed the life of the flowers, could they even flower at one time together, would not permit such painstaking and time-absorbing work. Apart from this, many of the flowers have an appearance of individuality, as if they had been arranged on the canvas, having been copied separately from studies, and there is no doubt that this is the solution to the galaxies of blooms depicted. In this way I feel the flowers lived in the artists' minds as beautiful apotheoses of the originals, and we must therefore forgive them for including so few of our favourite Old Roses, and for confusing the issue here and there by exaggerating the shape or using the wrong foliage. They are after all 'Flower Pieces', not botanical studies, and their beauty will at all times enthrall the beholder.

OLD ROSES IN PARIS

I NEED HARDLY repeat that the home of our Old Roses is in France. With very few exceptions the names are in French, and a visit to the gardens around Paris provides one with much food for thought.

In England the Old Roses are being planted again because they fit in with the modern trend of shrub gardening. They are barely represented in our parks and national gardens, though enthusiasm is growing for them in the gardens of amateurs. In Paris exactly the opposite obtains. The amateurs have no interest in them whatever, but in two of the public gardens, really large collections are to be seen.

A visit to one of the great gardens of Paris such as Bagatelle or the Roseraie de l'Haÿ is a step back in history. The visitor is carried back at least ninety years by comparison with our own gardening. The very roses that are now being grown in England because they are free-growing flowering shrubs are, in Paris, carefully pruned down to be kept as very dwarf bushes. A dozen flowers to each plant is the result, instead of fifty or a hundred.

The rose gardens of the Roseraie de l'Haÿ and Bagatelle are laid out in geometrical designs with a scope and exactitude such as we do not dream of over here. As a general rule the paths are of carefully raked shingle, bordered by grass or box edging. The lines are impeccably correct, the edgings perfect, and the grading of the plants most carefully effected by pruning and training.

The beds inside the grass edges are inevitably of carefully tended soil, but the beds surrounded by box edging contain, surprisingly often, grass, which is mown by scythe or sickle; these grass beds may be three or four feet wide, and along the centre small earth beds are cut about one foot wide, each containing one little rose bush, pruned to two feet in height or less. A series of these little beds will be broken by a pillar rose or a standard—again with impeccable straightness of stem—and at frequent intervals arches span the paths.

At the Roseraie de l'Haÿ by far the most extensive collection is to be found. The centre-piece, midway between the offices and museum, is a small geometrical pond, surrounded by long beds of decorative shape containing fine modern roses and also such old Hybrid Perpetuals as 'Frau Karl Druschki' and 'Ulrich Brunner'. As a background there is the great pergola and central arbour, all of which is completely covered with the Wichuraiana variety 'Alexandre Girault'. This perfectly trained tableau of rich glossy green bespangled all over with the warm, rosy-red flowers is a demonstration of what these old Wichuraiana Roses will do. It is strange how they became neglected, owing to the rise of the *Rosa multiflora* × *wichuraiana* Ramblers such as 'Excelsa' and 'Dorothy Perkins'.

From this central focal point paths radiate at every angle, with arched allées in some directions, crossed and subdivided at every point by less important vistas, which frequently meet at an ornamental architectural feature such as a temple, an urn, or a seat. And on every side above and below the eye are roses—roses on short little bushes; roses swinging on ropes between pillars; standard roses of all heights with solid bushy heads, or weeping from a perfect umbrella top; roses over arches square or rounded. Everywhere are blossoms and scent, giving just so much beauty as the careful treatment and severe training will allow.

There are Hybrid Teas and Hybrid Perpetuals, Dwarf Polyanthas and Floribundas; Chinas and Teas, Noisettes and Bourbons; Wichuraiana and Multiflora Ramblers, Climbers and species, Rugosas and Sweet Briers, and many an obscure hybrid and form which does not fit in anywhere in particular.

Very modern varieties are planted in some of the beds, but generally speaking this is a panorama of rose history. A new planting of rose species is to be seen on the large lawn away from the rose garden, and many large established bushes of species and near hybrids are in the borders surrounding the rose garden proper.

One of the triangular plots formed by the arrangement of the paths has beds filled entirely with the Old Roses. The outer beds contain large alphabetical collections of Gallica, Moss, Provence, and Damask Roses, with large central beds given to displays of one variety. Many old favourites are grown, and also a number of varieties almost unknown over here. Particularly does this refer to the collection of twelve Portland Roses.

During the war these gardens obviously became gravely neglected, and many labels were misplaced or lost, but it is wonderful what peace and work will do, and I fully believe it will not be long before the Roseraie de l'Haÿ will once more be a great centre of rose culture. The collection is unique, and in addition to the plants themselves and the nineteenth-century design, there is the Rose Museum, and also the Malmaison border. In this as many as possible of the roses grown by the Empress Josephine are collected, and one can walk along seeing plate after plate of Redouté's immortal drawings, come to life.

At Bagatelle the French hold their trials of new roses. Unlike the Roseraie de l'Haÿ, this is a large public park with orangery, lake, and many fine specimen trees; a tunnel of box; a long wall thickly planted with climbing roses and clematises, and a charming small formal garden of irises. Here again, as at l'Haÿ, the main rose garden is laid out in severe geometrical lines, offset by an occasional statue, or a yew clipped to a perfect cone. The gravel paths are mostly bordered by box edging, and the beds are nearly all sown with grass. The green setting for the little rose beds in these areas is very appealing, but the work entailed must be unending. Apart from certain beds being given over to the new plants on trial, a fairly representative collection of older roses is also grown, arranged botanically, and with the various beds attractively ornamented by half-standards and tall weeping standards. Some fine old Bourbons like 'Duhamel Dumonceau' and 'Giuletta' are grown, and many Gallicas and Mosses. All are, however, pruned down to small bushes.

Around the geometrical beds are some species, and some rare shrubby roses such as the *Rosa macrophylla* hybrid 'Auguste Roussel'; towards the north the ground rises to a Japanese temple set among trees.

My visit to these gardens was well worth while. The superintendents were most helpful and abounding in courtesy. The nomenclature was at the time of my visit (early June 1953) rather disappointing, and only here and there did I find correct names for some of my own foundlings. The difficulties in getting these Old Roses named correctly are very great, but not insurmountable. Comparing living specimens of my own with the German collection from Sangerhausen, and then seeing them all over again in France, has enabled me to sift many of the names thoroughly. The test comes when all the old books agree on the colour of a variety, which may be just the opposite of the plant we grow!

We realize then that we are wrong, and the search begins again, starting from a totally different angle. By degrees, through comparison and elimination, order is being restored, and the numerous examples I have been able to give of coloured plates of the older varieties prove how many are definitely and correctly named.

OLD ROSES FOR THE HOUSE

THE TRUE OLD ROSES have one great advantage over the Bourbons and all subsequent races when it comes to cutting for the house, for removal of whole branches bearing many buds and flowers will not spoil the bush. Rather will it be a good method of pruning, for there is no second crop of flowers to lose.

Roses are not the best of flowers for cutting if lasting qualities be the criterion, but at rose-time I like to have roses indoors as well as in the garden, to revel for the six or eight weeks in rich colours and scents, to meet roses on the table at meal times, and to let their beauty register deeply in the mind. Just two or three blooms at a time in a small vase, picked when half or fully open, are best for a gradual deepening of acquaintance with these gracious flowers. The pale colours, the whites and pinks, can safely be picked in exquisite bud and be allowed to open in water, but to savour the full tones of the violet and murrey roses they need to open fully in the air, and be brought in just at their most spectacular best. Their rich colours do not develop properly in the shade of the room.

I shall never forget my first introduction to these roses in a cut state. It was during my visit to see Constance Spry's collection in Kent. Before being allowed into the garden I was taken into the house, and on an oval marble table a satin cloth of palest spring-green was spread. In the centre was an almost overwhelming bowl of the most exotic violet, lilac, purple, and murrey roses spilling over the edges on to the cloth. An indescribably rich contrast was given by the dusky tones of the velvety petals, and the shining satin cloth. A few buds of Moss Roses appeared here and there, adding a delicate touch to the gorgeous qualities of 'Tour de Malakoff', 'Charles de Mills', 'Cardinal de Richelieu', and other famous varieties.

Once again the uses of contrasting foliage need stressing, and *Alchemilla* and *Hosta* leaves can play a successful part with roses of purple tones. Many roses have most decorative leaves: *Rosa glauca* (*R. rubrifolia*)—greyish-green suffused with plum purple—comes at once to mind; some have very dainty foliage; while the Bourbon 'Mme Ernst Calvat' produces in late summer the most handsome plum-coloured young shoots. Nor must we forget the decorative qualities of the heps; a few of our old roses, such as *R. gallica officinalis*, the Damask 'Gloire de Guilan', and *R. alba* 'Semi-plena', are very ornamental, but the pride of place in this character is given without hesitation to *R. moyesii* and its relatives.

When cutting roses for indoor decoration, it is advisable to cut in the evening or early morning, and to hammer or slit up the bases of the stems, as with all hard-wooded subjects. They will then last for several days in water, filling the room with fragrance. "The air of June is velvet with her scent, the realm of June is splendid with her state."[*] How very true are these words.

---

[*] V. Sackville-West: *The Garden.*

3

Old Roses in Cultivation Today

THE GALLICA ROSES

Prick not your finger as you pluck it off,
Lest, bleeding, you do paint the white rose red,
And fall on my side so, against your will.

Shakespeare, *King Henry VI*

THESE ARE AT ONCE the most ancient, the most famous, and the best garden plants among the Old Roses. They are also the ancestors in part of most other Old Roses, and their delicious fragrance is carried down through all their descendants.

Several characters are noticeable not only in the oldest garden forms such as *Rosa gallica officinalis* and 'Tuscany', but also in some of the most sumptuous of the nineteenth-century productions. First, their almost thornless stems: just a few prickles are present, which rub off at a touch of the finger, and abundant harmless tiny bristles; second, their leaves are rough, neat, dark green, and often poised upwards, unlike the large drooping leaves of the Provence Roses, and the Damask's and White Rose's grey tones. The buds are round and blunt, and the calyx does not as a rule project far. The most important character from a garden point of view is the poise of the flower. Almost without exception they form compact bushes with the flowers well disposed and held aloft, erect, on firm stalks. They lose the charm of the nodding flower thereby, but gain immeasurably in general value. Their colours embrace all the pinks and mauves, purples, murrey tints, and light crimsons imaginable, but I have found no white variety. This is rather surprising. I believe all the purplish varieties listed under *R. centifolia* probably owe their intense colouring to this species. Striped sports are numerous.

In addition, Gallicas are extremely prone to suckering. I have seen groups which have run over several yards of ground, and the result is a floral sight of very high order. They thrive with the absolute minimum of attention and are not so dependent on good soils as the Damask, Provence, and Moss Roses, thriving in poor, gravelly, sandy, chalky, or shaley soils, and annually giving a display that cannot but meet with satisfaction. Their performance on good soils is correspondingly and infinitely better.

As low hedging plants many varieties can be clipped annually with shears at the end of January. The result of this clipping is the formation of hundreds of fairly uniform flowering shoots, each bearing from one to four flowers upturned to the sky. (Fuller details are in Chapter 12.)

Without any pruning at all they can go on year after year flowering well, as their new shoots replace the old from the base. Dead wood can be cut away in the spring. Alternatively, by a little careful removal of flowering wood in July, after the flowering is over, an encouragement is given to produce better new growths, and they richly deserve and benefit from this treatment.

The group as a whole is well represented in gardens, and nomenclature is less confused than in other groups. On the other hand, a surprising lack of dates accompanies entries in the old books. A glance through a collection of varieties leaves no doubt in one's mind, however, that in *Rosa gallica officinalis*, 'Versicolor', 'Conditorum', and 'Tuscany' we are looking at unsophisticated early cultivated forms. The breeders' later perfection is probably found in 'Belle de Crécy', 'Gloire de France', 'du Maître d'École', and 'Duc de Guiche', while the influence of other roses than Gallica is found in 'Agathe Incarnata', 'Cardinal Richelieu', 'Hippolyte', and 'Violacea'.

The Frankfort Rose

I was for years puzzled over the identity of a pair of roses which I grew as 'Empress Josephine' and 'Pope Pius IX', and it was not until I was once again turning over the pages of Redouté's wonderful paintings in the Lindley Library that I suddenly realized I was looking at these two roses under different names. In Vol. I, Plate 127, was *Rosa turbinata*, Rosier de Francfort, almost identical to my 'Empress Josephine' except that the artist had indicated a bristly or hairy hep (Plate 10). Rehder lists this as *R. francofurtana*; it is also figured in Lawrance, Plate 69, and Roessig, Plate 11; Clusius in 1583 records it. It is an interesting hybrid, probably between *R. cinnamomea* and *R. gallica*, which has occurred from time to time on the Continent, and was named in the first instance from a specimen found in Saxony. Its garden forms include the variety 'Agatha', which appears to be identical with my 'Pope Pius IX'. There was an old specimen of this on the outside of the west wall of the University Botanic Garden at Oxford. The botanical portraits of *R. francofurtana* in old books (apart from Redouté) record a much less double and impressive rose, such as that in Jacquin's *Plantarum rariorum horti Schoenbrunnensis*, Plate 415, which depicts a very prickly type.

It is a strange fact that my plants of the 'Empress Josephine', which came to me originally from The Hon. Robert James of Richmond, Yorkshire, bore the simple designation 'Miss Willmott's rose'. Although *Rosa francofurtana* is given a short description in her *The Genus Rosa*, Miss Willmott did not have a portrait made of it. I suspect, therefore, that she may not have connected this rose with her description. The only roses named after the Impératrice Joséphine are of much later raising: Hybrid Perpetual, China and Bourbon varieties.

The Frankfort Rose is easily recognized by being practically thornless, with smooth greygreen twigs; by the very large stipules as much as half an inch wide; by the smooth, thin, greyish leaves noticeably corrugated by the veins, like those of an elm or hornbeam; and by the great turbinate hep. This most clearly seen in its early state under the bud, and is broader and bigger than that of any other rose at that time. The flowers have a papery quality, of rich Tyrian rose, flushed with lilac and purple, and veined exquisitely all over with a deeper tone (Plate 9). Fragrance is rather lacking in 'Empress Josephine', but in the form 'Agatha' it is as delicious and strong as any; the flowers of this form are, however, smaller, less shapely, and of more purple tone. 'Agatha' is a vigorous grower up to six feet, while the type hybrid is a lowly bush slowly making an effective plant up to three or four feet.

Gallica Roses

gallica (the French Rose or Rose of Provins). The title Provins is also found in the old name, *Rosa provincialis*, but must not be confused with the Provence Rose, *R. centifolia*. The wild type is a sprawling shrub up to 3 feet or so, with abundant suckers in light soils. There are few prickles of any size. The leaves are smaller and more rounded and of a lighter green than the Red Rose of Lancaster (*R. gallica officinalis*), and the flowers are simple, of true wild rose beauty, daintily shaped, and clear pink in colour. The colour is less intense around the circlet of yellow stamens, and the scent from this wildling, though sweet, is far less strong than that of many of the doubles. For colonizing poor soils this rose has its value, and the heps are quite ornamental in early autumn, but otherwise it cannot be classed for garden value with its more effective and richly coloured forms.

Redouté, Vol. 2, Plate 63. *Rosa gallica pumila;* Rosier d'Amour. This plate appears to portray exactly the only wild form in my collection, received from The Hon. Robert James of Richmond, Yorkshire.

Jacquin, *Flora Austriaca*, Plate 198, shows a similar rose.

'Agathe Incarnata'. Prior to 1815. An ancient variety probably hybridized with a Damask Rose. It bears considerable affinity with *Rosa damascena* 'Petite Lisette' and 'Omar Khayyám'. The grey-green downy leaves point to the Damask group, as also the prickly shoots up to 4 feet in height. It is a compact plant and extremely free-flowering. The bunches of buds open quickly to flat round flowers, composed of quartered, quilled petals, with distinct button eyes. Pale pink of even tone. I found this rose in the garden of W. B. Hopkins at Hapton, Norwich, and also in that of Major Roger Hog at Kirkliston, East Lothian.

Redouté, Vol. 3, Plate 77.

There were many 'Agatha' varieties of *Rosa gallica,* and they had usually fully double small flowers.

'Alain Blanchard'. Vibert, France, 1839. An open prickly bush, which thereby indicates its possible Centifolia parentage, with mid green, rather unattractive foliage. In spite of the date given I suspect that this is probably a very old type; it has cupped, nearly single flowers, rich in crimson tone, effectively lit by the yellow stamens in the centre. Very soon after opening the petals develop murrey shading in a mottled pattern; lastly they become purple with a mottling of light crimson. This, 'Marbrée', 'La Maculée', and 'La plus belle des Ponctuées' are the four most attractive spotted varieties I have come across; 'Royale Marbrée' is an unpleasant little double flower of unimpressive shape and colour. 5 feet.

'Alain Blanchard Panachée'. I received this beautiful and unique rose from Mrs Riall of Dublin, and it would appear to be a definite sport or the original of 'Alain Blanchard', being identical in every particular except the pattern of its colour. Instead of being spotted, its purple tones are striped and pencilled on the rich magenta-crimson ground. On cool days both varieties are full of an indescribable richness greatly enhanced by their yellow centres. I have lost this variety.

'Alexandre Laquement'. An ancient name, whose description denoted a purplish rose, spotted with red. Our present rose of this name has flowers loosely cupped, of light crimson flushed with purple; the reverse of the petals is lighter. A lax bush with some prickles and bristles and smooth rounded heps. It is very free-flowering and deserves to be included despite the doubt of its correct naming. Fairly well scented. 3 to 4 feet.

'Ambroise Paré'. Vibert, France, 1846. A vigorous upright bush with some prickles and bristles, and good Gallica foliage. From reddish buds the flowers open to full, quartered blooms with reflexing petals; deep rose-pink, veined and flushed with purple. Scent fair. 4 feet. (Plate 7.)

'Anaïs Ségales'. Vibert, France, 1837. In the old French books this rose is generally described as a crimson variety of *Rosa centifolia*. The colour we need not take too seriously, as true crimson was non-existent among roses of this type. The prickly stems do denote a parentage other than true *R. gallica*, but otherwise I think it fits best here. It forms a pleasingly branched small bush up to 3 feet or so, and the leaves are to scale, neat and light green. It may well be described as one of the most beautifully shaped among the Gallicas; every petal is held in place, and neatly rolled back, displaying a flat, well-filled bloom with a green eye. The colour at first is a rich mauve crimson, fading to pale lilac-pink at the edges in maturity. Very free-flowering.

'Antonia d'Ormois'. Fresh green growths appear with the flowers, and the plant shows a diversity of shoots and foliage. The flowers are late, and their warm blush colour and shape resemble the exquisite Alba variety 'Maiden's Blush'; at first cupped and later reflexing and fading to blush white at the edges. Has not proved free-flowering. 5 to 6 feet.

'Assemblage de Beautés' ('Rouge Éblouissante'). France, 1823. A compact bush with very few real thorns, and rich green leaves which make a hard contrast to the startling, extremely vivid blooms. At first they are of intense cerise-crimson, later becoming flushed with purple, and the multitudes of small petals reflex into a ball, revealing a small green point in the middle of a hard button eye. It creates an amazing picture in flower, and makes an excellent contrast to some of the softer tones, such as 'Anaïs Ségales', and intensifies the purple and murrey tones of 'Tuscany' and others of that tint. This is the rose one finds labelled 'Ponceau' in some collections. "Poppy-coloured" is a slight exaggeration, but it is certainly a vivid piece of colour. 4 feet.

'Beau Narcisse'. Mielles, France. Tall erect growth with some prickles and bristles; dark green, acutely pointed leaves, rounded hispid heps. The relatively small flowers are in large clusters, very double, quartered, of light crimson-purple. The petals have paler reverses and white centres. Button eyes. 5 feet.

'Bellard'. Prior to 1857. Sometimes spelt 'Bellart'. The fresh green pointed leaves on bushes of good growth are decorated with densely petalled flowers, quartered and with button eyes, some showing a green pointel. They are of clear pink with perimeter of blush or even white. The heps are hispid. Good scent. 4 feet.

'Belle de Crécy'. Roeser, France, prior to 1848. One of my favourites among the Gallicas; in fact, I consider it supreme for its soft parma-violet colourings—supreme among all Old Roses—and for fragrance it is hard to beat. Unfortunately it is not of sturdy habit, but with a little support among other bushes it is admirable and will then attain 4 feet, and is only slightly armed. The leaves tone well in their dull leaden green with the colours of the flowers, and are neat and well poised. On first opening the flowers give little indication of their ultimate colour, being of intense cerise pink freckled and veined with mauve. On exposure, and particularly in hot weather, they quickly begin to turn to softest violet, eventually being almost entirely lavender grey, with purple and cerise tints here and there. A perfect flower, of which there are many, opens wide, with reflexing and flat petals, leaving a pronounced button eye. With white roses such as 'Mme Hardy' the contrast is exquisite. (Plate 5.)

'**Belle Isis**'. Parmentier, France, 1845. One of the shorter Gallicas, seldom attaining 4 feet. Neat little light-green leaves, coarsely toothed; this character and the prickly stems denote possible Centifolia parentage, together with the winged and elegant calyx, but the flowers and flower stalks are pure Gallica. It is the only Gallica I have found in which an almost flesh pink colouring is found; this tint remains in the centre of the slightly reflexing full flowers after their edges have turned nearly white. Fat round buds. A pretty little rose bringing a distinct tint to the group.

'**Belle Virginie**'. The bristly stems have few prickles, good leaves and glandular heps. Lots of flowers are held upright in clusters on the bushy vigorous branches. Cupped buds open to cupped flowers reflexing with age; at first they are warm pink flushed with lilac, fading to a paler tint. Good scent. 5 feet.

'**Bérénice**'. Vibert, France, 1818. Large, full, globular blooms, opening flat but somewhat cupped and quartered. Reminiscent of 'Belle de Crécy' and equally well scented. Rich crimson-purple, fading to magenta with purple veining. Long sepals and hispid hep. The growth is vigorous but lax. 5 feet.

'**Camaieux**'. Vibert, France, 1830. One of the most remarkable of all striped roses, but unfortunately not a strong grower. It makes quite a healthy bush up to 3 feet or so, with somewhat arching growth and few prickles, and fairly typical sage-green leaves. The changes of colour in the petals are arresting and fascinating. The flowers are only semidouble when compared with some varieties, and have loosely arranged petals, which gently recurve. At first the blush-white of the petals is heavily striped and splashed with light crimson, which quickly flushes with violet-purple. Later the purple fades to magenta and eventually, just before falling on the third or fourth day, one can enjoy the delicacy of pale lilac-grey stripes on a white ground. The perfect complement at that stage to 'Belle de Crécy' and 'Mme Hardy'.
Gibson, Plate 3.

'**Cardinal de Richelieu**'. Laffay, France, 1840. One of the most famous varieties, which has qualities all to itself. It makes one of the best bushes up to 4 or 5 feet, with shiny green wood and very few prickles, and smooth, dark green leaves. The fat round buds are almost pink on first unfolding, and a partly open bloom shows a dome of balled petals of coppery rosy-lilac surrounded by the opening reflexing petals of indescribably rich velvety-purple, paling to almost white at the base. Later, when practically all the petals have reflexed, with conspicuously rolled edges, the whole ball-like flower is of a rich dark purple quality with the sumptuous bloom of a dark grape. This is a rose which well repays the best cultivation, and its most admirable companions are found in 'Céleste' and 'Maiden's Blush'. Little fragrance. (Plate 6.)

'**Charles de Mills**'. A compact shrub which makes one of the best displays every year. It is nearly thornless and the leaves are neat and fairly typical. The shape of the flowers is unique. They are extremely full-petalled, and when partly open they appear to have been sliced off in the bud, so flat and regular is the cupped formation. Later the petals open out, eventually resembling an African Marigold—but with much more quality! At this fully-expanded ball-like stage a pale green cavity is noticeable in the centre; one can see right into the receptacle, there being no button eye. As for colour, anything from richest crimson-purple to dark lilac and wine shades may be found on any bloom at any time. This is rather a coarse bloom, but splendid when planted with strong pink varieties. 5 feet. Little fragrance.

Gibson, Plate 3.

'**Charles Quint**'. Moreau-Robert, France. Though a welcome addition to the striped roses, this unfortunately has rather poor foliage. The bushes are compact and upright. From brownish-red buds the flowers open to blush pink with lilac stripes; in hot weather they are quite pale. Expanded shape; little scent; small hispid heps. 3 feet.

'**Complicata**'. I have been unable to find this name in any book, but it is widely known on the Continent. It is perhaps a *Rosa canina* or *R. macrantha* hybrid, with strong arching branches reaching to 5 feet in height and as much across, well clothed in large, pointed, clear green leaves. The large blooms, as much as 5 inches wide, are single, of pure brilliant pink, paling to white around the circle of yellow stamens. This is without doubt one of the most strikingly beautiful of single pink roses, and is a good hearty plant. I like it mixed up with yellows such as 'Lawrence Johnston', the two being strong in colour and able to vie with one another. When established among other shrubs it will ramble into trees to the height of 10 feet.

Thomas, 1991, pages 34, 35.

'**Conditorum**'. Dieck. My plant came from the University Botanic Garden at Oxford. The rose used in Hungary for attar and preserving. Recorded in 1900, but it is undoubtedly a very old form, rather than the result of late selection, for it approximates *Rosa gallica Officinalis* and 'Tuscany' in many ways. It forms a bushy plant with loose tousled flowers, semi-double, of rich, magenta-crimson tone, slightly flushed and veined with purple in hot weather, and showing yellow stamens. 3 to 4 feet.

'**Cosimo Ridolfi**'. Vibert, France, 1842. A compact little bush; a true Gallica with neat soft green leaves and upstanding flowers, each a model of perfection. The fat reddish buds open to little circular, cupped flowers of a sombre old rose, rapidly becoming flushed with parma violet, showing cerise veins and a button eye. One of the most exquisitely fashioned of Old Roses. Synonym 'Cosimo Ridolphi'. 3 feet.

'**Cramoisi Picoté**'. Vibert, France, 1834. An erect grower up to 4 feet or so, with daintily poised, neat, small dark-green leaves, and a charming companion for small striped varieties such as 'Georges Vibert' and 'Pompon Panachée', to which it is obviously closely related. The small compact blooms are very double, mere pompons, crimson in the bud, opening to a softer tone, and retaining a picotee edge of crimson. A pretty little flower, giving a vivid effect.

'**d'Aguesseau**'. Vibert, France, 1832. The most brilliant red I have found among the Gallicas. A vigorous plant up to 4 or 5 feet with big foliage of typical Gallica form. The flowers are very full, and open quickly to flat, quartered blooms, sometimes with button eyes; the outer petals reflex and develop a vivid cerise-pink, leaving the intense cerise-scarlet in the centre.

Paul, Plate 3. A rather faded portrait.

'Daphne'. The low sprawling growth marks this as appropriate for planting over low walls and banks. Heps bristly. The flowers open and remain flat, not reflexing, of rich crimson-purple fading to soft lilac. Name without foundation.

'Duc de Guiche' ('Senat Romain'). Prévost, France, 1835. This is undoubtedly a more recent variety, with a sophisticated beauty and perfect petal formation, comparable with 'Mme Hardy' and 'Belle de Crécy'. Extra well-filled flowers, opening cupped and reflexing into a ball, with a handsome moment when the outer petals are reflexed, leaving the centre cupped. The colour is intense crimson-magenta, minutely yet densely veined with purple in hot weather. It has a green eye, and is often quartered. 4 to 5 feet.

'Duchesse d'Angoulême' (the Wax Rose). Vibert, France, 1836. "*A pétales minces et transparents,*" as Max Singer so aptly puts it. This has indeed a delicacy which one does not expect among Gallicas; possibly *Rosa centifolia* has again been the refining influence, although the smooth, light green leaves, green smooth wood, and few prickles do not indicate this. It will grow to about 3 feet, but its growth is always arching and nodding—the flowers nod very much, and it is thus admirable as a standard. The shell-like transparent petals are pale blush-pink, tipped with crimson from the well-stained bud, giving a globular, exquisitely formed flower of very soft colouring.
Phillips and Rix, Plate 51.
Thomas, 1991, page 74.

'Duchesse de Buccleugh'. Robert, France, 1846. A robust shrub, almost thornless, with rich, green, luxuriant foliage, nearly as handsome as that of 'La Ville de Bruxelles'. It is one of the last to come into flower, and the first blooms are sometimes badly shaped. The flowers are exceptionally large, cupped, but opening quite flat, quartered, and with a button eye and tiny green centre. The intense magenta-pink, with crimson tones, fades slightly at the edges. 5 to 6 feet.

'Duchesse de Montebello'. Laffay, France. This is a charmer and cannot be omitted, although it does not appear to qualify for this name by which it is so well known. One can cut sprays a yard long from the lax bushes of free growth, and the neat greyish leaves provide just the right greenery for the sweet little blooms of clear blush-pink. It flowers early in the season, and makes a delightful picture when its sprays grow through one of the large purple-flowered varieties. 5 feet.

'du Maître d'École'. Although there is a French village called La Maître École, where Messrs Pajotin-Chédane used to grow a wonderful collection of the older roses, I like to think of this as the schoolmaster's favourite. Messrs Pajotin disclaim any connection with this rose. It is a practically thornless bush up to 3 or 4 feet, with good foliage. The growths are stout, but arch under the weight of the exceptionally large blooms, up to 5 inches across, and very double; from round reddish buds with long calyx lobes they open flat, later reflexing, often quartered, and with pronounced button eyes. A small green point is in the centre. The colouring is very soft, deep old rose, giving way to lilac-pink, with delicate mauve and coppery shadings. One of the great flowers of old days.

'Emilie Verachter'. Parmentier, France. A small upright bush with small leaves, large stipules and few prickles. Smooth rounded heps. Clear bright pink, full of quartered petals with green pointel. Little scent.

'Empress Josephine'. See "The Frankfort Rose," page 27.

'**Fleurs de Pelletier**'. Crimson-purple to deep lilac-pink with greyish shadows; full, flat flowers, quartered, showing stamens. A short bush with erect flowers, small prickles and bristles, heps glandular. A striking bush when in flower, with sharply pointed leaves. Good scent. 4 feet.

'**Fornarina**'. Vetillard, France, 1826. Synonym 'Belle Flore'. An unusual rose of erect and bushy growth, few prickles, and mid-green leaves. The flowers are particularly well and freely presented. The reddish buds open to muddled blooms with petals reflexed at the edges. There is a strong, rich, Tyrian pink in the centre of the flower, but pale tints develop around the circumference, the whole being mottled and spotted with blush. A poor bloom, but an effective bushy plant. 4 feet.

'**Georges Vibert**'. Robert, France, 1853. An erect-growing small bush up to 3 or 4 feet, with numerous small leaves, neatly poised, in dark green, on somewhat prickly shoots. The flowers are not large, although their narrow petals, opening flat and showing a green centre point, have a carnation-like charm in their neatly striped array. The blush-pink and dark crimson-pink stripes fade to paler tones. It is prettily quilled and quartered. It sometimes reverts to a uniform purplish tint.

'**Gloire de France**'. 1828. I had grown this beautiful form for many years before being sent it under the name of 'Fanny Bias' by Will Tillotson of Watsonville, California. The old French descriptions of either name would apply. It is a low-growing variety, covered with wonderfully double flowers, so filled with neat reflexing petals as to make a large pompon. The colour is a warm lilac-rose, the centre retaining its tone while the circumference rapidly fades to lilac-white. A pretty shrub up to 4 feet, and full of charm.

'**Henri Foucquier**'. 1811. This was received, like 'Fornarina', 'Nestor', and 'Marie Louise', from Will Tillotson of Watsonville, California. It has a rather procumbent habit, and is almost thornless; the flowers are large, very rounded, composed of many small petals, of rich uniform pink, reflexing and fading to lilac-pink. Button eye. 4 feet.

'**Hippolyte**'. A vigorous shrub, practically thornless, with neat small leaves, reaching some 5 or 6 feet. The long sprays bear beautiful flat little flowers, like rosettes, smooth-petalled, reflexing almost to a ball, with button eyes. An occasional cerise petal, or one of dove-grey, lights the many others, which are generally of soft violet. Not a typical Gallica.

'**Ipsilanté**'. 1821. William Paul speaks very highly of this rose, and it certainly produces some most handsome blooms. It is a vigorous plant up to 4 or 5 feet, with good foliage and wide flat blooms, quartered and quilled, of palest lilac-pink.

'**Jenny Duval**'. This has proved to be synonymous with 'Président de Sèze', q.v.

'**La Maculée**'. Dupont, France. Good upright growth. Brown stalks to the flowers, held above dark green leaves. The flowers are soft crimson-lilac passing to lilac-pink, veined or flecked with purple and with button eyes. Rounded hispid heps and good scent. 4 feet.

'**La plus belle des Ponctuées**'. It cannot be claimed that a spotting of pale pink on a rich pink ground can create a flower of any special beauty, although it may be interesting to examine. But this variety is fortunately blessed with a very vigorous constitution, and makes a fine shrub of luxuriant greenery, amid which the pink flowers shine in contrast. They are loose-petalled with muddled centres. Essentially a plant for garden effect. 6 feet.

'Louis Philippe'. The leaves are noticeably more rounded than most; glandular heps and few prickles. A variety with intense crimson-purple flowers with lighter edges to the petals, quartered, and with small green pointel. Vigorous, arching growth and good scent. 4 feet.

'Marcel Bourgouin'. Corboeuf, France, 1899. An old type of Gallica, nearly allied to 'Conditorum' and 'Tuscany' with loose semi-double flowers of dark purple velvet; the muddled centres show the lighter pink-toned reverses of the petals. Unfortunately in some seasons the flowers do not develop their full colour, and remain a flat magenta, but when at their best on good soils they are astonishingly sumptuous and richly coloured. Bushes of small growth to 3 feet, with dark green leaves. I have grown this variety under many names, including 'Belle des Jardins' and 'Le Jacobin'.

'Mazeppa'. Prior to 1848. A fine large bush with extra good large foliage. Heps rounded and hispid. The flowers are among the largest and most handsome, of full dark crimson-pink fading paler at the edges; they have large button eyes, reflexed, rolled and quartered petals. Fairly good scent. 5 feet.

'Nanette'. Few prickles grow on the upright stems reaching to 3 feet or so, otherwise it is a typical Gallica with good, small leaves, somewhat shiny. All the flowers are borne on stout stalks; they are small but of intense colouring. The vivid crimson petals are veined and streaked heavily, especially towards the centre of each, with purple, presenting a very rich effect when fully expanded. The colour becomes lighter on fading, but at all times the striping is evident.

'Nestor'. Prior to 1846. Fresh green foliage. The half-open blooms are cupped and the lilac-pink petals guard a heart of intense rosy-magenta. The quartering is very beautiful later, when mauve and grey shadows predominate. Few prickles. An extremely handsome rose. 4 feet.

'Nouveau Vulcain'. A large free-flowering bush with bristles and a few prickles; heps rounded, glandular. Distinctly Gallica leaves. The flowers are shapely and full, expanding flat with broad outer petals, of rich crimson heavily flushed and veined with purple. Sweet scent. 4 to 5 feet.

officinalis (*Rosa gallica maxima*). Sometimes called 'Splendens', this renowned rose is also known by the confusing name 'Red Damask', although it is obviously of pure Gallica development, and has given us the sport 'Rosa Mundi'. It is the Apothecary's Rose, and is also probably the Red Rose of Lancaster. A much-branched bush, of strong suckering proclivities when on its own roots, bearing abundant dark green, well-poised, acute foliage. Few prickles. The flowers do not open until the season is well advanced, and then create a most arresting display for some weeks, being held well aloft, over the bushes. They are semi-double, of light crimson, lit with yellow stamens. It is referred to in Prince's *Manual of Roses* (New York, 1846—a book closely following Rivers) as being much cultivated in Surrey for the druggists. It is probably the oldest cultivated form of *R. gallica*, and is right in the forefront of good garden shrubs, and very telling in the landscape. For a full explanation of the confusion over the name 'Red Damask', see Chapter 13. 4 feet.
Kingsley, facing page 40. Described as *Rosa gallica*, Red Damask (the Apothecary's Rose).
Bunyard, Plate 25. Bunyard elsewhere refers erroneously to this, the Apothecary's Rose, being fully double.

Redouté, Vol. 1, Plate 73. Le Rosier de Provins ordinaire.

Roessig, Plate 17. *Rosa gallica duplex*, Le Rosier de France semi-double.

Andrews, Plate 45. Officinal or French Red Rose. Fanciful.

Lawrance, Plate 16. *Rosa officinalis.*

Donnaud, Plate 14. Too dark.

Duhamel, Vol. 7, Plate 8.

Komlosy. *Rosa damascena rubra.* Poor.

'Ohl'. Vibert, France, 1830. Good dark foliage on a strong bush. The flowers are fully double, of dark crimson flushed with violet around the circumference. Very sweetly scented. 4 feet by 3 feet.

'Parvifolia'. The 'Pompon de Burgogne' is another favourite old miniature, also known as *Rosa burgundica* and 'Pompon de St François'. Perhaps figured by Tabernaemontanus in 1590. It no doubt occurred as a mutation. This is usually listed as a sport of *R. centifolia*, but I feel sure it must be of *R. gallica* derivation. The growths have few prickles, and are very erect and densely covered with dark, grey-green, acute leaves, a fastigiate mass of growth, setting off the tight rosette flowers, which are of dark Tyrian pink suffused with claret and purple, with paler centres. I have two distinct forms of this, one much more vigorous and larger in all its parts than the other. 3 to 5 feet.

Willmott, Plate 120.

Lawrance, Plate 44.

Roessig, Plate 4. Le Rosier de Bourgogne, *Rosa Burgundiaca.*

Redouté, Vol. 3, Plate 107. *Rosa Pomponiana.* There is no doubt about this figure, but it is somewhat confusing to find that Thory makes this rose synonymous with 'Le Petit de St François', 'Le Pompon de Reims' (Remensis), 'Le Rosier de Meaux' (Meldensis), 'Le Petit Provins Violet', 'Le Rosier de Champagne'. He was evidently in error here, as Miss Willmott points out. I have been unable to determine whether the title 'Pompon de St François' should refer to this rose or to 'de Meaux'; one author states that it belongs to *R. arvensis!*

Botanical Register, Vol. 6, Plate 452.

Andrews, Plate 56. *Rosa parvifolia.*

'Perle des Panachées' ('Cottage Maid'). 1845. Another of the 'Georges Vibert' family; this has light green leaves, small growth, with coppery foliage on the young shoots. The flowers are only semi-double, of rather loose shape, almost white with scattered pencillings of crimson, sometimes accompanied by a larger flake of colour. 3 feet.

'Petite Orléannaise'. A vigorous bush up to 5 feet, bearing many neat flat pink blooms with button centres. Rather too large a bush for the size of its flowers, which are individually perfect.

'Pompon Panachée'. The very small leaves on wiry erect branches recall 'Georges Vibert' in their shape, poise, and colour. Every short side-shoot bears one or two small double blooms striped with dark pink on a *cream* ground. It is the only striped variety that I have seen with this cream colouring on opening; it fades later to pale pink and white. An admirable companion for 'Cramoisi Picoté' or a contrast to some strong-coloured large flower like the Bourbon 'Prince Charles'. 4 feet. May be synonymous with 'Pompon', raised in 1856.

'Président de Sèze'. Prior to 1836. 'Mme Hébert'. One of the most remarkable of the two-toned, fully double Gallica roses. A bloom just fully open presents a combination of intense dark magenta-crimson in the centre and lilac-white around the circumference. The sudden change from the one to the other in the confines of the one flower is very striking. Even a fully open flower with its beautifully rolled petals still retains rich colouring in the centre, which is muddled and slightly quartered. The buds are soft pink and very beautiful. Altogether one of the "great" Gallicas, and a good sturdy bush with broad foliage. 4 to 5 feet.

'Royale Marbrée'. Erect vigorous shrub up to 4 or 5 feet. Shapely buds, opening cupped, later quite flat, quartered, and reflexing to a ball with rolled petals. Violet-crimson at first, later intense crimson-pink spotted with pink. Not of great garden value, and a poor flower.

'Sissinghurst Castle'. Ancient Gallica found by The Hon. V. Sackville-West at Sissinghurst, where it had held its own for many years among the brambles and nettles. It now grows, freely suckering, in a long bed, reaching 2 or 3 feet in height, and showing its semi-double flowers well above the plentiful, neat, pointed leaves. Few thorns. The rich plum-coloured petals have light magenta-crimson edges and are flecked with a similar tint, while their reverses are soft magenta-pink, and very telling in the half-open flowers. Golden stamens. I have been unable to find the suggested name 'Rose des Maures' in any old French book. 3 to 4 feet. (Drawing 1.)

'Sterckmanns'. Vibert, France, 1847. A good large bush with good foliage; rather late coming into flower. Prickles mostly small. Very full, handsome, flat flowers, quartered and with green pointel; rich dark pink fading to lilac pink. Very good. 5 feet. (Plate 8.)

'Sultane Favorite'. According to old French books this should be a small purplish rose. My present plant is far and away the most vigorous of the Gallica hybrids—a tall, swaying, leafy bush with abundant flowers in large upright trusses; they are small, cupped, double, quartered, clear pink fading paler. Sweet scent. Up to 20 flowers in a truss. Excellent for cutting long sprays. 5 to 6 feet.

'Surpasse Tout'. Prior to 1832. Vigorous, with distinct Gallica foliage, this variety is a good grower. The fat buds open slightly cupped, revealing a brilliant rosy crimson, passing to a vivid cerise-pink colouring. The petals reflex around a large button centre, and are delicately veined with a darker shade. A handsome rose. 4 to 5 feet.
Thomas, 1991, page 50.

'Tricolore' ('Reine Marguerite'). *c.* 1840. The stems bear some mixed prickles while the foliage is good, of Gallica type. The flowers are borne in small clusters or singly, cupped at first and later reflexed, vivid, rich magenta-crimson, quickly flushing with purple at the edges. A small white stripe is noticeable in the centre of each petal, thereby earning its name. 4 feet.
Thomas, 1991, page 138.

'Tricolore de Flandres'. Van Houtte, Belgium, 1846. Closely resembles 'Camaieux' at first glance, but it is proving a little more vigorous, with rather smoother leaves; the flowers have more petals and they are more distinctly reflexed and rolled. The striping is heavier and narrower, and the colour is a definite magenta-purple, with less of the rosy tint. A very desirable variety. Delightful as a contrast to the rich purples of 'Hippolyte' or 'Tuscany'.

It occasionally sports to the dark tone, presumably the original colouring, without the white stripes. 3 to 4 feet.
Komlosy. A good portrait.
Revue Horticole, 1847, Fig. 3. Poor colour.
Journal des Roses, Octobre 1881. Unrecognizable.
Flore des Serres, Vol. 11, Plate 155. Unrecognizable.

'Tuscany' (The Old Velvet Rose). One of the very best garden plants among the Gallicas, extremely effective in the colour and presentation of the flowers, but not quite so intensely fragrant as some. It will reach 4½ feet in good conditions, but is usually 3 to 4 feet. The small dark green leaves are well folded and curved, and the flowers are semi-double with rather flat petals, of intense dark murrey-purple, assuming maroon-violet tints, and offset in their richness by the yellow stamens. I think this is one of the older types of Gallicas; it bids fair to remain a favourite as long as any, being of such stalwart and bushy growth and thrifty on its own roots, when it will sucker freely.
Botanical Register, Vol. 6, page 448.
Andrews, Plate 43. *Rosa centifolia subnigra.*

'Tuscany Superb'. Correctly, 'Superb Tuscany'. Described by Paul in 1848. Of equally good growth to the original 'Tuscany', this has broader leaves and much larger flowers. They are extremely handsome, flat, and well filled, and make a better garden effect than 'Tuscany', but the doubling of the blooms results in fewer stamens, and in consequence some of the contrast of colour is lost. 4 feet. (Plate 4.)
Beales, Plate, page 165.

'Van Artevelde'. Narrow, rather folded light green leaves borne on a good bush, with prickles and bristles. Dark red buds emerging from viscous heps opening to clear crimson-purple flushed with slate and lilac, fading paler. Green pointel, surrounded by a cupped and quartered array of petals. Good scent. 3 to 4 feet.

'Versicolor' ('Rosa Mundi', *Rosa gallica* 'Variegata'). Recorded in the early seventeenth century. This, the most popular of the Old Roses, and found with 'Maiden's Blush' in many an old garden, is the most vivid of the striped roses, and cannot fail to arrest attention wherever it is planted. It is capable of making as brilliant a display as any other flowering shrub. It is a sport from *R. gallica officinalis,* and has the same admirable growth, few prickles, and good foliage; the same excellent presentation of its flowers, held well aloft, of light crimson splashed and striped with palest pink. The few petals are lit with yellow stamens and the astonishing display lasts well. Of first-class garden value. This rose has been frequently confused with the pink-and-white 'York and Lancaster', whose growth, leaves, and floral shape and colouring are completely distinct.

I think it can be said without reserve that this rose and its parent, *Rosa gallica officinalis,* are two of the most valuable hardy flowering shrubs for brilliant effect that are available for general planting today. Their floral shape is, happily, insufficiently formal to preclude them from association with species shrubs, but just sufficiently double to give them ease of entry into more sophisticated plantings. 4 feet.

Sir Thomas Hanmer in his *Garden Book* of 1659 states that it occurred, as a sport in Norfolk, "a few years since."
'Rosa Mundi', a name possibly signifying 'Rose-mouth' (Andrews, 1805).
Bunyard, Plate 23.

Lawrance, Plate 13.

Roessig, Plate 14. Rosier d'Yorck et de Lancastre, *Rosa versicolor.* The colouring of the flower shows that *R. gallica* 'Versicolor' was depicted, not *R. damascena* 'Versicolor'.

Andrews, Plate 46. *Rosa gallica variegata.*

Redouté, Vol. I, Plate 135.

'Violacea' ('La Belle Sultane', 'Gallica Maheka', 'Cumberland'). A difficult rose to place, both in a book and in a garden. It has undoubtedly many Gallica characters, but its vigorous arching growth up to 6 feet presents a problem. The stems are nearly smooth, and the leaves neatly rounded and drooping, suggesting a Damask inheritance; it has an early though rather short flowering season, but when in full flower presents a glorious burst of colour from its almost single blooms. At first they are rich deep crimson, rapidly assuming violet flushes, but the bases of the petals remain nearly white around the yellow stamens. It seems to be an old type of rose, with some of the characters found in 'Alain Blanchard'. The winged calyx suggests Centifolia influence. It is best grouped behind some such variety as 'Complicata' over which it can sprawl and create a mixed colour effect.

Keays, facing page 36.

Redouté, Vol. 3, Plate 78.

Willmott, Plate facing page 359. Described as *Rosa provincialis* and synonymous with *Rosa gallica officinalis* of Redouté! Two entirely distinct roses. This plate agrees with Redouté's.

Roessig, Plate 16. Le rosier semi-double velouté, *Rosa holosericea duplex.* This seems to have rather more petals than my specimen.

'Vivid' (sometimes called *Rosa gallica phoenicea,* 'Rose de Normandie'). Paul, U.K., 1853. A hybrid rose of great vigour, with prickly stems reaching to 6 feet, and shining leaves; probably related to the Centifolias. The flowers are very double, opening from dark crimson buds to vivid magenta-crimson, with a hint of cerise. Very well filled with petals reflexing to a flat circle, and becoming flushed with magenta in hot weather. Rather upsetting among the Gallicas, and best with such companions as 'Zigeunerknabe' and 'Adam Messerich', two newer Bourbon Roses. I have never felt that this rose was a real Gallica, and Jean Muraour of Mougins informed me that it was classed as a Hybrid Bourbon.

'Ypsilanté'. See 'Ipsilanté'.

THE DAMASK ROSES

And here I prophesy,—this brawl today
Grown to this faction, in the Temple garden,
Shall send, between the red rose and the white,
A thousand souls to death and deadly night.

Shakespeare, *King Henry VI*

THE DAMASK ROSES have proved the most elusive and most diverse of all these old types. There were fewer Damasks to be found in old gardens and their nomenclature has been, and still is, the most puzzling. This is partly because they comprise so many different types, which is not remarkable when we consider their probable parentage, so fascinatingly indicated by Dr Hurst in Chapter 13. It always strikes me as strange that some hybrids inclining more towards *Rosa moschata* have not been found. In view of this mixed parentage it is very difficult to fix on a particular rose as a type of the group; some of them are open and prickly like the Centifolias, while others incline to the Gallicas. *Rosa phoenicea*, one of the parents of the Summer Damasks, is not an imposing plant, but sprawling, with prickly wood and small single white flowers. Its characters are scarcely noticeable in its hybrids at first sight. The more compact Damasks show obvious Gallica affinity, but all the distinct Damasks do have a soft pubescence on the upper surface of their leaves; this is specially evident in 'Leda', 'Omar Khayyám', 'Petite Lisette', 'Quatre Saisons', and 'Versicolor'.

It is safe, therefore, to think of the Damasks as having downy grey foliage, with rather prickly wood and, in many instances, rather weak flower stalks. This is a character of the York and Lancaster Rose. In addition, the receptacle or hep is usually attenuated, by no means globose as in *Rosa gallica*, and the flowers are frequently borne in long bunches. Especially may this be noted in *R. damascena* 'Versicolor', 'Ispahan', and 'Celsiana'.

The Autumn Damasks were to me unknown until suddenly the rather poor 'Perpetual White Moss' sported to a pink, mossless rose. This gave me the clue and I realized I had had *Rosa damascena semperflorens* (*bifera*), the 'Quatre Saisons' Rose, for some years without knowing what it was. From that moment the White Mosses also fell into their places in my mind. (Plate 14.)

Dr Hurst's notes regarding the 'Scarlet Four Seasons' are of great use here, for they point to the probable origin of the race of Portland Roses. These are bushy roses, probably not exceeding 4 feet in height, and have one character which is very peculiar. In my own mind I always think of it as "high-shouldered": the blooms have very short stalks or "necks," and sit tightly upon a rosette or "shoulder" of leaves. They are mostly compact, quartered flowers, full-petalled, and keep on pushing up fresh flowering shoots through the season. (Plate 13.)

Once seen, these roses are unmistakable, and bear a remarkable resemblance to the Perpetual Moss Rose 'Mousseline'. In fact, this resemblance, and the finding of two similar Mosses at the Roseraie de l'Haÿ ('Marie Leczinska' and 'Mélanie Valdor', both raised in 1865), quite forcibly prove that the Autumn Damask Rose has played some part in the formation of the Mosses. The hard, almost woody moss of 'Quatre Saisons Blanc Mousseux' is undoubtedly encountered again in 'Mousseline' and 'Comtesse de Murinais'. The soft moss of *Rosa centifolia* 'Muscosa' is very different to the touch.

In cultivation the Summer Damasks need the same good attention as the Provence Roses; the same good soil and pruning. Their twiggy pieces should be removed early after flowering, and the long, strong shoots shortened by one-third in the winter. The Autumn Damasks, Perpetual Mosses, and the Portland Roses will only produce a really good succession of flowers provided they are pruned rather like Hybrid Tea Roses in December or January.

The 'Kazanlik' rose, too, had been a mystery to me for many years. I had received no fewer than three distinct roses under this name: one was a Gallica, one turned out to be 'Ispahan', and a third was identical with another rose I had been given labelled 'Professeur Émile Perrot'. This proved to be the real rose from Kazanlik, *Rosa damascena* 'Trigintipetala', the rose grown in greater quantity than any other in Bulgaria for the production of "attar." It is a similar type to York and Lancaster, *R. damascena* 'Versicolor', with spindly growth up to 6 feet or so, soft light green leaves, and rather small flowers, loosely double, of soft pink. In spite of its name this rose, over here at least, seldom has as many as thirty petals.

Through the kindness of Professor V. M. Staicov of the Bulgarian State Agricultural Institute for the Investigation of Medical and Aromatic Plants, who kindly sent me both herbarium specimens and, later, living material of the roses grown at Kazanlik, I have been able to elucidate the matter. The varieties are:

Rosa damascena. This appears to be almost if not quite identical with my R. damascena 'Trigintipetala'.

Rosa alba, with various numbers of petals. One is liable to get variation of this kind when raising R. alba 'Semi-plena' from seed.

'Stambulska' and 'Trendaphil', which I have so far been unable to identify with anything in this country.

Rosa rugosa 'Roseraie de l'Haÿ'. This variety is only on trial at Kazanlik and has not been used for industrial purposes.

Much further information about the rose fields and industry in Bulgaria will be found in "Fragrance," Chapter 12.

Miss Willmott's plate of Rosa damascena is, to me, unrecognizable.

The Summer Damasks

'Blush Damask'. Frequently labelled 'Blush Gallica'. I have a suspicion it may be a hybrid with a Scots Brier; it is certainly not a typical Damask. It forms a large, very twiggy bush, in time as much as 6 feet high and wide, bearing neat dark leaves, and is well covered in June with multitudes of nodding blooms. They are dark lilac-pink when half open, reflexing into a ball, lilac-white at the edges. A favourite of Gertrude Jekyll's; it grew well in her sandy soil, but has a rather short flowering season.
Bunyard, Plate 30.

'Botzaris'. A very pleasing little rose, probably owing its whiteness and distinct fragrance to Rosa alba; the hep is not of true Damask shape. Very double, opening flat, creamy white, even lemon-white in the centre, quartered and with button eye.

'Catherine Ghislaine'. A bushy variety with small prickles and bristles. Small light green leaves and typical narrow, hispid Damask hep. The flowers are blush-pink on opening, turning to creamy white, with muddled centres. Warmly scented. Good autumn crop. 3 to 4 feet.

'Celsiana'. Prior to 1750. A very beautiful rose, and it was a great pleasure to find it figured in Redouté after having grown it for years under the erroneous and misleading name 'Incarnata Maxima', which is only another way of saying 'Great Maiden's Blush'. With this rose it has, of course, no connection. 'Celsiana' is a graceful shrub with attractive light green leaves, smooth and greyish. The flowers are borne in typical clusters, and are wide and open, semi-double, revealing bright yellow stamens in the centre. When first open they are of a warm, light pink, fading later to blush. They are at all times extremely beautiful, in a loose informal way, with silky and folded petals. 4 to 5 feet.
Redouté, Vol. 2, Plate 53.
Gibson, Plate 4.

'Coralie'. A fine, arching shrub with somewhat prickly stems growing to about 4 feet, bearing small greyish leaves. The cupped blooms are of soft, warm pink, with rolled petals fading at the edges to blush. An attractive colour scheme.

'Gloire de Guilan'. Hilling, U.K., 1949. A most attractive sprawling shrub up to 3 or 4 feet, with fresh green leaves and small curved prickles. The cupped blooms soon open flat, being quartered, and with some petals remaining folded, in a particularly clear and beautiful pink. In the Caspian provinces of Iran, whence it was brought and named by Nancy Lindsay, this rose is used for making attar of roses.

'Ispahan' ('Rose d'Isfahan'). Also known as 'Pompon des Princes'. This is one of the first Old Roses to open and one of the last to finish, and creates a brilliant display for the whole period. It is a fine bushy, upright shrub, up to 5 feet or so, and extremely free-flowering in clusters, although its small rather shiny leaves suggest other parentage than pure Damask. Neat buds, and exquisite half-open blooms, reflexing loosely later, and at all times a clear and pretty pink. 'Ispahan' has possibly the longest flowering period of the Summer Damasks.

'La Ville de Bruxelles'. Vibert, France, 1849. A fine luxuriant shrub, with notably long and large leaves, well shaped and poised, and of clear light green. The flowers are among the largest of the Old Roses, and when fully open reflex at the edges from a large convex centre massed with short petals, with a button eye. The clear rich pink is constant. The individual flowering spray is of high quality, but the weight of the blooms tends to send the flowers downwards among the leaves—its only fault. 5 feet.

'Leda' (Painted Damask). Originated in England. This rose has certain qualities all of its own, particularly its luxuriant *dark* green rounded foliage and red-brown buds, which look bruised and battered, showing the colour of the petals long before they open. When the flower opens to an iridescent milky white just suffused with blush, the external red tones develop to crimson, remaining on the extremities of the outer petals, and giving the reason for its popular name. Most flowers have a pronounced button eye, and are well filled with petals, which reflex into almost a ball. 3 feet.
Smith, *The Florist's Museum,* page 113. Poor.
Gibson, Plate 4.

'Leda', pink form. There is little doubt that this is a sport from the above variety, or it may be that the Painted Damask arose from this pink type. They are identical apart from colour; in this form the colour is a soft uniform rosy-pink, darker in the bud, and again very fragrant. This form was apparently better known on the Continent, while the Painted Damask was more grown in Britain.

'Léon Lecomte'. A big strong bush with good, smooth leaden-green foliage. This points to Damask parentage, but the hep is rounded. The flowers are of rich warm pink fading paler and showing darker veins. Sweet scent. 5 to 6 feet.

'Mme Hardy'. Hardy, France, 1832. This rose, one of the most superlatively beautiful of the old white varieties, and having few peers among the coloured varieties, is not a pure Damask, but probably owes some of its beauty and vigour to *Rosa centifolia.* The bush is sturdy, up to 5 or 6 feet on good soils, with a variety of prickles and broad mid-green leaves showing little connection with the Damask Roses. The clusters of flowers do, however, show this affinity, while the perfect shape of the blooms is found again only in some of the Gallica Roses. There is just a suspicion of flesh pink in the half-open buds, emerging from their long calyces, and the flowers open cupped, rapidly becoming flat, the outer petals reflexing in a most beautiful manner, leaving the centre almost concave, of pure white, with a small green eye. 'Mme Hardy' was one of Dean Hole's favourites, with a reservation: "a true white, and a well-formed Rose, but alas! 'green-eyed' like 'jealousy'—envious, it may be, of Mme Zoutman, who, though not of such a clear complexion, is free from ocular infirmities." Personally I think the green eye is an additional charm. A bunch of these roses with some 'Belle de Crécy' among them gives to me the most satisfying complement imaginable. Both have exquisite form, and are sumptuous and ravishing. Paul mentions in 1848 that this one variety would suffice to make M. Hardy's name famous. What true words! This variety is still unsurpassed by any rose.

Bunyard, Plate 14. *Rosa centifolia alba.*

Bunyard in *New Flora and Silva*, Vol. 2, Fig. 1. *Rosa centifolia alba.*

Journal des Roses, Août 1880. Rather gross.

Komlosy. The plate obviously refers to the rose 'Mme Plantier'.

'Mme Zöetmans'. Moreau, France, 1836. The flowers are very much like those of the Gallica 'Duchesse de Montebello', but are much paler; they quickly fade almost to white with a faint blush centre, and are full-petalled with button eyes. The leaves are of fresh green, as opposed to those of the 'Duchesse de Montebello', which are grey-green. Early flowering. Graceful and free, growing to 4 feet. This has proved a first-rate variety.

Thomas, 1991, page 63.

'Marie Louise'. Grown at Malmaison in 1811. This rose has one of the most sumptuous flowers of the group. It forms a rather procumbent shrub, not only on account of its lax growth, but also because the flowers are so large and heavy. To lift up the leafy sprays and look steadily at the fully open blooms is a revelation—just another achievement of the rose. They carry no special promise in their buds but, when fully open, the uniform mauve-pink flowers are extremely full-petalled, reflexing into a ball, with large outer petals and pronounced button eye. 4 feet.

'Oeillet Parfait'. Foulard, France, 1841. It is important to remember that the other rose of this name was a striped Gallica. This variety probably owes its compact habit to *Rosa gallica*, but may suitably be grouped here for convenience. The uniform, rounded, small leaves are of soft green, covering a 3 to 4 foot compact twiggy bush with mixed prickles. Flowers in clusters of two or three, opening flat and very densely packed with shell-like petals from round fat buds, borne on stiff stalks. Later they reflex into almost a ball, being of rich, warm pink, fading slightly paler. I have found this rose under the name of 'Tour d'Auvergne'.

'Omar Khayyám'. An interesting, true Damask Rose, which has been propagated from Edward Fitzgerald's grave at Boulge, Suffolk, where it was originally planted in 1893, having been brought as seed from Omar Khayyám's grave at Nashipur. Light green wood and dark prickles and thorns; leaves small, downy, pale green. The flowers are not large but show a distinctive formation, having a pronounced button eye and folded and quartered petals, in soft light pink. Long sepals. 3 feet.

Phillips and Rix, Plate 53.

'Petite Lisette'. Vibert, France, 1817. This charming miniature variety has a few small prickles and green wood, and bears distinctly downy greyish foliage, small, rounded, and coarsely toothed. It is this cool colour which is so pleasant a complement to the clear blush pink of the neat flat circular flowers, perfectly formed, and well filled with folded petals, radiating from a pronounced button eye. 4 feet. At times I am tempted to think this is an original type of Damask Rose; it is closely related to 'Omar Khayyám', and also to the hybrid *Rosa gallica* 'Agathe Incarnata'.

'Rubrotincta' ('Hebe's Lip', 'Margined Hip', or 'Reine Blanche'). This hybrid of unknown origin makes a pretty picture when in flower and has much charm. Fresh green, coarsely toothed leaves make a good background to the cupped semi-double flowers of creamy-white, edged with rosy-crimson. The buds are particularly beautiful. It has a rather short flowering season. 4 feet.

Willmott, Plate facing page 375.

'St Nicholas'. Hilling, U.K., 1950. This very beautiful rose appeared spontaneously in the garden whose name it bears, owned by The Hon. Robert James at Richmond, Yorkshire. It forms a sturdy, erect bush with hooked prickles and good, dark-green foliage. The flowers are semi-double, of warm, rich pink, paler in the centre around the circle of golden stamens. It is no less beautiful when the petals open flat and the flower becomes paler all over, and the autumn heps are very showy. 4 to 5 feet.

Beales, Plate page 189.

'Versicolor' (York and Lancaster). A typical tall-growing Damask with the usual mixed prickles, green wood, and downy grey-green leaves of light tint. They are beautifully poised. On good soil and in cool conditions, as at Hidcote Manor, Chipping Campden, Gloucestershire, this rose can be very beautiful, the clusters of long-stalked flowers spraying outward, in blush white and light pink, over the soft foliage. They are loosely double, and not particularly shapely, but may be entirely of the paler or the darker colour, or flaked one with the other, or distinctly parti-coloured. They are never splashed and striped as in 'Rosa Mundi'. The impression given by Redouté is by no means exaggerated; it can be a fine rose when well grown. Interesting; raised prior to 1629. Possibly this is the rose which played so prominent a part in the "brawl . . . in the Temple Garden," between Yorkists and Lancastrians, which factions apparently later adopted *Rosa alba* 'Maxima' and *R. gallica officinalis* as their emblems. 5 feet.

Andrews, Plate 48. *Rosa damascena variegata.* Shows excellent variations.

Bunyard, Plate 23.

Lawrance, Plate 10.

Miller, Plate 221. *Rosa praenestina variegata plena.* York and Lancaster.

Redouté, Vol. I, Plate 137. *Rosa damascena variegata.*

Roessig, Plate 14. This portrait is of *Rosa gallica* 'Versicolor'.

Roessig, Plate 33. A true portrait. Rose d'Yorck et de Lancastre. *Rosa nubeculis rubentibus suffusa alba,* York et Lancaster dicta.

The Autumn Damasks

'Quatre Saisons' (*Rosa damascena semperflorens*) (*R. gallica* × *R. moschata*). A form of Autumn Damask Rose which I received from gardens in England and Ireland, and also from California, but without a reliable name. In 1950 I was interested to find it as a sport on my 'Perpetual White Moss' (Damask) (q.v., page 44), and this same sport was recorded also at Shrewsbury by Miss Murrell in the same year. It is notable not for the shape of its blooms but for its propensity for putting forth flowers from June to October; for its particularly pale yellowish-grey-green leaves, prolifically borne; and for its rich fragrance and long sepals. The flowers open from shapely buds, and are of clear pink, deeper in the centres, with few crumpled petals, sometimes quartered. Since this sported back from the 'Perpetual White Moss' it is presumably the original Autumn Damask. 5 feet. Also called the 'Alexandrian

Rose'. (Plate 15; fig. 2)

    Gordon Rowley finds the often used name *Rosa damascena bifera* invalid and proposes the use of the earlier *R. damascena semperflorens*.

Jamain et Forney, Plate 31. Rose de Quatre Saisons.

Roessig, Plate 8. Le Rosier de tous les mois. *Rosa omnium calendarum.*

Roessig, Plate 42. *Rosa bifera rosea persiana.* A good portrait.

Lawrance, Plate 5. *Rosa damascena*, the red monthly rose.

Revue Horticole, 1865, page 151. 'Quatre Saisons Ordinaire et Q. S. Mousseux Blanche ou Rose de Thionville'; growing on the same branch.

  Duhamel, Vol. 7, Plate 9. *Rosa damascena semperflorens.* Le Rosier de tous les mois.

  Andrews, Plate 51. *Rosa saepeflorens alba.* The White-flowered Monthly Rose.

'Quatre Saisons Blanc'. Mrs Gwen Fagan has recently sent me this rarity from South Africa, but I do not know from which rose it sported.

'Quatre Saisons Blanc Mousseux' (*Rosa damascena semperflorens* 'Albo-muscosa'). 1835. The 'Perpetual White Moss', 'Rosier de Thionville'. This interesting variety, recorded in *Production et Fixation des Variétés dans les végétaux* by E. A. Carrière, is undoubtedly a sport from the rose listed here as 'Quatre Saisons', since it reverted to that variety in 1950 and has done so many times since (Plate 28). The foliage is of the same colour, but bears mossy excrescences on the upper surface of the leaves on vigorous shoots. The moss on leaf, stem, and bud is brownish-green and the flowers are white with a faint blush tint on opening. Shapely buds, but poor flowers. Erect, vigorous, bushy growth. June to October. 5 feet.

Paul, Plate 10.

Carrière, as above.

Komlosy. The figure referring to *Rosa alba menstrualis* 'Mousseuse Blanche' does not match this rose so well as one captioned 'Princesse Adélaïde'.

The Portland Damasks

In Chapter 13 Dr Hurst gives a few brief notes on the Portland Rose, an historic link, presumably, between the Autumn Damask and the Hybrid Perpetuals. For some years I grew a rose given to me by Mrs L. Fleischmann, and also by Captain Robert Berkeley, and eventually identified it with Redouté's portrait of Le Rosier de Portland. It makes a low bush with erect twiggy growth, armed with small bristly prickles, and bright green foliage, rather reminiscent of the Red Rose of Lancaster. The flowers have the "high-shouldered" arrangement of the Autumn Damask, and are borne in erect clusters at the top of every shoot. They are bright crimson, rather darker and more intense than the Red Rose of Lancaster, but smaller, and semi-double, in shallow cup formation, opening well and showing yellow stamens. In hot dry seasons there is a long pause without flowers after the first flush at midsummer, but with good cultivation and reasonable moisture there are further flowers in autumn. It is not strongly scented. Heps long, of true Damask shape.

    This is *Rosa paestana*, or 'Scarlet Four Seasons'; its colour distinguishes it from all the old Autumn Damask variants, which were never more than pink.

Redouté, Vol. I, Plate 109. *Rosa damascena coccinea.*

Andrews, Plate 49.

Lawrance, Plate 5.

The Portland Roses received from the Roseraie de l'Haÿ some years ago have proved to be sturdy, erect plants and very free-flowering throughout summer and autumn. Some did not survive and are apparently no longer available in the Paris garden, but the following have grown well. Bearing the rich Old Rose fragrance, they are doubly welcome.

'**Arthur de Sansal**'. Cochet, France, 1855. A hybrid of 'Géant des Batailles'. A satisfactory, sturdy plant with good dark green leaves. Erect growth, producing large heads of small blooms in late summer, but in more or less continuous production from midsummer. Pretty buds of darkest murrey-purple. They open completely flat, very full of short petals, quartered, and of deepest murrey-purple-crimson, fading to a rich grape-purple. 3 feet.

'**Blanc de Vibert**'. Vibert, France, 1847. Yellowish-green soft Damask foliage. The cupped, double blooms are pure white with a hint of lemon in the centre when half open, becoming pure white. 3 feet.

'**Comte de Chambord**'. 1860. This is a first-class plant, always in flower, of sturdy erect growth, well clothed in pointed light green leaves. Most beautiful buds, opening with rolled petals to a densely filled flat flower, sometimes quartered, but always with reflexed and rolled petals around the edge. A full rich pink with lilac tones. Intense fragrance. 4 feet. (Plate 16.)
Gibson, Plate 17.
Thomas, 1991, pages 102, 103.

'**Delambre**'. Robert et Moreau, France, 1863. Good bush with few prickles and fresh green leaves. The flowers are in plentiful clusters, densely filled with petals, quartered, of deep lilac-pink, fading paler. Very sweet scent. Short hep. 3 to 4 feet.

'**Indigo**'. Laffay, France, c. 1830. Good upright bushes with smooth long leaves of good green. Hispid hep. This is a spectacular rich, dark purple rose, with expanded shape, flushed with dark crimson, showing a few stamens, and occasionally a white streak or mark. Warm scent. Fine display at midsummer and again later. Perhaps the richest and most effective of dark purple roses. 4 feet. (Plate 18.)

'**Jacques Cartier**'. Moreau-Robert, France, 1868. Compact and erect habit with plenty of light-green leaves, the terminal leaflet exceptionally long and narrow. Sepals often pronouncedly foliaceous. Flowers very full, quartered and with button eyes. Very fragrant. 5 feet.
   This rose has been, and still is, confused with 'Marquise Bocella' of 1842. However, since this is described as "very pale," "flesh coloured," and a dwarf grower, I feel confident that 'Jacques Cartier' is the correct name.
Gibson, Plate 17.
Thomas, 1991, pages 130, 131.

'**Mabel Morrison**'. According to *Modern Roses V,* this occurred as a sport from 'Baroness Rothschild' in 1878, which had been a sport from 'Souvenir de la Reine d'Angleterre'. It is classed as a Hybrid Perpetual. 'Baroness Rothschild' bore large flowers in, as far as I remember, the typical Hybrid Perpetual shape and style. 'Mabel Morrison', on the other hand, seems to have reverted to some inherent Damask influence, and conforms most nearly to the characters of the Portland Roses, having greyish leaves, neat erect habit, and the typical Damask hep and "high-shouldered" habit. The flowers are comparatively small for a Hybrid Perpetual, cupped, of a delicate blush pink becoming white, deliciously fra-

grant and borne recurrently. This rose was sent to me by Dorothy Stemler, who carried
on so well the collection started by my old friend Will Tillotson in California, and I regard
it as a most valuable addition to the all-too-few Portland Roses.

'**Marbrée**'. Robert et Moreau, France, 1858. A good, bushy plant well furnished with long-
pointed leaves. The narrow heps are covered with glandular hairs. The flowers are borne
in clustered heads, erect, from the tops of the branches, light crimson speckled with pale
pink. Attar scent. Good autumn crop. A valuable shrub. 4 feet. (Plate 17.)

'**Panachée de Lyon**'. Dubreuil, France, 1895. This is recorded as a sport from the 'Rose du
Roi'. It has small, pleated, flat flowers variously flaked or particoloured with pink and
crimson. An erect rather spindly plant; recurrent, but not prolific. 3 feet.

'**Pergolèse**'. Robert et Moreau, France, 1860. Mid-green leaves, a small upright plant. Comparatively small flowers opening quite flat and filled with petals, quartered, and often with
a green pointel in the centre. Bright cerise to magenta purple when freshly open, taking on
dark purple shadings like 'Duc de Guiche'. 4 feet.

'**Rembrandt**'. Moreau-Robert, France, 1883. A rather thin but erect bush. Sepals and heps
smooth, the latter narrow, leaves rounded. Small flowers, full-petalled, of light crimson,
veined and blotched. Good scent and autumn crop. 4 to 5 feet.

'**Sultane Favorite**'. A very vigorous, tall, arching shrub with light green small leaves. Some
prickles; smooth rounded hep. Very free flowering, rather late in the season, with rather
small, round, densely packed flowers of light pink, prettily quartered.

    Two varieties I have not seen are depicted in Jamain et Forney, 'Madame Boll' (Plate 39)
and 'Marie de St Jean' (Plate 36). The latter in particular shows the "high-shouldered"
character of this group. 'Madame Boll' is also in the *Revue Horticole* for 1865, page 111.

Two roses introduced by Miss Lindsay prior to the Second World War probably fit into the
Damask group. They are 'Rose de Resht' and 'Rose d'Hivers'. The former may well prove to
be the true 'Rose du Roi', as suggested by Brent Dickerson in *The Garden* for January 1989.
The proof would be to acquire 'Panachée de Lyon', which is reported to be a striped sport
from it. I found this unstable, liable to sport wholly to the red colouring, but could not compare it with the Resht Rose at the time, and have now lost it.

    Miss Lindsay's second rose is a twiggy little bush that may be a hybrid with *Rosa × alba.*
The flowers are dainty and of perfect shape, the large outer petals nearly white, guarding the
flesh-pink central petals, which remain in bud for several days. The flowers are said to retain
their shape when dried.

    I have it on good authority that the 'Rose de Resht' was in cultivation at Castle Howard,
Yorkshire, prior to the Second World War.

    Thomas, 1991, page 86.

THE WHITE ROSES

Then, for the truth and plainness of the case,
I pluck this pale and maiden blossom here,
Giving my verdict on the white rose side.

Shakespeare, King Henry VI

In Dr Hurst's notes (Chapter 13) it will be seen that he regards this race of roses as derived probably from *Rosa damascena* and a form of *R. canina*. It is a good thought that *R. canina*, the wild Dog Brier of Britain and other European countries, had a part in forming what must surely be the most beautiful and refined of all the old groups of roses. (Plate 19.) Many artists have undoubtedly preferred *R. centifolia* to the White Roses, but to me there is no rose scent so pure and refreshingly delicious as that of the 'Maiden's Blush'; no half-open bloom so lovely as 'Céleste', nor foliage so good; and few rose forms can compete with 'Mme Legras' or 'Koenigin von Danemarck'. The White Roses are supreme over all the other old races in vigour, longevity, foliage, delicacy of colour (for they embrace some exquisite pink varieties), and purity of scent.

Journeying through the countryside, whether it be in Cornwall or the home counties, west of the Marches or north of the Border, or over the sea to the Emerald Isle or France, certain White Roses, especially the 'Great Double White' and 'Maiden's Blush', are encountered wherever a rose has been suffered to live through the decades. Frequently they are remnants of plantings of a hundred years ago, so strong and self-reliant are they. Though sometimes crowded against a villa wall, their root run restricted by concrete pavement, or overhung by trees, or in a damp, cold, north-country garden, they thrive and flower well annually. They appear to resist all diseases.

They are one of the few types of roses that can actually be recommended for north walls; *Rosa alba* 'Maxima', 'Semi-plena', and 'Maiden's Blush' give a splendid display when trained up walls and allowed to spray outward. The smallest is the compact 'Jeanne d'Arc'; 'Félicité Parmentier', 'Koenigin von Danemarck', and 'Pompon Parfait' reach up taller, with 'Maxima' and 'Great Maiden's Blush' overtopping them. 'Blush Hip' is even taller and, with *R.* 'Complicata', and the two Moss Roses 'Jeanne de Montfort' and 'William Lobb', may be trained over hedges or into small trees, thence to grow downwards, with their flowers hanging at nose level.

Comparing them with other wild roses one notices at once their affinity with *Rosa canina*. The growth, prickles, bark, leaves, and heps of what we may term the typical form (*R. alba* 'Semi-Plena') are all very reminiscent of that species. But the habit is considerably more upright, and has earned them the name of "Tree Roses." These roses have an ideal habit for a flowering shrub. They are not so prone to run as the Gallicas, although they do spread slowly in that way when on their own roots, or when grafted plants are set rather deeper than usual. They make strong stems from the base, infrequently set with stout prickles on smooth green wood. As the years pass the stem branches more and more at the top, gradually arching over with the weight of growth, and after five or six years a well-built thicket of twigs is the result. Some of this should be removed each year after flowering, to encourage more basal growth, and this pruning will suffice when the bushes are grown as flowering shrubs in the mixed borders.

On the other hand, I feel that of all the Old Roses these Alba varieties respond best to close pruning. This should be done in December or January, spurring back all the previous year's small wood to three inches or so, and leaving the long shoots at one-third of their length. A superb display of good blooms all well set in even array will result.

Alba Roses blend happily with almost any colour; typically white or pink, their tone is clearer than that of many Old Roses, and they lack the purple shadings of many Gallicas and Centifolias. Their adoption as flowering shrubs for general use is therefore to be encouraged, and their grey-green foliage lends enchantment to almost any scheme. Only recently a friend decided on *Rosa alba* 'Maxima' to form a hedge in a white garden, where the foliage, after the flowering season is over, will help towards that coolness fostered by cream and other off-white tints.

Alba Roses

'À Feuilles de Chanvre' (*Rosa cannabina*). The Hemp-leaved rose. This is a very old form, having almost thornless stems and narrow, long, grey-green leaves supposedly like that of its namesake. The flowers are small, white, and semi-double. 3 feet or thereabouts.
Redouté, Vol. 2, Plate 47. *Rosa alba cimbaefolia*, Le Rosier Blanc à feuilles de chanvre.

'Belle Amour'. I was given this rose by Miss Lindsay, who had found it in an old convent at Elboeuf. In 1959 I saw it on the front of a cottage in Norfolk: an old-established bush, which must have been there for many years. This is the only rose in the old groups with such a salmon tone to its pink colouring; I suspect the influence of 'Ayrshire Splendens', an old rambler of the *Rosa arvensis* group, for not only is it precisely the same colour, but it has also the scent of myrrh; 'Ayrshire Splendens' was also known as the Myrrh-scented Rose. This theory may seem far-fetched, but it has a parallel in that the only other Old Rose with a hint of salmon—'Belle Isis'—has been used as a parent by David Austin; one of the seedlings, with a pronounced myrrh scent, we had the honour of naming after Constance Spry. It is, I feel, a fitting tribute to one whose help and influence were so great in re-establishing the Old Roses in popular favour.

'Blush Hip'. Raised about 1840, this rose was described as extremely vigorous, and a rose received from Mrs Salmon at Dublin conforms to the description. I use the name with some hesitancy, as it seems to be but another of the 'Maiden's Blush' derivatives; however, a scandent Alba variety growing to 12 feet is something of a novelty to us nowadays. The coarsely toothed leaves suggest *Rosa centifolia* as a possible parent, although otherwise it has most of the characters of 'Maiden's Blush'. The cherry-red buds open to well-formed, fully double flowers, of soft pink, with a button centre and green eye. William Paul, in 1848, mentions this rose as "new."

'Céleste' ('Celestial'). A delightful rose of true Alba qualities. Apart from the 'Rose d'Amour' and the earliest polyanthas like 'Mlle Cécile Brunner' I know of no rose of such exquisite charm when unfurling its petals. The bland clarity of tone in the flowers is unparalleled among pink roses. They are semi-double, of a pure, soft uniform pink, showing rich tones in the depths of the bud. As if this were not attraction enough the plant has leaves of particularly grey tint, the perfect foil to its floral colour, and the bush itself is strong and up-standing to about 6 feet. The flowers are enhanced by a circlet of yellow stamens, and as Gertrude Jekyll observes, it is "a rose of wonderful beauty when the bud is half opened." Redouté, following earlier authors, decided that certain characters warranted placing this rose among the Damasks, and calls it *Rosa damascena* 'Aurora', Le Rosier Aurore Poniatowska. It was apparently of Dutch origin at the end of the eighteenth century, and had become by no means common at the time of his writing. Redouté also mentions Rose Celestis, but refers this to 'Maiden's Blush'.

I had been told that 'Céleste' was the rose plucked by the men of the Suffolk Regiment after the battle of Minden; in fact, I have heard it called the Minden Rose. Being curious about the matter I wrote to the Officer Commanding, The Suffolk Regiment, and he kindly furnished me with the following particulars:

> ... Actually, no rose is figured in the badge of the Suffolk Regiment; but the following is an extract from *History of the 12th (The Suffolk) Regiment:*

1759
The Wearing of Roses

> All battalions of the Suffolk Regiment, on Minden Day (1st August), wear roses in their head-dress, and in the event of a parade, the colours and drums are similarly decked in honour of that memorable victory.
>
> As regards the selection of the rose, the accepted story is that when the regiment was following up the retreating French troops, they passed through a rose garden, and each man plucked a rose, which he fastened to his head-dress. Roses are also worn by the regiment on the Sovereign's birthday, in accordance with long-established custom.
>
> From the above it would appear that no one particular rose was worn during the battle, though the roses now worn by members of the Suffolk Regiment on Minden Day and on the Sovereign's birthday are red and yellow roses—the regimental colours being red and yellow. ....

It is difficult to see how any of the Old Roses could have been in flower as late as 1st August, apart from the Autumn Damask.

Redouté, Vol. 2, Plate 41. *Rosa damascena* 'Aurora'.

Willmott, Vol. 2, Plate facing page 413. *Rosa alba rubicunda.* The description following this figure unfortunately confuses this distinct rose with 'Maiden's Blush'.

Andrews, Plate 18. *Rosa erubescens* (Blushing or Celestial Rose).

Gibson, Plate 22.

'Chloris' ('Rosée du Matin'). Well-named 'Dew of the Morning', for its buds are only less beautiful than those of 'Céleste'. It is a good healthy bush. The prickles are few, the leaves leathery and dark green, held horizontally and flat. In the centre of the bud is a great depth of clear pink, the outer petals rolling backwards to the finely divided sepals. When fully open it reveals a soft 'Céleste' pink all over, reflexing and showing a button eye. A 'Maiden's Blush' type without the muddled centre. 5 to 6 feet.

'Cuisse de Nymphe'. Synonymous with 'Maiden's Blush'.

'Cuisse de Nymphe Émue'. A name sometimes given to particularly well-coloured flowers of 'Maiden's Blush'.

'Félicité Parmentier'. Prior to 1834. Reaching to about 5 feet, and being less upright than most of the Alba varieties, this shows a possible Damask affinity, and has light, almost yellowish-green leaves and twigs, with contrasting dark prickles. The peculiar yellow tone of

the buds vanishes when they open. No other variety in this section has such densely packed buds, opening to such full flowers of clear flesh pink. The petals reflex, a fully open flower being of exquisite beauty, shaped almost like a ball, and fading to cream at the edges.
Le Rougetel, page 31.
Gibson, Plate 15.

'Great Maiden's Blush'. Kew Gardens, U.K., 1797. One of the oldest favourites, and frequently found in cottage gardens, where its perennial good behaviour has commended it for safe keeping, in this country and on the Continent. 'La Royale', 'La Séduisante', 'Cuisse de Nymphe', 'La Virginale', 'Incarnata', and other fanciful names of free translation indicate its popularity. Specially well-coloured blooms were called 'Cuisse de Nymphe Émue'. It ranks very high among large shrub roses, having good, greyish foliage and stalwart growth up to 6 feet, thence freely branching and arching outwards to display the numerous flowers, of a delicate quality, and carrying a fragrance unequalled for pure sweetness. Its shape is informal, like that of *Rosa alba* 'Maxima'; it is a soft, warm blush-pink on opening, and the petals reflex and fade to a pale cream-pink at the edges, the Maiden's Blush remaining always in the centre. Redouté records this as *R. alba regalis*, Le Rosier Blanc Royale. "C'est la Great Maiden's Blush des Anglais, la Grosse Cuisse de Nymphe. C'est à-peu-près semblable à celle dîte 'La Cuisse de Nymphe Émue'." This is a rose that makes a really splendid display as an informal hedge, and as a shrub has particularly good garden value.
Redouté, Vol. I, Plate 97. *Rosa alba regalis.*
Roessig, Plate 23. *Rosa alba rubicunda plena,* Rosier Blanc incarnat à fleurs doubles. A remarkable portrait. Possibly the 'Small Maiden's Blush'. Plate 48. La Rose Rougissante, *R. rubicans.* Another excellent portrait, probably of 'Great Maiden's Blush'.
Mrs Gore, page 269, gives the following synonymy:
  'La Royale' = 'Cuisse de Nymphe'.
  'Cuisse de Nymphe Émue' = 'Cuisse de Nymphe' with glossy ovary.
  Small 'Cuisse de Nymphe' = *alba rubigens.*
Lawrance, Plate 32. 'Great Maiden's Blush Rose'. Buds excellent.
Andrews, Plate 16. 'Rosa Bella Donna', 'Maiden's Blush Rose'; good portrait but too much colour.
Plate 17. Ditto, var. flore minor; 'Maiden's Rose', small-flowered variety.
Gibson, Plate 22.

'Jeanne d'Arc'. 1818. Probably synonymous with 'Anglica Minor'. This may be described as a dwarf version of the 'Great Double White' ('Maxima'), forming a very dense bush up to 4 or 5 feet with typical, rather coarse, dark grey-green leaves. The flowers are well filled, with muddled centres, and are of a rich creamy-flesh on first opening, rapidly fading to ivory white.

'Koenigin von Danemarck' ('Queen of Denmark'). 1826. Like some of the later results of hybridizing in other groups, this variety has a perfection of form almost unequalled, and may be ranked with 'Mme Hardy', 'Duc de Guiche', and a few others, to show what the hybridizers of that day considered superlatively beautiful. The foliage is of dark blue-green, the leaves being extremely well cut and elegant; the buds are likewise perfect, and the partly opened flower reveals an intensity of vivid carmine unequalled by any other Old Rose. The flowers are at first cupped, but their multitudinous petals push outwards and reflex, by which time they are of a pale 'Céleste' pink, and are often beautifully quartered with a button centre. Its growth, though healthy and vigorous up to 6 feet or so, is some-what open and spindly; wall culture would undoubtedly help. (Plates 21, 22.)

Geoffrey Taylor of Dublin told me there was a China Rose of 1899 called 'Queen of Denmark'; but added that Rivers in his *Rose Amateur's Guide* of 1861 and earlier says, under *Rosa alba*, 'Queen of Denmark': "An old, but estimable variety, produces flowers of first-rate excellence as prize-flowers: so much was this esteemed when first raised from seed, that plants were sent from Germany to this country at five guineas each." The French synonym about 1900 was 'Naissance de Vénus'.

I must add a note regarding the origin of this famous rose, from O. Sonderhousen of Denmark. He kindly sent me a full account of an argument by the raisers and Professor Lehmann, director of the Botanic Gardens at Hamburg; the pamphlet was published at Altona in 1833 "in aid of the poor" and was written by John Booth. The complainants were James Booth & Söhne.

Under the motto *Nemo me impune lacessit* Booth states that a seedling of 'Maiden's Blush' flowered for the first time in his nursery at Flottbeck in 1816; that at first it was called the 'New Maidenblush' and as such distributed on a very small scale from about 1820 to 1821. After building up a good stock it was entered in their catalogue for 1826 as 'Königin von Dannemark' at a price of 12 marks. He obtained permission from the king to name it after the queen (i.e., the Danish queen, as in those days Denmark stretched down into Germany).

Then in 1828 Professor Lehmann claimed, in a list of plants in the Hamburg Botanic Gardens, that a rose named 'Belle Courtisanne', a cross between *Rosa centifolia* and 'Maiden-blush' and mentioned already in 1806 in a French catalogue, had been offered for sale re-cently under the name of 'Königen von Dannemark'.

On being tackled about this by Booth, Lehmann gave evasive replies, saying the rose was generally known in France and had been depicted by Redouté. Booth wrote thereupon to all the well-known rose breeders and Redouté, and their answers, quoted in full in the pamphlet, proved that nobody had ever heard of a rose called 'Belle Courtisanne'. The re-maining pages Booth devoted to a considerable crowing over Lehmann. Booth adds that

> even the probably best-known Rose collection in England in those days, viz.
> that in Hammersmith [Messrs Lee & Kennedy], eight years ago paid three
> guineas per plant for it before it had been entered in our catalogue, and men-
> tioned it in their garden list in 1830 as 'Queen of Denmark'.

'Koenigin von Danemarck' was undoubtedly a peerless rose then, as it is now, and it is not surprising to find the raiser standing up for himself in such circumstances.
Gibson, Plate 22.

'Mme Legras de St Germain'. Prior to 1848. "A superb White Rose," says William Paul at that date. This rose has made vigorous shoots up to 7 feet, almost thornless, bearing pale-green leaves. The flowers are perfection indeed, opening from a dainty bud to slightly cupped blooms of good size, later quite flat, and filled with regular petals. They are of glistening ivory white with a distinct pale canary-yellow flush in the centre, and in this col-ouring they are distinct from all other Alba varieties, until the Noisettes are considered. I can give no higher praise than to state that it is undoubtedly a rival in quality to 'Mme Hardy'. Petals suffer in wet weather.
Le Rougetel, page 27.

'Maxima' ('Great Double White'; Jacobite Rose; Cheshire Rose). A noble shrub with coarse, leaden-green leaves, borne mostly at the top of the big bushes, up to 7 or 8 feet in height. It is of rather gaunt habit, best for the back of the border or for training on walls, and has scattered large prickles. The flowers are informally double, with muddled centres, opening to warm creamy-blush, quickly passing to creamy-white. This is a noble Old Rose and the most common in old gardens of all the Old Roses. I have seen it in the east and west, and in Wales, Scotland, and Ireland, always doing well. Sported to *Rosa alba* 'Semi-plena', 1959. It was called the Common White Rose in the *Florists' Vademecum*, 1882, and must have been a double as the author compares it with 'Maiden's Blush', this "being the same, but blush." Kingsley, facing page 37, described as 'Rugosa'; *Rosa alba.*
Roessig, Plate 15. Le Rosier Blanc à fleurs doubles, *Rosa alba plena.*
Andrews, Plate 12. *Rosa alba flore pleno.*

'Pompon Blanc Parfait'. 1876. A stranger to this group in several ways. It is, however, a true 'pompon' type with delightful neat rosette blooms in palest lilac-pink, produced from fat, round, little buds. These are borne over a very long period, well into July. The growth is slender and erect, with few prickles, and the small, pale, grey-green leaves are perfectly in keeping with the miniature blooms. 5 feet.

'Semi-plena'. This is probably *Rosa alba suaveolens* or *nivea*, one of the roses grown for distilling attar at Kazanlik, where it frequently surrounds plantations of Damask Roses. Assorting well with true species roses on account of its refined air, this nearly single-flowered type may be regarded as an old form of this group, and it is one of the loveliest in growth, spraying its clusters of milk-white, golden-centred blooms over the ample grey-green foliage. In the autumn it carries a splendid crop of red heps. 5 to 6 feet. (Plate 20.)
Jekyll, facing page 14.
Bunyard, in *New Flora and Silva*, Vol. 2, Fig. 4 (The 'Maiden's Blush' Rose).
Willmott, Plate 136. *Rosa alba.*
Redouté, Vol. 1, Plate 117. *Rosa alba flore pleno.* Redouté records that the single variety has
  never been found wild, according to Desvaux.
Roessig, Plate 34.
Andrews, Plate 11. *Rosa alba semi duplex.*
Duhamel, Vol. 7, Plate 16. *Rosa alba*; this is *R. alba* 'Maxima'.
Lawrance, Plate 25. *Rosa alba* β, Double White Rose. This is *R. alba* 'Semi-plena'.
  Plate 37 shows the single *R. alba* (5 petals only).
Andrews, Plate 40, under the name of *Rosa glabra*, has a thornless double white rose, like
  'Mme Plantier' and 'Mme Legras de St Germain'.
Andrews, Plate 10. *Rosa alba*, single white type; "is in very few collections"; 5 petals only.
  This occurred at Mottisfont, 1980.

'Small Maiden's Blush'. With flowers only slightly smaller than the greater variety, this useful rose reaches only to 4 feet in height, but loses no charm thereby.
Bunyard, Plate 16.
Roessig, see under 'Great Maiden's Blush'.

THE CENTIFOLIA ROSES: THE PROVENCE ROSES

Loveliest of lovely things are they,
On earth that soonest pass away.
The rose that lives its little hour
Is prized beyond the sculptured flower.

William Cullen Bryant

IT IS ONLY in favourable conditions that the varieties of *Rosa centifolia* can be called good garden plants. More often than not their open thorny growth is anything but elegant, but when their full gracious flowers appear we can forgive them all their faults.

As a group their growth is generally lax and open, and the gaunt prickly stems need the support of stakes or close planting. *Rosa centifolia* and its varieties 'Cristata', 'Bullata', 'La Noblesse', and 'Variegata' are of similar habit and qualities. 'Petite de Hollande', 'Spong', and 'Unique' are much more bushy and able to stand on their own; 'Fantin-Latour', 'Blanchefleur', and 'Paul Ricault' are equally sturdy and taller growing. The two miniatures, 'de Meaux' and 'White de Meaux', are self-reliant also. 'Tour de Malakoff' is very prone to flop, and needs a wall or stake, also 'Robert le Diable', a smaller bush.

New shoots five feet long are not uncommon during the summer, and apart from any other pruning I think it is essential to reduce these by at least one-third or one-half in January. Otherwise, when the short flowering shoots appear during the following summer, the weight of the young growth will cause too much bending and arching, with the result that the stems will tend to become procumbent. By shortening the stems this evil may be avoided. Apart from this special treatment, pruning can be much the same as that recommended for the White Roses.

It would not do, however, to prune away all tendency to droop. Drooping is the very spirit of the Provence Roses. Their big leaves droop and likewise their buds and flowers, and far from their having just a weak neck, they appear deliberately to enhance their charm by gracefully arching their stalks and causing their admirers to lift their great luxuriant blooms. The big outer petals enfold the shorter "hundred leaves" which, not being affected generally by direct sunlight, retain a depth of colouring very telling in effect.

Let us therefore grow our Provence Roses for their nodding grace and fullness, and forget their prickly gawkiness and coarse leaves. Let us leave spring-like sweetness to the White Roses and revel in the full summer of the Provence varieties. A sun-warmed Centifolia has a richness of scent almost unbelievable.

F. J. Lambe of Totnes once sent me a semi-double rose that I recognised as very near to, if not identical with, Redouté's portrait of *Rosa centifolia anemonoides* (Vol. 2. Plate 115). This originated apparently about 1810, and has flowers of the usual pink, but the central petals are short and give what in horticulture is usually termed an "anemone centre." I have lost this variety.

Drapiez, Vol. 6, page 417. *Rosier aux centfeuilles*, var. Anemone.

Provence Roses

The Rose of a Hundred Leaves is also the Rose des Peintres in its best form, the Provence or Cabbage rose, and its poise, its shape, and its colour have been immortalized in many an Old Master. Its noted forms, *Rosa centifolia* 'Bullata', 'Cristata', and 'Muscosa', have the same long projecting sepals and rich drooping flowers, the same numerous petals—so closely curved round one another that the flower remains globe-shaped with a deep open centre—the same clear-pink colouring, and the delicious intense fragrance. *Rosa centifolia* itself is a wide-spreading, open, and tall shrub up to 5 feet in height, and its shoots, bearing prickles of mixed sizes and shapes from small spines to big hooked thorns, reach outwards to droop the next season with the weight of the big blooms, borne singly and in clusters. The large, rounded, drooping leaves are very coarsely toothed, and the whole plant has a lax air, yet it is sturdy. When wide open the flowers reveal a large button eye. The unfortunate title of "Cabbage" Rose has led to considerable confusion, as cabbages today more nearly approximate the incurved blooms of 'Mme Caroline Testout' or a modern Hybrid Tea Rose than the Rose des Peintres. Moreover, few people today think of *R. centifolia* when describing a rose as "cabbagy"—this term indeed more aptly describes the Hybrid Perpetuals, most of which have fallen out of cultivation. In fact, my experience has been that people who want to plant "cabbage roses" generally mean some coarse old Hybrid Perpetual rose of their childhood and seldom have any conception of *R. centifolia*.

The genuine *Rosa centifolia* can be traced in *European Flower Painters* by Peter Mitchell (A. & C. Black, 1973) to the early 1620s, in paintings such as those by Balthazar van der Ast. While similar roses occur in yet earlier paintings, they appear to be of a related type, but not true *R. centifolia*.

Kingsley, facing page 38.

Willmott. Plate facing page 345. Not recognizable; the material available was obviously incorrectly named, as Alfred Parsons captured all the grace of the Provence Rose in the 'Common Moss Rose'.

Redouté, Vol. I, Plate 25.

Jamain et Forney, Plate 15.

Roessig, Plate I.

Komlosy. Fair.

Duhamel, Vol. 7, Plate 12. A good portrait.

Andrews, Plate 15. Poor.

I have always considered the Rose des Peintres as simply *Rosa centifolia*, but some of the old writers praise it a good deal, apparently as a separate variety.

Choix des Plus Belles Roses. Plate 29. 'Rose des Peintres'. Raised by Verdier, France.

Roses et Rosiers, par des Horticulteurs et des Amateurs de Jardinage, Paris, 1872. Plate 48. 'Centfeuille des Peintres'. "Cette magnifique varieté fleuri de Juin à Août." *Centifolia* does sometimes linger in flower until August in cool districts.

'Blanchefleur'. Vibert, France, 1835. Not a typical form, but obviously a close relative, this rose has a vigorous open habit up to some 5 feet, with very spiny shoots and light-green leaves. The flowers have a rather cabbagy appearance, but are nevertheless very attractive in their creamy white, blushing in the centres of newly opened flowers, and with red-tipped buds. The blooms are often quartered and open flat, with rolled edges to the petals.

'Bullata'. Rose à feuilles de Laitue. This distinctive form originated about 1801, and apart from its leaves is a typical Provence Rose, with growth, buds, flowers, and scent like *Rosa centifolia*. But the leaves are remarkable and are in their way the most handsome in the genus. They undoubtedly resemble those of a lettuce—particularly 'Continuity'—in their puckered, bullate, and enlarged segments, hanging loosely from their stalks, and are richly tinted with mahogany while young. A rose of botanic and historic interest. 4 to 5 feet. (Plate 23.)

Willmott, Plate facing page 367. *Rosa provincialis bullata*.

Redouté, Vol. I, Plate 37.

Andrews, Plate 28. Poor.

'**Centifolia Alba**'. The rose figured under this name by Bunyard is the Hybrid Damask Rose 'Mme Hardy'. It is quite possible that 'Mme Hardy' has Centifolia parentage, but it is not fit to be classed as a true *Rosa centifolia* variety, and is usually found among the Damasks in old French books.

'**Cristata**'. Vibert, France, 1826. This is also called Crested Moss but, according to Dr Hurst's findings, is not an approach to a Moss Rose, but rather a parallel sport. The wings of the calyx are crested and enlarged to such an extent that the buds are almost enveloped in greenery. These buds are in fact of very great beauty, and impart to this otherwise typical *Rosa centifolia* a distinct charm. Fancy has added another title, 'Chapeau de Napoléon', as the winged calyx resembles a cockade. Records tell us that it was first found in 1820 in the crevice of an old wall at Fribourg in Switzerland, and may have been a chance seedling. The flowers are not quite so globular as *R. centifolia* itself. 4 to 5 feet. (Plate 25.)

Botanical Magazine, t.3475.

Keays, facing page 52.

Bunyard, Plate 20.

Hariot, Plate 60.

Paul, Plate I.

Willmott, Plate facing page 351 (not easily recognizable).

Journal des Roses, Avril 1885.

Phillips and Rix, Plate 61.

'**Decora**'. A mysterious little bush, obviously a sport from *Rosa centifolia*, midway between 'Spong' and 'de Meaux'. Light pink flowers which gradually turn light brown and remain on the bush. I have been unable to verify this variety, from Sangerhausen. 3 feet.

'**de Meaux**' (*Rosa centifolia* 'Pomponia'). This miniature is a charming little plant, with erect green shoots up to 3 or 4 feet, branched and twiggy in later years, bearing miniature Centifolia leaves of light green. The flowers are not of Centifolia shape, but are those of a pompon, opening flat, from exquisite buds, and of typical pink. It is much earlier flowering than the larger Provence varieties. The form known as 'White de Meaux' ('Le Rosier Pompon Blanc') is an albino with pink centres. 'Mossy de Meaux', introduced in 1814, I have not yet found. (Plate 24.)

Bunyard, Plate 28.

Willmott, Plate facing page 353.

Redouté, Vol. I, Plate 65. *Rosa pomponia*. Perhaps.

Lawrance, Plate 31.

Lawrance, Plate 50. 'White de Meaux' (Rosier de Pompon).

Roessig, Plate 24. Le Rosier de Dijon. Perhaps.

Roessig, Plate 37. Rose-pompon, *Rosa pomponia*.

Step, *Favourite Flowers*, Vol. I, Plate 78. *Rosa centifolia pomponia*; de Meaux.

Botanical Magazine, t. 407. The figure and description probably apply to 'White de Meaux'.

Gibson, Plate 23.

'Duc de Fitzjames'. Vigorous shrub up to 6 feet with good foliage and trusses of cupped blooms revealing green eyes. The petals are densely packed, showing very beautiful quartering, and fade to a soft lilac, being paler on the reverse. An effective plant, but the blooms are rather coarse.

'Fantin-Latour'. It is difficult to know where to class this splendid rose, as it clearly has Centifolia flowers, but the leaves show signs of China Rose smoothness. In growth and flower, however, it nearly approaches typical *Rosa centifolia*, and as it has one season of flowering only, it seems best included under this heading. It will make a large rounded bush, well clothed in handsome, broad, dark green leaves, 5 feet high and wide on good soils, and is one of the most handsome of shrub roses, particularly when in flower. Poised with Centifolia charm, the blooms have a circular, cupped shape when half open, of a bland pale pink, warmly tinted in the central folds with rich blush. Later the outer petals reflex, still leaving the centre cupped, and at this stage it is scarcely surpassed in beauty. It is a most satisfying rose in every way, and has a delicious fragrance. I found it in one garden where its name was unknown, labelled "Best Garden Rose," and as such it is worthily named after the great French artist. So far I have been unable to trace the name in any nineteenth-century book. (Plate 26.)
Le Rougetel, page 155.

'Foliacée'. Descemet or Vibert, France. 'Caroline de Berry'. Loosely double flowers of soft pink fading to lilac-white with a few darker petals; some flowers have button eyes. It is a free-flowering bush with clusters of erect buds. Few prickles; mid-green leaves, rather pointed for the Centifolia group. Probably incorrectly named, but a good variety with a good fragrance. 4 to 5 feet.

'Jeune Henry'. Vibert, France. An upright bush, unlike any in this group. Yellowish-green, small foliage. The flowers are fiery crimson fading to magenta-crimson, expanded, with muddled centres. Little scent. The hep is narrow with very small setae which might pass for moss. 3 to 4 feet.

'Juno'. Laffay, France, 1847. An arching shrub with soft, leaden-green leaves. It is grouped as a "*hybride non-remontant*," and it appears to fit this description; it is certainly not a Hybrid Perpetual, though it has some affinity with that group, and the flowers more nearly approach the exquisite form of the Provence Rose. The globular blooms of delicate blush open to a flat flower resembling 'Souvenir de la Malmaison', with a large button eye. Being lax in growth it would be very suitable for hanging over a low wall or growing as a standard. I place it in the front rank of Old Roses. 4 feet.

'Justine Ramet'. Vibert, France, 1845. A large, vigorous, rather lax bush, prickly, with good leaves. The hep is almost non-existent below the flower. Flowers of rich magenta-purple, quartered and sweetly scented.

'La Noblesse'. 1856. All stocks I have seen bearing this label are typical *Rosa centifolia*.

'Le Rire Niais'. Dupont, France, prior to 1810. There is little to support this name, but it is a good graceful bush with mid-green, rather pointed leaves. Very fragrant, warm pink flowers fading to lilac-pink, full-petalled and quartered, with green pointel. Few prickles. Heps hispid. 4 feet.

'Ombrée Parfaite'. Vibert, France, 1823. Vigorous but rather procumbent shrub, copiously clad in fresh green, folded, pointed leaves. The rather shapeless little blooms resemble those of 'Hippolyte', and show a similar remarkable diversity of tones, light-pink petals being placed next to those of intense dark maroon-purple. One of the darkest roses in my collection. 3 feet. A Gallica derivative.

'Parvifolia'. The foliage of this little shrub prompts me to place it among the Gallica roses, q.v.

'Paul Ricault'. Portemer, France, 1845. Like 'Blanchefleur', which it closely resembles, except in colour, this rose shows signs of hybridity. The rolled petals and densely packed flowers have considerable charm, and it is one of the most free-flowering among these old types. Soft, rich pink, and well scented. 5 feet.

'Petite de Hollande' ('Petite Junon de Hollande', 'Pompon des Dames', *Normandica*). While 'de Meaux' and the Gallica 'Parvifolia' are true pompons, this is just an exquisitely formed miniature Centifolia, every part reduced to scale, but of rather more bushy habit. The leaves resemble Centifolia leaves, reduced in size, but similarly coarsely toothed, and the calyx and flower are of typical colour and form, but borne with just a little more stiffness, which is the character of the bush. This imparts an air of distinction, and it is the best Provence Rose for smaller gardens. 4 feet.
This is probably the rose figured by Miss Lawrance, Plate 55.
Bunyard in *New Flora and Silva*, Vol. 2, Fig. 2.
Roessig, Plate 20. Le Petit Rosier à cent feuilles, *Rosa centifolia minor.*

'Robert le Diable'. A late-flowering, lax shrub, whose almost procumbent 4-foot prickly stems show their considerable beauties to the greatest advantage when allowed to spray over a low wall. The leaves are narrow and of dark green. It is by no means a typical Centifolia, and probably has Gallica derivation. The medium-sized flowers are most beautifully shaped, the half-open blooms having bold outer reflexing petals, and later all the petals reflex somewhat except those held centrally, which remain erect and poised outwards. An amazing number of tints is held in these flowers, a dark slatey lilac-purple predominating, shaded with violet-purple and lightened by vivid splashes of intense cerise and scarlet. Many of the petals have a minute veining of the same colour, and some of them fade to pale parma violet, eventually turning to dove-grey on exposure. This rose only develops its most arresting colours in dry, hot weather. 4 to 5 feet.

'Spong'. U.K., 1805. This interesting little bush, a typical form of *Rosa centifolia*, and midway in size between 'de Meaux' and 'Petite de Hollande', is very early flowering, and is generally over before the larger forms are in flower. The habit is bushy and upright, much branched, with rounded leaf segments and coarsely toothed margins. The flowers are cupped, opening flat; they are not very shapely, nor are they pompons, and their numerous petals stay conspicuously on the plants when the flowers have faded—an unfortunate habit of some of the older roses, but in none so objectionable as in this plant. In all other respects it is good. 4 to 5 feet.
Andrews, Plate 27. *Rosa provincialis hybrida.* Hybrid Provence Rose. "It is commonly known by the appellation of the 'Spong Rose' from having been first raised in quantities by a gardener of that name."

'The Bishop'. I suspect that this may be synonymous with the old French Gallica variety 'L'Évêque'. In the evening and after a hot day, when seen against the light and in shadow, this rose more nearly approaches blue than any other. The flat flowers, of closely packed rosette-form, and not at all like typical *Rosa centifolia*, have rolled petals of cerise-magenta.

They quickly turn to tones of violet and slatey grey-violet, and it is at this development that the blue shades appear so convincing. The grey tones only develop on parts of the flowers, cerise being present frequently with them. It forms a slender, rather erect bush, with neat leaves, rather polished, and showing affinity with 'Tour de Malakoff'. 4 to 5 feet.

'**Tour de Malakoff**'. Soupert et Notting, France, 1856. A very large bush of lax habit except on very strong fertile soils, where its colours and size of flower are wonderful. The smooth and rather small leaves are not in keeping with its other characters, and the tall stems, often up to 7 feet in height, should be supported, to show the flowers to best advantage. The buds are shapely and the reverses of the petals are of light lilac-pink; in a half-open bloom, somewhat cupped and not of formal shape, vivid magenta may predominate, but when the flowers receive full sunshine and the petals reflex, some petals turn to intense parma violet with many intermediate shades. All the magenta areas are veined and flushed with violet. Eventually, before falling, a cool lilac-grey assumes predominance over the 5-inch blooms, and a bunch of flowers of all tones is a startling revelation of what a rose can do. A few stamens light the centres. (Plate 27.)
Gibson, Plate 23.

'**Unique Blanche**'. Discovered at Needham, Suffolk, in 1775. The 'White Provence', 'Unique', or 'Vierge de Cléry' is a typical Provence Rose in growth, prickles, leaves, scent, and the texture of the petals. The buds, with long sepals, are red-flushed and almost burnished; a half-open bloom is cupped, the central petals being held together by those on the outside; later a distinct button eye is surrounded by a starry and effective display of creamy-white, glistening, transparent, narrow petals. At this stage it is arresting. On good soils it can be a very pleasing plant up to 4 or 5 feet. It flowers late in the summer season.
Redouté, Vol. I, Plate III. *Rosa centifolia mutabilis.*
Andrews, Plate 20. *Rosa provincialis alba.*
Roessig, Plate 41. Poor.
Lawrance, Plate 4. Excellent drawing.

'**Variegata**'. Introduced from Angers in 1845. This rose is found under many names in books and gardens: 'Belle des Jardins', 'La Rubanée', 'Village Maid', 'Cottage Maid', 'Panachée à fleur double', 'La Belle Villageoise', 'Dometil Beccard', and 'Dominic Boccardo' have been given to me at one time or another, and all have turned out to be not Gallica roses (to which these names should refer) but this old and fairly typical Centifolia. Miss Willmott, in *The Genus Rosa*, has a good portrait of it, and she wisely accords it the descriptive and safe name *variegata*. It is a vigorous bush, producing strong prickly shoots and good dark leaves, coarsely toothed. The flowers, borne singly or in clusters, are globular, filled with thin petals which do not resist wet weather and soon drop. But who can deny the beauty and freshness of those silky, creamy-white blooms so neatly striped with pale lilac-pink? It is very free-flowering. 5 feet.
Bunyard. 'Village Maid'.
Bunyard in *New Flora and Silva*, Vol. 2, Fig. 3. 'Cottage Maid'.
Willmott, Plate 122. *Rosa provincialis variegata.*
Journal des Roses, Août 1893. 'Dometil Beckart' (Beccard).
Andrews, Plate 25. *Rosa provincialis variegata*, Variegated Provence Rose. Rather highly coloured and too flat.

THE CENTIFOLIA ROSES: THE MOSS ROSES

Gather ye rosebuds while ye may
Old Time is still a-flying,
And the same flower that blooms today,
Tomorrow may be dying.

Robert Herrick

IN THESE FORMS of the Provence Rose the sepals assume great importance. These green segments enclosing the buds of all roses have interested mankind for a very long time; there is a Latin rhyme about them, one translation of which runs:

Five brothers take their stand
Under the same command.
Two darkly bearded frown,
Two without beards are known,
While one sustains with equal pryde
His sad appendage on one side.

The sepals are so arranged that some of their edges lie over and some under their neighbours, and they are always arranged in the same way. In *Rosa centifolia* 'Cristata' the beards are enlarged and leafy—or crested—while in the Moss Roses they have the effect of moss. What really happens is that the glandular projections all over the flower stalk and sepals—which add so much to the fragrance of many Old Roses—are enlarged and, at the apex of each sepal, a leafy, winged, and mossy elongation may be present. The "moss" is sticky and fragrant on one's fingers.

Dr Hurst's notes in Chapter 13 tell us all that we are likely to know about Moss Roses, but I refer the reader to my own conclusions regarding the white Mosses, given under *Rosa centifolia* 'Muscosa Alba'. The Mosses are really of comparatively recent occurrence, and, as they originated just when the China Rose was making its influence felt, it was inevitable that some of the later varieties should flower again, after the summer outburst is over. For these few late blooms we must be grateful, but the plants cannot really be called perpetual flowering. Direct evidence also may be found of the influence of the Damask Rose 'Quatre Saisons Blanc Mousseux' (page 44), not only regarding its perpetual flowering habit, but also in the quality of its "moss," which is hard and prickly, and very different from the soft moss of Centifolia varieties.

Generally speaking, the Moss Roses lack the exquisite quality of the true Provence Roses except in the few that are direct sports, e.g., *Rosa centifolia* 'Muscosa' and 'Alba'; the variety 'À longs pédoncules'; and a few other later kinds such as 'Louis Gimard' and 'Maréchal Davoust'. These have the grace and refinement we might expect; in fact I think the two first-named are undoubtedly the most beautiful, and I think that subsequent hybridization and selection did not succeed in giving us anything particularly good. This rather hard statement is, however, somewhat tempered by the thought of 'Comtesse de Murinais', 'Général Kléber', 'Henri Martin', 'Nuits de Young', 'René d'Anjou', and 'William Lobb'. These are certainly highlights among later Moss Roses.

In size the Moss Roses range from the dwarf varieties 'Little Gem' and 'Mousseline' to tall pillar roses like 'Jeanne de Montfort' and 'William Lobb', both of which are capable of reaching 8 feet. A number are really bushy, such as 'Pélisson' and 'James Mitchell'; some have grand flowers of considerable quality, like 'Eugénie Guinoiseau' and 'Mme Louis Lévêque'; 'Japonica' is a unique form, with mossy stems which are very elegant in their green moss contrasting with the rich amethyst tinting of the young foliage. But for really exquisite quality one must leave these and grow only the original sports.

Since 1900 a few Mosses have been raised that embody the vigour and mossy characters with rather modern colours. 'Gabrielle Noyelle' (1933) has flowers of orange-salmon with yellow base; 'Robert Léopold' (1941) is of similar colouring with attractive dark moss and brilliant green leaves. These are both good bushes up to about 5 feet, and with them we can grow the 'Golden' or 'Yellow Moss' (1930). This is rather shy-flowering. Their colours are somewhat fierce for growing with the Old Roses, but I feel their quality is a little lacking for inclusion among Hybrid Teas.

This proves once again that certain plants are best retained in their original state, with no attempt to bring them up to date by hybridizing. The Moss Roses fill a niche in the development of roses, and as such should be left alone, to be enjoyed with the Old Roses, and as period pieces particularly reminiscent of the "cosy" Victorian era. Although they are contemporaneous with many of the best Gallica roses, the Moss Roses alone have, to me, a specially Victorian quality. A few years ago I had a Valentine sent to me—from an unknown source, of course!—on which was a wonderful spray of Moss Roses in rich Victorian style. Underneath the sender had written, "Be my rose but not too old-fashioned." I feel that the Rose thereby soared to great heights of period quality and also humour, and I have many times been immensely tickled by the sender's kind thoughts for me. One could so easily become old-fashioned in such a pursuit as this!

In the garden, Moss Roses have the same values and qualities as the Provence Roses themselves, although on the whole they are of more robust and erect habit. Pruning will be the same as for the Provence Roses, always remembering that fairly hard spur-pruning in the winter will help to keep the more perpetual flowering varieties bushy and producing flowers through the summer.

Moss Roses

'**Muscosa**'. A great stir was made at the end of the seventeenth century, or at least by 1727, when the Moss Rose was introduced from the Continent. This sport from *Rosa centifolia* gave rise to several other forms, but it was not until after the single pink Moss Rose occurred at Bayswater in 1807 that seedlings were raised—none of which surpass the Common Moss in beauty. The fine foliage of mid-green, coarsely toothed, and long projecting calyx make a perfect foil for the lovely Provence blooms of clear pink, globular at first, opening flat, with button centre, and exquisitely fragrant. Only the white form and 'Gloire des Mousseux' have in my opinion buds which approach it in beauty. 4 feet.

William Paul, in his 9th edition, quotes the French raiser of roses M. Laffay as having said, in 1847, "from the moss roses we shall soon see great things." During the next forty years or so numerous varieties were introduced, running into several hundreds. Today but a handful remains and none has quite as much beauty as the Common Moss; none achieved high distinction but they are treasured because of their mossy buds and also, I need hardly repeat, their scent.

Niedtner, page 24. A pleasing portrait.

Jamain et Forney, Plate 45.

Botanical Magazine, t.69. Beautiful drawing.

Kingsley, facing page 39.

Keays, facing page 52.

Les Plus Belles Roses, facing page 98.

Willmott, Plate facing page 345.

Redouté, Vol. I, Plate 41. *Rosa muscosa multiplex.* He also shows the Single Moss, Vol. I, Plate 39.

Lawrance, Plate 14.

Roessig, Plate 6. Le Rosier Mousseux, *Rosa muscosa.*

Andrews, Plate 58. Depicts the Single Moss Rose, *Rosa muscosa simplex.*

Komlosy.

Hoffmann, Plate 2.

Phillips and Rix, Plate 65.

'Muscosa Alba'. Up to the present I have found it impossible to be quite certain about the typical white Moss Roses, but there is no doubt that this rose is identical with Redouté's beautiful portrait of *Rosa centifolia muscosa alba.* He calls this 'Shailer's White Moss', and refers also to 'White Bath' or 'Clifton Moss', which he says is rare in gardens and difficult to propagate. As there is apparently no coloured figure of the 'Clifton Moss' I am tempted to suggest that these sports were identical; in other words, that the White Moss was variously called 'Shailer's', 'Bath', or 'Clifton'; I therefore like to follow Redouté and use the botanical name. 'Shailer's White Moss' occurred in 1790. (Plate 29.)

This rose has the grace of pure *Rosa centifolia*, and is almost alone in this beauty, apart from the Common Moss and 'René d'Anjou'. The growth is lax and open, the leaves of soft green, well rounded and well poised, and the graceful flower stalks bear lovely buds with long, mossy calyces. The flower is less full than *R. centifolia*, but has the same papery delicate quality, and the blooms are flushed with flesh tint in the centre immediately on opening, passing to pure white, and reflexing quite flat with noticeable button eye. Occasionally a pink petal is produced. A delightful rose, very fragrant, probably reaching to 4 feet.

During the summer of 1954 I was interested to observe a flowering shoot of this double white Moss Rose producing perfect blooms in the typical pink of the Common Moss. On the spray the central bloom was pink, and the buds on the one side white, and on the other, pink. This also occurred at Mottisfont in 1980, and subsequently. (Plates 28, 30.)

Redouté, Vol. I, Plate 87.

Andrews, Plate 63.

Botanical Register, 102.

Both Andrews's and the *Botanical Register* figures are less easily recognized than Redouté's.

Phillips and Rix, Plate 65.

'Alfred de Dalmas'. See 'Mousseline', page 66.

'À longs pédoncules'. Robert, France, 1854. This extremely graceful rose, with its clusters of long-stalked flowers and pretty, neat foliage is worthy of more frequent cultivation. The leaves are of soft green, small and rounded, and the pale green mossy sheaves of buds open to small nodding pink flowers of a peculiarly soft tone of pink flushed with lilac. In spite of this lack of size it is recognizably a true Centifolia variety, and forms a vigorous plant. True Centifolia charm. 5 to 6 feet.

'**Angélique Quetier**'. Quetier, France, 1839. An upright, free-flowering bush, prickly and bristly, with narrow leaves. The hep is broad but the Moss denotes Damask derivation, and is of bright brownish tint. Full, dark pink flowers with paler edges, green pointel. Little scent. 4 to 5 feet.

'**Aristobule**'. Foulard, France, 1849. A very prickly and bristly bush with brownish young leaves. The moss is not plentiful, but is short and sticky. Flowers rich crimson-purple with purple flush in the centre, which is quartered; the petals are rolled and paler at the edges. 5 feet.

'**Baron de Wassanaer**'. Vendler, France, 1854. Vigorous shrub, of distinctive growth and good foliage. The buds are not conspicuously mossy, and the flowers are of globular or cupped shape, light crimson, but not very attractive. 4 to 5 feet. Rather modern in style. Phillips and Rix, Plate 63.

'**Blanche Moreau**'. Moreau, France. A fine white Moss, raised in 1880, the parentage being given as 'Comtesse de Murinais' and 'Quatre Saisons Blanc'. The latter was a Damask Rose, but I can see no sign of its influence in 'Blanche Moreau', apart from the occasional later flowers which may indicate Autumn Damask or China Rose parentage. It is a vigorous but slender, lax shrub up to 6 feet in height, with many prickles and dark, brownish-green moss; this dark colouring is noticeable on the leaf stalks also; truly a brunette among Mosses. The dark moss contrasts strongly with the small creamy-white flowers, very double, cupped or flat.

This is probably the rose on Plate facing page 349, Willmott, figured as *Rosa centifolia albo-muscosa*, which she states is the 'White Bath' or 'Clifton Moss'. The general appearance of the flower is so far removed from *R. centifolia* that her material was obviously wrongly named.
Journal des Roses, Septembre 1885.

'**Capitaine Basroger**'. Moreau-Robert, France, 1890. Vigorous and suitable for a pillar, or can be pruned to a bush. Very prickly, and the bulging buds are scarcely enveloped by the green mossy calyx, which has practically no wings at all. The flowers are not of classic shape, but have an intense, purplish-crimson colouring, and are cupped and reflexed. Produces a few late blooms. 6 feet.

'**Capitaine John Ingram**'. Laffay, France, 1856. A vigorous but dense bush up to 5 feet, with neat, dark leaves and many fine prickles. The blooms are pompon-like, opening flat and compact from tight, slightly mossy buds; the first colour is an intense, dark purplish crimson. This gives way to softer tones of purple, mottled with a variety of tints, and when fully open the button eye reveals the lilac pink of the reverse of the petals. This is the darkest and most velvety Moss Rose I have seen except 'Nuits de Young'. (Plate 33.)

'**Catherine von Wurtemburg**'. Robert, France, 1843. A slender, erect Centifolia bush reaching to about 6 feet, with small prickles, red-brown moss, and reddish young leaves, neat and pointed. The flat blooms are not particularly attractive; they are of soft lilac-pink, with muddled centres.

'**Celina**'. Hardy, France, 1855. This is a name which crops up now and again; the rose I grow has crimson and purple shades in each flower, clouded with murrey, and is semi-double. It gets mildew very badly, and is not a worthy variety.

'**Comtesse de Murinais**'. Vibert, France, 1843. A very beautiful and very vigorous white Moss. Long shoots up to 6 feet bear light-green leaves, curiously ribbed, and the moss is green and hard to the touch. The blush-white of the half-open flower fades, leaving a milk-white, well-formed bloom with a pronounced button eye. The petals open flat and are sometimes quilled or quartered. A superlative bloom. Of Damask Moss derivation.

'**Crested Moss**'. See *Rosa centifolia* 'Cristata', page 55.

'**Crimson Globe**'. An unsatisfactory, very dark crimson variety, often remaining 'balled'. Paul (catalogue) 1890. Very grandiose.

'**Crimson Moss**'. May be described as a fairly typical Centifolia, mossy, and crimson, with broad leaves. The flowers are so enveloped by their dark, murrey-purple outer petals that in all but the best weather they do not open properly. In the centre of the flower there is a rich mixture of crimson and purple. An unworthy variety. 5 feet.

'**de Candolle**'. Portemer, France, 1857. A bushy, upright grower, thorny and prickly, with small, light green leaves. Brownish Damask Moss. Open flowers of deep pink, fading paler, showing button eyes or stamens or pointel. 3 feet.

'**Deuil de Paul Fontaine**'. Fontaine, France, 1873. A noted variety, but not of great garden value. It was originally described as very vigorous, but has obviously lost some of its vigour. Hard prickly moss on the buds and globular flowers, very double, showing all tints from dark Tyrian rose through purple and murrey, to almost black, often with brown shadings. Quartered. 3 to 4 feet. June to October.
Journal des Roses, Août 1882. The portrait lacks the purple tones and is hardly "*nuancé acajou*," but is otherwise excellent, if a little overdone.

'**Duchesse de Verneuil**'. Portemer, France, 1856. One of the brightest and most effective of Moss Roses for the garden. It bears a close relationship to 'Général Kléber', in its pointed leaves of good green, and has flowers of a similar shape and purity. The clear, bright-pink petals are paler on the reverse and show this diversity in the button eyes. A delightful, bright, and healthy rose. 5 feet.

'**Eugénie Guinoiseau**'. Guinoiseau, France, 1864. Tall, erect bush up to 6 feet in height bearing very few real thorns. The leaves are rounded, dark, and rather shiny, and give a good effect in contrast to the large, full, velvety blooms. They are cupped on opening, reflexing with rolled edges, making a broad, rounded flower. Tints vary from the early vivid cerise-magenta, to soft grape-purple, fading to soft lilac-purple, but frequently maintaining a rich claret colouring in the centre. Produces blooms through the summer and autumn. Long, narrow hep, very little moss.
Journal des Roses, Novembre 1884.

'**Félicité Bohan**'. A pleasant shapely bush bearing very neat, small leaves of rich green edged in a young state with brown moss. The flowers are of medium size and of delicate flesh-pink, warming to rose in the centre, quartered and with button eyes, reflexing with age. 4 feet.

'**Général Kléber**'. Robert, France, 1856. A most desirable variety. It is the only Moss Rose I have seen which bears any resemblance to the clear and refined beauty of *Rosa alba* 'Céleste'. The double blooms are wide and of great quality, fragrant, in soft pure pink. A vigorous and attractive bushy plant, and the foliage and copious moss have a lettuce-green freshness. 5 feet.

Gibson, Plate 24.

'Gloire des Mousseux' ('Mme Alboni'). Laffay, France, 1852. A most attractive shrub, with sturdy growth and characteristic light-green leaves; likewise the moss is light in colour and, in keeping with the name, abundant, especially on the long sepals. Midsummer sees the only display of blooms, but they are large, full-petalled, opening well and reflexing, of clear bright pink, fading to paler tones, and long-lasting. Sometimes labelled 'Mme Louis Lévêque'. 5 feet.

'Goethe'. Lambert, Germany, 1911. A rather unsuccessful merging of two dissimilar parents, *Rosa multiflora* and a Moss Rose. Very vigorous, excessively prickly with much bristly brownish green moss. The panicles of flowers are borne freely; they are small, semi-double or nearly single, light crimson to pink, with some scent. 5 feet.

'Henri Martin'. Laffay, France, 1863. A particularly graceful plant, with wiry shoots bearing leaves and flowers of a dainty perfection. The foliage and rather scanty moss is of clear green. The flowers are by no means full, but are of the clearest and most intense shade approaching crimson among the Moss Roses that I know, fading to a deep rose shade. The petals are rounded and flat, and reflex with a camellia-like precision. I have seen this rose with flowers of gorgeous quality on a north wall, growing in moist deep soil. 5 to 6 feet.

'James Mitchell'. Verdier, France, 1861. Vigorous plant of bushy yet wide-spraying habit, with neat, pleated, bronzy leaves. The browny-green moss on the dainty little buds creates an exquisite picture and, when the whole bush is covered with flowers, borne singly or in clusters, a very fine garden plant is apparent. The intense magenta-pink of the buds fades to a soft lilac-pink in the flat, open flowers, each with a neat button eye. The flowers are small for the size of the bush, but their numbers and pompon-shape compensate for this. 5 feet.

Gibson, Plate 24.

'James Veitch'. Verdier, France, 1864. A compact low bush, excessively thorny and prickly, with bristly green moss. Leaves distinctly serrate. It is very free-flowering in both summer and autumn, and dead-heading is very necessary to encourage the later crop. The flowers open widely, of dark murrey colour fading to soft vinous, dusky magenta with slate tints. Quartered and with button eye. Faint scent. A useful front-line plant. 2 feet. (Plate 32.)

'Japonica' ('Moussu du Japon'). A slow-growing and interesting shrub whose young shoots are enveloped in clear green dense moss for their entire length; the moss spreads to the leaf-stalks and the surface of the pointed leaves, and is, of course, on the buds. The young foliage is frequently of metallic lustre, lilac and coppery hues appearing together. The magenta-rose flowers quickly reflex and fade to a soft grey-lilac, and are not unlike those of 'William Lobb', but are smaller and less intense in colour. 3 feet.

'Jean Bodin'. Vibert, France, 1846. A bushy upright plant, with young leaves brownish, later leaden green. Prickly Damask moss. Deep warm lilac-pink flowers fading paler towards the edges, quartered and with button eyes. Very sweetly scented. 3 to 4 feet. (Plate 31.)

'Jeanne de Montfort'. Robert, France, 1851. Perhaps the most vigorous Moss Rose, apart from 'William Lobb'; the bronzy mossy stems have shiny leaves and bear large clusters of flowers. The buds are very mossy, with long sepals covered with brown moss, in pleasing contrast to the clear warm pink of the blooms. They open well, are not over-filled with petals, and are lit with yellow stamens. An altogether pleasing rose where there is room for it. Occasional late blooms. 6 to 8 feet.

'**Lanei**'. 1845. A remontant Moss which is occasionally seen. It is a rather coarse variety, with big round buds and deep mauve-pink, very full blooms. Extremely vigorous lax growth. Not very mossy.
Journal des Roses, Mai 1880.

'**Little Gem**'. William Paul, U.K., 1880. A pretty little rose, which grows to 3 or 4 feet, well covered with small neat leaves. The buds are not very mossy, and enclose tightly-packed blooms of light crimson, opening to flat pompon blooms. The colouring is uniform. Also grown under the name of 'Validé'.

'**Louis Gimard**'. Pernet Père, France, 1877. Very hard, densely packed, cabbage-like buds open to rich lilac-cerise flowers, flushed and veined with lilac, flat with muddled centres, the petals being rolled at the edges. Neat, dark green pointed leaves. First-class, shapely blooms of rich appearance. 5 feet.

'**Mme Delaroche-Lambert**'. Robert, France, 1851. Purplish-rose flowers, of good size and vivid colouring, with beautifully rolled petals, centres muddled. The buds are particularly beautiful, with their green moss and long foliaceous sepals. The moss on the stems is brownish, and the leaves are soft, green, and rounded. A highly desirable plant whose flowers appear intermittently until the autumn. 4 to 5 feet.

'**Mme Landeau**'. Moreau-Robert, France, 1873. This compact bush has much to recommend it, but the name is suspect; the original was spotted with white. The stems bear prickles and bristles, the brownish moss is of the Damask persuasion. The leaves are brownish when young, turning to leaden green, contrasting well with the full, flat flowers of rich pink veined and speckled with darker pink. Large rounded buds; average fragrance. Good autumn crop. 3 to 4 feet.

'**Mme Louis Lévêque**'. 1898. A remarkable variety of stiff, upright habit, with long-pointed, bright green, copious foliage, and little moss. The flowers are larger than any others I have seen, and have probably been bred from a Hybrid Perpetual, for it is very markedly of re-montant habit. In wet weather the flowers are inclined to ball, but in dry, sunny times a large globular flower emerges, very fragrant, reflexing slightly, but at all times remaining a uniform pale pink. Bears some resemblance to 'Mrs John Laing' (H.P.). 4 to 5 feet.

'**Maréchal Davoust**'. Robert, France, 1853. A first-rate bush to 4 or 5 feet, with attractive pointed leaves. The buds, of perfect shape, have brownish moss, and on first opening show intense, deep, crimson-pink, with paler reverses. The petals reflex and have a button eye and green centre, retaining their colour well, a suffusion of cerise and purple mingling with the softer tones. This is particularly free-flowering and gives a rich general effect.

'**Marie de Blois**'. Robert, France, 1852. Vigorous and bushy plant with most attractive young shoots, the spines and moss being flushed with red among the fresh green leaves. The blooms are shapeless, but freely borne through summer and autumn, bright pink, frilled and muddled. 5 to 6 feet. A bush for garden effect, dense and floriferous. Suitable for hedging.

'**Monsieur Pélisson**'. See 'Pélisson', page 66.

'**Mousseline**'. Portemer, France, 1855. It is difficult to decide whether this name or 'Alfred de Dalmas', under which this variety is also sometimes found, should be used. The old writers are not definite in their descriptions. This variety makes an extremely compact bush up to 4 feet or so, with many short twigs and distinctive spoon-shaped leaflets; it flowers from June to October. The creamy-blush blooms are cupped and well filled, with high centres. Very free flowering, few prickles, but not conspicuously mossy. This variety seems to me to be obviously related to the Damask 'Quatre Saisons Blanc Mousseux', perhaps through the Portland Roses themselves.
Thomas, 1991, pages 68–69.

'**Nuits de Young**'. Laffay, France, 1845. Presumably named after 'Night Thoughts' by the eighteenth-century English poet, Edward Young. One of the most famous Mosses, and justly so, on account of its distinct habit and foliage, and the size and colouring of its flowers. It forms a wiry, thin bush up to 5 feet or so, with sparsely-disposed leaves, small and dark, yet beautifully burnished with metallic tones. The small flowers are of intense murrey-purple, dark and velvety, lit by a few yellow stamens. They are not very full, but reflex prettily and do not fade much. A gem. Midsummer flowering only. Selwyn Duruz, in his book *Flowering Shrubs*, points out that a yellow flower creates a most satisfying contrast.

'**Parmentier**'. Guillot Fils, France, 1860. Vivid pink fading paler but then revealing dark pink veins; the small flowers are globular on opening, with muddled or quartered centres, often with button eye or green pointel. It is a bush well furnished with narrow leaves. The moss is of Damask derivation. Good scent. Bushy. 4 to 5 feet.

'**Pélisson**'. Vibert, France, 1848. The plant I grow is notable for its coarsely toothed yet small leaves; its vigorous, dense, bushy habit; and for its symmetrical, very flat, fully double flowers, with fine button centres. In colour they are at first bright deep pink, fading paler, and at all times attractive. Greenish-brown moss in average quantity. 4 feet. A fine hedging rose.

'**Reine Blanche**'. Robert et Moreau, France, 1857. Foliage fresh, light green, making a pleasing contrast to the white flowers, which have a creamy-lemon intensity. The moss is copious and bright green, the sepals long and foliaceous. The flowers are fully double, inclined to nod, and have pronounced button centres. 4 to 5 feet.

'**René d'Anjou**'. Robert, France, 1853. Exhibiting the beautiful poise of the typical Centifolias, this variety has most charming buds, with brownish-green moss, opening to soft, warm pink flowers, passing to light lilac-pink, veined and crinkled and with muddled centres. Bronzy young foliage; bushy growth, probably to 5 feet. At all times beautiful.

'**Salet**'. Lacharme, France, 1854. A fairly perpetual-flowering, sturdy, reliable bush. The flowers are not of the very first quality, but are well filled with narrow petals, often quartered, with a muddled eye, and reflexing; clear pink, not very mossy. Soft, light-green leaves and few prickles. 4 feet.

'**Soupert et Notting**'. Pernet Père, France, 1874. A small twiggy bush of upright growth, with small leaves and little moss. The flowers are also small, densely filled with petals, neatly rounded and flat, with good fragrance and a second crop towards autumn.

'**Striped Moss**'. Verdier, France; for date, see Dr Hurst, Chapter 13. 'Oeillet Panaché'. Quaint little flowers of pale pink, striped and parti-coloured with vivid crimson, fading to softer tones. Not very sturdy growth; inferior to other striped roses. 3 to 4 feet. As can be seen from Dr Hurst's Table of Bud Variations (page 338), several striped mossy roses occurred at different dates.
Andrews, Plate 64. An excellent drawing.
Miller, Plate 221. The Striped Moss is depicted but the description does not apply.

'**William Lobb**' ('Duchesse d'Istrie'). Laffay, France, 1855. The 'Old Velvet' Moss. An amazing piece of colour. The freshly opened blooms, large and semi-double with muddled centres, have petals of dark crimson-purple with pale lilac-pink reverses; they fade the next day to a uniform lavender grey, lightened by the nearly white bases of the petals. The heavily green-mossed buds are borne in large clusters, on exceptionally strong shoots, reaching to 8 feet. Foliage small for the size of the plant, dark leaden-green. Best grown in a big group so that the branches of neighbouring plants interlace; or it can be trained up poles or on walls, or mixed with other vigorous roses. At Kiftsgate Court in Gloucestershire, it is used to great advantage with the rambler 'Albertine', which is of warm coral and salmon-pink tones.
Gibson, Plate 24.

PLATE 1. The species *Rosa gallica* L., in the parentage of all European roses ever raised. The single pink flowers are sweetly scented and are followed by red heps, on a freely suckering, short-growing plant. At Mottisfont.

PLATE 2. *Rosa gallica* 'Versicolor', the striped 'Rosa Mundi', was first recorded in 1665 and is here shown reverting to the original light crimson type, *R. gallica* var. *officinalis* Thory, which is believed to have been brought to France in the thirteenth century by the Crusaders. Both make compact bushes and flower freely at midsummer.

PLATE 3. The hedge of *Rosa gallica* var. *officinalis* and 'Versicolor' at Kiftsgate Court, Gloucestershire.

PLATE 4. 'Tuscany Superb' or 'Superb Tuscany' is an ancient Gallica Rose richer and fuller than 'Tuscany' itself. These very dark tones owe their being to *Rosa gallica*.

PLATE 5. 'Belle de Crécy' is an ancient Gallica Rose of exquisite softness of colour. Note the "button eye."

PLATE 6. 'Cardinal de Richelieu' is a renowned murrey-coloured Gallica hybrid, raised in 1840, of graceful arching growth.

PLATE 7. Raised in 1846, 'Ambroise Paré' is a good Gallica Rose, vigorous and upright and of fair scent.

PLATE 8. 'Sterkmanns'. Raised in France in 1847, this is a large-growing, rather late-flowering shrub of typical Gallica persuasion; note the green pointel in the centre of the flower.

PLATE 9. The plant known in English gardens as 'Empress Josephine', without foundation. Reputedly it was brought over, without a name, by the émigrés during the French Revolution. It bears a close resemblance to the Frankfort Rose (see Plate 10). One of the most gracious of Old Roses, but not overendowed with scent. Note the deeply veined leaves. Almost unarmed—a blessing.

Rosa Turbinata.

P. J. Redouté pinx.

Imprimerie de Remond.

Bossin sculp.

Rosier de Francfort.

PLATE 10. *Rosa × francofurtana* Muench. (*R. turbinata* Ait.). Believed to be a hybrid between *R. gallica* and *R. cinnamomea*. The rose we grow as 'Empress Josephine' is closely related in flower and other characters (*viz.*, hep, stipules, foliage and near-absence of prickles).

PLATE 11. The semi-double type of *Rosa damascena* 'Trigintipetala' as grown commercially in Saudi Arabia for the extraction of attar.

PLATE 12. *Rosa damascena* f. *versicolor* West., the York and Lancaster Rose. Some flowers are entirely white. Those wholly pink are reversions to *R. damascena* 'Trigintipetala' and the branch should be removed.

PLATE 13. 'Portlándica' or the Portland Rose, perhaps a hybrid between a Gallica Rose and the Autumn Damask Rose. It increases freely by suckering and produces more blooms after the main display. At Mottisfont.

PLATE 14. Perpetual White Damask Moss Rose sporting back to the original pink Autumn Damask [*Rosa damascena* var. *semperflorens* (Loisel.) Rowley or *R. bifera* (Poir.) Pers.]

PLATE 15. A white sport from *Rosa damascena* var. *semperflorens* (Loisel.) Rowley, preserved in South Africa by Gwen Fagan. At Mottisfont.

PLATE 16. 'Comte de Chambord', 1860, the best and most constantly in flower of the Portland group of Damask Roses.

PLATE 17. 'Marbrée' of 1858, a reliable and bushy Portland Rose showing its characteristic mottled petals; possibly a hybrid with a Gallica rose.

PLATE 18. 'Indigo', a superb, richly coloured Portland Rose which William Paul (1848) rated as "very distinct." Raised by Laffay, France, about 1830.

PLATE 19. It is considered that a white form of *Rosa canina* L. from the Middle East contributed to *R. gallica* to create *R.* × *alba* L. Here is *R. canina* from Britain in delicate pink. The characters of greyish foliage and large prickles are inherited in *R.* × *alba*.

PLATE 20. The White Rose of York, *R.* × *alba* 'Semiplena', a splendid large shrub that bears a good crop of red heps in autumn.

PLATE 21. 'Koenigin von Danemarck' ('Queen of Denmark'), a rose raised in 1826, probably a hybrid of a Damask Rose though with other characters denoting *R.* × *alba*. The greyish leaves tone beautifully with the clear pink of the flowers.

PLATE 22. *Rosa* × *alba* 'Koenigin von Danemarck' at Talbot Manor, Norfolk.

PLATE 23. *Rosa centifolia* 'Bullata'. Rose à feuilles de Laitue. An exact counterpart of the typical *R. centifolia* except for the enlarged and lettuce-like leaves. *Rosa centifolia* was and is much used by designers of patterned fabrics of all kinds on account of its deep-centred, voluptuous beauty.

PLATE 24. 'de Meaux'. A miniature sport of *Rosa centifolia* L., known since the eighteenth century or earlier. At the Royal National Rose Society's garden. The flowers are not more than 1 ½ inches wide.

PLATE 25. *Rosa centifolia* 'Cristata' or 'Chapeau de Napoléon'. Also known as the 'Crested Moss', though it is not a typical Moss Rose. The flowers are slightly smaller than those of *R. centifolia* itself but in all other ways its characters indicate a sport. Recorded about 1820. At Castle Howard.

PLATE 26. The rose known in English gardens as 'Fantin-Latour'. The name is without foundation; it is a somewhat hybridised version of *Rosa centifolia*, excelling in quality of foliage, flower, and fragrance.

PLATE 27. 'Tour de Malakoff'. 1856. A somewhat hybridized *Rosa centifolia* of strong though lax growth. The flowers are of the largest size.

PLATE 28. Sporting of Moss Roses. The top spray was cut from *Rosa centifolia* 'Muscosa Alba', and its lowest bud was pure white. The top buds and the main terminal flower were pink. It had reverted to *R. centifolia* 'Muscosa'. The roses on the right of the picture are of the 'Perpetual White Damask Rose' or *R. damascena* var. *semperflorens* 'Albo-muscosa' ('Quatre Saisons Blanc Mousseux'); it has reverted twice in the author's experience to the 'Perpetual Damask Rose' or *R. damascena* var. *semperflorens* ('Quatre Saisons'), which is shown in the lower left portion of the photograph. The difference between the long harsh moss of the Damask variety and the short soft moss of the Provence variety can be plainly seen; the long receptacle of the Damask is also very evident.

Rosa Muscosa alba.

Rosier Mousseux à fleurs blanches.

P.J. Redouté pinx.

Imprimerie de Remond

Langlois sculp.

PLATE 29. *Rosa centifolia* 'Muscosa Alba', which appears to be also known as 'Shailer's White Moss' or 'White Bath'. This portrait is by Redouté under the first name, 1817 to 1824; 'Shailer's' occurred in 1790, a sport from *R. centifolia* 'Muscosa' (prior to 1720). Redouté captured all the grace of 'Muscosa' in this portrait.

PLATE 30. This photograph, taken at Mottisfont, shows *Rosa centifolia* 'Muscosa Alba' sporting back to the Common Moss (pink). It occurs occasionally.

PLATE 31. The Moss Rose 'Jean Bodin' of 1846, showing good "mossy" buds and neat "button eyes," at Mottisfont.

PLATE 32. The Moss Rose 'James Veitch' of 1864, whose bristly "moss" indicates Damask Moss influence, as does its recurrent flowering habit. It is a compact, short-growing plant. From a water-colour by Siriol Sherlock.

PLATE 33. 'Capitaine John Ingram' is a Moss Rose of 1856 of remarkably dark, rich colouring. A good sturdy bush.

PLATE 34. *Rosa villosa* L. 'Wolley-Dod' or *R. pomifera* 'Duplex'. A fine sight with its semi-double flowers and later with its crimson heps. Greyish leaves.

PLATE 35. *Rosa glauca* Pourr. (*R. rubrifolia* Vill.) has the great merit of bearing dark coppery young foliage when grown in full sun, but light grey-green in shade. The single pink blooms are followed by bright red heps.

PLATE 36. Roses with greyish toned leaves: *Rosa glauca* Pourr. (*R. rubrifolia*), a native of southern and eastern Europe (top left); *R. fedtschenkoana* Reg. from Central Asia which flowers continually on young shoots; and the Hybrid Perpetual 'Reine des Violettes' of 1860, still the bluest rose ever raised.

Rosa Redutea glauca.   *Rosier Redouté à feuilles glauques.*

P. J. Redouté pinx.   Imprimerie de Remond.   Chapuy sculp.

PLATE 37. *Rosa redutea glauca* Thory as depicted by Redouté. It is a presumed hybrid of *R. glauca* and *R. pimpinellifolia*. Rediscovered in Ireland.

PLATE 38. *Rosa pulverulenta* Bieb., previously known as *R. glutinosa* Sibth. & Sm. The single pink flowers are followed by these showy heps, redolent of pines from the glandular hairs. At the Valley Gardens, Windsor Great Park.

PLATE 39. *Rosa multibracteata*, a species from China, with 'Cerise Bouquet', a hybrid with 'Crimson Glory'.

PLATE 40. *Rosa elegantula* Rolfe (previously known as *R. farreri* Stapf ex Stearn) 'Persetosa'. Farrer's Threepenny Bit Rose. It makes a wide-spreading dainty bush, the tiny foliage assuming burnished tones in sun. At Spetchley Park, Worcestershire.

PLATE 41. *Rosa moyesii* Hems. & Wils. is usually pink in the wild, or when raised from garden seed. 'Geranium', selected at Wisley by Brian Mulligan prior to 1937, is particularly brilliant in flower- and hep-colour and is the most desirable form for gardens.

PLATE 42. Colourful heps of the Cinnamomeae section. Top, *Rosa moyesii* 'Geranium'; left, *R. davidii* Crép.; bottom, *R. macrophylla* Lindl.

PLATE 43. The brilliant heps of *Rosa sweginzowii* Koehne. These heps and those in Plate 42 colour in late summer and early autumn.

PLATE 44. The plant known in gardens as *Rosa californica* 'Plena'. Though received under this name from a reputable U.S. firm in New Jersey, I suspect it is a double form or hybrid of *R. nutkana* Presl.

PLATE 45. *Rosa virginiana.* This very useful shrub excels not only in a late crop of bright pink flowers followed by bright red heps, but also in long-lasting autumn colour. It withstands wind and all vagaries of the weather.

Rosa Rapa.

Rosier Turneps.

P.J. Redouté pinx.

Imprimerie de Remond

Charlin sculp

PLATE 46. *Rosa rapa* Bosc. as depicted by Redouté. It had many characters which link it to our 'Rose d'Amour',
shown in pencil drawing 6.

PLATE 47. 'Rose d'Amour' trained up a wall at Wisley. The flowers are produced at midsummer and have a long season. From exquisite buds they open to shapely flowers. Numerous setae on the flowering stalks but few prickles. Its general appearance links it to *Rosa virginiana* and it has, like that species, good autumn colour.

PLATE 48. *Rosa hemisphaerica* J. Herrm. at Mottisfont. This was the only double yellow rose before the appearance of the Persian Yellow in 1838. It has small greyish foliage and produces good flowers in dry weather.

PLATE 49. *Rosa ecae* Aitch. An early-flowering species of special brilliance from northeastern Afghanistan and northwestern Pakistan.

PLATE 50. *Rosa foetida* 'Bicolor', or Austrian Copper Brier, sporting back to the original *R. foetida* J. Herrm., the Austrian Yellow, a native of Eastern Asia. It flowers early in the season and is in the parentage of all brilliant modern roses.

PLATE 51. *Rosa foetida* 'Persiana', the Persian Double Yellow, at Cambridge Botanic Garden. First used in hybridising in 1900 to produce vivid yellow roses.

PLATE 52. A photograph of *Rosa hugonis* Hemsl. at Hidcote, Gloucestershire, showing the grace and freedom of flowering of this Chinese species, flowering early in the season.

PLATE 53. Named 'Headleyensis' after Sir Oscar Warburg's garden near Epsom, Surrey, this hybrid is in my opinion the most satisfactory and beautiful of all the *Rosa hugonis* hybrids.

PLATE 54. *Rosa pimpinellifolia* L. (*R. spinosissima*), the Burnet Rose, growing in the sand dunes at Woolacombe Bay, North Devon. All its forms and hybrids sucker freely in sandy soils and flower early in the season. Their heps are very dark, almost black.

PLATE 55. 'Andrewsii', a well-known double form of the Burnet Rose, *Rosa pimpinellifolia.*

PLATE 56. 'Mrs Colville', probably a hybrid between *Rosa pimpinellifolia* and *R. pendulina,* indicated by its elongated plum-red heps. Freely suckering.

PLATE 57. 'Stanwell Perpetual', grown since 1838, and not surprisingly, for it is constantly in flower from late spring until early autumn, its clear blush-pink, intensely fragrant flowers making a delicious blend with its greyish leaves. A hybrid of *Rosa pimpinellifolia* perhaps crossed with an Autumn Damask Rose.

PLATE 58. *Rosa rugosa* Thunb. 'Roseraie de l'Haÿ', dating from 1901, at Barrington Court, Somerset. It flowers until autumn and has a rich clove scent.

PLATE 59. *Rosa rugosa* 'Fru Dagmar Hastrup' (1914) (top) and *R. rugosa* 'Roseraie de l'Haÿ' (1901), both deliciously redolent of cloves and fairly continuous in bloom until autumn. The first has large crimson heps.

PLATE 60. 'Fimbriata', a hybrid of *Rosa rugosa* with 'Mme Alfred Carrière'; of 1891, and still treasured for its fringed petals and sweet scent. At Rowallane, Co. Down.

PLATE 61. *Rosa rugosa* 'Fru Dagmar Hastrup' bears constantly flowers of a specially tender pink (see Plate 59) and blends them with the later crimson (not orange-red) heps. In the author's garden.

Rosa Berberifolia. *Rosier à feuilles d'Épine-vinette.*

P.J. Redouté pinx.   Imprimerie de Remond   Chapuy sculp.

PLATE 62. *Rosa persica* Michx. ex Juss. also known as *Hulthemia persica* (Michx.) Bornm. A rare dwarf species from eastern and central Asia, spreading by means of suckers.

PLATE 63. *Rosa roxburghii* Tratt. The Burr Rose, a native of China and Japan, gets its name from its large prickly green heps.

PLATE 64. *Rosa stellata* Wooton var. *mirifica* (Greene) Cockerell, the Sacramento Rose from New Mexico. It is quite hardy and in flower for many weeks. In the author's garden.

PLATE 65. *Rosa chinensis* Jacq. var. *spontanea* Rehd. & Wils. growing wild in Hubei, western China. It is a once-flowering, sprawling or climbing rose. Note that the flowers darken with age.

PLATE 66. Long known as 'Old Blush China' or 'Pallida', this is probably 'Parsons's Pink China', introduced from China in 1793, here depicted from a painting on silk a thousand years ago in China. Courtesy: Metropolitan Museum of Art, New York.

PLATE 67. 'Old Blush China' growing at Mottisfont. It is seldom out of flower. It is one of the old hybrids with *Rosa gigantea*, see page 314.

PLATE 68. The second of the old China Roses, 'Slater's Crimson China' introduced in 1794, as grown in Bermuda. It is not reliably hardy in England but is the source of true crimson in European roses raised in the nineteenth century and subsequently.

Rosa Indica.

La Bengale bichon

P. J. Redouté pinx.

Imprimerie de Rémond

Langlois sc.

PLATE 69. *Rosa indica* L. of Redouté, perhaps synonymous with 'Slater's Crimson China'.

PLATE 70. This charming little rose is known as 'Willmott's Crimson China', but is 'Chi Long Han Zhou' in China, signifying "Pearl in Red Dragon's Mouth." Constantly in flower, it achieves 2 feet or so in height.

PLATE 71. A good bush about 4 feet high and wide, of the China hybrid rose 'Bengal Crimson', sometimes called 'Sanguinea'. At Wisley.

PLATE 72. Introduced in 1809, this China Rose hybrid is known as 'Hume's Blush' and is the forerunner of Tea Roses. It will probably not exceed 2 feet in England unless trained on a warm wall. At Mottisfont

Rosa Indica fragrans.   *Rosier des Indes odorant.*
(*vulg. Bengale à odeur de thé.*)

P. J. Redouté pinx.   Imprimerie de Remond   Langlois sculp.

PLATE 73. 'Hume's Blush', depicted by Redouté. He called it *Rosa indica fragrans*.

PLATE 74. 'Parks's Yellow Tea-Scented China' is known in China as 'Danhuang Xianshui' ("The light yellow sweet-water Rose"). The fourth of the ancient Chinese Roses, it gave rise principally to the Noisettes and Tea Roses. In Hazel Le Rougetel's garden.

PLATE 75. 'Mutabilis', a China Rose hybrid of unknown origin. In warm districts its ascends to 8 feet high and an equal width and flowers more or less from early summer until autumn. At Mottisfont.

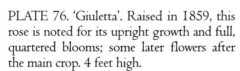

PLATE 76. 'Giuletta'. Raised in 1859, this rose is noted for its upright growth and full, quartered blooms; some later flowers after the main crop. 4 feet high.

PLATE 77. 'Héroïne de Vaucluse', a beauty of 1863. A large bush of lax growth, with good foliage. Some later blooms.

PLATE 78. A large bush of 'Honorine de Brabant' in the author's garden. The flowers are blush-pink, spotted and striped with lilac. Some later blooms after the main crop. Richly scented.

PLATE 79. 'Souvenir de St Anne's'. A semi-single sport from 'Souvenir de la Malmaison' of 1843. A good grower and almost constantly in flower, with a pronounced and delicious clove fragrance. In the author's garden.

PLATE 80. 'André Leroy', raised in 1860. A strong erect grower. Scented, with some later blooms after the first crop.

PLATE 81. 'Ardoisée de Lyon' of 1858 has a good scent and a good second crop. Slaty purple buds opening much paler.

PLATE 82. 'Georg Arends' is descended from 'Frau Karl Druschki' and 'La France' and thus is strictly a Hybrid Tea, but it fits best here. A highly decorative rose with a good scent, and repeat flowering. At Mottisfont.

PLATE 83. 'Jean Rosenkrantz' was raised in 1864 and has many good points including repeated flowering. An open, upright bush. Not much scent.

PLATE 84. A bushy, upright, branching plant is 'Lady Stuart' of 1851. Little scent, but a matchless bloom.

PLATE 85. A good scent and good autumn crop are the attributes of 'Magna Charta', a famous British rose of 1876.

PLATE 86. These exquisite blooms are of 'Paul's Early Blush', a famous British rose of 1893, a vigorous upright plant.

PLATE 87. 'Souvenir du Docteur Jamain', perhaps the richest and darkest of all Hybrid Perpetuals. Best trained on a west wall. Good repeat flowering and very fragrant.

PLATE 88. Reaching to 4 feet, 'Perle d'Or' of 1883 is justly famous for being in constant production and very fragrant. It foreshadowed the advent of the Polyanthas, being a hybrid of *Rosa multiflora* and a yellow Tea Rose. At Mottisfont.

PLATE 89. *Rosa gigantea* Collet ex Crép. A native of northeastern India, Upper Burma and Yunnan Province, flowering on the pergola at Mount Stewart, Co. Down. It is one parent of the four old Chinese roses that reached these shores between 1793 and 1824. Through 'Parks's Yellow Tea-Scented China' it gave rise to the first fairly hardy, large-flowered, yellowish climbers, the Tea Noisettes.

PLATE 90. On a sunny wall at Mottisfont: few can resist the charms of colour, shape, and scent of 'Céline Forestier', of 1842. The foliage is a pleasing light green and the plant is good at repeat-flowering.

PLATE 91. No climbing rose flowers more repeatedly through summer and autumn than 'Desprez à fleur jaune', a hybrid between 'Blush Noisette' and 'Parks's Yellow'. The perfume is fruity and unforgettable. Its early date (1830) makes it the more remarkable. At Mottisfont.

PLATE 92. While the bush form of 'Devoniensis' was raised in 1841, the climbing form did not occur until 1853. It is a sumptuous, very fragrant Tea Rose, and recurrent.

PLATE 93. Noisette Roses that are constantly in flower and very fragrant: 'Alister Stella Gray' (1894); below left, 'Blush Noisette' (*c.* 1818), and 'Céline Forestier' (1842).

PLATE 94. Nothing to approach it in size, voluptuousness, and Tea-fragrance had been seen before the famous Tea 'Maréchal Niel', in 1864, nor has anything like it been raised since. At Mottisfont.

PLATE 95. 'Lamarque' of 1830. It is of the same parentage as 'Desprez à fleur jaune', but leans more towards the second parent. At Dartington Hall, Devon.

PLATE 96. The fine, reliable old 'Gloire de Dijon', raised in 1853, can always be counted on to produce another and yet another bloom until autumn. On the gatehouse at Charlecote Park, Warwickshire.

PLATE 97. The climbing form of 'Lady Hillingdon' needs a high wall to take its tall growths. Its coppery foliage tones well with the flower colour and it is richly apricot- or tea-scented. In constant production. At Mottisfont.

PLATE 98. 'Mme Antoine Mari' of 1901 is one of the most reliable Tea Roses, making a good bush. Delicately scented.

PLATE 99. 'Blush Noisette'. Prior to 1817. The first fruit of the marrying of an ancient Chinese rose in North America with *Rosa moschata*, which led to numerous hybrids in Europe.

PLATE 100. The superb, dark green, shapely foliage and the late and continuous flowering of 'Aimée Vibert' mark this rose apart from all others. Not much scent. Vigorous.

PLATE 101. 'Fortune's Double Yellow', *Rosa odorata pseudindica* (Lindl.) Rehd., was introduced from China by Robert Fortune in 1845. It is here growing in a cool house in Ireland.

PLATE 102. 'Buff Beauty' is one of the most vigorous of the shrubby Hybrid Musk Roses and will convert to a climber on extra good soil. Tea-scented. Not good for cutting for the house.

PLATE 103. Hybrid Musk Roses 'Vanity' (1920) (top) and 'Pax' (1918); both are very fragrant and were raised by the Revd Joseph Pemberton.

PLATE 104. Hybrid Musk Rose 'Buff Beauty' (1939) (top) and five stages in the opening flowers of the China Rose hybrid 'Mutabilis'.

PLATE 105. 'Felicia' takes some beating as a scented shrub and, like 'Buff Beauty', repeats well if pruned after the main crop.

PLATE 106. 'Autumn Fire' is the name given to this brilliant rose and really refers to its astonishingly large heps (see pencil drawing 10) which are borne in autumn. There are also some late blooms after the main crop. A large, arching shrub.

PLATE 107. The summer display of 'Cerise Bouquet' from one plant at The Vyne, Hampshire. The autumn crop is not so prolific. See Plate 39.

PLATE 108. 'Complicata' is a fine, big, sprawling or semi-climbing shrub of unknown origin. It flowers once, at midsummer, and is a spectacular sight; fragrant.

PLATE 109. One way of growing 'Constance Spry' (Austin, 1961) is to train it on wall or fence. Very sweetly myrrh-scented, at midsummer. At Mottisfont.

PLATE 110. Another way of growing 'Constance Spry', trained up a support and allowed to hang down to nose level.

PLATE 111. A comparatively small-growing, re-peat-flowering shrub, 'Erfurt', 1939, with richly tinted young foliage. See Plate 113.

PLATE 112. 'Fritz Nobis', 1940, perhaps the most beautiful and graceful once-flowering shrub rose. Richly clove-scented. Lasting red heps. In the author's garden.

PLATE 113. Two brilliant modern Shrub Roses, continuous flowering: 'Golden Wings' a Burnet Rose hybrid of 1956, and 'Erfurt' of 1939.

PLATE 114. The light green leaves assort well with the soft-tinted Tea-scented flowers on a graceful shrub: 'Gold Bush' ('Goldbusch', Kordes, 1954) is to be recommended.

PLATE 115. The deliciously scented 'Nymphenburg' of 1954, which can be used as a shrub or climber.

PLATE 116. A unique hybrid between *Rosa roxburghii* and *R. sinowilsonii*, 'Roxane' was raised by Sir Frederic Stern. Once-flowering. At Highdown, Sussex.

PLATE 117. Fruits or heps of roses: top, 'Nymphenburg' (1954); mid-left, Hybrid Musk 'Penelope' (1924); mid-right, *Rosa moyesii* 'Geranium' (prior to 1937); bottom left, *R.* 'Fru Dagmar Hastrup' (1914); bottom, 'Ormiston Roy', a Burnet hybrid of 1953, and a small spray of *R. filipes* 'Kiftsgate'.

PLATE 118. 'Scarlet Fire' ('Scharlachglut', Kordes, 1952) is a lax grower, here seen trained on a wall at Sissinghurst Castle, Kent. The display of heps in autumn is nearly as brilliant.

PLATE 119. 'Heritage' (Austin, U.K., 1984). Few could resist the combination of Bourbon-perfection of shape coupled with lemon fragrance and lavish repeat blooming.

PLATE 120. 'Golden Celebration' (Austin, U.K., 1992). This has a specially good blend of yellow flowers and bright green foliage. Very fragrant; arching habit.

PLATE 121. 'The Prince' (Austin, U.K., 1990). Opening dark crimson, amid dark green leaves, the flowers quickly assume the richest imaginable purple velvet, with scent to match. A dusky effect.

PLATE 122. 'Redouté' (Austin, U.K., 1992). A free-flowering, bushy plant. A delicate pink sport from Austin's 'Mary Rose', with the same light fragrance.

PLATE 123. 'The Alexandra Rose' (Austin, U.K., 1992). A remarkably continuous-flowering rose, sweetly fragrant, of decided charm.

PLATE 147. 'Cramoisi Supérieur Grimpant'. The climbing sport is highly satisfactory on a sunny wall. Not much scent, but repeats well.

PLATE 148. William Paul crossed 'Frau Karl Druschki' with 'Maréchal Niel' to produce the unique 'Paul's Lemon Pillar' in 1915. The lemon hearts soon become creamy white. Here ascending *Cupressus arizonica* (*C. glabra*).

PLATE 149. 'Mme Grégoire Staechelin', another hybrid of 'Frau Karl Druschki', 1927, has a wonderful early summer flowering, loaded with sweet-pea perfume. It will even thrive on a north wall.

PLATE 150. The climbing form of 'Mrs Herbert Stevens' reveals the beauty of the nodding blooms—distressing in the bush form. Delicate Tea-scent. A good second crop follows. At Mottisfont.

PLATE 151. There is no rose of Hybrid Tea persuasion with so dark and rich a colour and velvety texture as 'Guinée'; it is pure, unfading, with intense red-rose fragrance. Dark foliage. A good first crop and many odd blooms later.

PLATE 152. 'Parade' on parade at the Royal National Rose Society's garden near St Albans, Hertfordshire. It is continually in flower, with good fragrance, and can be used with old or new roses.

PLATE 153. 'Aloha' can be used as a big shrub or on a pillar. The heavy repeat-flowering blooms are well scented.

PLATE 154. Graceful climbing sports of Tea Roses, 'Mrs Herbert Stevens' (1922), and 'Lady Hillingdon' (1927), both sweetly Tea-scented.

PLATE 155. The climbing sport of 'Gruss an Aachen' has a good second crop of these matchless old-style blooms with heavy fragrance.

Rose 'Lawrence Johnston' and Rose 'Cupid'

PLATE 156. A pair of modern-style climbers: 'Lawrence Johnston' (1923), and 'Cupid' (1915). The former is recurrent in early autumn and the latter has conspicuous heps.

PLATE 157. 'Meg' at Sissinghurst Castle, Kent. The dark stamens add something special to this warm-scented rose. Occasional later blooms until autumn.

Rosa 'Dream Girl'

PLATE 158. An excellent modern pillar rose, 'Dream Girl' (1944), fragrant and recurrent.

PART 2

Species Roses
and
Modern Shrub Roses

4

Rose Species in Nature and in the Garden

Would Jove appoint some flower to reign
In matchless beauty on the plain,
The Rose (mankind will all agree),
The Rose the Queen of Flowers should be.
                    Sappho, Greek poetess, born about 600 B.C.
            (from *The Book of the Rose*, by A. Foster-Melliar, 1894)

WILD ROSES MIGHT be described as prickly deciduous shrubs, with pinnate leaves and usually fragrant flowers borne singly or in clusters, from yellow and white through pink to dark red, normally with five petals; the achenes, or seeds, are contained in a fleshy, usually reddish hep. But how little can be conjured up from those bare phrases; how little they depict the wonderful and varied beauty to be found within the genus!

According to conservative botanists, about a hundred and forty species occur in the Northern Hemisphere, from as far north as Alaska and Siberia to Abyssinia and Mexico, but the greatest number come from China and neighbouring countries, and with very few exceptions all are hardy in the southern half of the British Isles. If we take our native Dog Brier, *Rosa canina*, as a yardstick we find about fifty species that are deserving of cultivation in our gardens. The Dog Brier is not usually grown as a garden plant; the reason being, I suppose, that it is too common in our hedgerows and too prickly to be manageable. Nobody will deny its beauty of flower, delicate fragrance, and colourful heps, but even so I would venture to say that all the other species roses that I have included in this book can make a greater appeal to us, through either their flowers or their heps, or both, for inclusion in our gardens. Many are just as thorny and unmanageable as *R. canina*, but their display makes them more valuable.

Some may ask why we trouble to grow wild species of rose when we have so many colourful garden hybrids; others may exclaim that the modern bedding roses are so overweening and vulgar that it is a relief to turn to nature's unadulterated beauty. In some districts and on some soils, species will grow where Hybrid Teas will not; in some gardens, anything but species would be out of place. Fortunately there is such a wide difference between the extremes of taste in gardening that there is enough demand even for the more obscure roses to warrant nurserymen growing them, although it is probably equally true that for every species that is sold, a hundred or more modern bedding roses find sales.

Some of us are brought up on Gilbert and Sullivan and develop later in life a taste for Bach. Whether the obvious is thrust on us or not, there comes a time in most people's lives when the discerning mind needs more than the obvious for its refreshment, and I know many gardeners who have graduated from dahlias and nasturtiums to species of flowering shrubs and lilies. But I should not like it to be thought that I have no use for the obvious, nor that I want all gardeners to grow species roses. When we are confronted by such variety as we find in the genus *Rosa*, only then can we say that there is a rose for every taste and every garden; and there is abundant latitude for all tastes.

Their Place in the Garden

As we study and seek to appreciate all kinds of roses so does our appreciation become deeper, finding more and more delight in colour, form, shape, scent, and all other characters that are spread before us. Gradually roses fall into fairly clearly marked groups in our minds—groups that are not botanical, nor of colour or size, but which bring together certain styles of roses. These styles become associated with styles of gardening and the gardens with styles of houses, and of course with types of people. Then there are the different areas of each type of garden to be considered. Thus, putting forth a few generalizations—however dangerous they may be—a small modern house in a new estate may suit Floribundas very well; but if the garden is large, the farther away from the house one goes the less prim one's ideas can become, and at the end of the plot wild species might not come amiss. Species can easily predominate in a country garden of large size, but I feel they are not happily placed near the house; that is where the Hybrid Teas can go, or China Roses; and to link one group with another there are the roses of sophisticated colouring, modern in tone, bright and perpetual-flowering, such as the Hybrid Musks and David Austin's English Roses, which can link the moderns with the species. And of course there is the period house around which only the Old Roses look well, with species appearing more and more frequently as one recedes farther into the depths of the shrub borders. I hope this does not sound fanciful. In my opinion, in this country today we are far too fond of collecting plants and not nearly careful enough over their placing. Our gardens are frequently like a junk shop where a bit of Old Chelsea lies cheek by jowl with a Japanese fan, an elephant's tusk, a piece of modern pottery, or a Roman coin. We are far more prone to go round the garden looking for a site for a new acquisition than to sit quietly and think out the best plant to give effect in a certain place. In the first instance the gardener is a *collector;* in the second he is a *selector,* and may well be an artist. Occasionally these two qualities are found in one individual.

Putting it simply, I like a slight sense of orderliness and prefer my Hybrid Teas, my Floribundas, or my Old Roses fairly near the house; they assort well with seats and paths, vegetable plots, formal lawns, and flower beds. At the other end of the scale are the species roses, breathing of fresh air and freedom and the wild countryside; appealing but not perhaps showy; of a beauty which needs other natural things around it in herbaceous or woody plants. Between the two extremes we are lucky in having today an ever-growing new category of roses, those which have perhaps modern colours but are big shrubs.

Having indicated the place in the garden generally that the wild species roses might occupy, let us now examine these roses and see what they have to offer us for our garden furnishing. No sweeping statements can be made. There is as much variety among them as is found in the majority of garden genera—in fact, *more.* They vary from little bushes of a couple of feet to climbers achieving a height of over 50 feet. They may grow into stalwart shrubs of 12 feet or may lie prone on the ground, exceeding that figure in length. They may make shrubs with a single woody stump giving off branches, or may colonize the ground with a thicket of ever-increasing suckering stems, and roots that travel as fast as couch grass. Some will do best climbing up into bushes and trees, others seem more at home sprawling downwards. Some are impossibly prickly; a very few are devoid of all thorns. Their lovely colours we have already sounded, and theirs is also the beauty of fruit: the heps may be tiny and round or long, bottle-shaped, and bristly. Given reasonably well-drained soil and freedom from dense overhead shade, there is not a position in any garden where a species rose would not thrive. Certainly they like full sunshine, but they will be beautiful in light shade, often taking on in such conditions a grace and delicacy not otherwise shown.

In this book I have felt it best to group the species botanically, following mainly B. O. Mulligan's key to the species in the Royal Horticultural Society's *Dictionary of Gardening*, incorporating recent changes in nomenclature from the eighth edition of Bean's *Trees & Shrubs Hardy in the British Isles* (1980). Every now and again one receives a jolt and finds that two species which one had always considered were alike, belong in fact to widely separated botanical groups! However, this once again demonstrates that gardeners and botanists do not think alike; it also demonstrates that the botanists' presupposed idea that all wild species should fall conveniently into botanical compartments is a hope without foundation. After all, why should they? They have been evolved through hundreds of thousands of years, and were successfully established denizens on this planet before mankind had invented anything, let alone a botanical "key" to the species. Various groups of species, shall we call them, had established themselves over the earth; as an example we may cite the Musk Roses which extend from Madeira through the Himalayas to Japan and, when introduced by seed from their native habitats, usually breed true to type. Geographical segregation is one of the factors which break up such an array of related plants into local species. When these "species," separated in nature by a varying terrain, are brought into cultivation and propagated by seeds over a generation or two, they may lose their identity; they may become one, or become totally different roses by hybridization with an unrelated species or garden hybrid.

This is what makes the study of species so difficult. Few of us can afford the time to refer to a pressed specimen in the British Museum, for instance, collected by a plant-hunter in western China, and have to be content with knowing the plant as grown in cultivation. Fortunately, variation of this kind can seldom be blamed upon the nurseryman. His long-practised method of reproduction has been by budding; he may be maligned when—on a wayward Dog Rose seedling that prefers a suckering life, or when his budding has been effected too high upon the "neck" of the stock and thus allows the latter to start life on its own—a rose comes up which is nothing like the plant that was sold; but he can at least claim that all his propagation has been to maintain the *status quo*. Much confusion has been caused in many genera of plants by the distribution of open-pollinated seeds of plants that inter-hybridize freely. One can sympathize with the keen amateur gardener who, having received seeds of some species from a noted botanical source, finds out after years of proud distribution of resulting plants to his friends that he has given away hosts of hybrid individuals, none of which is the true species which he tried to acquire. Roses interbreed so freely that seed-raising is not recommended; yet, let us remember the numerous seedlings that have been raised deliberately or under nature's care; I need only cite *Rosa* 'Highdownensis' as an example.

To return: as in the succeeding sections I have devoted some trouble to the grouping of the species botanically, I think this is the place to examine them horticulturally, so that when the artist goes into a brown study to find the right growth for his given spot he may perhaps be helped by the following notes, always remembering, however, that two seekers for quality in plants seldom see eye to eye. The beauty of plants is so infinite in its variety when nature has alone been the artist that we each discern different beauty on contemplation.

Ground-covering Species

It may be as well to start our review with a few completely prostrate roses, among which none is so flat and flowing as *Rosa wichuraiana*, and which has an added advantage among species: it is late-flowering. In the south of England the month of August usually arrives before the first flowers open. The dappling of creamy white small flowers over the close carpet of tiny, glossy leaves is a sight well worth waiting for, to say nothing of the fragrance. This is a rose which thrives well in sandy soil; it is a dense carpeter for any sunny slope or flat ground. Slightly higher off the ground is a hybrid between it and *R. rugosa*, 'Max Graf', which is a splendid colonizer, rooting as it goes. The next most important low ground-coverer is the vigorous and prickly *R*. 'Paulii'; this will cover 12 feet square in a few years, and not exceed 3 or 4 feet in height. Various hybrids of the true Wichuraiana Ramblers, such as 'Albéric Barbier' and 'François Juranville', are also excellent when allowed to grow flat. But lovely as they are when grown in this way, they are not sufficiently dense to smother weeds, and it is neither an easy nor a pleasant job hand-weeding among their prickly trails. So long as a rose can make a dense mass to exclude weeds I class it as a ground-cover plant; less dense roses are best used as ramblers and trained on supports.

There are several more rather higher-growing sprawling roses which make a dense covering; among the best are *Rosa* 'Macrantha' and its form 'Daisy Hill', 'Raubritter', and *R.* × *polliniana*. They all make wonderful hummocks of blossom, the first two being considerably stronger than the last two. One of the loveliest annual sights that I know is the flowering of a huge planting of 'Daisy Hill' at the back of a flower border. Practically no pruning is required. In the foreground of shrub borders, and on the fringe of woodland or grassy slopes and to cover low walls, these sprawling roses are invaluable. Many of them root as they go, and thus when suited will cover large areas of ground. This introductory list has been augmented of late years, as will be seen in Chapter 6, "Shrub Roses of the Twentieth Century."

Colonizing Species

In some gardens one sees an area devoted to heathers, which finish abruptly and give way to shrubs or other plants. As heathers are essentially plants of the wild, their surroundings should be made as harmonious as possible, and this is best done by planting dwarf rhododendrons (of which there are many that enjoy full sunshine), prostrate junipers, and dwarf brooms. Where the heathers are winter-flowering varieties or hybrids of *Erica carnea*, the ground may be limy and the rhododendrons must be excluded, but dwarf shrubby potentillas and some of the dwarf roses then come into their own, although they will of course do equally well, perhaps better, where there is no lime. The two really dwarf roses that are ideal for the heather garden and the outskirts of the rock garden are *Rosa nitida* and *R. pendulina* 'Nana'. They grow to only about 18 inches in height and are free colonizers, with single pink flowers and red heps, and with autumn colour from the first-named. Slightly taller and of similar uses are three little species, the first two with aromatic foliage: *R. pulverulenta*, *R. serafinii*, and *R. webbiana* var. *microphylla* (*R. nanothamnus*).

Rather taller, and suitable for use where the heathers merge into shrubs proper, some of the bigger colonizing roses, so thrifty on sandy soils, may be used; these are notably *Rosa pimpinellifolia* (*R. spinosissima*) in its many forms and colours, *R. virginiana*, *R.* × *reversa*, *R. foliolosa*, and *R. rugosa*. One or other of them would be flowering from the end of May till the end of September. I must repeat here a warning I have given under *R. pimpinellifolia*: that if you plant these roses you must be prepared for the nuisance of running roots. *Rosa rugosa* is considerably bigger than the others, but both thrive on light soils which are not usually given to roses, and even when the soil is really sandy—dunes or heathland—all these species will thrive amazingly. And in their likes as well as in their size and habit they are very suitable for the heather garden area. Many other species increase steadily at the root.

For Screens and Hedges

Many rose species will withstand the salt of the sea, but none makes so excellent a windbreak even on the dunes as *Rosa rugosa*. This hardy species in its typical forms is one of the best hedging roses we have. Its naturally bushy habit can be enhanced by clipping it every spring, and the clipping will result in a longer display of flower, for the best flowers are produced on the strong young shoots of the current year. Others which are dense and bushy and make good windbreaks are *R.* 'Coryana', *R.* × *micrugosa*, and 'Frühlingsanfang'. *Rosa virginiana* is lower and also excellent. Equally bushy is 'Felicia', a Hybrid Musk, and the great 'Nevada' is as good and dense as any. To create a really dense screen the first three and 'Nevada' should be planted at 4 feet apart, and the others at 3 feet, and they will all attain 5 to 7 feet in height. If greater sturdy height is needed from roses, I should interplant them at every 8 feet with one of the much taller types such as *R.* 'Highdownensis'. The riot of colour from such a mixture—and thorny tangle!—would be superb.

White on the subject of hedges I may perhaps call attention to some of the upright Gallica roses—*officinalis* and 'Rosa Mundi', 'Charles de Mills' and 'Tuscany Superb'—all will stand annual February clipping and will reach to about 3 or 4 feet. 'Great Maiden's Blush' comes to mind for an informal hedge, and many of the Hybrid Musks; in fact, any bushy rose is admirable for hedging. But let us return to the species.

Good Foliage

It is not generally realized what a big part roses can play in the colour schemes of the garden from the foliage point of view. *Rosa* × *alba*, *R. murieliae*, *R. fedtschenkoana*, *R. soulieana*, and *R. beggeriana* have grey-green leaves and white flowers. When they are in flower they give a nearly all-white effect. By grouping them with silvery foliage of other plants, santolinas, artemisias, *Elaeagnus argentea*, and the Cardoon, interspersed with white lilies, galtonias, and perhaps white phloxes and the rose 'Gruss an Aachen', a spread of cool colours can be achieved with very little trouble. To come upon such a planting round a bend in a path after a rich Byzantine mixture as visualized on page 101 would startle the most phlegmatic mortal. The two colour schemes could be linked together with another rose, *R. glauca*, whose leaves are greyish-green, overlaid with coppery-mauve. This is an invaluable species in the garden, being quite dusky and purplish in full sun, but pale and greyish in the shade. Other species have leaves which are variations in greens, though with considerable variety in shape, size, and texture, from the tiny foliage of *R. farreri* and *R. pimpinellifolia* to great limp leaves of *R. centifolia* 'Bullata' and *R. brunonii*. But all conform to a fairly regular pattern, except *R. sinowilsonii*, which grows well on a wall at Kew and in the open at Wakehurst, Sussex. This has wonderful lustrous, dark green leaves which are shining red brown beneath, and if I had a sunny wall available, it would have an honoured place. There is one variegated-leaved rose, *R. wichuraiana* 'Variegata', not very vigorous but producing dainty sprays of tiny leaves of shrimp pink turning to creamy white, with a few green flecks which become more prominent as the leaves age.

The genus is not noted for its autumn foliage colour, but there are a few species and varieties which make a decided contribution. Best known perhaps is the clear yellow of *R. rugosa*. The American species *R. virginiana*, *R. foliolosa*, and *R. nitida* can be brilliant in their red and orange, especially the first named. For more subtle and long-lasting tones 'Morletii' should be planted; its coppery pinks and soft orange will sometimes last in mild autumns until December.

Large Shrubs for Flower and Hep

Having combed out the dwarfs, the trailers, the dense low-growers, and the foliage roses, we now have left all the usual big bushes from 6 to 10 feet high and wide. The group headed by *Rosa moyesii*—*R. moyesii* 'Fargesii' and the forms 'Geranium', 'Sealing Wax', and others; *R. setipoda*, *R. davidii*, *R. sweginzowii*, and *R. macrophylla*—are all noted for their rather gaunt growth and magnificent flagon-shaped heps, which are at their best from August to October. Rather more bushy are three hybrids, *R.* 'Highdownensis', *R.* 'Hillieri', and 'Autumn Fire'. All of these must be expected to exceed 9 feet in height, and it is useless trying to keep them bushy by pruning. The more they are pruned the stronger they grow, and the less flower will be produced. It is best to encourage them to grow upright, and to make a wide ferny canopy over one's head, through which will appear the glowing flowers. The weight of the fruits will cause the branches to arch gracefully, and at that time nothing can surpass them for beauty in the garden. Small *Clematis* species like *C. macropetala* and *C. alpina* can be planted to grace their gaunt stems, and to add colour and interest in the spring.

This great group does not exhaust the fruiting roses. One of the most glittering and brilliant is *Rosa webbiana*, a very pretty, bushy, wiry shrub. And *R. canina* 'Andersonii', *R. eglanteria* (*R. rubiginosa*), *R. glauca* (*R. rubrifolia*), *R. × alba* 'Semi-plena', and some of the Hybrid Sweet Briers also are very good, but this group has the usual oval heps, not the striking flagon-shaped kind of *R. moyesii*. The main difference in the shape is that while both groups have oval heps, those of *R. moyesii* and its relatives have a persistent calyx which adds the flange, as it were, to the flagon. *Rosa rugosa* also has a persistent calyx, but its heps are rounded like tomatoes; *R. soulieana* has small orange heps. And apart from the species, several other roses are noted for their autumn fruits. 'Wilhelm' and 'Will Scarlet', two Hybrid Musks, hold their colour through the winter; 'St Nicholas', a Damask, and 'Cupid', 'Düsterlohe', 'Scarlet Fire', and many others come to mind.

From their size alone the big species would not be suitably placed in conventional beds. The fringe of woodland is an excellent place for them, or the back of wide shrub borders. They assort well with other shrubs and bring to a collection good late colour, just at a time when shrubs are looking most dull. I remember seeing a particularly happy grouping of *Rosa* 'Highdownensis' used behind *Brachyglottis* 'Sunshine', the arching sprays of red heps weeping over the grey-leaved hummocks of *Brachyglottis*; I have used *R. sweginzowii* behind the silvery grey of *Atriplex halimus*; the dark red of 'Marlena' (Floribunda) coupled with *Clematis* 'Royal Velour' is wonderful when lightened by the orange-red sprays of heps of *R. moyesii* 'Geranium'. Their period of beauty is so much longer when in fruit than when in flower that it comes to me more naturally to arrange schemes for that period. In May and June one welcomes every flower that comes to fill that glorious time, and all flowers contribute to the gaiety of the garden. But a display of certain colour in August and September is worth catering for: the weeks in the garden stand still, the flowers of the period are lasting, and all is poised in a quiet maturing way for the final autumn pageant. Even in July and August certain late-flowering species with only the one normal flowering period are at their best, notably *R. multibracteata*, *R. foliolosa*, *R. virginiana*, *R. davidii*, *R. setigera*, and the prostrate *R. wichuraiana* mentioned earlier in this chapter.

I have made no attempt in the following pages, devoted to species roses and their more immediate relatives, to describe the roses botanically. Full descriptions can be found in the standard works on the subject of woody plants. Rather, I have done my best to give a brief description of the garden merits, disadvantages, or peculiarities which may be of service to gardeners.

5

Species, Varieties, and Hybrids
Not Having Affinity to the China Rose

THE DOG ROSE AND ITS RELATIVES

OUR BELOVED native wild rose, *Rosa canina*, the Dog Brier, a fine tough shrub of great sweetness and beauty, is well enrolled among the most important ancestral species, for it will be recalled how it became united with the Damask Rose and produced a race we now call the Alba Roses. These I described at some length in Chapter 3. Of all the old races of roses, the Albas alone had large, widely spaced prickles, hard greyish leaves, excessive vigour, delicious fragrance, and clarity of colour, all of which characters can be traced back to *R. canina*. Although later varieties of Alba Roses became mixed up with all sorts of others, including no doubt the China Rose, no obvious influence of *R. canina* has transmitted itself to our newer groups. Its influence may be said to have died out, but we must always bless it for its part in producing a few roses of such great beauty and charm that they were, and still are in many ways, peerless.

All roses in our present group are natives of the Old World, and are mainly vigorous shrubs with scattered hooked prickles, and bear their flowers singly or in clusters; in nearly all species the heps become bald, that is, they lose their calyces on maturity. Many of the remaining species are not worthy of garden cultivation; in fact, if we take *Rosa canina* as our criterion, very many wild roses are ruled out, for this species sets quite a high standard of beauty. I have included two small species, *R. pulverulenta* (*R. glutinosa*) and *R. serafinii*, which are connoisseurs' plants and which add a leaf fragrance to their obvious charms. The most noted of all fragrant-leaved roses, the Sweet Brier, or *R. eglanteria* (*R. rubiginosa*), is similar in many outward appearances to *R. canina*, but with its brighter pink flowers, greater freedom of flower, and equal brilliance of hep, coupled with its delicious scent of flower and leaf, it would stand in my opinion very high in the ranks of flowering shrubs—if only it were not so frightfully prickly. It may well be that a thornless form will appear one day; thornless forms of *R. canina* have appeared from time to time—in fact it is usually considered that a thornless (or nearly so) form was the parent of *R. alba*—and today there are less prickly forms being developed as understocks for budding. If the Sweet Brier ever gives us this priceless boon, a new and very favoured flowering shrub will have arrived. Few shrubs have greater beauty at two seasons of the year.

Rosa villosa flowers early in the season, and I know of few more satisfying sights than the cool combination of clear light pink flowers scattered all over the pale jade-green leaves. Great bushes at Mottisfont and at Bone Hill flower wonderfully every year. But perhaps the most valuable rose in the group from a gardening point of view is *R. glauca*, on account of the colour—a soft greyish-green tinted with coppery-mauve. It is indispensable for colour schemes in the garden or home, but has been surprisingly little used for hybridizing. This species is widely separated botanically from *R. murieliae, R. fedtschenkoana,* and *R. beggeriana,* all of which have pale grey-green leaves and white flowers, but will hybridize readily with them, and herein may lie the germ of a series of grey-leaved roses of the future.

canina. Europe. The Dog Rose. Few wish to grow this species in their gardens; it is scarcely showy enough, and is such a common hedgerow wilding that it may well be left to grace the countryside. The Sweet Brier, *Rosa eglanteria,* has all its qualities coupled with fragrant foliage.

This species is raised by the million every year for the production of understocks for budding. It is not generally realized that when a "maiden" rose is bought—that is, a plant of one summer's growth—no fewer than four autumns have passed since the seed was picked to produce the understock. The seed needs stratifying for a year, and another year to grow; another summer passes when the rose is budded, and yet another year's growth for the scion. Looked at in this way, maiden roses are really four years old from the picking of the seed, and the price paid for the finished article has to cover these long years of patient and careful preparation by skilled workmen. First there is the harvesting, cleaning, and stratifying of the seeds, sowing and cultivating; next year lifting, grading, planting, cultivating, staking or tying, labelling, lifting, grading, and packing—and so to the customer's door. I wonder how many purchasers have any idea of all this work?

Roessig, Plate 21. Le Rosier canin.

Andrews, Plate 4. *Rosa canina,* the Dog Rose: "a title but ill adapted to designate wild nature's blushing maids."

Lawrance, Plate 81. Dog Rose or Hip Tree.

Duhamel, Vol. 7, Plate 11.

Schlechtendal, t.2629.

Bois and Trechslin, Plate 1.

Hoffman, Plate 1.

I grow three seedlings of *Rosa canina:*

—'Abbotswood'. Hilling, U.K., 1954. A seedling rose which cropped up in a hedgerow in the kitchen garden at Abbotswood, Stow-on-the-Wold, Gloucestershire; I subsequently named and distributed it. It is a vigorous plant, but more manageable than *Rosa canina* itself, and carries normal armature and light green foliage. The flowers are of true Dog Brier pink, fairly double, borne along the arching branches. Heps oval, orange-red, showy. Sweetly scented like *R. canina,* and a spray cut with half-open blooms can be very charming. 6 feet by 6 feet.

From the following illustrations it is obvious that chance hybrids or forms of this type must have occurred before:

Andrews, Plate 6, *Rosa canina* var. *flore pleno.* Very similar to 'Abbotswood'.

Lawrance, Plate 60, Double Dog Rose. Ditto.

—'Andersonii'. Known before 1912, when it was first recorded by Messrs Hillier, but of unknown origin. It is believed to be a hybrid of *Rosa canina* with one of the other diploid roses. Be this as it may, from the garden point of view it can be considered as a very worthwhile variant of the Dog Rose, for its flowers are not only considerably larger than those of that species, but of a rich and brilliant rose pink. Leaves dark, leaden green, long, pointed. Un-

like *R. canina*, its leaves are hairy beneath, while the heps are equal in brilliance and size to those of that species. It makes a wide arching bush, some 6 feet by 8 feet. Rich fragrance of raspberry-drops.
Willmott, Plate 379.
Paterson, Plate 177.

—'**Kiese**'. Kiese, Germany, 1910. 'Général Jacqueminot' × *Rosa canina*. A big, vigorous bush or semi-climber with dark green glossy leaves, and heads of semi-double or nearly single flowers, of bright cherry-red. 6 feet by 6 feet.

eglanteria (*Rosa rubiginosa*). Europe. The Sweet Brier, or Eglantine. One of the most treasured of English wild plants, and rightly so, for its flowers are clear pink, beautifully fashioned, and deliciously fragrant—a fragrance that has its richer counterpart in the aromatic foliage. It forms an arching shrub 8 feet or more high and as much through, and is very heavily armed with hooked prickles, so that it will make an impenetrable and beautiful hedge. In autumn the masses of glittering oval heps transform it into a vivid spectacle lasting well into the winter. It will make a dense hedge if pruned annually in spring, although thereby all the best flowering shoots will be removed; for this purpose it should be planted about 3 feet apart, and be allowed to make a mass some 6 feet wide. It is best to plant it to the south and west of the garden if possible, since its leaves release their fragrance most in warm moist wind. "Not even among the roses shall we find a more delicious perfume" (Dean Hole).

An interesting and beautiful hybrid is 'Eos', q.v.
Schlechtendal, t.2630.
Duhamel, Vol. 7, Plate 7. A small spray.
Andrews, Plate 109.
Lawrance, Plate 56.
Jacquin, *Flora Austriaca*, Vol. I, Plate 50.

Around 1800 several forms of Sweet Brier were growing, as recorded in old books, but very few of them have come down to us. I have found only two. And yet the Sweet Brier must have been a great favourite in old times, if only on account of its aromatic leaves. No form or hybrid that I have so far examined is as aromatic as the type species, and I have not yet seen a double pink form closely resembling the species with anything like the beauty of 'Abbotswood', a double *Rosa canina*. *Rosa eglanteria* seems to convey to its progeny a rather coarse appearance which is much at variance with its natural form.

—'**Janet's Pride**'. Introduced in 1892 by W. Paul and Sons, U.K., but Roy Shepherd tells us it was known prior to that date under the name of 'Clementine'. On the other hand, Miss Willmott records a statement by the Revd C. Wolley-Dod that this 'Janet's Pride' was found growing wild in a Cheshire lane, far from garden influence. It is thought to be a hybrid, perhaps with *Rosa damascena*, is less vigorous and prickly than *R. eglanteria*, and bears faintly aromatic foliage. The flowers are of fair size, with an extra two or three petals, bright cherry pink with nearly white centre, the pale colour running out into the pink in veins and occasional flashes, giving a charming effect. 6 feet by 5 feet.
Willmott, Plate 449.

—'**La Belle Distinguée**'. The Double Scarlet Sweet Brier. I have been unable to trace its origin, but it is no doubt a hybrid, for it is not very prickly, of dense rather upright growth to about 4 feet by 3 feet; leaves very dark green, tough, scarcely fragrant. Flowers flat, very double, deep cherry red, not very fragrant. It is a showy little bush. A few small dull red heps are produced.

Andrews, Plate 118. *Rosa eglanteria rubra*, Red-flowered Eglantine Rose. A similar, larger-flowered form, not identical to the above.

—'Manning's Blush Sweet Brier'. The excellent plate of this little double rose in Miss Lawrance's volume proves that it was in cultivation prior to 1797. Fortunately, although we know neither its origin nor its parentage, it inherits the fragrant foliage of *Rosa eglanteria*, but is very much more compact in growth, about 5 feet high and wide. It is really a minia-ture both in stature and in the size of the flowers, which are about an inch across, fully double, blush-white, with a flush of pink in the bud and half-open flower. Foliage small, rich green, on an arching fairly dense bush. Somewhat mossy calyx.

Andrews, Plate 115. The paler of the two depicted. Rather highly coloured.

Lawrance, Plate 41.

Lawrance, Plate 72. Depicts a double, mossy, Sweet Brier of dark colouring.

It is thought that the charming bright colouring of 'Janet's Pride' prompted Lord Penzance to start breeding with *Rosa eglanteria*, which he did about 1890, creating a fairly uniform group of vigorous shrubs by using pollen principally from Hybrid Perpetuals and Bourbons, and two others from *R. foetida* or its progeny. No fewer than fifteen hybrids were put on the market between 1894 and 1895, many of them rather similar. The two descended from *R. foetida*, 'Lord Penzance' and 'Lady Penzance', are not so vigorous as the others, which may frequently attain 10 feet in height and as much through; these are strong growers, therefore, suitable only for the largest plantings, where they will make a magnificent show at midsummer and not be without colour later from the heps, which most of them carry; those which I have examined have foliage somewhat aromatic, but of less potency than their parent.

Such hybrids might be placed in another section, but I prefer to list them here on account of their affinity to the Sweet Brier.

'Amy Robsart'. 1894. Deep rose pink, large, semi-double. Scarlet heps.

'Anne of Geierstein'. 1894. Dark crimson, single. Scarlet heps.

'Brenda'. 1894. Peach-blossom pink, single. I have not grown this variety.

'Catherine Seyton'. 1894. Soft pink, single. Aromatic foliage. I have not grown this variety.

'Edith Bellenden'. 1895. Pale pink, single. Aromatic foliage. Not in my collection.

'Flora McIvor'. White, flushed with pink, single. Aromatic.
    Mansfield, Plate 52.

'Greenmantle'. 1895. Rosy crimson, with white eye, single. Aromatic foliage.

'Jeannie Deans'. 1895. Brilliant crimson-scarlet, semi-double. Aromatic foliage.
    Kingsley, page 44.

'Julia Mannering'. 1895. Bright, clear, delicate pink, with darker veins; nearly single.

'Lady Penzance'. 1894. *Rosa eglanteria* × *R. foetida bicolor*. Single, bright yellow centre, with cop-pery-salmon flush over most of the petal area. Pretty arching growth, foliage somewhat aromatic. Scent of flowers reminiscent of *R. foetida*.
    Mansfield, Plate 52 (poor).

'**Lord Penzance**'. 1894. *Rosa eglanteria* × 'Harison's Yellow'. Single; rosy-fawn-yellow, lemon centre. Sweet scent; fragrant foliage.

'**Lucy Ashton**'. 1895. A distinct pink edge adds colour to the pure white, single flowers. Aromatic foliage.

'**Lucy Bertram**'. 1895. Dark, vivid crimson with white centre; single; aromatic leaves. Scarlet heps.

'**Meg Merrilies**'. 1894. Rosy crimson, nearly single. Aromatic foliage. Scarlet heps.

'**Minna**'. 1895. Clear salmon-rose with white centre. Sweet scent. Very aromatic foliage.

'**Rose Bradwardine**'. 1894. Rose pink, single. Aromatic foliage.

In 1916 Hesse, the German nurseryman, put on the market 'Magnifica', which was the result of "selfing" a seedling from 'Lucy Ashton'. It is a vigorous plant, with large, semi-double, deep pink, cupped blooms, deliciously scented, and has been used extensively by Wilhelm Kordes for the production of widely differing hybrids. Ann Wylie gave a very clear family tree in the Royal Horticultural Society's *Journal* for February 1955, showing all the derivatives, including Floribundas. We need only concern ourselves, however, with certain of the shrubby seedlings, one of which is of superlative beauty for general use, 'Fritz Nobis'. Kordes's aim is the production of bright Floribundas and others which will have greater hardiness and resistance to disease owing to the influx of new blood from *Rosa eglanteria*, and he has successfully launched several varieties and used the progeny for further experimentation. These newer shrubby types will be found included with others in Chapter 6, "Shrub Roses of the Twentieth Century."

glauca (*Rosa rubrifolia*). Mountains of central and southern Europe. *Rosa ferruginea*. Botanically, this rose is more suitably grouped with the species in the next section. There are very few shrubs with such distinctive garden value as this open-growing species, with no great pretensions apart from the colouring of its leaves. It is practically thornless, apart from the bases of the strong violet-coloured young shoots, and in winter imparts a warm red-brown effect, reaching up to 6 or 8 feet in height and as much through. The growth and leaves resemble somewhat the Dog Brier, but all the leaves, from spring till autumn, have a unique glaucous colouring; in shady cool places they are usually broad and luxuriant and grey-green, with a hint of mauve, while in sunshine they are smaller and suffused with a rich coppery-mauve tint. The flowers are borne in bunches, the long calyx-lobes creating a hairy effect around each bunch, and they open flat; they are of clear pink, enhanced by the white centre area which in turn is crowned by light yellow stamens. The buds and young wood are dark purplish-copper. Later the heps, of an unusual brownish-red, crop in bunches and give further colouring to the bush, as they are usually very free. Little scent. (Plate 35.)
Redouté, Vol. I, Plate 31. Le Rosier à feuilles rougeâtres.
Willmott, Plate 399. Beautiful and true to nature in every way.
Duhamel, Vol. 7, Plate 10.
Schlechtendal, t.2627. Does not show the usual white centre.
Botanical Register, Vol. 5, t.430. A poor little spray.
Andrews, Plate 92. *Rosa lurida*. A somewhat pithy comment on this fine portrait showing

an amazing number of flowers occurs in the *Botanical Register*: "Andrews has a figure of it in a most luxuriant state under the name of *lurida*, by which it is known in the nurseries." One might understand that nurserymen's flair for exaggeration was not unknown in those days.

Beales, Plate page 83, heps.

Gibson, Plate 15.

'Carmenetta'. (*Rosa* × *rubrosa.*) *Rosa glauca* (*R. rubrifolia*) × *R. rugosa.* Canada, 1930. Raised at Ottawa. This plant is very near to *R. glauca*, but from *R. rugosa* it inherits coarseness and prickles. On the whole I think it inferior to *R. glauca;* it has a stronger growth, equally good leaves, larger flowers in larger bunches, and the fruits are very similar. In some soils where for any reason *R. glauca* might not thrive—possibly those which are light and sandy— 'Carmenetta' should be tried. The leaves are glaucous blue-grey with violet tints above, grey-green beneath.

'Redutea Glauca'. Under this name Redouté records a rose which is manifestly a hybrid between *Rosa glauca* and *R. pimpinellifolia*. His painting is reproduced in this volume (Plate 37). Early in the nineteenth century a similar hybrid was grown in the garden of The (later Royal) Horticultural Society in London, and in 1838 a colony of the hybrid was found in the Haute Savoie. In one of his last catalogues Leslie Slinger, of the Donard Nursery, listed a white form of *R. rubrifolia* (*R. glauca*). Through the kindness of Philip Wood a plant eventually reached the garden of Dr E. C. Nelson, where we recognised it as this long-lost hybrid.

× hibernica. 1802. *Rosa canina* × *R. pimpinellifolia*. Mrs Gore, in *The Rose Fancier's Manual*, 1838, mentions that "the environs of Belfast produce an insignificant shrub, known as the Rose Hibernica, for the discovery of which Mr Templeton received a premium of fifty guineas from the Botanical Society of Dublin, as being a new indigenous plant." I have been amused by and not a little jealous of Mr Templeton's prowess; such a reward from such a quarter would be inconceivable today. It is a very pretty little shrub, now known to be a hybrid between *R. canina* and *R. pimpinellifolia*, thanks to Gordon Rowley's patient work. Mrs Gore refers to the difference in growth on poor or rich soil in her absurd remarks; with her it apparently varied considerably in vigour, but my plant, received from Lady Moore some years ago, has never departed from its normal appearance, which is in effect a large bush with greyish leaves and cream-pink single flowers, leaning considerably towards *R. canina*. It is recorded that this hybrid occurs occasionally in nature and may therefore vary in character, but the stock received from Lady Moore was the original. It has recently been resuscitated by Dr E. C. Nelson and is preserved in the grounds of the University, Belfast. About 6 feet by 10 feet.

Willmott, Plate 289.

× pokornyana is a name recorded for hybrids between *Rosa glauca* and *R. canina*.

pulverulenta (*Rosa glutinosa*). Southeastern Europe, western Asia. *Rosa dalmatica*. This rose is seldom seen, but should be in collections when possible on account of its aromatic foliage, which smells like a pine forest on a hot day. The odour comes from innumerable sticky

glands on both sides of the small leaves, which cluster the dense growth thickly. The twiggy shoots branch freely, bearing prickles of all sizes, and make a bushy plant up to 2 or 3 feet and as much wide. The flowers are small, of clear pink, and resemble those of the Sweet Brier, but the heps are large, of rich dark red, and covered with bristly hairs; the display of heps creates a more telling effect than that of the flowers. Tall forms are native to some localities. (Plate 38.)
Willmott, Plate 467.
Sibthorp, Vol. 5, Plate 482.
Botanical Magazine, t.8826. *Rosa glutinosa dalmatica*, a closely related geographical form with larger fruits.

serafinii. Mediterranean. *Rosa apennina*. An exceedingly dense twiggy plant, growing to about 3 feet in height, and copiously armed with small hooked prickles. The thin, wiry, short-jointed twigs interlace freely and bear numerous small rounded leaves with five or seven small rounded leaflets, densely glandular on the margin and stalk, and thus gummy and fragrant. Pretty little pale pink single blooms appear at midsummer, followed by a good show of small, bright red, rounded fruits. A gay little shrub suitable for planting in heath gardens and such places where a breath of the wild without unmannerliness is needed. *Rosa sicula* is very similar but has straight prickles. *Rosa biebersteinii* is an allied species.
Willmott, Plate 475. A good portrait.

sherardii. Northern and central Europe. *Rosa omissa*. This rose makes a well-filled shrub, covered with bluish-green leaves, up to about 5 feet high and wide. The shapely single pink flowers are of a particularly clear, fresh pink and contrast well with the foliage. This rose might be a good substitute in small gardens for the similarly coloured large-growing *R. villosa*. Bright oval heps.

villosa. *Rosa pomifera*. The Apple Rose. Europe, West Asia. This most beautiful species makes a large shrub, fairly compact, up to 7 feet high and rather wider. The large grey-green leaves are downy on both surfaces and give exactly the right contrast to the single flowers, which are of a particularly clear and lovely pink, and prettily crinkled. At flowering time it is not eclipsed in beauty by any other species. Through the summer the foliage remains greyish, although it loses its first cool freshness, and later makes another lovely foil for the huge heps, which turn from orange-red to rich plum-crimson, densely set with bristly hairs. Slightly fragrant. *Rosa tomentosa* is an allied species, likewise *R. mollis*, which is native to northern Britain and elsewhere.

Rosa villosa has been used as an understock for budding from time to time, and Dean Hole recalls in his *A Book About Roses* a hedge of it twenty years old at Kilkenny in 1834, belonging to a Mr Robertson, "about 8 or 10 feet high, which is a sheet of bloom every May, and throughout the rest of the season flowers with the Boursault, Noisette, Hybrid China, and other Roses which are budded on it." Andrews refers to a similar hedge 13 feet high with sixteen varieties of roses budded on it. All this might be a pointer towards bigger and better roses for the future.
Willmott, Plate 435. A rather poor flower. *Rosa pomifera*.
Andrews, Plate 34.

Lawrance, Plate 33. The single apple-bearing rose. Very highly coloured.

Botanical Magazine, t.7241. An admirable portrait of the flowers and remarkable fruits.

Schlechtendal, t.2632. A good portrait.

Roessig, Plate 30. Le rosier vélu ou à fruits épineux. *Rosa pomifera, R. villosa*. An excellent plate.

Duhamel, Vol. 7, Plate 15. *Rosa villosa*.

Redouté, Vol. 1, Plate 67. Le Rosier vélu.

—'**Wolley-Dod**'. *Rosa villosa* 'Duplex', *R. pomifera* 'Duplex'. A semi-double hybrid of the "Apple Rose" and of equal vigour, Wolley-Dod's Rose is undoubtedly a hybrid between *R. villosa* and a tetraploid garden rose, according to the chromosome count. The figure in Willmott's *Genus Rosa* was from the Revd Wolley-Dod's garden, and is therefore authentic. That this plant was an original seedling is not recorded by her, but semi-double forms were known earlier, witness two other plates cited. It has little scent; its chief merits are the exquisite blend of the flowers, and later the heavy dark red heps, with the leaves. It is not quite so free of fruits as the species. (Plate 34.)

Willmott, Plate 436. *Rosa pomifera* variety.

Andrews, Plate 34.

Lawrance, Plate 29. The double apple-bearing rose.

Beales, Plate, page 6; page 210.

Phillips and Rix, Plate 29.

THE CINNAMON ROSE AND ITS OLD WORLD RELATIVES

> The Canell or Cinnamon Rose, or the rose smelling like Cinnamon, hath leaves like unto those of Eglantine, but smaller and greener, of the savour or smell of Cinnamon, whereof it tooke his name, and not of the smell of his floures which have little or no savour at all.
>
> Gerard's *Herball*, 1597

THE MAJORITY of our garden rose species belong to what the botanists call the Cinnamomeae Group, exemplified by *Rosa majalis* (*R. cinnamomea*), a singular honour for a not very important small European species in a group comprising some forty species, including such horticultural giants as *R. rugosa* and *R. moyesii*. In botanical works, without which we should have difficulty in finding our way through the morass of species at all, mere size and colour of flower or hep are not so important as such obscure points as the shape of the style in the flower, the placing of the seeds in the hep, or the fusion of the stipules to the leaf-stalk.

I find it impossible to give a group of characters by which all species in this section can be distinguished. There are exceptions to every rule, but the section resolves itself fairly easily into several recognizable groups. There are *Rosa rugosa*, *R. kamtschatica*, and *R. acicularis* at one end, we might say, covered with prickles and bristles, whereas *R. pendulina* is thornless. Almost all species have persistent sepals, projecting erectly above the hep except in *R. willmottiae*. The great group of species allied to *R. moyesii* has long flagon-shaped heps, and does in fact constitute the bulk of the species included in this section, which is devoted to the Old World representatives of the Cinnamomeae Group, apart from *R. rugosa*, which has a section to itself. The New World species will be found in the next section.

beggeriana. Temperate Asia. The first alphabetically of a trio of roses with grey leaves and white flowers. From *Rosa fedtschenkoana* and *R. murieliae* it is separated by minor botanical differences; all provide an exceptional pale grey-green effect in the garden, and are thus valuable for colour schemes. This species is perhaps the least grey and the least ornamental of the three. Its hooked prickles distinguish it from the other two, and also from *R. soulieana*, another valuable grey-leaved rose which belongs to a separate group. The fragrant leaves are of medium size with 5 to 9 leaflets, and the flowers are borne in small clusters. They have a peculiar scent—reminiscent of *R. foetida*—and appear over a long period, the later ones having as companions dark-red heps from earlier flowers; these heps eventually turn to maroon, and lose their sepals—an exception to the rule. It is of tall, spreading habit, up to 8 feet high and wide. *Rosa gymnocarpa* and *R. albertii* are closely related.
Willmott, Plate 171.

davidii. Eastern Tibet, western China. A tall, open shrub reaching 9 to 10 feet in height, with erect but arching light green shoots and a few reddish prickles. The leaves are deeply veined, giving a corrugated yet matt effect, elegantly poised. The flowers do not appear until most species are over, and are borne in big bunches all the way up the stems, smelling of peonies, loosely nodding, with sticky, hairy stalks and long calyx lobes; their soft mallow-pink is a welcome change at that time from the vivid Floribundas. The resulting bunches of small, flagon-shaped heps are most attractive. A useful species on account of its late-flowering habit and slender grace.
Botanical Magazine, t.8679.

—**elongata**. A form with rather longer fruits in small clusters, and longer leaflets.

elegantula. Northwestern China. The wild species is not in cultivation.

—**'Persetosa'**. *Rosa farreri*. The Threepenny Bit Rose, so called because of the size of its flowers. This variety was noted by E. A. Bowles among a batch of seedlings of *R. elegantula* (Farrer No. 774), and was named *persetosa* because of its excessive crop of hair-like prickles, which occur all the way up the stems, and its richer colouring. The species makes a charming plant about 6 feet high and sometimes twice as wide, with graceful shoots set with the tiniest of leaves with 7 to 9 leaflets. It has quite an airy effect, like a veil, and when the clear salmon-pink flowers from coral buds appear it is a plant of great distinction. Small, orange heps follow.

It is the flimsiest of roses, like *Rosa willmottiae* but with leaves and flowers of half the size, and with the grace of *R. webbiana*. In the garden it appears to flourish best in cooler places, even in partial shade, when its ferny grace is the more apparent. In hot positions the foliage is frequently burnished or purple-tinted. (Plate 40.)
Botanical Magazine, t.8877.
Gibson, Plate 1.

fedtschenkoana. Turkestan. Shrubs with pale grey-green leaves are not many and for this reason alone this species has considerable garden value. It is similar to *Rosa beggeriana* and *R. murieliae* and also *R. soulieana* in this greyness, but noticeable characters separating it from all these are the hispid calyx tube and persistent sepals. Apart from these small botanical points it has another great attribute, for it produces its flowers continuously through the summer, one or a few together at the ends of short side-shoots; they are white, 2 inches across, with yellow stamens, and the later crop coincides with the earliest of the orange-red bristly heps. The scent of the flowers reminds me of that of *R. foetida*. It forms an erect bush up to 9 feet and about 6 feet wide, well filled with small branches, and spreads freely by underground shoots. The strong, young, grey shoots, covered all over with pinkish bristly prickles, are of great beauty. It is altogether a valuable rose, interesting and charming throughout the growing season. Leaflets 5 to 9.

Willmott, Plate 155. A good portrait.

Botanical Magazine, t.7770. A good portrait.

forrestiana. Western China. A vigorous bush, with strong, arching branches and straight prickles; fresh green, copious foliage, with 5 to 7 leaflets; very free-flowering, and a splendid sight both then and when in fruit. The flowers are deep carmine-pink, single, like *Rosa moyesii* in shape, with creamy-yellow stamens, very fragrant. They are borne on short side-shoots, but their stalks are almost absent, the flowers being clustered four or five together in a very tight bunch. The heps are large and hairy, bottle-shaped, bright red, and are framed in the persistent green bracts. 7 feet by 6 feet.

macrophylla. Himalaya. One of the largest of shrubby roses, reaching 15 feet in height and as much or more in width. An old plant in Cambridge Botanic Garden once achieved "18 feet in height by 25 feet—10 feet in excess of given height" (R. Irwin Lynch in the Royal Horticultural Society's *Journal*, 1915). It creates ferny shade, and often with the flowers above one it can be passed unnoticed, but the flowers when seen are not likely to be forgotten. They have much of the poise of those of *Rosa setipoda*, and are of warm clear pink, followed by bristly, long, flagon-shaped fruits. It is often without prickles, and the leaflets, from 7 to 9 in number, are hairy beneath. The whole plant is elegant and owes not a little to the beauty of the pruinose young shoots, and the maroon setae on the receptacle. Few roses have such an elegant poise of bloom. *Rosa saturata* is closely allied.

Two subsequent collections by Forrest (14958 and 15309) were named 'Glaucescens' and 'Rubricaulis' by Messrs Hillier. In the former the leaves are particularly glaucous, and in the latter the plum-like bloom on the dark reddish stems is a distinguishing feature. 'Rubricaulis' has not proved so hardy as the other forms in cultivation, but is of exceptional beauty, and richly coloured.

Willmott, Plate 157.

Wallich, Plate 117.

—**'Doncasteri'**. A form of *Rosa macrophylla* put on the market between the wars by Mr Doncaster of Messrs J. Burrell and Co. of Cambridge, but probably one of Dr Hurst's seedlings. It has narrower, darker green leaves than the type, with smaller, darker flowers, and a less free and graceful habit. Its chief glory is the sumptuous display of large, red, flagon-shaped heps in early autumn.

—**'Master Hugh'**. 1966. Raised by L. Maurice Mason from seed collected in China by Messrs Stainton, Sykes and Williams, No. 7822. Beautiful not only in its typical *Rosa macrophylla* flowers, but also in its splendid bottle-shaped fruits; both are of great size and quality. Probably 8 feet by 10 feet.

Other species related to these and allied to *Rosa moyesii* are *R. caudata, R. hemsleyana (Botanical Magazine,* t.8569), *R. banksiopsis;* all have some merit but I should not choose any of them in preference to the species I have described.

majalis (*Rosa cinnamomea*). Europe, northern and western Asia. Cinnamon or May Rose. Reaching 6 feet or so in height, this is a small-leaved shrub of no great merit for the garden. The flowers are of dark pink, up to 2 ½ inches across, borne in small clusters or singly. Stipules very wide. I have been unable to detect any cinnamon scent, though Gerard and Parkinson ascribe it to the foliage and to the flowers, respectively. Possibly "cinnamon" refers to the colour of the stems.
Willmott, Plate 141.
Andrews, Plate 96.
Schlechtendal, t.2626.
Redouté, Vol. I, Plate 133. *Rosa cinnamomea flore simplici,* Le Rosier de Mai à fleurs simples.

—'**Plena**'. Rose de Mai; Rose du Saint-Sacrement, Rose des Pâques. Miss Willmott claims that the original *Rosa cinnamomea* 'Plena' was of a much deeper colouring than her figure to which she gives the above synonyms. Probably doubling has occurred several times and slightly different colour forms have been the subject of separate records, but all that I have seen have had a dark lilac-pink tone, and I have not considered them of much value. It is true that it is one of the oldest recorded double roses, and as such is worthy of a place in a collector's garden. Mrs Gore, 1838, states "this sub-variety is a favourite in all gardens." It is extremely early-flowering, as its popular names suggest, and this may have been one of the causes of its popularity. About 4 feet by 3 feet.
Lindley, Plate 5. A good portrait of the flowers in bud.
Willmott, Plate 143. Possibly not authentic.
Lawrance, Plate 34. The Double Cinnamon rose.
Andrews, Plate 97. *Rosa cinnamomea multiplex,* the Double Cinnamon Rose, said to have been introduced from southern Europe in 1569.
Roessig, Plate 3. Le Rosier de Mai, *Rosa majalis.* Excellent.
Redouté, Vol. I, Plate 105. *Rosa cinnamomea majalis.* Le Rosier de Mai. A rather elongated drawing.

Michael R. Hayward informs me that there is a Damask Rose, grown in the commercial fields at Grasse in the south of France, also known as 'Rose de Mai'; further, that there is another with the same name, possibly a hybrid with *R. centifolia,* which is also cultivated to extend the harvesting season. Neither of these roses is connected with *R. cinnamomea.*

moyesii. Western China. This is not only a very fine species of unique qualities and colouring, but also a landmark in rose history. It was introduced into cultivation in 1908, and its intense red flowers and magnificent heps at once gave the growing of wild roses a fillip; *Rosa hugonis* had recently appeared in cultivation, and the two of them placed rose species well to the fore among flowering shrubs—a position to which the many rather insignificant pink species would never have brought them. It is undoubtedly one of the finest of all flowering shrubs, and one of E. H. Wilson's greatest treasures from the Far East.
Unfortunately it is of a gaunt, tall habit which at first might make it appear unsuitable for all but the largest of gardens, attaining as it often does 12 feet in height, the branches

above supported by relatively few, extremely stout, prickly stems. But where it thrives it forms a lofty canopy of small leaves with 7 to 13 leaflets of dark, rather bluish green, and the resulting broken shade provides the ideal conditions for plants that cannot stand full sunshine. The flowers are borne in small clusters, and are of intense blood-red colouring, with dark-coloured stamens. When seen against a blue sky their colouring is enhanced. This blood-red type is not the most common in its native habitat, but takes priority in naming. The pink form, to which seedlings often revert, is more common and is known as *R. m.* 'Fargesii'.

Although the flowers are of such wonderful colour I think that the heps were probably of more value in getting it the recognition it deserved: apart from its allied species, all introduced about the same time (except *Rosa macrophylla*), no other rose or shrub had such striking large fruits of so unusual a shape. They are bulbous at the base, narrowing above before widening again below the persistent calyx lobes, and thus shaped like a flask or flagon, with which they are often compared. The heps are at their best in August, and this applies to the allied species as well. Berried shrubs were not of much account in the nineteenth century, so that here again its introduction was most opportune, when the numerous new flowering shrubs were awakening the public to fresh beauty for their gardens.

The Garden, October 1916, page 514. Flowers and fruits; very fine.

Revue Horticole, 1926–7, page 334.

Botanical Magazine, t.8338. Poor.

Willmott, Plate 229. A splendid portrait.

Le Rougetel, Plate 39.

—'Fargesii'. This is so near to *Rosa moyesii* as not to be distinguished from a garden point of view, except in floral colour. It has rose-red flowers and the usual heps. On the other hand the chromosome count—it is a tetraploid—makes it a possible parent for 'Nevada' and other similar crosses, rather than *R. moyesii* itself, which is a hexaploid.

— 'Rosea'. *Rosa holodonta*. These two names are sometimes used for pink-flowered forms of *R. moyesii*. *Rosa holodonta* in reality relates to *R. davidii elongata*.

Botanical Magazine, t.9248. This is *Rosa sweginzowii*.

Garden Forms and Hybrids of Rosa moyesii

'Arthur Hillier'. Hillier, U.K., *c.* 1938. One of the type of seedling which occurs whenever either *Rosa macrophylla* or *R. moyesii* is grown. This excels in its semi-erect but arching vigour, lots of small dark leaves and bunches of rosy red flowers with prominent stamens. The display of bright red flask-shaped heps is equally brilliant, in early autumn. 10 feet by 6 feet.

'Autumn Fire'. Kordes, Germany, 1961. 'Herbstfeuer'. Having tested this for many years, I think it a worthy addition to autumn-fruiting roses, to say nothing of its midsummer display (with a few later) of dark blood-red blooms touched with scarlet and maroon. They are semi-double, borne along arching branches. In late autumn the heps take on red colouring; they are bottle-shaped, and the longest and largest in the genus. 6 feet by 9 feet. (Plate 106; heps, Drawing 10.)

'Fred Streeter'. Jackman, U.K., 1951. A seedling *Rosa moyesii* which originated at Petworth, Sussex, and was originally distributed as *R. moyesii* 'Petworth'. Considerably more bushy, with fine, dense, arching habit and fresh green leaves. The flowers are of bright cerise pink. Large flagon-shaped crimson-red heps. This is no doubt a form of *R. moyesii* 'Fargesii' and resembles 'Sealing Wax' and *R. wintoniensis*.

'Geranium'. 1938. This excellent form, raised at Wisley and selected by B. O. Mulligan, is of more compact growth than the type, with more copious, larger, fresh-green leaves. The flowers are a magnificent blazing red, and the heps are larger and smoother than those of the average *Rosa moyesii*, and of equally good colour. Undoubtedly the best type for the average garden, or at least for those gardeners who prefer a reasonably compact erect bush up to 10 feet by about 7 feet, rather than a gawky tree-like shrub creating overhead shade. It has few thorns. (Plate 41.)
Beales, Plate page 232 (heps).

'Sealing Wax'. 1938. A form or hybrid of *Rosa moyesii* 'Fargesii' of the same origin as 'Geranium', selected for its splendid scarlet heps. Vivid pink flowers in the *R. moyesii* style. Possibly a hybrid with *R. sweginzowii*.

Rosa moyesii crossed with 'Donald Prior' by Eddie in Canada produced two good roses of *moyesii* style but with larger flowers. 'Eddie's Crimson' (1956) is double, dark crimson followed by rounded red heps, and 'Eddie's Jewel' is also double, of bright red. It produces a later crop of flowers in good seasons. 9 feet by 6 feet.

The following are known or presumed to be hybrids of *Rosa moyesii*, but are sufficiently like a species rose to be included here.

'Eos'. Ruys, Holland, 1950. *Rosa moyesii* × 'Magnifica'. With two such vigorous parents a vigorous offspring would be expected, and this plant can achieve 12 feet in a few seasons after planting, sending up stiff yet arching shoots daintily set with small *moyesii* foliage in dark leaden green; the next spring they become wands of coral red, from the clusters of nearly single, flat flowers borne along their entire length. Stamens yellow. It is a most arresting sight; worthily named after the Goddess of the Dawn, for just those flaming tints appear at sunrise. No heps. For late May and early June display few roses can compete with its brilliance. It is best planted well behind other shrubs to cover its gaunt lower stems. Spiky red prickles.

'Highdownensis'. 1928. A seedling from *Rosa moyesii* which occurred in Sir Frederick Stern's garden at Highdown, Goring-by-Sea, Sussex. The original plant is still a fine sight on a chalky slope. Although it is less of a vivid red colour than a selected *R. moyesii*, it is in many ways a much more satisfactory and spectacular plant, being more bushy, and bearing elegant, deeply tinted leaves. The single flowers are borne in conspicuous clusters, of vivid cerise-crimson, and are followed by large flagon-shaped orange-scarlet heps. At both flowering and fruiting time it can hold its own with anything in the garden. Its general good behaviour and vigour recommend it for all large plantings of shrub roses; it makes a fine shrub of some 10 feet by 10 feet. The strongest shoots are very beautiful, with colourful prickles and bristles and coppery leaves. Little fragrance.
Gardeners' Chronicle, 6 January 1934.
Beales, Plate 233. Heps.

'Hillieri'. *Rosa hillieri*. Hillier, U.K., *c.* 1920. The darkest-flowered single rose, resembling *R. moyesii* in shape and type of flower, but the growth is more graceful, the branches forking and interlacing, making a large mass sparsely covered with small, pretty leaves. A few fine heps are produced, flagon-shaped, orange-red. It is best placed so that the sun shines through the murrey-crimson of the flowers, greatly enhancing their colour. Young wood glaucous green with few large thorns. 10 feet by 12 feet. Usually considered to be a hybrid between *R. moyesii* and *R. willmottiae*, but Gordon Rowley tells me that the chromosome count of *R. willmottiae* would preclude this cross. Sometimes classed under *R. × pruhoniciana*.

'Wintoniensis'. Hillier, U.K., 1928. *Rosa moyesii × R. setipoda.* A big, bushy, fresh green, leafy plant, whose foliage is scented, like that of *R. setipoda.* Single vivid cerise- to rose-pink flowers with paler centres, and the general appearance of *R. moyesii* 'Fargesii'. Has purplish setae on the young heps. 12 feet by 12 feet.

multibracteata. Western China. A vigorous shrub up to 7 feet and often more in width, sending up prickly stout shoots, green while young, with mahogany-coloured prickles which turn later to grey, on red-brown wood. These stout shoots branch freely in subsequent years, producing numerous fine zigzag twigs heavily set with tiny leaves of 7 to 9 greyish leaflets, rounded and grey-green, giving an effect of dots of green at a distance. The flowers are small but numerous, enshrouded with multitudes of grey-green bracts the same size as the leaves, in long arching, branching sprays; cool lilac-pink with creamy stamens, they are borne late in the season—often into August—and are thus doubly welcome. When growing vigorously it is luxuriant in its beauty, creating a curtain of flower and leaf. The scent is unusual, and related to that of *Rosa foetida.* Small bright red, cerise-tinted, rounded heps. *Rosa latibracteata* is closely allied. 'Cerise Bouquet' (q.v.) is a beautiful hybrid. (Plate 39.)

murieliae. Western China. The third of our trio of grey-leaved roses and larger than the others, making an arching shrub up to 6 or 8 feet and as wide, producing underground stems. The smaller shoots are drooping and make a dense curtain of foliage, pale grey-green, among which the small white flowers are disposed in clusters of 3 or 7. Leaflets 9 to 15, borne on downy, prickly stalks. The sepals have leafy tips and stay on the elliptical red heps, which are glabrous. In common with *Rosa fedtschenkoana* its strong young shoots are heavily armed with pinkish bristles, and a few prickles which are straight. It will grow to large proportions, arching and weeping to the ground and creating a beautiful effect, some 7 feet high by 12 feet wide.

oxyodon. *Rosa haematodes.* A native of the Caucasus, sometimes considered a variety of *R. pendulina* and, like that species, practically thornless, with reddish-purple stems. The leaves, composed of 7 to 9 leaflets, are of greyish-green with reddish stipules. It is not particularly striking when producing its clusters of single, deep pink flowers with yellow stamens and long sepals, but the bulky, flagon-shaped heps in dark red turn it into a thing of splendour in late summer. 4 to 5 feet.

pendulina. Central and southern Europe. *Rosa alpina.* This mountain shrub figures in all the illustrated Alpine floras, and it is surprising that it is found so seldom in gardens, being practically thornless. The reddish, sometimes purplish stems make an open, arching shrub up to 4 or 5 feet high and wide. As many as 11 leaflets sometimes occur but usually there are between 5 and 9, creating an airy effect. The flowers are about 2 inches across, of rich, light crimson with a purplish suffusion; stamens light yellow. The long fruit, more or less narrowed to a flask shape at the end, is bright red and decorative, but by no means as large as that of *R. moyesii*. It flowers very early in the season, and often provides good autumn colour too.

Among the progeny of *Rosa pendulina* are 'Mrs Colville' and *R. × reversa*. For years it has been claimed to be the ancestor of the old Boursault Roses (*R. lheritierana* or *R. × reclinata*); from chromosome counts taken at Bayfordbury, Gordon Rowley tells me that this is highly suspect and that some other species, perhaps *R. blanda*, is probably concerned in the parentage of this old group of roses.

Botanical Register, Vol. 5, t.424. Poor colour.
Lawrance, Plate 9. Good portrait, vivid colour.
Willmott, Plate 293.
Schlechtendal, t.2625. Light pink.
Andrews, Plate 88. *Rosa inermis*.
Jacquin, *Flora Austriaca*, Vol. 3, Plate 279.
Redouté, Vol. 1, Plate 57.

—**'Flore Pleno'**. See 'Morletii', Chapter 6.

—**'Nana'**. *Rosa pendulina pyrenaica*. This charming dwarf Pyrenean form was recorded in cultivation in 1815, and has enjoyed a certain amount of popularity among rock garden enthusiasts. It runs freely at the root and its plum-coloured stems ascend to about 1 foot. It is more prickly than the type species, but not heavily armed, and the scattering of single light crimson flowers can give a lovely effect among other plants. It has a densely glandular receptacle and calyx, giving a pine-like hint to a lemony fragrance, and later bears slender scarlet heps. Like all shrubs that are invasive, it can become a nuisance. It is easily grown in any well-drained soil in sun.

Jacquin, *Horti Schönbrunnensis*, Plate 416. Probably not a portrait of the dwarf clone described above.
Botanical Magazine, t.6724.

prattii. Western China. A shrub with small leaves and small, deep pink flowers in clusters, followed by small, long-shaped, red fruits.

sertata. Central and western China. A species up to about 7 feet with slender prickles and thin leaves, coppery-tinted while young. Clean pink flowers with white centres and creamy yellow stamens, above a glandular-hairy receptacle. The bottle-shaped heps are bright red and glandular-hairy. This often does duty in gardens for *Rosa webbiana*, a species to which it is closely related.
Botanical Magazine, t.8473.

setipoda. Western China. *Rosa macrophylla crasse-aculeata*. The individual bloom in shape, colouring, and poise can be supreme among wild roses. A few large, handsome, flat prickles beset the stout stems, which reach 9 feet in height and width, forming an open, arching shrub. Leaflets 7 to 9, rather long for this group, grey beneath; large stipules. The flowers are borne on hairy purple stalks with hairy purple calyx-tubes; the calyx lobes are long, with leafy tips enshrining a large, wide bloom of exquisite beauty. Perhaps the flower is nothing very great on its own, but I always feel its deeply notched petals, clear pink colouring fading to white in the centre around the creamy-yellow stamens, and the contrast of the purplish stalks and long calyces, are of special merit; and they are poised so beautifully. Very large flagon-shaped heps follow, in the *R. moyesii* tradition, freely set with sticky hairs. (Drawing 3.) The glandular-hairy flower stalks and calyx-tubes are redolent of pine, and the flowers of green-apple scent; in addition the leaves have a fragrance of Sweet Brier, but not so strong.

Botanical Magazine, t.8569.

soulieana. Western China. Although this species was introduced as long ago as 1896, it is still a rare plant in cultivation. It belongs to the entirely separate botanical group of Synstylae, all the others of which are great climbers, like *Rosa brunonii*; but as *R. soulieana* is a grey-leaved shrub, it fits best here horticulturally. In common with *R. fedtschenkoana*, *R. murieliae* and *R. beggeriana*, it has considerable value in the artistry of the garden. It is a large-growing rose of arching, sprawling habit, and possibly its scarcity in gardens is due to its size, for it can grow to 10 feet or so eventually, mounding itself up, and has an equal spread. I could take more interest in the beauty of the young grey stems set with yellowish prickles if the latter were not so numerous. Be this as it may, nobody can deny that the general effect is charming; the leaves are of cool, greyish green, usually with 7 leaflets, and the inch-wide white flowers are carried in bunches of several, emerging from ivory-yellow buds. When the crop of flowers is half open the plants are of extraordinary beauty, only equalled a few days later when the whole thing disappears under a snowy covering of petals, giving a rich, fruity fragrance. In the white garden at Kiftsgate Court, Gloucestershire, it is of outstanding merit.

It has a further unusual attraction, for the heps, which are small and round, are orange, not red, a tint which combines well with the deeper grey-green of late summer and early autumn.

It is not absolutely hardy; I have had strong growths of the summer killed to the ground by autumn frost, but it soon recovers, and I think it becomes hardier when its excessive early vigour has somewhat spent itself.

Willmott, Plate 57.

Botanical Magazine, t.8158. Rather too yellow.

Lancaster, Plate, page 351.

sweginzowii. Northwestern China, Kansu. A great shrub up to 12 feet and sometimes as wide, more bushy than *Rosa moyesii*, but armed with large, flattened prickles and many bristly thorns; the bases of the strong basal shoots are repellent. Leaflets 7 to 11, pubescent beneath, borne on prickly reddish stalks, and with prickly stipules; the prickles are glandular. The flowers are bright pink, carried singly or a few together, with glandular-hairy stalks and calyces. The hep is smaller and with less neck than that of *R. moyesii*, more or less hispid, but bright red and shining. As a garden plant it is more vigorous than *R. moyesii* 'Fargesii', and apart from its prickliness, more desirable. In common with all similar species, the heps are usually tarnished by the end of September. (Plate 43.)

Botanical Magazine, t.9248 (as *Rosa holodonta*).

—'Macrocarpa'. Sangerhausen, Germany; introduced by Kordes. A similar shrub to the type species, darker pink, with larger and more handsome heps. Fruits mature early. Superlative. Probably a hybrid.

wardii. Southeastern Tibet. The species is represented in cultivation by:

—culta (Kingdon Ward 6101). Although this form has been in cultivation since 1924, it has never become widely known. Probably a rose that acquired the nickname "white *moyesii*" would not be likely to become popular, but the beauty and refinement of the solid, creamy-white blooms with their rich mahogany red central disc and yellow stamens leave little to be desired. A.T. Johnson grew it well; it is of pretty, arching growth with light green leaves of *moyesii* persuasion, reaching perhaps 6 feet by 6 feet. Almost thornless.

webbiana. Western Himalaya. One of the prettiest of rose species, making dense bushes filled with arching, interlacing twigs, up to 6 feet high and wide. The wiry stems are of rich plum-brown with a purplish bloom when young, with scattered, long, straight, pale-yellowish prickles, mostly at the base. Leaflets tiny, 7 to 9. The pale lilac-pink flowers, up to 2 inches across and with yellow stamens, make a most charming, airy picture early in the season. As the twigs interlace so much many flowers are borne inside the bush, but the smallness of the leaves allows them to be seen. In late summer the bushes are once more alive with colour, for the narrow bottle-shaped heps are of brilliant sealing-wax scarlet and highly polished, with persistent sepals; it is one of the showiest of roses in fruit. In cold districts this species should be given a sheltered position. The flowers have a faint fresh scent. *Rosa webbiana* of gardens is, in all probability, correctly ascribed to *R. sertata*, a closely allied species with fewer prickles and longer leaves.
Willmott, Plate 233.

—var. microphylla (*Rosa nanothamnus*). China, central Asia. *Rosa webbiana microphylla* or *R. w. pustulata*. An extremely pretty small species, near to *R. webbiana* but only about 2 to 3 feet high, composed of small, freely branching twiggy shoots, straight prickles, and tiny leaves with serrations only on the upper third of the leaflets. The flowers, borne on very short flower stalks, are pink, single, small and dainty, but not unusual in any way; in fruit, however, the bush is really brilliant, with shining oval, scarlet heps.

willmottiae. Western China. I look upon *Rosa elegantula* 'Persetosa', *R. webbiana*, *R. willmottiae*, and *R. multibracteata* as four most exquisite and elegant species. *Rosa webbiana* is the smoothest and most wiry, *R. willmottiae* and *R. elegantula* 'Persetosa' have tiny bristles and prickles, while *R. multibracteata* is covered, as its name suggests, with many bracts below the flowers. All have pretty, tiny leaflets and comparatively small flowers, but make up for this in their plenteous crop.

   Rosa willmottiae forms a dense bush up to about 6 feet and considerably wider, every twig arching gracefully over the one below it. The young shoots have a pinkish effect from the tinted prickles and bear greyish, tiny leaves with 7 to 9 leaflets. The flowers, rich lilac pink with cream stamens, approach the size of *R. elegantula* 'Persetosa'. Later the small, pear-shaped heps of orange-scarlet decorate the bushes; they are very distinct from those of *R. webbiana*, since the sepals are deciduous.
Botanical Magazine, t.8186.

SOME AMERICAN WILD ROSES

FIVE SPECIES—*Rosa carolina, R. foliolosa, R. palustris, R. nitida,* and *R. virginiana*—are often classed in a group called Carolinae, but I feel it is simpler to group them with the remaining species of the Cinnamomeae—*R. blanda, R. californica, R. nutkana,* and *R. woodsii.* All are native only to the Western Hemisphere, and many have an obvious resemblance to one another, even to a non-botanist. The fairly constant botanical minutiae which support a separation of the Carolinae from the Cinnamomeae are that the sepals remain on the hep and curve over it—instead of remaining erect or dropping off—and that the seeds are usually attached only to the base of the receptacle, instead of to the bottom and sides.

Rosa californica, R. carolina, R. palustris and *R. foliolosa* are rather open-growing shrubs; *R. virginiana* is a dense-growing, wide, bushy plant; while *R. nitida* more nearly approaches the growth of *R. pimpinellifolia,* and is a dwarf. They all sucker freely. *Rosa nutkana* and *R. woodsii* are the most spectacular in fruit. *Rosa nitida, R. foliolosa* and *R. virginiana* are noted for their autumn leaf-colour: in fact, the last is unsurpassed among roses for its brilliant display, and takes a high place among shrubs in general which are noted for this asset. They do not stand high in garden value, apart from this autumnal brilliance, but some of them have charming double-flowered forms. The portraits of the Carolinae are much confused in old books, but I have done my best to sort them out.

blanda. Eastern and central North America. A nearly thornless species with limp, smooth, pale green leaves and clusters of single pink flowers. Its smooth hep, persistent sepals, and freedom from prickles place it near to *Rosa pendulina.* The hep is almost globose. Its most noticeable character is the very wide stipules, as much as an inch across. 5 feet. It has no great garden merit.
Willmott, Plate 307.

—**'Amurensis'**. Probably a hybrid of *Rosa blanda.* A name which has been used apparently without foundation; I believe it is traceable to the collection of Messrs Späth of Berlin, who listed it and distributed it before 1939. It forms a leafy bush of loose appearance owing to its light grey-green, limp, smooth leaves and very broad pale grey-green stipules and bracts. The calyx tube is pale green, and both this and the pedicel are slightly hairy. The flowers are semi-double, soft rose pink, loosely petalled, with yellow stamens, eventually fading to blush and reflexing. Sweet cucumber scent. Pear-shaped heps. A pretty bush of cool fresh appearance growing to about 6 feet by 6 feet.

californica. California. The single-flowered species has no particular garden merit, and makes a shrub up to 6 feet in height.

—**'Plena'**. One of the most free-flowering of the species-like roses, this makes a pleasing, leafy, dense yet graceful bush, freely set with fresh green somewhat hairy and folded leaves. The flowers are borne in arching sprays with conspicuous leafy bracts. They are rich dark pink with good yellow stamens. It is a splendid garden shrub. My stock of this rose was a gift from Mrs Fleischmann, and her plant came from Messrs Bobbink and Atkins, of Rutherford, New Jersey. Wood and thorns greenish when young; later the thorns are grey and the wood becomes a red-brown. 6 feet by 6 feet. In all probability this rose should be considered a hybrid of *Rosa nutkana,* not of *R. californica,* but it is well-established in gardens

under the latter name. 'Theano' (1894) was a similar rose. (Plate 44.)
Willmott, Plate 223. A doubtful portrait.

carolina. Eastern United States. *Rosa humilis, R. parviflora.* A shrub very variable in nature, often only 3 feet in height, bearing pairs of short, straight prickles at the junction of stem and leaf-stalk. The leaves are somewhat lustrous, composed usually of seven leaflets with fine serrations. The long calyx-lobes are characteristic, projecting well beyond the bud, and even showing well beyond the flower when it is wide open; flowers single, pink; receptacle usually glandular hispid.

Redouté, Vol. I, Plate 81. *Rosa carolina corymbosa;* shows a particularly large corymb of flowers.

Lawrance, Plate 24. *Rosa carolina.*

Andrews, Plate 100. *Rosa pennsylvanica.*

Andrews, Plate 103. *Rosa carolina pimpinellifolia.*

Willmott, Plate 201. *Rosa humilis.*

Jennings, Vol. 2, Plate 88.

Meehan, Thomas, Vol. 2, Plate 9. As *Rosa lucida.* Colour too flame in tone.

——'**Plena**'. In the 1950s Mr and Mrs Wilson Lynes of Taberg, New York State, rediscovered this exquisite little rose and kindly sent me plants. It is a double form of perhaps the smallest variant of this species and will reach probably no more than 2 feet in height; growth twiggy, dense, and bushy. My plants grew well after a very slow start, increasing by suckers. The leaves are smooth and dark green above, small, narrow, and pointed, freely serrated for three-quarters of their length, and the stipules are guarded by a pair of short, straight prickles. Flower-stalk, receptacle, and calyx are glandular-hairy, and the calyx lobes project well beyond the bud. The blooms are fully double, opening from pretty little shapely buds; they are of clear almost salmon pink, deeply coloured in the folded centre—often with a slight button eye—but rapidly fade on the wide outer petals, which become nearly white. It is exceedingly attractive; a half-open bloom surrounded by its five long wisps of calyx is very neat and strange. Unfortunately many buds do not open in our climate; they are best in hot summers. They come to perfection under glass—although the plants are quite hardy. (Drawing 4.)

Rosa carolina 'Plena' is a new combination devised by Mr Lynes, and the names in the following list of illustrations are synonymous with it. I am much indebted to Mr Lynes for so promptly sharing the results of his investigations with me.

Andrews, Plate 102. *Rosa pennsylvanica* var. *flore pleno.* The Pennsylvanian Rose, double-flowered variety. He states: "This delicate little rose is a most desirable variety . . . of dwarf growth . . . in dry weather the sun frequently extracts so much of the colour from the outer petals as to leave them almost bleached." A charming picture, true to nature.

Redouté, Vol. 2, Plate 73. *Rosa parviflora* var. *flore multiplici.* Le Rosier à petites fleurs; Rosier de Caroline; Rosier Caroline du Roi; Rosier de Virginie; Rosier Pennsylvanie à fleurs doubles, etc. Thory gives a long careful description finishing with the statement that the flowers have many rows of petals, paler in the centre than in the circumference of the flower, but the plate does not show this.

Lawrance, Plate 66. *Rosa carolina,* A; Double Pennsylvanian Rose.

foliolosa. Southeastern United States. Another species which suckers freely and thrives in light soil; but it does not usually make a dense thicket; the few rather weak stems are greenish brown, and bear narrow leaves with 7 to 9 leaflets, light in colour and fairly glossy above. The very long sepals project beyond the open flowers, which are of vivid cerise pink; they do not appear until well past midsummer, continuing into September, and have peculiarly short pedicels, thus distinguishing them from the others of the group. Small sub-globose red heps. Excellent autumn colour. 4 feet. There is a white form.

Botanical Magazine, t.8513. Very vivid colouring.

Willmott, Plate 219.

Beales, Plate, page 212.

nitida. Eastern North America. In many ways this little shrub resembles the Burnet roses — in its dwarf, twiggy habit, seldom exceeding 2 feet in height, its masses of slender prickles and bristles all the way up the freely suckering reddish stems, and in its 7 to 9 leaflets; but here the similarity stops, for the leaflets are narrow and pointed, shining green above, and turning to vivid scarlet in the autumn. In addition the flowers are of bright deep pink with yellow stamens, and the heps red and bristly, without the persistent sepals of the Burnets. The young basal shoots are of great beauty, for the masses of prickles are of rich reddish colouring.

In the wild it grows in low-lying, often marshy, places, but in the garden seems happy in ordinary soils, including sand and heavy loam, although it has usually taken some time to settle down under my care. I should feel this to be an attractive rose for a dwarf bushy hedge were it not for its questing roots. It is, however, one of the very best of dwarf shrubs for autumn colour and is therefore valuable for the foreground of shrub beds and borders, for heath and wild garden areas.

Unfortunately the true plant is very scarce; more vigorous, erect, poor hybrids do duty for it.

Willmott, Plate 215.

Lawrance, Plate 36. Upright Carolina Rose. From its prickles this may be intended for *Rosa nitida*.

nutkana. Western North America. A species closely related to *Rosa blanda*, growing to 5 feet. The fairly wide single pink flowers are pleasing, but the main horticultural value of this open-growing shrub is found in the heps, which are rounded and persist on the bush until the severe frosts of winter cause them to decay.

—**'Cantab'**. 1927. This hybrid, *Rosa nutkana* × 'Red Letter Day', was raised by Dr C. C. Hurst while working on the genetics of the rose at Cambridge University Botanic Garden. It is in effect a vigorous, species-like rose with normal prickly stems and has 7 to 9 small, lead-green leaflets. The flowers are big and single, of deep pink, lilac-tinted, with creamy stamens, and create a good display at midsummer. Fragrant. The large, oval heps last through the winter, in bright orange-red, with persistent calyces. 7 to 8 feet by 6 to 7 feet. On good soil it can make an impressive and colourful bush at two seasons of the year.

palustris. Eastern North America. In spite of its name this rose will grow and flower well in poor, sandy, dry soil. It has few garden merits apart from the production of its bright yet deep pink flowers in July, when most species are over. It forms an erect sparse shrub up to

6 feet high.
Redouté, Vol. I, Plate 95. *Rosa hudsoniana.*
Willmott, Plate 211. *Rosa carolina,* but I think applies to *R. palustris.*
Addisonia, 1923, page 275. The Swamp Rose. A good example of flowers and heps.
Jennings, Vol. 2, Plate 87.
Phillips and Rix, Plate 28.

setigera (*Rosa rubifolia*). Prairie Rose. Eastern United States. A species with procumbent stems, arching and capable of climbing into shrubs and small trees. The branches may reach 12 feet or so, bearing along their length clusters of single mallow-pink flowers with broad petals which are very fragrant, in spite of numerous statements to the contrary. In nature, I am told, this varies from white to crimson in colour, but over here I have never seen anything but pink forms. It increases freely in the wild by suckering and self-layering the tips of the arching branches; thus quite large areas may be covered by a single clone. Its own peculiarity is that it has only 3 leaflets.

From its habitat one would think this rose would thrive particularly in sandy soils. It has been a parent of several climbing roses. It is not spectacular, but is useful as it does not flower until after most species are over, together with *Rosa davidii, R. multibracteata,* and *R. wichuraiana.* These are thornless forms. This species belongs to the Synstylae group, which are mainly climbers, but as it is a sprawling shrub rather than a climber, it fits best horticulturally here.
Willmott, Plate 71.
Meehan, Thomas, Vol. 8, Plate 5.
Phillips and Rix, Plate 34.

virginiana. Eastern North America. The synonym, *Rosa lucida,* calls attention to the shining leaves, a very lovely attribute of this plant. Frequently the young foliage is richly tinted, soon covering up the thicket of suckering stems, which are fairly free of prickles except at the base; in the autumn the leaves become beetroot-coloured with the approach of cold weather, and later turn to vivid orange-red, those in the centre of the bush frequently turning to yellow only, thus adding to the very brilliant display. Usually 9 leaflets.

In July appear the pointed vivid buds opening to cerise-pink flowers, with paler centres crowned with yellow stamens; together with others of this group, *Rosa setigera, R. wichuraiana, R. moschata,* and the Noisette 'Princesse de Nassau', it is one of the latest roses to flower and continues well into August. Bristly receptacle. By October the clusters of blooms have given rise to bunches of glittering rounded heps, which last long after the leaves have fallen. In winter these and the red-brown twigs give a warm glow. There are few shrubs in any genera which have such manifold attractions, and it therefore must be reckoned with the very best, being suitable for almost any soil, but particularly those of a light nature, where it will colonize the ground freely, making an ever-spreading thicket up to 5 feet high. Although sometimes recommended for hedges, its suckering habit makes it rather too wide for this purpose except where ample space is available. It is very wind-resistant. (Plate 45.)
Redouté, Vol. I, Plate 45. *Rosa lucida.* Le Rosier luisant.
Duhamel, Vol. 7, Plate 7.
Andrews. The portrait of *Rosa lucida* (Vol. 2, Plate 78) refers to a totally different species, *R. bracteata,* also with very glossy leaves.

Willmott, Plate 197. Unfortunately Miss Willmott's paragraphs are confusing: on page 198 she mentions the double form in the second paragraph; the last paragraph on the same page also refers to this double form, but the intervening two paragraphs obviously refer to the single-flowered species, except for the line in the fourth paragraph where she mentions the fading of the outer petals; this reference I take to refer to the double form.

Lawrance, Plates 54 and 68. No prickles. These plates are not definitive.

Gibson, Plate 15.

—'Alba'. A beautiful white-flowered rose, having less shiny leaves than *Rosa virginiana*. The whole bush reveals its albinoid derivation, even carried as far as the stems, which are green instead of brown; the foliage is also light green. So far it has remained compact with me, but that is no doubt because I have it only as a budded plant on a rootstock of *R. canina*. The heps, in common with those of the species, lose their calyces, but are surmounted by a tiny tuft of grey-white hairs. The foliage does not colour much in autumn. Its various characters suggest that it may be a hybrid with *R. carolina*.

Willmott, Plate 198.

—'d'Orsay'. For many years I considered this rose to be synonymous with 'Rose d'Amour', and a pencil drawing of it was wrongly captioned under the latter name in the earlier editions of my book *Shrub Roses of Today*. There was, however, at Hidcote Manor, a moribund plant labelled 'd'Orsay' which when revived proved to be quite different from 'Rose d'Amour'. (The two are illustrated by pencil drawings in this book, Figures 5 and 6.) 'd'Orsay' is a compact shrub to 4 or 5 feet in height with smooth, somewhat leaden green leaves with pairs of prickles below each leaf, possibly indicating affinity with *Rosa carolina*. The name 'd'Orsay' came from Nancy Lindsay, but may well not be the original. (Count d'Orsay, "the last of the dandies," died in 1852 at the age of 51.)

I pointed out the distinctions between the two in the Royal National Rose Society's *Annual* for 1977 and added the following paragraph:

"According to my old friend Gordon Coe of Elgin, Morayshire, there is at Lochloy, Nairn, a plant of 'Rose d'Amour' which was given to the then owner of the property, Miss Burnaby, in the late eighteenth century by George Washington."

—'Mariae-Graebneriae' (*c.* 1880) is a repeat-flowering hybrid of *Rosa virginiana*, probably with *R. palustris* or *R. carolina*.

—'Rose d'Amour'. I distributed this double-flowered rose wrongly for years under the name of *Rosa virginiana plena*; it is also known as St Mark's Rose. The last name refers to its flowering in Venice on St Mark's Day, 25 April, a statement of Miss Willmott's which I find hard to believe, since it flowers so late in the summer season with us. I have never been able to find authentic portraits of it in the old books, but Wilson Lynes did a lot of research, and kindly sent me his findings. It is probably a hybrid because, while it bears much resemblance to *R. virginiana*, it has thin terete prickles and less lustrous leaves; perhaps *R. carolina* was the other parent. On account of the broad hep, a similar hybrid was known as *R. rapa*, or Le Rosier de Turneps, and this may be found figured in Redouté, Vol. 2, Plate 7. With the usual allowance one has to make with Redouté's portraits, the magnificent rose depicted can perhaps be our little 'Rose d'Amour'. (Plate 46.)

Though it has small flowers, the 'Rose d'Amour' is not a small shrub. At Wisley in sandy soil it has achieved 10 feet in height on a wall, and great bushes may also be seen at

Kiftsgate Court in Gloucestershire, at Mellerstain, Berwickshire, and elsewhere. It is practically thornless; the leaves are composed of 5 to 7 leaflets, neat and serrated, with very wide stipules. It does not start flowering in Surrey until mid-July, and in cool seasons and districts may still be in flower in early September. The exquisite buds, with long calyces, are slender, neatly rolled, and remain in half-open form for a few days in cool weather, eventually opening with wide outer petals and revealing a fairly well-filled centre. They are of deep pink in bud, the outer petals fading to pale pink, those in the centre retaining their colour well. In the fullness of midsummer the flowers are packed with petals, often causing a button eye. (Plate 47.)

I know of few roses that can compare in daintiness with this flower; 'Céleste' has perhaps an even more beautiful bud, but is less good on opening; the only others which approach it in beauty of bud are the 'Mlle Cécile Brunner' group; and *Rosa carolina* 'Plena', which is neater when fully open. It cannot be called a spectacular plant, but its freedom of flower over a long period and its vigour should ensure its continual popularity. A well-flowered bush can create a good pink effect for some weeks. This 'Rose d'Amour' must not be confused with the single-flowered Gallica rose depicted by Redouté: Vol. 2, Plate 63. There is a good photograph in Jekyll, between pages 74 and 75.

woodsii. Central and western North America. Inferior to *Rosa woodsii fendleri.* Reaches 6 feet or so, flowers pink, sometimes white, small rounded heps. Of little garden value. *Rosa arkansana* and *R. pisocarpa* are related.
Willmott, Plate 235.
Willmott, Plate 236. White form.
Botanical Register, Vol. 12, t.976.

—fendleri. Of rather more southerly distribution than *Rosa woodsii* itself, extending from British Columbia to Mexico. A most pleasing, graceful variety, with greyish leaves and clear, soft, lilac-pink flowers with cream stamens, borne very early in the season. Few prickles, reddish, on smooth green wood. The brilliant, rounded, red heps, the size of marbles, last into late autumn or winter; their weight causes the slender branches to hang vertically, and the result is like a series of strings of large red currants. 6 feet by 5 feet. It produces many suckers.
Willmott, Plate 175.

NOTE: A useful survey of these species by E. W. Erlanson occurred in the *American Rose Annual* for 1932.

DRAWING I. The Gallica Rose 'Sissinghurst Castle'. The dark plum-coloured petals have light edges and are flecked with magenta, with paler reverses. (Reproduced at 85%.)

DRAWING 2. *Rosa damascena* J. Herrmann var. *semperflorens* (Loisel.) Rowley. Four Seasons or Monthly Rose, Autumn Damask. Pink. (Reproduced at 95%.)

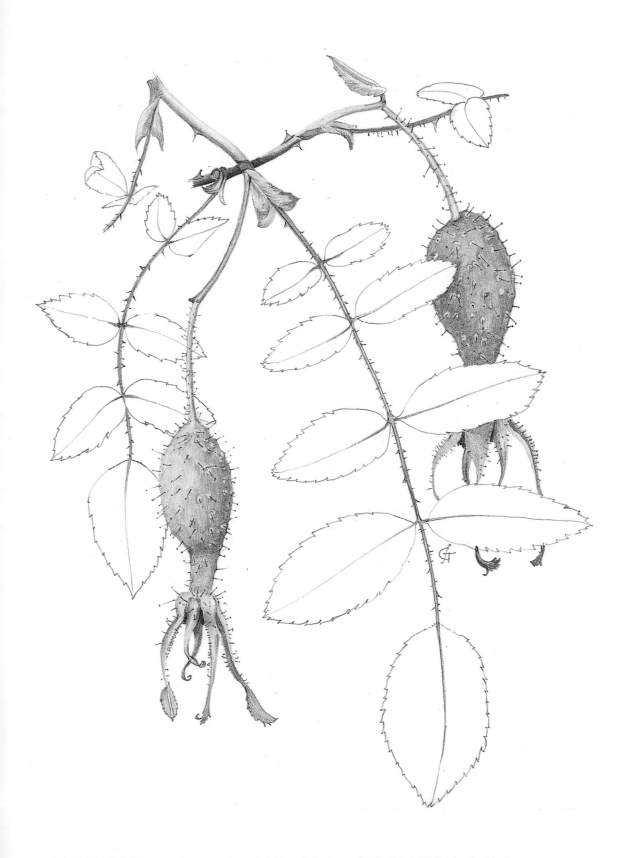

DRAWING 3. The very large orange-red fruits of *Rosa setipoda* Hemsl. & Wils. develop in late summer.

DRAWING 4. *Rosa carolina* L. 'Plena'. A small bush with delicately coloured pink flowers. Only for a dry climate.

DRAWING 5. Old Rose 'd'Orsay', probably a hybrid of *R. virginiana*. Rich pink, fragrant; the flowering period extends into late summer.

DRAWING 6. 'Rose d'Amour', another Old Rose and probably a hybrid of *R. virginiana*. Its flowers are rich pink, fragrant, and the flowering period extends into late summer.

DRAWING 7. The rare Sacramento Rose, *Rosa stellata* Wooton var. *mirifica* (Greene) Cockerell, from the Sacramento Mountains in New Mexico. Lilac-pink with cream stamens.

DRAWING 8. 'Mlle Cécile Brunner', a miniature of 1881. It might be ranked among early Poly-poms. Delicate pink, scented.

DRAWING 9. The Rose known in British gardens as 'Bloomfield Abundance', though the original of this name was a large-flowered Hybrid Tea raised in the United States. Note the elongated calyx-lobes which at once distinguish it from 'Mlle Cécile Brunner'. It reaches 6 to 7 feet in height. Delicate pink, scented.

DRAWING 10. Heps of 'Autumn Fire' ('Herbstfeuer'). Orange-red.

DRAWING 11. The blush-pink 'Fimbriata' (1891), a *Rosa rugosa* derivative
of earlier raising than the Grootendoorst varieties.

DRAWING 22. The creamy white, repeat-flowering, climbing species *Rosa gigantea*.
It is a tender rose from Upper Burma, etc., which gave the Tea-scent and long petals
to hybrids of the last century and more.

DRAWING 23. The climbing, Tea-scented Rose 'Vicomtesse Pierre de Fou'
of 1923, showing the typical "quartering" of the petals in old-style varieties.
Flowers coppery orange passing to coppery pink. Well scented.

Rambling roses planted round a tetrapod and trained to form a bow or shamrock. At the Roseraie de l'Haÿ, near Paris.

A rose trained from under a low-swung rope and up to the top of the supporting poles, each of which is clothed in a pillar rose. At the Roseraie de l'Haÿ, near Paris. Rose growths lend themselves more naturally to training in this way, rather than persuading them to grow down the swags with a sharp bend at the top of the pole.

THE WILD YELLOW ROSES AND RELATED SPECIES

The Yellow Rose (as divers do report) was by Art so coloured, and altered
from his first estate, by grafting a wilde Rose upon a Broome-stalke; whereby
(say they) it doth not only change his colour but his smell and force.

Gerard's *Herball*, 1597

IT SO HAPPENS that most of the few yellow-flowered wild roses fit botanically into a convenient group, the Pimpinellifoliae, which includes two white-flowered species, and these few
species are distributed only through the Old World, from Eastern Europe to China. So far
only two of them—*Rosa foetida*, the Austrian Brier, and *R. pimpinellifolia*, the Burnet Rose—
have been used to any extent by hybridizers, and possibly untold advances in yellow roses are
at hand through some of the other species.

These roses form a rather diverse group from a garden point of view, but botanically they
are governed by a few characters common to them all. They are erect-growing shrubs, with
straight or almost straight prickles; leaves small, with anything from 5 to 19 leaflets; stipules
narrow and joined to the petiole for about half their length; bracts absent; the sepals are vertical and stay on the heps, which are rounded and orange, red, or maroon.

It will be seen, therefore, that we have ordinary shrubs with small leaves to deal with; no
great attraction in the heps, only in the colour of the flowers, but there is no doubt that the
species in this group do add something very valuable, not only to roses in general, but to the
whole of horticulture. For where would our early summer shrub display be without the
dainty grace of *Rosa hugonis* or *R.* 'Cantabrigiensis', or without the glory of 'Frühlingsgold'?—
to say nothing of our modern roses, which owe almost their entire yellow and flame colouring to *R. foetida* and its latent characters.

In the garden all these roses except *Rosa ecae*, and also *R. foetida* and its varieties, blend happily with everything else, their tones being cool and refreshing; the soft mauves of lilacs and
rhododendrons or the flaming colours of azaleas are all the better for a few pale yellow or
white roses; likewise, irises and peonies are enhanced by big bushes of pale yellow behind
them.

A very different approach is needed for *Rosa foetida* and its more startling varieties; I do not
feel happy with them in any combination of roses apart from their own derivatives. Their
yellow is so harsh and insistent that it needs the rich background of a copper beech hedge to
add tone. The gorgeous warmth of the Austrian Copper Brier is equally difficult to place with
other roses, but it is such a glorious personage itself that I prefer it on its own. Against varied
greenery or copper leaves it can be the focal point for the whole garden for its few brief weeks
of flowering, then sink into insignificance for the rest of the season. Even so, I prefer to lead
up to such brilliance as this with other brilliant plants, such as potentillas and geums, which
diffuse the dazzling colour in a kaleidoscopic mixture, and through their varied warmth and
overlapping flowering periods prolong the display so that the given spot can retain a barbaric
splendour through the summer. I referred briefly to this colouring in the Introduction, and
at risk of repeating myself would like to enlarge upon it here as, among species roses, *Rosa
foetida* and *R. f.* 'Bicolor' do need such careful placing in the garden, and need to be approached
in colours of gathering strength. This method is indeed practised in several famous gardens
today, and excellent examples may be seen in the purple-and-orange garden at Crathes Castle,
Kincardineshire, in the red-and-purple borders at Hidcote Manor, Gloucestershire, in the
red-and-yellow borders at Tintinhull, Somerset, and in beds of gorgeous colour assortments

at Sissinghurst Castle, Kent, Newby Hall, Yorkshire, and Blickling Hall, Norfolk. Let it not be thought, however, that roses provide necessarily the bulk of colour in these blends. Probably the reverse would be true. But there is no doubt that the Austrian Copper and some of its near relatives can add very greatly to such displays. I need only call attention to 'Réveil Dijonnais' and some of the flame-and-yellow Hybrid Teas and vivid Floribundas to conjure up some wonderful 'hot' colour schemes.

This type of colour work cannot depend upon normal greenery for its ultimate success. As I mentioned earlier, the copper foliage of a Beech, *Prunus,* or *Berberis* hedge is to my mind almost essential to give the grouping warmth and richness, and provides of course the inestimable asset of permanent colour through the various flowering seasons.

ecae. Afghanistan. The strange name commemorates Mrs Aitchison—E. C. A.—the wife of the botanist who named it. This rose is unique; slender, upright growth with long reddish twigs set with reddish prickles and small, smooth, dark green leaves. It is quite startling when in flower, for the blooms are of intense, deep buttercup-yellow. 5 feet by 4 feet, or considerably more on good soil. Needs full sunshine and well-drained soil, and contrasts well with blue spring-flowering ceanothuses. (Plate 49.) *Rosa kokanica,* from central Asia, is closely related.
Willmott, Plate 277. Wrongly captioned *Rosa xanthina.*
Botanical Magazine, t.7666. Ditto.
Phillips and Rix, Plate 16.

foetida. Western Asia. The Austrian Brier. Although marked by an intensity of yellow bordering on the colour of sulphur, a scent that one could hardly call attractive, and possessing a name which calls attention to its heavy odour, this rose had a profound influence on our modern garden roses, mainly through its famous variety *Rosa foetida* 'Persiana'. In the old books the species was called *R. lutea,* and it was known and grown before 1600. The shining, rich brown stems are set with straight grey prickles, and bear small leaves of intense parsley green. The wide-open flowers create a very startling effect. In my experience, despite the fact that it is a native of hot, arid districts, it appears to thrive best in the cooler counties of Britain; this is also true of other roses from the Middle East. Pruning seldom improves the results. 5 feet by 4 feet. The quotation at the head of this section applies to this rose.
Lawrance, Plate 12. Excellent portrait.
Botanical Magazine, t.363.
Roessig, Plate 2. Le Rosier jaune, à fleurs simples couleur de cire.
Revue Horticole, 1865, page 191. Not exact.
Andrews, Plate 120. *Rosa lutea.*
Willmott, Plate 267. Good colour.
Schlechtendal, t.2622. Poor.
Redouté, Vol. I, Plate 69. Le Rosier Eglantier.
The Garden, January 1898, page 22. Artist's impression showing *Rosa foetida* and *R. f.* 'Persiana'.
Phillips and Rix, Plate 15.

—**'Bicolor'**. *Rosa lutea punicea.* The famous Austrian Copper Brier has been known since before 1590. The reverse of the petals is much the same colour as that of *R. foetida,* but shows through the thin texture some of the intense nasturtium-red of the face of the flower.

Occasionally this dazzling rose reverts on an odd branch or two to the vivid yellow of the species. (Plate 50.) In the garden it grows best in the same conditions as *R. foetida*, and both of them, on account of their colour, should be kept well away from the many roses which flower with them early in the season, and which have those soft tones of mauve pink which are so prevalent in the genus. Miss Willmott tells us it is known in France by the name of Rose Capucine and used to be known as Rose Comtesse. I wish we could find the double form, which was apparently recorded in 1815 or thereabouts—although it could scarcely be an improvement on the single. In most of the portraits cited the artists have obviously been carried away with the unusual colouring of the flowers; we can imagine what a relief it must be to have a rose to paint of such brilliance when so many are mauve-pink.

Paul, 9th edition, Plate 8. Rather exaggerated.

Roses et Rosiers, Plate 5. Rose Eglantier variété couleur ponceau. The name of Eglantine was given to this rose erroneously by Linnaeus. Poppy-coloured is one of its best descriptions. Good portrait.

Roessig, Plate 5. Le Rosier à fleurs couleur d'orange ou de feu. *Rosa punicea.*

Journal des Roses, Février 1890. Rose capucine jaune bicolore. A colourful impression.

Step, Vol. 2, Plate 81. Very good.

Trechslin & Coggiatti. Superb.

Revue Horticole, 1865, page 191. Not exact.

Andrews, Plate 120. *Rosa lutea bicolor.*

Lawrance, Plate 6. *Rosa lutea bicolor.* Very good, but colour too brown.

Botanical Magazine, t.1077, *Rosa foetida bicolor.*

Willmott, Plate 269. Excellent portrait.

Redouté, Vol. 1, Plate 71. Le Rosier Eglantier var. couleur Ponceau.

Duhamel, Vol. 7, Plate 14. Rose Eglantine.

Harvey, Plate 1.

Phillips and Rix, Plate 15.

Beales, Plate, page 135.

—'**Persiana**'. The Persian Yellow Rose was introduced to this country by Sir Henry Willock in 1838, and was welcomed by growers as the most brilliant and satisfactory of the double yellow roses for the garden. To us, with so many fine yellow roses around us, it is difficult to imagine a time when the only double roses of this colour were the little Burnet hybrids and *Rosa hemisphaerica*. The latter seldom produced flowers worth looking at except in good weather, so we can appreciate with what enthusiasm Persian Yellow must have been greeted. In the *Gardeners' Chronicle* for 1843 plants were advertised at 15 shillings each, a fabulous sum in those days for a new rose. Eventually its pollen was used to produce fine yellow modern roses, such as had never been seen before. 5 feet by 4 feet. (Plate 51.)

The famous nurseryman of Lyon, Pernet-Ducher, made a determined effort in 1883 and subsequent years, pollinating thousands of Hybrid Perpetuals with 'Persiana', and eventually succeeded in raising two seedlings, one of which subsequently gave rise to 'Soleil d'Or', the first of the Pernet race of roses. They have since been merged into the Hybrid Teas and, with the brilliant colouring of *Rosa foetida* 'Bicolor', have also given us the two-tone effect which occurs in the Austrian Copper.

Jamain et Forney, Plate 55. Not representative.

Journal des Roses, Mars 1882. Exaggerated flower.

Komlosy. Yellow too dark, but a good drawing.

Paul, 8th edition, 1881, Plate 4.
Choix des Plus Belles Roses, Plate 36.
Flore des Serres, Vol. 4, Plate 374.
Trechslin & Coggiatti. Superb.
Phillips and Rix, Plate 15.

hemisphaerica. Western Asia. *Rosa sulphurea, R. glaucophylla.* The Sulphur Rose. Known and grown before 1625. A famous rose which is not really suited to the British climate, but prior to the introduction of 'Persiana' it was the only large double yellow rose in cultivation. On account of its size of bloom it was often called the Yellow Provence Rose, although in growth and general appearance it bears no resemblance to the true Provence Rose, *R. centifolia.*

Its synonym, *Rosa glaucophylla,* gives us the key to its foliage, which is of a distinctly greyish hue, and it has hooked prickles, distinguishing it again from *R. foetida,* even without the flowers. It is of rather loose habit, and the twigs droop with the weight of the large globular blooms, filled with petals, of a brilliant sulphur yellow, and sweetly scented. Unfortunately, except in particularly warm, dry weather, and in the right conditions, it seldom gives perfect blooms. They tend to "ball" and decay without opening. It grows and flowers at Mottisfont, Hampshire. Gordon Rowley suggests that this rose derived as a sport from a single-flowered species, *R. rapinii.* As, however, the double-flowered rose was named first, the name of this single-flowered species would be *R. hemisphaerica rapinii.* This species is native of Asiatic Turkey to northwestern Iran. About 4 feet.

There is a very full account of these roses, and an excellent plate, in Miss Willmott's book *The Genus Rosa.* The double variety was depicted by van Huysum and others in some of the great Dutch flower pictures of the seventeenth century, and its vivid colour and occasionally superb blooms made it greatly prized. (Plate 48.)
Willmott, Plate 273. Very good.
Andrews, Plate 91. *Rosa sulphurea.* A splendid spray, showing the buds well.
Lawrance, Plate 77. The Double Yellow Rose.
Komlosy. *Rosa sulphurea;* the colouring is too dark, but an excellent portrait.
Roessig, Plate 43. *Rosa glaucophylla.* Poor flower.
Botanical Register, Vol. 1, t.46.
Redouté, Vol. 1, Plate 29. *Rosa sulphurea.* Le Rosier jaune de Soufre.
Phillips and Rix, Plate 15.

hugonis. Central China. With *Rosa moyesii* this is one of the two famous roses which, being brought from the Far East at the turn of the century, revolutionized the horticultural appraisal of the wild roses. An established plant is nearly thornless, but the bases of the young shoots are often crimson, with bristly hairs and prickles. (Some forms collected in Kansu have large flattened prickles reminiscent of *R. sericea;* such plants may represent the origin of 'Hidcote Gold' and 'Earldomensis'.) This exquisite species has tiny, smooth leaves, creating a fern-like effect on a shrub some 7 feet high and wide. The flowers are charmingly disposed along the arching wiry twigs, and are of cool butter-yellow, with a hint of primrose; they seldom open fully, remaining in a cupped shape, crinkled and silky. (Plate 52.) Surpassed by some of its offspring. It is at its best on its own roots, when it will thrive even on chalky soils. The small maroon-coloured heps are not conspicuous, but the foliage often turns to purplish brown in the autumn.

A semi-double hybrid, raised in 1926, was named 'Dr E. M. Mills'; its flowers of creamy pale yellow do not open fully, and it is not of much garden value.
Willmott, Plate 279.
Botanical Magazine, t.8004. Scarcely recognizable.
Bois and Trechslin, Plate 4.

omeiensis. See *Rosa sericea.*

primula. Turkestan to northern China. The Incense Rose is so called because of the rich aroma which emanates from the young foliage, which is dark green, smooth, narrow, and of a somewhat glaucous tint. Some leaves have as many as 15 leaflets. The plants are upright, and a pretty sight when in flower, the tone of yellow being very pale and transparent, like that of a primrose. It can make a fine effect when loaded with flowers; at Highdown, Sussex it has reached some 6 feet by 10 feet. Heps reddish, not conspicuous, but the young growth is reddish brown with red prickles.
Phillips and Rix, Plate 15.
Gibson, Plate 15.

sericea and **omeiensis.** Separated as they are only by minor botanical differences, it is best to class these two species together for our present purpose. They are the only roses which have four petals instead of the usual five. They make tall, rather open shrubs up to some 9 feet high and wide; the stout young shoots are often densely bristly, giving way to almost smooth wood, which is irregularly set with wide, flattened, triangular prickles, most evident in the variety *Rosa sericea pteracantha.* Numerous rich green leaflets give the plant the ferny appearance peculiar to several of these roses. In August and September in a good season the bushes are brilliant with small pear-shaped glossy heps in bright scarlet; in *R. s. omeiensis* they have a thickened yellow stalk. In addition, *R. s. omeiensis* has nearly glaucous leaflets up to 17, whereas those of *R. sericea* are silky-pubescent beneath, and not more than 11. In spite of all this it is considered, from Dr Hurst's hybridizations and from observations on living material, that these roses should be united under *R. sericea.*

These are attractive shrubs for the garden, giving the unsophisticated effect that is the prerogative of dainty wild species, and are really exquisite in flower. The petals are beautifully shaped and slightly veined, remaining in a wide cup formation for most of their short life. The flowers are normally white.

sericea. Himalaya, introduced 1822.
Willmott, Plate 163.
Botanical Magazine, t.5200.
Gibson, Plate 1.

omeiensis. Szechwan, western China, introduced 1901. This name is used to denote forms with fleshy, coloured pedicels to the heps, together with leaflets in excess of eleven. In the event of selections of the species with numerous leaflets but without fleshy pedicels, the name *Rosa sericea* var. *polyphylla* is used.

sericea 'Chrysocarpa'. A form with beautiful yellow heps.

—**'Denudata'.** A thornless form.

—'Heather Muir'. A superb form, named after the creator of the Kiftsgate Court garden, who purchased it many years previously as a seedling from E. A. Bunyard. A most beautiful large shrub with extra large white flowers produced over a long period, followed by orange-red heps on orange-red stalks. In flower May to July. 9 feet by 9 feet.

—var. **polyphylla**. *Rosa sericea inermis glandulosa, Rosa sericea omeiensis.* A form with numerous leaflets, and not many prickles.

—var. **pteracantha**. *Rosa omeiensis pteracantha.* A rose well known for its large, flattened prickles. These are borne on stiff, straight stems, being sometimes so numerous and wide that they make a vertical line of red among the small ferny leaves. Some prickles are an inch or more wide at the base. The flowers are white, and the plant is much like the species, but less graceful. In the garden this variety should be placed so that the sun can shine through the prickles, giving a rich colour effect. In their second season the prickles become grey; thus pruning to encourage constant new shoots is desirable. Introduced from western China in 1890. 8 feet by 6 feet.
Botanical Magazine, t.8218. Shows the thickened red stalk to the fruit.
The Garden, 2 June 1906, Vol. 69, page 300. Showing thorns and foliage only. Excellent picture.

xanthina. This, the double-flowered form, has been cultivated for over a hundred years in northern China and Korea, and has been known in Britain as *Rosa slingeri.* The growth is less free than that of its single parent and the flowers, though a good colour and fairly double, are less beautiful and effective. 6 feet by 6 feet. Unlike 'Canary Bird', which is sometimes called *Rosa xanthina spontanea*, it has prickles.
McFarland, *Roses of the World*, page 285.

—var. **spontanea**. Northern China and Korea. Although this was introduced in 1907 it has never become widely known, having been overshadowed by 'Canary Bird' (q.v.). It is vigorous, reaching 8 to 9 feet, with the usual light green, ferny foliage of the group, and large light-yellow single flowers.

Hybrids of the Yellow Roses

'Canary Bird'. At one time distributed as *Rosa xanthina spontanea*, under the impression that it was the wild type of *R. xanthina*, this has since been considered a hybrid, perhaps *R. hugonis* × *xanthina* or *pimpinellifolia*. I have found no record of its origin. The richly coloured brown stems have a few prickles towards the base, and are noticeably warty, i.e., covered with tiny excrescences. The leaves are of bright, fresh green, luxuriant but small and fern-like; they are hairy beneath, and also in the folds above. The flowers open wide, and are of clear, bright yellow, creating a really splendid effect on the arching young branches and small twigs. Unfortunately it is subject to "die back," like *R. hugonis*, and it is therefore best to propagate it from cuttings or layers. It appears to be most at home in the drier parts of Britain on well-drained soils. Heps maroon or blackish, not conspicuous. 7 feet by 7 feet. Reputedly raised at Osterley Park.
Le Rougetel, page 39.

'Cantabrigiensis'. U.K., 1931. A chance seedling which occurred at Cambridge Botanic Garden. I regard this and *Rosa* 'Headleyensis' as the most satisfactory of the species-like yellow roses. *Rosa* 'Cantabrigiensis' makes an erect bush 7 feet by 6 feet or more, densely covered in tiny hairy bristles on strong young growth, but without winglike prickles; with the same ferny leaf effect of its parents, but of a shapely, well-filled habit. The five-petalled flowers are very slightly paler than those of *R. hugonis*, but still a good clear yellow, and are far more shapely and open wider than those of that species. Extremely free-flowering and a wonderful sight in full bloom; small orange-red heps in late summer. Fragrant. Not subject to "die-back" in my experience, where it scores over *R. hugonis* and 'Canary Bird'.

'Earldomensis'. Page, U.K., 1934. *Rosa pteragonis pteragonis. Rosa hugonis* × *R. sericea pteracantha*. Raised in Courtenay Page's garden, Earldom, Haywards Heath, West Sussex, where the National Rose Society's trials were held for many years. Forms a bushy, thorny shrub with some of the reddish flattened prickles of the second parent. Small, pretty foliage and bright yellow single flowers early in the season. 6 to 7 feet high and wide.

'Golden Chersonese'. Raised by E. F. Allen, Ipswich, U.K., 1963. 'Canary Bird' × *Rosa ecae*. This good hybrid inherits the fern-like prettiness of *R. ecae* and also its deep yellow colouring, coupled with the larger bloom of 'Canary Bird'. Like its parents it flowers delightfully, early in the season. Fragrant. Erect growth. 8 feet by 6 feet.

'Headleyensis'. This was raised at Boidier, then the home of Sir Oscar Warburg, at Headley near Epsom, Surrey, about 1920. The seed parent was *Rosa hugonis*, presumably pollinated by *R. pimpinellifolia altaica*. This vigorous and healthy plant, about 9 feet high by 12 feet wide, has the general ferny appearance of the parents, as one would expect, with particularly handsome creamy yellow single flowers. Very fragrant. I consider this is the most ornamental of all the hybrids of *R. hugonis* that I have seen so far; its wide flowers, graceful growth, and clear soft colouring make it an important garden plant, and it is amazing that it has remained so long in obscurity. (Plate 53.)

A rose of similar parentage is 'Albert Edwards'; Hillier, 1938.

'Helen Knight'. Raised U.K., 1966. F. P. Knight collected seeds from *Rosa ecae* at Wisley, which had presumably been crossed with *R. pimpinellifolia* 'Grandiflora' (*R.* 'Altaica') of gardens, since this was growing nearby. The dark wood and dainty foliage of *R. ecae* are repeated in this plant, but the flowers are larger and of bright pale yellow, 1 ½ inches across, slightly cupped. Early. Faintly fragrant. 7 feet.

'Hidcote Gold'. 1948. Apart from the fact that this plant has been growing for many years at Hidcote Manor, Gloucestershire and was apparently raised there, I have no records of it. It is possibly a hybrid of *Rosa hugonis*, and the other parent is no doubt *R. sericea pteracantha*, since it bears conspicuous flattened prickles very like those of this species. It is a vigorous, graceful bush with long wand-like branches and drooping twigs studded with good, clear yellow, single, five-petalled flowers and plenty of small foliage. An attractive shrub combining the five petals of a yellow rose with the striking armature of *R. sericea pteracantha*. 7 feet by 7 feet. See also under *R. hugonis*, page 104.

THE WILD BURNET ROSES AND THEIR GARDEN FORMS

The Pimpinell Rose . . . groweth . . . in a pasture as you goe from a village
hard by London called Knights bridge unto Fulham, a village thereby.

Gerard's *Herball,* 1597

FROM THE ABOVE early reference, no doubt, Linnaeus's name of *Rosa pimpinellifolia* sprang. Botanists have differed over the desirability of using one or two names for these roses. Miss Willmott decided to call them *R. spinosissima* and *R. s. pimpinellifolia,* using the latter for those forms without glandular hairs on the peduncles.

Nowadays they are usually grouped under one or the other species, and for our purpose I will adopt *Rosa pimpinellifolia,* as being accepted by most botanists today. This species has the widest distribution of any, and it will be readily understood therefore that a great variation occurs in nature, since it grows from Iceland to eastern Siberia, and as far south as the Caucasus and Armenia. Around the coasts of Britain it grows in sandy dunes, often only reaching 9 inches in height, while the tallest variants may achieve 6 feet. This species is included in the botanical group Pimpinellifoliae, together with the roses in the previous section.

The species spreads freely by underground stolons, or suckers, and bears an excessive number of straight prickles accompanied by multitudes of fine bristles, and has small leaves divided into 7 to 9 leaflets. The flowers are also small, and are borne singly on short stalks from the leaf axils; they appear in spring, usually in May or very early June, and are followed in late summer by nearly black heps, round and shining like huge black currants, with the characteristic of retaining the old calyx lobes. Towards autumn these dark fruits often add to a remarkable display of sombre leaf colour; grey-brown and plum-colour vie with maroon and dark red in intensity, with an orange or yellow leaf here and there. The wide hummocky bushes thus contribute something unique to the autumn pageant, and I know gardens where this contribution is greatly valued.

It is of course their floral display that has been the main attraction to gardeners through the centuries. They are nearly as prolific of their flowers as they are of their leaves and prickles. A bush in full flower is a wonderful sight, the wiry shoots bending under the weight of the blossoms, and the whole creating a brilliant effect. Mere plenitude would not be enough, however; they fortunately have a sweet charm all of their own, an exhilarating fresh scent—like Lily of the valley in its revivifying purity—and they flower in early summer just when we are ready to welcome roses, before the hot days of midsummer bring forth the greater garden varieties. There is no doubt, either, that their extreme hardiness and thriftiness have made them favourites, for they will grow and luxuriate in the poorest of sandy soils and do not suffer from any extremes of cold that we experience in Great Britain.

Looking back through the history of gardening we find that these roses reached a high popularity for a brief period rather before the middle of the nineteenth century, over two hundred forms, supposedly distinct, being listed by Scottish nurserymen. They did not meet with such favour in England; in 1848 William Paul listed only seventy-six, all with fancy names and descriptions of two or three words only. They found even less favour in France. They are easy to raise from their abundant seed and this no doubt contributed to the multitudes of named varieties, but unfortunately very few of the plants growing today can be authentically connected with the names published in the lists nearly a hundred and fifty years ago. No careful descriptions appear to be available. Today it is more usual to be given a root that the owner calls "double red" or "single pink," or knows by some proprietary name that serves to record its finding in a district or garden, than to find a plant bearing an authentic name such as 'William III'. The laxity in this matter is so great that varieties are known by different names in different counties and countries today, and nomenclature could not be more vague or unfathomable.

Their flowers run to no striking floral style, being just single, or with extra rows of petals, and almost always showing the bright yellow stamens; fully double forms usually remain fairly globular. Their colours range in strange mixtures from white to pink and dark plum-crimson, and from pale to dark yellow, with a few biscuit tones thrown in. Some are mottled or two-toned, and frequently there is a marked difference between the colour on the front of the petals and that of the reverse. I suspect that all yellow forms are really hybrids with *Rosa foetida;* in some the scent proves this without doubt. I have not found yellow variants growing wild.

pimpinellifolia. Europe, Asia. This species has been given much attention by artists:
Botanical Register, Vol. 5, t.431.
Roessig, Plate 9. Le Rosier blanc à fleurs de pimprenelle, single, white, smooth peduncle.
Andrews, Plate 121. *Rosa spinosissima*, single white; excellent portrait.
Schlechtendal, t.2623.
Lawrance, Plate 48. *Rosa spinosissima*, the Common Scotch Rose. Good.
Lawrance, Plate 19. A tall form.

—**'Grandiflora'**, of gardens; also known as 'Altaica', but not *Rosa pimpinellifolia altaica*, botanically. This beautiful rose is well represented in gardens, even where roses are not usually grown, for it is a very thrifty plant, freely increasing underground and of vigorous upright habit, with comparatively few, large prickles. The leaves also are larger than those of the species. In the full glory of its short flowering season few shrubs are more attractive, the branches drooping beneath the numerous wide, creamy-ivory flowers, suffused on opening with primrose yellow. It flowers concurrently with lilacs, with which it makes a delightful contrast and underplanting. The heps are conspicuous, of dark shining maroon-black. 6 feet. 'Dunwichensis', a form found growing at Dunwich, Suffolk, is very free-flowering, with flowers the same colour as 'Grandiflora' but smaller; it is a good garden plant, compact and bushy. It does not differ from a horticultural point of view from *R. p.* 'Grandiflora', only in a slight difference in chromosomes. 'Grandiflora' has produced many good hybrids, including some of the 'Frühlings-' group, also 'Karl Foerster'. See Chapter 6, "Shrub Roses of the Twentieth Century."
Willmott, Plate 257.
Lawrance, Plate 19. *Rosa spinosissima*, The tall Scotch rose.
The Garden, 1898, Vol. 53. An artist's impression.
Botanical Register, Vol. 11, t.888. *Rosa spinosissima grandiflora.*
Rosa pimpinellifolia 'Grandiflora':
Le Rougetel, page 158.
Beales, page 141.

—**'Hispida'**. Siberia. Noted for its bristles, rather than prickles, which densely cover the branches and twigs. This was a great favourite of A. T. Johnson's, and indeed it is as beautiful as *Rosa pimpinellifolia* 'Grandiflora', which is giving high praise. It is not so bushy nor so free of its suckers, however, which possibly accounts for its scarcity, but the almost furry branches with few hurtful prickles, and opaque, soft creamy-yellow flowers, are very appealing. 5 feet.
Botanical Magazine, t.1570.

Willmott, Plate 259. Incorrect, probably *Rosa pimpinellifolia* 'Luteola', since it lacks the numerous hair-like prickles.

The Garden, 1899, Vol. 56, page 398. An artist's impression, showing no prickles. The accompanying article, by W. J. Bean, states that it breeds true from seeds and was cultivated as far back as 1781 at Islington.

—'**Lutea Maxima**' (*Rosa spinosissima* 'Lutea'). On account of its scent, and apart from any other characters, it is probably a hybrid with *R. foetida*. This is also a well-known rose and, if we except *R. ecae* and *R. foetida*, is the brightest of the early yellow single roses. The dark wood and few prickles, twigs somewhat tortuous and weak, leaves downy beneath, and vivid canary-yellow of the flowers, are all characteristic of it. It is a most satisfactory garden plant, the copious bright green foliage giving a lush appearance with the flowers. Fruits black. 4 feet. Spreads fairly freely.

Redouté, Vol. 3, Plate 19.

—'**Luteola**'. Russia. *Rosa pimpinellifolia ochroleuca*. Of more open habit and taller than the last two, this has pale flowers which often remain in a half-open state. It is hardly worth cultivating, for it cannot compare with *R. hugonis, R.* 'Cantabrigiensis', and others. 6 to 9 feet.

Willmott, Plate 255.

—var. **myriacantha**. Spain and France to Armenia. *Rosa myriacantha*. An interesting and constant variant which even in this prickly group is noted for its dense mass of long, sharp, straight prickles. It makes a twiggy shrub not more than 3 feet in height, and its flowers and fruits are much like those of the type species, in creamy white. The dark prickles add to its attraction. A noticeable feature is the glandular under-surface of the leaves. A slow spreader.

Willmott, Plate 261.

Lindley, Plate 10. A very good portrait.

Redouté, Vol. 3, Plate 11. Le Rosier à mille Épines. Thory states that it has been in cultivation a long time. An excellent portrait.

Garden Forms of the Burnet Roses

Sabine records how Robert Brown and his brother transplanted some wild plants of the Burnet rose from the Hill of Kinnoul into their neighbouring nursery garden near Perth. One bore flowers tinged with red, and subsequent seedlings from this started the fashion in selecting colour variants of this rose in Scotland and England.

The most extraordinary thing about these garden variants is that in the largest list of them, in an old catalogue of Messrs Austin and McAslan of Glasgow—kindly lent to me by H. Stewart-Paton—there is no mention of any of the names which are found today. The list of two hundred and eight varieties, with colour descriptions reduced to one or a combination of two adjectives, of which there were only eleven used, is surely the best example of economy ever produced in a nurseryman's catalogue! There is an account of these roses in the Royal Horticultural Society's *Journal* for 1822, by Sabine, but here again there are no useful descriptions. All of them spread freely.

'**Andrewsii**'. Miss Willmott records that this is the most commonly found in French gardens. In England it is less common, there being several double pink varieties extant, but no others have I encountered with the clarity of colour found in this variety. It grows particularly

well in my sandy soil in Surrey. The semi-double or double, somewhat cupped, flowers are as large as any, of clear rose-pink without a trace of blue. Being of dense, bushy growth it makes an excellent hedge. 3 to 4 feet. (Plate 55.)
Willmott, Plate 263.

'Bicolor'. There were many bicolour and tinged varieties; mine is of rosy-lilac, reverse paler, fading to lilac-white at the edges. Yellow stamens. Semi-double. 3 to 4 feet.

'Double Blush'. Rich blush centre, fading outwards, and with nearly white reverse. A charming pale pink variety, probably reaching to 4 feet.

'Double White'. This is perhaps 'William IV' (recorded by Rivers) or 'Duchess of Montrose' (listed by Austin and McAslan) and is a well-known garden plant, very free in growth, reaching 4 to 6 feet. The double flowers have much longer petals than most of these little roses, and do not open so widely, and thus are more cup-shaped, or even goblet-shaped. Pure white with the most wonderful, penetrating, delicious scent, as fresh as Lily of the valley. A splendid, vigorous plant, exceedingly free in flower. Andrews's portrait of a double white (Plate 122) shows a very dwarf plant.

'Falkland'. I regard this as one of the most beautiful. It has greyish leaves, making a charming soft background to the semi-double, shapely flowers, which are of the softest, palest pink imaginable, with a hint of palest lilac. It fades nearly to white in hot sunshine. 4 feet.

'Glory of Edzell'. An unrecorded name which denotes an early-flowering, tall-growing form, perhaps a hybrid, with clear, light pink, single flowers. 6 to 7 feet.

'Irish Rich Marbled'. Rounded, soft pink buds opening deep cherry pink with lilac-pink reverse; the colour fades towards the edges. Semi-double, three rows of broad petals, the outer ones reflexing conspicuously. Yellow centre around the stamens. Probably 4 feet.

'Loch Leven'. This name indicates a form found growing in the castle garden at Loch Leven, Kinross-shire (Tayside), where Mary Queen of Scots was imprisoned. It is very free-growing and flowering, with semi-double, creamy-blush flowers, heavily mottled and delicately pencilled with rose pink. Probably 4 to 5 feet.

'Mary Queen of Scots'. A most beautiful form grown by Lady Moore in Dublin; the story goes that it was brought from France by the queen and eventually reached Northern Ireland, where it is found in many gardens. Lady Moore found it in 1921 in Antrim. The grey-lilac buds open to fairly double blooms, the surface of the petals being nearly as richly plum-tinted as in 'William III'. The grey-lilac and the plum make a fascinating contrast, a souvenir of a sad life. Probably 4 feet.

'Purpurea Plena'. Soft mallow-purple or deep old rose with mauve tint, fading to lilac pink, reverse pale pink. Double. Creamy yellow stamens. 3 to 4 feet.

'Single Cherry'. Bluish-green foliage. The bright rose-pink buds open to vivid single flowers of intense cherry red; the colour is splashed and flushed so thickly on a blush ground that it appears uniform. Probably 3 to 4 feet.

'Townsend'. A tall-growing, very prolific plant. Almost double, blush-pink fading to ivory, base of petals yellow. It is not of clear colouring, and creates rather a dirty effect. Small black heps. 5 to 6 feet.

'William III'. Very dwarf, but vigorous. Grey-green leaves densely covering the dense thicket of tiny twigs. Semi-double flowers showing a few yellow stamens, magenta-crimson changing to rich plum-colour and fading to dark lilac-pink. Reverse paler. Black heps. I to 2 feet.

I have come across a few portraits of coloured garden forms of the Burnet roses, and although I do not feel anything very definite can be achieved in nomenclature it may be worth recording them here.

Roses et Rosiers, Plate 30. A double pink.

Botanical Cabinet. Vol. 7, Plate 687. *Rosa spinosissima picta.* Single, murrey-splashed.

Andrews, Plate 121. White, also touched pink.

Andrews, Plates 122–8. Various colour forms, dwarf and tall.

Lawrance, Plate 78. 'Marbled Scotch.' Single, dark, maroon-veined.

Lawrance, Plate 15. 'Striped Scotch'.

Lawrance, Plate 62. A good plate of single red variety.

Nestel's Rosengarten shows two plates of rather highly coloured and enlarged forms.

Hybrids of the Burnet Roses

These being mostly old and not generally related to the China Rose, I consider they should be included in this chapter.

'Allard'. *Rosa xanthina allardii.* Originated in the Botanic Garden at Lyon, France; listed by Messrs Hesse in 1927. I suspect it to be a seedling of *R. × harisonii,* or of similar parentage, and it probably has no affinity with *R. xanthina.* It has similar leaves to *R. × harisonii* and thorny dark wood; a bristly, squat receptacle, glandular calyx, and small down-curved prickles on the pedicel. The flowers are nearly double, with petaloid centre and yellow stigmata; true, bright yellow and a fresh scent. Probably 4 feet.

× harisonii. 'Harison's Yellow'. *Rosa spinosissima harisonii.* Rehder adds further synonymy: *R. lutea hoggii,* 'Hogg's Double Yellow Briar': *Horticulture,* Vol. 5 is cited, but in this I have found no coloured plate as stated, only a short note in regard to a seedling of 'Harison's Yellow'. Bunyard states that this rose was raised by George Harison of New York in 1830. 'Hogg's Double Yellow' was obtained, according to Sweet's *The British Flower Garden,* 1838, Series 2, Vol. 4, page 410, from Thomas Hogg, a nurseryman of New York, and it had been raised from seed of the "single yellow rose." I have been unable to trace the origins further, but it is quite possible that Harison's and Hogg's plants were the same. In those days the only yellow rose which could have been used was *R. foetida,* the Austrian Brier, and it is probably a hybrid of this species and *R. pimpinellifolia.* It is quite distinct from 'Williams' Double Yellow' (*R. pimpinellifolia lutea plena,* q.v.) in that it has yellow stamens, whereas 'Williams'' has green carpels, in the centre of the flowers. 'Harison's' is free-growing and free-flowering in brilliant sulphur-yellow, loosely double and somewhat cupped, and has a gaunt, upright habit, reaching 6 feet. It does not sucker freely. It bears the scent of *R. foetida.* A useful, erect rose for planting among other more bushy shrubs, creating a brilliant effect in early summer. Has been used freely in hybridizing: 'Rustica', 'Sonnenlicht', 'Wildenfels Gelb', and others: see Chapter 6, "Shrub Roses of the Twentieth Century."

Sweet, 1838, Series 2, Vol. 4, Plate 410. 'Hogg's Double Yellow'.

Beales, page 140.

× **involuta**. *Rosa tomentosa* × *R. pimpinellifolia*. *Rosa rubella* of Smith. A spontaneous hybrid recorded first in 1800 from the Hebrides. Has much of the appearance of *R. pimpinellifolia* and is a rapid runner underground. Single, usually white, flowers, richly tinted with pink in the bud. Long reddish heps. 3 to 4 feet.

'**Mrs Colville**'. No doubt a hybrid with *Rosa pendulina*, indicated by its rather smooth red-brown wood, and long, plum-red heps. Nearly single, of intense crimson-purple with a white zone round the yellow stamens. Suckers freely. 3 to 4 feet. (Plate 56.)

'**Ormiston Roy**'. Doorenbos, Holland, 1938. 'Allard' × *Rosa pimpinellifolia*. Mr Doorenbos tells me that this rose of his often produces blooms late in the summer as well as at the normal time. It appeared in the F2 generation and was named after a friend in Montreal. The well-formed, clear yellow, single flowers are beautifully veined. Large black-maroon heps and pedicels. Compact habit, about 4 feet. It is a parent of 'Golden Wings', q.v.

× **reversa**. Prior to 1820. *Rosa pimpinellifolia* × *R. pendulina*. *Rosa rubella*. A neat little bush with obvious leanings towards *R. pimpinellifolia* in its suckering thicket of prickly stems and profuse, fresh green, small leaves. The form I grow is a very bright plant and has rich carmine pink blooms, single, followed by dark red heps, oval and nodding as in *R. pendulina*; they are produced in late summer. *Rosa malyi* is of similar parentage. 4 feet.
Schlechtendal, t.2624.

'**Stanwell Perpetual**'. A most treasured possession, and is likely to remain in cultivation as long as roses are grown, for it is perpetual-flowering and has a very sweet scent. It was a chance seedling in a garden at Stanwell, Middlesex, and was put on the market by the nurseryman Lee, of Hammersmith, in 1838. That is all that is known about it; but presumably it owes its perpetual habit and floral style to one of the Gallica group, probably an Autumn Damask. In good soil it makes a lax, thorny, twiggy bush up to 5 feet or so, with greyish small leaves resembling those of *Rosa pimpinellifolia*, which is no doubt its other parent. The flowers are of pale blush-pink, opening flat, with quilled and quartered petals. (Plate 57.) The main display is at midsummer, but it is never without flowers. Favoured by Miss Jekyll.
Kingsley, Plate 45. Exquisite portrait.
Willmott, Plate 253. Rather fewer petals than usual.
Trechslin & Coggiatti. Very good.
Phillips and Rix, Plate 107.

'**Williams' Double Yellow**'. *Rosa pimpinellifolia lutea plena*. This was raised about 1828 by John Williams of Pitmaston near Worcester (U.K.), from seeds obtained from the single yellow rose (*R. foetida*). It is thus of the same parentage as *R.* × *harisonii*, but the present Old Double Yellow Scots Rose, as it is often called, is very distinct. It would seem to be much nearer to the Burnet Roses than to *R.* × *harisonii*, making a freely suckering, branching, prickly bush about 4 feet high, with neat leaves and loosely double, bright yellow flowers. These have a bunch of green carpels in the centre; 'Harison's Yellow' has yellow stamens, and this at once distinguishes them, apart from other characters. The heavy scent of *R. foetida* pervades them both. In shape the flowers are inclined to reflex, and the petals stay on the bush for a long time after turning brown, a sad disadvantage. It is used effectively with the clear lavender of *Nepeta* × *faassenii* (*N. mussinii*) against the yellow-brown stone of Upton House near Banbury, Oxfordshire, a property of the National Trust. It is often encountered in

gardens in the Western Highlands, where it is known as 'Prince Charlie's Rose'.
Sweet, 1838, Series 2, Vol. 4, Plate 353. *Rosa spinosissima lutea plena;* 'Williams' Double Yellow'.

THE JAPANESE OR RUGOSA ROSES

The Plant of Roses, though it be a shrub full of prickles yet it had been more
fit and convenient to have placed it with the most glorious floures of the
world than to insert the same among base and thorny shrubs.

Gerard's *Herball,* 1597

THIS NOBLE GROUP of hardy floriferous shrubs has two major disadvantages. First, nearly
everyone who hears the word *rugosa* conjures up a mental image of the so-called *"Rosa rugosa"*
which is used as an understock specially for standard roses, and which is a hybrid of *R. rugosa*
(its accepted name is *R. rugosa* 'Hollandica'); and, second, that *rugosa* varieties do not lend
themselves well to cutting, and thereby lose a lot of publicity at shows and in the home. They
have, however, so many assets that these few disadvantages are greatly outnumbered.

The species is a member of the group Cinnamomeae and is a native of north-eastern Asia,
of northern China, Korea, and Japan, and was first recorded in Europe in a botanical way by
Thunberg in 1784. E. A. Bunyard relates how the Chinese in particular portrayed this rose
as far back as A.D. 1000, and the China Rose even earlier. As it was also grown in Japan, it
was understandable that it should reach us from those shores first; in 1796 it was introduced
as a novelty by Lee and Kennedy of Hammersmith, but did not prove very popular. It was
scarcely a type of rose that would have been given an honoured place then, for it brought no
new colour to roses; the craze for Chinoiserie was over, the day of the flowering shrub had
not been thought of, and the blooms were comparatively shapeless.

Looking at *Rosa rugosa* today we find a rose with few faults. It is extremely hardy; it is bushy;
and it thrives on sandy and other soils, though it is not so successful on heavy clay and chalk,
where it develops chlorosis. It flowers from the end of May onwards into autumn, bears heps,
and gives autumn colour. It has a variety of colours, and an excellent fragrance. From its petals
the Chinese, so W. J. Bean records, made a kind of pot-pourri, and its heps have been used
in Europe for making preserves. I have seen no disease on it or on its varieties, and pests do
not make any impression on it. It would be very difficult to give a longer recital of merits to
any other shrub, and yet this rose and its varieties can hardly be described as popular, although a definite trend towards increased favour has been noticeable in the last quarter-century.

It grows freely enough, sets quantities of seeds which germinate well, and hybridizes
readily with almost any rose growing near by. Its disadvantages are the lack of form in the
double-flowered varieties, though the singles are as beautiful as any; the short duration of
each flower; its suckering proclivities; and its excessive prickliness. Unfortunately, the last
character is nearly always handed on—often with interest—to its progeny. On light soils the
suckers can become a nuisance, but only to clumpy herbaceous plants and small shrubs which
cannot stand being invaded. It is just a question of giving it enough room, and I can think of
many shrubs that, in a given area, would not provide half so much enjoyment as one of the
Rugosas.

The Rugosa Rose existed for the best part of a hundred years in Europe before much attention was paid to it. And then, when the transformation enacted among popular roses had
begun to pall, rose-growers began to accord it some attention. Many crosses with popular

garden roses were made and a few good hybrids cropped up, but there the matter stopped, for in the main the hybrids were sterile or incapable of handing on the tremendous vigour and scent of the parent. They were raised mostly in France and the United States.

During this century it has attracted much more interest. It became recognized as a rose that could withstand extreme cold, and some of the varieties raised around the turn of the century in Germany have proved useful in central Europe; the same thing has happened in the northern United States and Canada, where many of the China Rose derivatives cannot stand the extreme weather.

One asset has not yet been exploited, that of its adaptability in sandy soils, and especially in maritime districts. My attention was called to a thriving, dense, suckering colony of it, which had been seen by Mrs C. C. Hurst on the shore at West Wittering; I have also noticed it established in sandy soil near Newmarket. It would be a wonderful rose for consolidating windbreaks on dunes, for it would, I imagine, make such dense growth, with a rootstock like a woody bracken, that it would be proof against wind-drift. It might perhaps be an unpleasantly prickly neighbour for a party of bathers, but the scent, wafting over the sun-warmed sand, would perhaps outweigh the inconvenience of an occasional scratch. The "Ramanas Rose" is a term often used in conjunction with *Rosa rugosa*, without explanation: Desmond Clarke, in editing *Rosa* for the eighth edition of Bean's *Trees & Shrubs Hardy in the British Isles*, suggests that it may be derived from the Japanese *Hamanashi*, or "Shore Pear." *Rosa rugosa* is frequently found by the sea—but its heps are rather far removed from a pear.

There are of course the big public parks in our coastal towns to be considered; *Rosa rugosa* is surely the right plant for them, a carefree bush that likes the sea air, flowers during the whole of the holiday season, and repels small children and dogs. It is undoubtedly *the* park rose, and great quantities are grown annually in Europe for sale to municipal bodies.

The species is now well on the way to make history. A usually sterile hybrid named 'Max Graf', probably between *Rosa rugosa* and *R. wichuraiana*, was raised in 1919 in the United States, and in the early 1940s, in the hands of Wilhelm Kordes, a seedling from it spontaneously doubled its chromosomes and became fertile. Ann Wylie wrote about this in the Royal Horticultural Society's *Journal*, February 1955, and went on to tell how Kordes at once perceived his opportunity and raised many hybrids from it. He crossed it with the Wichuraiana climber 'Golden Glow' and with Floribundas, and has achieved a remarkably hardy, disease-resistant race. They are, however, mainly climbers, and do not concern us here.

Today the species and its hybrids present a mixed lot. This is inevitable, when breeders get busy, with any genus or species. I have already mentioned the understock *Rosa rugosa* 'Hollandica', which is possibly a hybrid with 'Manettii' (Phillips and Rix, Plate 101). It is supposed to have originated in Holland and, in spite of its weakness, its suckers, and its comparatively short life, it is nowadays the most popular stem with nurserymen for standard roses. It is best to get rid of this rose from our shrub category. It is never planted deliberately, but often a dense yet lanky thicket may be found in a garden where a budded scion has succumbed to its embrace. The nearly single, light mallow-pink flowers, produced throughout the growing season, could be tolerated, even enjoyed, if one could feel happier about the spreading root and the lanky stems. On some waste railway bank or gravel pit, or in some sooty backyard, its disadvantages may be forgiven, but the genus *Rosa* and *R. rugosa* in particular have better to offer.

Rosa rugosa varies considerably in nature, and a nearly related species, hybrid, or variety, *R. kamtschatica*, has been confused with it by writers during the years; it is not of much garden value. My laudatory remarks at the beginning of this chapter refer almost entirely to the typical forms and close hybrids of *R. rugosa*. Its natural colours make it a harmonious companion for Old Roses, and it starts flowering even in advance of these, usually by the end of May in Surrey, in all its forms.

The garden forms and hybrids fall fairly clearly into two groups: those which are actual forms or very near hybrids of *Rosa rugosa*; and big lusty hybrids with other roses. Together with a few others, including the prostrate 'Paulii' and 'Max Graf', all of them will be found in Chapter 6, in the section "Shrub Roses of the Twentieth Century."

The following are all forms or such near hybrids that from a gardening point of view they are practically identical, except for their floral variety. They form dense rounded bushes, usu-ally nearly as wide as high, covering the ground with many shoots, well set with large and small prickles and bristles, making them impenetrable; the leaves usually have 7 or 9 leaflets and are neatly shaped, glossy, deeply veined or corrugated, and covering the bushes with a mantle of rich dark green which turns yellow in the autumn. The flowers are borne singly or in small clusters on small shoots produced very freely early in the season; later, strong shoots appear bearing up to a dozen or so flowers. The singles and semi-doubles show creamy yellow stamens, much paler than in many species, and this colour assorts particularly well with the floral tones. The buds are beautiful, long and pointed with a mass of pale green bracts around the larger clusters. In fact the pale green wood, prickles, bracts, and calyces make an excellent contrast with the flowers and leaves. (Plate 59.) The doubles are loosely knit, somewhat shapeless, open quickly from the bud, and are at their best the first day. In hot weather they last only two days, but a long succession is maintained. The scent is delicious, redolent of cloves, and carries well on the air. The heps retain their projecting calyx lobes and are very handsome, large, round, and shining.

Very little pruning is required; the plants grow bushy naturally, but if they become old and gaunt due to overcrowding they can be cut back severely. No rose benefits so much from being allowed plenty of space to create its naturally well-balanced, rounded shape. To ensure a long flowering season the doubles may be clipped over in early February. The singles may be treated likewise, but the formation of heps on them is inclined to prevent the formation of later crops of flowers, and a choice has to be made between flowers and heps.

They make splendid sturdy hedges, and can be kept in shape by pruning or clipping to about 4 or 5 feet high by 3 or 4 feet wide; for such a hedge they should be planted at 3 feet apart. Supports would be necessary on less fertile soils to take a hedge to greater heights. As suckers are part of the natural Rugosa traits, due consideration should be given to ultimate spread at the time of planting, particularly on light soil. Some plants may become 8 feet wide after six or more years of cultivation, and if suited there is no limit to what they can do. It will be understood therefore that unless some pruning of shoots and roots is contemplated they are not suitable for small borders.

rugosa. *Rosa rugosa rugosa*. It is difficult to pin down one form as the type of so variable a spe-cies, and when raised from seed this form itself is variable. Vigorous growth, less upright than *R. rugosa* 'Alba' and 'Roseraie de l'Haÿ'; excellent foliage. Its only disadvantage is the unpleasant contrast between the violaceous carmine of the flowers and the bright tomato-red heps, which it produces freely. This wild type is the best for dune-planting, especially as it is more often available on its own roots from nurseries. 5 feet.
Andrews, Plate 129. A magnificent drawing.
Lawrance, Plate 42. *Rosa ferox*; Hedgehog Rose. *Rosa rugosa*.
Botanical Register, Vol. 5; t.420. *Rosa ferox. Rosa rugosa*; a good portrait.
Siebold, Vol. I, t.28. Excellent.

—'Alba'. *Rosa rugosa albiflora*. Pure white single flowers, blush-tinted in the bud. The white in Rugosa varieties is much purer than in most other roses. An exceptionally vigorous form, very bushy and well covered with fresh, dark green leaves. Particularly effective in late summer when the crops of large, shining, orange-red heps appear, contrasting with the later flowers. 6 to 7 feet. When well grown will make a magnificent large rounded bush.

The Garden, Vol. 9, page 452. A very fine portrait.

Journal des Roses, Août 1906.

Rosenzeitung, June 1907.

McFarland, *Roses of the World*, page 237. With heps.

Beales, page 239.

Phillips and Rix, Plate 101.

—'Rubra'. This is a splendid horticultural clone, also known as *Rosa rugosa* 'Atropurpurea'. In growth and foliage and fruit it follows *R. rugosa* but in colour it is wine-crimson, against which richness the creamy stamens show to advantage.

Austin, page 238.

Garden Forms and Hybrids of Rosa rugosa

'Belle Poitevine'. Bruant, France, 1894. Although I have failed to find exact details of parentage, this is usually reported to be a hybrid of *Rosa rugosa*, raised by Georges Bruant. The foliage is not so glossy as the most typical forms, such as *R. r.* 'Alba' and 'Rubra', and the growth is not quite so lush. It does, however, make a similarly good bush. The flowers are loosely double, opening rather flat, four inches across, showing creamy stamens; pale magenta or mallow-pink. Good heps. 5 feet by 5 feet.

Park, Plate 189.

'Blanc Double de Coubert'. Cochet-Cochet, France, 1892. The parentage given, *Rosa rugosa* × 'Sombreuil', is very doubtful. Shows little trace of hybridity except that it is much less bushy and lush than *R. rugosa* 'Alba'. The pure white blooms are loosely semi-double, less flat than others of this group, slightly blush-tinted in the bud. 6 feet by 5 feet. The best-known rose in this group; those who have grown only this variety should try some of the others.

Journal des Roses, Février 1897.

Trechslin & Coggiatti.

'Calocarpa'. See "Shrub Roses of the Twentieth Century," Chapter 6.

'Delicata'. Cooling, U.S., 1898. An American, and probably a hybrid. The least vigorous and bushy of this group and seldom a satisfactory plant in the garden, or in the nursery, where it seems very difficult to propagate. The flowers are semi-double, resembling 'Belle Poitevine' but of a delightful cool lilac-pink. Foliage fairly good. Perhaps 5 feet when growing well, though usually about 3 feet.

Phillips and Rix, Plate 101.

'Fru Dagmar Hastrup'. Hastrup, Denmark, *c.* 1914. A seedling from *Rosa rugosa*. A most satisfactory plant, of compact growth, dark green foliage, and exquisite single flowers of clear, light pink entirely lacking the purplish shade of the others. Fortunately the heps are rich crimson, not the usual orange-red of the other singles, and as a consequence they harmonize with the flowers. The cream stamens are conspicuous, and the buds are rich deep pink. 5 feet by 5 feet. Its slightly lower and very compact growth make it one of the few ideal roses for hedges. (Plate 61.)

Gibson, Plate 33.

'Hansa'. Schaum, Holland, 1905. A very tough, free-flowering bush with typical growth and foliage. It is greatly valued and planted in northern and central Europe, but I find it much less appealing than the less-known 'Roseraie de l'Haÿ'. The flowers are fully double, well formed, of deep crimson-purple of rather a harsh tone, and the foliage shows signs of hybridity. 5 feet by 4 feet.

Les Plus Belles Roses, page 182, has a portrait of 'Souvenir de Pierre Leperdrieux', which I have not seen. This portrait with its excellent heps is very near to 'Hansa'.

'Roseraie de l'Haÿ'. Gravereaux, France, 1901. Reputed to be a sport from or hybrid of *Rosa rugosa rosea,* which is difficult to believe; it is of normal growth, slightly more erect than *R. rugosa* 'Alba', but equally fresh and luxuriant, the lovely narrow foliage densely covering the whole bush. The buds are particularly long and pointed, scrolled like a perfect 'Céleste' or Hybrid Tea, and of dark purplish red; they open to 4½ inches wide, fairly full, glorious blooms of intense rich crimson-purple, with cream stamens lighting the centre, from which radiate folded petals. It is much looser, more velvety, and of brighter, richer colouring than 'Hansa'. Few heps. A superb rose, admirable with blue hydrangeas. 6 feet by 5 feet. (Plate 58.)

Journal des Roses, Août 1906.

Rosenzeitung, June 1907.

Les Plus Belles Roses, page 116. Somewhat exaggerated, but the true colour.

Park, Plate 191. Too pale.

Gibson, Plate 33.

'Scabrosa'. Prior to 1939. I have been unable to trace the origin of this splendid form, which is extra vigorous, bears large leaves, and makes a wide handsome bush, of typical appearance. The single flowers are also large, 5½ inches across, of violaceous crimson, with the usual cream stamens, and are followed by immense orange-red heps. Certainly the grossest development so far among the forms and near hybrids of the species, in leaf, flower, and fruit. 5 feet by 5 feet.

While I doubt if it applies, Andrews's Plate 129 is similar to this variety.

Park, Plate 190.

'Souvenir de Christophe Cochet'. Cochet-Cochet, France, 1894. Records state that this is *Rosa rugosa alba simplex* × 'Comte d'Épremesnil'; it is very similar to 'Belle Poitevine', but the foliage and flowers are less attractive. 'Comte Épremesnil' was a Rugosa seedling, which had double pinkish flowers, and bore fruits. 6 feet.

Journal des Roses, Septembre 1894. A grandiose portrait. Rather too bright.

Rosenzeitung, 1893.

'Souvenir de Philémon Cochet'. Cochet-Cochet, France, 1899. This was a sport from 'Blanc Double de Coubert', and I have noticed it recurring from time to time in recent years. It differs in floral shape only, being very double, the mass of small central petals and wide outer petals producing a flower not unlike a double hollyhock. The faint blush tinting of the bud is usually preserved in the centre when the flower is full blown. 4 feet to 5 feet.

Phillips and Rix, Plate 103.

It is very difficult to decide, where learned botanists differ, how to group the Kamchatka Rose, by some treated as a distinct species, *Rosa kamtschatica*, and by others as a variety of *R. rugosa*. It is not important horticulturally, being inferior in value to *R. rugosa* in every way, but the many figures of it, to the exclusion of *R. rugosa*, in old books make me think that *R. rugosa* may sometimes have been depicted and captioned in error. It was introduced in 1770. Also known as *R. r. ventenatiana*.

Botanical Magazine, t.3149. *Rosa rugosa kamtschatica*.

Duhamel, Vol. 7, Plate 10. *Rosa kamtschatica*.

Botanical Register, Vol. 10, t.419.

Redouté, Vol. 1, Plate 47. Probably *Rosa rugosa*.

Roses et Rosiers, Plate 44. Probably of this species.

SOME STRANGE SPECIES AND THEIR HYBRIDS

Among all floures of the worlde the floure of the rose is cheyf and beeryth ye pryse. And by cause of vertues and swete smelle and savour. For by fayrnesse they fede the syghte: and playseth the smelle by odour, the touche by softe handlynge. And wythstondeth and socouryth by vertue ayenst many syknesses and euylles.

Bartholomaeus Anglicus, *De Proprietatibus Rerum*,
translated by John de Trevisa, 1398

THE HEPS OF MANY roses are bristly but only a very few are actually prickly, like those of a Horse Chestnut, though smaller. There are three species in cultivation with this peculiarity. Two of these are closely related, *Rosa stellata* and *R. mirifica*; in fact the latter is sometimes classed as a variety of the former. The other species, *R. roxburghii*, also known as *R. microphylla*, is totally distinct. While the first two are small wiry shrubs, *R. roxburghii* is a mighty plant, and is placed separately by botanists in the sub-genus *Platyrhodon*, while *R. stellata* is in the sub-genus *Hesperhodos*.

roxburghii. The Burr or Chestnut Rose (Rose Châtaigne). A native of China and Japan, and introduced to cultivation in 1908. It makes a large rounded bush, the stiff angular-branching stems having flaking, buff-coloured bark which adds to its attraction in winter. It is a particularly unpleasant rose to handle, being rigid and armed with pairs of straight prickles below the leaves. As many as 15 leaflets occur, narrow and arranged in compact ladder-like fashion; the flowers are variable in colour from nearly white to deep rose, and are supported by stalks, calyx tube, and calyx, all prickly and very distinct. The resultant hep is an inch or more across, rounded, with persistent, conspicuous, broad calyx lobes and covered with stiff prickles. It so happens that the double form, *Rosa roxburghii roxburghii*, was introduced many years before the single wild type, in 1824, and the figures in old books are naturally of this double form. In consequence the forms are classed as follows:

—var. **normalis**. China, whence it was introduced in 1908. The single type of the Chestnut Rose. The four-inch-wide flowers are very beautiful but evanescent, and rather hide themselves under the leaves. The value of this plant in gardens is better gauged by its foliage, stance, and interest than by its floral effect. In poor sandy soil it has attained some 9 feet in height and width. (Plate 63.)

Botanical Magazine, t.6548. This shows the Japanese form *Rosa roxburghii hirsuta* or *hirtula,*
    whose leaves are pubescent beneath, thus differing from *R. r. normalis,* the Chinese form;
    introduced before 1880.

Iwasaki, *Phonzo Soufou,* Vol. 84.

Gault and Synge, Plates 45 and 46, flowers and fruits.

Phillips and Rix, Plate 19.

Lancaster, page 296, flowers and fruits.

Gibson, Plate 34.

—var. **roxburghii.** *Rosa roxburghii plena, R. microphylla.* An ancient cultivated form of the Chest-
    nut Rose which is presumably of Chinese origin. Miss Willmott tells us how its portrait
    in a collection of Chinese drawings resulted in Lindley mentioning it in his monograph,
    and it was found to exist in the Calcutta Botanic Garden, whence it was introduced by Dr
    Roxburgh from Canton. It flowered first in Britain in 1824.

    In my experience it is not so vigorous nor so hardy as the single type, and is much
    smaller in growth. The flowers have large, pale pink outer petals making a frame for the
    mass of short central petals, which are of intense deep pink with a lilac tint. Slightly
    scented. 4 feet.

Journal des Roses, Septembre 1874. *Rosa microphylla,* pourpre ancien. A fanciful flower and colour.

Botanical Magazine, t.3490. A splendid portrait.

Willmott, Plate 135. Half-open flowers only.

Le Rougetel, page 38.

Iwasaki, *Phonzo Soufou,* Vol. 84.

Botanical Register, Vol. 11, t.919. A flower of rather exaggerated perfection.

Reeves' Drawings of Chinese Plants. Very good.

The Chestnut Rose has given some hybrids which, while not in the front rank of garden value,
are interesting, beautiful, and perhaps an indication of what may follow; they are 'Coryana',
'Jardin de la Croix', 'Roxane', and × *micrugosa,* which will be found in Chapter 6 in the section
"Shrub Roses of the Twentieth Century."

'Triomphe de la Guillotière'. Guillot, France, 1863. The raiser's name will immediately
    quash any suspicion that this rose is connected with the guillotine! An extremely interest-
    ing hybrid of *Rosa roxburghii* (*R. microphylla*) and one that may well be used again in our
    search for "different" roses. The dainty leaves, pinnate or divided into neat small leaflets,
    indicate its ancestry. It flowers well on a west wall at the Roseraie de l'Haÿ; borne singly
    and in clusters, the flowers are light rose-pink and fragrant, about 3 inches across, tightly
    filled with petals in the Old Rose style, with button eye. Buds large, round, downy; bark
    smooth. This is certainly a rose on its own, for preservation, and it should be quite hardy.

stellata. Western Texas to northern Arizona. *Hesperhodos stellatus.* This dwarf plant is distin-
    guished by having *only 3* leaflets—hairy, deeply toothed and at first sight rather like those
    of a gooseberry—and minute stellate hairs on the stems. Grey-green stems, bearing short,
    sharp prickles of ivory colouring when young, form a wiry thicket up to about 2 feet; in
    flower it is silky like a cistus, the colour being a deep vinous pink of a subdued tone, with
    yellow stamens; it is in flower for a long time. Coming as it does from so far south, it needs
    all the sun we can give it and thrives best in a well-drained position against a south wall.
    The heps are rounded, of dull red colouring. I have not found it so vigorous as *Rosa stellata*

mirifica, but both can be of equal vigour when raised from seed.
Willmott, Plate 305.

—var. **mirifica**. New Mexico, U.S. The 'Sacramento Rose', so called because of its growing in the Sacramento Mountains, New Mexico; closely related to *Rosa stellata* although sometimes classed as a separate species. It is perhaps of stronger growth and more readily adaptable to British garden conditions, forming a dense bush, filled with wiry, arching stems freely branching and set with small sharp prickles in the manner of *R. stellata*, but with smooth stems. The leaves usually have 3 to 5 leaflets and are more or less smooth. It is more free in flower and slightly longer in petal and of paler colouring, but is also silky and like a cistus.

Again it is reputed to love all the sun we can give it, and a well-drained soil, though in my own garden in poor sandy soil it has ascended to 4 feet on a wall, practically without any sunshine. This is a useful and unusual little rose of charm and interest to the plantsman. No hybrids are known. (Plate 64, Drawing 7.)
Botanical Magazine, t.9070. A poor plate.
Mansfield, Plate 2.
American Rose Annual, 1932, photograph.

persica. The remaining species to be considered is *Rosa persica* or, classified as it is now in a separate genus, *Hulthemia persica* (*Lowea berberifolia, Rosa berberifolia*). It is a strange little shrub, only a few inches high, succeeding best in extremely warm, well-drained positions such as at Highdown, Sussex, where it used to spread by underground runners, throwing up small shoots bearing simple—not pinnate—grey-green leaves. The flowers are a brilliant buttercup yellow with a scarlet blotch at the base of each petal, reminiscent of *Halimium*. (Plate 62.) It is very difficult to propagate and establish.

While some spontaneous hybrids have been reported from the former Soviet Union, the only one I have come across is that now known as × *Hulthemosa hardii* (*Rosa hardii*), presumed to be a cross between *Hulthemia persica* and *Rosa clinophylla*. The latter is closely related to *R. laevigata* and a far cry, botanically, from *Hulthemia persica*. It appeared in the Jardins de Luxembourg, Paris, in 1836, probably from seed of *Rosa persica*. The fact that it has remained in cultivation for so long cannot be attributed to its vigour as we know it, for it is notoriously difficult and short-lived, though more tractable than *Hulthemia persica*. Its colour has endeared it to us, for it has retained the brilliance of *H. persica*, but has a larger flower, 2 inches across, and larger red blotches. For many years a plant grew successfully in the University Botanic Garden at Cambridge, but I expect the best one ever grown was at Berkeley Castle, Gloucestershire, where it achieved 9 feet by 9 feet, against a wall. There is no doubt it is a spectacular plant when in full flower, and plants on their own roots should be tried in favoured places against sunny walls in the southeastern parts of England. As *H. persica* is a native of areas from Iran to Afghanistan, both it and its hybrids are probably best suited to the sunnier districts of England. Where they thrive, *Rosa stellata* and *R. mirifica* would also be expected to thrive.

It is a pleasant thought that J. A. Hardy, who was no doubt a keen plantsman and rosarian, should be commemorated in this remarkable plant, while his wife has to her credit the famous white Damask Rose 'Mme Hardy'. Neither is likely ever to go out of cultivation from popular neglect, so long as they retain vigour.
Botanical Magazine, t.7096. *Rosa persica*.

Duhamel, Vol. 7, t.14. *Rosa berberifolia*. Poor.
Willmott, Plate 1. *Rosa persica*.
Botanical Register, Vol. 15, t.1261. *Lowea berberifolia*.
Willmott, Plate 2. *Rosa hardii*.
Journal des Roses, Juin 1881. *Rosa hardii*.
Paxton's Magazine of Botany, Vol. 10, Fig. 195. *Rosa hardii*.
Phillips and Rix, Plate 19.

A great effort was made by J. L. Harkness of Hitchin, Hertfordshire to raise new hybrids, using *Rosa persica* derived from native-source seeds. Crosses were made with several modern roses but all proved to be sterile, so there the breeding stopped. The red blotch was present in most. Edward Hyams found a red-blotched hybrid in Iran, and similar hybrids have been found in Russia. All the hybrids so far seen have pinnate leaves, as opposed to the single blade of *R. persica*.

Breeding continues, and if once the longed-for amalgamation takes place we may see a strain of roses with the fetching red eye of *Rosa persica*. To date Messrs Harkness have named 'Tigris' (*R. persica* × 'Trier'), 1985, a dwarf bush with double yellow red-eyed flowers; and 'Euphrates' (*R. persica* × 'Fairy Changeling'), 1986, a low, lax grower with single, reddish-salmon flowers with scarlet eye. These were followed in 1989 with two more: 'Nigel Hawthorne' (*R. persica* × 'Harvest Home'), salmon-rose with red eye, a small prickly little bush; and 'Xerxes' (*R. persica* × 'Canary Bird'), single, bright yellow, small flowers with crimson eye, early-flowering and non-prickly. I am indebted to Jack Harkness for these particulars. While none of the varieties can truly be called a shrub rose, it is good to be able to focus attention on great endeavour along entirely fresh lines.

6

Shrub and Other Roses
Having Affinity to the China Rose

THE INFLUENCE OF THE CHINA ROSES

As this blind rose, no more than a whim of dust,
achieved her excellence without intent,
so man, the casual sport of time and lust,
plans wealth and war, and loves by accident.

Humbert Wolfe

THE CHINA ROSE is the foundation species upon which all our modern roses are built, whether they be bedding roses or shrubs or perpetual-flowering climbers. Its influence in rose-breeding over nearly two hundred years has been so great, so overwhelming, and so potent that it is difficult to see where we should have been without it. We are so used to thinking of roses in terms of Hybrid Teas and Floribundas that we are apt to forget that these are, comparatively, very new and specialized, and they owe more than half their success and *éclat* to the China Rose.

In 1891 William Paul thought very highly of China Roses and included four in his twelve best roses for freedom, constancy of bloom, and for massing: 'Fabvier', 'Cramoisi Supérieur', 'Common (Old Blush) China' and 'Fellemberg'. They still rank among our most free-flowering roses.

Rosa chinensis was the name given in 1768 to a pressed specimen in Gronovius's Herbarium, which in 1733 he had called Chineeshe Eglantier Roosen. It was a crimson form. In 1751 the rose was seen growing in the gardens of the custom house at Canton by Peter Osbeck, a pupil of Linnaeus. The single-flowered wild species was not discovered until 1885, and thus our rose history in regard to this species really starts with four garden roses, possibly hybrids with the Tea Rose, as recorded by Dr Hurst in Chapter 13. His "four stud Chinas" were 'Slater's Crimson China' introduced in 1792, 'Parsons's Pink China' (1793), 'Hume's Blush Tea-scented China' (1809), and 'Parks's Yellow Tea-scented China' (1824). The first is a double crimson China Rose that may have been in cultivation in Italy since the middle of the seventeenth century. Thus was the initial work already done for us in China, and enthusiasts in Europe were thereby provided with *perpetual-flowering* roses ranging through pink to true dark crimson, salmon and pale yellow, for hybridizing. Nor was this all. I have already said how these roses flowered through summer and autumn; they also had a new shape, a new texture, a dwarf habit, totally different leaves and twigs from any other in cultivation, and a different fragrance. The wild *Rosa chinensis* (now called *R. chinensis spontanea* to distinguish it from garden forms or hybrids discovered previously) was found by Dr Augustine Henry in glens near Ichang in central China. He devoted a long article to it in the *Gardeners' Chronicle* for 23 June 1902, describing it as a climber, growing like *R. banksiae*, with 3 to 5 leaflets, and solitary flowers (single), generally deep red but sometimes pink. We have single-flowered China Roses such as *R. chinensis* 'Mutabilis', 'Miss Lowe', and 'Bengal Crimson', but just what these are derived from we do not know. The fact that they, and all the double-flowered Chinas which we grow, are perpetually in flower proves that they are either sports or otherwise derived from ancient hybrids of *R. chinensis*. (Once-flowering climbing roses tend to produce perpetual-flowering dwarf sports, as recorded by Hurst; 'Little White Pet' and 'The Fairy' are further examples. The reverse is also true sometimes.)

By great good fortune I managed to persuade my friend Mikinori Ogisu, a Japanese botanist working in China, to hunt for *Rosa chinensis* var. *spontanea* in the Ichang Gorge of the Yangtse Kiang River in Hupeh, western China. He was successful and sent me the photograph on Plate 65, the first ever published in the western world. It has appeared in *The Rose* and *The Garden*, journals of the Royal National Rose Society and the Royal Horticultural Society respectively. As described by Dr Augustine Henry all those years ago, it is a big, sprawling or climbing rose with three leaflets, and single flowers of rich pink maturing to dark crimson, flowering probably only once at midsummer. In addition to photographs, Mikinori also collected seeds, and at the time of writing the resulting plants are being nursed at the Savill Garden in Windsor Great Park, and elsewhere.

Our garden China Roses are shrubs of small to medium growth, according to the local climate, and have smooth wood, reddish when young and sparsely set with small, handsome, dark red prickles. The leaves are also sparsely borne, with 3 to 5 pointed segments; they are smooth, richly tinted with red-brown when young, and contribute greatly to the general colour of the plants. (This leaf-colour is reproduced in its most intense richness in such roses as 'Donald Prior' and 'Rosemary Rose', both modern Floribundas.) The flowers have five or more rather limp petals of silky texture, making rather a shapeless flower after their first opening, especially in the singles. I have grown and seen China Roses in different districts and in exposed open places; on poor soils they may barely reach 2 feet in height, while the same form or variety in good rich soil, away from ground frost or against a wall, may reach 9 or 10 feet.

'Old Blush'. For our present purpose we may take the 'Monthly Rose' as our standard for comparison. It is a well-known garden plant and identical to 'Parsons's Pink China', introduced in 1793. It has been known and grown in China for more than a thousand years and is there known as 'Yue Yue Fen' or 'Monthly Pink'. This information, together with Chinese names for other old Chinese roses, has been most kindly supplied by Professor Chen Junyu of Beijing Forestry University. Being pink and with a plain China Rose scent and of compact habit, it may perhaps be nearly unadulterated *Rosa chinensis*, whereas probably all the coppery named forms are infused with the Tea Rose. There is a single-flowered pink sport. (Plates 66, 67.)

There are few garden plants of so great value in cultivation today as the 'Old Blush', and it can well take its place with the Winter Jasmine, the *Forsythia*, the Lilac, and other favourites without which no garden is complete. It is a perfect bedding rose and needs little pruning, and in common with all China varieties it roots easily from cuttings. It seems to thrive in any soil, and will reach 10 feet on a sheltered wall, while for a dwarf flowering hedge of about 3 feet it is almost unequalled. The scent is like that of sweet peas, and the petals are exquisitely veined. A noticeable character of all true China Roses is that the colour of the petals deepens as they age, instead of fading, as with all other species. Tom Smith, the famous nurseryman of Newry, Co. Down, Northern Ireland, used to claim this to be the 'Last Rose of Summer' of the Irish poet, Thomas Moore, and a plant often provides me with buds at Christmas, after a mild autumn.

Willmott, Plate 79. A splendid portrait.

Andrews, Plate 66. The Pale China Rose. A rather poor portrait; exaggerated.

Lawrance, Plate 26. *Rosa semperflorens.* Bad.

Duhamel, Vol. 7, Plate 18. *Rosa semperflorens.* Probably 'Old Blush'. Very poor.

Redouté, Vol. 1, Plate 51. *Rosa indica vulgaris,* 'Parsons's Pink China'.

Gibson, Plate 5.

'Slater's Crimson China' ('Semperflorens'). Similar to 'Old Blush' but of rich crimson colouring and open in growth; smaller, more richly tinted, pretty leaves and flowers, loosely open and delicately scented. It is not generally realized that true dark crimson was quite unknown among garden roses before the introduction of this plant. No Damask or Gallica rose was darker than light crimson, except where overclouded with purple. To this introduction, then, in 1792, we can trace back all our favourite dark red roses. In China it is known as 'Yue Yue Hong' or 'Monthly Crimson'. This rose had been lost for many years, but has been traced and obtained from Bermuda. Dr Hurst found it to be a triploid. Gordon Rowley found a similar but much dwarfer, diploid plant (which also grows at Wisley) in a Hertfordshire garden (Plate 68), identical with the plate on page 89 in Willmott's *The Genus Rosa.* (See 'Willmott's Crimson China'.)

Andrews, Plate 72.

Lawrance, Plate 28. Bad.

Step, Vol. 2, Plate 80.

Jacquin, *Horti Schönbrunnensis,* Vol. 3, Plate 281.

Drapiez, Vol. 6, page 418. Le Rosier du Bengale toujours fleuri.

Botanical Magazine, t.284. Shows an unusually prickly stem for a China Rose.

'Hume's Blush Tea-scented China'. Introduced in 1809. Unfortunately this hybrid appears to be extinct in Europe, but its portrait confirms that it must have been a hybrid between *Rosa chinensis* and *R. gigantea.* It was probably not very hardy, but it was an important ancestor of the Tea Roses. The names given by Andrews and Redouté are interesting, denoting the distinct fragrance derived from the Tea Rose. Dr Hurst recalls that 'special arrangements were made by both the British and French Admiralties for the safe transit of plants of this new Tea-scented China to the Empress Josephine at Malmaison, in spite of the fierce war that was raging between England and France at that time' (See Chapter 13). Thus does horticulture transcend the petty bickerings of mankind. (Plate 73.) A plant obtained from Sangerhausen does not appear to be true to name and exhibits little of the Tea Rose character, but the genuine plant has been obtained from the Bermuda Rose Society, and tallies exactly with Thory's description and Redouté's painting. It is a weak grower, to about 3 feet. (Plate 72.)

Andrews, Plate 77, *Rosa indica odorata.*

Redouté, Vol. 1, Plate 61. *Rosa indica fragrans,* 'Hume's Blush'.

Botanical Register, Vol. 10, Plate 804.

'Parks's Yellow Tea-scented China'. Introduced in 1824. Probably of similar parentage to 'Hume's Blush', but leaning more towards the Tea Rose in colour and in scent, this was found, probably in a Southern Hemisphere garden, by Peter Beales. It has been established at Mottisfont and in Hazel Le Rougetel's garden, both in Hampshire, and produces its gracious flowers sparingly, except after a hot summer. (Plate 74.) It is a vigorous grower. In China it is known as 'Dànhuang Xianshui' ('The light yellow sweet-water rose'). By union with the Noisettes this rose became the ancestor of the famous yellow climbing Tea Roses such as 'Gloire de Dijon' and 'Maréchal Niel', which are often classed as Noisettes. Redouté, 3rd edition, 1835, Vol. 3. *Rosa indica sulphurea*, 'Parks's Yellow'. Poor.
Le Rougetel, page 43.

In the Lindley Library of the Royal Horticultural Society there are some volumes of beautiful Chinese paintings collected by a Mr Reeves. Their probable date is 1812 to 1831. In the second volume are the following Chinese roses: *semperflorens*; Double Dark Red Monthly; Monthly Blush; Indica double white. Plate 32 is possibly 'Parks's Yellow'.

The following may be considered as fairly near hybrids of the China Rose.

'Bengal Crimson'. A name given by Nancy Lindsay to a strong-growing single crimson variant of great garden value. Considering that so many roses from Chinese gardens reached Europe via India and Madagascar the name seems perfectly reasonable, but it would be good to know its Chinese name. It has grown very satisfactorily in the sandy soil at Wisley for many years in an exposed sunny position and has achieved 4 feet by 4 feet. It flowers continually from summer until autumn; the flowers are single, light crimson maturing to dark crimson, with a delicate scent. Dark leaden green leaves and few large prickles. It is a thoroughly worthy rose for our gardens. Sometimes labelled 'Sanguinea' or 'Rose de Bengale'. (Plate 71.)

'Cramoisi Supérieur'. Cocquereau or Plantier, 1835. 'Agrippina'. The true deep crimson of 'Slater's Crimson China' pervades this beautiful free-flowering variety. It is *petite* in its growth, with small wiry twigs gradually building up into a small bush; dark green small leaves richly tinted when young, and cupped double blooms borne singly or in small clusters in summer and in large heads on the strong young shoots later. It is remontant, and a glorious colour. Like all China Roses it does best in sunny, sheltered positions. 3 feet. The climbing form 'Cramoisi Supérieur Grimpant' (Plate 147) is a magnificent plant for a sunny wall; Tom Smith mentioned in his catalogue for 1912 that he had "seen the whole front of a two-storey house completely covered with the Climbing Cramoisi," whose flowers "are continually produced all the season through." I have not found it so perpetual as the bush form, but China Roses do not grow satisfactorily in my area. Not very fragrant.
Curtis, Vol. 2, Plate 11. Good.
Jamain et Forney, Plate 54. Poor.
Journal des Roses, Août 1883. Good.

'Hermosa'. Marcheseau, France, 1840. 'Armosa', 'Setina', 'Mélanie Lemarié', 'Madame Neumann'. Occurred as a seedling with four different breeders between 1834 and 1841; Dr Hurst called this a China-reversion. In some works 'Hermosa' is classed as a Bourbon, but it is very near indeed to the 'Old Blush' in habit and other characters. It is of a particularly bland lilac-pink, much fuller of petals—which are rolled at the edges—than 'Old Blush'.

It is also much more prickly, and produces a round hep, whereas 'Old Blush' has an oval hep. It is equally vigorous but usually rather more compact, and I generally observe that it is not quite so continuous. But a bunch of 'Hermosa' blooms leaves little to be desired; their form and colour are perfect, and it is fairly fragrant. As a rule the bush form does not exceed 3 feet.

There is a climbing form, known as 'Climbing Hermosa', that originated with Henderson in 1879, but like most climbing sports of free-flowering dwarfs, it is not so perpetual, few flowers being produced after the long first flush. 'Hermosa' used to be a great favourite. George Paul, writing in the Royal Horticultural Society's *Journal* in 1896, says it "is *par excellence* the dwarf hedge rose."

Choix des Plus Belles Roses, Plate 38.

Jamain et Forney, Plate 34. Poor.

Curtis, 1850, Vol. I, Plate 7. 'Armosa'.

Thomas, G. C., page 114.

Beales, Plate, page 324.

Gibson, Plate 5.

'**Miss Lowe**'. This is a name given to a single crimson of good colour and shape but of a very small growth. It is free-flowering, growing in good soil perhaps to 4 feet, but with me it is usually 18 inches. It is light crimson turning to dark crimson, with rather quilled petals.

The Garden, 1887, Vol. 2, page 128. An excellent portrait from a painting by Miss Lowe, a friend of E. A. Bowles, at Wimbledon.

'**Mutabilis**'. 'Tipo Ideale'. Writing in the *Revue Horticole* for 1934 (page 60) Henri Correvon, the celebrated Swiss alpine gardener, stated that it was given to him forty years previously by Prince Gilberto Borromeo. Later he saw it growing in Milan, but as nobody appeared to have a name for it, M. Correvon called it, very aptly, *mutabilis*, although there had been a *sempervirens* variety of this name previously. E. A. Bunyard mentioned a portrait of it by Redouté in the Jardin des Plantes, Paris, but this portrait is the Centifolia Rose 'Unique Blanche', which is also called 'Mutabilis'. It is sometimes called *Rosa* 'Turkestanica', which is a rose in the Pimpinellifoliae section, and quite distinct.

It is a slender but vigorous and robust rose, with dark plum-coloured young wood, reddish thorns, and handsome coppery young foliage. In sheltered gardens where it really thrives, as at Kiftsgate Court, Gloucestershire, it is a magnificent shrub reaching 8 feet high and wide with stout stems an inch or more in diameter, in the open border. On sunny walls in Kent it is an equal success, but very often in lowland gardens it reaches only 3 feet in height and is more like a bedding rose.

The colour of the flowers is remarkable: they open from slender pointed buds of vivid orange, flame-coloured where the sun strikes them; on opening they are. of soft pale chamois-yellow within, while the flame of the bud continues to mark the outside. The second day, after pollination, they change to soft coppery pink, and on the third day as they wrinkle and fall the colour deepens to coppery crimson. The colours are deepest in hot weather; the countless blossoms resemble flights of butterflies. (Plate 75.)

As a bedding rose this variety has great assets, particularly its long season of flowering, from early June until the autumn, and its varied tones, which enable it to fit into almost any colour scheme. It flowers early enough to plant it with the blue hardy geraniums such as *Geranium himalayense* and *G.* 'Johnson's Blue', which create an especially good contrast. Its flame tones and coppery leaves assort well with combinations of red, orange, and yellow, while its general effect is soft enough to create a pleasing complement to grey foliage. Its possibilities are endless, and it is so free that it might well find its way into our public parks as a bedding plant.

Willmott, page 81. "The variety known as Miss Willmott's *indica* is a garden form." There is no further description and no particulars of origin. Although this does not show all the variations of colour I consider it applies to *Rosa chinensis* 'Mutabilis'; at least it shows colouring fairly near to the orange-pink in the original painting.

Revue Horticole, 1934, page 60. Excellent plate showing all colours.

Trechslin & Coggiatti. Good.

Gibson, Plate 5.

'Serratipetala'. 'Oeillet de Saint Arquey', 'Fimbriata à pétales frangés'. Roy Shepherd states that this rose was found in France in 1912 under the above synonym. It is a vigorous bushy plant, considerably wider in growth than others of these more typical varieties, with widely branching angular stems building up into a good bush, but sparsely leaved. The leaves are of a leaden green, and the flowers small, long-lasting, borne freely in angular clusters or singly. Each petal is fringed like those of a pink. In hot weather it is a rich crimson but in cooler weather nearer to pink, especially on the smaller, very fringed central petals. It is fairly double, with little fragrance. Young shoots and leaves are plum-coloured. 4 feet by 4 feet. It cannot be described as a striking garden rose, but more of a curiosity with some value for small bouquets, like the Green Rose. It is not as perpetual as the other China Roses, but produces a few late flowers. The leaden-coloured leaves and flower tints denote close affinity with *Rosa chinensis*.

'Viridiflora' (*Rosa* 'Monstrosa'). The Green Rose. With similar growth to 'Old Blush', this is a free-flowering and otherwise normal plant, but has all its floral parts transformed into greenish scales. The result is a beautiful oval bud, quite small, of soft blue-green, and at that stage it is acceptable. Unfortunately, on opening it becomes loose and tawdry, splashed with brown, and cannot be called beautiful. 3 to 4 feet. It is a curiosity, and demonstrates the extraordinary variability found in the China Rose. Roy Shepherd records that it was in cultivation as early as 1743; August Jäger states 'Bambridge and Harrison, 1856', but Geoffrey Taylor sent me a cutting as follows:

> There is a note in Henry Bright's *Year in a Lancashire Garden*, 1879, quoting a letter to the *Gardeners' Chronicle* from Mr Buist of the Rosedale Nurseries, Philadelphia: "There appears to be some uncertainty in regard to the origin of this rose. It is a sport from *Rosa indica* (the China Rose of England and Daily Rose of America). It was caught in Charleston, South Carolina, about 1833, and came to Baltimore through Mr R. Halliday, from whom I obtained it, and presented two plants to my old friend Thomas Rivers in 1837."

I have been unable to trace Mr Buist's letter.

Flore des Serres, 1856, Vol. 11, Plate 1136.

Roses et Rosiers, Plate 19.

Journal des Roses, Septembre 1908.

Rosenzeitung, June 1908.

L'Horticulteur Français, 1856, Plate 19.
Phillips and Rix, Plate 69.

'Willmott's Crimson China'. This is a charming little rose, known in China as 'Chi Long Han Zhu' or 'Pearl in the Red Dragon's Mouth'. The flowers are well-rounded, small, dark crimson. (Plate 70.) It grows to about 18 inches in Surrey. Hazel Le Rougetel brought another small-growing, double crimson China from gardens in the north of that country; as yet we have no name for this, but it should prove quite hardy, and like 'Chi Long Han Zhu' is floriferous. It is about midway between this little rose and 'Cramoisi Supérieur'.

Apart from 'Mutabilis', which may be derived partly from the Tea Rose, the above seven varieties are of almost pure China derivation. Now, reverting to Dr Hurst's "four stud Chinas," we can pass to the second two (presuming that the first two gave rise to the pink and red varieties); they are 'Hume's Blush Tea-scented China' and 'Parks's Yellow Tea-scented China'. Both were derived from *Rosa chinensis* crossed with *R. gigantea,* the Tea Rose, and may have arisen in Chinese gardens hundreds of years prior to their introduction to England.

While it cannot be proved that the following, which are usually classed as China Roses, were derived directly from these two Chinese hybrids, it is more than likely; they are far removed from other classes of roses which were being raised at the time, and certainly are near to the Chinas in growth and many other characteristics, while showing also the influence of the Tea Rose in their colour and scent.

They all make twiggy, bushy plants with coppery-tinted young shoots and leaves, and bear loosely semi-double flowers with limp silky petals. I find they have a splendid habit of producing three main bursts of bloom, the first at the end of May and through June; then, after a pause, another in August; while from mid-September onwards they are continually in flower until winter comes. As Hybrid Teas and Floribundas flower most profusely in July and September, the happy way in which these Chinas fill in and keep the colour going can easily be perceived. It is worth noting that the yellowish varieties among the following roses fade as they mature, and therefore are markedly different from the purer China Rose varieties.

'Comtesse du Cayla'. Guillot, France, 1902. Brilliant coral-flame, fading to salmon pink, with yellow-tinted reverses to the petals; tea and sweet-pea scent. Young shoots and foliage bloomy purple. 4 feet.

'Fabvier'. Laffay, France, 1832. 'Mme Fabvier' or 'Général Fabvier'. A short-growing variety approaching the form of a Polyantha Rose, but with typical China Rose stems, prickles, leaves, and lack of scent. The small flowers are borne singly or a few together, and have rather more than a single row of brilliant scarlet-crimson petals, often showing a white streak. It is a gay little plant, always in flower, but it is difficult to fit into the garden. It would be admirable in small formal Victorian beds, or can be given a place in front of modern roses. Leaves richly tinted when young, turning to dark leaden green. Almost scentless. 18 inches.
Komlosy. Very good.
Choix des Plus Belles Roses, Plate 21. Very good.

'Némésis'. Is another miniature variety; see later section in this chapter, "The Poly-poms: An Interlude."

'Le Vésuve'. Laffay, France, 1825. 'Lemesle'. (Not to be confused with 'Vesuvius', a single crimson Hybrid Tea.) I found this rose many years ago in the garden at Ronans, Bracknell, Berkshire, and it was named for me by Courtney Page and Walter Easlea. It shows the noteworthy habit of the China Rose in the deepening colour of the fading flowers. In my light Surrey soil it has never been much more than pink with a few richer tones on the outer petals, but at Ronans the great old bush that I knew had reached 5 feet in height and the older flowers turned to a warm coppery carmine. On opening it has a peculiarly soft, creamy tone of pink, not far removed from the Redouté portrait of 'Hume's Blush'. The sturdy, prickly plant gradually builds up into a criss-cross of branches bearing elegant, pointed, rather grey-green leaves. The flowers are fully double, of Tea shape, with rolled petals and delicious soft tea-scent. It is constantly in flower. There was a climbing sport recorded in 1904.

Journal des Roses, Mai 1891. Misleadingly rich colouring.

Les Plus Belles Roses, Plate 92. A poor portrait, but showing the typical colour of the mature flower.

Phillips and Rix, Plate 69.

'Mme Eugène Résal'. Guillot, France, 1894. Vivid nasturtium red with yellow base, quickly fading to pink. A sport from 'Mme Laurette Messimy'. 4 feet. I do not think this is in cultivation in Britain.

Journal des Roses, Avril 1895.

'Mme Laurette Messimy'. Guillot Fils, France, 1887. ('Laurette Messimy'.) 'Rival de Paestum' × 'Mme Falcot'. Clear bright salmon-pink, shaded copper and yellow and with yellow base, fading to dull salmon-pink. Young shoots glaucous. 4 feet.

The Garden, 24 October 1891, page 378. Very good.

'Purpurea'. Chenault, France, 1930. A small bush, with fairly typical leaves and growth for a China Rose; indeed, the flowers and general appearance conform to this group. But I cannot help thinking it must have been hybridized with a Gallica or Bourbon to produce this rich, glowing, purplish crimson colour. 18 inches.

Andrews, Plate 80. *Rosa indica purpurea*. As the plant I describe above was raised in 1930, this cannot refer, but the constant striving after a blue rose is still with us, even from those early days. Andrews wrote:

> The purple variety is said to have been first imported from China about the year 1810, to the gardens of Lord Milford, under the appellation of the Blue Rose. . . . This Rose of expectation, when its blooms unfolded, no heavenly blue disclosed, but a red purple, which as it faded off became paler, less brilliant, but of a bluer or colder purple, which gives to the fresh-opened blossoms a very different appearance contrasted with those retiring; and although the blue's celestial tint is wanting, it is nevertheless a graceful and very abundant flowering rose.

The portrait shows a pink rose, slightly flushed with lilac!

'Rival de Paestum'. G. Paul, U.K., prior to 1848. Young shoots, prickles and leaves rich glaucous plum colour. Long creamy buds are borne erect, but nod to open into loose, semi-double, ivory-white blooms. Gracious and floriferous. Slight tea-scent. 4 feet.

Four other roses are related to the China Rose and sometimes grouped with it:

'Fellemberg'. Omitted from this section as I consider it fits better with the various Noisette
Roses; see the section "The Noisette and Tea Roses" later in this chapter.

'Five-coloured China Rose'. This is a remarkable plant discovered by Robert Fortune during
his journeys in China for the then Horticultural Society of London, recorded in his book
Three Years' Wanderings in the Northern Provinces of China, of 1847. It has been treasured for many
years in Bermuda, whence came my plants, which seem to be hardy. A slender grower with
small leaves and flowers, it produces flowers of red, pink, parti-coloured or white on the
same bush throughout the growing season.

In China, Professor Chen Junyu tells me, it is known as 'Wu Se' Quaing Wei', and is to
be found in Wan Xiang-jin's *Encyclopaedia of Flowers* (1620) and in the *Thesaurus of Flowers*
edited by Wang Hao (1708).

'Gloire des Rosomanes'. Vibert, France, 1825. A China × Bourbon hybrid. Used extensively
in California as an understock, where it is called 'Ragged Robin', and also as a hedging
rose, 'Red Robin'. An historic rose, and one of the founders of the Hybrid Perpetual
Roses. Not of great garden value today. Large, double, crimson, fragrant flowers borne in
large and small clusters. 4 feet.
Choix des Plus Belles Roses, Plate 12.

'Gruss an Teplitz'. See later section, "Shrub Roses of the Twentieth Century."

THE BOURBON ROSES

THE ROSES IN this section represent some of the first fruits of hybridizing certain Old Roses
with, probably, the Old Blush China. The China Roses over the years destroyed the perfec-
tions of the Old Roses, but the varieties here listed still have much of the fullness of the Old
Roses and their colouring and scent, coupled with the smoother leaves and repeat-flowering
habit of the China Roses. They eventually gave rise to the Hybrid Perpetuals.

The name Bourbon was given to the race because the first plant was a chance seedling
found on the Île de Bourbon (Île de Réunion) in 1817, growing in close proximity to both
its parents. It became known as 'Rose Edward' in the adjacent island of Mauritius. Seeds were
sent to Paris and presumably the best one raised was called 'Le Rosier de l'Île Bourbon'. The
full story is told by Dr Hurst in Chapter 13. In its second generation it was named and distributed in France around 1823, reaching England about two years later. Dr Hurst writes:

> Mendelian segregation had given it a double dose of the China gene for con-
> tinuous flowering, and it was a beautiful semi-double Rose with brilliant
> rose-coloured flowers, and nearly evergreen foliage. From its Damask grand-
> parent it inherited a delicious fragrance which was particularly marked in the
> late autumn months.

Practically all the Bourbon varieties I am describing flower more or less through the summer, and they give the Old Rose garden a little colour at an otherwise dull time. Fortunately
their colours blend happily with all other Old Roses.

In view of their gradual development as so clearly described by Dr Hurst, it was inevitable
that many types of habit and flower should evolve, and I therefore cannot dispose of them as
a class in a few words. Every now and again through the years a "new" Bourbon Rose is raised;

such as 'Adam Messerich' (1920), a flaunting beauty in warm Tyrian rose and admirable for a wall or pillar; the showy red 'Parkzierde' (1909), a martyr to black spot; and the more famous and useful 'Zigeunerknabe' or 'Gipsy Boy' (1909). This is a great bush bearing hundreds of rich purple roses at midsummer, and is a useful and showy shrub for general planting. But these new varieties have not inherited even the rather diverse and indeterminate characters of the more authentic varieties. They lack the true Bourbon's floral qualities and charm.

The old Bourbons have, all of them, much charm; the lovely shape of the Old Roses coupled with the silky petal of the China Rose puts them high in the floral delights of the genus. Two roses often classed as Hybrid Perpetuals can very well be grouped with the Bourbons, as they so nearly approach them in all characters. They are 'Reine des Violettes' (1860) and 'Souvenir du Docteur Jamain' (1865). Both are fine, large shrubs up to 5 or 6 feet with good foliage, that of the former having a greyish sheen assorting well with the flowers, which at times I place first among the purple roses. My pen will not do justice to the regular and beautiful arrangement of the incurved petals forming a wide, flat, quartered flower with button eye. From a pale blush-mauve centre the petals flush to a rich parma violet, with a touch of cerise and purple here and there. Against these 'Souvenir du Docteur Jamain' gives extra velvety, dark wine-red flowers, whose colour intensifies with age to darkest murrey-purple.

These two shrubs, together with the true Bourbons like 'Honorine de Brabant', 'Variegata di Bologna', both growing to about 6 to 7 feet high and wide, the smaller 'Boule de Neige' and the great 'Mme Ernst Calvat' and 'Mme Isaac Pereire', can produce superlative blooms in August and September. In fact, these roses do their best at that time of the year, the earlier blooms frequently being of poorer quality. The slender 'Mme Pierre Oger' and 'Reine Victoria' are most suitable for putting among other roses, where on good soil they will grow to 5 or 6 feet, taking up surprisingly little room, especially if staked. It is sad that the superlative 'Mme Lauriol de Barny' flowers only in early summer.

This brings me to pruning. It will be obvious that these roses need rather different attention from the Old Roses, as they flower on the current year's growth as well as on that produced the previous season. Pruning away all short, twiggy growth as soon as it has flowered will again be beneficial, as it will help to encourage fresh flowering shoots to appear. But some thoughtful winter pruning must also be done, much in the same way as is advocated for modern roses, although these Bourbons are all vigorous bushes, and it is little use trying to keep them down. In December all small wood can be spurred back to three eyes, and long vigorous shoots reduced by one-third of their length. The best blooms will be produced on really vigorous shoots which grow up after the first flush of flower is over.

Bourbon Roses

'Blairii Number 2'. Mr Blair, of Stamford Hill, raised his Number 1 and Number 2 seedlings in 1845, and both grow at Hidcote Manor, Gloucestershire. Number 2 is a most beautiful climbing rose up to 15 feet, and is admirable on a wall or pillar, the long, arching shoots bearing elegant mahogany-tinted foliage. The flowers are very large, fully double, retaining the rich pink centre while the outer petals develop a paler tone, the fully-open flower being of rare beauty, richly veined. Excellent for planting among shrubs through which its long shoots can thread their way. Little pruning is needed. 'Blairii Number 1' has very shapely, neater flowers of lighter tint and is rather less vigorous.
Thomas, 1991, pages 78, 79.

'**Boule de Neige**'. Lacharme, France, 1867. A vigorous, erect bush reaching to 4 feet or so, constantly thrusting forth fresh shoots of bold, leathery, dark foliage, and bearing from June to October heavy blooms in small clusters. The buds are hard and round, tinted with crimson, and open to flowers of the old perfection, densely packed and formal in shape, of creamy white. They reflex almost to a ball. This is a rose to plant among those of lower bushy habit, for it is slender and erect in growth, although I have known old compact heads on standards.

Illustrierte Rosengarten. Plate 5.

Jamain et Forney, Plate 32. Poor.

Hariot, Plate 59.

Journal des Roses, Octobre 1902. I wish mine grew so magnificently.

'**Bourbon Queen**' ('Reine de l'Île Bourbon'). Breon-Mauget, France, 1835. An old cottage favourite, still seen up and down the country, displaying its semi-double magenta and pink flowers mainly in June. They are cupped and loose, and the petals are crinkled and beautifully veined with a darker shade. Reaches some 10 or 12 feet as a climber, but can be pruned to a shrub. The leaves are leathery, mid green, and distinctly toothed. Judging by a portrait of this rose in Komlosy I have doubts about my plant being true to name, but it is well established in various collections in this country. Sometimes known as 'Souvenir de la Princesse de Lamballe'.

'**Champion of the World**'. 1894. This high-sounding variety is quite a meek little rose! It belongs to the more refined 'Louise Odier' type, of rather dainty bearing, with light-brown prickles and small, light-green, neat leaves. The crimson buds expand, giving medium-sized, reflexed blooms of soft pale-pink with a faint lilac tinting. It is similar in growth to 'Louise Odier', and is constantly in flower during summer and autumn. 5 feet.

'**Charles Lawson**'. 1853. A vigorous plant, needing some support; useful for fences and pillars. The flowers only appear at midsummer, and are large, loose, of soft pink shaded with a darker tint. 6 to 8 feet.

'**Commandant Beaurepaire**' ('Panachée d'Angers'). 1874. This is one of the most spectacular of striped roses, containing in its flowers tones of light carmine-pink, splashed and striped with rose-madder, carmine, and purple, and an occasional blazing scarlet splash on the inner surfaces. It has an elegant growth, and the arching shoots often display a score of blooms open at one time, when their glorious colours need to be seen to be believed. The flowers are round and cupped. In marked and delightful contrast to the flowers, the leaves are long-pointed, undulating, and of a peculiarly light yellowish-green. Prickly. The flowers appear at midsummer. Only careful and selective pruning will prevent it from becoming an overcrowded mass. 5 feet. 'Panachée d'Angers' applies to the repeat-flowering original.

Journal des Roses, Mai 1882. A poor and exaggerated portrait lacking the purple colouring.

The specimen was given the name 'Commandant Beaurepaire' in error.

'**Coupe d'Hébé**'. 1840. Of rather coarse growth; bright green leaves on tall, pale-green shoots, reaching to about 8 feet. The flowers are of soft pink, borne in clusters, and have a somewhat modern appearance. They are sometimes slightly quartered, and fade very little. Best on a pillar or with other support. Midsummer only.

Paul, Plate 6.

'**Ferdinand Pichard**'. Tanne, France, 1921. I have been unable to ascertain whether this was raised from seed or occurred as a sport. It is obviously closely related to 'Commandant Beaurepaire', but is of more compact growth, with similar light green though more pointed leaves. The flowers on freshly opening are clear pink heavily dotted, splashed, striped and flaked with vivid crimson; on the next day the pink turns to blush and the crimson to purple. Cupped and fairly double. The most important point is that it constantly produces flowers through summer and autumn, after the first glorious flush is over. Probably 4 to 5 feet. Thomas, 1991, page 45.

'Giuletta'. Laurentius, France, 1859. Upright growth, broad leaden leaves and long, smooth heps. Camellia-like blush pink flowers with creamy centres, the petals elegantly rolled. Little scent. A companion for 'Boule de Neige'. 4 feet. (Plate 76.)

'Great Western'. This ship was the second mail steamship to cross the Atlantic, in 1838. She arrived only a few hours after the *Sirius* which had left four days earlier, so our rose is duly honoured. A free and vigorous variety but rather lacking in quality. Large rounded flowers, well quartered, of vivid magenta-crimson, flushed with purple. It has only one season of flowering. 5 feet.

'Héroïne de Vaucluse'. Robert et Moreau, France, 1863. A large bush of lax growth, with good foliage. Red buds and smooth Damask heps. The flowers are of dark lilac-crimson fading to lilac-pink, cupped and quartered; the petals have rolled edges. Fair scent. 5 to 6 feet.

'Honorine de Brabant'. An extra vigorous, well-filled shrub up to some 6 feet, showing a relationship with 'Commandant Beaurepaire', but larger and coarser in all parts. Green wood, with a few large prickles and good foliage of mid green, large and leathery. The main crop of flowers is borne at midsummer, but it is seldom out of flower, and the later blooms retain their colour better. Their shape is informally cupped and quartered, of pale pink daintily spotted and striped with much darker tones, varying from mauve to violet. (Plate 78.)
Gibson, Plate 16.

'Kathleen Harrop'. See under 'Zéphirine Drouhin'.

'Kronprinzessin Viktoria von Preussen'. This sport of 'Souvenir de la Malmaison' is recorded in August Jäger's *Rosenlexicon,* Leipzig, 1960, as originating with Vollert, and being introduced by the nurseryman Späth of Berlin in 1888. It came to light some years ago, having been treasured in the garden at Smallhythe, Kent, a property of the National Trust. It makes a compact bush, and is in effect a pure white sport, showing lemon tinting in the bud and half-open flower, and is unique in bringing this tint to the Bourbon Roses.

'Leveson Gower'. Beluze, France, 1846. A sport of 'Souvenir de la Malmaison', also known as 'Malmaison Rouge'. A wide-branching bush with smooth mid green leaves and smooth large heps; few prickles. From shapely buds the flowers open to rich pink flowers with a slight coppery-purple flush; they are loosely formed with recurved petals, muddled in the centre. 4 feet.

'Louise Odier'. Margottin, France, 1851. 'Mme de Stella'. A most valuable rose, being of vigorous growth up to about 6 feet, and fresh green in leaf, and bearing a constant succession of flowers from June to the end of October. This is a Bourbon with the old-world perfection of shape; each half-open bloom shows a flat face which appears to be made up of circles, so closely and so truly are the petals laid together. The warm pink, shaded softly with lilac, is delightful.

Hariot, Plate 16.

Journal des Roses, Juin 1883.

Jamain et Forney. Plate 50. Poor.

Choix de Plus Belles Roses, Plate 40.

'**Mme Ernst Calvat**'. Vve Schwartz, France, 1888. This very vigorous pillar rose can be pruned to encourage bushy growth if required. It is unique among roses in the rich crimson-purple of the leaves on the strong shoots. This colour makes a wonderful foil for the globular cabbagy blooms, which appear constantly through summer and autumn, of warm flesh pink, with darker reverses. The blooms are frequently and characteristically quartered. Of rare beauty in many ways. 7 to 8 feet. In view of the dates of introduction of this rose and 'Mme Isaac Pereire', and the fact that the latter occurred as a sport on the former in Father Curtis's garden near Dublin, it seems that 'Mme Ernst Calvat' was originally a sport from 'Mme Isaac Pereire'.

'**Mme Isaac Pereire**'. Garçon, France, 1880. 'Le Bienheureux de la Salle'. Possibly the most powerfully fragrant of all roses; the flowers are enormous, of intense rose-madder, shaded magenta, bulging with rolled petals, quartered, and opening to a great saucer-face. Big, bold foliage on a fine big bush up to 6 to 8 feet. It can also be trained upon supports with advantage. The blooms are produced in several bursts; those appearing early are frequently misshapen, but the September blooms are unbelievably fine and large. When it is well grown, on good deep soil, it has no peer.

Journal des Roses, Avril 1893.

Jekyll, facing page 6.

Hariot, Plate 44.

Le Rougetel, page 150.

Gibson, Plate 16.

'**Mme Lauriol de Barny**'. Trouillard, France, 1868. For several years I had a rose called 'Lauriol de Barny', but have been unable to trace it satisfactorily in old books. Singer states that the name applies to a 'currant-red' Hybrid Perpetual, but I find he also lists 'Mme Lauriol de Barny' with flowers *rose charmant*. I think this must be our rose, which I trace back to the Bunyard collection; it is one of the most beautiful, producing early in the season, but seldom later, large fully double blooms of light silvery pink, rather after the style of 'Mme Isaac Pereire'. With the smooth foliage they are set along the arching stems. It is a first-class variety, suitable for growing as an open bush up to about 5 feet, or as a pillar rose, 6 to 7 feet.

'**Mme Pierre Oger**'. This favourite variety originated in 1878 as a sport from 'Reine Victoria', and has become more popular than its parent, although it is identical in every respect except colour. When first open on a cool day 'Mme Pierre Oger' is of a soft, warm, creamy flesh-colour, and in dull weather may remain so; in sunny weather the sun warms the petals or the portions of them that it touches to a clear rose, and in very hot weather a really intense colour develops. These two roses have petals of shell-like beauty, and are of a dainty and formal perfection unique among roses. Dark prickles. 6 feet. June to October.

Bunyard, Plate 17.

Hoffmann, Plate 14. Showing rich colouring from hot sun.

Rosenzeitung, 1889.
Journal des Roses, Juillet 1885.

'Mme Souchet'. Souchet, France, 1843. A prolific, upright bush with good foliage. Blush-white flowers, full-petalled. A good rose of neat growth.

'Mrs Paul'. Paul & Son, U.K., 1891. (Not to be confused with 'Mrs William Paul' (1863), a dark crimson Hybrid Perpetual—see *Florist & Pomologist,* 1863, page 121.) A seedling from 'Mme Isaac Pereire', raised by George Paul of the Old Nurseries, Cheshunt. Occasionally, usually in September, I have seen blooms as good and large as those depicted in *The Garden,* but in the summer they are not up to the standard of 'Mme Isaac Pereire'. A vigorous rose with good foliage, and very free-flowering; needs the support of a stake or a wall, and of similar growth to 'Mme Isaac Pereire'. It makes a good trio with its parent and 'Mme Ernst Calvat', and is equally fragrant. Pearly white suffused pink and a soft peach shade; best in the autumn.
The Garden, 1890, page 484.
Jekyll, facing page 128 (photograph).

'Prince Charles'. A vigorous, nearly thornless rose, and a counterpart to 'Bourbon Queen' in its growth and the veined and crinkled quality of its flowers. Big, broad, dark-green leaves are well disposed, and the flowers are borne in the usual clusters or singly, but I have not known flowers to appear after midsummer. They are loose and not very double, dark madder-rose on opening, quickly attaining maroon tinting, and fading to lilac-magenta, when the veining of crimson-purple becomes more noticeable. These rich tints are accentuated by the pale, almost white, bases of the petals. 4 to 5 feet.

'Queen of Bedders'. Raised at Sunningdale, U.K., by Noble, 1871. A shrub of short growth, unlike most Bourbons, and it thus impressed Charles Noble as a suitable plant for bedding before roses were much used for this purpose. Good dark foliage. The flowers are crimson, fading to purplish, expanded and quartered. Good raspberry fragrance. 2 feet.

'Reine Victoria'. 1872. This variety has achieved much fame through giving rise to the lighter-coloured sport 'Mme Pierre Oger', which has acquired much greater popularity. Both make slender, erect bushes to about 6 feet in height, constantly sending up fresh shoots which bear flowers from June to October. They are borne well aloft, over elegantly poised leaves of soft green. The flowers are full and very rounded, retaining their cupped shape until the last; each petal is like a thin shell, of intense rose-madder where the sun lights upon it, but far paler within and at the base. I know of no other roses with more delicate charm. They are unique period pieces. 'La' should not be included in the name of this rose.

'Sir Joseph Paxton'. Laffay, France, 1852. This has little scent, but is a showy rose reminiscent of 'Mme Isaac Pereire'. A bushy plant with leaden green leaves, large prickles and smooth heps. The large, full flowers are of light, bright crimson, inclined to nod, the petals paler at the edge of the flower, quartered. 4 feet.

'Souvenir de la Malmaison'. The date 1843 refers to the introduction of the bush, and original, form. I saw this at La Malmaison, very appropriately, occupying a bed on the lawn. During hot summers this rose excels itself, producing enough flowers to make a Floribunda wilt. Roy Shepherd tells us that it was the Grand Duke of Russia who, obtaining a plant for the Imperial Garden at St Petersburg, gave it its name. Delicately fragrant and constantly in flower until the autumn. Pale flesh-pink fading paler on exposure, often distinctly quartered and always very full. There was a pink variety, which is illustrated in Verschaffelt: *L'Illustrations Horticole*, 1860; perhaps this was a sport and may occur again.

Choix des Plus Belles Roses, Plate 2.

Hoffmann, Plate 4. Very good.

Paul, Plate 15.

Curtis, Vol. 2, Plate 17.

'**Souvenir de la Malmaison, Climbing**'. Bennett, U.K., 1893. Reaching 10 to 12 feet in height, and with handsome large leaves and prickles, when in bud this notable variety might be taken for a vigorous, modern, climbing Hybrid Tea Rose. The big, strong shoots need some support, but it can also be pruned and kept to neater proportions. The half-open flowers are cup-shaped, expanding later to very large flat flowers some 5 inches across, distinctly and regularly quartered. The colour is a very soft flesh-pink, fading to paler tints on exposure, and the flowers have a peculiarly soft and unusual perfume, probably derived from a Tea ancestor; they are produced in two large crops at midsummer and in September, with a few blooms in between. As with so many roses of more than one flowering season, the flowers produced in the cooler weather of September are unsurpassed for quality and colour.

Kingsley, facing page 124 (bud only).

Hariot, Plate 16.

Komlosy.

'**Souvenir de Mme Auguste Charles**'. Moreau-Robert, France, 1866. A lax grower but vigorous, needing support. Smooth round heps; small flowers, tightly packed with petals, quilled and quartered, reminiscent of a camellia. It is of clear, light pink, early flowering and with a good autumn crop, but has only a faint scent.

Thomas, 1991, page 139.

'**Souvenir de St Anne's**'. Prior to 1916. This originated in Lady Ardilaun's garden—St Anne's, near Dublin—and was carefully preserved by Lady Moore at Willbrook House, Rathfarnham, Dublin, for many years. A nearly single sport of 'Souvenir de la Malmaison', it has all its characteristics, except the full, quartered blooms. The petals are slightly deeper on the reverse side, and have a very rich quality in their delicate tints and beautiful sculptured shapes. Richly fragrant, and constantly in flower until the autumn. The scent emanates from the stamens, not the petals, a trait inherited from *Rosa moschata*, one of its parents. Lady Moore suggested the name for this rose; I have so far found no reference to any such sport in old books. It makes a bushy plant up to 6 feet, slowly building up its branches. (Plate 79.)

'**Variegata di Bologna**'. Bonfiglioni, Italy, 1909. This comparative newcomer has all the attributes of the older Bourbon Roses. On deep, good soil it will reach up to 10 feet in height, producing strong shoots with neat, narrow, pointed foliage, but it is much less vigorous on poorer soils, where it is subject to black spot. I believe it would do well on a north-west wall, where a cool root run would probably help it. There is no doubt that it is a most spectacular rose when in flower, and fortunately it produces a few blooms through late summer and autumn, apart from its midsummer crop. The blush-tinted, almost white, petals are numerous and unfold to make a rather globular flower, very neatly striped with vivid crimson-purple. A yard-long spray of blooms makes a striking picture when placed next to 'Commandant Beaurepaire'; the shapely buds and blooms of each are so different in every way. Fortunately, like other Bourbons it can be kept as a bush by pruning. This has sported to what was presumably its original, a dark crimson-purple rose, but I have not yet found its name.

'Zéphirine Drouhin'. Bizot, France, 1868. This has been the most popular of the Bourbon Roses over many years, partly on account of its prickle-free branches and partly, no doubt, due to its vivid cerise-pink flowers, very sweetly scented, borne for so many summer and autumn months. It is best classed as a climber, up to some 12 feet, but is suitable for use as a large bush if kept within bounds by pruning. The beautiful leaves are of rich green, and of coppery-purple tint while young, and the flowers have a loose, semi-double formation. The sport 'Kathleen Harrop' occurred in 1919, and is in my experience not so vigorous, but makes a very pleasing bush with flowers of bright, light pink, the petals being much darker on the reverse side, and beautifully marked with transparent veins. It is reported that this sport was found in Turkey.

THE HYBRID PERPETUAL ROSES

He who would have beautiful roses in his garden
must have beautiful roses in his heart.

Dean Hole, *A Book about Roses,* 1870

THE OLD SAYING about "not eating our cake and having it" does not apply, among roses, to the Bourbons and the Portland Roses: they give us the lovely colours, scents, floral style, and vigorous growth of the Old Roses, coupled with the perpetual-flowering habit of the China Rose.

For about forty-five years the Bourbon Roses were very important in rose gardens. They provided a welcome change from the solely summer-flowering roses, and also from the varieties known as Hybrid China Roses. These were similar crosses, which were named and put into commerce in quantity although they only flowered once. Mendelian laws were not understood in those days and these by-blows were therefore tolerated and even encouraged.

In 1825 'Gloire des Rosomanes' appeared. It was the first really rich red rose, and must have been a great acquisition at the time. It became the chief ancestor of the red Hybrid Perpetuals and carried with it through the breeding the rich Damask fragrance inherited from its original forbear. Its colour was no doubt derived from its China parent.

Now let us retrace our steps a little. Various Old Roses grew in Italy, where the China Rose had been treated as a hardy plant long before it was trusted outside in England, and it is thought that a special seedling of brilliant red colouring arose in the neighbourhood of Paestum. Legend has it that the Duchess of Portland obtained it and brought it to England, where it was much treasured on account of its vivid colouring and became known as the 'Portland Rose', or *Rosa Paestana*, from its supposed origin in Italy. Redouté has a good figure of it (Plate 109, Vol. I). I had seen this rose for years in several collections (notably in Mrs Fleischmann's garden at Chetwode Manor, Buckinghamshire; and at Blickling Hall, Norfolk and Spetchley Park, Worcestershire), not realizing what it was. The 'Portland Rose' was eventually taken to France, and from it was subsequently raised in 1819 the 'Rose du Roi', which became famous for its influence in breeding. In later times breeders looking back on this rose dubbed it the first Hybrid Perpetual.

And so the Bourbons and the H.P.s arose at approximately the same time, and ran a fairly parallel course for many years. The non-perpetual seedlings raised from both these groups were, as I have said, very numerous and were called Hybrid Chinas, and a lot of them no doubt went right back to the Old Rose types such as 'Cardinal de Richelieu', 'Tour de Mala-koff', and 'Paul Ricault', which have unusually smooth leaves for their floral type. Probably in many instances the Bourbons and Hybrid Perpetuals were intermarried and their charac-ters became merged, but whereas production along Bourbon lines eventually ceased, the Hy-brid Perpetuals soared ahead. They incorporated all the best traits available in the China Rose hybrids over fifty years or so, to emerge later as a recognizable race. They took their place in horticultural history as the first race of roses to appear in quantity yearly from different rais-ers. The selection in those days, when the characters and colours were considerably limited and no National Rose Society Trials were held, must have been much more difficult than now, when the same state has been reached by later groups.

By about 1845, the H.P.s had fairly come into their own, with large flowers and ever more brilliant colourings. Raisers had acquired enough knowledge to produce really repeat-flowering plants. Some had long flowering periods; others merely gave a few flowers in the autumn. "Few resume their former glory in autumn," said Dean Hole in 1870. None that I grow today can really be called perpetual, i.e., flowering throughout the summer and into the autumn, and on the whole I think the French gave a better title to this group than we did: they called them Hybride Remontant, changing to this from Damas Perpetuelle. William Paul states that his own breeding of Hybrid Perpetuals started with seedlings from the purplish 'Princesse Hélène', which itself was "the first strongly marked divergence from the Damask Perpetuals from which it sprang." In three years he had twenty varieties from its seed. This was in 1837. In 1863 he says "now the number is legion and they take the same place in gardens as the French roses did twenty-five years ago." By 1869 he was complaining of loss of vigour among the newer roses, no doubt due to too much China and Tea influence.

Until about the end of the century the H.P.s were all-powerful. Books and catalogues teem with names. In 1859 'Victor Verdier' appeared, and this has sometimes been called the first Hybrid Tea. From this and 'La France', raised in 1867, a small group of varieties was raised, carrying strong Tea influence into the Hybrid Perpetuals. 'La France' was H.P. 'Mme Victor Verdier' × Tea 'Mme Bravy'. By the turn of the century new roses called Hybrid Teas had taken command and the power of the Hybrid Perpetuals was broken.

Today there are very few of the thousands of H.P.s still in cultivation and perhaps it is as well, for many were undoubtedly only fit for the bonfire. George Paul, writing in the Royal Horticultural Society's *Journal* for 1896, emphasizes this: "I will not weary you with the earlier H.P.s. They played their part and do not want recalling." Even in 1890 the term "Garden Roses" was used to designate the Gallicas and their relatives; so many Hybrid Perpetuals were fit for nothing but the greenhouse and show bench. Dean Hole and the Revd Foster-Melliar mentioned this failing. 'Rose du Roi' was called 'Lee's Crimson Perpetual' in Britain; 'Rose du Roi à fleur pourpre' occurred in 1819. The next oldest to come down to us is 'Baronne Prévost' (1842), and in 1852 the still famous 'Général Jacqueminot' appeared, descended from the Bourbon 'Gloire des Rosomanes'; the 'Général' ushered in a wonderful race of vivid red colouring.

It must have puzzled many why most of the rose names of the nineteenth century should be French, at a time when the rose had become well established as the English national emblem. Mrs Gore, in *The Rose Fancier's Manual,* 1838, makes the matter clear.

> The high price of fuel [in France] places the cultivation of the tender exotics (by which English amateurs are chiefly engrossed) almost out of the question; and as the French adhere to the wise custom of repairing to their country seats in May and quitting them in December, their attention and money are appropriated to the improvement of such plants as adorn the flower garden during the summer season. They care little for any that cannot be brought to perfection in the open air; and precisely the same motive which promotes the cultivation of the dahlia in England has brought the rose to greater perfection in France. The extent of importation is, however, a convincing proof that though the more opulent classes of our countrymen are induced to pass the midsummer days of the rose season in London, a sufficient number of amateurs remain in the country [for the promotion of rose-growing].

The French at that time had a highly organized horticultural department. Mrs Gore adds that "The Chamber of Peers . . . have lately rendered the rose school of the Luxembourg nursery secondary [only] to the school of vines." The word in brackets is mine.

In the garden the very strong growers, such as 'Hugh Dickson' and 'Ulrich Brunner Fils', make the best display when the long shoots are tied down to the base of a neighbouring bush.

Hybrid Perpetuals

'Alfred Colomb'. Lacharme, France, 1865. A seedling from 'Général Jacqueminot'. A bushy, vigorous plant, leafy and producing a few autumn flowers. Flowers are globular when open, fully double, rich scarlet crimson with darker shadings and fading slightly towards purple. Very fragrant. Also known as 'Marshall P. Wilder'. There was a climbing sport in 1930. 4 to 5 feet.
Hariot, Plate 19.

'André Leroy'. Pradel, France, 1860. Strong erect growth and large leaflets. Long heps. The old books record flowers of pale pink, but mine have a rich pink colour fading to lilac-pink; large, full, flat flowers showing some stamens. It has some scent and produces some late flowers after the summer crop. 5 feet. (Plate 80.)

'Archiduchesse Élisabeth d'Autriche'. Robert et Moreau, France, 1881. Having grown 'Vick's Caprice' (often mis-spelt 'Wick's') for several years, a gift from Will Tillotson, I was disappointed to find it reverting to a lilac-pink rose, without the stripes. However, judge of my delight when I came across its portrait in the *Journal des Roses,* with the statement that it occurred in Mr Vick's garden in 1892, on a bush of 'Archiduchesse Élisabeth d'Autriche'. Thus was the name of this plain pink rose found; it is exactly like Vick's striped form, q.v., except in colour. Bushy, about 3 to 4 feet.
Thomas, 1991, page 94.

'Ardoisée de Lyon'. Damaizin, France, 1858. A strong, compact bush with brown prickles and big coarse foliage, pale green while young. Long heps, hispid. From buds of slaty purple emerge large full flowers, opening flat and quartered, dark mid-pink with greyish tint. Subject to mildew. Good scent and good autumn crop. 5 feet. (Plate 81.)

'**Baron Girod de l'Ain**'. Reverchon, France, 1897. It recurred in 1901 and was provisionally christened 'Royal Mondain'. By a strange coincidence I had this rose growing next to 'Eugène Fürst' and had noticed the similarity in everything except colour. And then, browsing through the *Journal des Roses*, I found a plate of the Baron's Rose, with a note that it was a sport from 'Eugène Fürst'. By such chances are we able to check nomenclature; the statement proves that both roses are correctly named—which is something one can never be too sure about with these ancient varieties. The 'Baron' is a fine upstanding bush with green wood and few prickles, bearing broad, rounded leaves, and is constantly in production in the summer, sparingly so in autumn. The flowers are a bright, true crimson, with white deckle edges; less richly coloured and marked than the better known 'Roger Lambelin', but a better grower. It has a pretty habit of retaining most of the petals in cup-formation and reflexing the outer ones; at that stage it is exceptionally handsome. 5 feet.
Journal des Roses, Mars 1906. Very poor portrait.
Gault and Synge, Plate 106.

'**Baronne Prévost**'. Desprez, France, 1842. "Flowers clear, pale rose, glossy, very large and full; form compact. Habit, erect; growth, robust. A superb kind. Raised by M. Desprez of Yèbles. One of the largest." Thus William Paul catalogued this famous and unique rose in 1848. Like many others it was available in the United States and reached me from Will Tillotson, but it appeared to be extinct over here. It has grown well and is a free-flowerer and, being so very early in the Hybrid Perpetual tradition, retains the Old Rose form: the flat, wide bloom, the quartering and button eye which are so appealing. The blooms are often 4 inches across, of rich pink suffused lilac, produced throughout summer and autumn. I see no reason why it should not go on for another hundred years. 4 to 5 feet. There was a striped sport, carmine on bright rose, called 'Baronne Prévost Marbrée' (recorded in *The Florist and Pomologist*). Not seen, but I record it here in case it occurs again.
Curtis, Vol. 2, Plate 9. Poor portrait.
Jamain et Forney, Plate 25. Poor portrait.
Journal des Roses, Octobre 1879.

'**Captain Hayward**'. Raised at Shepperton, U.K., in 1894 by Henry Bennett, the creator of many famous varieties including 'Mrs John Laing'. A plant of loose, open growth with good, large foliage; long smooth heps. A brilliant variety in its day. Vivid crimson-scarlet fading to lilac-pink, loosely formed and showing some stamens. Some scent. 6 to 7 feet.

'**Comtesse Cécile de Chabrillant**'. Marest, France, 1858. This is a strong, prickly bush with rather dull leaves; long heps. Full, rounded flowers of rich lilac pink with darker veining; the petals are much paler on the reverse—a lovely contrast—and have rolled edges. Very sweet scent and good autumn display. 6 to 7 feet.
Roses et Rosiers. Poor.

'**Directeur Alphand**'. Lévêque, France, 1883. A vivid rich crimson fading to rich purple, fully double flowers of good shape with muddled centres, showing a few stamens. They are held over a short, dense, prickly bush, with a more or less continuous display. Good leaves, narrow heps. 5 feet.

'**Duchesse de Cambacères**'. Fontaine, France, 1854. A lax bush with prickly stems, flower stalks with prickles and bristles; hep narrow, hispid. The broad leaflets are coarsely toothed. The flowers are in large clusters, full and cupped; of light crimson, edges of petals lilac pink, all with darker veining. Very sweet scent and good autumn crop. 5 to 6 feet. Jamain et Forney, Plate 8.

'Duke of Edinburgh'. W. Paul, U.K., 1868. Fairly good scent from flowers which occasionally "ball." Rich crimson-purple veined with dark red, inclined to burn in hot sun. It is a good, upright grower with fine broad leaves. Smooth heps. 4 feet.

'Empereur du Maroc'. Bertrand Guinoisseau, France, 1858. A hybrid of 'Géant des Batailles'. At first sight this might be considered a weakling, with its small dark leaves and growth resembling an old Hybrid Tea, but it is a healthy, free-flowering plant. It is of historic interest, being as far as I can ascertain the first really dark red with no purple shadings. It is of intense dark crimson with velvety maroon flush, and no doubt inherits its rather spindly growth and gorgeous colouring from 'Slater's Crimson China' somewhere back in its pedigree. No Gallica is richer than 'Duc de Guiche' and no reliable rose had apparently been raised among Bourbons, Hybrid Chinas, and Hybrid Perpetuals of such magnificent colouring. Its petals are small, often quilled and quartered, arranged in flat array. Intense fragrance. 4 feet.

'Erinnerung an Brod'. Geschwind, Hungary, 1886. 'Souvenir de Brod'. Brod is a town in Bosnia. Supposed to be a hybrid between *Rosa setigera* (*R. rubifolia*) and 'Génie de Châteaubriand'. I think it doubtful whether there is really any *R. setigera* in its parentage; it is a fairly typical Hybrid Perpetual. Double flowers, of Old Rose style, quartered, pleated, opening flat, and with green pointel; any shade from cerise-pink to dark crimson-purple is found in each flower. Good, Old Rose fragrance. Vigorous, reaching 8 feet.
Journal des Roses, Octobre 1907. A fine plate.

'Eugène Fürst'. Soupert et Notting, France, 1875. 'Prince Eugène', 'Général Korolkov'. The original from which 'Baron Girod de l'Ain' sported in 1897, and of equal vigour and general garden value, making a good plant with good foliage. The short-petalled flowers are well-formed, cupped, with outer petals soon reflexing, and of intense carmine flushed with maroon, rich and velvety; reverses paler. Delicious fragrance. A hybrid of 'Baron de Bonstetten'. 5 feet.
Journal des Roses, Avril 1883.

'Fisher Holmes'. Verdier, France, 1865. A hybrid of 'Maurice Bernardin'. A splendid old variety which I found at Kew, with a whole bed devoted to it. It is hard to beat as one of the better Hybrid Perpetuals, with its vigorous growth, good leaves, and recurrent blooms of velvety rich, scarlet-lake, heavily shaded crimson, and borne on strong stalks. Good scent. William Paul placed 'Fisher Holmes' among his best twenty-five in 1868. 4 feet.

'Frau Karl Druschki'. Lambert, France, 1901. 'Reine des Neiges', 'Snow Queen', 'White American Beauty'. This has always been an indispensable white rose but its name has been against it, and thus names more euphonious to other tongues have been coined. Had it always been known as 'Schneekoenigin' ('Snow Queen'), as was originally proposed, its popularity would have increased greatly. In many ways it is the most beautiful white rose ever raised, but it lacks scent. It is a vigorous bush with good but coarse light-green leaves and erect growth. Every stout shoot bears one or more superb high-centred blooms through the summer, with elegantly rolled petals; they are of purest white with a lemon flush at the heart and more or less carmine-tinted on the bud. 5 to 6 feet.

It has an interesting pedigree. On the seed-bearing side it probably owes its existence far back to *Rosa centifolia*, through 'La Reine'. Seed from this famous large silvery pink gave the blush 'Souvenir de la Reine d'Angleterre', and two progressively whiter sports produced 'Merveille de Lyon' which, crossed with 'Mme Caroline Testout', produced the 'Frau'. 'Mme Caroline Testout' was the result of 'Mme de Tartas', a Tea, crossed with 'Lady Mary Fitzwilliam', which again has a Tea ('Devoniensis') in its parentage, together with a Hybrid Perpetual ('Victor Verdier'). Thus 'Frau Karl Druschki' is not a Hybrid Perpetual but a Hybrid Tea, but in general appearance it certainly conforms fairly well to our present group.

It is a wonderful rose for colour schemes in the garden or in the house, and its long, strong stems make it ideal for cutting and grouping with similar roses such as 'Conrad F. Meyer' and 'Mrs John Laing'.

Darlington, page 138.

McFarland, *Roses of the World*, page 87.

Journal des Roses, Août 1902.

Hoffmann, Plate 20.

'**Général Jacqueminot**'. Roussel, France, 1853. Possibly a hybrid between 'Gloire des Rosomanes' and 'Géant des Batailles'. Be this as it may, at its time of introduction this was a brilliant red rose. Nowadays I feel it is outclassed in form and colour. Rich crimson flowers, fully double, large and cabbagy, very fragrant, borne on good stems. The bush is vigorous with good, fresh green foliage. The main display is in the summer with a few blooms later. A famous plant and ancestor of 'Liberty', 'Richmond', 'Étoile de Holland', 'Crimson Glory', etc. Reaches 6 feet on good soils. Synonyms: 'La Brillante', 'Richard Smith', 'Triomphe d'Amiens', and 'Mrs Cleveland'.

McFarland, *Roses of the World*, page 92.

Komlosy. Too dark.

Jamain et Forney, Plate 60. Fanciful.

Niedtner, page 256.

'**Georg Arends**'. Hinner, France, 1910. 'Frau Karl Druschki' × 'La France'. In view of the parentage this should be classed as a Hybrid Tea. If it had been, I think it would have been more often grown; Hybrid Perpetuals have a way of being neglected. For a Hybrid Tea it is a little on the coarse side, while as a Hybrid Perpetual it is of superlative beauty. I cannot improve on the description in my *Manual of Shrub Roses*:

> No other pink rose raised before or since has flowers of similar beauty; each petal rolls back in a beautiful way, and the flower, from the scrolled bud to the blown bloom, retains its clear strawberry-ice pink; the cream is mixed in the reverse of the petals. 'Druschki' growth and foliage. Delicious scent.

Nearly thornless. 5 feet. (Plate 82.)

'**Gloire de Chédane Guinoiseau**'. Chédane and Pajotin, France, 1907. A hybrid of 'Gloire de Ducher'. An extra handsome and vigorous variety with dull, dark-green leaves. The blooms are large, full, well-shaped, of very bright crimson-red, and are produced freely at midsummer, with a few later: sweetly scented. 5 to 6 feet.

'**Gloire de Ducher**'. Ducher, France, 1865. 'Germania'. A lanky grower best trained on a wall or pillar, or supported by other shrubs or pegged down. Apart from the summer flowers on side-shoots, great autumnal blooms are produced at the ends of vigorous new wood.

They are of large size, rich and velvety, dark crimson-purple, with darker shadings; some petals are quilled and folded, and there is usually a button eye, revealing the paler reverses of the petals. Well clothed in good foliage. 7 feet. Very fragrant. One of several good roses that were preserved by Constance Spry during the Second World War.
Jamain et Forney, Plate 43. Very poor.
Journal des Roses, Juillet 1881. Rather gross.

'Gloire d'un Enfant d'Hiram'. Rose Vilin, France, 1899. A vigorous plant, rather sparsely covered with good leaves, and a few large prickles. The flowers are the nearest to pure glowing crimson, with brighter red in bud, fading slightly to a purplish tone, but at all times arresting. Splendid, shapely, full flowers. Large heps. 6 to 7 feet.
Journal des Roses, Août 1900. Good.
Thomas, 1991, page 122.

'Gloire Lyonnaise'. Guillot Fils, France, 1885. 'Baronesse Rothschild' × 'Madame Falcot'. A good upright grower, the dark green foliage contrasting well with the loosely double flowers of creamy white, opening flat. Well scented. Few prickles.
Beales, page 361.
Journal des Roses, Août 1886.

'Glory of Steinforth'. See 'Ruhm von Steinfurth'.

'Henry Nevard'. F. Cant, U.K., 1924. A good dark-red, full, shapely, very fragrant rose, with sturdy, erect growth and large, leathery, dark-green leaves. A handsome plant and flower. 4 to 5 feet.

'Her Majesty'. Bennett, U.K., 1885. Stout, short, upright bush with abundant prickles and good leaves. Immense double blooms, full of petals of two tones of pink. Good autumn crop. Little scent. 3 feet.
Rosenzeitung, 1886, Plate I.

'Héroïne de Vaucluse'. Robert et Moreau, France, 1863. A large bush of lax growth, with good foliage. Red buds and smooth Damask heps. The flowers are of dark lilac-crimson fading to lilac-pink, cupped and quartered; the petals have rolled edges. Fair scent. 5 to 6 feet.

'Hugh Dickson'. H. Dickson, U.K., 1905. Descended from 'Gruss an Teplitz', which is no doubt the source of its good colouring. An extraordinarily vigorous plant, for which reason people sometimes ask for 'Climbing Hugh Dickson'; a climbing sport was announced in California in 1914, but I have not seen it. However, the bush form has no difficulty in reaching 10 feet in good soil. Unfortunately these long shoots, which are exceptionally well clothed in bright-green leaves, unless pegged down flower only at their extremities. The flowers may be in clusters and should be disbudded; they are large, fully double, well shaped and high-centred, of brilliant scarlet crimson, fairly fragrant. Its vigour is against it, but when suitably trained it can give a magnificent show.
Darlington, Frontispiece.

'Jean Rosenkrantz'. Portemer, France, 1864. A shrub with an open but upright habit; large smooth heps. Little scent but a good autumn display, repeating the summer crop of large flowers with many rolled petals creating a high centre, particularly shapely when half open. Full rich crimson fading to dark pink. 3 to 4 feet. (Plate 83.)

'John Hopper'. Ward, U.K., 1862. 'Jules Margottin' × 'Mme Vidot'. Extra-double flowers in the old style; well-serried ranks of rolled petals, but rather loose; vivid cerise-pink to light crimson, with mauve sheen on fading. Very fragrant. A vigorous healthy plant, bearing erect prickly wood with refined foliage. A few blooms in autumn. 5 feet. A real old 'cabbage' in its usually understood sense.
Floral Magazine, 1862, Vol. 2, Plate 110.
Journal des Roses, Mai 1881.
Hariot, Plate 38. Magnificent.

'Jules Margottin'. Margottin, France, 1853. A great parent in the past, but not of much account now, as it is a coarse, prickly plant, and is not truly perpetual, nor very decisive in its colour. Extra double flowers, opening flat and somewhat quartered, of carmine rose. Not very fragrant. 6 feet.
Hariot, Plate 40. Very fine.
L'Horticulteur Français, 1853, Plate 18. Too bright.
Journal des Roses, Décembre 1880.

'Lady Stuart'. Portemer, France, 1851. A bushy, upright, branching plant with large and small prickles, small heps, and leaden green leaves. The shapely flowers are blush-pink fading to white, cup-shaped, quartered and usually with green pointel. Little scent. (Plate 84.)

'Le Havre'. Eudes, France, 1871. A big strong plant resembling 'Ulrich Brunner', with a few prickles and smooth heps. The leaves are of light green, folded and narrow. The large, loosely cupped flowers are a rich cherry-crimson flushed with purple, paler outside. It has a sweet scent and a good autumn crop. 5 to 6 feet.

'Mabel Morrison'. Broughton, U.K., 1878. Reported to be a sport from 'Baroness Rothschild', which was a sport from 'Souvenir de la Reine d'Angleterre'. Though classed as a Hybrid Perpetual, it more closely resembles a Portland Rose, and I have accordingly included it in Chapter 3 in the section "The Damask Roses."
Jekyll ('White Baroness'), between pages 106 and 107.

'Mme Gabriel Luizet'. Liabaud, France, 1877. A hybrid of 'Jules Margottin'; vigorous, somewhat recurrent. Large double blooms of bright silvery pink, paler at the edges and inclined to be cupped. Fragrant. 5 to 6 feet.

'Magna Charta'. W. Paul, U.K., 1876. Vigorous plant with mid-green leaves and smooth narrow heps. The large flowers are borne in clusters; they are large and shapely, the petals rolled at the edges and inclined to "ball." Clear pink with dark veining. Good scent and good autumn crop. 5 to 6 feet. (Plate 85.)

'Marie Baumann'. Baumann, France, 1863. 'Général Jacqueminot' × 'Victor Verdier'. I have not seen this rose, but it is occasionally listed. A globular carmine-red variety, vigorous.
The Garden, 1883, Vol. I, Plate 516.
Hariot, Plate 50.

'Mrs John Laing'. Bennett, U.K., 1887. Ancestry includes 'La Reine'. Hundreds of pink roses have been raised and named since the appearance of this, but none has that bland, old-world, uniform tone of pink with its faint lilac flush. Nor have many roses so excellent a constitution, which enables it to thrive in poor sandy soils and to excel in good soils, where its upright habit and stiff flower-stalks provide some of the best blooms anyone could

want, on plants up to 6 feet. The flowers are large, fully double, with high outer petals, rather shorter within, opening from an exquisite bud to a well-filled, cupped flower. It is one of the most satisfying roses to grow and cut, and has a glorious scent. Foliage plentiful, of soft, light green, dull and smooth. Nearly thornless. For one who was brought up smelling this rose—and even complaining of its ubiquity in a small garden—this is a conservative estimate of its attractions. Dean Hole was much more lavish: "Not only in vigour, constancy, and abundance, but in form and features, Beauty's Queen."
Darlington, page 40. Shows the typical deeper colouring on the outer petals.
Journal des Roses, Mars 1914. Poor.

'Paul Neyron'. Levet, France, 1869. 'Victor Verdier' × 'Anna de Diesbach'. Another descendant of 'La Reine' and an extra vigorous plant up to 6 feet, with copious, large, glossy foliage in mid green. The stiff shoots bear truly enormous flowers, rather like 'Peace' in size and shape, but flatter, sometimes quartered and more filled with petals; deep rosy pink with lilac flush, paler on the reverse. Of no special ornament in the garden, and of no attraction to the nose, but a luxury to cut. Big peonies are larger, but they are over by the time the rose appears, and it is remontant. Few prickles.
Jamain et Forney, Plate 19. Small and poor.
McFarland, *Roses of the World*, page 204.
Illustrierte Rosengarten. A poor portrait and too dark.
Journal des Roses, Septembre 1877.

   In the *Revue Horticole*, 1898, page 288, is an astounding portrait entitled 'Panachée de Bordeaux', with the statement that M. Abel Chatenay considered this to be a sport of 'Paul Neyron'; I wish it would occur again.

'Paul's Early Blush'. G. Paul, U.K., 1893. Sport from 'Heinrich Schultheis'. A vigorous, upright plant with many large prickles and fresh green leaves. The long, smooth hep is supported by a pedicel covered in setae. The pointed buds are borne in clusters, opening to full and rounded flowers with rolled and reflexing petals, still remaining cupped in the centre, sometimes quartered. Soft blush pink. Scent faintly cinnamon, good. 4 feet. (Plate 86.)

'Paul Verdier'. E. Verdier, France, 1866. Very vigorous, prickly plant with good broad foliage and smooth heps. The fine large flowers are well rounded, of bright pinkish crimson fading paler. Very fragrant.

'Prince Camille de Rohan'. E. Verdier, France, 1861. 'La Rosière', 'Souvenir d'Auguste Rivoire', 'Edouard Dufour'. Descended through 'Maurice Bernardin' from 'Général Jacqueminot'.

> Although not a full rose, possesses the qualities of distinctness in an eminent degree; the flowers are dark velvety maroon, shaded towards the circumference with blood red: it is not more than average size, but the colour is exceedingly rich and beautiful.

So wrote William Paul in 1863. I find it has a weak flower stem, but a bushy branching habit unlike many other H.P.s, and on good soils it is a splendid leafy bush. 'Roger Lambelin' is a sport from it. Prolific in flower through summer and again in autumn. 4 feet.
Hariot, Plate 55. Good.
Komlosy.

'**Reine des Violettes**'. Millet-Malet, France, 1860. Although this is always classed as a Hybrid Perpetual it has little connection with their accepted style and is near to the Bourbons. First, it makes a large graceful bush, often as wide as high, well covered with leaden green leaves of smooth texture, and having the "high-shouldered" effect under the blooms that I connect with the Autumn Damasks. Second, the blooms have the flat expanded shape of the old Gallica Roses, well filled with rolled and quartered petals, and with button eye. Third, it partakes more nearly of the Old Rose purple colouring than any other which I have seen having China parentage. There is nothing like it; it is the apotheosis of the Old Roses, with an invaluable habit of flowering through the summer and again, freely, in the autumn. On half opening to a deep cup from unpropitious buds, the blooms are of dark, soft grape purple. The next day they open widely and are paler but with still rich colouring; later they fade to softest parma violet, and at all times in the open flower the velvety upper surface contrasts with the lighter silky reverse of the petals. This is a rose to be treasured for all time. It needs a rich soil to bring it to perfection. 6 feet by 5 feet.
Gibson, Plate 6.
Thomas, 1991, page 95.

'**Roger Lambelin**'. Vve Schwartz, France, 1890. It occasionally sports back to its parent 'Prince Camille de Rohan' and, like the Prince, has a weak stalk and is only a success on good soils. I have seen bushes 5 feet high and wide, full of foliage and bloom on good soil as at Bayfordbury, Hertfordshire, but more often than not it is stunted and cankerous. And a poor flower is not worth having when one compares it with a first-class bloom; then the fairly full effect is of crimson-purple velvet of gorgeous quality, deckle-edged with white. As the blooms fade the crimson turns to murrey-crimson. Much more bizarre than 'Baron Girod de l'Ain' but less sure. Very fragrant.
McFarland, *Roses of the World*, page 231. Rather fewer petals than normal.
Journal des Roses, Mai 1895.
Phillips and Rix, Plate 75.
Beales, page 362.

'**Rose du Roi à fleur pourpre**'. 1819. 'Mogador'. A sport from 'Rose du Roi', which was a descendant from the Autumn Damask through the Portland Rose and is generally looked upon as the first of the Hybrid Perpetual Roses. It has not grown very high with me, but produces fairly constantly medium-sized blooms with surprisingly high centres for its period. They are shapely, of richest vinous crimson, fading to a wonderful purple tone in good conditions. Richly scented, small leaves. 3 feet. It was a gift, an heirloom, from George Salmon of Dundrum; and the bloom he showed me was as remarkable as any I have seen.

Writing in 1950, Mr Salmon recorded that his mother obtained the stock from an old garden in Northern Ireland in 1893, and that he had never seen the variety elsewhere. He found it more or less perpetual.

It is doubtful whether this rose is correctly named; it bears no resemblance to 'Rose du Roi'. The original 'Rose du Roi' was raised at Sèvres in 1819 and is figured in Jamain et Forney, Plate 58, showing the typical "high-shouldered" effect, with the top leaf immediately under the flower.

'**Ruhm von Steinfurth**'. Weigand, Germany, 1920. 'Red Druschki'. 'Frau Karl Druschki' × 'General MacArthur'. A fine strong-growing rose with flowers similar to 'Mrs John Laing' but larger and more richly coloured. For some reason it has never found favour; although it is really a Hybrid Tea, it certainly resembles the Hybrid Perpetuals and so I take the liberty of including it here. 4 to 5 feet.

'Sidonie'. Vibert, France, 1847. A good bushy plant with small and large prickles, heps slightly bristly. Long narrow leaflets. Densely double flowers in clusters, clear, light pink, flat and quartered. Very free summer and autumn crops. 4 feet.

'Souvenir de Brod'. See 'Erinnerung an Brod'.

'Souvenir de Jeanne Balandreau'. R. Vilin, France, 1899. Very vigorous and almost prickleless with broad, bright leaves. The large opulent blooms are of rich crimson fading to madder, somewhat striped. Long-lasting and fragrant. Might be likened to a paler 'Hugh Dickson'. 5 to 6 feet.

'Souvenir du Docteur Jamain'. Lacharme, France, 1865. 'Général Jacqueminot' × 'Charles Lefèbvre'. A somewhat temperamental plant needing good soil and an aspect away from the sun, or at least facing west, for the petals "burn" and turn brown in hot sunshine. But it is worth all trouble to get those matchless, velvety, dark wine-coloured blooms clouded over with murrey-purple. Very fragrant, and flowers again in autumn. We owe the preservation of this remarkable rose to The Hon. V. Sackville-West, who found it at Hollamby's Nurseries, Groombridge, and generously distributed it. A great success on good soils, where it will attain 10 feet on a wall. (Plate 87.)

'Star of Waltham'. W. Paul, U.K., 1875. Very fine, rich crimson flowers, fading to magenta, borne in clusters. Occasional white stripe. Smooth heps and decisive broad leaves. Some scent. Good autumn crop on a compact bush. 4 to 5 feet.
Journal des Roses, Mars 1882. Good.
Paul, 10th edition, 1903.

'Tom Wood'. Dickson, Newtownards, U.K., 1896. A short, sturdy plant with acutely pointed flat green leaves. Few prickles. The flowers are cupped, cherry red, fading paler, with a sweet scent. 4 feet.

'Triomphe de l'Exposition'. Margottin, France, 1855. The foliage is pointed, dark green; the young leaves are yellowish. An attractive flower, well filled with petals, button-eyed, and quartered, opening fairly flat; light carmine-crimson with deeper shadings. An old type of rose, sweetly scented. 5 feet.
Journal des Roses, Mai 1884.

'Ulrich Brunner Fils'. Levet, France, 1882. One of the lusty, upright, smooth-leaved ordinary Hybrid Perpetuals, carrying rather vulgar, light-crimson, vivid cerise or rosy-red flowers, flushed lilac. Rich fragrance. Often has foliaceous sepals. 8 feet. August Jäger says it is a seedling of 'Anna de Diesbach', but Max Singer states: "issue de 'Paul Neyron'."
McFarland, *Roses of the World,* page 275. Rather dark.
Kingsley, page 115. Very good.
Journal des Roses, Juillet 1888. A flattering colour.
Leroy, Plate 3.

'Vick's Caprice'. Vick, U.S., 1897. A sport from 'Archiduchesse (or Impératrice) Élisabeth d'Autriche' which occurred in Mr Vick's garden at Rochester, New York. Its chief claim to preservation is that it freely produces soft old-rose-pink flowers striped and flecked variously with white or palest pink, from dark-red buds. The blooms are fully double, like those of 'Mrs John Laing', but with shorter petals and shorter stalks, and very fragrant, produced on a compact leafy plant. Few thorns. Inclined to "ball," and also to revert to the original. 3 to 4 feet.

Journal des Roses, Mars 1898. Flowers very good.

Gault and Synge, Plate 117.

'**La France**'. Guillot, France, 1867. Usually classed as the first Hybrid Tea Rose. The climbing form was introduced by Henderson, U.S., 1893. There are many good portraits of this famous rose:

Niedtner, Plate 96.

Hariot, Plate 41.

Journal des Roses, Mars 1879.

Les Plus Belles Roses, page 76.

Hoffmann, Plate 9.

Bois and Trechslin, Plate 5.

THE POLY-POMS: AN INTERLUDE

WHEN I started this book, it did not occur to me that I should need to write a section, even a short one, on the Poly-poms, or Dwarf Polyanthas, in order to complete it. Writers of today about modern roses often ignore them: they are overshadowed by the triumphant Floribundas, and few people grow them. But are they outclassed? For continuous colour-giving coupled with a short growth, they have never been surpassed. Their undoing has been brought about by their small scentless flowers, in the same way that their parent 'Crimson Rambler' and its breed have lost popularity among climbers. A rose must have a "soul" if it is to survive, and to my mind these have none. Yet we have only to go to Blickling Hall, a National Trust garden in Norfolk, to find 'Locarno' (1926) and 'Paul Crampel' (1930) in a mixed planting creating as good a show of colour as could be desired. The plants sport back and forth, and a kaleidoscope of tints combines to give a richness that could not otherwise be achieved, and is just what is desired to offset the neighbouring beds of brightly coloured yellow and red herbaceous plants. Just occasionally, then, I find these dwarf roses are exactly right for certain schemes, and I hope that such as 'Cameo', 'Ideal', 'Yvonne Rabier', 'Paul Crampel', and several of the others may survive into the future.

But they cannot be called 'Shrub Roses', and I must now make some excuse for this section. The excuse is that the Poly-poms include a very few varieties which are exquisite and small (not weak) and need championing, and one of which needs a deal of clarifying. These few are outlying roses, we may say, on the fringe of the Poly-poms, but not really belonging to them, and as there is nothing like them in the world of horticulture, I feel that my excuse will be accepted. Nobody who has contemplated 'Mlle Cécile Brunner' could possibly let it become lost, and this is only one of them.

The first two Poly-poms were sister seedlings, the second generation from a hybrid between the Japanese *Rosa multiflora* and a Chinese rose, as recorded by Dr Hurst; they were

'Paquerette' and 'Mignonette', and appeared in 1873, being distributed in 1875 and 1881 respectively. It is possible that the Chinese rose was the Dwarf Pink China which we now call *R. chinensis* 'Minima' or 'Lawranceana', and which had been raised in England in 1805 and is reputed to be *R. chinensis* × *R. gigantea*. So that 'Paquerette' and 'Mignonette' carried great potentiality in their parentage, and indeed the latter was the parent of many famous Poly-poms through several well known varieties; among them was 'Mme Norbert Levavasseur', whose name is always cropping up in rose ancestry. Since pinks and whites came apparently easily, it is not surprising that a Tea Rose was pressed again into service in order to achieve yellow, having regard to what had happened in other, older groups of roses.

'Mme Falcot', a large double nankeen-yellow Tea, was therefore used for crossing one of the seedling Poly-poms, or *Rosa multiflora* itself, and 'Perle d'Or', the result, appeared in 1884. A pink Tea, 'Mme de Tartas', was used on a Poly-pom, and 'Mlle Cécile Brunner' was named in 1881. Thus 'Mlle Cécile Brunner' can claim to be the first Tea-Poly-pom, and after a hundred and more years of useful life is in danger of slipping quietly away. Instead of allowing them to go, others should be raised until we have a whole race of these quintessential varieties, which have never been surpassed; nor have they any rivals, because there is nothing like them except one extraordinary chance hybrid or sport, known erroneously as 'Bloomfield Abundance'. They are small to medium bushes, quite healthy and vigorous, incessantly in flower, and every flower is a perfect miniature of a Covent Garden bloom of 'Lady Sylvia' or 'Mme Butterfly', with the same perfection of scrolled and sculptured bud and yet of a size to go into a thimble. Anything more finished, fragrant, and dainty for buttonholes, corsages, and small sprays could not be imagined.

These are not roses for park bedding. They do not provide enough colour. But in small beds they are most attractive, especially where the scale of the rose garden is comparatively small. Both 'Mlle Cécile Brunner' and 'Perle d'Or' achieve a high degree of continuity and are always admired. Is there not here a pointer: in the smaller garden of today does not the smaller flower, provided it is well-turned, have a new value? And is it too much to hope, therefore, that we may even yet have a race of these miniatures in all colours, including silvery mauve and maroon, white and orange and crimson, for the delight of what undoubtedly would be a large admiring public? The only good newcomer is 'Jenny Wren', a hybrid of 'Mlle Cécile Brunner' but, alas, considerably larger.

Here I must add a further paragraph to explain the difference between these roses and the tiny Lawranceanas that have been raised in such quantity during the last twenty years or more. The roses I am writing about are stalwart bushes, reaching to 2 to 4 feet but with sprays of miniature blooms, that are fit for general garden use; they are not fussy little pieces to be set about with miniature rockeries, imitation lawns, trees, and gnomes. I leave these roses where they are most suited, in the greenhouse and on the show table.

'Mlle Cécile Brunner'. Ducher, France, 1881. A seedling Poly-pom × 'Mme de Tartas' (a pink Tea). Also called 'Mignon' (not 'Mignonette'), 'Cécile Brunner', or 'The Sweetheart Rose' (not 'Sweetheart', a climber). A small-wooded H.T. with small, dark green, rather shiny leaves, and very few prickles. The tallest plants I have seen were about 4 feet in height, but it is usually nearer to 2 feet. Besides the small, leafy side-shoots, each bearing one bloom, it throws up, particularly in late summer, sturdy shoots bearing branching heads (not in an elongated panicle) containing up to about 12 blooms. These shoots are devoid of prickles. It should be noted that they are smooth, devoid of bracts, and that the calyx is short and *never extends into a leafy lobe* beyond the bud. The blooms are of beautiful

Hybrid Tea shape, but less than two inches across when fully expanded, clear, pale silvery pink, warmer in the centre. It is constantly in flower, and is the most shapely of all these little beauties. (Drawing 8.)

Journal des Roses, Février 1885.

Rosenzeitung, September 1886. 'Mdlle Cécile Brunner'; enlarged.

Trechslin & Coggiatti.

Murray Hornibrook told me he had a lemon-white sport of 'Cécile Brunner' growing in his garden in France, and fortunately managed to send me material before he died. It is usually called 'White Mlle Cécile Brunner', and originated in France (Fauque et Fils) in 1909. The climbing form, 'Climbing Mlle Cécile Brunner', is noted in the next section, "The Noisette and Tea Roses." It is not so constantly in flower.

Gibson, Plate 10.

'**Mme Jules Thibaud**'. A sport from 'Mlle Cécile Brunner', very near to it, but of peach colour rather than pink. I have been unable to trace its origin.

'**Perle d'Or**'. Dubreuil, France, 1883. *Rosa multiflora* (or dwarf form or hybrid) × 'Mme Falcot', a yellow Tea Rose. This is a more vigorous, leafy plant than 'Mlle Cécile Brunner', and old plants achieve 4 feet in height and width. I have seen particularly good ones in Cambridge Botanic Garden and in Walberswick churchyard, Suffolk. The wood is rather more prickly and more stout, the leaves rather richer in colour, the flower-heads have stouter stalks and more, larger flowers with more petals. (Plate 88.) In shape this rose does not quite equal 'Mlle Cécile Brunner', although it is exceedingly good. The buds have not the H.T. perfection of outline and the inner petals, of which there are many, are narrow and often folded. In colour the young bud is rich, warm yolk-orange opening to a paler salmon shade heavily mixed with cream. Deliciously scented. The colour and the narrow central petals are the main distinguishing features from 'Mlle Cécile Brunner'.

Journal des Roses, Septembre 1887. Poor.

Rosenzeitung, January 1887. 'Perle d'Or' and others. Poor.

Kingsley, page 129.

Trechslin and Coggiatti.

'**Bloomfield Abundance**'. The original plant was raised by George C. Thomas in the United States in 1920, a hybrid between 'Sylvia' and 'Dorothy Page Roberts'. It was an undoubted Hybrid Tea, with normal large flowers. Since that date an imposter—though a very beautiful one—has intervened, with a close resemblance to 'Mlle Cécile Brunner' in its miniature flowers. Several people have claimed that it is a sport from 'Mlle Cécile Brunner' and this is quite possible and likely, but nobody I have met or written to has actually observed a plant of either sporting to the other. In the United States there is a variety called 'Spray Cécile Brunner', but I have yet to see this.

The plant we are growing as 'Bloomfield Abundance', while young, or starved, is much like 'Mlle Cécile Brunner'; the flowers have less colour in a less-filled centre, but have larger outer petals. The same beauty of bud is apparent. When established the plant will throw up great summer shoots perhaps six feet high, without leaves except for a few on the main stem. The wiry side-branches are devoid of leaves, but have a few bracts and make wonderful airy panicles with one flower at every extremity. The panicle may be 2 feet long and a foot wide, with perhaps two or three dozen flowers. There is nothing like it. Apart from these airy sprays, flowers are produced singly and in clusters from every old shoot, the whole building itself into a bush 7 feet high and wide. As will be seen from the pencil sketches, Figures 8 and 9, our 'Bloomfield Abundance' has elongated, leafy calyx lobes, absent in 'Mlle Cécile Brunner'.

Huge bushes of 'Mlle Cécile Brunner' described by enthusiastic cultivators always turn out to be our 'Bloomfield Abundance'. Both can be propagated readily from cuttings, and when a small plant of the latter changes hands and is without a name it is natural that someone should recognise it as 'Mlle Cécile Brunner'. It is a mystery that needs clearing up. It is obvious that our plant is wrongly named—witness photographs of the original in the *American Rose Annual* for 1920 and 1928, and another in McFarland, page 24.

Though they are not related to the above roses, and not strictly Polypoms, I feel this is the place to mention the following:

'Improved Cécile Brunner'. Duerhsen, California, 1948. 'Rosy Morn'. 'Dainty Bess' × 'Double Gigantea'. Flowers 3 inches across. If breeders think *this* is the way to get beautiful roses, let them carry on; they may achieve victory some day. But why drag in the name of Cécile Brunner?

'Little White Pet'. Henderson, U.S., 1879. 'White Pet'. This has nothing to do with China Roses or Poly-poms, but horticulturally fits in best here. It is a dwarf perpetual-flowering sport of 'Félicité Perpétue', a Sempervirens Rambler raised at the Château Neuilly in 1827. The plant seldom reaches more than 2 feet high, and is seldom without a cluster of its beautiful dense rosette-blooms, of creamy white touched with carmine in the bud. Possibly the most free-flowering rose apart from the Chinas.
Garten-Zeitung, 1880, t.28.

'Némésis'. Bizard, France, 1836. A dwarf pompon-type of China Rose, which fits best in this group. Dainty small leaves on a dwarf, twiggy bush. The flowers are double, quite small, of rich plum-crimson with coppery shadings, borne in small clusters early in the summer and in great heads on the strong young shoots later. Not much scent. 2 to 3 feet.

'Opal Brunner'. Marshall, California, *c.* 1948. Classed as a climbing Floribunda, this has the colouring of the Hybrid Musk 'Cornelia', slightly richer, but with smaller flowers and prettier buds. Though certainly not a China Rose, it is mentioned here to keep the 'Brunner' varieties together; at the same time, as with 'Improved Cécile Brunner', I feel it is an insult to link it with that variety. Parentage unknown.

THE NOISETTE AND TEA ROSES

> I have loved flowers that fade,
> Within whose magic tents
> Rich hues have marriage made
> With sweet unmemoried scents.
> Robert Bridges, 1844–1930

THEIR SIZE, vigour and habit of growth would seem to place the Noisettes among the Climbers and Ramblers of Part 3, but their close affinity with the China Rose makes me feel they are more suitably included at this point in our survey.

In the next section I explain the derivation of the Hybrid Musk Roses, how they probably owe their fragrance to *Rosa multiflora* and how successfully they have retained the power of floating their fragrance in the air—a propensity very noticeable in *R. multiflora* and others of the Synstylae Section. What we know as the original group of Noisettes is believed to be of practically the same parentage; they may be crosses between China × Tea hybrids and *R. moschata*. Such a hybrid was the double pink 'Champneys' Pink Cluster', whose full story can be read in Dr C. C. Hurst's dissertation in Chapter 13. This rose I have not seen, but it is comparable in parentage to several others of the China Rose hybrids with members of the Synstylae Section.

I have never been quite happy about the rose figured in early editions of Bean's *Trees and Shrubs* as *Rosa noisettiana*. It appears to be very near to *R. moschata*. However, there is a photograph of the same plant, presumably, in *The Garden*, Vol. 71, page 335, showing a rounded bush some 10 feet across and 6 feet high, bearing single white flowers. The contributor, W. D[allimore], states that it is beautiful for about a fortnight, and that its glossy leaves show affinity to the China Rose.

In the second generation the plants are apt to be perpetual or recurrent flowering. A friend of John Champneys in Charleston, South Carolina, was Philippe Noisette, a nurseryman, who sowed seeds of the Champneys' rose, and raised a plant perpetually in flower through the summer and autumn. He sent it to his brother in Paris, Louis Noisette; it was figured by Redouté in 1821 under the name of *Rosa noisettiana*, and was distributed in France and no doubt sent to England in due course.

My first acquaintance with what I believe to be this rose was at Nymans, Sussex, now a National Trust garden but then the home of Lieutenant-Colonel Leonard Messel; his gardener James Comber had a plant of considerable age on his cottage and it still grows there. Roses, particularly the old varieties, were especially treasured at Nymans by Mrs Messel, and hours were spent turning the pages of Redouté's great volumes trying to identify some of those which had reached the garden from various sources. Comber's eye picked on Plate 77 in Vol. 2 as the original portrait of his rose, and when I visited the garden before the Second World War I was shown the 'Blush Noisette'. Though I have seen this rose here and there in old gardens through the south of England, I have not met anyone before or since who has had an inkling of its name and history.

Considering its original importance, its continued long life in the face of neglect, its floriferousness and scent, it is most extraordinary that this rose escaped the notice of all the writers of rose books earlier in this century.

Also at Nymans were 'Aimée Vibert' and 'Fellemberg', both comparable varieties combining the vigour and small, clustered flowers of the Musk Rose group with the perpetual flowering habit of the China Rose. 'Aimée Vibert' is recorded variously as a sport from the Noisette 'Repens' and also as a hybrid between 'Champneys' Pink Cluster' and *Rosa sempervirens*. If the latter be true, this may account for its being poorly scented. These small-flowered cluster roses were the originals of the Noisette group, and were "much improved by the Tea Rose" (William Paul). Others are reported to have derived purplish colouring from *R. multiflora*, but up to the present I have traced none of these.

There is an interesting account in the *Florist and Pomologist* for September 1878 about hedges of the Noisette Roses 'Aimée Vibert' and 'Fellemberg', with a few 'Gloire de Dijon' and 'Duchesse de Cazes' to give variety of colour. They were grown from cuttings and provided delicious scent in the evening.

It will be seen that so far the Tea Rose had had little influence in Noisettes, in spite of its possible presence to a small degree in the parentage. But around 1830 the 'Blush Noisette' was crossed with 'Parks's Yellow Tea-Scented China', and the first yellow garden roses were raised, starting two new races, the dwarf or shrubby Tea Roses and the yellow Tea-scented climbing Noisettes. The latter soon disappeared as a race, and became Climbing Tea Roses, owing no doubt to the constant crossing with yellow Tea Roses—and one can well understand the enthusiasm for this, in gardens stocked almost entirely with roses of white, pink, mauve, and allied shades.

With the appearance of the first yellowish Noisettes, 'Lamarque' and 'Desprez à fleur jaune' in 1830, a new standard had been reached, and these together with their descendants 'Céline Forestier' (1842) and 'Gloire de Dijon' (1853) provide us with great beauty. I would go further and say that 'Jaune Desprez' (as it is also known) and 'Gloire de Dijon' are among the most free-flowering climbing roses which are grown today, and this and their scent will surely make them treasured for ever. It is rather remarkable, considering the undoubted excellence of these and similar roses, that some breeding has not been done among them more recently, for they were so epoch-making in their colouring and vigour. It would be more profitable than with many yellow roses that have been raised since, and fortunately these old yellow Tea hybrids are still available.

It is manifest that the Noisette Roses form a very mixed group, about which there can be little generalization. In cultivation they grow best on sunny walls in warm districts, as one would expect from their ancestry. 'Lamarque', indeed, is best grown under glass in cold districts.

Although it departs from normal alphabetical progression, I think it best to arrange the roses in this section in four groups. First, the original Noisette and closely allied varieties, derived probably from *Rosa moschata* and China Roses or Bourbons. (Full details of *R. chinensis* and its hybrids will be found in the first section of this chapter, "The Influence of the China Roses.") Next comes *R. gigantea* itself, followed by the Tea-Noisettes with yellow colouring in them, derived from the Tea Roses. These are followed by a few comparatively new, large-flowered climbers derived from *R. gigantea* and modern roses, and a selection of Tea Roses which, while they are not all actually climbers, deserve the shelter of a wall.

Original Noisette Roses

'**Blush Noisette**'. Philippe Noisette, U.S., prior to 1817. In previous writings this has often been given in error the name of 'Champneys' Pink Cluster', which was the original cross between the Musk and the China from which seeds were taken giving rise to the first Noisette, called 'Blush'. It is a beautiful lax shrub covered with copious leaves of mid green, rather dull, borne on nearly prickle-free green wood. The flowers are borne in small or large clusters from midsummer onwards on smooth plum-coloured shoots; they are small and cupped, with several rows of petals— about three-quarters double—and show yellow stamens. In bud they are deep old-rose, fading to creamy lilac-pink, and they have a rich clove fragrance.

It may be grown as a bush, and one sees it frequently so, peeping over a garden wall, or sometimes it is grown up a house wall to 15 feet. It is often referred to in disparaging terms, but is never discarded, on account of its scent and freedom of flower. It was grown by Tom Smith of Newry as 'Blush Cluster', and Mrs Gore called it 'Flesh-coloured Noisette'. Miss Willmott adds greatly to the confusion over this rose; her plate does not conform to the text, although it may well be a portrait of a cross between the two species.

As this pretty rose is found so freely up and down the country in old gardens, and 'Blush Noisette' would have been so popular in old days owing to its recurrent habit, I feel there is no doubt now about the identification of this fragrant plant, and illustrations add corroboration. (Plate 99.)

Redouté, Vol. 2, Plate 77. Le Rosier de Philippe Noisette. Exquisite.

Drapiez, Vol. 4, page 260.

Andrews, Plate 106.

Andrews, Plate 95. Very similar and of the same derivation.

Willmott, Plate 93. This is possibly a portrait of the original hybrid, but not of 'Champneys' Pink Cluster' nor of 'Blush Noisette'.

'Aimée Vibert'. Vibert, France, 1828. 'Bouquet de la Mariée'. As this is derived from China, Tea, Musk, and Evergreen Rose parentage it is a little difficult to place, but it was raised from a Noisette crossed with *Rosa sempervirens* about the time when Noisettes were creating a stir, being the *first perpetual-flowering climbing roses*, and so I feel it should appear here. It is a climber to 15 feet when trained on wall or shrub, but can well remain as an arching loose bush, covered with some of *the most beautiful of all rose foliage*, dark green, deeply veined, glossy, long-pointed and serrated, and gracefully poised. Great, branching, nearly thornless, brownish shoots are thrown out during the summer, bearing a truss of blooms at the end, and clothed well in leaves. The buds are pink-tipped, opening to fairly full white flowers, showing yellow stamens, with a peculiar scent, rather like that of 'Souvenir de la Malmaison'. Superb for cutting; a clean white; and the flowers are produced from about mid-July on bushes in the open, until autumn. This late flowering is partly because it is slightly tender, losing many of its flowering shoots in hard winters. On a sheltered wall a much earlier crop is given, in June or late May, on well-ripened shoots; the big late crops of flowers are no doubt an inheritance from the original *R. moschata*. There is a remarkable photograph between pages 36 and 37 in Miss Jekyll's *Roses for English Gardens*, and another facing page 55. A glance at these will make us all want to grow it; it is, after all, the only perpetual-flowering white rambler of any quality. (Plate 100.)

Jamain et Forney, Plate 59.

Roses et Rosiers, Plate 15.

Willmott, Plate 94. Flowers not full enough.

Journal des Roses, Février 1881. Rather gross.

Journal des Roses, Mai 1905. 'À fleur jaune'. I have not seen this form, probably a sport, raised 1900, introduced 1904. Salmon-orange in colour.

Komlosy.

Choix des Plus Belles Roses, Plate 5. Very good.

'Fellemberg'. Fellemberg, France, 1857. 'La Belle Marseillaise'. Sometimes classed as a China Rose, this rather obscure but well-known rose is, according to Miss Willmott, a hybrid between *Rosa chinensis* and *R. multiflora*. I think this is doubtful, for it would not then be recurrent. It does, however, conform reasonably closely to the larger-growing China Roses and the 'Blush Noisette', and thus I place it here. It is far removed from the dwarf original Chinas.

'Fellemberg' makes a large, open, angular-branching bush up to 8 feet high and wide on any soil. It takes some time to build itself up, and is never dense. The young shoots are of glaucous green or purplish and bear reddish prickles; the young leaves have much the same colour, maturing to dark green, and are small and pointed. Small and large clusters of flowers appear, emerging from crimson buds and opening to rich warm pink or light lilac-crimson, fading to lighter pink as they age, semi-double, cupped, showing stamens, with sweet-pea fragrance. Sometimes the central petals remain balled, some are quilled, and the flowers seldom exceed 2 inches in width.

It is one of the few shrubby roses to have been given the Award of Garden Merit by the Royal Horticultural Society, an honour it richly deserves, for flowers are produced so long as the weather is mild, right into the autumn. It assorts well with the Hybrid Musk Roses, or can be used with white Rugosas and other flowering shrubs, but (as a shrub) should never be placed near the front of the border on account of its somewhat leggy habit. Two yards back, enhanced perhaps by *Caryopteris clandonensis* or lavenders, or ceanothuses of the 'Topaze' persuasion in the foreground, it comes into its own as a very beautiful and useful shrub. Alternatively, it is a constant flowerer if pruned as a bedding rose, achieving about 3 feet annually.

Choix des Plus Belles Roses, Plate 33. 'La Marseillaise': rather light in colour.

Willmott, Plate 97. Seldom have I seen it in such magnificent form.

Gibson, Plate 5.

'Mme Legras de St Germain', 1846, and **'Mme Plantier'**, 1835. The parentage of these two roses is obscure, but they could be called non-recurrent hybrids of Noisette derivation. (See the section "Old and New Garden Ramblers" in Chapter 8.)

'Manettii'. Raised in Italy at Monza Botanic Garden by Dr Manetti; brought to England by Rivers, the Sawbridgeworth nurseryman, in 1835. A bush with reddish erect shoots and smooth, pointed leaves. Semi-double, light pink flowers about 2 inches in diameter produced singly and in small clusters. No particular garden value, but included here in view of its supposed parentage; much used for an understock, and as a consequence it lingers in gardens long after its scions have died. Susceptible to black spot.

Bailey, Vol. 3, Fig. 3441. Pen drawing.

Rosa gigantea and Its Influence on the Noisettes

Rosa gigantea, "the giant rose"—we might say the queen, the empress of wild roses—ascends in nature to a height of 40 feet or more by means of its strong shoots and hooked prickles, with large elegant drooping leaves and great lemon-white silky flowers 5 inches across. They lent their poise and length of petal, their texture and their fragrance, to the old Tea Roses of the last century, which became merged with the Hybrid Teas and are now seldom seen. It is scarcely surprising that this luxuriant inhabitant of south-west China and Upper Burma, where the monsoon spends itself in the mountains, should not take kindly to the British climate. We can perhaps give it the rain it needs, but not the sun's ripening power, and in consequence its sappy stems get cut by autumn frosts, and really cold winters will raze it to the ground or kill it outright. In greenhouses and on the Riviera the tale is different, and superb blooms have been picked under glass. For some years Mrs Nigel Law grew large plants in the open in her garden at Chalfont St Peter, Buckinghamshire, but they were killed in a cold winter; they flowered well in warm summers. There are records in the 1939 *Annual* of the National Rose Society, page 177, of its growing and flowering well in such varied districts as Chepstow, Monmouthshire; Hinckley, Leicestershire; Hayward's Heath, Sussex; and in Suffolk. It grows and flowers well on the pergola at Mount Stewart, Northern Ireland, a property of the National Trust.

This regal rose was introduced from the Far East in 1888; there appears to be more than one form in cultivation in this country: a white-flowered plant with rather small leaves and flowers, and a much larger plant with large leaves and large lemon-white flowers. The former grew well on a sunny wall at the John Innes Institute, Hertfordshire; the latter was my first introduction to this species when it flowered in the corridor of the greenhouse range at the University Botanic Garden, Cambridge, in 1929. An account of this particular form is in *The New Flora and Silva*, Vol. I. The smaller type would appear to be more hardy, but could certainly not be called regal. It is possible that the larger type may be that which Collet called *macrocarpa*.

We must, I am afraid, write this rose off as a garden plant for general use in England. But if what Dr Hurst called his "Four Stud Chinas"—or at least two of them—were descended from the China Rose and this species, it has had a profound influence on modern rose-breeding. 'Parks's Yellow Tea-Scented China' in particular, and 'Hume's Blush Tea-Scented China', are both looked upon as of *gigantea* derivation, if only on account of their scent. They were, presumably, Old Roses in China before being brought over here. These China hybrids produced flowers throughout summer and autumn, and *Rosa gigantea* gave them what yellow colouring they had, together with long petals and a silky texture.

All this and more is fully explained in Dr Hurst's notes in Chapter 13. Here we are concerned with how these two "Stud Chinas" became linked with a species of the Musk Rose Section to give several roses of diverse characters which later became known as Tea-Noisettes or Climbing Teas.

It has been stated that the fragrance of the Tea Roses resembles that of crushed leaves of the Tea plant (*Thea sinensis*), but I have not found this so. On the other hand, the flowers of several of them smell exactly like a freshly-opened packet of gentle China tea—not the fully "tarry" quality, but "slightly tarry." This delicate and delicious aroma is found in several roses, one of the best known being 'Lady Hillingdon', and another 'Mons. Paul Lédé'. The source of this delicate fragrance is *Rosa gigantea* itself. (Plate 89.)

The Parental Species of the Tea Roses

gigantea. Southwestern China, Burma. Introduced in 1889. Discovered by Sir Henry Collet in the Shan Hills in northern Burma, and subsequently found in neighbouring states. Sometimes called *Rosa odorata gigantea*, but I prefer to consider it a species, whereas *R. odorata* correctly refers to garden hybrids introduced from China and called Tea Roses. Like the China Rose, it belongs to the Indicae Section. A pink form or hybrid is called *R. gigantea erubescens*.
Willmott, Plate 99. Splendid portrait.
Botanical Magazine, t.7972. Poor.
Lancaster, page 146.

Climbing Tea-Noisettes

'Alister Stella Gray'. Raised by Gray, introduced by George Paul, U.K., 1894. Synonym 'Golden Rambler' in the United States. For the back of the border, where it will make an open shrub up to about 8 feet, or for a wall with any aspect where it will climb to 15 feet or more, this is one of the most perpetual of roses. Perhaps, because I have known it since a child, I look upon it with over-fond appreciation, but there was seldom a day from July to October when my father could not pick one of those perfect, scented buds for his buttonhole; and who, with this memory and the vigour and fragrance of the plant before him, could neglect to grow it?

At midsummer all the short zigzag shoots, with their horizontally poised glossy leaves and few prickles, produce one or several flowers at their extremity; opening, a day or two later, from the tightly scrolled, yolk-yellow bud, to a silky, double, flat flower about 3 inches across, quartered and with button centre. These small sprays are excellent for cutting. Later on the plants throw up great shoots which, no matter how woody or strong, produce huge branching heads of bloom, even into the autumn. Then they have less colour, but just as much scent. It is ideal behind Hybrid Musk Roses or at the back of flower and shrub borders. On a wall with a sunless aspect it has not much colour. It received an Award of Merit from the Royal Horticultural Society in 1893 when exhibited by the raiser. Delicious sweet scent, with a suspicion of tea.

Journal des Roses, Août 1903. ⎱ Identical plates. Fanciful.
Rosenzeitung, June 1903. ⎰
Le Rougetel, page 48.

'Céline Forestier'. Trouillard, France, 1842. Although this is the result of 'selfing' one of the earlier yellowish Noisettes, its Tea ancestry has come considerably to the fore, particularly in its colouring and scent. In view of its parentage and its flat, Old Rose shape, I prefer to retain it among the Noisettes. It is a tough old variety, happy when settled, but slow in building up. The prickly wood and light green, limp leaves are pleasing, but no particular asset to the flowers, which are of especially high quality. Tight buds borne singly or in small clusters open out to a perfect circle of flat petals, with quartering and pronounced button eye, silky, and of refreshing creamy pale yellow with peach tones in the centre on opening. Spicy Tea-rose fragrance, powerful, delicious, and intense; always in flower. This is a rose to treasure on a warm wall. 8 to 10 feet. (Plate 90.)
Journal des Roses, Octobre 1880. A splendid portrait.
Floral Magazine, 1861, Plate 64. Rather exaggerated.

'Cloth of Gold' ('Chromatella'). Coquereau, France, 1843. Descended from the famous 'Lamarque' and similarly rather tender, needing usually a warm wall. The soft sulphur-yellow flowers are fully double and deeper in colour in the centre. Pronounced tea-scent. 12 feet.

'Crépuscule'. Dubreuil, France, 1904. A shrubby semi-climber which is rather tender, and best grown against a sunny wall. The loosely double flowers are silky, of several tones of apricot and yellow, sweetly scented, and the plants are seldom without an odd bloom or two after the main flush. Young foliage coppery from dark brown stems, turning later to light green. 8 feet.

'Desprez à fleur jaune'. Desprez, France, 1830. 'Jaune Desprez'. A hybrid between the 'Blush Noisette' and 'Parks's Yellow Tea-scented China'. The name indicates that it may have been a yellow sport from 'Desprez', but I have been unable to trace any information about it. We could not, however, wish for anything more beautiful; and I think it is wonderful that this rose, raised so long ago and without probably any idea in the raiser's mind as to what might materialize, should remain one of the most perpetual of all roses. I received this treasure from W. B. Hopkins of Hapton House, near Norwich; on the sunny front of his house was a luxuriant old plant reaching to some 15 feet, its strong branches trained

up and all subsequent growth allowed to arch and fall outwards and downwards. It has few prickles, and is well clothed in rather light green leaves. The shoots, both small and large, have a zigzag turn at every node. One or a few flowers are borne at the end of every shoot, and the display is kept up unceasingly. They are silky, about 2 inches across, double, showing a few stamens, of creamy-tinted apricot-pink, with peach and yellow flushes, quite indescribable, and with an amazingly delicious, powerful fruity scent of equal charm. The only other rose really like it is 'Princesse de Nassau' (formerly grown erroneously as *Rosa moschata* 'Autumnalis', which was the name under which it reached me from Daisy Hill Nurseries, Northern Ireland), and until these have been seen no satisfactory image can be conjured up. If these roses could be bred again, and given more colour, they would take the world by storm. Prince, in his *Manual of Roses*, 1846, wrote: "It is so powerfully fragrant that one plant will perfume a large garden in the cool weather of autumn." (Plate 91.)
Choix des Plus Belles Roses, Plate 35. Very good portrait.
Jamain et Forney, Plate 51. A very poor copy of the above in reverse.

'Duchesse d'Auerstädt'. Bernaix, France, 1888. Jäger says this is a hybrid of 'Rêve d'Or'; Mc-Farland, 1952 (V), claims it to be a sport from the same. I found it growing and flowering well at the Roseraie de l'Haÿ, producing large blooms, full of petals of the 'Gloire de Dijon' persuasion, and of similar colouring. Handsome foliage. This is a valuable variety.
Journal des Roses, Octobre 1887.

'Gloire de Dijon'. Jacotot, France, 1853. Far removed from the original Noisettes, and as near to a Tea Rose as 'Lamarque'; it was the result of crossing a vigorous Tea Rose with the Bourbon 'Souvenir de la Malmaison'. It certainly seems to have derived some vigour and fullness from the Old Roses. It is the most popular and satisfactory of all old climbing roses; in constant flower in sun or shade, admirable for wall training, and the giver of a rich fragrance from its deep buff-yellow flowers suffused in warm weather with pink and apricot. It is rather leggy in growth, but this can be dealt with by planting with it a small-growing *Clematis*, or growing it between two shrubs on the wall; it certainly needs support. With its many assets it was indeed an epoch-making rose, at a time when yellow roses were tender, or drooping, or pale. 15 feet. (Plate 96.)

Dean Hole, in *A Book about Roses* (1870), ranked it as his favourite and most successful climbing rose. With so much competition from climbing Hybrid Teas, Ramblers and many newcomers, we cannot quite place it first among climbers today, taking all things into consideration, but it is certainly no back number, and is in many respects the best yellow climber still. In my experience it still retains its vigour. 'Bouquet d'Or', raised in 1872 and a descendant of 'Gloire de Dijon', is of similar colouring to its parent. There is a good plate of it in *La Belgique Horticole*, 1879.
Jamain et Forney, Plate 28. Poor.
Roses et Rosiers, Plate 17.
Hariot, Plate 4. Very full-coloured.
L'Horticulteur Français, 1856, Plate 10.
Komlosy. Very good.
Flore des Serres, Vol. 9, Plate 39. Too pink.
Hoffmann, Plate 5. Good.

'Jaune Desprez'. See 'Desprez à fleur jaune'.

'Lamarque'. Maréchal, France, 1830. Originally known as 'Thé Maréchal', having been raised by M. Maréchal and grown as a window plant, subsequently named in honour of Général Lamarque. This, with 'Desprez à fleur jaune', was one of the first yellowish Noisettes raised. It is of the same parentage as the Desprez rose, but leans more towards the Tea Rose. It is a plant only for the warmer west outdoors, but is a success under glass. At Dartington Hall, Devon, it grows on a sunny wall to perfection; its few limp light green leaves and large lemon-white flowers against the varied pattern of stone and moss and lichen provide a picture that could not be improved upon. The flowers are nodding—a well-known trait of the Tea Roses—very double, flat, with quilled and quartered petals, and pass from fresh lemon-white to nearly white, with a most exquisite tea-scent. A great treasure. 8 feet in our cool climate. (Plate 95.)

In *The Floral World*, 1874, page 118, occurs the following amazing description:

> The mammoth rose-tree of Santa Rosa is, we think, of sufficient importance to justify its being noticed in these pages. This immense rose-tree, now clothing the cottage of a Mr Rendall, of Santa Rosa, is an example of our old friend Lamarque, one of the finest of Noisette roses. It covers an area of four hundred superficial feet, and in due season is fairly loaded with flowers. Indeed, so profusely does it bloom, that it has had no less than four thousand fully expanded roses and twenty thousand buds at one time. It appears to have been planted fifteen years since, and so vigorous has been the growth from the first, that it now extends over the roof of the house, and when in bloom it presents a magnificent sight.

How I long for a warm climate!
Choix des Plus Belles Roses, Plate 30. Excellent portrait.
Jamain et Forney, Plate 17. 'Général Lamarque'. Poor.
Journal des Roses, Juillet 1905. A good but flattering portrait.
Jekyll. Facing page 80 (photograph).

'Ley's Perpetual'. A strangely neglected seedling of 'Gloire de Dijon', of lighter colour and delicious tea-scent. Raised in Germany early in this century. 15 feet.

'Mme Alfred Carrière'. Vve Schwartz, France, 1879. Very far removed from our original Noisettes, but a wonderful plant and as perpetual as any. It can be treated as a large shrub, some 10 feet high and wide, like the old plant that grew at Kiftsgate Court, Gloucestershire, or as a climber reaching 18 feet, as at Sissinghurst Castle, Kent. It remains one of the more popular old climbing roses to this day, and can compete on equal terms with modern roses in every respect, if we do not cavil at its pale colouring. The leaves are of light fresh green on green stems. The flowers are large, fully double, rather globular when opened from the pretty scrolled buds, creamy blush fading to blush-white, sometimes quartered or with muddled centres. The scent is more like that of a modern rose than an old Noisette.
Journal des Roses, Avril 1886. Excellent portrait.
Rosenzeitung, February–May 1907.

'Mlle Cécile Brunner, Climbing'. Hosp, U.S., 1894. This occurred as a sport from the original bush form in California. It is a vigorous, handsome, leafy plant, somewhat larger in leaf and flower than the bush, and will reach 20 feet in height on wall or tree. (The original bush form is described in the preceding section.) A fine plant in the University

Botanic Garden at Oxford annually covers itself with hundreds of flowers of the same exquisite shape as the original, but rather richer in colouring. Each bloom is like a miniature
Hybrid Tea Rose, of a size to go in a thimble, of clear pink, deeper in the fully double
centre. Unfortunately the climbing form flowers only very sparsely after midsummer.
Sweetly fragrant.

It is worth recording that a plant of this was sent to the Royal Horticultural Society's
garden at Wisley some years ago; the plant came from Malta, where it is prized commercially and is known as 'Fiteni's Rose'. It has also been distributed as 'Climbing Bloomfield
Abundance'.

I never lose an opportunity for extolling the qualities of 'Mlle Cécile Brunner'; my sole
excuse for including the climbing form in this section is that it does not fit the others any
better, and bears some resemblance to 'Alister Stella Gray'. It is not a Noisette.

'**Mlle Claire Jacquier**'. Bernaix, France, 1888. Although its parentage is not recorded, it is no
doubt of similar derivation to 'Alister Stella Gray', which it resembles closely in its flowers.
It is, however, more hardy and much more vigorous, achieving 25 to 30 feet on a wall. This
it has done as far north as at St Nicholas, Richmond, Yorkshire, and covers the east end
of the exposed house with luxuriant greenery, bearing a copious crop of flowers at midsummer and a few later. It is not so continuous as 'Alister Stella Gray', but its vigour brings
us a *tall* yellow climber, with neat double yolk-yellow blooms like those of 'Alister Stella
Gray', and delicious perfume. Its leaves are more pointed, with coarser toothing.
Gault and Synge, Plate 200.

'**Mlle** (or Mme) **de Sombreuil, Climbing**'. The bush form, raised in 1850 and introduced
by Robert, was a hybrid of 'Gigantesque', a pink Hybrid Perpetual. The climbing form
produces good flowers of wonderful beauty, somewhat reminiscent of the flat, quartered
character of 'Souvenir de la Malmaison', but infinitely more refined, of creamy white with
flesh tint in the centre, which is filled with multitudes of small petals. Delicious tea-scent.
To be treasured for all time. Perhaps 12 feet on a warm wall, and repeatedly in flower.
Hariot, Plate 12.
Nestel's Rosengarten. 'Mme de Sombreuil'. Claimed to be very hardy.
Le Rougetel, page 86.

'**Maréchal Niel**'. Pradel, France, 1864. Said to be a seedling of 'Cloth of Gold'. What exciting days they were, when 'Gloire de Dijon', that robust, coppery-yellow garden rose, was
followed eleven years later by the wonderful 'Maréchal Niel'! Nothing so yellow, so voluptuous, so fragrant of tea had been seen before, and it has more good portraits in colour
than any other rose of its kind, some so flattering that one might think it was sunflower-
yellow rather than its own softer buttery tone. Unfortunately it has a weak flower stalk,
and a loose nodding bloom, of long Tea-rose shape, and does not last well in wet weather.
Its growth and foliage are excellent. Whether it has deteriorated I do not know; I have
grown it in the sunny angle created by two sheds facing south-west, and it grew well to
10 feet, and flowered fairly freely. It flowers well at Mottisfont in warm summers. Decidedly a specialist's rose, but one that we cannot afford to lose. It is in effect a climbing
Tea Rose, with *Rosa moschata* in its parentage, though rather far back.

There is no doubt that in warmer climates it could be a glorious rose; sunny positions
in south Devon might suit it. Abroad it should still be grown; anyone who has read C. M.
Villiers-Stuart's *Gardens of the Great Mughals* will remember the passage in her description of
the Shalimar Bagh in Kashmir on page 175: "But the loveliest roses in the garden are the

Maréchal Niels which climb the grey green walls of the Hall of Public Audience and hang their soft yellow globes head downward in clusters from the carved cedar cornice."

It is excellent for greenhouse culture, so long as its root is in the open soil, outside like that of a vine, with its branches on a framework under the sloping glass. (See *The Rose Annual*, 1931, page 166—The National Rose Society.) When in stale borders in the house or in pots or tubs it does not thrive for long. There are some wonderful pictures of it in various books, thriving under glass, and I cannot think of any species of any genus for which I would be more ready to give wall space under glass. (Plate 94.)

Paul, 9th edition, Plate I.

Jamain et Forney, Plate 22.

Roses et Rosiers, Plate 6.

Niedtner, page 144. Good.

Hariot, Plate 8.

Journal des Roses, Mars 1877.

L'Horticulteur Français, 1864, Plate 20.

Nestel's Rosengarten, 1866. Very good.

Komlosy. Too dark a colour.

The Garden, 1883, page 426. Excellent portrait.

Floral Magazine, 1865. Plate 237.

Hoffmann, Plate 8. Excellent.

'**Mons. Paul Lédé, Climbing**'. Low, U.K., 1913. A sport from the bush original bred by Pernet-Ducher and introduced in 1902. It is surprising how rare this rose is. One would expect its delicious tea-scent to have warranted its more general use. It is a vigorous plant with good foliage and is satisfactory in every way, producing a big initial crop and subsequent blooms until the autumn; full-petalled, yellowish-buff with deep carmine flush in the centre; like a deeper-coloured, even more fragrant 'Gloire de Dijon'. And this must be my excuse for its inclusion here; none of the normal check-lists even mentions it. 15 feet.

'**Rêve d'Or**'. Ducher, France, 1869. 'Golden Chain' in the United States. A seedling from 'Mme Schultz'. A vigorous plant for warm, sunny gardens; beautiful rich green glossy leaves, coppery-tinted while young, and loose semi-double flowers of deep buff-yellow suffused with salmon fading to butter-yellow, with dark yellow stamens; the petals are often quilled. An excellent rose, constantly in flower until the autumn, but best on a warm wall. Slight tea-fragrance.

Journal des Roses, Décembre 1882. Exaggerated.

'**William Allen Richardson**'. Ducher, France, 1878. A sport from 'Rêve d'Or'; richer in colour, but of less vigorous and graceful growth. I doubt whether this rose would have remained in cultivation except for its vivid orange colouring, as rare then as it is today. The young shoots and foliage are richly coloured with a dark mahogany tone; prickly on strong growth, but almost thornless on small twigs. The flowers are borne singly or two or three together, rather shapeless, double, of intense orange/yolk-yellow colouring, quickly fading to near white in sunny weather. Slight tea-scent. An awkward angular plant for sunny walls, where its extraordinary colour, arising from unattractive buds, can be tolerated, but more of an historic piece than one of great beauty unless exceptionally well grown. 12 feet.

Hariot, Plate 14. Exaggerated.

Journal des Roses, Mars 1886. Poor.

Florist and Pomologist, 1883. Rather flattering.

Kingsley, Plate 71, Poor.
Garten-Zeitung, Berlin, 1883. Exaggerated.
Hoffmann, Plate 13. Good.

The following Tea Rose hybrids are tender except in favoured parts of England, but are popular in California and the south of France. In districts suited to them they are a great success and very strong-growing. A number of similar hybrids have been raised in Australia by Alister Clark, and I have grown 'Flying Colours', 'Kitty Kininmonth', 'Lorraine Lee', 'Nancy Hayward', and 'Pennant', but our summers do not ripen their wood sufficiently to make them flower. I hear of 'Lorraine Lee' as a spectacular hedge-plant in Australia.

'Belle Portugaise'. Raised in the Lisbon Botanic Garden by Henri Cayeux, 1903. *Rosa gigantea* × 'Reine Marie-Henriette', a cherry-red Hybrid Tea. A fine old plant of this vigorous rose used to grow on the laboratory in the Royal Horticultural Society's gardens at Wisley, Surrey. It has large, elegant, drooping leaves and large gracious flowers emerging from long pointed buds—in the true Tea fashion, in fact. The loosely double flower is composed of silky quilled petals, rolled at the edges, creamy salmon with deeper reverse. Delicious tea-scent. One magnificent season of flower. Requires a warm wall and does best in sheltered districts; it is obvious from the Wisley plant that it is vigorous enough to thrive on sand. 15 feet. A hybrid of this, 'Susan Louise', is a prolific large bush in California.

'La Follette'. Raised at Cannes, France, by Lord Brougham's gardener, Busby, about 1910. It resembles 'Belle Portugaise', but is much richer in colour, rose pink with cream, but dark coppery salmon-pink to crimson on the reverse. A beautiful flower of loose, long-pointed shape. A plant used to grow and flower well in the walled garden at Nymans, Sussex. In an article in *The Rose*, Vol. 10, No. 3, Peter Harkness described a stupendous plant growing in a greenhouse at Southill Park, Bedfordshire, producing annually between fifteen hundred and two thousand flowers during the early months of the year. It had stems about 18 feet high and then spread out horizontally aloft covering an area about 48 feet by 30 feet. Out of doors in England it may achieve 18 feet on a warm wall; it is vigorous but needs a warm sunny wall in England; on the Riviera it flourishes.

'Sénateur Amic'. Nabonnand, France, 1824. *Rosa gigantea* × 'General MacArthur'. Vivid cerise-crimson, nearly single flowers from long, pointed buds. This is a satisfactory wall plant in sandy soil at Wisley, Surrey, and annually provides a brilliant display in June. 15 feet.

Tea Roses

Notes on a few varieties

There remain the Tea Roses, and I wish my cultivation of them were more successful so that I could hand on plenty of first-hand experience. They do not thrive in my bleak part of Surrey. One has to go to sheltered, rich gardens in the heart of Sussex or in the west of England, or in Ireland—or to France, New Zealand, or South Africa—to see them really thriving. And yet every now and again one comes across a grand old plant making a great show in the most unexpected place. These old Tea Roses are best grown against a wall; they should be encouraged to build up slowly, with light pruning, and should be given protection in winter with mats or evergreen branches and a good deep mulch.

I think we can claim that all the China Roses of flame or yellowish colouring are really hybrids of the original Tea Roses, which are presumed to be old Chinese garden hybrids between *Rosa chinensis* and *R. gigantea*, and known botanically as *R. × odorata*. I include some true climbers, and also the climbing forms of 'Lady Hillingdon' and 'Mrs Herbert Stevens'; the former is a true Tea, the latter has one parent a Hybrid Tea. They give us the loose Tea-rose shape, unfolding from long shapely buds, and the delicious perfume of the Tea Roses, coupled with a reasonable hardiness.

Writing in the Royal Horticultural Society's *Journal*, in the account of the Society's Rose Conference in 1889, the Revd C. Wilks, a noted rosarian of that time, gave a list of what he considered the hardiest Tea Roses: 'Mme Lambard', 'Marie van Houtte', 'Anna Olivier', 'Souvenir d'un Ami', 'Gloire de Dijon', 'Rubens', 'Franzisca Krüger', 'Homère', 'The Hon. Edith Gifford', 'Jean Ducher', 'Caroline Kuster', 'Catherine Mermet', 'Mme Willermoz', 'Mme Bravy', 'Mme Berard'. Most of these I have seen or grown, and they are very free-flowering. It would seem worth while for someone to try to collect these together and grow them in a sheltered garden. In those days they found *Rosa canina* the best understock. I wish I had a large, slightly heated greenhouse to accommodate them. They are too good to lose forever; the gentle elegance of bygone days is preserved in them. It is good to find that so many of them are grown in the southern hemisphere.

'Anna Olivier'. Ducher, France, 1872. A vigorous, branching bush with pointed leaves of mid-green. Beautiful blooms, high centred and shapely, the petals flesh-pink with dark pink reverse. Delicate tea-scent. 3 feet by 3 feet.

'Baronne Henriette de Snoy'. Bernaix, France, 1897. Flesh-pink petals with dark pink on the reverses make up impressive high-centred blooms produced continually. Sweetly scented.

'Catherine Mermet'. Guillot Fils, France, 1870. One of the famous Teas. A beautiful shapely bloom, delicately scented, of clear lilac-pink. This needs nurturing against a warm wall. Coppery-tinted foliage of good quality.

'Devoniensis, Climbing'. Introduced in 1858, while the original bush form was introduced in 1841, by Lucombe, a nurseryman at Exeter, famous for the hybrid oak bearing his name. Known as the Magnolia Rose. Large double, well-shaped flowers of creamy white, tinged with carmine on the bud, and with a warm flush of apricot in the centre on opening, flat and well-filled, with many small quilled petals in the very centre. Richly tea-scented and recurrent. Perhaps 12 feet on a warm wall. (Plate 92.)
Paxton, t.169.
Curtis, Vol. I, Plate I.
Hibberd, page 167. Poor.
Le Rougetel, page 126.

'Duchesse de Brabant'. Bernède, France, 1857. 'Comtesse de Labarthe'. A reliable leafy bush with clear pink shapely flowers, freely produced.

'Fortune's Double Yellow'. *Rosa odorata pseudindica* or 'Beauty of Glazenwood'; 'Gold of Ophir'. Introduced by Robert Fortune from China in 1845. This was the most brilliant rose of its time, and will make people blink even today. It is not a strong grower except in favoured climates, such as that at Mount Usher in Northern Ireland, where it covers a wall some 9 feet high. The loose semi-double flowers are bright coppery-yellow, heavily flushed with coppery-scarlet, borne singly or in small clusters at midsummer. (Plate 101.) It was already an old garden plant when Fortune discovered it in a "rich Mandarin's garden at Ningpo," and for five or six years after its introduction its pruning was so misunderstood that growers everywhere cut away its flowering wood. Eventually beautiful plants were grown and flowered without pruning—except after flowering—by Messrs Standish and Noble, the then proprietors of Sunningdale Nurseries. This is recorded in *The Botanical Magazine*, t.4679.

Komlosy.

Willmott, Plate 85. Good.

Flore des Serres, Vol. 8, page 53.

Nestel's Rosengarten, 1866.

Le Jardin Fleuriste, Vol. 4, Plate 361. Poor colour.

Botanical Magazine, t.4679. Pale.

Journal des Roses, Mai 1877. Exaggerated colour.

'Francis Dubreuil'. Dubreuil, France, 1894. One of the mysteries among roses is why this superlative, unfading, darkest-crimson variety has been neglected for almost a century. The shapely, fragrant blooms occur in midsummer and again later amid good foliage on a compact bush. 3 feet by 2 feet.

Rosenzeitung, 1896, Plate 3.

'Général Schablikine'. Nabonnand, France, 1878. A thrifty, hardy, vigorous plant with beautiful plum-coloured shoots and elegant leaves. Produces three big flushes of bloom, but is seldom out of flower. Flowers borne on a characteristic somewhat nodding but firm stalk, each one scrolled and shapely; deep coppery carmine-pink, opening well and fading but little. Delicate fragrance. A bush, 5 feet or so, but higher on a wall.

'Lady Hillingdon, Climbing'. 'Papa Gontier' × 'Mme Hoste', both Tea Roses. The original was raised by Lowe and Shawyer (U.K.) in 1910, but the climbing sport did not occur until 1917. This and the climbing form of 'Mrs Herbert Stevens' are precious, hardy, vigorous climbing roses in the Tea tradition. A most beautiful plant, with plum-coloured young wood and prickles, darkest green leaves, plum-tinted when young, and gracious flowers, loosely double, from long shapely buds of softest apricot yellow. Delicious fragrance of a freshly opened packet of tea, with a hint of apricots. It is in constant production from midsummer until the frosts stop it, and a wonderful plant for sunny walls, where it will reach some 20 feet, its blooms nodding down at one and shedding its rich scent. It is vigorous, and will thrive even on poor sandy soils. Wing-Commander Young, in the American *Rose Annual* for 1956, placed this and 'Zéphirine Drouhin' right in the top rank for continuous production. (Plates 97, 154.)

Gibson, Plate 18.

'Mme Antoine Mari'. Mari, France, 1901. Quilled petals, creamy blush with reverse of rosy lilac to carmine; deep pink buds; large and full-petalled. Plum-coloured wood and prickles. A bush of some 4 feet; satisfactory in reasonably sheltered districts, but considerably stronger when trained on a warm wall. Delicate perfume. (Plate 98.)

Journal des Roses, Février 1904. Good.

'Mme Falcot'. Guillot Fils, France, 1858. Rich nankeen-yellow, fading paler, with somewhat quilled petals. Large double flowers. A bush, perhaps 5 feet on a wall. Jäger calls this a "subspecies" of 'Safrano'.

Roses et Rosiers, Plate 46. Pale.
Niedtner, facing page 48. Good.
Journal des Roses, Juin 1880.
Jamain et Forney, Plate 49.

'**Mme Jules Gravereaux**'. Soupert, France, 1901. One of the most satisfactory Teas, of mainly apricot colouring but with lighter and darker tints in the shapely flowers. A strong grower with good foliage. Sweetly tea-scented.

'**Mme Wagram, Comtesse de Turenne**'. Bernaix, France, 1895. Despite the unaccountable name this is a good garden plant with good growth and foliage. The large rounded flowers are pink with rosy-red reverses to the petals, and their yellow bases shine through the blooms.
Journal des Roses, Mai 1899. Very good.
Rosenzeitung, 1899, Plate I.

'**Mlle Franziska Krüger**'. Nabonnand, France, 1880. 'Catherine Mermet' × 'Général Schabli-kine'. Long treasured by James Comber at Nymans. A fairly tough Tea Rose, pale yellow and pink, very double. Rather weak stem. A bush, perhaps 7 feet on a wall.
Journal des Roses, Février 1888. Good.
Hoffmann, Plate 15. Too yellow.

'**Maman Cochet**'. Cochet, France, 1893. A famous old variety, bushy, with dark green leaves. The lemon-yellow centre shines through the well-open pale pink flowers unfolding from globular buds.

'**Marie van Houtte**'. 'Mlle Marie van Houtte'. Ducher, France, 1871. 'Mme de Tartas' × 'Mme Falcot'—distinguished parents which have produced many a good rose. This is no exception, and it is perhaps the most satisfactory of all Tea Roses. Beautiful, shapely, high-centred, full blooms of creamy yellow, intensifying in the centre, and tinged with rose around the perimeter. Handsome foliage. This grew well to 4 to 6 feet in the lee of an old wall at Oxford Botanic Garden. Delicious tea-fragrance.
Hariot, Plate 9. All the grace is captured.
Journal des Roses, Avril 1880. Good.
The Garden, 1879, Vol. 16, Plate 221.
Brougham, 1898. In an account of roses growing at the Château Éléonore, Lord Brougham and Vaux shows a photograph of a bush some 10 feet high by 70 feet circumference, densely bushy and flowering freely.
Paul, 9th edition, Plate 14. Might be mistaken for a portrait of 'Peace'!
Hoffmann, Plate 10. Very good.

'**Mrs Herbert Stevens, Climbing**'. 'Frau Karl Druschki' × 'Niphetos'. The climbing sport of this famous 1910 McGredy (U.K.) rose occurred with Pernet-Ducher in France in 1922. It is a rose all on its own today, when so few Tea Roses remain to us. Vigorous stems and good foliage always producing exquisite tea-scented blooms of creamy lemon-white with long bud and scrolled petals. The thin quality of the petals suffers occasionally in wet weather. Even so, it is well worth growing, giving flowers singly and in clusters. Some of the delicacy of the old Tea Rose 'Niphetos' is preserved in this hardy hybrid, but it is infinitely more fragrant. A splendid vigorous plant which grows well even in poor sandy soil, and is recurrent. 15 feet. (Plate 154.)

'Niphetos'. Bougère, France, 1843. The climbing form was introduced in 1889. Lemon-white, drooping flowers closely resembling 'Maréchal Niel' except in colour. A delicate beauty needing a cool greenhouse and there worthy of every attention. Delicate tea-scent. A beautiful photograph is in *Favourite Flowers* by Constance Spry, page 52 (Dent, 1959). Hariot, Plate 11. Excellent portrait.

'Papa Gontier'. Nabonnand, France, 1883. The climbing form was introduced in 1904, and is reputedly of better substance. Semi-double, bright coppery pink, deeper reverse.

'Reine Marie-Henriette'. Levet, France, 1878. 'Mme Bérard' × 'Général Jacqueminot'. Two famous ancestors, bringing in 'Mme Falcot' and 'Gloire de Dijon', and there is indeed plenty of Tea-quality in the colour, shape, and fragrance. Large cupped flowers of deep cerise-crimson on a vigorous plant with plenty of foliage. Classed correctly in works of reference as a Hybrid Tea, but just suitable for inclusion here. 15 feet.

'Rhodologue Jules Gravereaux'. Fontes, France, 1908. With such distinguished parents as 'Marie van Houtte' and 'Mme Abel Chatenay' it would be surprising to find this anything but a fine rose. A shapely pink, two-toned and delicately scented. A vigorous, good bush, and free flowering.

'Rosette Delizy'. P. Nabonnand, France, 1922. This hybrid between 'General Gallieni' and 'Comtesse Bardi', both reddish varieties, has given rise to a rose of high quality, reasonably hardy. The deep cadmium-yellow, high-centred flowers have apricot reflexes and are flushed with brick-red and carmine.

'Safrano'. Beauregard, France, 1839. A historic old piece, giving a good account of itself in a sheltered position. Pointed buds opening flat and filled with petals and scent; buff-yellow with apricot tints.

'Solfaterre'. Boyau, France, 1843. A seedling from 'Lamarque' and resembling it in habit. Large double flowers, light sulphur yellow, full, graceful; free-flowering. Very fragrant. Comparatively hardy, and a rose to keep. Vigorous in warm climates.
Curtis, Vol. 2, Plate 1.

'Souvenir de Mme Léonie Viennot'. Bernaix, France, 1898. Beautiful shapely buds of coral-red opening to blooms showing clear yellow colouring, heavily flushed with clear coppery-pink and coppery-red, the whole losing colour with age, but always pleasant. Loosely double, silky petals; delicious tea-scent. Recurrent flowering. Good foliage. Will probably achieve 15 to 20 feet on a warm wall.
Le Rougetel, page 86.

'Souvenir d'un Ami'. Bélot-Defougère, France, 1846. 'Mme Tixier'. A delicate beauty worth all the care we gardeners can bestow upon it in the way of a sheltered wall, good soil, and protection in winter—or to be grown under glass. Incurved petals of warm, light coppery-pink enfold yellow stamens; a large cupped flower, semi-double. A fragrance to which one returns again and again. A bush, perhaps 5 feet on a warm wall. This is very near to 'Hume's Blush Tea-Scented China'.
Choix des Plus Belles Roses, Plate 18. "The most beautiful bright flesh that it is possible to see." Excellent portrait.
Curtis, Vol. 2, No. 13. Poor.
Jamain et Forney, Plate 44. Poor.

Hariot, Plate 13. Poor colour.
Nestel's Rosengarten, 1868. Exquisite.

'Vicomtesse Pierre de Fou'. Sauvageot, France, 1923. 'L'Idéal' × 'Joseph Hill' (a yellowish-red Noisette and a yellowish-orange Hybrid Tea, respectively). A magnificent, strong-growing climbing rose with broad glossy leaves and two good crops of flowers. They are large, full, dusky coppery-orange passing to deep coppery-pink, quite unusual, the rolled, quartered, and somewhat quilled petals making an elegant flower, nodding always at the admirer underneath. Delicious tea-fragrance. Will achieve 18 feet even in poor soil. An extraordinarily good rose which has been unaccountably neglected. (Drawing 23.)

'William A. Smith'. Bagg, U.S., 1909. A good, compact plant which produces many loosely double, blush-white flowers with warm yellow at the bases of the petals.

THE HYBRID MUSK ROSES

... Rose of the World; th' embroidered Tuscany;
The scented Cabbage, and the Damascene;
Sweet Briar, lovelier named the eglantine;
But above all the Musk
With classic names, Thisbe, Penelope,
Whose nectarous load grows heavier with the dusk
And like a grape too sweetly muscadine.
V. Sackville-West, *The Garden*, 1946

IN 1904 PETER LAMBERT, a German nurseryman, put upon the market a rose called 'Trier' which was destined to be the forerunner of a new group of roses. It was descended from a seedling of 'Aglaia', reputedly crossed with 'Mrs R. G. Sharman-Crawford', but genetical research suggests that the fusion with the latter did not take place. 'Aglaia' was a rambler or loose shrub which Lambert had introduced in 1896. It is rather similar to the well-known rambler 'Goldfinch' but considerably more refined, and although it does not flower so freely, it retains its pale yellow colouring better. One still comes across it, hanging over old garden walls. 'Aglaia' has as parents *Rosa multiflora* and 'Rêve d'Or'; the latter was a Noisette raised in 1860, with considerable Tea influence, and with *R. moschata* some way back in its pedigree, through the older Noisettes.

'Trier' has so little Musk Rose influence that the group of roses we are about to discuss has very little claim to be called Hybrid Musks, or hybrids of *Rosa moschata*, but that is the name they have been given and will no doubt, through long usage, keep. Their parentage from 'Trier' backwards contains strains of all garden races, and the actual crosses which produced the Hybrid Musks were mainly with Hybrid Teas, but most of them contained 'Trier' or something near it. They are in fact a thoroughly mixed bag and the title is rather far-fetched. On the other hand, it is no more far-fetched than the term Noisette, by which they are known on the continent.

Be that as it may, certain very fine garden shrubs have come to us along these lines and from several sources, and they have, strangely enough, sufficient similarity to bind them together in a horticultural group. Most of them are remarkably fragrant. 'Trier' is deliciously scented, and it is a scent derived I am sure from *Rosa multiflora*; this Japanese species, to my nose, is powerfully and richly fragrant with a fruity odour, as are so many of its relatives. Moreover, it is considered a complementary species to the great Musk Rose chain that extends in a line over almost the whole of the Old World from Madeira to Japan, with *R. brunonii* and allied species through the Himalaya and China. Yet again this scent is especially "free in the air," as Francis Bacon describes it; and some of the Hybrid Musks can be savoured far off on warm, damp days. This is indeed a wonderful attribute; their scent can be detected yards away, a glorious perfume and a tremendous asset to any garden. The blend at that time of the year with the fragrance of Mock Orange or *Philadelphus* can be sublime; and fortunately the mock-oranges provide good white flowers, so valuable in any grouping of shrub roses. The Hybrid Musks are indeed splendid types for our new ideal: perpetual-flowering, fragrant, large-flowered, vigorous shrub roses. But let us look further into their development.

Lambert had been growing 'Trier' for only a year or two before he crossed it with other roses, and from 1909 until 1922 he produced a small series which became known as the 'Lambertiana' roses. Only one of these is not connected with 'Trier', and in one 'Aglaia' was used instead, but they make a fairly uniform collection. They are more rightly described as recurrent, small-flowered (Poly-pom) pillar-roses or semi-climbers than as shrubs; they made loose bushes 6 to 8 feet high. Their foliage was also of the Poly-pom style. I grew them all at one time, but discarded the lot as they were neither large in flower nor decisive—some were not even beautiful in colour, and they lacked personality. Possibly they had some other attribute, such as greater hardiness, which would have appealed to a German raiser. In the following pages I give a list of all the varieties I have grown, for the purpose of recording this step towards the perpetual-flowering shrub roses.

Meanwhile the Revd Joseph Pemberton had been busy in his garden at Havering-atte-Bower, a village in Essex where Queen Elizabeth I had a "locked garden of trees, grass and sweet herbs." In the extremely mixed group he produced it is difficult to see any definite plan of hybridizing if the parentage given in the records available is correct, but he evidently had a high regard for scent, and probably discarded all seedlings which were unworthy in this respect. Some two dozen roses were named by Pemberton and put on the market by J. A. Bentall. Of these, nine have practically disappeared, six are just in cultivation, and a further nine have taken their place in the forefront of roses, and indeed of flowering shrubs. After Pemberton's death Bentall carried on and produced six more varieties, only two of which still linger in cultivation. This was a remarkable memorial to the two raisers, but I doubt whether many realized at the time what actually had been achieved. The few excellent swans were overwhelmed by the geese, and also by popular opinion, which was still rabidly doting on Hybrid Teas and dwarf Polyanthas; the achievement was also somewhat overshadowed later by the Poulsen group. The Hybrid Musks received a place in many catalogues but the demand was small, and they had not found their niche in the gardening world.

Coloured plates of Hybrid Musk Roses are conspicuous by their absence. Apart from one poor picture of an over-coloured 'Felicia' in the National Rose Society's *Annual* I have found no good portrait other than that recorded for 'Danaë'. This almost complete absence helps to show how much too soon they were evolved—before anyone was really looking for shrub roses, though this was the avowed aim of Pemberton. Those wishing for further details of this far-seeing rosarian may like to turn to my article in the *Rose Annual* for 1968, and to Hazel Le Rougetel's *A Heritage of Roses*, 1988.

After the Second World War shrub roses became more appreciated, and are now indispensable for creating fragrance and colour in shrub and mixed borders in July and onwards. They flower when the species and the Old Roses are fading, and thus open at a useful time from the garden planning point of view, spilling their bounty to the eye and nose with the deutzias and philadelphuses, weigelas and escallonias and all the shrubs of their kind which burst forth at midsummer. That at least is what they do in Surrey; and after their first glorious display is over, the new shoots continually push and produce later blooms until cold weather finally calls a halt. In fact 'Vanity' has received both its awards from the Royal Horticultural Society in the month of October, at which time no shrub of any kind has so much beauty and scent.

A further claim to garden value is made by a few varieties, particularly 'Penelope' and 'Wilhelm', together with its sport 'Will Scarlet': these retain their heps through the winter, or at least until a long spell of arctic conditions spoils them. The heps are produced in such quantity that they create a rich glow of colour over the bushes.

Let us first glance through the Lambertiana group; they are chronologically first, and a resting-place on the way to ultimate perfection, but are no longer grown in Britain.

Lambertiana Roses

'Arndt'. 1913. 'Hélène' × 'Gustav Grünerwald'. An open-growing bush or semi-climber with dark burnished coppery foliage and dark brown wood. The flowers are small and double, borne in Poly-pom style in summer and again in autumn; the bud is well coloured with red and orange, opening to subdued flesh pink. Sweetly scented. 'Hélène' and 'Aglaïa' in its immediate ancestry, also 'Crimson Rambler'. 6 feet.

'Chamisso'. 1922. 'Geheimrat Dr Mittweg' × 'Tip Top'. Descended from 'Trier' through both its parents. Similar in general appearance and value to 'Arndt', of clearer pink, centre yellowish white. Dark foliage, recurrent bloom. 8 to 10 feet.

'Excellenz von Schubert'. 1909. 'Mme Norbert Levavasseur' × 'Frau Karl Druschki'. Richly coloured foliage; small dark pink or light crimson flowers in Poly-pom clusters. Recurrent, vigorous.

'Heinrich Conrad Söth'. 1919. 'Trier' is a quarter-parent. A pretty, shrubby rambler with small, dark, glossy leaves. Flowers in large pyramidal trusses, small, single, pink with white eye. Recurrent. 6 feet.

'Hoffmann von Fallersleben'. 1917. 'Geheimrat Dr Mittweg' × 'Tip-Top'; both parents are descended from 'Trier'. Deep salmon pink, yellowish shadings, in small or large clusters. Vigorous.

'Lessing'. 1914. 'Trier' × 'Entente Cordiale'. Light green leaves and trusses of small, single Poly-pom flowers, blush-rose, yellow-centred, and sometimes having white streaks.

'Trier'. 1904. 'Aglaïa' seedling × 'Mrs R. G. Sharman-Crawford'. A fairly erect bush or climber with small leaves, and tiny, nearly single flowers of light creamy yellow, pink flushed. 6 to 8 feet. An important parent, but uninteresting horticulturally.
Rosenzeitung, August 1907. Flattering.
Amateur Gardening, 4th June 1910.

'Von Liliencron'. 1916. 'Geheimrat Dr Mittweg' × 'Mrs Aaron Ward'. Dark glossy leaves; small double flowers, light yellowish rose, deeper reverse. Seldom flowers much after the summer crop. 'Trier' is once again in the ancestry.

Hybrid Musk Roses

(mostly raised by the Revd Joseph Pemberton)

'Aurora'. 1928. 'Danaë' × 'Miriam'. Nearly single, canary yellow passing to milky white. Not very tall-growing but produces large sprays. 3 feet.

'Autumn Delight'. 1933. Foliage fresh dark green, rather dull and leathery, practically thornless. The buds are pointed, apricot yellow, opening to a nearly single flower of extreme beauty, of soft creamy buff-yellow. In hot weather they fade to creamy white but in cool autumn are especially good, always retaining a cupped shape. Beautiful stamens. A good display in summer from side-shoots, and magnificent heads of blossom in autumn. 5 feet by 4 feet. A delightful cool-coloured effect and admirable for giving lightness to a grouping of flaming floribundas.

'Ballerina'. 1937. Large clusters of small flowers, of clear pink, single, with white eyes. From being rather a Cinderella on account of its small single blooms, this variety has leapt to popularity during recent decades. It makes a tremendous display at midsummer and produces several later trusses towards autumn. 4 feet.
Beales, page 264.

'Bishop Darlington'. Raised in California by Captain G. C. Thomas in 1926. 'Aviateur Blériot' × 'Moonlight'. A rose sent to me by Mrs Stemler of Will Tillotson's Roses, California, and a pleasant addition to the group, with the true musk fragrance. Large, semi-double, creamy flesh-coloured flowers, opening from shapely coral-coloured buds. The large zone of yellow at the base of the petals lights the whole flower. Perhaps 5 feet.

'Buff Beauty'. 1939. It has an excellent habit, with arching branches gradually building up into a good graceful bush; more sturdy and compact than 'Pax' but similar in general growth. Very good dark green, broad leaves, bronzy when young. The flowers, as in all others, are borne singly or in small clusters at midsummer, but in long panicles as the strong new shoots produce them in late summer and autumn. They are large, shapely, fully double, rich apricot yellow fading slightly, tinted coral in the bud, with a most delicious scent, leaning towards the Tea Rose quality. Red-brown young stems. (Plate 102.) The whole plant is excellent and it is continuous-flowering; admirable as a 6-foot by 6-foot shrub or trained on a wall, when it will grow higher in good soil. Not good for picking for the house.
Le Rougetel, page 119.

'Callisto'. 1920. A seedling from 'William Allen Richardson'. Greenish-brown stems and prickles and mid green, crinkled leaves. It is very near in general appearance to 'Cornelia', with similarly shaped flowers and truss, but the colour is soft, warm buttery yellow from small, round, deep-yellow buds touched with apricot, fading to near white. Rich fragrance of oranges. 3 to 4 feet or higher.

'Charmi'. 1929. Small Polyantha-like leaves, dark wood, and prickles with fringed stipules and glandular pedicels. Single pink flowers, with the usual yellow stamens. Fresh scent of apples. Rather lacking in character. 4 feet.

'Clytemnestra'. 1915. 'Trier' × 'Liberty'. Deep coppery-salmon buds open to small, crinkled, salmon-yellow flowers, fading to chamois, excellent in autumn. Dark leathery leaves. An attractive, richly coloured variety. Spreading, bushy. 3 to 4 feet.

'**Cornelia**'. 1925. Parentage unrecorded, but it so well conforms to the accepted style of these roses that we may presume 'Trier' or 'Aglaia' is in its ancestry, if only on account of its scent, which is pronouncedly soft, rich, and musky. A splendid, vigorous bush, with shining, dark green, smallish leaves. Even the small, summer flower-sprays arch gracefully, bearing tight, unattractive buds developing into small rosette blooms with yellow stamens, of soft coppery apricot fading to creamy pink. The big sprays which appear late in the growing season are particularly good in bud, being of rich, warm, coppery coral, and a far better colour when open than in the summer. These autumnal sprays may be 18 inches long and are superlative for cutting. 5 feet by 7 feet as a bush, higher if trained on a wall. The scent is especially pervasive.
Beales, Plate, page 265.

'**Danaë**'. 1913. Reputedly 'Trier' × 'Gloire de Chédane Guinoisseau', but it is more probably 'Trier' selfed. Rich green, shining foliage, mahogany-tinted when young. When opening the flowers are of deep yolk-yellow, fading to ivory in hot weather. This has not made a large bush with me, but is quite healthy. 4 feet by 3 feet.
The Garden, 1913, page 254. Rather heavily coloured, but a splendid portrait.

'**Daybreak**'. 1918. 'Trier' × 'Liberty'. Chocolate-brown stalks and stems with dark red-brown young foliage turning later to dark green. Rich yellow buds opening to loosely double or semi-double light yellow flowers with dark golden stamens. Rich musk fragrance. 3 to 4 feet.

'**Eva**'. Kordes, Germany, 1933. 'Robin Hood' × 'J. C. Thornton'. The first parent was a Pemberton Hybrid Musk, with a Polyantha in its ancestry, and this variety may well be likened to an immense Polyantha, with stout stems bearing heads of single flowers like 'American Pillar'. Showy, but it has never appealed to me as a garden plant. Good foliage. Fairly fragrant. 6 feet. It was the first tetraploid to occur in this group and in consequence it was speedily used to good effect by its raiser to produce various strong-growing shrub roses, many of which are Floribundas.

'**Felicia**'. 1928. 'Trier' × 'Ophelia'. This is in every way an ideal plant. It is compact and bushy, with good broad foliage, and may be pruned suitably for bedding, when it can rival any Floribunda of its colouring in general display. But lest comparison with Floribundas may be taken as disparagement, I must add that if left to itself it builds up into a fine bushy plant and is admirable for hedging. The flowers inherit some of the beautiful shape and colouring of 'Lady Sylvia', being warm apricot-pink in the bud, opening to tones of silvery pink, most charmingly blended. This seems to me one of the most perfect of shrub roses for beauty and continuous display. I have seen ten-year-old plants about 5 feet high and 9 feet through so smothered with bloom in July that no other shrub could surpass them for effect. (Plate 105.)

'**Fortuna**'. 1927. 'Lady Pirrie' × 'Nur Mahal'. A compact plant with nearly single flowers of roes-pink becoming paler, with conspicuous anthers. Rich fragrance. 3 feet. I have no experience of this variety.

'**Francesca**'. 1922. 'Danaë' × 'Sunburst'. Dark red-brown wood and prickles, with glossy, long, dark green leaves, creating a fine, luxuriant, leafy bush of graceful habit and inclined to Tea influence in leaf, flower, and scent, but quite hardy and vigorous. The arching, but not weak, stems support loose, nodding, apricot-yellow blooms, of long shape in the bud, fading in hot sun to butter colour. At all times beautiful and richly tea-scented. Has very much the air of a Noisette or early Tea Rose, and is a valuable garden shrub. 6 feet by 6 feet.

'Galatea'. 1914. Flowers in rosette shape, small, soft, buff-white edged pink, borne in clusters. Neither this nor 'Havering' is in my collection.

'Havering'. 1937. Borne in small clusters, the flowers are of soft pink, large and semi-double. Sturdy upright growth. About 3 feet.

'Kathleen'. 1922. 'Daphne' × 'Perle des Jardins' (?). A very vigorous, branching shrub with long-stemmed clusters of small, single, blush-pink flowers from apricot buds. Coppery young shoots and leaves, turning to green; narrow leaflets. Pronounced musk scent. The petals unfortunately suffer from "spotting" after rain. 5 feet by 4 feet.

'Moonlight'. 1913. 'Trier' × 'Sulphurea'. Dark-brownish wood, with reddish prickles, supporting a mass of branches clothed with upturned, small, dark, shining leaves. In summer, multitudes of flowers are borne in small sprays; cream buds, opening white, small, semi-double, and with their yellow stamens making a splendid contrast to the foliage. In the autumn, on the great new shoots, I have had heads 18 inches across containing many dozens of flowers, rivalling in effect 'Vanity' itself. 'Trier' has certainly had abundant influence with this rose, for it is musk-scented as well. It is an excellent rose for garden effect, shrubby yet graceful, and can be used as a pillar rose or allowed to ramble through low trees or over hedges, since its branches will reach 10 feet or more in length if encouraged.

'Nur Mahal'. 1923. 'Château de Clos Vougeot' × seedling. Plentiful leathery, dark leaves on a compact, low-branching, sturdy bush, resembling 'Penelope' in growth and in the semi-double, wide-open flowers. The colour is soft dark carmine-red in the bud, becoming a soft, light mauve-crimson, with showy stamens. This is one of the most satisfactory of the Hybrid Musks, suitable for hedging or as a shrub or, suitably pruned, for bedding. Its colour is rather subdued but just what is wanted to act as a connection between the Old Roses and the musks. Musk fragrance, but not very strong. 4 feet by 5 feet.

'Pax'. 1918. 'Trier' × 'Sunburst'. The most lax in growth of all the Hybrid Musks, making a large, arching bush which is laden with drooping masses of bloom, borne in small clusters in summer and in later months in long sprays. Creamy yellow pointed buds develop into loose, semi-double, creamy-white, wide flowers with pronounced dark golden stamens; the petals are shapely, rolled at the edges, making a beautiful flower. The foliage is red-brown turning to dark green and the stems dark brown in effective contrast. Musk and tea-scent richly blended. Equally good when trained over an arch or hedgerow or allowed to achieve shrub dimensions by the gradual building up of the arching stems; 6 to 8 feet high.

'Penelope'. 1924. 'Ophelia' × seedling. The excellent bushy growth and broad, ribbed leaves at once put this rose into the front rank. In flower it is as free as any, bearing wide, semi-double blooms in small and large clusters. The buds are salmon-orange, quickly losing their bright colour on opening, but making a delightful contrast in the half-open spray; on expanding in cool weather the colour remains a delicate creamy pink, fading nearly to white in full sunshine. Good stamens. Magnificent trusses appear in autumn. This is one of the very best roses for creating a white effect without being white, and grown with grey foliage and pale-coloured flowers, particularly pale blue, it can be really exquisite. Rich, musky fragrance. I have seen it 8 feet high in special conditions, but it is usually about 5 feet by 4 feet.

By late November the heps develop their soft colouring; it is a delightful diversion from the usual red, glossy berries of most shrubs to find these heps are dull and bloom-covered, and change from cool green to coral pink, slowly. The warmer the autumn the more highly coloured they become, and they last for many weeks. I know of no other shrubs with berries approaching this soft colour.
Gibson, Plate 12.

'Pink Prosperity'. 1931. I doubt whether this was a sport from 'Prosperity'; it was more likely a seedling. Green wood; fresh, rich green foliage often folded upwards, on an erect plant like a very large Polyantha, and bearing flowers rather in the same style. They are, however, larger than those of the average Polyantha, each one being a perfect, double rosette of warm, clear pink. Small summer trusses are followed by heavier ones in autumn. Highly fragrant. 6 feet by 4 feet.

'Prosperity'. 1919. 'Marie Jeanne' × 'Perle des Jardins' (?). A fine, upstanding bush with glossy, dark leaves, but like 'Pink Prosperity' more of a giant Polyantha than a true-to-type Hybrid Musk. The trusses of bloom cover the bush and after opening become ivory white, with a lemon flush in the centre, losing their creamy-pink bud tint. A very effective garden plant, and sweetly scented. 6 feet by 4 feet.
Gibson, Plate 12.

'Robin Hood'. 1927. Seedling × 'Edith Cavell'. A vigorous plant, like a Polyantha, in cherry red, with small double flowers in large clusters. This is not a favourite of mine, being dusky and dusty in tone, rather soulless and scentless, but it has played its part well in rose-breeding, being very fertile and a parent of 'Eva' and 'Wilhelm'. 4 feet by 3 feet.

'Sammy'. 1921. A hybrid of 'Gruss an Teplitz', the seed being borne by a 'Trier' hybrid. A glossy-leaved plant producing pleasing, large Polyantha clusters of light carmine, semi-double blooms. Thornless. 4 feet. Rather too near to a Poly-pom to be effective as a shrub.

'The Fairy'. 1932. 'Paul Crampel' × 'Lady Gay'. Vigorous, sprawling dense habit with a generous supply of sprays of small, double, clear pink flowers, not scented. Graceful and exquisite for cutting. 3 feet by 6 feet. Ground cover, or will make a large standard.

'Thisbe'. 1918. 'Marie Jeanne' × 'Perle des Jardins' (?). It is fortunate that this variety has such a pronounced Musk fragrance, otherwise in spite of its colour I should be inclined to neglect it. Semi-double rosette blooms open from rich buff-yellow buds, fading later to creamy buff, enclosing rich golden stamens. Erect growth and light green leaves; the later sprays of bloom resemble those of 'Cornelia' in shape. This is near to the Lambertiana group but on account of its fragrance should never be forgotten. 4 feet by 4 feet.

'Vanity'. 1920. 'Château de Clos Vougeot' × seedling. A most remarkable plant, but not suitable for a small garden. One plant will put up a fair display but will probably be ill-balanced and shapeless. It is essentially a rose for growing several together, planted about 3 feet apart, when the long, angular shoots will interlace and compensate for the open habit, and create a great thicket. In summer it will cover its widely-spaced leaflets with short trusses of bloom, and later the 5-foot autumnal shoots will arise. Their stalks are glaucous green and support branching heads perhaps 2 feet across, open and leafless, but displaying the flowers to advantage, like a flight of butterflies. They emerge from pointed crimson buds, are almost single and of good size, of clear rose pink with a tuft of yellow anthers. Rather a harsh colour in high summer, but softer with the approach of cooler weather; this is because its China Rose ancestry causes the petals to deepen in hot sunshine. Their scent is sweet-pea-like, very sweet and strong. A wonderful shrub, continually in bloom, reaching 8 feet in height and width on good soils.

'**Wilhelm**'. Kordes, Germany, 1934. Known as 'Skyrocket' in the United States. 'Robin Hood' × 'J. C. Thornton' (H.T.). A sister seedling of 'Eva'; similarly a tetraploid, and useful as a parent. This splendid, vigorous, and showy shrub rose has one disadvantage: it is very slightly scented. To some eyes—the eyes of a modern rose-lover—it also has a disadvantage in its colouring, which is a deep crimson with plum shadings. But we do not all want flaming scarlets, and I find 'Wilhelm' satisfying to a great degree; it gives a mass of rich colour which is heavier in tone than most other shrub roses, and is sumptuous when used with pink and light colours. The flowers are semi-double, opening from intense maroon, pointed buds, and borne in large and small trusses. Around the yellow stamens is a lighter zone, paling to lilac-pink. A faded flower is dark mauve-crimson. It is one of the few comparatively new shrub roses which can be used as a meeting point between the Old Roses and the moderns.

As a shrub it leaves nothing to be desired; stalwart, bushy, with few prickles on the great green shoots, and handsome dark-green leaves in plenty. The bright orange-red heps with persistent grey calyces do not colour before November and last through the winter. As a pillar rose, and with suitable pruning, it could be taken up to 10 feet or so. Usually 6 feet by 5 feet.

'**Will Scarlet**'. Hilling, U.K. A sport which occurred on a plant of 'Wilhelm' under my care in 1947 and was introduced in 1950. It is identical to its parent in all respects except colour and scent, and brings to the Hybrid Musk group a splash of real scarlet in some lights. The tone of the petals is pale in the centre, brightening to vivid rose and true "hunting pink" on the freshly open flower, emerging from brilliant scarlet buds. In hot weather a faint suffusion of lilac appears in the centre. It presents a dazzling display and may well be used to link the shrub roses to the Floribundas. As valuable as 'Wilhelm' for its winter display of glossy orange-red heps. Delicate fragrance. 6 feet by 5 feet.

SHRUB ROSES OF THE TWENTIETH CENTURY

> Rose, shut your heart against the bee.
> Why should you heed his minstrelsy?
> Refuse your urgent lover, rose,
> He does but drink the heart and goes.
>
> Humbert Wolfe

IN THIS SECTION are grouped varieties which in the main are comparatively new and do not owe their derivation directly to the Old Roses. That is the only general claim I can make about them; their parentage and characters are extremely diverse. Most of them have been the results of deliberate crosses, and it is interesting to find that few of the yellowish ones owe their colour to modern Hybrid Teas or Floribundas, but to *Rosa foetida* and *R. pimpinellifolia* directly. *Rosa rugosa*, being the fecund parent that it is, is concerned in the ancestry of a great number. A learner may find it disconcerting to be confronted with such a heterogeneous collection, so I will do my best to arrange them into groups, having more regard to horticulture than to botany.

First, there are the once-flowering shrubs, which are mostly pink or white and assort well with the Old Roses. There is the renowned 'Complicata' itself, together with the taller *Rosa* 'Dupontii'. Similar but sprawling types, suitable for wild gardening, banks, ground cover, or flinging over stumps, bushes, and hedgerows, are *R. × polliniana;* 'Macrantha' and its forms or hybrids, 'Daisy Hill', 'Harry Maasz', 'Raubritter', and 'Dusterlohe'; 'Lady Curzon', 'Schneelicht', 'Paulii' and 'Paulii Rosea', with 'Max Graf' the most prostrate of the lot, and nearly as prostrate as *R. wichuraiana* itself.

I am never sure about the placing in the garden of the three modern-coloured Moss Roses, 'Gabrielle Noyelle', 'Golden Moss', and 'Robert Leopold'; their colours are upsetting among the Old Roses—though they possess some of their fragrance—and they are not reliably recurrent.

Some of the most substantial shrubs—descended as might be expected from *Rosa rugosa*—are *R. × micrugosa* and its relatives, the 'Grootendorst' varieties and 'Schneezwerg'; similarly fine shrubs are 'Adam Messerich', 'Fritz Nobis', 'Zigeunerknabe'; with them we must remember the Hybrid Musks from the preceding section. 'Nevada' and its sport remain unchallenged as recurrent-flowering shrub roses of the largest size. To this category we might add 'Golden Wings' and 'Aloha'; no doubt others will materialize in the future.

For the back of the border, so that their gaunt lower growths become hidden, I would choose the tall 'Refulgence', 'Conrad F. Meyer', and 'Nova Zembla', 'Sarah van Fleet' and 'Mme Georges Bruant'.

Famous early-flowering roses are the several 'Frühlings-' varieties, a series of Burnet Rose crosses, among which 'Frühlingsgold' stands out as a really splendid shrub for spring display; all of these have a tendency towards yellow, likewise the *rugosa* hybrid 'Agnes'. I am watching the performance of some of the newer crosses in this colour, such as 'Gold Bush', 'Windrush', 'Oratam', and the *rugosa* hybrid 'Vanguard'.

Now, taking them more botanically, we find that *Rosa rugosa* provides a rich assembly. While they do not resemble very much the forms of the species described in Chapter 5, most of them have the unmistakable stamp of *R. rugosa*, particularly in its prickly wood. Few can be called refined; 'Schneezwerg' has charm, and also 'Fimbriata', while the flowers of 'Sarah van Fleet' and 'Mme Georges Bruant' approach the shape of a Hybrid Tea. In the garden I find that 'Agnes', 'Carmen', 'Fimbriata', 'New Century', 'Mrs Anthony Waterer', 'Mme Georges Bruant', 'Sarah van Fleet', and 'Schneezwerg' all inherit, with the Grootendorst varieties, something of the round, bushy habit of *R. rugosa*, although very inferior to it. It may be asked, therefore, why these roses are still grown. Certainly they have few real assets, and I do not think our gardens would be much poorer without them. They are, however, fairly productive; some, like 'Schneezwerg', 'Fimbriata', and the Grootendorst varieties, are charming and constantly in flower. And then it comes back to scent; all except the 'Grootendorsts' are fragrant, some exceedingly so; in addition, many are very hardy, owing to their *R. rugosa* ancestry.

It is difficult to discern any real trend in the above hybrid production. Some were probably the opposite of what was expected, but were considered to be too good to discard. Several species have entered the lists, apart from the hybrids recorded earlier in this book, and important crosses resulting in attractive roses are 'Cerise Bouquet' (*Rosa multibracteata* hybrid); 'Auguste Roussel' (*R. macrophylla*); 'Fritz Nobis' (*R. eglanteria*); 'Moyesii Superba' (*R. moyesii*);

'Scarlet Fire' (*R. gallica*); and finally 'Golden Wings' and the 'Frühlings-' varieties (*R. pimpinellifolia*).

Among the progeny of Hybrid Teas and Floribundas crossed with roses of Hybrid Musk and Sweet Brier derivation—mostly raised by Wilhelm Kordes—a striving after hardy big shrubs with shapely Hybrid Tea-style blooms is more apparent. Even these, I suspect, will give way in due course to something more floriferous and shapely. There are some good plants among the extra vigorous Floribundas, such as 'Chinatown' (large, yellow), 'Escapade' (rosy-lilac, white centre), 'Frensham' (dark red), 'Iceberg' (white); some which are more dwarf but which still do not conform to a Floribunda style are 'Gruss an Aachen', 'Magenta', and 'Lavender Lassie', all exceedingly fragrant.

A few Hybrid Teas can be classed as Shrub Roses when well grown. For back planting, where its gawky stems are covered by lower bushes, 'President Herbert Hoover', raised in 1930, cannot be beaten as a free-flowering plant up to 6 or 8 feet, loaded with bloom at mid-summer and again later. It can be seen all over the country, tall enough to show over garden fences, a rich blend of flame, pink, and orange, while its equally vigorous sport in coppery rose, 'Texas Centennial', has never become popular. Among vigorous varieties are 'Buccaneer', 'Fred Howard' (both 1952), 'Helen Traubel' (1951), 'Queen Elizabeth' (1954), and 'Uncle Walter' (1963).

Looking at the bulk of roses in this section as a group, while there are some superlative roses among them, we must realize that they do not compare with the true Rugosas and 'Nevada' in growth and floriferousness. 'Nevada', though not so free as the true *Rosa rugosa*, is a landmark in shrub rose hybridization, but is unfortunately sterile. It occupies the same position among shrubs as that other splendid sterile rose 'Mermaid' does among climbers. Taken altogether, they present an interesting array, and I think we may conclude that some progress has been made towards perpetual-flowering shrub roses with fragrance and with all modern colours, though much has yet to be done.

We are much concerned with ground-cover plants today, one of the best and most satisfactory ways of preventing weeds from appearing, and it is good to feel that the rose can contribute effectively. No rose is more suitable than *Rosa wichuraiana* and its descendant 'Sanders' White Rambler' (see Chapter 8). Some excellent roses have been developed which have dense, sprawling growth; the first was, I think, 'Max Graf' in 1919, and then came 'The Fairy' in 1932 and the unique 'Raubritter' in 1936.

These were all happy chances; of recent years, deliberate breeding has resulted in new ground-coverers from several countries. The pale pink 'Grouse' and 'Pheasant' and white 'Partridge' are to the fore, speedily giving an 8-foot spread only about 2 feet high. Rather higher for their width are 'Ferdy', 'Pink Wave', 'Red Blanket', 'Rosy Cushion', and 'Smarty'. Quite small, a dense carpeter is 'Snow Carpet'. Much vaunted 'Nozomi' looks all very well in the perfection of newly opened pearly pink single flowers, but it soon fades to a dirty white. Among David Austin's roses are some remarkable wide, bushy roses constantly in flower from summer until autumn. 'Dapple Dawn' and 'Red Coat' are single-flowered, pink and crimson respectively. 'Francine' is rather more upright but still of a spreading nature, and bears lots of small, double, white flowers. These are all new concepts among roses and will need several years of assessment; no doubt other and perhaps better ones will come upon the market, now that the Rose has proved itself capable of entering this new field. But it should be emphasized that no rose can be considered for ground-cover unless it totally excludes weeds. The thought of extracting weeds from among prickly stems is discouraging, to say the least!

'Adam Messerich'. Lambert, Germany, 1920. 'Frau Oberhofgärtner Singer' crossed with a hybrid between a 'Louise Odier' seedling and 'Louis Philippe'. The last was a purplish Centifolia. The result is a fine, upstanding bush with stout, green wood bearing few prickles, and leaves of modern appearance. The flowers are semi-double, cupped, silky, retaining their warm, deep-pink colouring well, produced in a heavy summer crop and intermittently later. Rich raspberry fragrance. Supposed to be a Bourbon, but fits better here. 6 feet by 5 feet.

'Agnes'. Saunders, 1922. Raised at Ottawa, Canada. *Rosa rugosa* × *R. foetida* 'Persiana'. A fairly erect bush gracefully spraying its prickly twigs outwards, heavily covered with small parsley-green leaves which in general characters are between the two parents. Early in the season a great crop of flowers appears, strongly reminiscent in shape and colour of the Persian Yellow; fully double, even crowded in the centre, with a mass of small petals, of rich butter-yellow tinted with amber. It usually produces a second crop of flowers in late summer. Bristly receptacle. Unusual and delicious scent. 6 feet by 4 feet.

Although it is effective at a distance when in full flower, this rose should be enjoyed at close quarters to appreciate its rich, intriguing scent and old-world shape.

Sitwell and Russell, page 24. A poor representation.

McFarland, *Roses of the World*, page 2.

Phillips and Rix, Plate 103.

'Aloha'. Boerner, U.S., 1949. 'Mercédès Gallart' × 'New Dawn'. Although classed as a Hybrid Tea this has made more of a sturdy upright bush or pillar rose with me. The foliage is dark and glossy and the main mass of blooms is succeeded by many later crops. Each flower is full of petals—really crammed—of good rose-pink with deeper reverses and a warm shading of orange-pink in the centre. Fragrant. Perhaps 7 feet by 4 feet.

'Altissimo'. Delbard-Chabert, France, 1967. Usually classed as a climber, but with pruning it can be kept as a large shrub, up to about 7 feet. Single blazing scarlet flowers are borne repetitively over good foliage. Little scent.

'Angelina'. Cocker, U.K., 1976. An involved parentage, including 'Frühlingsmorgen', has given us a useful, compact bush bearing particularly clear pink flowers, fragrant, borne in clusters almost continuously. The clarity of the flower-tint is enhanced by yellow stamens. 4 feet by 3 feet.

'À Parfum de l'Haÿ'. Gravereaux, France, 1903. *Rosa damascena* × 'Général Jacqueminot'. For some reason, probably because of its name and association, this rose has become renowned for its scent, but I have never discovered anything exceptional about it, finding it just fairly well-scented when comparing it with other Rugosas and allied roses. It is undoubtedly a good rose in hot climates, and is liked in California. With me it is a second-rate rose as far as quality of bloom is concerned, producing on weak stalks clusters of cupped, semi-double flowers of light crimson, distinctly lilac-flushed. The plant is prickly, and set fairly freely with leaves of modern appearance. 5 feet.

Journal des Roses, Février 1903.

Revue Horticole, 1902, page 64. Pale colour.

Trechslin & Coggiatti. Exaggerated.

'Auguste Roussel'. Barbier, France, 1913. *Rosa macrophylla* × 'Papa Gontier'. This unusual cross seems to have led nowhere, though the result is elegant and free-flowering. Imagine an open-growing, arching bush with leaves and growth rather like its first parent, and bearing pretty, semi-double to nearly double, sophisticated blooms in clear, light pink with well-formed broad petals. They are borne in clusters at midsummer only and are sweetly scented. 6 feet by 8 feet.

'Berlin'. Kordes, Germany, 1949. 'Eva' × 'Peace'. A rose of rather modern appearance, as might be expected from the parentage, with large red thorns and handsome, dark, leathery leaves. The flowers are single, of blazing orange-red with a pale almost white centre, turning pink after pollinating; yellow stamens. Petals thick and leathery. Although sometimes classed as a Hybrid Musk, I think this is very misleading. It has no character in common with the established members of that group, and is best considered as a strong-growing Floribunda. 4 feet by 3 feet.

'Bonica'. Meilland, France, 1984. Almost continuously in flower after the very free main crop. Pretty, little, shapely double flowers of two tones of clear pink, sweetly scented. 3 feet by 6 feet.

'Calocarpa'. Bruant, France, 1895. *Rosa rugosa* × *R. chinensis* hybrid. A perpetual-flowering hybrid that also bears a handsome lot of heps. Large, single flowers of rich lilac-crimson, with creamy yellow stamens. Perhaps a useful shrub, but not an improvement on either parent; nearly pure *R. rugosa*. 4 feet.
Willmott, Plate 189. Good.
Journal des Roses, Août 1906. Depicts a double rose.
The Garden, 1897, page 384. A good picture by H. G. Moon, but doubtful.
Rosenzeitung, June 1907. Depicts a double rose.

'Cardinal Hume'. Harkness, U.K., 1984. A very involved parentage has produced a low shrub, usually broader than high, with plentiful dark foliage. The flowers are also dark, of rich crimson purple, opening flat with muddled centres, showing a few stamens. Good fragrance. Constantly in flower after a late start.

'Carmen'. Lambert, Germany, 1907. *Rosa rugosa rosea* × 'Princesse de Béarn', which was a red H.P. As a young plant this has some charm, especially in its pure dark crimson single flowers with their cream stamens. Unfortunately its foliage has a diseased appearance, and it seldom flowers after midsummer. 6 feet by 4 feet.
Rosenzeitung, October 1906.

'Cerise Bouquet'. Tantau, Germany, 1958. *Rosa multibracteata* × 'Crimson Glory'. From *R. multibracteata* it derives a strong, graceful, arching habit, small greyish leaves, and lots of grey-green bracts. The large flowers, which are borne in clusters, are derived more from its other parent; they are of intense crimson in the tightly scrolled, shapely bud, opening to fairly flat, nearly double blooms, brilliant cerise-crimson, offset by the yellow stamens. (Plate 107.) A rich raspberry fragrance contributes to what is a splendid and interesting addition to summer-flowering shrub roses, and it usually has another crop towards autumn. 9 feet by 12 feet.
Beales, page 236.
Gibson, Plate 29.

'Chianti'. Austin; Sunningdale, U.K., 1966. *Rosa* 'Macrantha' × 'Vanity'. A modern shrub rose with good foliage and growth and velvety flowers of intense rich wine-purple, full of petals and a lovely shape. A useful fragrant addition for midsummer. 5 feet by 5 feet.

'**Complicata**'. I mentioned this rose in Chapter 3 in connection with the Gallicas. In the light sandy soil in my garden, in close competition with a privet hedge, it has succeeded with a little help in climbing up to 10 feet into an apple tree, and creates a superb display every season. It should be in every garden where shrubs are grown, and will make a handsome, solid bush if left to its own devices. Flowers 5 inches across, single, shapely, of bright, clear pink, borne on large arching sprays. Sweetly scented. When in full flower, no shrub is more spectacular. Normally about 5 feet high and 8 feet wide. (Plate 108.)

'**Conrad Ferdinand Meyer**'. Müller, Germany, 1899. A hybrid between 'Gloire de Dijon' and 'Duc de Rohan' crossed with *Rosa rugosa* 'Germanica'. This is one of the most popular of the *R. rugosa* derivatives, and deservedly so, for it is vigorous and produces, in common with its sport 'Nova Zembla', fine, large flowers of good shape. The plant is very prickly, making a gaunt, upright plant frequently bare of branches for 4 feet, which can scarcely be called a shrub. Above this the good, large foliage is borne, and a huge crop of blooms appears in early summer and again in September. Most attractive red-thorned, stout stalks support the big blooms, too rounded and filled to be called H.T.s, but a credit to the more substantial H.P.s, of soft silvery pink, with petals rolled at the edges and opening beautifully, revealing a 'muddled' centre. Glorious scent. The blooms of the later crop are usually superb. On account of its habit it is best grown well behind good bushy roses or shrubs up to 4 feet or even 5 feet. 8 to 9 feet by 4 feet.
Kingsley, page 46.
Journal des Roses, Mai 1902.

'**Constance Spry**'. 1961. Raised by David Austin of Wolverhampton; a cross between 'Belle Isis' (Gallica) and 'Dainty Maid' (Floribunda). An interesting and beautiful hybrid which my friend David Austin and I think is worthy to be named after one who did so much for the Old Roses. It is a vigorous plant, probably reaching 7 feet high and wide, well covered in good dark green leaves. The flowers are double, of clear, bright rose pink, cupped at first and opening to 4 inches in width when well grown. A magnificent bloom, in the grand Centifolia tradition, filled with petals and with a sweet fragrance of myrrh. This vigorous, arching rose is best supported by hedge, fence or wall. (Plates 109, 110.)
Beales, page 280.
Gibson, Plate 29.

'**Coryana**'. 1939. A seedling of *Rosa roxburghii* probably hybridized with *R. macrophylla*, raised from open-pollinated seed from Kew by Dr C. C. Hurst at Cambridge (U.K.) in 1926. This has many good points, but inherits from its first parent the unfortunate habit of hiding its flowers among its leaves. The growth is vigorous, stiff, and rather horizontal, with copious rich green, fern-like leaves, and the plant when fully grown is usually wider than high and densely branched to the ground. The deep rose-pink flowers have the perpendicular poise of *R. macrophylla*, and are wide and flat like *R. roxburghii*. Bright yellow stamens. Little scent. 8 feet by 10 feet. The bark peels as in *R. roxburghii*.

'**de la Grifferaie**'. Vibert, France, 1846. Possibly a hybrid of *Rosa multiflora* with one of the Old Roses, bearing clusters of fully double, pompon-like, magenta-cerise blooms fading to lilac-white, deliciously scented, on long arching branches.
    This is one of the most usual Old Roses to be sent in for naming. It is a thrifty old hybrid and, having been used for many years as an understock, often survives long after the scion has died. The colouring is certainly reminiscent of the Gallica Roses, but its

frayed stipules and coarse, rounded leaves soon identify it. It is not to be despised for the show it puts up, and is useful for adding height to a border of Old Roses. Nearly thornless. 6 feet by 5 feet.

'**Dentelle de Malines**'. Lens, France, 1985(?). This might be described as a small, pink 'Kiftsgate', but is of bushy, arching growth, and wide-spreading fragrance. The large trusses of small single flowers make an impressive display at midsummer. 4 feet by 5 feet.

'**Dupontii**'. Raised prior to 1817 by M. Dupont, the founder of the Luxembourg rose-garden, whom the Empress Josephine commissioned to help her assemble her collection at La Malmaison. It is a shrub of extreme beauty, nearly thornless, bearing pale grey-green, dull leaves which tone beautifully with the blush-tinted milk-white of the flowers. These are borne singly or in clusters along the arching stems, and are of perfect, rounded outline. It has a rich fragrance of bananas, and bears a few orange-coloured, slender heps. The chromosome count does not confirm the suggested parentage, i.e., *Rosa moschata* × *R. damascena* or *R. gallica.* 7 feet by 7 feet.

Botanical Register, t.861. *Rosa moschata nivea.*
Willmott, Plate 43. Excellent.
The Garden, 1895, page 62. Poor.

'**Düsterlohe**'. Kordes, Germany, after 1931. The present plant was derived from 'Dance of Joy' × 'Daisy Hill' and is not a hybrid of *Rosa venusta pendula*, as is sometimes stated. A prickly, sprawling rose, with neat, dark green leaves. The flowers are borne singly and in clusters all along the arching branches, semi-double, of Tudor Rose shape, each petal raised and distinct from the others, of bright, clear rose-pink with paler centre and yellow stamens. Can be a very showy garden plant at midsummer. The large pear-shaped heps are bright orange with persistent calyx, and are conspicuous through the winter. Slightly fragrant. 4 feet by 8 feet.

'**Elmshorn**'. Kordes, Germany, 1950. 'Hamburg' × 'Verdun'. Glossy, pointed leaves of mid green. Clusters of double cherry-red flowers, small, scentless, and soulless. Can be a showy plant at midsummer and again when the big, new shoots arrive later. 5 feet by 4 feet.

'**Erfurt**'. Kordes, Germany, 1939. 'Eva' × 'Réveil Dijonnais'. Vigorous, building up slowly from a low, bushy plant with plentiful, attractive foliage, richly tinted when young. The arching, branching stems bear large wide-open flowers, singly and in clusters, from beautiful long rosy-red buds; semi-double, lemon-white around the yellow stamens, deeply flushed with brilliant pink. (Plate 111.) One of the best of the newer perpetual Shrub Roses, giving a splendid effect of clear pink in the garden. Old Rose scent. 5 feet by 6 feet.

'**Escapade**'. Harkness, U.K., 1967. Although usually grown as a bedding rose, this will build up—with light pruning—into a graceful shrub. It seems never to be without flowers, well displayed and softly fragrant. The semi-double blooms are borne in large and small clusters and have a delicate blend of tints of light lilac-tinted pink with creamy centres. 4 feet by 3 feet.

'**Fimbriata**'. Morlet, France, 1891. *Rosa rugosa* × 'Mme Alfred Carrière'. It seems that *R. rugosa* has a tendency to produce flowers with fringed petals, when one considers the Grootendorst varieties, which have different parentage. The Noisette 'Mme Alfred Carrière' has had little effect on *R. rugosa* in the production of this rose; it is a fairly good shrub with slightly rugose foliage, but in general is rather sparsely branched and leaved. Besides being

known under the above name, it is sometimes found under the Irish name of 'Phoebe's Frilled Pink'; also 'Dianthiflora'. 'Phoebe' was Phoebe Newton, who remembered an old plant growing at Killinure House. I have been unable to ascertain whether the word 'Pink' refers to the colour or the shape of the flower, but 'Dianthiflora' leaves us in no doubt, and indeed the flowers are much like those of a carnation or pink. They are not very double, but the petals are shorter in the centre, and the edges of all are serrated, or fringed. It is a rose to grow for intimate use, scarcely for garden effect, although I remember a conspicuous bush of it at Rowallane, Northern Ireland, which was covered with flowers; there, in a cool climate, it had grown well. In hot, dry Surrey it is not so successful. It is fragrant and occasionally has a few rounded, red heps. 5 feet. (Plate 60, Drawing 11.)
Journal des Roses, Septembre 1896.

'F. J. Grootendorst'. De Goey, Holland, 1918. *Rosa rugosa rubra* × 'Mme Norbert Levavasseur' (a Poly-pom rose whose ancestry is strongly Multiflora, through 'Crimson Rambler' and 'Gloire des Polyanthas'). Like its sports 'Pink Grootendorst' and 'Grootendorst Supreme' it has no scent and is therefore for ever damned by some people, and I must agree that this is a great disadvantage, for which the cheap prettiness of the flowers and their unpleasant contrast with the foliage do nothing to compensate.

On the other hand, it makes a bushy, prickly plant, healthy and vigorous, well covered with leaves somewhat in the Rugosa tradition, and bears bunch after bunch, large and small, of flowers throughout summer and autumn. These are small, fringed like those of a pink, and well swathed in light green bracts. The colour is a dull crimson-red, fading to magenta-crimson. 5 to 8 feet by 5 feet. I do not think it would be grown where other roses are hardy, except for the pretty fringed effect and its prolificity, for it is seldom out of flower. I do, however, consider this superior to its darker-coloured sport, 'Grootendorst Supreme', which has unhealthy, yellowish foliage.

'Fritz Nobis'. Kordes, Germany, 1940. 'Joanna Hill' × 'Magnifica'. Undoubtedly a valuable garden rose, and the one which has achieved most popularity among the three results of the cross; the other two are 'Max Haufe' and 'Josef Rothmund'. It inherits great vigour from both parents, 'Joanna Hill' being a H.T. which grew up to 6 feet even on poor soil at Wisley; from this plant also come the beautifully shaped semi-double flowers, opening from 'Ophelia'-like buds. They are clear pink in two tones, reveal a few yellow stamens, and are deliciously scented of cloves. The strong zigzag stems have a splendid lot of broad, dark green leaves. An exceptionally fine shrub up to some 6 feet high and wide and of wonderful beauty at midsummer. Round, dull-reddish heps, which last into the winter. (Plate 112.)
Gibson, Plate 29.

'Frühlingsanfang'. Kordes, Germany, 1950. 'Joanna Hill' × *Rosa pimpinellifolia* 'Grandiflora'. Very few of the newer shrub roses, or the species themselves, make such a luxuriant shrub as this; the copious leaves create a mantle of dark greenery against which the spring display of flowers is conspicuous. The flowers are of ivory-white, single, sumptuous, and open wide and flat. In the autumn handsome maroon-red heps are produced, at which time the leaves usually turn to rich colours. 8 feet by 9 feet.

'Frühlingsduft'. Kordes, Germany, 1949. 'Joanna Hill' × *Rosa pimpinellifolia* 'Grandiflora'. This is the only one of the set that has fully double, almost modern H.T. flowers, having inherited these and much of their colour from 'Joanna Hill'. They are shapely, with rolled petals, of a strange lemon-creamy-white, flushed with pink, with deeper apricot tones in the centre. An extremely rich fragrance is its proudest possession. Makes a vigorous leafy bush, 6 feet by 6 feet.

'Frühlingsgold'. Kordes, Germany, 1937. 'Joanna Hill' × *Rosa pimpinellifolia* 'Hispida'. There is no doubt that in this rose we have a superlative plant which can hold its own in charm, fragrance, freedom of flowering, and growth with any flowering shrub. At the peak of its flowering period there is nothing more lovely in the garden, and fortunately it thrives in any soil. Its great arching branches, freely but not densely set with leaves, carry along their length large, nearly single flowers of warm butter yellow, with richly coloured stamens, fading in hot weather to creamy white. It has a glorious, far-carrying fragrance. In some seasons it produces a September crop of flowers, but is usually only spring-flowering. Its spiny stems recall its *R. p.* 'Hispida' parentage. 6 feet by 7 feet.

'Frühlingsmorgen'. Kordes, Germany, 1941. A hybrid of 'E. G. Hill' × 'Cathrine Kordes' crossed with *Rosa pimpinellifolia* 'Grandiflora'. I hesitate to claim that this is the most beautiful of all roses with single (five-petalled) flowers: there are so many claimants. But appraising a flowering spray can easily suggest that here is a rare example of the breeder's art which equals if it does not eclipse nature's best efforts. Apart from the beauty of the clear rose-pink large petals which pass to clear, pale yellow in the centre, the flowers have the incomparable attraction of maroon-coloured filaments and anthers. It usually gives a crop of flowers in late summer as well as the generous mass in the spring. The bush is on the sparse side, leaves leaden green. 6 feet by 5 feet. A few large, maroon-red heps are produced.
Austin, page 258.

'Frühlingsschnee'. Kordes, Germany, 1954. 'Golden Glow' × *Rosa pimpinellifolia* 'Grandiflora'. This has not developed strongly with me; the foliage is of a slightly greyish tinge, borne freely on arching branches. Beautifully scrolled buds of creamy yellow open to large, loosely semi-double, nearly white flowers. Fragrant. 5 feet.

'Frühlingstag'. Kordes, Germany, 1949. 'McGredy's Wonder' × 'Frühlingsgold'. This has not impressed me. The clusters of semi-double, golden yellow flowers are produced in early summer. Very fragrant.

'Frühlingszauber'. Kordes, Germany, 1941. The same parentage as 'Frühlingsmorgen', but of less good growth; with me, it is weak and awkward, never making a shrub, but creates a vivid though somewhat vulgar display in flower. The blooms are 3 to 4 inches across, semi-double to nearly single, of a flashy cerise-scarlet with yellow centre on opening, fading to pink. A few large maroon-red heps. 6 feet.

'Gabrielle Noyelle'. Buatois, France, 1933. 'Salet' × 'Souvenir de Mme Krüger'. The first, in alphabetical order, of three yellowish Moss roses; the others are 'Golden Moss' and 'Robert Leopold'. Bright flesh pink to deep salmon is in the shapely small buds; they open to rich, creamy salmon with yellow base; semi-double, of starry shape. Free-flowering and showy. Attractive foliage. 5 feet by 4 feet.

'Gold Bush'. Kordes, Germany, 1954. 'Goldbusch'. 'Golden Glow' × *Rosa eglanteria* hybrid. This makes a freely branching, low bush, and has light, yellowish-green leaves assorting well with the well-formed, deep peach-yellow flowers, semi-double to double, showing yellow stamens. The shapely buds are coral-coloured. Rich tea fragrance. Produces a good second crop, and may reach 5 feet by 9 feet. Full of beauty. (Plate 114.)

'**Golden Moss**'. Dot, Spain, 1932. All strains of modern roses, apart from Floribundas and Poly-poms, are gathered together in this 'Blanche Moreau' hybrid. A lanky bush with dark green leaves, dark brown-red moss. The apricot buds open to well-filled, rather flat flowers of canary-yellow, fading paler, and with peach tones in the centre. 6 feet by 4 feet.

'**Golden Wings**'. Shepherd, U.S., 1956. An interesting and beautiful hybrid raised by Roy Shepherd. *Rosa pimpinellifolia* and the nearly related form or hybrid of it, 'Ormiston Roy', unite in the parentage with 'Soeur Thérèse', which is Hybrid Perpetual combined with Pernetiana. The result is a free-flowering and perpetual plant, no doubt of considerable hardiness; free-branching, compact habit; light green leaves of Hybrid Tea persuasion, but not glossy. The blooms are borne singly or in clusters, with five to ten shapely petals making an exquisite large bloom. Clear, light canary yellow, fading slightly, contrasting with mahogany-amber stamens. Long, pointed buds. Deliciously scented. I have been highly impressed with its continuous performance, colour, and fragrance, but it may be eclipsed by David Austin's 'Windrush', q.v. 6 feet by 5 feet.
McFarland, *Modern Roses* 5, frontispiece.
Beales, page 143.

'**Gruss an Teplitz**'. Geschwind, Germany, 1897. ('Sir Joseph Paxton' × 'Fellemberg') × ('Papa Gontier' × 'Gloire des Rosomanes'). Owing to this fine battle of names in its parentage, this rose does not fit well into any group. From a horticultural point of view it may be classed as a Bourbon. The dark crimson flowers often show intensification of colour after hot sunshine, which confirms the considerable amount of China Rose in it. The flowers are borne in small clusters at midsummer, but the strong, arching shoots later in the season may bear up to a dozen nodding blooms. Purplish young foliage becoming green but usually retaining a dark edge on a strong bush reaching up to 6 feet or so, or 12 feet with support. Rich spicy fragrance. Perpetual. An admirable rose for many purposes, assorting well with new or old varieties, and useful for informal hedges.
Rosenzeitung, 1899.
Journal des Roses, Septembre 1899. 'Salut à Teplitz'. Poor.
Hoffmann, Plate 19.

'**Harry Maasz**'. Kordes, Germany, 1939. 'Barcelona' (H.T.) × *Rosa* 'Macrantha Daisy Hill'. In garden effect this may be described as a crimson-flowered variant of *R.* 'Macrantha'. The yellow stamens show up beautifully against the paler centre of the light crimson flower, which deepens in colour towards the edges of the petals, emerging from pointed, dark crimson buds. These flowers are borne along the trailing stems and create a vivid display. The foliage is dull, dark leaden green. It would be superb trailing through some grey-leaved shrub. Shoots 10 feet long are produced in a season, and it is less bushy than *R.* 'Macrantha' and so is suitable for training on fences, over hedges, into low trees, etc. Well scented.

'**Hon. Lady Lindsay**'. Hansen, U.S., 1938. 'New Dawn' × 'Revd Page Roberts'. This might be described as the first shrub rose raised with H.T. flowers. It has plum-red prickles and handsome growth, glossy dark leathery leaves of medium size, on a branching plant usually wider than high. The blooms have a 'Chatenay' freshness, double but showing stamens, of a delightful, two-toned, pale salmon pink; darker on the reverse of the petals. *Wichuraiana* scent, tempered with Tea. I find this a fairly good grower, and a free flowerer in hot summers. 4 feet.

'Hunter'. Mattock, U.K., 1961. *Rosa rugosa* 'Rubra' × 'Independence'. Unusually glossy leaves for a rose of Rugosa parentage; they are of dark green and the flowers of rich crimson, double, well-filled and fragrant. A useful dusky-toned shrub. It flowers on until autumn, in clusters. 4 feet by 3 feet.

'James Mason'. Beales, U.K., 1982. 'Scharlachglut' × 'Tuscany'. A lovely, vigorous hybrid having two doses of Gallica in it. The leafy bushes display nearly single blooms of crimson with a purplish flush, and showing good yellow stamens. 5 feet by 4 feet.
Beales, page 159.

'Jardin de la Croix' was raised at Roseraie de l'Haÿ (France) in 1901, and one parent was *Rosa roxburghii*. A very interesting hybrid, showing unmistakably the influence of this species. It grew well at the Roseraie, with good foliage and double pink flowers, but now seems to be extinct.

'Karl Foerster'. Kordes, Germany, 1931. 'Frau Karl Druschki' × *Rosa pimpinellifolia* 'Grandiflora'. A most interesting cross, making a strong bush with medium-sized green leaves. The scentless, double, white flowers inherited from 'Frau Karl' are shapely in the bud and when open. Effective in the garden. Recurrent. 5 feet by 4 feet when growing well.

'Kassel'. Kordes, Germany, 1957. 'Obergärtner Wiebicke' × 'Independence'. Classed as a climber, but makes a good arching shrub with plentiful, dark, glossy leaves. Vivid flowers in the 'Bonn' persuasion, but brighter and of better form. Brilliant cherry-red, with cinnabarred and flame overtones, large, semi-double; profuse at midsummer, and intermittently later. Probably 12 feet on a wall but about 7 feet as a shrub. Rather gawky, needs support. Some fragrance.

'Lady Curzon'. Turner, U.K., 1901. An exceptionally vigorous, prolific hybrid between *Rosa rugosa* 'Rubra' and *R.* 'Macrantha'; if left to itself it makes a mound of tangled branches some 8 feet high and wide, but its prickly, far-reaching and arching growths can climb through bushes and low trees. The dark green, rough foliage shows signs of both parents. The single, crinkled, light pink, wide-open flowers are produced in the utmost profusion, completely smothering the branches for a few weeks. Beautiful stamens; good scent. I remember my first sight of this at Nymans, Sussex, where its branches were effectively interlaced with the tiny violet-purple flowers of the Rambler 'Violette'.
Gault and Synge, Plate 174.

'Lafter' ('Laughter'). Brownell, U.S., 1948. 'Général Jacqueminot' and 'Dr van Fleet' are in its parentage, mixed up with modern roses. Of sufficient vigour and grace to be included here, though classed as a Floribunda. Starts flowering late in the season and has successive crops; the clusters of semi-double flowers on arching shoots have brilliance and charm. They are of medium-sized, loosely-cupped shape, semi-double, rich salmon-flame fading to salmon rose, with apricot reverse, yellow base, and yellow stamens. The light green leaves and red prickles complete a pleasing picture. Growth vigorous and will probably attain 5 feet by 4 feet. Rich *wichuraiana* scent of green apples and lemon.

'Lavender Lassie'. Kordes, Germany, 1960. Though launched as a Floribunda, if pruned lightly this will grow into a tall, graceful, open shrub and is always in flower, its large and small trusses of soft lilac-pink flowers, sweetly scented, blending with many gentle colour essays. Good dark glossy foliage, disease-proof. 8 feet by 4 feet.

'Macrantha'. One of the most prolific and thrifty of shrubs, making an intricate tangle of arching branches set with small prickles and bearing neat leaves. The flowers are borne in small clusters and are large, single, of cream-pink fading to nearly white from a pink bud, with conspicuous stamens. In full flower it is an arresting sight, and deliciously scented. It is, being procumbent and arching, an ideal shrub for foreground planting, clothing banks, stumps, and hedgerows. The round, red heps create a display later. 5 feet by 10 feet. This rose of uncertain garden origin is sometimes made a variety of *Rosa waitziana*, the name for the cross between *R. canina* and *R. gallica;* but if that is so our present plant is some generations removed from the original cross.
Willmott, Plate 403.
Revue Horticole, 1901, page 548. Poor.
The Garden, 1897, page 464.
Beales, page 195.

'Macrantha Daisy Hill'. Similar in all respects to *Rosa* 'Macrantha', of which it is supposedly a hybrid, but with an extra two or three petals. This results in the flowers remaining open better in dull weather. Conspicuous in flower and later, when bearing round, red heps. A thoroughly satisfactory garden shrub, mounding itself into a large dense mass, and exceedingly fragrant. 5 feet by 12 feet.

'Magenta'. Kordes, Germany, 1954. Yellow Floribunda seedling × 'Lavender Pinocchio'. A beautiful rose, in effect a tall Floribunda with old-style flowers. The far-away connection with the Hybrid Musk group may be the reason for the excellent foliage, resembling that of 'Penelope'. Red prickles. Trusses of double flowers, opening from beautifully coiled lilac-pink buds to coppery lilac-pink with cerise shadings. Full-petalled, often quartered. Delicious scent of myrrh. 4 feet.

'Maigold'. Kordes, Germany, 1953. 'McGredy's Wonder' × 'Frühlingsgold'. Something between a climber and a shrub, this rose has really excellent foliage, rich, glossy and profuse. The flowers appear at the beginning of the rose season, of deep buff yellow, reddish in the bud, semi-double, showing a bunch of golden stamens. Powerful, delicious fragrance. Repeats in late summer on tips of new shoots. As a shrub, about 5 feet by 10 feet.

'Marguerite Hilling'. Sleet, 1959. A sport from 'Nevada' which occurred about 1954. The same colour form occurred at the Sunningdale Nurseries some years previously and also in Mrs Steen's garden in New Zealand in 1958. It promises to make as good a plant as 'Nevada' and the colour is a pleasing deep flesh-pink.

'Martin Frobisher'. Department of Agriculture, Canada, 1968. This seedling from 'Schneezwerg' has proved not only a good grower, making a graceful leafy bush, but very hardy and prickly. The clusters of shapely double pink flowers are rather small but are borne intermittently until autumn after the summer crop. Sweetly scented. 5 feet by 5 feet.

'Max Graf'. Bowditch, U.S., 1919. *Rosa rugosa* × *R. wichuraiana.* 'Lady Duncan' was of similar parentage. For many years lingering in obscurity, this rose has sprung into the limelight for two reasons. First, because it spontaneously produced tetraploid seeds, the progeny qualifying for specific status as *R. kordesii.* It had been sterile for years but the fertile tetraploid has been the ancestor of many new roses raised by Kordes. Secondly, because we now welcome roses that are satisfactory, attractive, weed-smothering ground-covers. It makes a dense mat of trailing branches, seldom reaching above 2 feet until thoroughly mounded up with its own growths, and well covered with bright green leaves. I have grown two forms, presumably sister-seedlings, one with rather dull leaves and the other with more glossy leaves of darker green: the two appear to lean toward either parent in this respect. Although they flower only once, it is a very long season, and the contrast of the nearly single pink blooms with white centres and yellow stamens over the greenery is pleasing, and they are sweetly scented of green apples.

It is a most valuable plant, rooting as it goes and creating a dense mantle over the ground; presumably with unlimited scope there would be no stopping it, for its subsidiary layers would ever produce new and vigorous plants. No weeds come through it. It is ideal for the fronts of shrub borders, for clothing banks and for hanging down walls, and no doubt could also be trained upwards, on banks and fences.
Gibson, Plate 36.

× **microgosa**. Raised prior to 1905 at the Strasbourg Botanical Institute. *Rosa rugosa* × *R. roxburghii* (*R. microphylla*). *Rosa vilmoriniana, R. wilsonii.* This combines the very bushy habit of both parents, leaning towards *R. rugosa* in its prickles and crisp foliage, while the flowers are single and flat, similar to *R. roxburghii,* and held in a similar way among the leaves, but do not last long. It is a very dense bush, and would make an excellent impenetrable hedge. Will probably exceed 5 feet by 6 feet. Heps rounded, bristly, orange-green. The prickly bark does not peel.
Gartenflora, Vol. 59, Plate 1581. Unrecognizable.
Revue Horticole, 1905, page 144. Fruits, very fine.

× **microgosa 'Alba'**. Raised by Dr C. C. Hurst at Cambridge, U.K.; a second generation from the original cross. Slightly more erect in growth, with lighter green leaves and white flowers. Heps similar. The flowers are more fragrant than in the pink type, and successive crops are produced; a valuable asset.

'Mme Georges Bruant'. Bruant, France, 1887. *Rosa rugosa* × 'Sombreuil', which is a creamy-white Tea Rose, and the result is what one would expect from such a cross: a big, strong, prickly, upright bush with glossy yet slightly rugose foliage in rich green. The flowers emerge from very shapely Tea Rose buds, creamy white, fading to white, fairly double and silky, scented, showing yellow stamens. They are borne singly and in clusters, in great profusion at midsummer and in autumn, and intermittently meanwhile. It creates a specially good contrast of floral and foliage colours; seen against a dark yew hedge, as at Spetchley Park, Worcestershire, it can be magnificent. Unfortunately the flowers are often poorly shaped. 6 feet by 4 feet.
Rosenzeitung, October 1906.

'Morletii'. Morlet, France, 1883. *Rosa inermis morletii.* Also found under the name of *R. pendulina plena,* which is of doubtful authenticity. It is beautiful in spring, with richly tinted young foliage, which later becomes greyish green with reddish veins and stalks. Early in the flowering season it produces many clusters of double, small to medium-sized, magenta blooms. Densely glandular calyx and smooth receptacle. Dark, plum-coloured wood, devoid of prickles, making an elegant, arching shrub. Foliage develops prolonged autumn colour, coppery-orange and red tones predominating. In spite of its lack of scent, this is one of the best shrub roses for continued effect, giving as it does colour in spring and autumn as well as at flowering time. 5 feet by 5 feet.

'Morning Stars'. Jacobus, U.S., 1949. With 'Autumn Bouquet', 'Inspiration', and a double dose of 'New Dawn' in its being this is a fresh-looking, small shrub with glossy, dark green leaves, and produces lemon-white, semi-double, modern flowers singly or in clusters through the season, showing yellow stamens. Delicious penetrating lemon scent. 5 feet by 4 feet.

'Moyesii Superba'. Van Rossem, Holland. A dusky beauty with the elegant growth of *Rosa moyesii*, but much more compact. Dark green foliage; plum-coloured stems, calyx and receptacle. Flowers are semi-double, in the *R. moyesii* persuasion, but of very dark crimson. It unfortunately has no scent and does not produce heps. A large bush should create an impressive sight, and may reach 7 feet in height. Reported to be *R. moyesii* × 'Gustav Grünerwald', but the chromosome count does not support the inclusion of the Hybrid Tea rose.

'Mrs Anthony Waterer'. Waterer, U.K., 1898. 'Général Jacqueminot' × hybrid of *Rosa rugosa*. A vigorous bush with red prickles and dull, dark green leaves, making usually a mound of arching growths. In early summer a luxuriant crop of flowers is produced, and a few later, but in my experience it does not have an effective autumn crop. The flowers are loosely double or semi-double, cupped, of rich, bright crimson flushed with purple, borne usually in small clusters or singly. Richly scented. This rose was given a special bed at Kew and was a splendid sight every summer; on a bright day the flowers fade, but the blend of colour over the bed is always satisfying. 4 feet by 7 feet.

'Mrs Oakley Fisher'. Cant, U.K., 1921. In the gardens of those who admire single-flowered roses, in constant flower through the season, borne on a large shrub, this exquisite variety is not overlooked. Shapely buds open into 5-petalled blooms of soft buff-yellow, deliciously fragrant. At Sissinghurst Castle, Kent, it achieves some 5 feet by 5 feet. Strictly a Hybrid Tea, but it fits well with roses in this chapter, providing much-needed yellow, or would assort with Hybrid Musks.

'München'. Kordes, Germany, 1940. 'Eva' × 'Réveil Dijonnais'. One of the several perpetual-flowering shrub roses which have a distant connection, through 'Eva', with the Hybrid Musks; the influence of *Rosa foetida*, through 'Réveil Dijonnais', is not noticeable. It is a robust shrub with good, dark, glossy green leaves. The flowers, borne in clusters, are loosely semi-double from pointed maroon buds and are of intense dark garnet-red, with an occasional white streak, but little scent. Large greenish heps with persistent calyx. A sister seedling to 'Erfurt', and valuable for the depth of tone it imparts to any collection. 8 feet by 5 feet.

'Narrow Water'. Daisy Hill Nurseries, Ireland, *c.* 1883. A vigorous Noisette-type of rose producing sprays of blooms late into autumn. Probably related to 'Blush Noisette'; it has the same narrow buds opening into semi-double flowers showing beautiful stamens. Sweetly scented. 9 feet by 6 feet.

'Nevada'. Dot, Spain, 1927. 'La Giralda' × tetraploid relative of *Rosa moyesii*. 'La Giralda' was a cross between 'Frau Karl Druschki' and 'Mme Édouard Herriot', and the result is about what one might expect from a fusion of the H.T. type and *Rosa moyesii*. From the latter are inherited the great spraying branches flowering along their length; the leaves are light green, midway between the parents; the flowers are 4 inches across, nearly single, creamy white with blush tints, emerging from reddish buds. In hot weather the colour becomes more pink, with sometimes a red splash. (Drawing 12.)

This is one of the most spectacular of all flowering shrubs when in bloom, hundreds of flowers being littered all over the bush, almost obscuring the foliage, at early midsummer; later in August if the weather be warm a smaller crop matures; in good weather subsequent flowers appear until autumn. In dull summers a lack of continuity is noticeable and the colour fades nearly to white. It flowers with the Rugosa roses, and with them makes a large, rounded shrub some 7 feet high and even wider, shoots sometimes of 8 feet in length being studded with flowers for their entire length.

Doubts have been cast by leading geneticists on the published parentage of this rose, since *Rosa moyesii* itself is a hexaploid; possibly one of the tetraploid forms or related species, such as *R. moyesii* 'Fargesii' or *R. holodonta*, was used. Pink sports have occurred and one has been named 'Marguerite Hilling', q.v.
Gibson, Plate 35.

'New Century'. Van Fleet, U.S., 1900. *Rosa rugosa* 'Alba' × 'Clothilde Soupert'. This and 'Sir Thomas Lipton' were raised from the same cross, but have little in common. 'New Century' makes a fine bush, rather in the Rugosa tradition, but less prickly and with smoother leaves. The flowers are saucer-shaped, with several rows of petals of cool lilac-pink fading at the edges, and having a heart of creamy stamens. Very fragrant. At times the blooms have the fullness and shape of *R. centifolia*. 4 feet by 4 feet.

'Nova Zembla'. Mees, U.K., 1907. A sport which appeared in 1907 on 'Conrad F. Meyer'. It is in all respects identical except for the colour of the flowers, which are nearly white, with a delicate pink flush. Like 'Conrad Meyer' it produces its best blooms in early autumn, and at that time few flowers can touch it for shape, purity, and exquisite tint. Sweetly scented. 8 to 9 feet by 4 feet.

'Nymphenburg'. Kordes, Germany, 1954. 'Sangerhausen' × 'Sunmist'. Vigorous, semi-climbing stems fork freely but do not make a good bush. Foliage large, glossy, dark green. The flowers are nearly double, of warm salmon-pink shaded cerise-pink and orange, with yellow bases to the petals, emerging from apricot buds. Extremely delicious green-apple scent, of penetrating intensity. Recurrent bloom until autumn. After hot summers the plants are resplendent in autumn with large turbinate heps of orange-red. Probably 6 by 8 feet. (Plate 115.)

'Nyveldt's White'. Nyveldt, Holland, 1955. *Rosa rugosa* 'Rubra' × *R. cinnamomea* crossed with *R. nitida*. This shows more affinity to *R. rugosa* and makes a large, arching shrub with fresh green leaves. The flowers are borne in clusters, single, of cold, pure white; recurrent. Fragrant. Heps orange-red.
Austin, page 239.

'Oratam'. Jacobus, U.S., 1939. *Rosa damascena* × 'Souvenir de Claudius Pernet'. An unexpected rose to have Damask parentage. It has dark, broad, glossy leaves and fully double luxurious flowers, salmon, with yellowish reverse and centre. A rather vulgar rose, and one which I find rather difficult to assess for garden value, but it may well be useful among the modern shrub roses. Resembles the Rugosa hybrid 'Vanguard'. 5 feet by 4 feet.

'Paulii'. George Paul, U.K.—prior to 1903. *Rosa rugosa* × *R. arvensis*. *Rosa rugosa repens alba*. Excessively prickly, with *rugosa*-like foliage and flowers. The vigour and trailing habit of

R. arvensis are added to characters which are otherwise near to those of *R. rugosa.* The shoots grow to about 12 feet long and lie flat on the ground, successive shoots gradually mounding up to 3 feet in height, but it is at all times a vigorous, dense ground-cover, and very thrifty. Flowers slightly clove-scented, like those of *R. rugosa;* petals deeply notched, crinkled, with a bunch of yellow stamens; many pale green bracts.

This trailer, with 'Max Graf', the *Rosa* 'Macrantha' forms, and *R. wichuraiana* itself, are the best ground-covering roses, and of them all *R.* 'Paulii' is the most prickly and dense. When in flower it looks like a *Clematis montana.*
Gibson, Plate 36.

'Paulii Rosea'. Prior to 1912. Rather less vigorous than the all-conquering white type, this has a beauty of flower unexcelled by other single pink roses. The petals are deeply notched, pleated, silky, of clear and beautiful pink, but white around the yellow stamens, giving each bloom a very fresh appearance. I have heard of *Rosa* 'Paulii' producing pink sports, and therefore conclude that this form was originally one such. Equally fragrant.
Les Plus Belles Roses, page 44. *Rosa gallica × rugosa:* unmistakably 'Paulii Rosea'.
Trechslin & Coggiatti. Very good.
Phillips and Rix, Plate 101.

'Pink Grootendorst'. Grootendorst, Holland, 1923. Like 'Grootendorst Supreme', this was a sport from 'F. J. Grootendorst' and, in spite of its chocolate-box prettiness and complete lack of scent, it is a favourite with many. It resembles in every way its parent, and is seldom out of flower during the summer and autumn. The bunches of flowers are of brilliant, light cerise-pink, in marked contrast to the leaves, and create a good effect in the garden. It is excellent for cutting and adds character to many a bowl of mixed roses. It is curious that both the sports are less vigorous and healthy than the original; a darker variant is often less vigorous than a pale rose, but here both are decidedly inferior to 'F. J. Grootendorst' in vigour and foliage. There is also a white sport, 'White Grootendorst'.
McFarland, *Roses of the World,* page 211. Rather exaggerated; a good colour photograph.
Park, Plate 203. A good photograph.
Bois and Trechslin, Plate 9.
Gibson, Plate 33.

'Pleine de Grâce'. Lens, France, 1985. This forms an immense, arching, dense bush smothered in thousands of small single white flowers in small as well as large trusses at midsummer. The fragrance is wonderful and all-pervading. In the autumn the tiny orange-red heps make an equally impressive display. 8 feet by 12 feet.

× polliniana. Cultivated since 1820, this is a hybrid between *Rosa arvensis* and *R. gallica.* No doubt it has occurred many times—and both colour and habit would vary—but this particular clone seems well known in horticulture and is accurately portrayed by Miss Willmott. It is a low, sprawling shrub, gradually making a mound about 10 feet wide and 4 feet high, with prickly shoots which would climb through shrubs and into trees. Small olive-green leaves; the whole plant is decorated for a short period by the small clusters of large, single roses, clear rose-pink in the dainty buds and opening to blush, with yellow stamens and delicious scent. Young twigs are purplish coloured, with coppery leaves, partaking of *R. arvensis.*
Willmott, Plate 333.

'**Poulsen's Park Rose**'. Poulsen, Denmark, 1953. 'Great Western' (a Bourbon) × 'Karen Poulsen'. Stout, reddish, prickly stems make a fine, big shrub with two great bursts of flower, of high quality in dry, warm weather: the petals are rather thin, and are not resistant to rain. Large and small clusters of blooms, long-pointed in the bud, opening to shapely, nearly double blossoms, of Hybrid Tea quality; soft pink. Fragrant. 4 feet by 5 feet.

'**Raubritter**'. Kordes, Germany, 1936. *Rosa* 'Macrantha Daisy Hill' × 'Solarium' (Rambler). A pretty, sprawling shrub for foreground and bank planting, eventually mounding itself into a hummock about 7 feet across, 3 feet high, with somewhat prickly, interlacing branches and small dark leaves. The flowers are borne in clusters, of clear, fresh pink, semi-double, but remaining prettily incurved, recalling the old Bourbon Roses. Each bloom stays in beauty for a week and the plants are beautiful for several weeks at midsummer. No other rose that I have met has such irresistible charm, with its low branches laden with ball-like blooms. Beautiful with all purple-flowered plants and grey foliage. Liable to mildew.
Phillips and Rix, Plate 107.
Thomas, 1991, page 38.

'**Refulgence**'. W. Paul, U.K., 1909. A big, gaunt plant descended from *Rosa eglanteria*, with strong, prickly shoots 8 feet high, sparsely leaved but bearing refulgent scarlet-crimson, semi-double flowers. A showy plant which is best placed behind others to cover its ugly growth below. A few round to oval heps.

'**Robert Leopold**'. Buatois, France, 1941. Very vigorous Moss Rose hybrid with bright green leaves and dark prickles and "moss." The shapely, brilliant apricot buds open to coppery-apricot, loosely double flowers of rounded outline fading to lilac-rose in full sun. Sweetly scented. 5 feet by 3 feet.

'**Rosenwunder**'. Kordes, Germany, 1934. 'W. E. Chaplin' × 'Magnifica'. A lax bush with richly coloured reddish twigs, nearly thornless; pretty, coppery young foliage; good, glossy summer leaves and attractive flowers followed by red heps. The flowers are loosely semi-double, cupped, coppery light crimson, with a rich scent of ripe gooseberries. 6 feet by 6 feet.

'**Roxane**'. Raised by Sir Frederick Stern (U.K.), the result of crossing *Rosa roxburghii* with *R. sinowilsonii* At Highdown this reached about five feet in height. It has pleasant foliage of light green and flat, deep pink flowers, both more reminiscent of *R. roxburghii* than of the other parent. Green prickly heps. (Plate 116.)

'**Ruskin**'. Van Fleet, U.S., 1928. *Rosa rugosa* × 'Victor Hugo' (H.P.). This is a coarse, unmanageable hybrid making very prickly shoots 10 feet or more long, and bearing plentiful, good foliage of rough texture. Like the little girl in the nursery rhyme—"when she was good she was very, very good, but when she was bad she was horrid"—the blooms can be sumptuous, of H.P. fullness and of a gorgeous crimson scarlet and with delicious scent. Sometimes, more often than not, one only has the scent. It can be made into a reasonable bush by pruning, or can be pegged down, or trained on wall or fence, and is very free-flowering at midsummer, with a few blooms later.

'**Rustica**'. Barbier, France, 1929. 'Mme Édouard Herriot' × 'Harison's Yellow'. In both parents is a strain of *Rosa foetida*, and this rose certainly leans towards them in its smooth brown wood and grey prickles, rich green leaves, wide receptacle, and peculiar fragrance. The flowers are fully double though loose, coral- or salmon-tinted yellow. It flowers early in the season and is a beautiful plant when well grown, its arching branches being in flower for their whole length. 4 feet by 4 feet.

'**Sarah van Fleet**'. Van Fleet, U.S., 1926. *Rosa rugosa* × 'My Maryland' (H.T.). Few flowering shrubs of any kind make such a dense mass of erect, prickly stems; they are covered with good leaves except at the base. It is ideal for a tall screen, or for planting at the back of the border, and is always in flower, creating a massed effect at midsummer; the September crop appears on longer stems with elegant prickles and foliage. The flowers are in clusters, with two or three rows of petals, opening from pointed buds to shallow cups of cool pink with a hint of lilac. Young foliage and shoots are bronze-tinted. Suitable for the largest plantings. 8 feet by 5 feet. 'Mary Manners', from the Leicester Rose Company, U.S., in 1970, is a white-flowered close relative, perhaps a sport. Equally prickly.

'**Scarlet Fire**'. Kordes, Germany, 1952. 'Scharlachglut'. 'Poinsettia' × *Rosa gallica* 'Grandiflora'. A great arching shrub with smooth brown wood and prickles and plenty of normal green leaves. During its one flowering season, which is long, it is a most spectacular plant. Each flower—and they are borne in clusters all along the branches—is well shaped, 3 inches across, composed of five perfect, lustrous, velvety petals of intense blazing scarlet-crimson, lightened by a neat centre of yellow stamens. Large, long-lasting, pear-shaped red heps with persistent calyx. A really splendid shrub of large dimensions, probably 7 feet by 7 feet or wider, which takes time to build itself into a firm bush. Admirable when trained on a wall, as at Sissinghurst Castle, Kent. (Plate 118.)

'**Schneelicht**'. Geschwind, Hungary, 1896. Reported to be *Rosa rugosa* × *R. phoenicea*. Good foliage, fairly typical of *R. rugosa*, of rich dark green, which shows up the pure white flowers, opening from pointed, blush-white buds; they are single with yellow stamens. The bush is composed of many arching branches, and the flowers are borne Rambler-fashion all along the branches in clusters. Good, fairly light green foliage. Makes a really splendid mound, comparable to *R*. 'Paulii', less prostrate but with better flowers, 5 feet by 8 feet.

'**Schneezwerg**'. Lambert, Germany, 1912. *Rosa rugosa* hybrid. A most pleasing bush, of good shape, fairly dense and twiggy, bearing pairs of grey prickles, and dark, shining green, rugose foliage. The creamy buds are perfect, likewise the flowers—opening flat like an anemone, and with two or three rows of pure white petals and creamy-yellow stamens; they are produced without stint through the season, and the later crops coincide delightfully with the small orange-red heps. I have never clipped it, but think it would respond well and make a good hedge. One of the few hybrids of *R. rugosa* that approach the first-class category. 7 feet by 5 feet. It was originally reported to be *R. rugosa* × *R. bracteata*, and this seems quite possible from its appearance.

'**Scintillation**'. Austin, Sunningdale, U.K., 1966. *Rosa* 'Macrantha' × 'Vanity'. Decorated by yellow stamens, the scintillating mass of petals from the clusters of semi-double blush-pink flowers creates an effect at midsummer which one cannot forget. It is a vigorous sprawler for covering stumps and hedges and for climbing into small trees. Leaden green foliage. Very fragrant. 5 feet by 10 feet.

'**Sir Thomas Lipton**'. Van Fleet, U.S., 1900. *Rosa rugosa* 'Alba' × 'Clothilde Soupert'. Although of different parentage, it is a similar large bush to 'Mme Georges Bruant', with green young wood and fairly good foliage. The blooms are creamy white, borne singly or in clusters, in early summer and intermittently onwards, semi-double to fully double. When a good one appears, it can be as shapely as a camellia. 6 feet by 4 feet.

'Soleil d'Or'. Pernet-Ducher, France, 1900. 'Antoine Ducher' × 'Persian Yellow'. This cannot be described as a shrub rose, but it is such an historic piece that I feel I must mention it. The bulk of our flame and orange modern roses have this rose in their ancestry, for it was the first Pernetiana rose; unfortunately it is a martyr to black spot. Double, rich orange-yellow; the influence of *Rosa foetida* is found in its scent and foliage.
Revue de l'Horticulture Belge, 1900, Plate 109; also 1905, Plate 13.
Journal des Roses, Juin 1900.

'Sophie's Perpetual'. An old garden rose found by Humphrey Brook without a name. He gave it this name in the absence of any other, but its true one may yet be found. It can be grown as a loose bush, or as a climber, in which case it will achieve 15 feet or more. Good dark green foliage on stems almost without prickles. The flowers are fairly double, somewhat cupped, of a clear light pink flushed on the outer petals with cerise-crimson. Scented, and almost constantly in flower.

'Thérèse Bugnet'. Bugnet, Canada, 1950. An involved parentage includes several doses of *Rosa rugosa* derivatives. Very hardy. Large, loose crimson flowers, fading paler, sweetly-scented, on a vigorous bush. 6 feet by 6 feet.

'Vanguard'. Stevens, U.S., 1932. A hybrid between *Rosa wichuraiana* and *R. rugosa* 'Alba' was crossed with 'Eldorado', an H.T. of Pernetiana descent from 'Mme Edouard Herriot'. This remarkable hybrid is in a way a foretaste of the *kordesii* roses. It is a vigorous plant, making stout wood and bearing large, shining, green leaves, with large orange-salmon flowers, rather shapeless but fully double. It can be treated as a bush or a pillar rose, but is very upsetting in the garden except among roses of its own colouring. 5 feet by 5 feet.
McFarland, *Roses of the World,* page 276. A good representation.

'Windrush'. Austin, U.K., 1984. Descended from the noted 'Golden Wings', this bids fair to supersede it in every way—in bushiness, light green foliage, and a constant succession from early in the season of light yellow, single blooms showing good stamens. It has a re-freshing Burnet Rose scent. 4 feet by 4 feet.

'Zigeunerknabe'. Geschwind, Hungary, 1909. 'Gipsy Boy'. A seedling of 'Russelliana', which is possibly descended from *Rosa setigera*. One of the most thrifty roses in my collection, making dense, graceful bushes 5 feet high and nearly twice as wide, composed of arching, prickly stems. Both stems and foliage are reminiscent of *R. rugosa*. It creates a magnificent effect in flower at midsummer, when it is covered with small clusters of fair-sized blooms, semi-double, flat and reflexing, of intense crimson purple, white towards the centre. Rather lacking in quality as a flower, but splendid as a shrub. Orange-red heps. A little fragrance.
Park, Plate 177.

THE NEW ENGLISH ROSES

WE NOW COME to a new epoch in the development of the Rose. For almost thirty years David Austin has been working along his own preconceived ideas of what our roses should look like. Not for him are the stereotyped small upright bushes producing garish colours—flame, orange, and blatant yellow predominating—which are the prerogative of Hybrid Tea and Floribunda enthusiasts. These are bred to provide brilliant colour in beds on lawns and in formal rose gardens. David's ideals were altogether different; in fact, in many ways he sought to carry on some of the ideas of Pemberton and his Hybrid Musks. But the English Roses have gone further, and while they are certainly more consistent in their production of bloom from summer until autumn, they are mostly smaller shrubs. David's ideal was to produce good healthy bushes of graceful growth bearing flowers in the unsurpassed style of the Old Roses of the nineteenth century, full of petals and fragrance and in a variety of soft tints. Was not this a worthy idea? Just how successful he has been may be realized from the descriptions of the roses in this section, all except one of his own breeding.

It has been a fascinating exercise to make an annual pilgrimage to Albrighton, near Wolverhampton, to see his thousands of seedlings under trial, to watch the growth, and to admire the rich or delicate (not strident) colours, the wonderful shapes, and the satisfying fragrance. Full well has he achieved his purpose, and of late years his display-ground of established bushes has taken over where the Old Roses left off. It is not likely that anyone will start breeding these again; the earlier pages of this book demonstrate that probably enough varieties have, thankfully, come down to us through many years of almost total neglect. We can enjoy them and revel in their unique qualities, and at the same time take to our hearts all these new productions of David's which give us just as shapely blooms, with a rich array of colours and scents from midsummer until autumn.

Nobody could expect to please all rose growers in a programme of rose breeding along these lines. One hears criticisms in regard to lack of colour. But every colour offered by the rose is there, except for flaming reds and oranges. While I would guarantee to make up an assortment of tints of flowers and leaves in which the blatant tones of, for instance, 'Super Star' would look at home, I should not want it in my garden. Nor do I want strong cocktails every or all day; rather, mellow wines of varied vintage and colours. Several people have told me that the English Roses are inclined to droop their flowers to the ground. This is usually because they are insufficiently well nurtured, or wrongly pruned. It is customary with the well-known rather drooping 'Victoria' Plum to prune to an upward eye, and this would help to improve the shape of some of David's more lax bushes. The rose which he was kind enough to name after me did not receive an award in the trials at Bone Hill; the Committee for New Seedlings of the Royal National Rose Society considered it "too lanky." But they judged it for only three years, and then discarded it. A shrub rose requires four or five years to assess, and 'Graham Thomas' has been a resounding success throughout the rose-growing world now that it has had sufficient time to prove itself. The same may be said of all the English Roses—they are small to medium shrubs, not what we term "bush" roses for beds, though several of the smallest would prove admirable for this purpose. But to return: a large, graceful and shapely bush must be lanky in its youth.

It is important to realize that these roses have been bred with several ideals in mind—growth, scent, and floriferousness among them—but one main ideal is that the open flowers of most shall be well filled with petals, in the old tradition. The Old Roses were beautiful throughout their life, and so are all of David's breeding. The fact that most lack the scrolled buds of the Hybrid Teas is amply compensated for by their many other delights.

There is also the matter of perfume. Here David has had the extraordinary good fortune to give us, by pure chance, a new perfume in many of his roses—the scent of myrrh. It occurred first some two hundred years ago in the old so-called Ayrshire Rambler 'Splendens'. Somehow, without its being related in any obvious way to this Rambler, the Old Rose 'Belle

Amour' (for which we have neither date nor parentage) has it too, and it may be detected in one or two Floribundas. None of these is in the parentage of 'Constance Spry' (David Austin, 1961), so it appears that this is a hybrid fragrance which crops up frequently in the English Roses. It cannot be traced to one original occurrence, as can the fierce colour pelargonidin (see the Introduction to this book).

David Austin has named over 60 varieties of his own raising; some appeal to me more than others, and only time will tell which are to be permanently in the gardens of those who love roses of all kinds. The following selection is partly mine and partly David's.

'**Abraham Darby**'. Austin, U.K., 1985. 'Yellow Cushion' × 'Aloha'. These two modern roses have produced a splendid, large, arching bush with good foliage and deeply cupped blooms loosely filled with petals, peach-pink with light yellow reverses, flowering well throughout the summer and autumn. These warm tints fade with age, but it is at all times beautiful, and richly scented. The growth is unusually shapely, rounded and tidy. It would also be useful when trained on a wall. 5 feet by 5 feet.

'**Belle Story**'. Austin, U.K., 1984. 'Iceberg' is in the parentage, and gives freely of its influence in foliage and prolificity. Pretty, loose flowers with petals neatly incurving over the lovely stamens. Sweetly scented. 4 feet by 4 feet.

'**Brother Cadfael**'. Austin, U.K., 1990. 'Charles Austin' × seedling. Very large, globular, almost peony-like flowers of soft pink with a rich fragrance. Substantial bushy growth, about 3 ½ feet.

'**Charles Rennie Mackintosh**'. Austin, U.K., 1988. ('Chaucer' × 'Conrad Ferdinand Meyer') × 'Mary Rose'. A good pink, overlaid with lilac in the old tradition. The powerful fragrance from the cupped flowers adds much to its value as a tough bushy plant; 3 ½ feet by 3 feet.

'**Country Living**'. Austin, U.K., 1991. 'Wife of Bath' × 'Graham Thomas'. Wonderful, well-filled flowers of typical Old Rose charm, delicate pink fading almost to white with age, but at all stages near perfection. Sweetly fragrant; a small shrub of upright growth. 3 feet by 2 feet.

'**Cymbeline**'. Austin, U.K., 1982. This is the first, alphabetically, of the myrrh-scented English Roses. The wide-open, quartered flowers are densely filled with short petals of a soft grey-pink. A fine graceful bush with arching growth. Always in flower. 4 feet by 5 feet.

'**English Garden**'. Austin, U.K., 1986. 'Lilian Austin' × (seedling × 'Iceberg'). Opening flat, full of quartered petals, giving an overall clear yellow effect but with apricot tones in the centre. The flowers tone well with the light green leaves on an upright bush. 3 feet by 2 ½ feet.

'**Evelyn**'. Austin, U.K., 1991. The apricot and yellow of the folded petals form a rich centre to the large cupped blooms, gradually reflexing. 3 ½ feet by 3 feet.

'**Gertrude Jekyll**'. Austin, U.K., 1986. 'Wife of Bath' × 'Comte de Chambord', an old Portland Rose. The result is a rich pink rose of beautiful shape in the bud, opening into well filled shapely flowers. Very fragrant.

'**Glamis Castle**'. Austin, U.K., 1992. 'Graham Thomas' × 'Mary Rose'. A superb white rose with wide, cupped flowers, well filled with petals of typical Old Rose charm. Rich myrrh fragrance. Short growth, bushy, flowering with abundance and continuity. 2½ feet by 3 feet.

'**Golden Celebration**'. Austin, U.K., 1992. 'Charles Austin' × 'Abraham Darby'. Deeply cupped flowers, large and filled with petals of brilliant canary-yellow flushed with soft orange. The bushy plants are of rounded, arching habit covered in particularly bright, light green foliage, harmonising well with the flower colour. Exceptionally fragrant. 4 feet by 4 feet. (Plate 120.)

'**Graham Thomas**'. Austin, U.K., 1983. In the field full of seedlings from which we chose this there were very few yellows, and no other with so rich and deep a colour as this. The only rose that in any way approaches its rich tint of apricot in the bud is 'Lady Hillingdon', a Tea Rose of 1910. The splendid loosely-filled blooms expand to a deep butter yellow, richly tea-scented. It builds up into a fine graceful bush or can be used as a short climber. I have seen it as a shrub up to 6 or 7 feet, but it is usually about 4½ feet. Repeats well. (Plate 124.)

'**Gruss an Aachen**'. Geduldig, Germany, 1909. Bred long before English Roses or Floribundas were even thought of, but it fits well with all these others. It has 'Frau Karl Druschki' and other famous roses of Tea ancestry in its bloodstream. It can hold its own in size of bloom and floriferousness with any today, and is deliciously fragrant. Creamy pale apricot-pink fading to creamy white, well filled with petals and of the flat Old Rose shape. A few discerning gardeners knew it and grew it, such as Major Johnston at Hidcote Manor, Gloucestershire. One day I want to plant it with 'Magenta'. It is well illustrated in Strassheim's *Rosenzeitung* for March 1912, and in the *Journal des Roses* for August 1912. Climbing and pink sports have occurred.

'**Heritage**'. Austin, U.K., 1984. Another superlative variety with good growth and foliage, descended in part from 'Iceberg'. The soft blush-pink flowers are of open, cupped formation with varied ranks of shell-like petals. Rich fragrance with a hint of lemon. A fine bushy plant to 5 feet by 4 feet. (Plate 119.)

'**Jayne Austin**'. Austin, U.K., 1990. 'Graham Thomas' × 'Tamora'. An excellent rich yellow, even more apricot-tinted than my own namesake, with good Tea fragrance from the shallow cupped blooms, which often have button eyes. Light green foliage on an upright bushy plant. Free-flowering. 3½ feet by 4 feet.

'**Kathryn Morley**'. Austin, U.K., 1990. 'Mary Rose' × 'Chaucer'. A short, bushy shrub, ideal for smaller gardens. Shapely cupped blooms of soft pink, filled with petals and fragrance. Free-flowering. 2½ feet by 2 feet.

'**L. D. Braithwaite**'. Austin, U.K., 1988. 'Mary Rose' × 'The Squire'. The brilliant crimson flowers, fully double and quartered, often showing a few stamens, are in evidence through the season and have a good Old Rose scent. Good bushy plants, 3½ feet by 3½ feet.

'**Leander**'. Austin, U.K., 1982. This is a really large, bushy shrub with excellent foliage. The deep apricot-tinted flowers are of full rosette-shape with a rich fruity fragrance. It is a fine shrub, mainly for summer display. 5 feet by 5 feet.

'**Lucetta**'. Austin, U.K., 1983. A fine, arching shrub bearing a wealth of soft blush-pink flowers fading paler, at all times lovely, and sweetly scented. 4 feet by 4 feet.

'**Mary Rose**'. Austin, U.K., 1983. A prolific flowerer with excellent bushy growth. Sweetly scented flowers, large and full of petals, of warm pink. A reliable bush. 4 feet by 4 feet.

'**Perdita**'. Austin, U.K., 1983. Like its namesake, a rose of refinement, and particularly well scented. The quartered blooms are of blush-pink tinted with apricot, held well above dark green foliage on bushy growth. 3½ feet by 3½ feet.

'**Redouté**'. Austin, U.K., 1992. A delicate pink sport of 'Mary Rose', with light fragrance and freedom of flowering over a good bushy plant. (Plate 122.)

'**St Cecilia**'. Austin, U.K., 1987. Creamy buff, cupped blooms, sweetly scented of myrrh, produced repeatedly on a good, fairly erect bush. 3½ feet by 2½ feet.

'**Sharifa Asma**'. Austin, U.K., 1989. 'Mary Rose' × 'Admired Miranda'. The shallowly cupped blooms reflex to form a perfect rosette. Delicate blush-pink, fading paler around the perimeter, coupled with a pronounced fragrance. A short, rather upright bush. 3 feet by 2½ feet.

'**Sweet Juliet**'. Austin, U.K., 1989. Excellent upright yet graceful growth, continuously in flower. The rich apricot tint is held well in the full cupped flowers, paling at the edges. 3½ feet by 3 feet.

'**The Alexandra Rose**'. Austin, U.K., 1992. 'Shropshire Lass' × 'Heritage'. This should really be listed among the Modern Shrub Roses. It is a remarkably continuous-flowering shrub producing single, fragrant blooms of clear coppery pink. 4½ feet by 4 feet. (Plate 123.)

'**The Countryman**'. Austin, U.K., 1987. Rich Old Rose fragrance and Old Rose shape, of clear pink. Many petals. A low, arching shrub with two good crops of blooms during the year, though seldom without a flower. It has the same connection with the Portland Rose as 'Gertrude Jekyll'. Unassuming but beautiful. 3½ feet by 3½ feet.

'**The Dark Lady**'. Austin, U.K., 1991. 'Mary Rose' × 'Prospero'. Rich Old Rose fragrance from large, dark crimson, loosely-formed flowers. The wide bushes are of graceful habit. 3 feet by 3½ feet.

'**The Prince**'. Austin, U.K., 1990. 'William Austin' × 'The Squire'. Although a comparatively small grower it is good and bushy, but I am really including it because of its unrivalled colour. It is the only modern rose with the rich dark violet-purple of the best of the Old Roses. The petals, opening a dark crimson, quickly assume the richest imaginable purple velvet, and scent to match. Glossy dark leaves give a dusky effect. 2 feet by 2½ feet. (Plate 121.)

'**Wife of Bath**'. Austin, U.K., 1969. This was one of the first to exhibit the myrrh scent. A small upright bush with lovely cupped flowers of soft pink, constantly in flower. 3 feet by 2 feet.

'**Winchester Cathedral**'. Austin, U.K., 1988. This most distinguished white sport of the famed 'Mary Rose' can hardly fail to please. Highly satisfactory and well scented. 4 feet by 4 feet.

PART 3

Climbing Roses Old and New

7

Ramblers and Climbers Old and New,
Their Characters and Uses

You violets that first appeare,
By your pure purple mantles known,
Like the proud virgins of the yeare,
As if the spring were all your owne,
What are you when the Rose is blown?
Sir Henry Wotton, 1568–1639

I LIKE TO PASS ON the pleasures I have enjoyed by growing all sorts of roses. It is not until one can hold in one's hand such diverse beauties as 'Mlle Cécile Brunner', 'Mme Hardy', 'Reine des Violettes', 'Spek's Yellow', the double white Burnet, 'Mrs John Laing', 'Roseraie de l'Haÿ', 'Lady Hillingdon', 'Lilac Charm', *elegantula,* 'Mme Abel Chatenay', 'Souvenir de la Malmaison', 'Frühlingsmorgen', 'Josephine Bruce' . . . but I had better stop (I could with little trouble name another fourteen of equally divergent beauty); it is not until we contemplate such a handful that we can claim to know THE ROSE. These fourteen vary in width of bloom from one inch to five inches; in colour, from white through yellow, salmon, pink, crimson, murrey, purple, and lilac; in scent, indefinable and indescribable; in shape, rounded, globular, angular, cupped, flat or reflexed, single with five petals only, or double with sixty or more; so that we may say they cover the principal variations of the rose, in both wild and cultivated forms.

The above are bush or shrub roses. It will be quite easy to name fourteen climbers and ramblers with as much variation: 'Adélaïde d'Orléans', 'Guinée', 'Gloire de Dijon', 'Sanders' White', the single yellow Banksian, 'Violette', 'Mermaid', 'Mme de Sancy de Parabère', 'Alister Stella Gray', ' Mrs Herbert Stevens', 'Étoile de Hollande', 'Mme Alice Garnier', 'Kiftsgate', and 'Danse du Feu'. Here are scramblers—in more ways than one—for every position and task; to the categories of qualities listed above they add a further variation, for in height they may achieve from six feet to forty feet on supports, and an equal width.

I like to grow these varying kinds because only by so doing can I feel that I am appreciating to the full the bounties offered by the genus. Of what use is it to be so besieged by novelties and bright colours that one has neither time nor space to grow the established favourites? And by this I do not mean the favourites of yesterday, but of the last hundred and fifty or more years, the best of which stand out like lightships in the drowning waste of the thousands of second-rate varieties that have come and gone. It is a shattering thought that we mortals have made and named during the last hundred and seventy-five years some ten to fifteen thousand varieties of roses that are completely lost and forgotten.

Raisers of roses have always named their best seedlings and distributed them; just a few have achieved such popularity that they have been preserved through changing fashions— ready for emergence when some new fashion or economic or social change brings them forth again. This is what happened to the Old Shrub Roses after the Second World War. It may well happen all over again when good-style roses become neglected. It is illuminating to read how Dean Hole, the celebrated rosarian of the late nineteenth century, and founder of our National Rose Society, cast aside the old ramblers. He was mainly interested in the bigger and better roses of the day for the show-bench; he loved the brighter and more spectacular roses which were then founding the race of Hybrid Teas. His 'Maréchal Niel', 'Gloire de Dijon', and 'Charles Lefèbvre' were to him the apotheosis of the rose; he gracefully recalls (in 1870) how "many years have passed since I laid 'The Garland', as an Immortelle, upon the tomb of 'Madame d'Arblay'." Thirty-two years later, with the turn of the horticultural tide from artificiality to a truer appreciation of natural beauty, Gertrude Jekyll found them just the thing to create graceful festoons of scented blossom over her arches, walls, and shrubs. The principal message of her excellent book *Roses for English Gardens* (1902) is this use of the carefree rambler.

As far as I am aware, no book devoted solely to rambling and climbing roses appeared in Britain until my first essay on the subject: *Climbing Roses Old and New* first appeared in 1965 and had two new editions. This work has been thoroughly revised and brought up to date in the following pages. It is no longer fashionable to address the "gentle reader," but we must be gentle, open-minded, and appreciative of all grace and beauty in assessing both wild species and man-made hybrids. As with all plants we must also be patient, waiting for the soil and the weather to help our roses to give of their best. When our culture is right and the weather perfect, and above all when the placing of the plants and their companions is right, then, at a certain moment of the year, for perhaps a day or two or even a week, any rose in our gardens can be so beautiful that we shall stop weeding and fussing and drink deeply of that unfathomable, incalculable "rich power that breeds so many and many a flower." Though that moment may never come again with the same rose plant, it will enrich our lives with a precious memory of welcome colour, intangible fragrance and natural grace— qualities which seem to become yearly more scarce. And it is to the wild species and certain ramblers that we must turn for the greatest refreshment, with their supreme contributions of grace, fragrance, and plenitude of flower.

There comes a day in June when the popular rose 'Chaplin's Pink' begins to open, and all over the south of England at least its vivid cerise-pink shows over garden walls. Because of its brilliance and ubiquity it heralds the beginning of the rose season. With it two much older but less spectacular roses usually open, 'Paul's Carmine Pillar' and 'Gloire de Dijon'. Apart from some early flowering species of *Rosa*, such as the Banksian and certain shrub roses, these are the first. They are closely followed by 'Albertine', 'American Pillar', and 'Paul's Scarlet', and later by 'Dorothy Perkins', 'Excelsa' and 'Dr van Fleet'. What household words these have become! And what sheets of bloom they give, effervescing up house walls, foaming over arches and garden fences, and even cascading down banks or surmounting the wrecks of posts or trees that they have overpowered!

They come at a time when we have already feasted on the season's fullness. The rhododendrons and azaleas, the cherries, lilacs, laburnums, and many other favourite genera are over, each adding to the year's pageant of beauty. The rose can easily hold its own with them, and particularly is this true of the ramblers and climbers; each plant can give a greater quantity of blossom at one time than any other type of rose. Most of them bring a wonderful perfume—and also prickles. (A list of roses without prickles is given in Chapter I I, for the benefit of the less courageous.)

But first let us consider our terminology and define what is meant by the horticultural groups "ramblers" and "climbers." According to the dictionary they are the same, but they have come to mean two quite different classes of roses, and are comparable in their looseness and synonymy with the two terms for lower-growing roses—"shrub" and "bush." Just as shrub roses have come to mean the wild species and bigger roses bred closely from them, and the bush or bedding roses mean the highly bred, large-flowered Hybrid Teas and Floribundas, so among the taller roses the ramblers are the wild species and closely allied garden forms—flowering once only in the summer, as is normal with most species—and the climbers are the large-flowered, highly bred, mainly repeat-flowering varieties.

These are very superficial terms. To begin with, no rose really climbs in the sense that self-clinging or twining plants like ivy or honeysuckle will climb. The rose, like the blackberry, usually bears hooked prickles which help to secure its branches to the support, but almost all roses need tying and helping upwards or outwards. The botanists term them "scramblers"; we might call them drooping roses, or roses that need support. These terms might be mis-understood, and so throughout this book I shall adopt the accepted distinctions as outlined above.

Fifty years ago it would have been comparatively easy to describe the difference between the two groups of roses, the ramblers and the climbers, but with increased hybridization they come nearer together in the search for a large-flowered rose that will bloom through the summer and into autumn, be hardy, fragrant, and graceful. A few, like 'Mermaid', 'New Dawn', and 'Pink Cloud', are getting near to this ideal.

Species and Hybrids

This book is concerned as much with species of roses as with garden hybrids, and a list of the wild species mentioned in these pages which can be classed as ramblers or climbers is given below, arranged in their taxonomic sections. All roses mentioned in these chapters owe part of their parentage to one or more of these species; they are all natives of the Old World, except one, and mostly of the Far East.

Synstylae
Rosa arvensis
   brunonii
   cerasocarpa
   crocacantha
   filipes
   helenae
   henryi
   longicuspis
   luciae
   maximowicziana

Rosa moschata
   mulliganii
   multiflora
   phoenicea
   rubus
   sempervirens
   setigera
   sinowilsonii
   soulieana
   wichuraiana

Laevigatae
Rosa laevigata

Banksianae
Rosa banksiae

Bracteatae
Rosa bracteata

Indicae
Rosa chinensis
   gigantea

The species of the Laevigatae, Bracteatae, and Banksianae Sections have made little groups on their own, and have had no appreciable influence on our garden ramblers and climbers; moreover, together with *Rosa gigantea*, they would not be reliably hardy, except on sunny walls, in the warmer parts of Great Britain. Therefore we turn to the members of the Synstylae Section, and among these the most prolific of hybrids has been *R. wichuraiana*, with *R. multiflora* and the old *R. moschata* a good second and third. *Rosa phoenicea* and the old *R. moschata* are believed to be parents of the Old Shrub Roses, and *R. arvensis* and *R. sempervirens* had their little day as founders of a few old ramblers grown some two hundred years ago; the last two species are not grown in gardens and their hybrids are now seldom seen. The pages devoted to each Section contain fuller details.

The members of the Synstylae, the Laevigatae, and the Banksianae are all once-flowering ramblers; likewise *Rosa chinensis* var. *spontanea* (the wild species) and *R. gigantea*. *Rosa bracteata* flowers from summer till autumn and therefore qualifies, in this abstract horticultural classification, as the only "species-climber." Practically all the climbers in cultivation owe their status to four original hybrids of *R. chinensis* and *R. gigantea* which were introduced as garden plants from China between 1792 and 1824, as outlined by Dr Hurst in Chapter 13.

The wild roses of the Synstylae Section are, almost all, pre-eminent in fragrance, on account of both their strength and their carrying power in the air. With a richness unsurpassed among roses, and indeed in the floral world, in this character they are nearly unique. In spite of the size of growth of so many of them and their short season of flowering, their fragrance should ensure their being planted everywhere. They take their place with the Linden and the *Philadelphus*, the clover and the bean, bringing midsummer to a climax of scent which is not equalled during the rest of the year out of doors.

Before we consider hybrid ramblers and climbers, I will recall those roses of lax growth which are perhaps not of sufficient length of shoot to be classed as ramblers, and which are also probably too bushy for training on supports. These can be classed as sprawling shrubs— even carpeters—and all those which create dense ground-cover, either flat or mounding themselves up into wide hummocks, have been described in Chapter 6. If a climbing or rambling rose has no support it will obviously make either a loose arching shrub or collapse on the ground, according to how sturdy are the branches; if it is dense in growth it qualifies for a position among labour-saving ground-covering plants. But if it does not make a dense mass, however beautiful it may be sprawling about, it will not make satisfactory ground-cover, and to try to weed or otherwise tend the ground among trailing and arching prickly growth is not a desirable occupation; the growths should be given proper support and kept under control.

So far the classification seems obvious and easy, but when it comes to hybrid climbers it is a very different matter. The oldest recurrent or perpetual hybrid climbers belong to the Noisettes and Bourbons; somewhat later in the general trend are the Tea-Noisettes and Hybrid Perpetuals. 'Blush Noisette' and 'Aimée Vibert' are two important originals, showing the first-fruits of the combined influences of the China and the Musk Rose towards perpetual-flowering climbers.

In addition to the great bulk of large-flowered, recurrent, climbing sports of Hybrid Teas belonging to this century are the repeat-flowering climbers in their own right, so to speak— varieties raised from seed like 'Allen Chandler' and 'Golden Showers'. Conversely, some climbing sports are very shy of later blooms, like 'Peace', and there are some splendid large-flowered climbers, raised from seed, which flower only at midsummer. We also have climbing sports of bush Polyanthas and Floribundas, and I know of a plant of 'Frensham' which has reached some 12 feet in rich soil against a wall, yet it has not produced a climbing sport. This is just an example of how, with the warmth and protection of a wall, shrub and other roses may grow to unexpected heights.

We are dealing with such a complex race of plants that anything may happen when new varieties are raised from seed. The China Rose hybrids are at the back of everything; to them may be traced not only practically all our perpetual or recurrent-flowering climbing roses of today, but the overwhelming majority of hybrid shrub roses and dwarf bush roses as well. Only two or three wild species are recurrent, and these have not yet entered into the parentage of our modern roses, except recently through *Rosa kordesii*. Those roses which flower from June to October, among which may be numbered several Old Roses and many new, raise the genus *Rosa* to a high pinnacle among hybridized genera. Glad we may be of this, but the mere recurrence of flower should not blind us to the beauties of the wild species and the many well-tried favourites which give to our gardens unsurpassed grace and free fragrance. Very few of the large-flowered climbing roses make any pretence of shedding fragrance to the degree achieved by the species in the Synstylae group.

Scent and grace, to me, are important points. When they are combined, as occasionally happens among the ramblers, then I choose them in preference to a graceless plant with big double blooms. There is something a trifle vulgar about having huge growth *and* huge blooms, however desirable it may appear at first sight; and yet I have only to meet a big plant of some climbing Hybrid Tea sport, smothered with fragrant, large, beautiful flowers, to realize that I would rather have those than any number of small blooms *without scent* on a graceful rambler. And it must be admitted that a few ramblers have no scent, or have only an apology for it.

A knowledge of the various groups mentioned above is necessary when it comes to pruning, though it is better not to prune climbers and ramblers at all than to prune them wrongly. I have included some hints in Chapter 12; the elementary rules are easy to grasp.

Uses of Ramblers and Climbers in Gardens

This brings us to another point: how do we most enjoy our ramblers and climbers? Their use in our gardens really depends upon whether we are tidy—or, shall I say, untidy—gardeners; putting it perhaps more subtly, it depends on whether we impose our will on the roses or let them display their personalities to us.

The first method entails training and pruning so that the stiffer, more modern varieties with their large blooms may make a curtain of blossom one foot from a house wall or trellis, so that the shorter-growing varieties may make a cylinder of close bloom up a post or pillar; and so that the strong pliant ramblers may be trained to outline neatly the curve of arch or swinging chain or rope. In these ways the roses become part of the architecture of the garden, and give neat displays, often more closely smothered with bloom than any other garden plant. The best place to see a display such as this is at Bagatelle or at the Roseraie de l'Haÿ, near Paris, as I have described in Chapter 2. The endless variety of cross vistas and the great treillage of ramblers is an example of floral gardening which it would be hard to surpass. Moreover, it is an example of English and French gardening of more than a hundred years ago.

Two of the best English displays of ramblers and climbers are found in or near London. At Queen Mary's Rose Garden in Regent's Park, very high and widely spaced pillars connected with swinging ropes taxed the resources of the Superintendent to the full—only the best cultivation and careful selection of most vigorous varieties have made it the success it is. At the Royal Botanic Garden, Kew, we can see a pergola of stout brick pillars connected with beams above, providing homes for many varieties. Here again, on gravel as opposed to the clay of Regent's Park, the size of the arches is proving a test in covering the pergola success-fully. The Royal National Rose Society's Gardens of the Rose, near St Albans in Hertford-shire, display a considerable range of short climbers and tall ramblers. At Wisley, on poor sandy soil, larch poles with their side-shoots left at a discreet length provide wide pillars of blossom, and a similar method is used at Powis Castle in mid Wales, while at Polesden Lacey, Surrey, on shallow soil overlying chalk, an Edwardian rose garden has a long larchwood per-gola covered with roses of the period—'Dorothy Perkins', 'American Pillar', and all their clan. The effect is delightful but, of course, fragrance is mainly lacking. At Bodnant, in North Wales, the climbers and ramblers are mixed with other things, which is how I prefer them.

I prefer my climbing and rambling roses growing in a natural way, their main shoots se-cured for safety to firm supports, and their branches spilling forward and weighed down with beauty; most of my experience, my thought and aim in growing such roses, has been with this style in mind. This is one reason why I like the older varieties; from my remarks in Chapter 9 in connection with the large-flowered Hybrid Tea-style climbers, it will be understood that hybridization in the main has given us the recurrent-flowering habit at the expense of grace.

There is a great variety of suitable supports for rambling and climbing roses, and I have tried to make their selection and erection easier in Chapter 11. In addition to the more for-mal supports, there is the simple stout post about six feet high to which one ties the main shoots of a rambler; thereafter it is allowed to grow outwards and downwards, making a lax bush or fountain of blossom.

Ramblers are useful plants to cover unsightly sheds and fences and stumps and stems of dead trees, but none of these methods, neat or natural, on artificial or existing supports, can rival the beauty of a rose trained on a living support, allowing it freedom of growth. A rose can grow through a living tree without harming it, giving it midsummer beauty.

It is the *falling spray* of ramblers that is most beautiful, not those which are trained upwards. This is the lesson I have learnt and want to try to pass on, and some of the methods described above may help. To see and smell the long trail of blossoms hanging from a growing leafy host-tree is one of the great pleasures of summer.

This brings me away from the garden varieties and hybrids of ramblers back to the species themselves. The gardening public has not yet realized what giants these wild roses can be. It is no good putting them into the usual ornamental or fruit trees of our gardens; *Rosa brunonii*, *R. rubus*, and *R. helenae*, together with 'Kiftsgate', 'La Mortola', and 'Paul's Himalayan Musk', are tremendous growers and suitable for really big supports. I have enlarged on this in the section devoted to them. It is enough to say here that there is a wealth of garden beauty and fragrance available in strong and very strong rambling species and varieties to add greatly to our gardens in June and July.

So far we have been considering the uses of ramblers and once-flowering allied roses. The hybridized climbers require rather different treatment. Some are manageable and easy to train, and will make great lax bushes like those visualized above; others, particularly the climbing sports of Hybrid Teas, are stiff and awkward to train and are apt to get lanky at the base. I think these stiffer-growing roses have two main uses; to grow up high walls so that their blooms look in at the bedroom windows, while below we can plant something smaller to hide their nakedness; or to grow as lanky shrubs among the greater inmates at the back of large borders, with a stake or two to make them safe. I especially like the combination of a great Hybrid Tea flower growing mixed with a small-flowered rambler; the two different types of growth support one another. When fully established, the big wood of the climber would support some of the rambler's trails, while the latter, as the years go by, develops a thicket of growth and helps to bolster up the climber. Almost all pruning would be omitted, leaving the general effect to be enjoyed, rather than quality of bloom. Personally, in a large garden I like a *smother* of roses, a great mounding up of blossom and scent, contrasting in shape and size, using the stiff shrubby growers to provide solidity for a tangle of ramblers; it is all in keeping with summer's bounty.

It will be understood from what I have written that my favourite methods of growing climbing and rambling roses are not suitable for very small gardens. This should not, however, discourage owners of such from growing them; they will reap great enjoyment when their roses are trained over arches and along fences. A rose is always beautiful, anywhere.

8

Ramblers Derived from the Musk or Synstylae Section of the Genus Rosa

THE SYNSTYLAE: THE WILD RAMBLERS OF THE MUSK ROSE SECTION, AND A FEW CLOSE HYBRIDS

I know a bank where the wild thyme blows,
Where oxlips and the nodding violet grows,
Quite over-canopied with luscious woodbine,
With sweet musk-roses and with eglantine.

Shakespeare, *A Midsummer Night's Dream*

THE NAME MUSK crops up in many garden flowers, denoting a special scent supposed to be like that obtained from the male Musk Deer. The little Musk plant was a strain of *Mimulus moschatus* which ages ago developed this fragrance and which it has since lost. *Rosa moschata*, the Musk Rose,* is a noted member of the Synstylae Section and, in fact, many of the roses of this Section are so closely related in general appearance and in their sweet fragrance that they may well be termed collectively the Musk Roses, especially as another species, *R. arvensis,* is, I consider, the original English Musk Rose of the poets (see "The Mystery of the Musk Rose").

The roses of this Section grow wild in a chain of countries and districts across the Old World, extending from Madeira, North Africa and southern Europe, western Asia (*Rosa moschata* itself) to the Himalaya (*R. brunonii*) through western and central China (*R. longicuspis, R. mulliganii, R. helenae,* etc.), to Japan and Korea (*R. multiflora*), while *R. setigera* is the sole representative in the New World. (Details of this last species will be found in Chapter 5.) Except for poor forms of *R. multiflora* and its sport *watsoniana,* all are of considerable beauty, some superlatively so.

All wild species of roses are best classed as shrubs except those enumerated in this part of the book, and it so happens that practically all the roses of our gardens—and particularly the ramblers—owe all or part of their ancestry to the species in this botanical Section, the Synstylae (if one is ready to accept that *Rosa phoenicea* is a parent of the Damask Roses). The term at once indicates their botanical character—their speciality of having their little bunch of styles in the very centre of each flower tightly aggregated into a brief column, not spread out as in other species. (The Old Roses sometimes have a green pointel in the centre, but this is quite a different phenomenon.)

---

* Quite distinct from *Rosa centifolia muscosa,* the Moss Rose—all very confusing to the novice.

208

Though the Section as a whole is so distinct, its members are not so easily separated. If I wanted to give someone a life-task, I would assign to him the botanical unravelling of these roses; I would ask a good friend to do it, for the fragrance and beauty of these Musk Roses are unsurpassed, and would be a wonderful companionship for full enjoyment over the years. The task would consist of importing plants or seeds of these roses from their native countries, and from as many districts in those countries as they are to be found; to grow them for some years to maturity in a warm and sunny field, and to write us a new botanical key to the Section. On the completion of this task, he should then be able to decide to what species belong all the numerous roses that masquerade in our gardens under the specific names contained in this Section.

I must confess I find them more confusing and difficult to name than all the other species and, being mostly such large plants, they are seldom seen about the country; moreover, they germinate well from seeds and hybridize very easily in cultivation; many hybrids are found in gardens. Only by fresh importation and study can we be certain, I think, of correct identification. While some of the species, i.e., *Rosa setigera*, *R. soulieana*, *R. arvensis*, *R. sempervirens*, and *R. sinowilsonii*, are readily recognizable, many of the others seem to merge into one another. There are several more closely related species enumerated in botanical books: as they are rare and obscure and not seen in gardens, I have omitted them; among others they include *R. maximowicziana*, *R. leschenaultiana*, *R. glomerata*, and *R. crocacantha*. These four are natives of the Far East.

The descriptions in botanical works are based on the original specimen—usually in a herbarium—collected by the discoverer. The plants we grow in our gardens may have been propagated vegetatively from first or second or later generations of seed, and may be more or less hybridized. The resulting plants will grow quite differently in varying soils and conditions, and the particular plants we know under various established names may be different from those grown in another country. Be this as it may, the plants I grow and describe are all distinct horticulturally; all have been propagated vegetatively from established specimens, and these clones have been widely distributed.

All of the species in this Section, then, are ramblers achieving anything up to 40 feet with support—some only 12 feet, perhaps—with clusters of flowers borne rambler-fashion on short shoots all along last year's long summer growths; the flowers are single, with five petals only, creamy white with yellow stamens and a delicious fragrance; the only exceptions in colour are *Rosa setigera* and *R. multiflora*, and the plant known as 'Betty Sherriff'. All normally have seven leaflets. *Rosa soulieana* and *R. setigera* are shrubby in growth rather than climbers, and accordingly I included them in Chapter 5; they are, however, excellent when allowed to clamber through and over bushes, low trees, and hedgerows. The remainder need much space and are unsuitable for small gardens. Those who look for less rampageous ramblers with equally fragrant single flowers and the "wild" look, should choose 'Kew Rambler' and 'Francis E. Lester'.

Taking the smallest first, there is little *Rosa watsoniana*, which is more of a curiosity than a plant of garden value. The next least vigorous of those in the present chapter are *R. multiflora* and *R. wichuraiana*. The former has rather small flowers but an unforgettable scent; in addition it has value in other ways which I will mention under its own heading later in this section. *Rosa wichuraiana* is a most valuable plant for many purposes, for ground-cover on banks and borders, or as a dense rambler, and it does not flower until summer is well advanced and the eucryphias are in flower. *Rosa luciae* is closely related, or synonymous.

Some of middle strength are *Rosa helenae*, *R. henryi*, *R. longicuspis*, *R. mulliganii*, and *R. sinowilsonii*, together with a few hybrids such as 'Wedding Day' and 'Polyantha Grandiflora'. We can expect all these except one to climb at least 25 feet; *R. sinowilsonii* is somewhat of an exception as it is not really hardy in England and needs the shelter of a wall, where its magnificent foliage, the best provided by any rose, will create more beauty than its flowers. The Old Musk Rose *R. moschata* is probably all the better for a wall also. This leaves us with *R. brunonii*, *R. rubus*, and *R. filipes*, all achieving 40 feet in favourable conditions. *Rosa sempervirens* and *R. arvensis* are not normally grown in our gardens, but I have included them as they are ancestors of some garden ramblers.

Some of these great roses may be seen smothering small trees in certain gardens, as at Kiftsgate Court, Gloucestershire; at Highdown, Sussex, they have even seeded themselves in the chalk cliff, and give visitors an excellent example of their use in a bold way in the landscape; many are trained up trees at Knightshayes Court in Devon, and at Sissinghurst Castle in Kent and Hidcote Manor in Gloucestershire.

In his book *On the Eaves of the World*, Vol. 2, Reginald Farrer gives a description of one of these musk roses growing wild in Kansu, western China. We do not turn instinctively to Farrer for information on roses, but his pen is one of the very few that can give us a real picture of the prolificity and all-pervading fragrance of these roses. He writes of *Rosa filipes* ('Barley Bee' is his adaptation of the name of the local village):

> In June Barley Bee has yet a further attraction, for all its hedges are filled with a gigantic rambler rose, which casts abroad twelve-foot slender sprays (beset with rare but very vigorous and ferocious thorns), which in their second season are bowed into arches by the weight, all along their length, of huge loose bunches of snow-white blossom unfolding from buds of nankeen yellow; and carrying on their glory far into the early winter in showers of round berries, finer than the finest mountain ash, that ripen of a rich orange and develop to soft crimson-scarlet with a delicate, faint bloom. But this is not its chief merit when it submerges Barley Bee in a surf of snow, for now the scent is so keen and entrancing that all the air quivers with the intoxicating deliciousness of it for half a mile round the village in every direction, and the toils of the climb ended sweetly indeed, as I lay out upon the flat roof through the soft summer dusk and dark, lapped in waves of that warm fragrance, staring up to where the dim bulk of the mountain overhead again and again leapt into a vivider darkness, with the wide flares of sheet-lightning flickering out behind. . . .

This is not as fanciful as it sounds. If any English village had a dozen plants of *Rosa filipes* growing over its barns and hedgerows, an equally all-pervading fragrance would hang in the air.

Looked at historically, some natives of the Old World have been in cultivation a long time. *Rosa moschata* is recorded in books from the sixteenth century onwards; *R. arvensis* is a native of Britain and gave rise to the Ayrshire roses, dating from the early nineteenth century. *Rosa sempervirens* was mentioned first in the seventeenth century, and has given rise to a few hybrids also. *Rosa brunonii* reached us in 1822, while *R. multiflora* arrived from eastern Asia in 1862; from this species stem all the early ramblers like 'Crimson Rambler', 'Goldfinch', and 'Blush Rambler'. The other most potent species, *R. wichuraiana*, which provided the hybrids of the 'Dorothy Perkins' clan and, intermarrying with the Tea Roses, the far superior strain modelled on 'Albéric Barbier', arrived with *R. soulieana* just before the turn of the century.

With the great plant collectors busy in China during the first two decades of our century, a flow of new species arrived: *Rosa sinowilsonii, R. helenae, R. rubus, R. filipes, R. longicuspis, R. mulliganii*, and others.

It is believed that, prior to all of this, in days before history started—perhaps aided by man, who may have grown them together and was thus instrumental in the exchange of pollen—*Rosa phoenicea* from Asia Minor and the old original *R. moschata* of Herrmann, from south Europe and North Africa, were ancestors of the Summer and Autumn Damask roses. The old *R. moschata* enters our strains again through the Noisettes, and perhaps, together with *R. multiflora*, through the Hybrid Musks. This last species is also a parent of the Dwarf Polyanthas, and thus through to the Floribundas and our newest roses. The older species of the Synstylae therefore have played a considerable part in the production of garden roses through the centuries, and it remains to be seen what effect the comparatively new introductions will have.

arvensis. A native of Britain and Europe, rare in Scotland, and a characteristic of many of our hedgerows, where it flowers rather later than the Dog Brier, *Rosa canina*, in the hotter weather of July. Then its creamy, wide-open flowers with their rich yellow stamens are most welcome, as the grasses fade and we reach high summer. It is *very fragrant*, the flowers being borne in small clusters along the lengthy, trailing branches. In their first year these branches are sparsely leaved and of purplish hue, and this tone together with the dark leaves and creamy flowers puts it into a class of its own. (Plate 131.) The fruits are oval or rounded, bright red. It is not to be recommended for any but the wildest of gardens, for it makes long, unmanageable trails, eventually creating a dense thicket, but its influence may be sought among the so-called Ayrshire Roses, of which a few linger in old gardens. For these please see the section "Old and New Garden Ramblers," and for its possible connection with the Musk Rose see "The Mystery of the Musk Rose."

> Then will I raise aloft the milk-white Rose,
> With whose sweet smell the air shall be perfumed.
>> Shakespeare, *2 Henry VI*

Redouté, Vol. I, Plate 89.

Andrews, Plates I and 2. White and pink forms. Unnatural. Plate 3. Double pink Ayrshire.

Willmott, Plate 11. Excellent.

Lawrance, Plate 86. The White Dog Rose. Poor.

Botanical Magazine, t.2054. The figure is of *Rosa arvensis*, and hence the editor's inability to distinguish the Ayrshires from *R. arvensis*.

Journal des Roses, Décembre 1907. 'Thoresbyana', a double white Ayrshire.

Sowerby, Vol. 3, Plate 476.

The Garden, Vol. 56, page 233. A good monochrome photograph of a spray and also a plant in full flower.

Jekyll, photograph of a plant in full flower, facing page 30.

Hybridized with a China rose, *Rosa arvensis* gave *R. ruga*. This was a beautiful rose, according to illustrations, but I have found it to be scentless.

Botanical Register, t.1389.

Willmott, Plate 55.

brunonii. The Himalayan Musk Rose. It is a native of the Himalaya and, according to Miss Willmott, is found from Afghanistan to Kashmir, Simla, Garhwal, Kumaon, and Nepal. It flowered in this country in 1823 and was originally classed as a variety of *Rosa moschata*, *R. m. nepalensis*. It is a very vigorous species with big hooked prickles, sending canes over a building or into trees up to 30 or 40 feet. The leaves are greyish, downy, of extreme drooping elegance, with narrow leaflets. The flowers are borne on downy stalks in a rather tight and inelegant corymb. The heps small, oval. Heavy fragrance. Apt to suffer in cold winters. (Drawing 13.)

This rose could not be confused with *Rosa moschata* of Miller and Herrmann, and I am at a loss to know why there should ever have been any doubt as to its identity. The picture became confused in later years, and today the old *R. moschata* is practically unknown, its place having been taken by the Himalayan Musk Roses. (See under *R. moschata*.)
Willmott, Plate 37.
Andrews, Plate 82. *Rosa napaulensis*. Possibly incorrect, as the prickles shown are straight instead of hooked.
Botanical Magazine, t.4030.
Botanical Register, Vol. 10, Plate 829. *Rosa moschata nepalensis*, the Nepal Musk Rose. The information given is controversial.
Flore des Serres, Vol. 4, Plate 366. Reverse of plate in *Botanical Magazine*.

—**'La Mortola'**. 1954. A particularly fine form of *Rosa brunonii*, which was brought by E. A. Bunyard from the famous garden whose name it bears; I secured it from Kiftsgate Court, Gloucestershire, where Mrs J. B. Muir had planted it, and introduced it, with her permission, under this name. Over a wall and outbuilding at Kiftsgate it made a splendid mound some 30 feet high by 40 feet across. Foliage long, limp, greyish, and downy; large pure white flowers in good clusters, the petals having distinctly mucronate apices; medium-sized oval heps. Richly fragrant. Apt to suffer in cold winters. Unquestionably the most ornamental of the *brunonii* group. (Plate 125.)

cerasocarpa. Introduced in 1914. Discovered by Augustine Henry in the district near Ichang, central China, where also grows *Rosa chinensis*. Long, pointed, rather leathery leaves and panicles of small white fragrant flowers borne on markedly glandular pedicels. Globose fruit, dark red. I have not grown this.
Botanical Magazine, t.8688. Shows attractive flowers.

filipes. Western China. Introduced in 1908. Though seldom seen in gardens, this species should take a high place. The only form that I have grown or seen is one secured, probably from the Roseraie de l'Haÿ, by E. A. Bunyard, but I have found no record of it in his writings. A plant was purchased from him by Mrs Muir about 1938, and still grows strongly at Kiftsgate Court. It makes shoots 20 feet long in a season, is about 100 feet wide and is steadily invading bushes and trees within reach, including a Copper Beech, in which it has achieved a height of about 50 feet. I have heard of another old plant of this growing in Yorkshire. The young shoots are richly tinted with brown and copper, and the leaves are of light green with 5 to 7 leaflets. When in flower or fruit it is a most astonishing sight: the corymbs of blossom may be 18 inches across, composed of a hundred or more small, cupped, creamy white flowers with yellow stamens, borne on thread-like stalks. These slender stalks give it the name of 'filipes'. Small oval heps. Its fragrance is equally remarkable, and it is undoubtedly a very fine type, which should be grown wherever space can be given to it.

This particular form is being distributed by nurseries as 'Kiftsgate', thus distinguishing it from other possibly inferior forms of *Rosa filipes*, and also drawing attention to the garden where it thrives so well. Together with *R. mulliganii* it flowers rather later than most in this group, often remaining in beauty until late July in the south of England. It takes some years to become established, and disappoints the impatient; for them I recommend *R. mulliganii*, but for those who garden on good soil in a reasonably sheltered area, I should choose 'Kiftsgate' provided there is room for it. (Plate 126; Drawing 16.)

Botanical Magazine, t.8894. A plate and description of the wild species. The Kiftsgate rose appears to be very near if not identical.

Beales, page 256.

helenae. Central China, whence it was introduced in 1907. Reaching 15 or 20 feet, this is another of the big scrambling roses for growing over hedgerows and trees; its main characters, to distinguish it from its relatives, are the strong hooked prickles, and leaves having 7 to 9 leaflets pubescent beneath, or at least on the veins. The flowers are creamy white, borne in a fairly regular, round-topped, umbel-like corymb. The dark green of the leaves shows up the flowers to great advantage, and it is as fragrant as any. It is spectacular when in bloom, as the flowers are in dense snowball-like heads, and is a plant of extraordinary beauty in fruit, the closely held bunches of small, oval heps being conspicuous at a distance. Though the flowers are held aloft, the fruits droop in graceful bunches from their own weight, and are extremely attractive in late autumn.

Hu, Vol. 2, t.77. A line drawing.

R.H.S. *Journal*, Vol. 47, Plate 195. (Monochrome photograph.)

Phillips and Rix, Plate 36.

Le Rougetel, page 146.

henryi. Central and eastern China. Introduced in 1907. Introduced in 1907. Bears some resemblance to *Rosa helenae*, but has glabrous leaves and orbicular fruits. For many years I have grown what was given to me as *R. gentiliana* (*R. henryi*) and distributed it, but on examination my plant proved to be the hybrid 'Polyantha Grandiflora', q.v. under *R. phoenicea*.

Lancaster, page 396.

longicuspis. Prior to 1915. Sometimes considered synonymous with *Rosa sinowilsonii* and *R. lucens*. For many years I have been guilty of distributing a plant under this name which was in reality *R. mulliganii*. *Rosa longicuspis* has leaves nearly as large as those of *R. sinowilsonii*. A useful late-flowering species, bearing large heps. *Rosa lucens* has particularly shining dark leaves and a more shrubby growth. It grows at Mount Stewart, Northern Ireland.

moschata. The Musk Rose. Its native countries are variously given as Madeira, North Africa (Barbary), Spain, and southern Europe to western Asia, and it is supposed to have been brought to England in the early years of the first Elizabethan Age, as recorded by Hakluyt. Its name was recorded by Bauhin in 1671, and it was described by Herrmann in 1762 and by Miller in 1768. It grows to about 12 feet, has glabrous leaves, oval rather than elliptic, with downy stalks and downy veins on the reverse, and downy flower stems and calyx. The flowers are borne in branching heads, cream, single, the petals reflexing often by noon on the day of opening, deliciously fragrant (of Musk), and *are not produced until late summer*, carrying on until autumn. Thus it is an outstanding and valuable garden plant, and as a progenitor of our garden roses and for further hybridizing it is noteworthy. Redouté records that it was used for distilling perfumes in Tunis. Miller records that it "varies with double flowers." (Plates 129, 130; Drawing 14.)

Andrews, Plate 93. A good portrait.

Lawrance, Plate 64. The Single Musk Rose. Not unrecognizable.

Redouté, Vol. I, Plate 33. Good.

Gibson, Plate 1.

As I recount in the next section, "The Mystery of the Musk Rose," this rose became almost extinct, its place in botanic gardens having been taken by a well-known species, *Rosa brunonii*, q.v. This *R. brunonii* has been widely distributed by nurseries, and is a spectacular garden plant.

This plant has greenish brown young wood, nearly straight prickles, limp, long, attenuated leaves, glabrous above, downy on the midrib below, somewhat purplish when young but turning to grey-green or light green later, with 5 to 7 leaflets. Flowers usually in corymbs of about seven, 2 inches wide, followed by small oval heps. The scent is powerful and delicious, particularly in the evening, and carries well in the air. The colour of the leaves and the white of the flowers gives a cool, fresh appearance to this rose, which is lacking in others of the Section, excepting *Rosa soulieana*. Its lightness makes it particularly suitable for growing over yew or holly trees, or other shrubs of dark colouring. It should be given full sunshine and a position somewhat sheltered from cold winds, as its long summer growths continue to grow until the autumn, and are sometimes spoiled by winter frosts.

Willmott, Plate 33. This portrait has the general appearance of the old *Rosa moschata* of
　　Herrmann, but lacks the reflexing petals and the oval leaves.

—'Plena'. *Rosa moschata semi-plena, R. m. minor flore pleno.* This, the "Coroneola that beareth in Autume" of Parkinson's *Theatrum Botanicum*, is recorded by many old writers as indistinguishable from the single type, except by its extra petals; Herrmann states that it also differs from the type in not having semi-pinnate calyces; Thory, not quite so strong-growing and with smaller prickles; Andrews, that it is a sport occasionally produced by the single type. As recorded in the next section, my double form occurred on one-year-old plants propagated from the old type plant at Myddelton House, Enfield, Middlesex, which had produced only five-petalled flowers during the previous season. I am satisfied that this present sport, if such it be, is identical with the Redouté drawing.

Thory in Redouté describes it as a native of Indostan. He records as historical fact a legend found in many books, that the Mogul Princess Nur Jehan was the first to notice an oily substance floating on a stream of rose-water which had been made to flow through the royal garden at a time of fête, and from this discovery started the industry of extracting attar or otto of roses. By attributing this discovery to *Rosa moschata plena* Thory poses a query: Had this rose been introduced from Europe to Kashmir and was it grown commercially to produce rose-water in copious quantity, or should we understand that *R. brunonii* was used, a native of northern India?

Redouté, Vol. I, Plate 99. *Rosa moschata flore semi-plena*. A superlatively beautiful and accurate portrait of the Double Musk Rose, showing the characteristic reflexing of the petals, which is not shown in the following drawings.

Andrews, Plate 94. The Double Musk Rose. A good drawing, but flowers are not characteristic.

Lawrance, Plate 53. The Double Musk Rose. Poor.

Jacquin, *Horti Schönbrunnensis*. Exaggerated.

Roessig, Plate 27. Le Rosier Musqué. A semi-double form, described as *Rosa corymbifera alba hispanica*—a doubtful and confusing appellation. A poor drawing.

—'**Nastarana'**. *Rosa pissartii*. A geographical form of *R. moschata* Herrmann, reputedly introduced from Persia in 1879, and always described as more vigorous than *R. moschata*. The plate in Willmott's *The Genus Rosa* shows a semi-double form, although I have found no mention of this doubling elsewhere. I have not seen this rose.

Willmott, Plate 39. Semi-double. Highly doubtful.

Revue Horticole, 1880, pages 314, 315. Line drawing and account, showing a single-flowered rose.

—'**Princesse de Nassau'**. This came to me from Daisy Hill Nursery, labelled *Rosa moschata* 'Autumnalis', a name which occurs in their catalogue of 1912, but is not in any book that I have consulted. It is strange that it is so little known, for it is a pretty plant, with a few hooked prickles and light yellowish-green small leaves, limp and matt, and does not flower until August, carrying on until the autumn. Dainty sprays of small semi-double blossoms on softly downy stalks; silky petals, deep creamy buff on opening from pink-tinted yellowish buds, fading to cream, with yellow stamens and a delicious fragrance. It is apt to be damaged in hard winters and should be given the shelter of a wall. The thornless branchlets proceed in zigzag fashion from leaf to leaf. Possibly a Noisette of very early origin, such as 'Muscate Perpetuelle', although I incline more and more to the likelihood that this rose is really Mrs Gore's 'Princesse de Nassau' of 1897, see my notes in the Royal National Rose Society's *Annual* for 1983. (Drawing 20.)

mulliganii. Introduced from western China in 1917–19. A beautiful rose similar to *Rosa rubus, R. longicuspis*, and others, equally fragrant and floriferous. Like the Kiftsgate *R. filipes*, this species flowers after most of these Musk Roses are over, and is therefore doubly valuable. Its young shoots are reddish, becoming green, extremely vigorous, reaching 20 feet in length in one season, with hooked prickles and bearing, rather sparsely, dark green glossy, leathery leaves with 7 leaflets. Like all these roses, in the second year the flower shoots appear in every leaf axil, bearing in this species large open corymbs containing up to one hundred and fifty blooms on the principal shoots. The flowers are deep cream in bud opening to milk-white, with conspicuous yellow stamens and a glorious fragrance of bananas. A very satisfactory garden rose, often growing well where 'Kiftsgate' will not thrive. Abundant small heps. 25 feet. (Plate 127; Drawing 15.)

multiflora. *Rosa polyantha, R. multiflora thunbergiana*. Japan, Korea. Recorded by Plukenet in 1696 and introduced in 1862, this species has had a profound influence on garden roses in many ways. Though I had known it as a stock for nursery budding for many years, my first real acquaintance with it as a garden plant was at Nymans, Sussex, where it had been allowed to grow naturally, arching its smooth long stems over the path, and bearing freely the narrow somewhat pubescent leaves with, usually, 9 leaflets and pyramid-shaped trusses of tiny blooms which are so well known throughout the old Rambler group of roses, of which it was the main ancestor. The flowers are single, creamy fading to white, with bright yellow stamens and a powerful fruity fragrance, which is carried freely in the air. It can best be described as an arching shrub, although its shoots will ramble into trees as high as 20 feet. Normally it makes a dense thicket of interlacing lax shoots, much like a blackberry. So dense is it, indeed, that when planted closely as a hedge it is rabbit-proof, and so thickly do its stems grow that it is becoming increasingly popular in the United States and also in Britain as a roadside plant, for its resilient thicket can hold a car which runs off the road. What a use for a rose! On the other hand, how lucky we are to be able to provide so pretty and sweet a shrub for such a use. It is claimed in America that it is "horse high, bull strong and goat tight," and Roy Shepherd records that over five hundred miles have been planted in Ohio alone. It is not a greedy shrub; it is a haven for wild life, prevents erosion, holds embankments, and serves as a windbreak or snow-fence.

After the clusters of flowers are over in July, the heps develop, reaching maturity in late summer, and lasting through the autumn into winter. They are about the size of a small pea, bright red, very dainty, and most useful for cutting. The long arching sprays may be cut in flower or fruit without damaging the plant, just as one may cut any rambler, thus encouraging fresh strong growth which will flower in later years. There are few easier roses for growing in semi-wild parts of the garden, and certainly nothing cheaper. If interspersed with something more flamboyant, like *Rosa* 'Highdownensis' or *R. moyesii*, a hedge of interest for a very long period will be achieved, with crops of flowers and fruit of the respective plants alternating through summer and autumn.

It is very often seen in gardens without the owner having any idea of its identity, except that they know it is an understock which has remained at the expense of its scion; and of course it is utterly unsuited for a rose bed. The forms known as *Rosa multiflora japonica* (prickly) and *R. m.* 'Simplex' (prickle-less) are those used most often as understocks for budding, and differ but little from a horticultural point of view; either will make a charming plant, but both are rather small-flowered. Another understock, 'Cress and Danieli', is undoubtedly the best of all forms to grow for its beauty. The flowers, trusses, and foliage are all of a high order. It was raised in the United States.
Willmott, Plate 23. Excellent.
Step, Vol. 2, Plate 79.
Botanical Magazine, t.7119.

Yet another understock, known as *Rosa multiflora* 'de la Grifferaie', is also sometimes used for budding, and as a consequence it is also often seen in gardens, having outlived its scion. See Chapter 6, "Shrub Roses of the Twentieth Century." It is lusty, vigorous, prolific, and highly scented—qualities which will ensure its remaining in cultivation long after it has been completely given up as an understock. I have been unable to trace its origin; it may not be related to *R. multiflora,* in spite of its name, but possibly connected with *R. setigera.*
Jamain et Forney, Plate 52. Poor.
Leroy, Plate 2. Excellent.

—'**Carnea**'. A double form of *Rosa multiflora* 'Cathayensis', which I have not seen but which was introduced in 1804 and was a favourite for many years.

Botanical Magazine, t.1059. Poor.

Redouté, Vol. 2, Plate 67. Exquisite.

Roses et Rosiers, Plate 41. A poor copy of part of the Redouté portrait.

Duhamel, Vol. 7, Plate 17.

Drapiez, Vol. 2, Plate 113. Poor.

Reeves, Vol. 2, Plate 38 possibly refers.

—'**Cathayensis**'. A variant with single pink flowers which was brought from China in 1907. Like its type-species it is vigorous and thrifty, and these characters together with its scent might keep it in cultivation. White flowers, blush-tipped; downy-backed leaves of dull blue-green, rather coarse and reminiscent of 'Seven Sisters'.

Journal des Roses, Juin 1886. Nos. 3 and 4 may apply.

Hu, t.76. A pen drawing.

Lancaster, page 388.

—'**Nana**'. I have found no record of its origin, but it is available from seedsmen as *Rosa multi-flora polyantha* or *R. carteri*, flowering in two months or so from date of sowing the seeds. A pretty, dwarf, bushy mutant or hybrid, not climbing, bearing sprays of palest pink or creamy-white single blooms all the growing season, followed by tiny red heps. The white is usually taller than the pink; both are sweetly scented.

—'**Platyphylla**'. 'Seven Sisters Rose'. *Rosa cathayensis platyphylla.* A double pink rose introduced by Sir Charles Greville from Japan between 1815 and 1817, and probably a hybrid of *R. multiflora*, of which it is not likely to be a chimerical sport on account of its fringed stipules. In the days when there were no coloured ramblers it was highly prized, and it is still grown on account of its origin, floriferousness, vigour, and charm of colouring. Its very name re-calls its supposedly 7 flowers in the truss (usually many more), each of a different tint ac-cording to age; they open a bright deep cerise-purple, and fade to palest mauve or ivory white before dropping. Large, broad, light green leaves. It is somewhat fragrant, in the *R. multiflora* tradition, but with an admixture of the "fresh-apple" fragrance of *R. wichuraiana*. Although a vigorous plant achieving 18 feet in a season, its canes sometimes suffer from early autumn frost, and it does best in full sun on a wall. It shows affinity with 'Crimson Rambler'. The name 'Seven Sisters' is sometimes erroneously given to 'Félicité Perpétue'. Like all Multifloras, it roots easily from cuttings.

Journal des Roses, Juillet 1886. A Japanese portrait, but too bright a colour and not showing the normal variation.

Botanical Register, Vol. 16, Plate 1372. Shows the varying colour well.

Redouté, Vol. 2, Plate 69. Flowers not typical.

—'**Watsoniana**'. This strange little rose can scarcely be considered as an ornament for gar-dens, rather as a curiosity. It carries very narrow leaflets, almost linear and spotted and marbled with grey, on its trailing or arching stems, and makes a plant rather like a weak *Rosa multiflora*, of which it is counted a chimerical mutant or sport. Small flowers, single, pale pink, and round red fruits seldom containing fertile seeds. It was first recorded from a garden near New York in 1870, but is also grown in Japanese gardens, and is therefore probably a Japanese cultivar.

Willmott, t.53. An admirable portrait.

phoenicea. Turkey, Syria. Tiny flowers and a rambling habit like that of *Rosa multiflora.* Its only claim to fame horticulturally is that it is thought to be a parent of the Damask Rose. It is not hardy in Surrey.

rubus (*Rosa ernestii*). Central and western China. Like *R. helenae,* to which it is closely related, it was introduced in 1907 and is even stronger-growing, with large hooked prickles; leaflets usually 5, more or less pubescent beneath, and flowers 1½ inches across, in dense heads. The buds are often pinkish in colour, deep cream when open with a suffusion of orange-yellow towards the base of the petals. As the stamens are of orange, a freshly open spray gives a richer colour effect than other roses in the Section. Powerful *multiflora* fragrance. Early-flowering in this Section. Small oval heps. 30 feet.

There are two fairly distinct types of *Rosa rubus* in cultivation, one quite glabrous and the other downy. According to the latest classification, they should be distinguished as *R. rubus rubus* (*R. rubus velutescens*) for the original downy type, while the glabrous form, which is the superior garden plant described above, should be called *R. rubus nudescens* (*R. rubus*). *Rosa rubus velutescens* has long-pointed leaves and a short flowering period.

Willmott, Plate 507. Line drawing.

sempervirens. From southern Europe and North Africa, this rose is seldom seen in our gardens, being somewhat tender, nearly evergreen, white-flowered, and only slightly fragrant. Leaflets 5 to 7. Its evergreen character has been transmitted to a race of old ramblers of which we still find in gardens 'Félicité Perpétue', 'Spectabilis', and 'Adélaïde d'Orléans' (see this chapter, "Old and New Garden Ramblers"). They are freely pictured in *Roses for English Gardens* by Gertrude Jekyll. Supposedly a parent of the Ayrshire Roses.

Redouté, Vol. 2, Plate 15.

Redouté, Vol. 2, Plate 49. *Rosa sempervirens latifolia.*

Roessig, Plate 32, Rose toujours verte. *Rosa sempervirens.*

Willmott, Plate 5.

Andrews, Plate 89.

Lawrance, Plate 45. Good.

Botanical Register, Vol. 6, Plate 465.

Duhamel, Vol. 3, Plate 13. Poor.

setigera. The Prairie Rose of the eastern United States. A shrubby species which I have described in Chapter 5. Being of considerable hardiness it was used by breeders, notably Horvath in the United States, in an effort to obtain hardy climbing roses for cold districts, but they are mostly insufficiently distinct to be popular for the British climate. I have grown 'Doubloons' (a good yellow), 'Jean Lafitte', and 'Long John Silver'; Komlosy has illustrations of two older hybrids, 'Beauty of the Prairies' and 'Queen of the Prairies'; to these may be added 'Baltimore Belle'. 'American Pillar' also has *Rosa setigera* in its parentage.

Willmott, Plate 71. The colour is far too near to salmon, and shows none of the mauve tinting of the original.

Meehan's Monthly, Vol. 8, Plate 5. Poor.

Redouté, Vol. 3, Plate 71. *Rosa rubifolia.* This is not recognizable.

sinowilsonii. Western China. Considerable confusion surrounds the botanical status of this rose and *Rosa longicuspis*. They have been considered synonymous, but as grown at Kew, at Bodnant in Wales, and at Wakehurst and Borde Hill, Sussex, *R. sinowilsonii* is quite distinct from any other rose I have seen. The plant is most conspicuous in the summer on account of its shining red-brown angled shoots, prickles of the same colour, and the seven broad but long-pointed leaflets, deeply veined and corrugated and coarsely toothed, of lustrous dark green above while beneath they are of glossy, rich, purplish red-brown. The flowers are white, borne several together, but not in the first rank of beauty. *No rose is so handsome in leaf,* and it would be worth a place on any warm sunny wall for this character alone; it is not particularly hardy, and will only otherwise thrive in sheltered gardens. Introduced in 1904.

soulieana. A Chinese species with greyish leaves and white flowers, and bushy growth. Described in Chapter 5, as it is more of a shrub than a climber—though it can produce shoots 12 to 15 feet long in a season when established.
Willmott, Plate 57.
Botanical Magazine, t.8158. Too yellow.

wichuraiana. *Rosa luciae* of some authors, also *R. luciae* var. *wichuraiana*. According to the latest taxonomic ruling, if one considers the two species as synonymous the name *luciae* takes priority; but because *wichuraiana* is so well known, it will be simplest to continue using it in the following pages. This trailing evergreen rose has had great influence on rose-breeding during this century but as a species it has remained in obscurity, usually being found only in botanic gardens in this country. It was introduced in 1891 from Japan, but is also found wild in Korea, Formosa, and eastern China. Known as the 'Memorial Rose' in the United States, owing to its use in cemeteries.

It lies prostrate on the ground, which it covers with trailing stems, rooting as they grow, and bears numerous small, shining, dark green leaves, with 7 to 9 blunt-ended leaflets. These make a splendid ground-cover and background to the clusters of flowers, which are small, single, white with rich yellow stamens, borne in small pyramid-shaped clusters, very sweetly scented, and do not appear until late summer, usually in August. The flower branches bear 3-lobed leaves and numerous bracts. Tiny heps follow. It can of course be trained upright on supports, and its few hooked prickles help it to scramble through bushes and trees up to 15 feet or so, after which, if left to itself, it will form cascades of trailing shoots. (Plate 128; Drawing 17.)

During decades when roses were judged only for the size and brilliance of their flowers, it is remarkable that this insignificant plant was ever deemed worthy for hybridization. But today, when a new appreciation of plants—as opposed to flowers—is developing, it is obvious that this species is one of very great garden value. For instance, it is most unusual to be able to number a rose among first-class ground-covering plants, and especially an *evergreen* rose. Then again, few roses are at their best in August. I know only three others that do not actually start to flower until that month, and those are *Rosa moschata*, 'Aimée Vibert', and 'Princesse de Nassau'. The scent of *R. wichuraiana* is delicious.

Conspicuous among descendants of this rose are the rambling roses of the 'Dorothy Perkins' and the 'Albéric Barbier' groups, and *Rosa wichuraiana* has a further claim to fame,

having been one of the parents of the new tetraploid species *R. kordesii.*
Revue Horticole, 1898, pages 105, 106. Line drawings.
Willmott, Plate 19. Very good.
Botanical Magazine, t.7421 (*Rosa luciae*). Exaggerated.
Journal des Roses, Mai 1902. Poor.
Jekyll, facing page 7 (photograph), as a ground-cover.
Phillips and Rix, page 35.

—'**Variegata**'. I have been unable to trace the origin of this pretty little plant. So far it has
not flowered with me, and it is very much less vigorous than the species. The shoots of
my plants have not exceeded 3 feet. The dainty leaves and the growing stems show much
creamy variegation, some extremes of the branches being wholly without green colouring,
and the growing tips and unfolding leaves are often coral-pink. Delightful for cutting, but
hardly a good garden plant, and requires a sheltered position with a little shade at the hottest time of the day.

THE MYSTERY OF THE MUSK ROSE

I saw the sweetest flower wild nature yields,
A fresh blown musk-Rose 'twas the first that threw
Its sweets upon the summer; graceful it grew
As in the wand that Queen Titania wields
And, as I feasted on its fragrance,
I thought the garden rose it much excelled.

John Keats, 1795–1821

WHEN I BEGAN to study the Synstylae Section, I had no idea that there was any real mystery
about the identity of the Musk Rose, *Rosa moschata.* I had always accepted that the great rose
which used to achieve some 40 feet on the pine stems in the University Botanic Garden at
Cambridge, and the old giant of the rose dell in the Royal Botanic Garden at Kew, were, both
of them, *R. moschata,* THE Musk Rose, described in all the books and a well recognized and
noted ancestor of the Damask and Noisette races of roses. But this Musk Rose is a summer-
flowering rose with long narrow leaves; one great crop of bloom and all is over: the Musk
Rose of the ancient herbals was an autumn-flowering rose with oval leaves. Then there was
the difficulty of reconciling either of these to the native Musk Rose of Shakespeare, Keats,
and other poets. Lastly there was the indeterminate fragrance: What *was* musk, anyway? Why
should a rose smell of it, and why should the little musk plant (*Mimulus moschatus*) have lost
its scent?

As so often happens in trying to unravel horticultural problems, botanical niceties—
useful though they may be—were not of such value as the more outstanding characters of
the various roses concerned. Let me make it clear that we are concerned in this mystery with
no fewer than three distinct roses—one for Shakespeare, one for the herbalists, and one for
the botanic gardens. Though the first and last are identified, I doubt whether we shall ever
know the origin of the second.

Let us start with the English Musk of the poets. I think there is no doubt that both
Shakespeare and Keats described in their well-known lines (at the heads of the preceding section, and this one) a native rose, and, bearing everything in mind and allowing a little poetic

licence (not much is needed), I am sure their rose was *Rosa arvensis*. It is a native of this country, frequents copses and bosky hedgerows, flowers with the honeysuckle, and is deliciously fragrant. Shakespeare refers to a summer-flowering plant (not autumn-flowering), as does Bacon, mentioning specifically the month of July, which is the normal time of flowering for *R. arvensis* in the south of England. To me, this trailing rose with purplish stems, neat leaves, and clusters of creamy, scented flowers is as appealing and freshly delightful as *R. canina*, the Dog Brier, which flowers rather earlier and is by comparison a coarse prickly shrub.

Turning next to the herbalists' rose, the true (foreign) *Rosa moschata* of Elizabethan and Jacobean days did not flower until the late summer or autumn. John Gerard, in his *Herball* of 1597, says that "the Muske Rose flowereth in Autumn, or the fall of the leafe: the rest flower when the Damask and red Rose do." John Parkinson, in *Paradisi in Sole Paradisus Terrestris*, 1629, describes *R. moschata simplex* and *multiplex*:

> The Muske Rose, both single and double, rise up oftentimes to a very great height, that it overgroweth any arbour in a garden, or being set by an house side, to bee ten or twelve foote high, or more, but more especially the single kinde, with many green farre spread branches, armed with a few sharpe great thornes, as the wilder sorts of roses are, whereof these are accounted to be kindes, having small darke green leaves on them, not much bigger than the leaves of Eglantine: . . . the double bearing more double flowers, as if they were once or twice more double than the single, with yellow thrummes also in the middle, both of them of a very sweete and pleasing smell, resembling Muske.

He adds that the single and double do not flower until the end of the summer and autumn.

John Ray wrote the second volume of his *Historia plantarum* in 1688 and mentions *Rosa moschata minor*, the Musk Rose, growing to a height of 10 or 12 feet with leaves like those of *R. alba*, glabrous above, hairy beneath; also *R. moschata major*, a bigger plant flowering in June. This, he says, on account of its flowering time can scarcely be considered the true and genuine *R. moschata* species, which flowers not before the end of summer and the beginning of autumn.

Johannes Herrmann's *Dissertation inauguratis botanico medica de Rosa*, 1762, gives a full description in Latin of *Rosa moschata* and states that it flowers in autumn. Philip Miller produced the 8th edition of his *The Gardener's Dictionary* in 1768; he calls his Musk Rose *R. moschata*, with a synonym *R. moschata major*. The latter is a name used in a vague description by J. Bauhin in 1651 (*Historiae plantarum universalis*). Likewise Aiton, *Hortus Kewensis*, 1789; Jacquin, *Plantarum rariorum horti Schönbrunnensis*, 1797; we may go on, looking at Roessig, 1802–20; Andrews, 1805; Dumont de Courset, 1811; Redouté, 1817–24; and lastly at Loudon's *Hortus Britannicus*, 1830: all repeat the late season of flowering and, where such particulars are included, all state the oval leaf and the height roughly from 7 to 12 feet—sometimes not specifically given but compared with the Sweet Brier—and the native habitat is variously ascribed to Spain, Madeira, Barbary. Although many of the drawings are not recognizable and the descriptions are not careful in the oldest books, I think the above all amounts to a fairly clear picture of a Musk Rose imported from south-western Europe, North Africa, or Madeira, grown in gardens for its sweet scent and late-flowering character and being used to cover arbours or to make a fair-sized shrub. Apart from a few Autumn Damask roses this would have been the only rose to have flowered late in the season, and as such would have been greatly treasured. To this we must add that *R. moschata* in any form was the only rose that could be called "climbing" in those early days of gardening in Britain, for none of its Far East relatives had been introduced, and *R. phoenicea, R. arvensis,* and *R. sempervirens,* if cultivated, were of little value, though the second was well known in the hedgerows. It was therefore a very important garden plant, and was listed by nurserymen; W. Masters of Canterbury (1831) mentions the double form flowering in September and October, and William Paul (1848) writes of "abundant blooms, especially in the autumn"; Thomas Rivers (1843) includes *R. moschata* in his "autumnal rose garden." He adds some further details, stating that there was in the early days of the French Republic a rose tree at Ispahan (Iran), called "the Chinese Rose Tree, fifteen feet high . . . seeds were sent to Paris and produced the common Musk Rose . . . large and very old plants of the Musk Rose may sometimes be seen in the gardens of old English country houses." Other writers also mention this plant. Though it could have been a hybrid, it is more likely to have been the original Musk Rose.

It is here that the mystery makes itself so greatly felt. It will be noted that up to the present there has been no mention of a gigantic climbing rose whose shoots reach 30 to 50 feet, bearing long drooping leaves and a spectacular midsummer burst of large white fragrant blossoms, which is the type of rose commonly found in rose collections today under the name of *R. moschata.*

E. H. Wilson, the famous gardener, botanist, and plant collector, writes: "The original Musk rose, *Rosa moschata,* appears to have been native of the Pyrenees, but has long been lost to cultivation, and its name applied to a vigorous climbing rose (*R. brunonii*) . . . whose flowers have the odor of Musk." This I culled from his book *If I were to make a garden* (1931), prompted by Mrs F. L. Keays in her *Old Roses.* She gives us the American picture, and adds that the Musk Rose of Gerard "may survive in some old gardens"; further, "while *R. moschata* continues blooming until frosts cut it, after once started, *R. brunonii* is summer flowering only." Bailey's *Cyclopedia,* also American, mentions that "the Musk Rose of the older writers, known since the sixteenth century, seems to have at present almost disappeared from cultivation; the plant generally cultivated under this name is *R. brunonii* . . . ."

Rosa brunonii was introduced in 1812 from Nepal. It is quite obvious that under *R. moschata* Miss Willmott was describing *R. brunonii*—a native "from Afghanistan to Kashmir, Simla, Garhwal, Kumaon, and Nepal." From these extractions we can I think conclude that what I have called the gigantic climbing Musk Rose is a nearly glabrous form or hybrid of *R. brunonii.* Just when and where it originated and usurped the position of the Old Musk Rose is still a mystery to me. Willmott's portrait appears to be of this usurper, with its long drooping leaves.

I had looked at many gardening books in the hope of further elucidation, and also with the hope of finding a plant of this Old Musk. Almost the last book I looked at was *My Garden in Summer,* by E. A. Bowles, 1914. Here I found:

> The true and rare old Musk Rose exists here [Myddelton House, Enfield,
> north of London], but in a juvenile state at present, for it is not many years
> since I brought it as cuttings from the splendid old specimen on The Grange
> at Bitton, and I must not expect its deliciously scented, late-in-the-season
> flowers before it has scrambled up its wall space.

Now, whatever other opinions we might consider, I was prepared to treat Mr Bowles's with the greatest respect. He was an erudite, observant, and highly trained gardener; he had seen Canon Ellacombe's plant flowering late in the season, as he was a frequent visitor to that garden, and he would not have given just "its wall space" to an enormous grower such as *Rosa brunonii,* which would need the whole house.

I visited Myddelton House in late August 1963. And there on a cold north-west facing wall of the house was a rose just coming into flower. It was without doubt the Old Musk Rose. A pencil drawing of this plant is reproduced (Drawing 14).

Besides making a drawing of Bowles's Musk Rose, I pressed a specimen; both were compared with Herrmann's description and Linnaeus' specimens by my old friend Dr W. T. Stearn of the Botany Department of the British Museum, who pronounced them all one and the same. Both Herrmann and also Miller, whose names are used in various books as the authority for the naming of *Rosa moschata*, take the species' name from prior publication by Caspar Bauhin, 1671. So far, so good.

The propagating material secured in 1963 was used partly for budding on brier stocks and partly for cuttings. The latter did not flower in their first summer under my care, but the three budded plants produced several flower heads, and judge of my surprise when every bloom turned out to be double! Here was a further puzzle: had I by chance used a twig for budding which during its year of growth had sported to the double form, or was the plant given to producing single and double blooms irregularly but constantly? John Rogers, head gardener since Mr Bowles's day at Myddelton House, assured me he had seen only single flowers on the old plant; certainly the terminal flowers which I saw in the first place were simply five-petalled.

After carefully looking at portraits of double forms in old books, I feel sure that my double compares exactly with the best illustration, that of Redouté. Other portraits are stylized and obviously inexact. I therefore conclude that the double form which has occurred in this unexpected way is a repetition of Parkinson's "Coroneola"; in his *Theatrum Botanicum* of 1640 he states that "the Coroneola that beareth in Autume is generally held by all writers to be the Double Muske Rose, which cometh only at that time and is very sweet."

On referring again to Andrews, we read that the double form "may justly be called the prototype of the former [single]; more especially as upon the single plant double flowers have sometimes been found, but not frequent." Miller says that the Musk Rose varies with double flowers.

The actual status of the double form is extremely important in considering the origin of the Damask and other roses (see Dr Hurst's notes, Chapter 13). Nobody has yet explained how the Autumn Damask originated; why should a union of *Rosa moschata* with *R. gallica* produce flowers again in the autumn if both parents were summer-flowering only? The rediscovery of the Old Musk Rose will undoubtedly shed light here. Hurst put forward the idea that the Autumn Damask, grown in Roman days and still in existence, owes its recurrent habit to *R. moschata*. He had little but theory to confirm this, but he recorded having in his possession a dwarf sport of *R. moschata* which was recurrent. This I have not seen. While the old writers had always observed and described the true old *R. moschata* under that name, towards the end of the nineteenth century French botanists decided that *R. brunonii* was in fact the type of *R. moschata*; hence the subsequent confusion in botanic gardens. In fact, having examined Dr Hurst's herbarium specimens at the University Botanic Garden, Cambridge, I find that he accepted *R. brunonii* as *R. moschata*, and that all his observations therefore apply to the former species. It is possible that the recurrent-flowering habit of the old *R. moschata* (*R. brunonii* was not found and named until 1822) was transmitted not only to the Autumn Damask but also to the first Noisette, 'Champney's Pink Cluster'. Further notes of mine occur in the Royal National Rose Society's *Annual* for 1983.

Many old books mention *Rosa moschata nivea*, which is none other than *R. dupontii*. It is surmised that this is *R. moschata* × *R. gallica*, and therefore is, technically speaking, an Autumn

Damask, but it flowers only at midsummer. It is very downy, which might point towards *R. brunonii*, but its date of raising (1817) seems to preclude that. Another name we find is *R. moschata damascena alba*, which appears to refer to a double white form or hybrid of *R. cinna-momea*.

It is not likely that *Rosa chinensis* had an influence in the old Musks if they were hybrids, for in old pictures their stems and leaf veins are distinctly shown as pubescent, and as a general rule China Rose derivatives tend towards glabrousness, and early- as well as late-flowering. But we cannot altogether rule out its influence, since, through Eastern trade routes, Far East roses may have crept into Europe, married and died out long before our rose histories lead us to believe.

We are left with the description "Musk scented." A fact which is little known today was observed by Parkinson, mentioned above, that the Musk Rose bears its scent in its filaments—the threads that bear the anthers, or stamens: "some there be that have avouched, that the chiefest scent of these roses [the Musk roses] consisteth not in the leaves [petals] but in the threads of the flowers" (*Paradisi in Sole*, etc.). I have found that all species of the Synstylae Section have this character; what the connection between it and their free-floating fragrance is, I cannot say; one would need to test all flowers likewise to reach even a comparative conclusion.

We can but conclude that the name Musk was given to this one rose because of its resemblance to genuine musk scent. Here Dr Stearn again came to my help: the source of genuine musk is a scent gland, known in the perfumery trade as a "pod," taken from the little antlerless male Musk Deer (*Moschus moschiferus*) of central and eastern Asia. This over-hunted animal is solitary and far from prolific; genuine musk is accordingly very costly. The little phial of tincture of musk which accompanied his letter was sampled and it certainly resembles very closely the delicious penetrating odour of the species of the Synstylae Section. "Muskiness" seems nowadays to be applied to a heavy odour that one meets in Crown Imperials and Mollis azaleas, rather than the true, refreshingly sweet musk of the deer and the rose. I was born too late to take note of the fragrance of the little Musk plant before it lost it, and so can offer no observations on this unfortunate occurrence.

OLD AND NEW GARDEN RAMBLERS

As explained in 'The Synstylae' earlier in this chapter, certain species of roses belonging to this Section that have been in cultivation a long time are the foundation of our garden varieties of rambling roses. A hundred and fifty years ago the only rambling roses grown were descendants of *Rosa arvensis, R. sempervirens,* and *R. moschata,* and the last-named, later uniting more with Shrub and China Roses, tended to produce large-flowered climbers rather than ramblers.

Apart from the few double forms or hybrids which were growing long before, *Rosa arvensis* produced a little group of double ramblers, mainly white, of great hardiness and excessive vigour but unfortunately with little or no scent. One still comes across old plants of these so-called Ayrshire roses, which must be 'Bennett's Seedling' ('Thoresbyana'), 'Dundee Rambler', or some other old variety. Wilhelm Kordes found 'Venusta Pendula' and made it available again, but none of these is likely to be considered worth growing today. "Since perfume is the soul and spirit of a flower" (Alphonse Karr), the only variety that *I* value is 'Splendens', the Myrrh-scented Rose. Its scent is of a rare quality, and found (so far as I know) only in 'Belle

Amour' and the newer roses 'Constance Spry' (and others of David Austin's breeding) and 'Pink Chiffon'.

There is a long account of the Ayrshire roses in the *Transactions of the Horticultural Society* for 1822, by Joseph Sabine, in which he states that seeds of *Rosa arvensis* were sent from eastern North America to the Earl of Loudoun at Loudoun Castle, Ayrshire, and there raised. The results were hybrids of *R. arvensis* showing a possibility of hybridity with a garden rose perhaps descended from *R. sempervirens*. He further observes that the information given in the *Botanical Magazine*, t.2054, is incorrect, and the figure refers to *R. arvensis* itself. A good picture of a double white Ayrshire rose is in *Roses et Rosiers*, Plate 3; and in a photograph of a plant in Jekyll's *Roses for English Gardens* between pages 56 and 57.

These "Ayrshires," as they became known, apart from their hardiness, have perhaps two attributes which might still recommend them for use today. One is that they are prostrate unless given support, and would presumably make a good weed-proof ground-cover; the other is their value for climbing into trees. William Paul, as long ago as 1888, suggested them for this purpose—before wild gardening as such became a vogue—and they have an additional advantage over modern ramblers in that they will *thrive and flower in thin woodland*. *Rosa arvensis* itself is just as much at home in shade as in full exposure. New hybrids might be attempted, with better flowers but incorporating the greater hardiness and tolerance towards shade.

Whatever its influence may have been towards the Ayrshires, the Evergreen Rose, *Rosa sempervirens*, created another little group of superior quality, mainly at the hands of M. Jacques, who was in charge of the garden of the Duc d'Orléans at Château Neuilly in France from 1824 to 1832; 'Adélaïde d'Orléans' and 'Félicité Perpétue' are two very beautiful varieties having some of the evergreen trait of the main parent. Their scent is delicate and reminiscent of primroses, and they have well-formed flowers. Others of this group which I have collected are 'Flora', 'Princesse Louise', and 'Spectabilis', the last being less vigorous than any so far mentioned. No gardener who wants a reasonably good representation of Old Roses can afford to neglect the Myrrh-scented rose, 'Adélaïde d'Orléans', and 'Félicité Perpétue'; they are unique; nothing like them has been raised since.

Another little group was derived from *Rosa setigera*, the American representative of the Synstylae Section; seeds were sown from open-pollinated flowers, and 'Baltimore Belle', 'Beauty of the Prairies', and 'Eva Corinna' resulted in the nursery of Messrs Feast in Baltimore in 1873. These are all exceptionally hardy, useful ramblers and are later-flowering than most, two attributes of which greater use might be made in present-day hybridizing. 'Erinnerung an Brod' was another hybrid of *R. setigera*, deriving from Hungary; it is classed as a Hybrid Perpetual.

'Madame d'Arblay' and 'The Garland' were, Roy Shepherd records, raised from the same hep, the result of a cross between *Rosa moschata* and *R. multiflora*, occurring at Tunbridge Wells, Kent. Whatever their parents, they are fragrant blush-white charmers, prolific and vigorous. With them we may group the tremendous plant that is called 'Paul's Himalyan Musk'.

We owe the ramblers of more recent raising in great part to *Rosa multiflora*, a Japanese species introduced in 1862, though hybrids or forms of it were introduced from Far East gardens earlier in the century—such as 'Seven Sisters' and the double pink *R. multiflora* 'Carnea'; botanically this is now *R. multiflora multiflora*, being regarded as the type species, introduced in 1804. 'Laure Davoust' is one of these early roses, but the main type is of course 'Crimson Rambler'. This is a double crimson garden hybrid of *R. multiflora* which created quite a stir, in spite of being scentless, dull in colour, and subject to mildew. It was the first of several

Multiflora ramblers to achieve considerable popularity, among which none was more free and fragrant than 'Blush Rambler'. The most important contribution of the group to gardens to-day is the little collection of purple ramblers, three of which are probably hybrids of *R. wichuraiana*. They are 'Veilchenblau', well scented and early-flowering; 'Rose-Marie Viaud', almost pure *R. multiflora*, scentless and late flowering; the remaining two, 'Violette' and 'Bleu Magenta', flower in between, are scentless, and are noted for their rich dark purplish-crimson colouring. They are invaluable for gardens of old or new roses, for they alone (with one exception) provide purplish colouring among ramblers to act as a contrast to all the other tints, which are mostly pale. The exception is 'Amadis', an old Boursault, which flowers before 'Veilchenblau' has really opened. With all five, one can have this colour represented in the garden for five or six weeks in a normal season.

Next we have three creamy yellow varieties, 'Aglaia', the noted great-grandparent of so many Hybrid Musks, but otherwise rather pale and ineffective; and 'Goldfinch', stalwart, prolific, and full of scent, but fading rapidly in sunlight to nearly white. I have also included 'Phyllis Bide', since, though repeat-flowering and of mixed parentage, it is nevertheless a small-flowered rambler.

With the arrival of *Rosa wichuraiana* all was due to be changed, and its glossy leaves have contributed to the foliage of most of its descendants; its late-summer-flowering propensity has also had some effect, and the true Wichuraiana ramblers do not usually flower until the Multiflora varieties are over. In the United States, between 1901 and 1920, a string of ramblers was raised by M. H. Walsh in Massachusetts, and several, like 'Excelsa', 'Hiawatha', 'Minnehaha', and 'Lady Gay', became favourites. The equally famous 'Dorothy Perkins' also appeared in 1901. None of these would take high marks for fragrance, which is their main point of difference from the Multiflora ramblers, apart from their more glossy leaves. Personally, I would grow 'Débutante' in place of 'Dorothy Perkins', extending a hand towards the latest addition—the beautiful 'Crimson Shower'—and welcoming with open arms 'Sanders' White', that most beautiful and fragrant of all the group, fit to be in any garden of roses. 'Blushing Lucy' is another *R. wichuraiana* charmer, and might be described briefly as 'Dorothy Perkins' without the mildew but with recurrence of its fragrant flowers.

A tendency is noticeable among these Multiflora and Wichuraiana ramblers to lack prickles, or scent, or both. While *Rosa multiflora* certainly produces forms without prickles, and might account for the lack of these in its offspring, both this species and *R. wichuraiana* are extremely fragrant. Therefore it would seem that lack of fragrance must be the responsibility of the other parents.

While that is a general history of the development of ramblers—bearing in mind the other group of *Rosa wichuraiana* crosses which, to give them due importance and to keep them quite separate from the above, I have placed in Chapter 9—there are a few odd varieties which go with them, though they are not perhaps closely related. They are isolated hybrids without a real home in these pages, so I include them here. 'Francis E. Lester' and 'Kew Rambler' are both exceptionally fragrant, and that is the only thing they have in common. The second variety brings in *R. soulieana* as a parent, with its greyish leaves and orange heps transmitted in part to the hybrid. 'Una' is a charming hybrid of *R. canina* and a rose of Tea derivation, and 'Russeliana' a purplish crimson, very prickly rambler which is possibly derived from *R. setigera*. 'Rambling Rector', 'Thalia', and 'Seagull' are closely related to *R. multiflora*; 'Lykkefund' and 'Helen Patricia', both hybrids of *R. helenae*, complete the selection, with 'Wedding Day' and 'Bobbie James'.

This little survey has been written so that the roses described in the following pages may be sorted out, but I want to stress again the overriding importance of the dark purple colouring of the few *Rosa multiflora* ramblers. If *R. multiflora* had contributed nothing else but these, it would have earned our undying gratitude. 'Dorothy Perkins' and its clan are included to complete the historical picture, although to see an arbour or pergola covered entirely with roses of this popular class is to realize that even these soulless, scentless roses must be given their due, and can look right in the right surroundings.

At the present state of rose hybridization we have to choose, when we want rambling and climbing roses, between the grace of the summer ramblers or the comparative lack of grace of those which flower recurrently. I should never allow the ramblers to be excluded, since they have a quality not provided by anything else. Fortunately a few Old Roses like 'Blush Noisette' and 'Alister Stella Gray', and some newer varieties like 'Mermaid' and 'New Dawn', show that grace and recurrence of bloom can be combined.

Why have I omitted 'Chaplin's Pink Climber' and 'American Pillar' from the following list? Because they are blatant, almost scentless, and would not be included in my own garden, however large, mainly owing to their growth and size of flower. I have throughout used the accepted name of *Rosa wichuraiana* as the parent of all these roses; my remarks in the first section of this chapter will elucidate the matter of the choice of title.

'Adélaïde d'Orléans'. France, 1826. This appears to be synonymous with 'Léopoldine d'Orléans' (the two names commemorate the daughters of the then Duc d'Orléans); both were raised by the duc's gardener M. Jacques. 'Adélaïde d'Orléans' is a hybrid of *Rosa sempervirens*, and like 'Félicité Perpétue' is partially evergreen. It is vigorous, with long slender shoots, reddish prickles, and neat, small, dark green leaves. The flowers are borne profusely at midsummer only, opening to loosely double flowers from small shapely buds. They hang in clusters, exquisitely, like those of a double Japanese cherry, for which reason it is particularly suitable for training over arches and horizontal supports. I know of no other rose with this lovely quality. The buds are of deep, creamy rose-pink, the colour remaining on the outer petals, while those inside are blush-white. Yellow stamens. Delicate primrose scent. 15 feet. (Plate 135.)

'Aglaia'. Schmitt, France, 1896. *Rosa multiflora* × 'Rêve d'Or'. This was the first yellow-flowered rambler ever raised. In effect it is like any other Multiflora rambler, but is not so free-flowering as the later, paler 'Goldfinch', though it has a longer flowering season. The flowers are semi-double, cupped, pale canary-yellow with a hint of primrose and fading to lemon-white, with an intense fragrance. Young wood greenish brown; fresh bright green leaves. Occasionally seen hanging over old garden walls, but scarcely worth growing today except for its part in the ancestry of the Hybrid Musk Roses. About 12 feet.

'Aglaia' was one of the Three Graces, the others being 'Euphrosyne' and 'Thalia'. All were used as names for his roses by M. Schmitt of Lyon, France, and it is sad that all have become 'back numbers' as far as roses are concerned; but are they not immortal in all roses—as Grace, Gentleness, and Beauty?

'Amadis'. Laffay, France, 1829. In the days when there were no crimson ramblers, this was called the 'Crimson Boursault'; today, when we have several true crimson varieties, we can place this spectacular plant with the purple ramblers. It is a useful addition, for its display occurs before the earliest of these opens. It is thornless, with long, strong shoots, green at first becoming purplish-brown with age, smooth green leaves, and abundant flowers in small and large clusters. In some seasons it produces another crop later. The flowers are semi-double, cupped, deep crimson-purple with an occasional white streak or deformed

petal, and showing stamens. It is unfortunately practically scentless, but its other characters outweigh this. A valuable shrubby rambler, ideal for contrast with 'Frühlingsgold',
'Agnes', *Rosa* 'Cantabrigiensis', and other early-flowering yellow roses. It is best trained
upon poles or a high hedge, and then allowed to hang down in festoons. Will achieve
16 feet. (Plate 137.)

The Boursault roses include 'Morletii', which, as a shrub, I included in Chapter 6;
'Mme de Sancy de Parabère' occurs in Chapter 9, with a note about the race; and 'Blush
Boursault'. All are very early flowering.

'Baltimore Belle'. Feast, U.S., 1843. All books acknowledge it to be a hybrid of *Rosa setigera*
(*R. rubifolia*), but are not unanimous about its other parent. I found this many years ago at
Walberswick in Suffolk under the name 'Princesse Louise', and have only recently found
its correct name in Paris. It is valuable because it flowers late in the rambler season, often
lasting into August, and is very hardy. Reddish buds opening to palest flesh-pink, fully
double, somewhat incurved flowers, fading to ivory white, often with a button eye. Drooping clusters, pretty growth, fresh green foliage. 10 feet. 'Eva Corinna' is another raised at
the same time, which grows at Roseraie de l'Haÿ.

'Belvedere'. I listed this in the 1983 edition of *Climbing Roses Old and New* as 'Princesse Marie'
in error. It was a spontaneous seedling which occurred in the garden of Belvedere, near
Dublin, Ireland. It is a mighty grower, to at least 40 feet; the foliage resembles that of *Rosa
canina*, but the pretty double pink flowers are borne in large panicles. It fades badly when
grown on poor soils in hot places.

'Betty Sherriff'. A clear pink, single rose of great vigour. The original seeds were collected
by George Sherriff in western China, and indicate that some species or hybrids of the Synstylae Section may be pink in the wild.

'Bleu Magenta'. This rose reached me from the Roseraie de l'Haÿ near Paris, but I have been
unable to trace the name anywhere. This is unfortunate, since it is the largest in flower and
the richest in colour of the purplish ramblers. Fully double flowers in dense clusters, darkest violet-crimson fading to dark parma-violet and grey, with an occasional white fleck.
Practically scentless. Shining dark green leaves on nearly thornless green wood. An effective garden plant. About 15 feet. The last to flower of the purple ramblers. (Plate 136.)
Thomas, 1991, page 128.

'Blushing Lucy'. A. H. Williams, U.K., 1938. A good free-growing rambler with small glossy
leaves and sprays of small, semi-double flowers of clear pink with a white eye; very fragrant. Its chief merit is that it flowers repeatedly until autumn.

'Blush Rambler'. B. R. Cant, U.K., 1903. 'Crimson Rambler' × 'The Garland'. A vigorous
rambler, almost thornless, with light green leaves. Flowers cupped, semi-double, light
pink, in large or small trusses and deliciously fragrant. Still occasionally found in old gardens; it appears to be of almost pure *multiflora* breed. 15 feet.
Kingsley, pages 58, 59.

'Bobbie James'. Sunningdale Nurseries, U.K., 1960. An unnamed foundling which it was my
privilege to name in memory of one of the grand old men of gardening, The Hon. Robert
James, a friend and correspondent of many years, who preserved many lovely roses and
other plants in his beautiful garden at St Nicholas, Richmond, Yorkshire. It is the type of

extremely fragrant rose which he would have appreciated, and it would have contributed nobly to his "garden of roses, not a rose garden," as he used to say. It is extremely vigorous, with large, long-pointed, fresh green, glossy foliage and large heads of creamy white flowers, inclined to have an extra row or two of petals, with the usual glorious fragrance of the Synstylae Section. Bright yellow stamens surround the united styles. Small oval heps. Will probably achieve 25 feet. A really splendid luxuriant and prolific plant, probably related to *Rosa multiflora* and deserving the strongest of supports. (Drawing 18.)

'Brenda Colvin'. Colvin, U.K., 1970. A self-sown seedling, probably from 'Kiftsgate', which occurred in Brenda Colvin's garden at Filkins, Gloucestershire, and which I distributed from Sunningdale Nurseries in 1970. It has the same immense vigour but the flowers are light pink, fading paler. Leaves often purplish tinted. Very pervasive scent. 30 feet.

'Crimson Rambler'. See 'Turner's Crimson Rambler'.

'Crimson Shower'. Norman, U.K., 1951. A later-flowering, richer-coloured 'Excelsa'; suitable for the same positions as that variety, 'Dorothy Perkins' and the fragrant 'Sanders' White'. Small glossy leaves. Unlike most ramblers, this excellent variety does not start flowering until well past midsummer and continues into September. Almost scentless. 15 feet.

'Débutante'. Walsh, U.S., 1902. *Rosa wichuraiana* × 'Baroness Rothschild' (1868). At first sight similar to 'Dorothy Perkins', but infinitely more beautiful, of better colour and not subject to mildew. Dark green, rounded, neat foliage, similar to *R. wichuraiana*, and long dainty sprays of bloom set with pale green bracts. Flowers cupped at first, later reflexing with quilled petals; clear rose-pink fading to blush. A charming rambler for all purposes, and delightful for cutting. Delicate primrose fragrance. Undoubtedly the best pink rambler in its section. 15 feet.

Journal des Roses, Juin 1908. ⎫
Rosenzeitung, September 1908. ⎬ Identical illustrations, poor.
Thomas, 1991, page 129. ⎭

'Donau'. Praskac, Czechoslovakia, 1913. 'Erinnerung an Brod' × a pink hybrid of *Rosa wichuraiana*. This was once sent to me as a purple rambler; it is in fact cerise-pink, but with little scent, and subject to mildew.

'Dorothy Perkins'. Jackson Perkins, U.S., 1901. *Rosa wichuraiana* × 'Madame Gabriel Luizet' (an old pink Hybrid Perpetual which is still worth growing, raised in 1877). Too well known to need description; rather subject to mildew, and little scent. I prefer 'Débutante'. Can create an exquisite Edwardian effect, and is one of the essentials for gardens with arches and trellises where more modern roses are grown, together with 'Excelsa', 'Crimson Shower', 'Hiawatha', 'Evangeline', and the fragrant 'Sanders' White'. Well represented at Polesden Lacey, a property of the National Trust in Surrey, in the Edwardian rose garden. Small glossy leaves. 18 feet. 'Lady Godiva' is a sport of paler, more pleasing colouring, and is not so subject to mildew.
Journal des Roses, Juin 1908.
Darlington, Plate 5.

'Evangeline'. Walsh, U.S., 1906. *Rosa wichuraiana* × 'Crimson Rambler'. A very pretty, fragrant, single, light pink variety, sweetly scented. Richer in colour than 'Francis E. Lester'. It is to the pale pinks what 'Hiawatha' is to the crimsons. 18 feet.

'**Excelsa**'. Walsh, U.S., 1909. Known as the 'Red Dorothy Perkins', this rose has no recorded parentage. Except for its colour, which is clear bright crimson, it resembles 'Dorothy Perkins' and has the same uses. Small glossy leaves. Surpassed by 'Crimson Shower'. 18 feet. Leroy, Plate 13. A good photograph in colour of a weeping standard.

'**Félicité Perpétue**'. 1827, raised by M. Jacques, gardener to the Duc d'Orléans. It is the most evergreen descendant of *Rosa sempervirens* and will retain some leaves through a mild winter. They are small, neat, dark shining green, plum-coloured when young. It is very bushy, making masses of shoots, and is therefore best grown as a wide bush or over a stump, low wall, or hedgerow; pruning is of little use, and does not promote flowering. It is completely covered at flowering time with perfect rosette-like double flowers of milk-white from crimson-touched buds, with slight button eye. Delicate primrose fragrance. A rose all on its own, and never to be forgotten when once one has seen a large plant. Very hardy, thriving in windswept Welsh and Scottish upland gardens; flowers well even in shade on north walls; late in the Rambler season. 12 feet. (Plate 135.)
Journal des Roses, Avril 1884. Grossly exaggerated.
Revue de l'Horticulture, Belge et Étrangère, 1890. Plate 18. Good.
Rosenzeitung, 1889. Poor.

'**Flora**'. Some authors give this as synonymous with 'William's Evergreen', which was a blush-white rose (1855). The reddish stems are best when trained up wall or fence and the subsequent growths allowed to fall forward, covering the plant with a sheet of bloom. Dark green pointed leaves. The flowers have a shape reminiscent of *Rosa centifolia*, being cupped, very full, of lilac-pink with dark old-rose in the centre. Delicate perfume of primroses. 12 feet. Miss Jekyll has a good photograph in *Roses for English Gardens* between pages 54 and 55. (Plate 133.)

'**Francis E. Lester**'. Lester Rose Gardens, U.S., 1946. Seedling from 'Kathleen', a Hybrid Musk. In the dark green leaves, neatly pointed and usually with an edging of maroon serrations, and the profuse, rather bushy growth, it has something in common with 'Félicité Perpétue'. Reddish young shoots and flower stalks. The bunches of flowers, borne rambler-fashion, cover the plant and fill the garden with an intense fragrance of oranges and bananas. The buds are clear pink, opening like apple-blossom, fading to white, with good yellow stamens. Few roses give more flower and scent at midsummer. Excellent as a lax bush or supported by a stump or hedgerow. About 14 feet. Small, oval, orange heps.

'**Ghislaine de Feligonde**'. Turbat, France, 1956. A shrubby rambler, descended from 'Goldfinch'. It is scarcely prickly, with good broad foliage. The clusters of flowers are warm yellow in the bud, fading paler on opening and developing a pinkish flush.

'**Goldfinch**'. George Paul, U.K., 1907. A hybrid of 'Hélène', which was the result of a Hybrid Tea crossed with a hybrid between 'Aglaia' and 'Crimson Rambler'. Thus there are two doses of *Rosa multiflora* in it, and indeed it is almost pure *R. multiflora* from a garden point of view. It is practically thornless, with fresh shining green leaves; buds yolk-yellow fading to milk-white in hot sunshine after opening, with dark yellow stamens. Powerful scent of oranges and bananas. If it did not fade so much it would be the more prized, but if cut in bud and opened indoors the flowers remain full of colour. Useful as a sprawling bush or trained on stump or hedgerow. (Plate 136.)

'**Hiawatha**'. Walsh, U.S., 1904. 'Crimson Rambler' × 'Paul's Carmine Pillar'. On the lines of

'Evangeline', but crimson with white centre. Not fragrant. 15 feet.
Darlington, Plate 2.

'Kew Rambler'. Raised at Kew in 1912. *Rosa soulieana* × 'Hiawatha'. The only pink seedling resulting from the cross; an account appears in the *Gardeners' Chronicle* for 27 July 1918, page 32. The prickles and greyish dull leaves are reminiscent of *R. soulieana*. It is a vigorous true rambler with pointed, bright pink buds opening to beautiful single flowers, light rose pink with white zone around the yellow stamens, and thus it resembles 'Hiawatha'. Large trusses of blossom late in the season, exhaling a rich Multiflora scent. An attractive and useful plant for many purposes, but perhaps best in a tree, where it will reach about 18 feet. Small, round-oval, orange heps. The use of *R. soulieana* apparently provides greyish foliage, and breeding along these lines might be very attractive, especially if plants bearing purple flowers could be raised, to tone with the leaves.

'Lady Gay'. Walsh, U.S., 1905. *Rosa wichuraiana* × 'Bardou Job'. Very similar to 'Dorothy Perkins' but slightly larger in flower, deeper in colour, and not so subject to mildew.

'Laure Davoust'. Laffay, France, 1843 or 1846. Smooth stems and long-pointed mid green leaves, with abundant flowers, leaning more towards *Rosa sempervirens* than to *R. multiflora*, with which it is usually grouped. From magenta-pink buds the flowers open almost flat, yet with cupped formation, quilled and quartered petals, and green pointel in the centre. They are soft lilac-rose fading to lilac-white. Sweetly scented. Jäger says it will grow to 15 feet or more, but my plants have not exceeded 8 feet.
Choix des Plus Belles Roses, Plate 20. Good.
Jamain et Forney, Plate 53. Poor.
Journal des Roses, Juin 1878.
Komlosy.

'Lykkefund'. Olsen, 1930. A "lucky find" from Denmark. A seedling from *Rosa helenae* (Barbier's form); the pollen-parent is stated to be 'Zéphirine Drouhin'. It bids fair to make a vigorous rambler, and the raiser reports that a five-year-old plant had grown to 20 feet by 13 feet. It has one great display at midsummer, but no heps. Arching habit with small, dark green, glossy leaves and nearly single flowers in panicles of 10 to 30, creamy yellow with a salmon tinge fading nearly to white, with orange-yellow stamens and the delicious fragrance peculiar to the Synstylae Section. It is thornless, and is admirable rambling through a tree, or making a dense arching mass.

'Mme d'Arblay'. Wells, U.K., 1835. *Rosa multiflora* × *R. moschata*, the reverse cross to 'The Garland' and by the same raiser, Mr Wells of Tunbridge Wells, who apparently has no other roses to his name. A graceful, vigorous rambler with long trailing branches, somewhat sparsely leaved and like the Sempervirens class. Dainty, long-stalked clusters of bloom, half filled with short petals, creating open rosettes; palest blush passing to near white. Sweet fragrance. 18 to 20 feet. (Mme d'Arblay: *née* Frances Burney.)
Le Rougetel, page 91.

'Mme de Sancy de Parabère'. See Chapter 9.

'Marjorie W. Lester'. I received this from the Lester Rose Gardens, California, together with 'Francis E. Lester', but it turned out to be synonymous with the old rambler 'Laure Davoust'.

'Minnehaha'. Walsh, U.S., 1905. *Rosa wichuraiana* × 'Paul Neyron'. A deep pink, non-fading version of 'Dorothy Perkins', than which it is bolder, more effective, and flowers later. Almost scentless. Small glossy leaves. 15 feet.

'Patricia Macoun'. Ottawa, Canada, 1945. A hybrid of *Rosa helenae* made by the Central Experimental Farm in an effort to breed hardiness into rambling roses, in which they were certainly successful with this one. It is described as "a fine white for severe climates." In the south we should all prefer 'Sanders' White', but it is an interesting hybrid and is smothered with double, cupped flowers of snow white at midsummer. Vigorous. Glossy leaves. Fragrant. Small orange heps. 20 feet.

'Paul's Himalayan Musk'. Browsing through old books one day I came across the description of this rose, but unfortunately have no record of it. It was given to me by Ashley Slocock, of Woking, and a plant is growing on trees at the west end of Seven Acres in the Royal Horticultural Society's Garden at Wisley. It is a tremendous grower, and could therefore be linked with the vigorous species of the Synstylae Section, but as it has coloured double flowers I prefer to include it here. It will make growths 30 feet or more in length, thin and trailing, and is admirable to grow into trees, when its dainty sprays will hang down in festoons of bloom at midsummer. Each flower, on thread-like stem, is a little rosette of blush-lilac-pink, exhaling a sweet *Rosa multiflora* scent. Narrow pointed leaves. Dark wood and prickles. It is possible that this is a hybrid of *R. filipes*, on account of its thread-like flower stalks; many flowers have united styles. Its vigour and prickles enable it to creep from one tree to another, enveloping all in a mantle of beauty. Very small oval heps.

'Phyllis Bide'. Bide, U.K., 1923. The parentage is stated to be 'Perle d'Or' × 'Gloire de Dijon', but Gordon Rowley tells me that the number of chromosomes (fourteen) would preclude the possibility of this cross. Whatever the parentage, it has produced good results, though *Rosa multiflora*, through 'Perle d'Or', is most in evidence. Small leaves and small rambler-type flowers in constant succession until autumn. Double, clear yellow flushed with salmon pink, in clusters. Sweet scent. 10 feet.

'Polyantha Grandiflora'. Bernaix, France, 1886. The name is certainly descriptive, but is not really permissible since it infringes the International Code of Nomenclature; *Rosa polyantha* is a synonym of *R. multiflora* and is, besides, used as a group-name for the Poly-poms. I have for many years distributed this rose as *R. gentiliana* in error; it is probably *R. multiflora* hybridized with a garden rose—a common occurrence where that species is concerned—as its styles are not united. In all other respects it might be taken for a species in the Synstylae Section; the leaves are smooth, lustrous, richly tinted while young, becoming deep green, with rather deep veins, laciniate stipules, and prickles on the reverse. It bears a few large reddish prickles on its trailing stems, which will reach 20 feet or more, climbing into trees. At midsummer it is covered with creamy white single flowers, opening from creamy yellow buds and with conspicuous orange-yellow stamens, borne on glandular-hispid flower stalks, in clusters of a dozen or so. It has a powerful fragrance of orange. Bunches of medium-sized, oval, orange-red heps last usually through the winter, creating a greater show than any of the true species in the Section except *R. helenae* and *R. lucens.* In spite of the information given in several books, this rose bears little resemblance to *R. moschata* or *R. brunonii.*

Willmott, Plate 34. This does not show the glandular-hispid flower stalks, and the drawing of the heps seems grossly exaggerated.

Journal des Roses, Mars 1887.

'**Princesse Louise**'. 1829. This is of the same origin as 'Félicité Perpétue' and 'Adelaïde d'Orléans', q.v. The flowers are between the two in shape and fullness, opening creamy blush-white from pink buds. Equally hardy and floriferous.

'**Rambling Rector**'. Almost pure *Rosa multiflora* but semi-double, and bears a superficial resemblance to 'The Garland' but is coarser in all its parts; its flowers are creamy on opening, and the flower stalks do not grow perpendicularly, as in that variety. The leaves are long with lacy stipules, downy beneath, the flower stalks densely glandular-hairy; the flowers fade to white, borne in large heads with yellow stamens which quickly turn dark on maturity—its only fault. It is dense-growing, mounding itself rapidly into a large bush, or will scramble over hedges or into trees, and is prickly and impenetrable and un-prunable; quite overpowering in flower, from both the quantity of blossom and the delicious *R. multiflora* fragrance. It was included in the Daisy Hill Nursery catalogue for 1912. Small oval heps.

'**Rose-Marie Viaud**'. Igoult, France, 1924. A seedling from 'Veilchenblau' and like that variety almost thornless, except for a few bristles at the bottom of strong basal shoots. The stems are stout enough for it to make a large arching shrub, but are also of sufficient vigour to climb 15 feet into trees and to hang down in festoons. Its lack of prickles makes it easy to manage. The leaves are broad, beautifully shaped, and coarsely toothed. Flowers in typical large bunches, fully double like little rosettes; they are from vivid cerise to lilac on opening, turning to pure parma-violet and fading still paler, giving an exquisite range of cool tones. This is one of the last purplish ramblers to flower, and coincides with the flowering of 'Kew Rambler'; they look very beautiful when growing together. Unfortunately it is scentless and prone to mildew on the flower stalks—but it is worth it!—and the mildew is seldom noticed owing to the colour of the flowers. (Plate 136.)
Gault and Synge, Plate 222.

'**Russeliana**'. 1840. An Old Rose which is generally classed with *Rosa multiflora* varieties, but possibly it is more nearly related to *R. setigera* or *R. rugosa*. It was variously known as 'Russel's Cottage Rose', 'Scarlet Grevillea', 'Old Spanish Rose', and more recently 'Souvenir de la Bataille de Marengo' has been added to this list of synonyms. Its name 'Scarlet Grevillea' points to its having perhaps been brought from the Far East by Sir Charles Greville (together with *R. multiflora* 'Platyphylla'), and I suppose by comparison with that pale rose its intense colouring might in those days be called 'scarlet'. In these days it certainly would not, being of intense cerise-crimson flushed crimson-purple, fading to magenta; flowers very double, small, in clusters. Dark green, obovate leaves. Stems densely covered with small prickles. A hardy, floriferous rose making a good colour effect at midsummer, but rather coarse. Will reach to 20 feet and appears to be imperturbably hardy. Old rose scent. Possibly related to 'de la Grifferaie', a shrub rose frequently used as an understock.

'**Sanders' White Rambler**'. Sanders, U.K., 1912. A beautiful white rose similar to 'Dorothy Perkins' and its group, except for colour. Small glossy leaves. Assorts well with varieties like 'Dorothy', but as it has no upsetting colour it can be used with any class of rose, especially as it has a delicious fruity fragrance. Flowers late in the rambler season. 18 feet.

'**Seagull**'. Pritchard, U.K., 1907. A wonderful sight in flower, this may be likened to a large-flowered version of *Rosa multiflora*, possessing many characteristics of that species, including its amazing perfume. Semi-double white flowers borne profusely in large trusses with bright yellow stamens. See also under 'Thalia'.

'**Sir Cedric Morris**'. Beales, U.K., 1979. A seedling which occurred in Cedric's garden at Benton End, Hadleigh, Suffolk, growing near to *Rosa glauca* (*R. rubrifolia*) and *R. mulliganii*, though there is nothing to prove that these were the parents. It has much of the vigour and plenitude of flower of the second species, and the young foliage is distinctly purplish. Flowers single, strongly scented, followed by small orange heps. 30 feet.

'Spectabilis'. Prior to 1848. 'Noisette Ayez'. A *Rosa sempervirens* hybrid which flowers after the others of its class are over. Greeny-brown wood and dark prickles; leaves slim, pointed. Globular buds opening to regular, incurved, fully double rose-pink flowers, with a lilac tint, reflexing into a perfect rosette. A dainty little rose of similar perfection in flower to 'Félicité Perpétue' but not so vigorous. Will reach 10 feet. There are few roses of any class with such exquisite buds and blooms, reminiscent of the most perfect of rosettes; the whole plant is refined and delightful. Sweet primrose fragrance. (Plate 132.)

'Splendens'. 'Ayrshire Splendens' or 'Myrrh-scented Rose'. A *Rosa arvensis* hybrid with small dark green, pointed leaves borne on long trailing shoots, freely branching and making a thicket. The buds show reddish plum colour, but open to loosely double, cupped flowers of creamy colouring, with yellow-orange stamens, borne singly or in small clusters. This rose has a delicious and pronounced fragrance of myrrh and is, therefore, worth retaining, particularly because it will thrive in the shade of trees.

'Tea Rambler'. W. Paul, U.K., 1904. This pleasing hybrid between the old 'Crimson Rambler' and a Tea Rose has limp, long leaflets. The flowers are borne early in the season, fragrant, of salmon-pink to yellowish tone, touched with flame.

'Thalia'. Schmitt, France, 1895. Known as 'White Rambler', this and 'Seagull' were for many years the best fragrant white ramblers, until the coming of the later-flowering 'Sanders' White'. 'Thalia' was a hybrid between *Rosa multiflora* and 'Paquerette', one of the earliest Poly-poms or Dwarf Polyanthas. Small double white flowers in big clusters on a vigorous plant achieving 12 feet or more. Very fragrant.

'The Garland'. Wells, U.K., 1835. *Rosa moschata* × *R. multiflora*. A renowned old rambler which proves once again how scent can be paramount in our affection for roses. One of its characteristics is the green wood with dark purplish-brown prickles; another is that at whatever angle the flower trusses grow, the actual flower stalks grow erect, resulting in all the flowers being held in an upright position. This is clearly shown in the photograph facing page 21 in Miss Jekyll's *Roses for English Gardens*. Vast multitudes of flowers are produced in large and small clusters; buds creamy-salmon opening to cream with a faint blush and quickly fading to creamy-white, flat, with quilled petals giving a daisy-like effect, with some yellow stamens. Dark green, smallish leaves. Rich orange perfume, carrying well in the air. An ideal rose for new or old gardens, where its bushy vigour will suit it for a number of uses, even as a loose shrub. Small oval red heps. 15 feet. (Plate 134; Drawing 19.)

'Thelma'. Easlea, U.K., 1927. *Rosa wichuraiana* × 'Paul's Scarlet Climber'. The soft colouring, luxurious flowering, and fragrance all commend this pale pink rambler for continued cultivation. Less vigorous than most others in this section, and suitable for a pillar. Nearly thornless. 10 feet.

'Treasure Trove'. Treasure, U.K., 1979. Presumed to be a seedling from 'Kiftsgate', with beautiful reddish young foliage. The flowers are borne in great profusion and are of good size, semi-double, cupped, of warm creamy apricot, fading paler. Delicious fragrance. Needs a sheltered position. 30 feet.

'Turner's Crimson Rambler'. Introduced to western gardens in 1893. Affectionately known as 'Crimson Rambler', 'The Engineer', 'Shi-Tz-Mei', or 'Ten Sisters', this was once a popular plant, but it is very subject to mildew, scentless, and should be discarded in favour of 'Crimson Shower'. Dusky dark red. It was imported from Japan, and is probably a hybrid of *Rosa multiflora* × *R. wichuraiana*. A landmark in the development of rambling roses, having a profound influence on rose breeding, but otherwise not worth growing today.
Revue Horticole, 1894, page 156.
Hoffmann, Plate 12. Very good.
Journal des Roses, 1886.

'Una'. George Paul, U.K., 1900. A Tea Rose, perhaps 'Gloire de Dijon' × *Rosa canina*. Hooked prickles and dull green leaves sharply serrated, inherited from *R. canina;* young foliage bronzy. The flowers are borne in small clusters and are nearly single—with two or three extra petals—creamy white opening from creamy buff buds about 3 inches across; delicious primrose scent. One crop of flowers only. Usually grows to 12 feet or so, but can achieve 18 feet on a wall. Large round heps which usually remain green.

'Veilchenblau'. Schmidt, Erfurt, Germany, 1909. 'Crimson Rambler' × 'Erinnerung an Brod'. Almost thornless green wood bearing smooth, fresh green leaves, long and pointed. It is of typical rambler growth with flowers in generous clusters. Buds crimson-purple, petals opening violet, streaked with white (not variegated but, seemingly, a character connected with the central vein in each petal); semi-double, incurved, with a few small petals around the yellow stamens. White centre. The colour verges to murrey later and fades on the third day to lilac-grey. Sweetly fragrant of green apples. Excellent on a shady wall, where the colour remains fairly uniform. It flowers early in the rambler season, and achieves 12 feet. (Plate 136.)

'Venusta Pendula'. An old *Rosa arvensis* form or hybrid, rediscovered by Herr Kordes. A complete smother of blossom, but practically scentless. Pink buds, opening blush white, fading to creamy white, with yellow stamens. 15 feet.

'Violette'. Turbat, France, 1921. This flowers just after 'Veilchenblau' opens, early in the rambler season. Thornless and vigorous with green wood and dark green leaves, rather recurved and bluntly serrate. Large trusses of flowers with buds and freshly open flowers of intense crimson-purple, and occasionally a white streak, intensifying to murrey-purple and fading to murrey-grey, with subtle brownish tints; yellow stamens; very slight scent of apples. Will attain 15 feet on good soils. (Plate 136.)

   I first saw this rambler at Nymans, interlaced with the large pink single flowers of 'Lady Curzon'; the contrast of size and colour was admirable. 'Complicata' and other large pink varieties would do equally well; another favourite companion is 'Goldfinch'.

'Wedding Day'. Stern, U.K., 1950. This is a hybrid of *Rosa sinowilsonii* raised by Sir Frederick Stern at Highdown, Sussex. Green wood and scattered red prickles; rich green, glossy leaves, slightly serrated and gracefully poised. The trusses of flowers are very large; each bloom emerges from a yolk-yellow bud, opening to creamy white with vivid orange-yellow stamens around the united styles. Each petal is broadly wedge-shaped with a mucronate apex, giving a starry effect. Exceedingly fragrant of oranges. A prolific grower and flowerer, it will cover barns, hedgerows, and trees, probably achieving a maximum height or length of 35 feet, creating a billowy mass of leaves and flowers; it can also be used to cover the ground. Unfortunately the petals are inclined to "spot" after rain, becoming blotched with pink when fading, which spoils the effect.

'White Dorothy'. Inferior to the excellent 'Sanders' White'.

'Wichmoss'. Barbier, France, 1911. *Rosa wichuraiana* × 'Salet', a pink Moss Rose. This effort to produce a rambling rose with mossy buds is only partially successful, for it lacks decisive colour and the mossy buds are invariably covered with mildew. However, it is a true rambler, with fairly glossy leaves and double small blooms of blush white. Fragrant. 15 feet. I include this as evidence that we could have mossy buds on ramblers, and hope that it may be raised again and be free from mildew.

'Wickwar'. A seedling of *Rosa soulieana*, raised and introduced by Keith Steadman of Wickwar, Gloucestershire, U.K. It retains the vigour, greyish leaves and delicious fragrance of *R. soulieana*, but has clear pink single flowers and a more tractable climbing habit.

9

Ramblers and Climbers Derived from the Musk Rose or Synstylae Section Intermarried with the Offspring of the China and Tea Roses

LARGE-FLOWERED RAMBLERS

THIS RACE OF ROSES is, I consider, in the top rank of beautiful, fragrant, graceful ramblers, and further hybridization, along the same lines but using more modern parents, might give splendid results. No ramblers or climbers raised before or since surpass their prodigality of bloom, extreme fragrance, and beautiful foliage, coupled with ease of training.

The most popular of this group is 'Albéric Barbier', and as so many of the varieties were raised by Messieurs Barbier et Cie of Orléans, France, I think they need a special title. They are usually classed with 'Dorothy Perkins' and others related to *Rosa multiflora* and *R. wichuraiana*, but with these varieties our present roses have nothing in common. They are as different as Hybrid Teas from Floribundas.

The preceding chapter was devoted to hybrids between the Old Roses, with non-glossy foliage and no yellow in the flowers, and *Rosa multiflora* or *R. wichuraiana*. The roses in this section all have flowers verging towards yellow or salmon coupled, usually, with extra glossy foliage: two characters which result from using Tea Roses crossed with *R. wichuraiana*. In the two editions of my book *Climbing Roses Old and New* I wrongly attributed these present note-worthy characters to the influence of *R. luciae*, as stated by their French raisers; but botanically, *R. luciae* and *R. wichuraiana* are synonymous.

The roses under consideration here do not produce long straight canes bearing in the next season stiff heads of small flowers, as do the varieties in the previous chapter. Rather do they produce, with their free-branching and luxuriant glossy dark greenery, a mantle of richness following the contours of whatever they cover in a free and continuous way, further encouraged by the fact that they do not depend on annual summer pruning to give of their best. The flowers are borne singly or in graceful small clusters, and are anything from two to four inches across, mostly fully double in the old floral style, extremely sweetly-scented with the "fresh green-apple" fragrance which is their own contribution to this addition to the visual delight of roses. They flower mainly at midsummer, but most of them produce odd blooms until the autumn, especially if not parched or starved; in fact, a thorough soak after flowering will often start them into bud again.

In this group we are for the first time dealing with roses of modern colouring. Only 'Alexandre Girault' and 'May Queen' have a touch of the soft mauve tone of the Old Roses, with 'Gerbe Rose' and 'Mary Wallace' a neutral pink; all the others verge towards salmon and

copper or creamy yellow. Some are therefore hardly suitable for growing with the Old Shrub
Roses, but their old-style quartered blooms and fragrance endear them to lovers of the Old
Roses, while their somewhat recurrent flowering habit and more modern colouring give them
pride of place among graceful ramblers for the modern rose garden; the creamy white varieties
will of course blend with anything.

The group really starts, as far as we are concerned—by which I mean the varieties I have
collected together—with hybridizing by W. A. Manda of New Jersey in the United States.
In 1898 and the year following he launched 'May Queen', 'Gardenia', and 'Jersey Beauty',
lilac-pink and double and single creamy yellow, respectively. These are seldom recurrent, but
create a wonderful display at midsummer and are extremely fragrant. The Barbier firm produced 'Albéric Barbier', 'Paul Transon', 'René André', 'Léontine Gervais', 'François Juranville',
'Alexandre Girault', and 'Auguste Gervais', in that order, between 1900 and 1908. Meanwhile
Fauque et Fils, also of Orléans, introduced 'Gerbe Rose', 'La Perle', and the little charmer
'Mme Alice Garnier'. 'Gerbe Rose' is not quite so graceful as the rest of them, while 'La Perle'
equals any in vigour. The Barbier and the Fauque seedlings are all somewhat recurrent. H. A.
Hesse of Ems, Germany, brought out 'Fräulein Oktavia Hesse' in 1909, which is very similar
to 'Albéric Barbier'. In 1918 Benjamin Cant introduced 'Emily Gray' which, with 'Albéric
Barbier', has remained very popular in public esteem; and the last of the group, 'Mary Wallace' and 'Breeze Hill', came from van Fleet in the United States in 1924 and 1926 respectively. These have less glossy foliage than the bulk of earlier varieties.

There is no doubt that these make a most attractive group. All those with salmon or yellow
tints have as their other parent a China × Tea hybrid, and the others go back to Bourbons or
Hybrid Perpetuals. None is connected with *Rosa multiflora*.

It is unfortunate that these lovely ramblers are not so hardy as many of the Multiflora
types. This precludes their use in very cold countries except on sheltered walls, a use for
which they are well suited. Unlike many of the other ramblers they are not prone to mildew;
they thrive excellently in all manner of positions, and are hardy throughout England.

Although the varieties in this chapter make a homogeneous group I have included two
well-known varieties, 'Albertine' and 'Mary Wallace', which would in some ways be better left
until the later section, "The 'New' Climbers."

'Albéric Barbier'. Barbier, France, 1900. *Rosa wichuraiana* × 'Shirley Hibberd' (a small yellow
Tea Rose). Right in the forefront of beautiful rambling roses, and a splendid sample for
its relatives in this section. The flowers are large, opening from pretty, pointed buds to
starry flowers of soft yellow expanding to creamy white, many-petalled and quartered. Extremely sweet green-apple scent. Almost dense enough for ground-cover, and constantly
produces scattered late flowers until the autumn. 20 feet or more.
Gibson, Plate 26.

'Albertine'. Barbier, France, 1921. *Rosa wichuraiana* × 'Mrs A. R. Waddell', a coppery Hybrid
Tea. Not uniform with the other roses in this chapter. This is a shrubby climber or a lax
bush, for while it is usually made to climb or ramble, it creates such a thicket of stems that
it is far nobler when allowed to do as it likes among shrubs. Glossy leaves. Coppery pink,
two-toned, loosely double, but too well known to need description. Creating an unforgettable midsummer display, with or without pruning; the rich fragrance carries well in the
air. 18 feet on a wall or 6 feet high by 15 feet across if unsupported.
Le Rougetel, page 111.
Gibson, Plate 26.

'**Alexandre Girault**'. Barbier, France, 1909. *Rosa wichuraiana* × 'Papa Gontier' (a pink Tea Rose). Dark glossy leaves, very vigorous growth. Pretty buds of deeper colour open to almost scarlet flowers, nearly filled with rather quilled petals but showing white centre, green eye, and yellow stamens; the colour deepens to lilac-carmine, but remains paler on the reverse of the petals. This strange mixture of colours blends into a deep coppery carmine at a distance and is very satisfying, so much so that it has been given an important position at the Roseraie de l'Haÿ near Paris, where it covers a long high trellis around the formal pool. Rich green-apple scent. Few prickles. 20 feet. (Plate 142.)

'**Auguste Gervais**'. Barbier, France, 1918. *Rosa wichuraiana* × 'Le Progrès', a yellow Hybrid Tea. First-class foliage and large flowers for this section; coppery flame-pink on the reverse which makes a splendid contrast to the bland creamy-apricot on the inside of the petals. Considerably paler but always beautiful in hot weather, and, as usual with these varieties, deliciously fragrant. Has a long flowering season and odd blooms later. 20 feet. (Plates 139, 142.)

'**Aviateur Blériot**'. Fauque, France, 1910. Though summer-flowering only, this has the attraction of large flowers, inherited from 'Le Progrès' of 1903, of warm apricot-yellow fading to creamy white, and extra fragrant. Shining dark leaves. 12 feet.
Beales, page 317.

'**Breeze Hill**'. Van Fleet, U.S., 1926. *Rosa wichuraiana* × 'Beauté de Lyon', a coral red Hybrid Tea. This variety has not such glossy foliage as the others in this class, and G. A. Stevens suggests that it may be a seedling of 'Dr van Fleet' which had *R. soulieana* as one parent. The rounded foliage could certainly have come from such a hybrid; otherwise the large flowers conform to the normal and are a warm creamy apricot-rose, fading to buff-cream. Good scent of green apples. Perhaps achieving 12 feet, but can be grown as an arching bush.
McFarland, *Roses of the World*, page 27. Rather dull.
Stevens, page 106. The same plate as above.
American *Rose Annual*, 1927. Plate 1.

'**City of York**'. Tantau, Germany, 1945. A hybrid between 'Dorothy Perkins' and a Hybrid Tea, 'Professor Gnau'. Though of rather more involved parentage than most, the *Rosa wichuraiana* in 'Dorothy Perkins' accounts for the general appearance, and this glossy-leaved vigorous rose may be likened to 'Albéric Barbier', but has larger, semi-double, cupped flowers of creamy white. So far it has had no later crop with me. Also known as 'Direktor Benschop'. Fragrant.

'**Emily Gray**'. Williams, U.K., 1918. 'Jersey Beauty' × 'Comtesse du Cayla'. A favourite for many years, to which the beautiful glossy foliage, richly tinted while young, contributes greatly. Clusters of warm buff-yellow nearly single flowers with good stamens and fragrance. Seldom flowers after midsummer. Strong grower, reaching 20 feet.

'**François Juranville**'. Barbier, France, 1906. *Rosa wichuraiana* × 'Mme Laurette Messimy', a salmon-pink China Rose. The next in popularity to 'Albéric Barbier' and 'Emily Gray', with slightly less glossy, smaller leaves and slightly smaller flowers, but equal vigour and charm. Flat double flowers filled with quilled and quartered petals, opening rich coral rose fading to light rose, base of petals yellow. Sweet fresh-apple scent. Adds grace and beauty to whatever it grows upon. Inclined to be "leggy" at the base. Not suitable for walls, where it sometimes gets mildew. 25 feet. (Plate 140.)

'Fräulein Oktavia Hesse'. Hesse, Germany, 1909. *Rosa wichuraiana* × 'Kaiserin Augusta Viktoria'. Similar to 'Albéric Barbier', which is a superior rose. This variety is nearer to white and less fragrant, but has well-formed flowers at first cupped and creamy, later reflexing flat and passing to white. Sweet apple scent. One crop only.
Rosenzeitung, December 1909.

'Gardenia'. Manda, U.S., 1899. *Rosa wichuraiana* × 'Perle des Jardins', a yellow Tea Rose. Similar to 'Albéric Barbier' with small dark green glossy leaves. The flowers are very double, quartered, rather cupped, of creamy white deepening to yolk-yellow in the centre, fading to nearly white in hot sun. True apple scent. 18 feet. It grows luxuriantly over the treillage at Bodnant, North Wales, and is extra free-flowering.

'Gerbe Rose'. Fauque, France, 1904. Of the same parentage as 'Débutante', but further removed from *Rose wichuraiana*; in fact it approaches the 'Albéric Barbier' group, with its larger, glossy dark leaves. It is not a vigorous rambler, but rather a robust pillar rose, with almost thornless reddish shoots. The flowers are large, loosely double, petals cupped, quartered and crinkled, soft pink with a hint of lilac and cream, with a delicious fragrance of white peonies particularly noticeable in the evening. Apart from its main crop it is seldom without flowers until the autumn. 12 feet. (Plate 138.)

'Jersey Beauty'. Manda, U.S., 1899. *Rosa wichuraiana* × 'Perle des Jardins'. A luxuriant plant which will densely cover its support with excellent glossy foliage. Single creamy yellow flowers with deep yellow stamens at midsummer. Very fragrant. 12 feet.
Kingsley, page 62.

'La Perle'. Fauque, France, 1904. *Rosa wichuraiana* × 'Mme Hoste', a pale yellow Tea Rose. Similar to 'Albéric Barbier', but more vigorous, and with less glossy leaves; the young foliage has a red-brown tinge. The buds are also brown-touched, opening to a cupped globular bloom of greenish creamy white with a lemon-yellow centre; later becoming flat with some quilled petals. Deliciously intense fragrance of green apples, lemon and tea. Extremely vigorous, reaching 30 feet.

'Léontine Gervais'. Barbier, France, 1903. *Rosa wichuraiana* × 'Souvenir de Catherine Guillot'. In all respects very similar to 'François Juranville' except the colour, which inclines towards copper and orange. As 'Paul Transon' (q.v.) has a much longer flowering season, I prefer it. 25 feet.

'Little Compton Creeper'. Brownell, U.S., 1938. Though the parentage is not recorded, this is obviously related to the others in this section, with highly polished dark green leaves. The flowers are single, reminiscent of 'Emily Gray', but of warm coppery flesh-pink, with cluster of stamens. Orange-red fruit. Multiflora scent; short flowering period and does not repeat, but is an attractive plant at all times. Medium to large red heps. 18 feet.

'Mme Alice Garnier'. Fauque, France, 1906. *Rosa wichuraiana* × 'Mme Charles', a yellow Tea Rose. A miniature in growth, leaf, and flower, making a sprawling bush or a short climber, set with neat dark leaves. The flowers are flat rosettes of quilled and quartered petals, bright rose with yellow centre, passing to light pink, giving a creamy-apricot effect. Extremely fragrant of green apples. Perhaps 10 feet.

'Mary Wallace'. Van Fleet, U.S., 1924. *Rosa wichuraiana* × a pink Hybrid Tea. A lovely graceful plant, less full of foliage than the others, and less glossy. Large, loose, semi-double, rose-pink flowers, sweetly fragrant. Seldom repeats. 20 feet.

'May Queen'. There were two roses of this name raised in the United States in 1898, and that introduced by W. A. Manda of New Jersey is *Rosa wichuraiana* × 'Champion of the World'; the van Fleet hybrid is *R. wichuraiana* × 'Mme de Graw'; in both, the second parent is a Bourbon. Our plant could be either; it has green wood with a few reddish prickles and fresh green leaves somewhat glossy, bluntly serrate. The flowers are clear rose-pink on opening, taking on a delicate flush of lilac similar to 'Champion of the World'; slightly cupped on opening, they become flat and reflex, filled with quartered petals and often a button eye. Few roses create such a sheet of blossom; I have seen it equally good on south, east, and north walls. It can also be grown as a dense, arching bush, since it is not so prone to make long shoots as the other varieties, but creates more of a mass of interlacing twigs. Delicious green-apple scent. 15 feet. (Plate 141.)

'Paul Transon'. Barbier, France, 1901. *Rosa wichuraiana* × 'l'Idéal', a coral-red Tea Rose. Purplish shoots and prickles, shining small leaves with acute serrations, richly tinted when young. The little buds are coppery-orange opening to salmon-coral, fading to creamy salmon with yellow tints in the centre. Semi-double to double, flat, with pleated petals. Well scented of green apples. A very charming free-flowering variety which produces so many late flowers that it might be called recurrent; in fact I find it as free with later blooms as 'Albéric Barbier'. 15 feet.

'René André'. Barbier, France, 1901. *Rosa wichuraiana* × 'l'Idéal'. Exceptionally lax, and will climb into trees to 20 feet or more, hanging down in slender festoons, with small flowers of soft yellowish apricot flushed with pink, loosely double and somewhat cupped. Sweet apple scent.
Journal des Roses, Octobre 1903. Very large and of too brilliant colouring.

As a result of a visit to the Paris rose gardens I noted the following worthy varieties:

'Élisa Robichon'. Barbier, France, 1901. Small salmon-pink flowers and small shiny leaves. A vigorous grower, but subject to mildew on a wall.

'François Foucard'. Barbier, France, 1900. Lemon yellow.
(The above two are the result of *Rosa wichuraiana* × 'l'Idéal'.)

'Madame Constans'. L'Haÿ, France, 1902. Soft pink.

'Valentin Beaulieu'. Barbier, France, 1902. Lilac pink with darker centre.

LARGE-FLOWERED CLIMBERS OF HYBRID TEA STYLE

> See how the flowers, as at parade,
> Under their colours stand display'd:
> Each regiment in order grows,
> That of the tulip, pink, and rose.
> Andrew Marvell, 1621–1678

So far this book has proceeded with only botanical and historical difficulties; enough, certainly, in a genus so involved in hybridity as *Rosa* to daunt us all, but nothing compared with the difficulty we must all experience in making a selection from among countless favourites. The whole book is, however, a selection—*my* selection—and it so happens that in horticulture, and maybe in other walks of life too, the odd variety which does not conform to the general style becomes neglected. Our more favourite genera are littered with these individuals: good varieties on their own which have been unaccountably passed by. The catalogues seem to like to offer to the public solid groups of varieties which vary in colour but not in other particulars. I have always championed the odd varieties because I like individuality, and if Mr A grows 'Garnette', his neighbour 'Pink Garnette' and Mrs B down the road buys 'White Garnette', I certainly would not choose a 'Yellow Garnette'; I would have the unique 'Mlle Cécile Brunner'—without individuality we shall all be levelled down to the least common denominator and our gardens will all be the same.

Among climbing roses there are many isolated varieties which do not conform to the main stream. This is because very little attention has been given by hybridists to the raising of climbing roses, and because there are few available compared with the thousands of bush varieties. The good new varieties of ramblers raised since the Second World War are less in number than the fingers on one hand, and if we put the number of good, equally new, strong-growing, perpetual-flowering climbers at two handfuls, we shall not be far wrong. But the bushes are counted in hundreds over the same period. If it were not for the climbing sports of Hybrid Teas we should indeed be suffering from a scarcity of climbers—and yet they are just the roses which can give the greatest display of all. There is much research needed and much has to be done to bring our climbing roses up to the standard of the Hybrid Teas and Floribundas.

Many climbing sports of Hybrid Teas have arisen but have not become popular, since they were not sufficiently prolific of blooms later in the season. Sometimes a more recurrent sport arises after the original, but it is manifest that climbing sports are only likely to be selected from the more modern varieties in commerce today, though it is equally true that some of the oldest are among the very best. Ann Wylie describes in the Royal Horticultural Society's *Journal* for January 1955, following observation by D. Morey, how it is possible that these climbing mutants or sports are similar in origin to certain graft hybrids (periclinal chimeras) like +*Laburnocytisus adamii*. If so, this would account for the readiness of some of the less stable to revert to the original bush form when propagated from root cuttings.

This section, then, contains my selection of Climbing Hybrid Teas, together with a number of similar quality and a few isolated gems which are not recurrent but which we cannot afford to lose.

To help intending planters we will discuss the collection, and can at once dispose of a few which need not be referred to again in these pages, since they have had their due in earlier chapters. They are the extra-strong-growing varieties of Bourbons and Hybrid Perpetuals, which will reach anything up to 8 feet without support, or even more if trained on wall or fence. As their colours are all soft, being on the blue side of red in the spectrum, they are valuable with many of the old ramblers for providing climbing roses to decorate a garden or border devoted to Old Roses. They include some really excellent, fragrant plants, such as 'Blairii Number 2', the perpetual-flowering 'Zéphirine Drouhin' and its sport 'Kathleen Harrop', and 'Climbing Souvenir de la Malmaison'. The climbing China Roses were described in Chapter 6. Lists of these and others will be found in Chapter 11.

There are a few descendants of *Rosa wichuraiana* for this section. With some hesitation I included 'Albertine' and 'Mary Wallace' in the previous section; they do not conform to those fairly uniform Ramblers, but they would not really have fitted here, though 'Mary Wallace' might be considered as a step towards 'New Dawn'. Equally, they link with 'Dream Girl' and 'Purity' in the next section, where 'Albertine' might have been included. All of these roses have the glossy leaves and some of the fragrance of *R. wichuraiana*. I have omitted 'Dr van Fleet', since though it makes a superlative contribution annually in flower and fragrance, it is not recurrent, and I therefore prefer the otherwise identical though rather less vigorous 'New Dawn'.

Next we have a few really splendid climbing roses, not sports of Hybrid Teas, and not recurrent. Oldest is 'Mme de Sancy de Parabère', one of the Boursault Roses, thornless and very early-flowering. It has a shape unlike any other double rose, but little fragrance. Even so, I would retain it for the wonderful early display. 'Cupid' is a pretty, large-flowering single with large heps in autumn. The three most magnificent varieties in this little set are 'Easlea's Golden', yellow; 'Paul's Lemon Pillar', lemon-white; and 'Mme Grégoire Staechelin', rich pink. All are exceptionally fragrant, large-flowered, and early-flowering, but not recurrent. They are indispensable.

There are two recurrent varieties which are alike only in name: 'Gruss an Aachen' and 'Gruss an Teplitz', both full-petalled in the old style, creamy pink and crimson respectively.

Now we can look at the sports of Hybrid Teas, and roses similarly shaped and recurrent. As suggested earlier, even these are not without disadvantages. While I like a rose of the Hybrid Tea persuasion to be erect and carry its flower well aloft on a good stem so long as it is a bush, I am certain that this is a disadvantage when a climbing sport occurs. We train the shoots along and up the wall, or, if they will bend, over an arch—and what happens? The flowers are produced on side shoots, mostly erect with their flowers at the top, and as a rule most of the flowers will be well up the wall or over the top of the arch. The result is that, unless one looks out of an upstairs window, the flowers cannot really be appreciated, except for their show of colour. This applies to the bulk of the Hybrid Tea climbing sports. In other words, I do not like my climbing roses to be without grace, even when the flowers are large and recurrent. The great joy of a climbing rose is when its flowers nod down or at least are poised outwardly from the wall or support. There are just a few modern-type, large-flowered, recurrent-flowering climbers that do this, and among them I would cite 'Souvenir de Claudius Denoyel', 'Crimson Glory', 'Mme Édouard Herriot', 'Shot Silk', and 'Ena Harkness'.

Let us look at pure pink varieties first. Few of superlative worth have been raised recently; my first choice, historically, would be 'La France', one hundred years old, with 'Mme Abel Chatenay' and 'Mme Caroline Testout', both raised in the last century, followed by one of the 'Ophelia' breed—'Ophelia' itself, 'Mme Butterfly', or 'Lady Sylvia', dating back to the original in 1912—with the addition of 'Shot Silk'. The 'Ophelia' breed are very stiff but extra recurrent, and probably produce more flowers in a season than any of the other climbing Hybrid Tea sports. It is astonishing how all these grand old varieties still stand unrivalled, but it is partly because breeders have been interested in extraneous colours like red and yellow and their intermediates. 'Michèle Meilland', 'Picture', 'Souvenir de la Malmaison', and 'Lady Waterlow' might also be chosen, with the pretty, single 'Dainty Bess'.

Among the true reds and crimsons are two very dark-coloured roses, 'Château de Clos Vougeot', 1908, containing all the oldest wine, and 'Guinée', 1938, made of the darkest port-wine-coloured velvet. The first to flower is generally the bright crimson 'Souvenir de Claudius Denoyel' followed by the two stalwarts 'Étoile de Hollande' and 'Crimson Glory', and 'Ena Harkness', if a third be wanted. Of equal value for effect is 'Allen Chandler'.

There are practically no white varieties; for this colour we must turn to the ramblers and 'Purity', 'Mrs Herbert Stevens', 1910, a Tea to be found in Chapter 6, and 'McGredy's Ivory', 1930, hold the field still among large-flowered climbers; the climbing form of 'Frau Karl

Druschki' seems to have died out, only the bush remaining in cultivation.

The dates I have given above indicate when the original bush form was raised, and it is interesting to see how well these climbing sports—for most of them are such—hold their own through the decades.

Lovely and appreciated as are the best climbing Hybrid Teas and these few others, this type of rose cannot be considered as the ultimate goal. Already surpassing them in freedom of flowering are a few new climbers of bright modern colours. These are to be found in the next section. If it is the aim of the breeders to produce strong-growing climbers of graceful growth and good foliage giving Hybrid Tea-type fragrant flowers at midsummer and with later crops, then one of the few varieties which approaches this ideal is 'New Dawn'. When a race of these superlative roses is available there will be no need to cherish the ungainly sports of Hybrid Teas, unless like 'Ophelia' and its breed they are really recurrent. One reservation should be made here: a climbing rose can often be given a suitable position in a garden, fitting in with any design, whereas bush Hybrid Teas, needing individual cultivation, generally in isolated beds, may be felt out of place. Therefore we should retain the best Hybrid Tea climbers, because there is no substitute for the perfection of their blooms.

I have found it difficult to describe the scents of the roses in this section and the next. The Hybrid Tea is of such mixed parentage that its fragrance is often composed of different characters, and frequently their smell in the evening is quite different from that in the morning.

'**Allen Chandler**'. Prince, U.K., 1923. A hybrid from 'Hugh Dickson' and a really excellent red rose, with greater brilliance, better texture and shape—though nearly single—and larger flowers than 'Paul's Scarlet', showing yellow stamens. It is a sturdy climber with good foliage, and is seldom without flower after the main crop. Produces a copious and lasting display of large orange-red heps; valuable as these may be in late autumn, if they are removed as they develop more flowers are the result. 12 feet.

'**Allen's Fragrant Pillar**'. Allen, U.K., 1931. 'Paul's Lemon Pillar' × 'Souvenir de Claudius Denoyel'. With two such distinguished parents this is justly good. Large loose blooms, cerise pink, with yellow base giving a touch of brilliance. Delicious scent, glossy foliage, and very vigorous. Recurrent. 8 to 10 feet.

'**Apeles Mestres**'. Pedro Dot, Spain, 1925. 'Frau Karl Druschki' × 'Souvenir de Claudius Pernet'. A beautiful rose, owing its long shapely bud to 'Druschki'; pale clear yellow, sweet-scented. A good strong grower producing flowers mostly at midsummer. 12 feet.

'**Blush Boursault**'. Prior to 1848. 'Calypso', 'Rose de l'Isle', 'Florida'. A vigorous, thornless, early-flowering variety, similar in growth and style and size of flower to 'Mme de Sancy de Parabère', but without the large outer petals. Fully double, palest blush pink, but much deeper in the centre. An old plant grows and flowers well on the west wall of Melford Hall, a National Trust property in Suffolk. 15 feet.

'**Château de Clos Vougeot, Climbing**'. Morse, U.K., 1920. A sport from the bush form, 1908. Open, short-petalled flowers of darkest red with nearly black shadings, fully double. No purple tints. Normal Hybrid Tea foliage. A vigorous plant, will thrive on light soils, and gives blooms after the main display. Fragrance as deep and powerful as the colouring. 12 feet.

Journal des Roses, Août 1908.

Rosenzeitung, February 1909.

'Colcestria'. B. R. Cant, U.K., 1916. A strangely neglected rose which has a good first crop and repeats modestly later. It has good foliage and is vigorous. It is the flowers that are remarkable: silvery rose-pink, very full, with rolled petals. Very fragrant. A worthy companion to 'Paul's Lemon Pillar'. It is usually classed as a Hybrid Tea.

'Crimson Glory, Climbing'. Kordes, Germany, 1935. 'Catherine Kordes' seedling × 'W. E. Chaplin'. The climbing sport was introduced in 1946. This magnificent, very fragrant, deepest crimson rose gives a number of later blooms after the main crop. Those who object to purplish tints should place this variety where it is protected from the hottest sun. 10 to 12 feet.
Leroy, Plate 8.
Baird, page 48.

'Cupid'. Cant, U.K., 1915. Strong prickly shoots with brownish-tinted foliage when young, turning to dark green. The flowers are light peach pink, very large and nearly single, with crinkled petals, showing good stamens. One season of flowering, but the heps are large, rounded, orange-red with persistent calyces and last in beauty well into the winter. I like it best when planted among other shrubs, so that it can grow through and over them, as it is never overpowering. Sweet raspberry scent. Probably 15 feet. (Plate 156.)
Austin, Plate page 297.

'Dainty Bess, Climbing'. Introduced in 1935, from the original bush raised in 1925 by Archer, U.K. 'Ophelia' × 'K. of K.'. Exquisite single pink variety, deeper on the reverse, and with lovely red-brown stamens. The petals are often divided or fringed, but not so much as in 'Ellen Willmott', a descendant of 'Dainty Bess'. Fragrant. 8 to 12 feet.

'Easlea's Golden Rambler'. Easlea, U.K., 1932. The best-known rose raised by Walter Easlea, who was a keen rosarian and appreciated the Rose in all its forms. It is a pity this was called a Rambler, since this conjures up a small-flowered rose. It does certainly ramble, but would be better described as a once-flowering climber. The foliage distinguishes it from all other roses—rich green and glossy, broader at the end than at the middle, and distinctly corrugated by the deep veins. Large, lovely flowers filled with petals of rich butter-yellow touched with red in the bud, borne singly and in clusters early in the season. Glorious fragrance. 12 to 15 feet.
McFarland, *Roses of the World*, page 166.
American *Rose Annual*, 1934, page 40.
Phillips and Rix, page 97.

'Ena Harkness, Climbing'. The original was raised by Norman, U.K., and introduced in 1946. 'Crimson Glory' × 'Southport'. The climbing sport occurred in 1954. I have never been very fond of this rose, but its crimson blooms are large and somewhat fragrant, and have the advantage of nodding down at one. 15 feet.

'Étoile de Hollande, Climbing'. Verschuren, Holland, 1919. 'General MacArthur' × 'Hadley'. The climbing sport was introduced in 1931. A superlative old crimson rose with amazing rich fragrance. Vigorous, 18 feet, and recurrent. Splendid under glass, but quite hardy.
Gibson, Plate 30.

'Golden Dawn, Climbing'. Grant, Australia, 1929. 'Élégante' × 'Ethel Somerset'. The best

climbing sport is that introduced by LeGrice in 1947. A delicious tea-scented, fully double, light yellow rose of power and persuasion. Some later blooms. Good foliage. 12 feet.

'Gruss an Aachen, Climbing'. A sport from the bush form, which occurred at Sangerhausen
and was introduced by Kordes in 1937. The parentage is reputedly 'Frau Karl Druschki'
× 'Franz Deegen', but chromosome numbers suggest otherwise. Both of these are Hybrid
Teas, so that it is strange that 'Gruss an Aachen' should be cluster-flowered, and classed as
a Floribunda in spite of its having been raised in 1909 (by Geduldig, Germany), long before the term was invented!

   The climbing form is a good grower and is recurrent-flowering, but is not as free after
the main display as the bush form. Its delicate ivory-white tone enriched with apricot-pink
and its rich fragrance and full-petalled shape make it too good to neglect. Probably 12
feet. (Plate 155.)

'Gruss an Teplitz'. Described in Chapter 6, "Shrub Roses of the Twentieth Century," since
it is more of a shrub than a climber, though it can be trained up to some 8 or 10 feet.
Gorgeous crimson without purple, recurrent, and fragrant. This has much of the true dark
crimson of the 'Slater's Crimson China' which I guess is in its pedigree. A climbing sport
was named 'Catalunya'.
Hoffmann, Plate 19.
Rosenzeitung, 1899.
Journal des Roses, Septembre 1899. 'Salut à Teplitz'. Poor.

'Guinée'. Mallerin, France, 1938. Owing its dark colour to 'Château de Clos Vougeot', this
rose is of mixed modern parentage, but its colour resembles the most dusky of Hybrid
Perpetuals, such as 'Souvenir du Docteur Jamain': deepest murrey with crimson centre,
pure, unfading, without purple; beautiful shapely flowers and intense red-rose fragrance.
A vigorous, satisfactory plant which has no peer in its colour class among old or new roses.
Foliage good. 18 feet. Needs a light background and does not show up against greenery.
A good first crop and many odd blooms later. (Plate 151.)

'La France, Climbing'. Henderson, U.S., 1893. Presumed to be 'Mme Victor Verdier' ×
'Mme Bravy'. While the climbing sport is not nearly so free-flowering as the original bush
form (Guillot Fils, France, 1867), it does give me an opportunity to mention this exquisite hardy fragrant rose, one of the first Hybrid Teas raised. Grow the bush by all means,
but do not let us lose this delightful charmer. The climber will reach 12 feet or more.
Gibson, Plate 8.

'Lady Forteviot, Climbing'. Cant, U.K., 1928. The climbing sport occurred in 1935. Its rich
scent and soft orange-apricot suffusion over the yellow of the petals warrant its inclusion,
though it is not very recurrent, but vigorous and with good foliage.

'Lady Sylvia, Climbing'. Stevens, U.K., 1926; a sport from 'Mme Butterfly'; produced climbing sport in 1933. The deeper of the two well-known and exquisite descendants of
'Ophelia'. 20 feet.

'Lady Waterlow'. Nabonnand, France, 1903. 'La France de '89' × 'Mme Marie Lavalley'. Full
blooms of very clear pink, with salmon shadings; beautifully-veined petals. Clean, sweet
fragrance. Many later blooms. 12 feet. A gem.

'**Mme Abel Chatenay, Climbing**'. The climbing sport originated in 1917 from the original raised by Pernet-Ducher in 1895. 'Dr Grill' (Tea) × 'Victor Verdier' (Hybrid Tea). The bush form is extremely good and there is no need to grow the climber but, as with 'La France', it does allow me to include this outstandingly beautiful and highly productive rose. The flowers are very full, with quilled petals, light pink deepening towards the centre, and with deeper reverse. A poor description for an exquisite flower, unsurpassed for its neat fullness and its revivifying, penetrating, delicious fragrance. 15 feet.
Journal des Roses, Juin 1913. A poor portrait.
Revue Horticole, 1906, page 64. Fair.
Hoffmann, Plate 9.

'**Mme Butterfly, Climbing**'. E. G. Hill Co., U.S., 1918. 'Ophelia' sport, from which the climbing sport was introduced in 1926. Delightful pale pink. Regularly recurrent. See also 'Ophelia'. 18 feet.

'**Mme Caroline Testout, Climbing**'. Pernet-Ducher, France, 1890. 'Mme de Tartas' × 'Lady Mary Fitzwilliam'. The sport was introduced in 1901. Little fragrance, and the flowers are apt to "ball." Even so it is, after all these years, one of the most prolific and recurrent of climbing sports. Clear silvery pink with rolled petals. Mid green leaves. It has had an immense influence on the breeding of roses. 18 feet.
Kingsley, page 97.
Gibson, Plate 30.

'**Mme de Sancy de Parabère**'. Bonnet, France, prior to 1845. The largest-flowered and most beautiful of all the old Boursault Roses. Clear, soft pink flowers of large size, 5 inches across; as a rule the outer petals are far larger than those in the middle, which are inclined to make a central rosette. Gentle scent. Free-flowering very early in the season on long shoots which are completely thornless. 15 feet.

I think the floral style of this rose is unique and, coupled with its early season and freedom from prickles, makes it well worth growing. The smaller-flowered crimson-purple Boursault 'Amadis' is also sometimes seen; it is included in Chapter 8, "Old and New Garden Ramblers." (Plate 137.)

'**Mme Édouard Herriot, Climbing**'. Pernet-Ducher, France, 1913. 'Mme Caroline Testout' × a Hybrid Tea, from which the climbing sport was introduced in 1921. '*Daily Mail* Rose'. A noted favourite; nothing quite like it in colour has been raised since. Buds deep flame-pink, opening coral pink, loosely double, starry. Early-flowering, with a few blooms later. Fragrant. 15 feet.

'**Mme Grégoire Staechelin**'. Dot, Spain, 1927. 'Spanish Beauty'. 'Frau Karl Druschki' × 'Château de Clos Vougeot'. It is unfortunate that this handsome rose flowers only once, but what a flowering it is! Early in the season with 'Easlea's Golden', 'Blairii Number 2', and others, it coincides with the flowering of the Bearded Irises and makes a most glorious display, with delicious sweet-pea fragrance. Large generous flowers, semi-double, glowing flesh pink with much deeper reverse. Dark glossy leaves. An indispensable rose which will thrive on a north wall, as at Tintinhull House, Somerset, a property of the National Trust. 20 feet. (Plate 149.)
McFarland, *Roses of the World*, page 172. } The same picture.
Stevens, page 154.

In my earlier books I followed the usual authorities in describing the Boursault roses as hybrids between *Rosa pendulina* and *R. chinensis.* Gordon Rowley tells me the chromosome count of *R. pendulina* renders this improbable and that it is likely that some other diploid thornless species was concerned, such as *R. blanda.* The three varieties I have found are only slightly fragrant, but this and the others, the shrubby 'Morletii' and 'Amadis', are worth retaining for their other attributes.

Redouté, Vol. 3, Plates 79 (*Rosa reclinata*) and 80 (*R. reclinata sub multiplici*). These plates show prickly roses which cannot be reconciled with any Boursault known today.

Redouté, Vol. 3, Plate 21. *Rosa lheritierana.* Also prickly!

'New Dawn'. A perpetual-flowering sport of 'Dr van Fleet' which occurred in the United States (1930). Justly famous for its glossy foliage and deliciously fragrant, light silvery pink small flowers, of exquisite shape in bud and when open; they are produced freely in clusters, just past midsummer usually, for many weeks, and later crops occur. Lovely with old or new roses. Will achieve 20 feet on a wall, but is superb when allowed to grow as a lax bush, or trained loosely over a stump or hedge, with *Lonicera americana.* Less vigorous than its once-flowering parent, 'Dr van Fleet'.
Stevens, page 208.

'Ophelia, Climbing'. W. Paul, U.K., 1912. Parentage unknown. The climbing sport was introduced in 1920. This exquisite blush-pink rose, of beautiful scrolled shape in bud and ideal for cutting on strong stems, has produced two equally valuable darker sports, 'Mme Butterfly' and 'Lady Sylvia'. All are first-rate and very recurrent and fragrant. Good under glass but quite hardy. 20 feet.

An interesting account by Ann Wylie of sports and hybrids from this prolific parental rose will be found in the *Journal* of the Royal Horticultural Society for January 1955.

'Paul's Lemon Pillar'. William Paul, U.K., 1915. 'Frau Karl Druschki' × 'Maréchal Niel'. Distinguished parents have produced a unique once-flowering rose, and its crop of huge scented blooms in early midsummer will excuse it from its failure later. The flowers are extra large, filled with petals rolled at the edges, and of sumptuous quality and fragrance, clear lemon-white with a slight primrose-green tint in the centre. In spite of its Tea parentage, it has not suffered from cold in the open with me, but should be given a warm wall in cold districts, where it may reach 15 feet. There is nothing like it. (Plate 148.)

'Picture, Climbing'. McGredy, U.K., 1932. Parentage unknown. The climbing sport was introduced ten years later. In the 'Ophelia' tradition, but smaller in flower. Dusky deep pink. Fragrant. Recurrent. 15 feet.

'Shot Silk, Climbing'. Dickson, U.K., 1924. 'Hugh Dickson' seedling × 'Sunstar', the sport from which was introduced in 1931. Beautiful, rounded, deep warm salmon-pink blooms with yellow base. Fragrant. Recurrent. 12 feet. Early flowering.
Gibson, Plate 30.

'Souvenir de Claudius Denoyel'. Chambard, France, 1920. A hybrid of 'Château de Clos Vougeot', and possessing its informal, somewhat cupped flowers. Vigorous, with large mid green leaves. A great crop of flowers is borne at midsummer, early in the flowering season of Hybrid Teas, the whole plant becoming a sheet of bright crimson, of unfading quality; repeats in less quantity in later months. Lovely loose flowers of old style; intense sweet fragrance. 18 feet.

'**Souvenir de la Malmaison, Climbing**'. Bennett (the raiser of 'Mrs John Laing'), Shepperton, Surrey, 1893. A climbing sport of the original bush form, described in Chapter 6, "The

those in September are always best. A flat, double, blush rose of great size in the old tradition. Useful for sunny or shady walls. 12 feet.

THE "NEW" CLIMBERS

Oh, how much more doth beauty beauteous seem
By that sweet ornament which truth doth give!
The rose looks fair, but fairer we it deem
For that sweet odour which doth in it live.

Shakespeare, Sonnet 54

IF THE ROSES in the last section may be called "Hybrid Tea climbers," denoting a large, formal style of flower, those in this chapter might well be dubbed "Floribunda climbers." There is a lot of variation in size and shape among them, but in the main they are loosely double or semi-double and of informal shape. Some are actually climbing sports of Floribundas and, with the vast quantities of these roses in current cultivation today, we can expect to see their numbers increased every year.

As with earlier sections, there are some outlying varieties, some quite old, which have to be included simply because they do not fit elsewhere.

First there are a few derived from descendants of *Rosa foetida*, the Austrian Brier: 'Star of Persia' (1919) and 'Réveil Dijonnais' (1931); the former inherits the peculiar scent of *R. foetida*, and seldom is recurrent, while the brilliant 'Réveil' is more recurrent, with a sweet fragrance. Many class these both as shrubs, but they are the better for some support. 'Lawrence Johnston' and 'Le Rêve' were raised in 1923, and the former is one of our most brilliant and earliest, somewhat recurrent yellow climbers with medium-sized flowers; the same might be said of 'Paul's Scarlet Climber' (1916) among those of that colour.

A rose raised by George Paul, 'Paul's Single White', is seldom seen today, but for those who prefer quietness and charm to brilliance and splendour it is worth growing, and is always in flower.

Rosa wichuraiana intrudes through 'Purity'—an excellent pure white—'Dream Girl', and several others. The last is of salmon-pink tone, and I regard it as one of the best and most fragrant of recurrent pillar roses in this colour, while 'Dr van Fleet', and its perpetual sport 'New Dawn' (see preceding section) might well be included in this category.

One of the best of perpetual-flowering shrub roses, *Rosa rugosa* has produced a lot of hybrids but, owing to its character of being unable to transmit fertility to succeeding generations, it has never entered into the main stream of garden roses. However, as noted in Chapter 5, "The Japanese or Rugosa Roses," in the care of Wilhelm Kordes seed of the hybrid 'Max Graf' (raised in 1919, *R. rugosa* × *R. wichuraiana*) ripened in the early 1940s with spontaneously doubled chromosomes and produced tetraploid seedlings. One of these has been named *R. kordesii*, and is in effect a new fertile species, combining great hardiness and disease resistance, and has been used as a parent with various roses, resulting in many new perpetual-flowering climbing roses, including 'Dortmund', 'Hamburger Phoenix', 'Leverkusen' and 'Parkdirektor Riggers'. These and the bulk of new varieties are red, flame, or yellow in tone.

With these introductory remarks we may now cursorily go through the roses in this section; taking the yellows first, 'Leverkusen' is a delightful creamy lemon colour, 'Casino', soft
yellow, and 'Magic Carpet' is brighter, with the distinction of having extremely attractive
well-filled flowers with petals quilled and quartered in the old·style. 'Golden Showers',
'Alchymist', and 'Royal Gold' are clear, bright yellows of varying tones. 'Climbing Allgold' is
a vivid deep yellow—and, to judge from how well the parent Floribunda does in the wetter
west, this rose should be a reliable grower where rain and black spot abound. It appears to be
resistant to both!—but the climbing sport is at present rather shy-flowering, unfortunately.
'Maigold' is a very deep and lovely buff yellow, nearly single with splendid dark foliage, a
character in which practically all these modern roses excel.

Next we have one rather on its own, the nearly single 'Meg' in rich peach and apricot tones,
and the double 'Schoolgirl' and 'Compassion' of similar warm colouring.

Really flaming scarlet is found in 'Soldier Boy'—comparable with 'Scarlet Fire' among the
shrubs—and 'Kassel', which has a coppery sheen. 'Danse du Feu' and 'Danse des Sylphes' I
have omitted from this chapter of personal choices; the former dies off with contrasting
tones of purplish-red against the orange-red of the freshly open flowers.

Darker reds are 'Dortmund', 'Hamburger Phoenix', 'Sweet Sultan', 'Raymond Chenault',
and 'Sympathie'; 'Sweet Sultan' verges towards murrey. Less intense, with a good deal more
crimson or carmine in it, is 'Étendard', descended direct from 'New Dawn', while the splendid 'Parade' in light crimson brings us to the pinks. My favourite is 'Dream Girl', mentioned
above; 'Nymphenburg' I deal with in Chapter 6, "Shrub Roses, of the Twentieth Century,"
though it could be grown as a climber equally well. This leaves us several good pinks: 'Ritter
von Barmstede', 'Climbing Ballet', 'Bantry Bay', 'Handel', 'Coral Dawn', and 'Pink Perpétue'.
These are in the forefront of modern climbing roses and it is to be regretted that, while in
cool weather they are so delightful, several of them—and others mentioned above—fade
disagreeably.

All on its own is 'Ash Wednesday', or 'Aschermittwoch'; its light lilac-grey fades on expansion to grey-white, and the flower is in the old style, well filled with petals and quartered.
This and 'Leverkusen' are good varieties for cooling down the welter of orange-red varieties.

None of these varieties is likely to exceed greatly 12 feet in height. It is misleading in books
and catalogues today to read of their being "rampant growers"; this term is best reserved for
such enormous plants as the 'Kiftsgate' *Rosa filipes, R. rubus,* 'Mermaid', 'Albéric Barbier', and
'Mme d'Arblay', to name but a few. It is disconcerting to find the term "rampant grower"
immediately followed by a recommendation of the variety being described for growing on a
pillar. Really rampant growers are quite unsuited to such a use, as very hard pruning results
in few flowers, and the average pillar (usually of wood) in our gardens does not exceed 8 feet
in height. I should like to grow all these modern varieties—and all the Climbing sports of
Hybrid Teas—in one field, with identical cultivation. Then it would be possible to assess
their relative merits, vigour, fragrance, and most particularly their proclivities towards perpetual flowering. Only then could we make a choice with any degree of accuracy. Unfortunately
I have been unable to grow all these roses, and neither the Royal National Rose Society nor
the Royal Horticultural Society is able to institute so space-taking a trial; only a few have
been given any really studied reports from a disinterested body. One therefore has to rely on
raisers' original descriptions, coupled with one's observations on seeing odd varieties in various gardens. My descriptions must therefore be taken as an indication only of the qualities
of each variety.

First let us look at three older varieties derived from *Rosa foetida* in early days which still have their values, and at the unique 'Single White' of George Paul.

'Lawrence Johnston'. Raised in 1923 by Pernet-Ducher, this rose was out of the same cross as 'Le Rêve' ('Mme Eugène Verdier' × *Rosa foetida persiana*). For some reason it did not appeal to the raiser, while 'Le Rêve' was put on the market. It languished unappreciated until Major Lawrence Johnston saw it, bought the original and only plant, and transferred it to his garden at Hidcote Manor, Gloucestershire, some time between the First and Second World Wars. There it was christened 'Hidcote Yellow' (but distinct from 'Hidcote Gold', which is related to *R. sericea pteracantha*), and was distributed to a few favoured gardeners, eventually finding its way into my hands. I thought so highly of it that I asked Major Johnston if I could exhibit it; he assented, and asked that his name should be put on it. It received the Royal Horticultural Society's Award of Merit, 1948. It outclasses 'Le Rêve'; the growth is stronger, the foliage equally good, the yellow warmer and richer, and the flowers are better formed, with larger petals. The scent is just as rich and powerful. Fortunately it flowers with equal abandon in June and also goes on producing flowers intermittently through the summer. Shoots may grow to 20 feet. The original plant still grows at Hidcote Manor, and young ones have been planted there. (Plate 156.)
Gibson, Plate 7.

'Réveil Dijonnais'. Buatois, France, 1931. This spectacular rose owes its brilliant colour to 'Constance', a Pernet-Ducher rose with 'Rayon d'Or' in its parentage; the other parent was 'Eugène Fürst', a splendid dark red Hybrid Perpetual. The result is a vigorous plant with good, light green foliage richly tinted when young, producing semi-double or nearly single flowers at midsummer and a few later through the growing season; brilliant cerise-scarlet with wide yellow centres and yellowish reverse, obviously inherited far back from 'Austrian Copper'. Useful for "hot" colour schemes. Branches achieve about 12 feet, but it is best used as an open shrub; not so suitable for pillars or confined wall spaces, since it is bushy. Pleasant sweet scent, without trace of *Rosa foetida*.
McFarland, *Roses of the World*, page 223.
American *Rose Annual*, 1935, page 201.

'Star of Persia'. Pemberton, U.K., 1919. *Rosa foetida* × 'Trier'. No doubt this was an attempt to get a really yellow Hybrid Musk, but the result is too near to *R. foetida* in foliage and wood; lanky in growth and without the Hybrid Musk scent, leaning more towards that of *R. foetida*. Semi-double, brilliant yellow. Hardly worth growing, but included here because it has never entirely lost favour. 8 to 10 feet.
Stevens, page 149.

'Paul's Single White'. George Paul, U.K., 1883. Seldom seen today, George Paul's rose does not compare with William Paul's 'Paul's Scarlet'. It is a plant achieving 6 to 8 feet, with good foliage and a constant production (a few at a time) of single, blush-white flowers in clusters. Sweetly scented. Makes a pleasing foil to larger, double blooms. There is a good monochrome photograph of this in Miss Jekyll's *Roses for English Gardens*, facing page 11. In the days when ramblers flowered only at midsummer, this must have been greatly prized; today it is unique, and that is all one can say, though a range of colours on plants like this would be acceptable. At least it is perpetual, which is a rare attribute. A close relative of *Rosa moschata*.
The Garden, 1886, Vol. 29, Plate 526, facing page 28.

Modern Floribunda Climbers

I have all but omitted references to coloured illustrations from the descriptions of these newer roses. There is a wealth of such illustrations today, some good, some bad, in catalogues and books; but very few show more than a bloom or two, omitting all details of growth, foliage, and armature, and so their citing loses point.

'Alchymist'. Kordes, Germany, 1956. 'Golden Glow' × *Rosa rubiginosa* hybrid. Though not recurrent, this is well worth a place in the garden for the sake of its very full-petalled, old-style, double, fragrant flowers, of clear light yellow warmed by orange in the centre. Excellent bronzy foliage. Fragrant. 12 feet.

'Allgold, Climbing'. Gandy, U.K., 1961. Rather shy-flowering until well established. Clear yellow, double. Some fragrance. Glossy foliage. About 12 feet.

'Aloha'. Boerner, U.S., 1949. 'Mercédès Gallart' × 'New Dawn'. From famous antecedents in the previous generation 'Aloha' gives a lot of the quality of the big, full roses of the past. Clear rose-pink with much deeper reverse to the petals; the blooms are coppery in the centre, and thus they blend with almost any colour association. Not really a climber, but suitable for a pillar or for use as a shrub. Delicious Tea-fragrance. Possibly 8 feet. (Plate 153.) Park, Plate 48.
Gault and Synge, Plate 230.

'Altissimo'. Delbard-Chabert, France, 1967. Though often classed as a climber, it is equally suitable for growing as a large shrub, when its brilliant red, single blooms and matt foliage create a wonderful picture. Little scent.
Gault and Synge, Plate 231.

'Aschermittwoch'. See 'Ash Wednesday', below.

'Ash Wednesday' ('Aschermittwoch'). Kordes, Germany, 1955. *Rosa rubiginosa* hybrid. Grey-lilac buds develop into large, full, grey-white flowers borne in bunches. Abundant bloom at midsummer. 12 to 18 feet.

'Ballet, Climbing'. Kordes, Germany, 1962. 'Florex' × 'Karl Herbst'. The fully double flowers are beautifully coiled in the bud, opening with rolled petals. A very good warm pink; fragrant. Matt foliage. This does well on sandy soil at Wisley, and is recurrent. 10 feet.

'Bantry Bay'. McGredy, U.K., 1967. Semi-double flowers, opening flat, of rich deep flesh pink, produced recurrently. Good glossy foliage. Sweet brier scent. 10 feet.

'Blossomtime'. O'Neal, U.S., 1951. 'New Dawn' is one parent, the other being an unnamed Hybrid Tea. It has derived good from both parents, being a lax shrub or low climber with good foliage and bearing Hybrid Tea-style flowers of clear pink, deeper on the reverse, in clusters. The first crop is followed by numerous later flowers. It has much of the beauty of the old 'La France'. Very fragrant. 6 to 8 feet.

'Casino'. McGredy, U.K., 1963. 'Coral Dawn' × 'Buccaneer'. The large double flowers are of soft yellow, paling with age, fragrant, with dark green, glossy, abundant foliage. Frequent later blooms. 10 feet.

'Compassion'. Harkness, U.K., 1974. 'White Cockade' × 'Prima Ballerina'. Beautifully scrolled buds, of warm apricot orange, opening to soft salmon-pink. Splendid dark glossy foliage and vigorous growth to 8 feet. Very fragrant and continuous.

'Coral Dawn'. Boerner, U.S., 1952. A 'New Dawn' seedling × unnamed yellow Hybrid Tea, crossed with unnamed orange-red Polyantha; anything might happen!—but a very charming rose is the result. Large blooms, cupped, of rich coral pink. Leathery foliage. Fragrant. 7 to 9 feet.
Gault and Synge, Plate 238.

'Dream Girl'. Jacobus, U.S., 1944. A seedling of 'Dr van Fleet'. Lambertus C. Bobbink sent me this rose with very high recommendations, which it has upheld to the full. Seldom reaching more than 9 feet, it is suitable for fence or pillar, and would, I believe, with suitable pruning make a shrub. It flowers after midsummer; large, fully double, warm coral-pink flowers, fading paler, in branching clusters, with delicious penetrating aroma. The flowers resemble those of the old shrub roses and are often quartered; and it has dark glossy leaves. (Plate 158.)

'Dreaming Spires'. Mattock, U.K., 1977. 'Buccaneer' × 'Arthur Bell'. A welcome addition to the warm deep yellows, with orange flush, fading paler, contrasting well with the dark stamens. Handsome dark foliage, neatly veined. Constantly in flower. Fragrant. Perhaps 12 feet.

'Étendard'. Robichon, France, 1956. Also known as 'New Dawn Rouge', this was produced by crossing 'New Dawn' with a seedling, and the result is very successful. Dark, leaden green, glossy leaves and clusters of deep carmine flowers in the 'New Dawn' tradition. Fragrant. Very free-flowering in summer and through till autumn. Perhaps 12 feet.

'Golden Showers'. Lammerts, U.S., 1956. 'Charlotte Armstrong' × 'Captain Thomas'. Good, glossy foliage and erect growth, making with a little support almost a shrub, but probably best as a pillar or wall rose. The flowers are large, loosely semi-double, emerging from shapely buds, bright clear yellow, fragrant. This rose bids fair to be as floriferous as any throughout the summer and autumn. 8 to 10 feet.

'Handel'. McGredy, U.K., 1965. Exquisite buds and scrolled half-open blooms of creamy white with pink picotee edge. In hot weather the picotee increases in area over the expanding petals, and deepens in colour. Lovely in autumn, it is constantly in flower after the main crop. 8 feet. Some fragrance.

'Iceberg, Climbing'. Cant, U.K., 1968. This Kordes rose, raised in 1958, sported ten years later to give us an excellent white, fragrant climber, which when well established is constantly in flower. 10 feet.

'Karlsruhe'. Kordes, Germany, 1957. Of *Rosa kordesii* derivation, and a vigorous glossy-leaved rose with fully double old-type flowers of deep rose-pink. Very free at midsummer and intermittently until autumn. Some fragrance. 10 to 12 feet.

'Leverkusen'. Kordes, Germany, 1954. *Rosa kordesii* × 'Golden Glow'. Glossy light green leaves blend well with the light yellow blooms, large and double. Its grace, glittering foliage, pleasing colour, and lemony fragrance, a main crop and frequent later sprays of blooms, add up to a fine rose. Freely branching, can be used as a shrub or hedge with suitable training and pruning. Will achieve 10 feet or more on a wall.

'**Maigold**'. Kordes, Germany, 1953. 'McGredy's Wonder' × 'Frühlingsgold'. From its parentage this is obviously a shrub, but it appears disposed to climb. Like 'Nymphenburg' it lies between the two classes, and is perhaps best treated as a sprawling shrub, or used to cover low hedges or supports, as is so excellent for 'Albertine'. This rose has really excellent foliage, rich and glossy and profuse. The flowers appear early in the season and are of deep buff-yellow, reddish in the bud, semi-double, showing a bunch of yellow stamens. Powerful, delicious fragrance. Repeats occasionally through the summer. 12 feet.

'**Meg**'. Gosset, U.K., 1954. Probably 'Paul's Lemon Pillar' × 'Mme Butterfly'. These two classic parents have produced an unclassical but beautiful child. It is almost single—about ten petals—with large blooms of apricot-pink with yellow base and dark stamens; borne in clusters. Fragrant. A vigorous climber to 10 feet with good foliage. Occasional later blooms after the main crop. (Plate 157.)
Gault and Synge, Plate 250.

'**New Dawn**'. See preceding section.

'**Nymphenburg**'. Kordes, Germany, 1954. 'Sangerhausen' × 'Sunmist'. This splendid rose is described in Chapter 6, "Shrub Roses of the Twentieth Century." Being a lax grower with long, strong shoots it would make an admirable climber, probably achieving 18 feet with support, but is also ideal for covering a shed or tree stump or hedgerow. Clear salmon-pink, shaded cerise-pink and orange with yellow base. As perpetual as any.

'**Parade**'. Boerner, U.S., 1953. 'New Dawn' seedling × 'Climbing World's Fair'. A brilliant and free-flowering rose bearing two big crops of bloom and odd blooms in between. A deep rich crimson-pink, cupped, on good stems. Good fragrance. 12 feet. (Plate 152.)

'**Paul's Scarlet Climber**'. William Paul, U.K., 1916. The most popular of all climbing roses, though 'Chaplin's Pink' and 'Albertine' run it close. The three together usher in the summer rose season on countless garden walls throughout Great Britain. The bright crimson-scarlet of Paul's splendid rose, together with its unsophisticated shape, make it suitable for association with the older roses as well as the new. Slightly fragrant. Later blooms are most plentiful when it is not pruned after the first crop. 20 feet.
The Garden, 1897, Vol. 2, page 464.

'**Pink Perpétue**'. Gregory, U.K., 1965. 'Danse du Feu' × 'New Dawn'. The most popular pink, repeat-blooming climber. Rich warm pink, double flowers, in clusters, well set off by glossy foliage. Fragrance of green apples, derived from *Rosa wichuraiana* far back in its parentage. 10 feet.

'**Purity**'. Hoopes, U.S., 1917. The unnamed seedling which was crossed with 'Mme Caroline Testout' must have been of *Rosa wichuraiana* parentage, judging by its offspring's glossy leaves, reminiscent of 'New Dawn'. Pure white flowers, loosely double, showing yellow stamens. Delicious fragrance. A vigorous, prickly plant. Seldom repeats. 12 feet.

'**Rosy Mantle**'. Cocker, U.K., 1968. 'New Dawn' × 'Prima Ballerina'. A good repeat-flowerer with dark glossy foliage, and considerable fragrance. Rich silvery pink, flushed cerise on opening, fairly full flowers with quilled petals. 9 feet.

'**Soldier Boy**'. LeGrice, U.K., 1953. Seedling × 'Guinée'. Blazing scarlet, single shapely blooms with yellow stamens. For brilliance this pillar rose would be hard to beat. The main crop is succeeded by frequent later blooms. 8 to 10 feet.

'**Swan Lake**'. McGredy, U.K., 1968. 'Memoriam' × 'Heidelburg'. A beautiful white rose, with rosy flush in the centre. Full, large flowers, shapely, borne singly and in clusters through the season. Glossy leaves. No fragrance. 10 feet.

'**Sympathie**'. Kordes, Germany, 1964. Velvety, shapely, double, dark red blooms borne repeatedly among glossy foliage. Some fragrance. 10 feet.

In spite of their tendency towards strident colouring and lack of scent, I find many of these newer "Floribunda climbers" of real value when designing mixed borders for colour effect. They assort well with shrubs and plants and, either as a background trained on a wall, or allowed to hang over a big evergreen shrub or otherwise to be enjoyed as informal loose shrubs themselves, they are in the main an asset to present-day horticulture. Very few would be suitable in a garden of the older roses, but I think we could include 'Aloha', 'Étendard', 'Dream Girl', and 'Parade'; 'Leverkusen' and 'Magic Carpet' if yellows are wanted; while the white 'Purity' and 'Paul's Single White' and grey 'Ash Wednesday' would have right of entry on account of colour.

It has been extremely difficult to try to divide all these Hybrid Tea- and Floribunda-types of climbers into two sections, and every now and again I have felt the shrubby character of one or another was so much to the fore that they might well have been included in Part 2 of this book. Today there are no clear-cut races of roses, except the three main divisions: BEDDING ROSES, SHRUB ROSES, and CLIMBERS (including Ramblers). Breeding proceeds apace and roses of every conceivable variation in growth, shape of flower, style, and colour are being raised, mainly among bedding and shrub varieties, and it is inevitable that the old group-names should become unsuitable to cover all this diversity. The range of varieties will increase with every fresh species that is pressed into service for hybridizing.

While it should not be necessary to abandon the old group names (such as the Old Roses, the Noisettes, the Hybrid Musks, and others) for *roses already raised*, it cannot be pretended that new varieties will necessarily fit into these groups, which are genealogical rather than functional. I very much hope that some may be raised along the old lines, for these old groups give us something which we can ill afford to lose: perpetual production, fragrance, and vigour are at their best in some of the old Noisettes; grace and vigour and Edwardian charm in some of the old Ramblers; foliage, fragrance, vigour, and old-style flowers in what I have called the Large-flowered Ramblers.

But today, with an ever more complex race evolving, the term Bedding Roses should cover all those bush varieties suitable for pruning low, to make a pattern of colour, up to say 3 feet in height in formal or informal bedding: these would include as subdivisions the small-flowered Poly-poms (at one time classed as Dwarf Polyanthas), the Hybrid Teas, and the intermediates, the Floribundas. It would be quite right to retain these group names for roses which have been raised and conform to one group or another. As, gradually, bush roses are bred infusing all these types, which seems the obvious and inevitable trend, they can be termed simply Bedding Roses.

With the shrubs, in which might be included certain Bedding Roses which make good bushy plants of 4 feet or over, once again the old group names should be retained for such distinct strains as the true Rugosas, the Old Roses, and the Hybrid Musks, and, as for the Bedding Roses, when new perpetual- or recurrent-flowering varieties of mixed parentage are raised, they could simply be termed Shrub Roses, recurrent.

And so with climbers—retaining old terms like Ramblers and Climbing sports of Hybrid Teas, and using simply a term such as Climber for all the new kinds.

These terms would be all-embracing, or as nearly so as possible, and would make for ease of reference and selection in the future, until some species of untold potentiality is pressed into service. None of the groups above specifically makes provision for ground-covering varieties, but these are, of course, Ramblers which are used without supports.

It may well be that, in addition to the three big group names, the need will be felt for some new terms for new groups, when raised. For instance, supposing recurrent-flowering Ramblers are produced, where would they be classed? While obviously still coming into the category of Climbing Roses, they would not fit with the modern Floribunda-climbers any better than with the once-flowering Ramblers. A new group name would have to be coined. It is quite possible that, using 'Aimée Vibert', the Old Musk, 'Paul's Single White', *Rosa setigera*, 'Crimson Shower', and a few more, hybridizing might result in a race of Ramblers flowering *from July onwards.*

Several paragraphs in earlier sections have been devoted to roses of the future, and I venture to suggest once again some lines of breeding which would greatly increase the breadth of rose-appreciation. As I am not a breeder myself, this may seem presumptuous, but my re-iterated thought is that until one delves deeply into roses—all kinds of roses—one cannot realize the almost limitless array of characters available; breeding along stereotyped lines is quite unnecessary. Breeders today generally know what they want. As a rule it is size and brilliance, coupled with stout stalks, hard shiny foliage, and vigour. Fragrance, grace, and charm are not qualities which are given so much thought today, although David Austin is an exception in this, as in his choice of soft colours. A few breeders, such as E. B. LeGrice, saw beauty in single roses as originally contrived by nature. As the fragrance in the Synstylae species is in their stamens, there is no need in rambling roses to increase the petals to provide more fragrance. In short, I should like to see breeders bringing in the stamen-borne fragrance of the Synstylae species, the superb foliage of 'Albéric Barbier' and 'Mermaid', and also the Tea fragrance and pale and apricot yellows—coupled with their perpetual-flowering habit—of the best Noisettes; uniting the purple colouring of the main Ramblers of that colour with good characters of other groups; creating late-flowering Ramblers, and re-creating our favourite Ramblers so that they are all fragrant.

As I have said earlier, compared with the effort that has gone into the production of Bedding Roses, little has been done for Climbers and Ramblers, and I like to think that one day breeders will turn their attention to a greater variety of colour, fragrance, and charm than is apparent today in the ceaseless stream of red, scarlet, and flame.

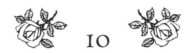

10

Some Rare Species and Their Forms and Hybrids

Oh love (the more my wo) to it thow art
Yeven as the moysture in each plant that growes
Yeven as the soonn unto the frosen ground
Yeven as the sweetness to th'incarnate rose
Yeven as the Centre in each perfait rounde.

Sir Walter Raleigh, ?1552–1618

THE BANKSIAN ROSES

THERE IS NO DOUBT that where they can be grown, the forms of the Banksian Rose give unique beauty. They are exceedingly vigorous ramblers producing their small flowers in clusters in spring, and figures have been quoted in gardening journals giving the number of flowers on large plants as fifty thousand. I can well believe it, after looking at some of the pictures in these old books. In the list of Roses at the Château Éléonore, Cannes, compiled by Lord Brougham and Vaux in 1898, there is a photograph of a plant of the double yellow form covering an olive tree with countless trails and branches, creating a mound of blossom some 30 feet high. An article in *Arizona Highways* for January 1956, kindly sent to me by W. L. Hunt of North Carolina, describes a tree, in Tombstone, Arizona, of the double white form supported as a canopy and covering 4,620 square feet; it produces hundreds of thousands of blooms. To be there at flowering time and to smell the fragrance of violets floating from it must be among the greatest floral experiences of the world.

In England this exuberance is not achieved. These are roses that need lots of sunshine to ripen their wood, and a corresponding absence of severe frost. There is no doubt that proper ripening of the wood enables them to resist winter cold, and on sunny walls in the south of England the double yellow form may be expected to thrive and flower freely.

The various forms flowered first in Europe during the nineteenth century and just into the present century, and their discovery provides an interesting sequence of events.

A celebrated gardener at the turn of the century, E. H. Woodall, whose name is remembered best perhaps in the fine form of *Carpenteria californica* that bears his name, must have been very delighted and even thrilled in 1909 when he first saw flowers on an unknown rose in his garden. He had obtained cuttings from Megginch Castle, Strathtay, Scotland, where it had grown for many years, having been brought from China with various other plants, so the story goes, by one Robert Drummond, in 1796; he had cruised to the Far East with his brother the Admiral. This intriguing rose had lived at Megginch for all those years without a flower, having been cut back annually by the severe winter weather. It was thornless, with neat small leaves. Its flowers, produced at Nice for the first time, were small, single, white, with a pronounced fragrance, and I think we can say that this was the first time this wild form of *Rosa banksiae*, known as *normalis*, had flowered in Europe.

Meanwhile, in 1803 William Kerr was sent to China by the Royal Society to look for good garden plants to bring home, and among others he found in a Canton garden the double white form of the species, which arrived in England in 1807 and flowered at Isleworth, being named after Lady Banks, the wife of the then director at Kew. This is now known botanically as *Rosa banksiae banksiae*, the type-species, though most usually called *R. banksiae* 'Alba Plena'; it also is deliciously scented.

A little later, the Royal Horticultural Society sent J. D. Parks (the introducer of 'Parks's Yellow Tea-scented China Rose') on a trip to Asia, and his instructions included the obtaining of the double yellow Banksian rose which had been reported at Calcutta Botanic Garden. It had been brought from China; it was collected successfully and flowered here in 1824, and is now known as *Rosa banksiae* 'Lutea'. It is delicately fragrant.

In 1870, plants of the single yellow form were introduced to England by Sir Thomas Hanbury from his famous garden at La Mortola, Menton, though I cannot find out whence he obtained it. It is called *Rosa banksiae* 'Lutescens' and is as sweetly-scented as the single and double white forms. This rose and its varieties had presumably been favourites in Chinese gardens for a long while; most of the Europeans collecting in China had not penetrated far into the mainland, but had found many plants in gardens around the coastal towns. In the wild state it occurs mainly in western China, in the mountain ranges between Yunnan and Shensi and as far east as Hupeh. In these areas the wild forms are found at altitudes of around five thousand feet.

This rose and its forms have no immediate relatives among other species of *Rosa* except *R. cymosa*. In cultivation they are practically thornless, with long green flexible canes bearing the small pointed smooth leaves with three to five leaflets, and the stipules fall away very early in the season. When the plants get old the bark becomes flaky and brown, and very thick trunks are produced. It is important to retain all the young wood, up to six or seven years old if possible, because the flowers are produced in greatest quality and quantity on the two- to three-year-old side-shoots growing off the long trails. Consequently, pruning should consist of removing, occasionally, very old wood. This is always difficult because usually there are strong young shoots coming from it, which should be allowed to arch gracefully from the wall. But if a percentage of, say, five-year-old shoots is removed each year, there will usually be plenty left to produce flowers. When the plant is young no pruning is required, but hampered as we are by having to give the rose wall-space, some limit will be reached and some pruning must be done from time to time. I would much prefer to see it covering a tree in its loose and graceful way, but this could be successful only in really warm sunny gardens, where little or no frost occurs.

The double yellow is a splendid free-flowering plant, and it is unfortunate that this most popular Banksian variety has less scent than the others. Contrary to the statements in many books, and to the usual opinion, I find it is not by any means scentless. The other three forms do not flower so freely in England in my experience, though they grow and flower at Leonardslee and at Highdown, Sussex, and also at Powis Castle, Montgomeryshire, a property of the National Trust. At Kiftsgate Court in Gloucestershire the soft buttery yellow of *Rosa banksiae* 'Lutea' creates a lovely picture with *Clematis montana rubens*. Both colours are particularly tender in quality, and assort well together against the stone wall.

It grows and flowers freely in the south of France and other Mediterranean districts where the climate is congenial. It is easy to grow from cuttings and has been used as an understock. In severe winters in Surrey, I have known the young wood to be killed.

banksiae. The single forms are considered to be variants from the wild. All will achieve 20 feet or more in good conditions.

—**banksiae** ('Alba Plena'). Double white flowers densely packed with small petals, making a neat rosette, very fragrant: "having a sweet perfume as though it had just returned on a visit from the Violet" (Dean Hole).
Redouté, Vol. 2, Plate 43.
Botanical Register, Vol. 5, t.397. *Rosa banksiae flore pleno.*
Andrews, Plate 76.
Drapiez, Vol. 1, page 71. *Rosa banksiana,* double white.
Roses et Rosiers, Plate 21. Le Rosier Banks épineux. Perhaps *Rosa fortuniana.*
Botanical Magazine, t.1954. Poor.

—**'Lutea'.** Small, double, yellow; fragrant. (Plate 143.)
Paul, 9th edition, Plate 9. Too bright.
Roses et Rosiers, Plate 8. Le Rosier Banks à fleurs jaunes. Good.
Botanical Register, Vol. 13, t.1105.
Willmott, Plate 35. Excellent portrait.
Florist and Pomologist, Plate 28. Very good.
Reeves, Vol. 2, Plate 33.

—**'Lutescens'.** Small, single, yellow, very fragrant.
Botanical Magazine, t.7171.
Botanical Cabinet, t.1960.
Phillips and Rix, page 30.

—var. **normalis.** Small, single, white. Very fragrant.

William Paul records several varieties or hybrids which are no longer grown in this country, including a large double yellow (*lutescens spinosa*—presumably prickly and a hybrid); 'Jaune Sérin'; and *rosea,* with vivid pink cupped flowers. It would be interesting to know if these are still grown in Europe or elsewhere.

anemoneflora (*Rosa triphylla*). A double-flowered garden rose, introduced from eastern China in 1844, about whose origin we cannot be certain. It has been described, variously, as a hybrid between *R. banksiae, R. laevigata,* and *R. multiflora;* it bears considerable resemblance to the first, has the hispid pedicels and three leaflets of the second, while the styles are united in a column like those of all Synstylae Section roses, of which *R. multiflora* is a member. It suffers in cold winters, but breaks forth from the old wood as Miss Willmott's illustration shows. Leaves slender and pointed, neatly serrate, glaucous beneath. Flowers small, fully double, in small clusters pink in the bud fading to nearly white, central petals narrow and often with frayed edges. Pretty, but not in the first flight of Ramblers; a connoisseur's plant, to be grown on a sheltered wall. (Plate 144.)
Willmott, Plate 67. Very good.
Revue Horticole, 1849, page 15.

cymosa. China. A species closely related to *Rosa banksiae* and probably equally tender. The stock at present in cultivation stems from seeds collected on the Great Wall of China by Keith Rushforth. It is somewhat prickly, with 3 to 5 glossy leaflets, which when young can be of dark beetroot tint. The small, scented flowers are single, creamy white, arranged in clusters like those of May or *Crataegus*. They are followed by small, dark heps.

× **fortuniana.** A hybrid, presumed with *Rosa laevigata*, introduced from Chinese gardens by Robert Fortune about 1845. It should not be confused with 'Fortune's Double Yellow' (*R. odorata pseudindica*). It does not flower very freely in England, but I hear of it as a success in warmer climates. The growth and foliage resemble the Banksian roses, but it is larger in all parts, while the flowers are fully double, creamy white, somewhat like 'Albéric Barbier' but less well formed. The flower stalk inherits the glandular hairs of *R. laevigata*. Apart from ornamentation it is also used in southern Europe as an understock, for which purpose it is said to be admirable and to transmit its vigour to the scion.

Flore des Serres, Vol. 7, page 256. Line drawing.

Willmott, Plate 36.

Roses et Rosiers, Plate 21. Possibly this is *Rosa fortuniana*.

Beales, page 400.

THE MACARTNEY ROSE, *Rosa bracteata*

This aristocratic and altogether splendid rose was introduced from China by Lord Macartney in 1793. Not being quite hardy, it has remained a rare rose in England, but has so many admirable qualities that it should be attempted more often. It is usually a success against a sunny wall in the more favoured parts of the country. As an evergreen wall shrub with a long flowering period it has few peers. The sturdy twigs are covered with brown-grey down and bear pairs of stout, hooked prickles as well as scattered smaller ones. The leaves raise it to a very high level among shrubs, being glossy, of darkest green and divided into 5 to 9 leaflets, which are often blunt at the apex—most unusual in a rose. The name *bracteata* refers to the leafy bracts surrounding the flowers, which are usually about 3 inches across, pure white—lustrous and of silky appearance like those of a cistus—with bright orange-yellow stamens. They appear on exceedingly stout shoots from midsummer until autumn, singly or in clusters, and have a rich scent of lemons. (Drawing 21.)

When growing well it may reach to 15 feet in height, but is always dense and more like a shrub than a climber. It has become naturalized in the southern states of North America, and root so readily in the ground as it grows as even to be considered a nuisance in some districts. It grows well at Trelissick, a National Trust garden in Cornwall, and I remember a splendid plant at Wormley Bury, Hertfordshire. It has proved particularly resistant to black spot fungoid disease, but this character has not been transmitted to its noted hybrid 'Mermaid'.

bracteata.

Botanical Magazine, t.1377.

Willmott, Plate 125.

Duhamel, Vol. 7, Plate 13.

Andrews, Plate 78. *Rosa lucida.*
Lawrance, Plate 84. *Rosa lucida,* Single White China Rose.
Redouté, Vol. I, Plate 35. Very good.
Braam, Plate 10. Chinese painting, excellent.
Hu, t.78. A pen drawing.
Paul, 9th edition, page 77. Excellent line-engraving.

As is understandable with a rose that has been in cultivation for so many years, this species has produced some hybrids, and Miss Willmott recalls several of rich colouring which apparently have died out, at least in England. A double white is still grown, sometimes called *alba odorata* and sometimes 'Marie Léonida', but according to the latest ruling it is now *Rosa × leonida.* It is unfortunately not a success in England, since its flowers seldom open properly, although they are freely produced on a vigorous plant. In warmer climates it is splendid. Miss Willmott's Plate 127, a semi-double flowered hybrid between *R. bracteata* and *R. laevigata,* does not appear to be this double variety. Other doubles have also been recorded and various raisers have tried to make hybrids, but with little success apart from the splendid climber 'Mermaid', a hybrid with a yellow Tea Rose.

—'**Mermaid'.** William Paul, U.K., 1918. This grows best in England on sunny walls, but flowers very freely even on north walls. In less sheltered districts it is liable to be killed to the ground in severe winters. It may be evergreen or deciduous, according to climate and situation. The leaves and flowers and freedom of growth are all greater than in *Rosa bracteata,* and the colour is a warm soft canary-yellow. After the petals have fallen the stamens remain in beauty for some days. In really sheltered districts on sunny banks it may be allowed to make a great sprawling bush, but however it may be grown it remains an outstandingly beautiful plant. In frost-free sunny climates it develops a strength and magnificence far surpassing anything we see in Britain. It flowers after midsummer and on into autumn. 25 feet.
McFarland, 1937, page 159.
American *Rose Annual,* 1931, Plate 12.
Park, Plate 217. Flowers only.
Austin, Plate page 296.

Another hybrid, supposedly of *Rosa bracteata × R. rugosa,* is the shrub 'Schneezwerg', for which see Chapter 6, "Shrub Roses of the Twentieth Century."

clinophylla. A tender rose, native to Bengal, Nepal, and China, introduced from India in 1917; synonymous with *Rosa lyellii, R. involucrata,* and *R. lindleyana.* I have not seen this rose, but it is a close relative to *R. bracteata,* and is figured in the *Botanical Register,* t.739. William Paul, in his ninth edition, shows a superb double form or hybrid, which he calls *R. lucida duplex.* The large full flowers are pure white with a rosy flush in the centre. Even though this may not be hardy everywhere, it should be reintroduced. In *Plant Hunting on the Edge of the World,* Kingdon Ward describes how in Burma, forty miles from Myitkyina, "the botanist gets his first thrill. Here the long ribs of slate rock, which in March are exposed in the river bed, are covered with wild Roses (*R. bracteata*) and crimson Azalea (*Rhododendron indicum*)." But apparently it was *Rosa clinophylla* which Kingdon Ward found in Burma, not *R. bracteata.*

THE CHEROKEE ROSE, *Rosa laevigata*

It is quite an achievement, I think, for a wild rose of China to become so established and naturalized in the United States that it has acquired the name of 'Cherokee Rose', and has, moreover, been accepted as the state flower of Georgia, U.S. Yet such is the fortune of *Rosa laevigata*. Nobody knows when it arrived in America.

Known also as *Rosa sinica*, *R. cherokeensis*, and *R. camellia*, it is a strong-growing rambling species for mild climates; when grown on a warm wall or in a warm district it is nearly evergreen, with only three leaflets, glossy and coarsely toothed, of dark shining green. It is a beautiful plant even when out of flower. The green stems are set with red-brown prickles, large and small, which diminish into mere bristles below the flower and all over the receptacle and calyx. The large, single, well-formed flowers are creamy white with broad rounded petals and beautiful yellow stamens. Deliciously scented. The flowers appear in late May and June. I fear that few of us would give it the 25 feet square of space that it needs on a warm wall, owing to its short flowering period, and for this reason it remains uncommon.

laevigata.
> *Botanical Magazine*, t.2847.
> *Botanical Register*, t.1922. Very good.
> Willmott, Plate 117. Very good.
> Stevens, page 186. *Rosa laevigata*, 'Anemone', and 'Ramona'; the portraits give very little idea of the beauty of these three.
> Braam, Plate 19. Chinese painting, very good.
> Reeves, Vol. 2, Plate 39.
> *Journal des Roses*, Août 1886.

—**'Cooperi'** (*Rosa odorata* 'Cooper's Variety'). R. E. Cooper sent seeds from Lady Wheeler Cuffe's garden at Maymyo, near Rangoon, to Glasnevin in 1923. From this sending are believed to derive all the 'Cooperi' plants in cultivation. It is closely allied to the species and has similar but dark reddish twigs and prickles. The leaves have mostly three leaflets and are of dark shining green against which the single, pure white flowers are conspicuous. Unfortunately the yellow stamens turn black after pollination. A vigorous grower for a warm wall.

Two very beautiful coloured descendants of *Rosa laevigata* are in cultivation, and it is presumed that the other parent was a Tea Rose; however, as they very closely resemble *R. laevigata*, I think it best to include them here.

—**'Anemone'**. *Rosa sinica* 'Anemone', *R. anemonoides*. Schmidt, Erfurt, Germany, 1895. Known as the 'Anemone Rose', though I can see no reason for this descriptive name. Usually the term "anemone-flowered" refers to a double flower with petaloid stamens, but there is no suggestion of anything like this in the shapely, wide, single blooms of this rose, so very much like *R. laevigata* except in colour. Presumably it is thought to resemble a Japanese anemone. The soft, clear pink is veined with a deeper shade, but paler on the reverse. The growth, buds, and foliage all resemble those of *R. laevigata*, but it is by no means such a luxuriant rambler. 'Anemone' is hardy in all but the most severe winters (I have seldom known it hurt on a wall) and is rather angular, sparsely-leaved, and open-growing. Starting early in the season the flowers appear over many weeks, and are some 4 inches across. (Plate 145.)

Revue Horticole, 1901, t.548. Poor.

Willmott, Plate 121.

——'Ramona'. A deeply-coloured sport of 'Anemone' which originated in California in the nursery of Dietrich and Turner in 1913. Exactly resembles its parent except that its colour is an intense glowing cerise-crimson, with effective greyish tint on the reverse. Again, it has an early and long flowering season, and sometimes a few blooms appear in September. (Plate 146.)

Phillips and Rix, page 33.

'Silver Moon'. Van Fleet, U.S., 1910. *Rosa wichuraiana* × *R. laevigata* is usually given as the parentage, but it is highly likely that a hybrid rose also was used, and the latest supposition is that it was 'Devoniensis'. A very vigorous, noble rose, creating a curtain of handsome dark glossy leaves, and bearing clusters of large creamy white semi-double flowers at midsummer, opening from butter-yellow buds, and with yellow stamens. Rich fragrance of green apples. Glaucous stems set with a few purplish prickles. An unforgettable sight at Kew growing into trees, where it attained about 30 feet.

Addisonia, 1917, page 61. Poor.

II

Ramblers and Climbers: Their Selection and Display

SELECTIONS FOR VARIOUS POSITIONS AND PURPOSES

THE FOLLOWING lists, I hope, will help intending selectors who might otherwise waste hours searching for what they want for a given purpose. There are so many roses available that none of us, given a little care, need choose a variety unsuitable for its position. One must consider height, foliage, style, tractability, season, fragrance, and colour, and also the background and complementary planting, in order to select the ideal variety.

The varieties selected are, in my opinion, the best in their groups. Every variety mentioned in this book is not necessarily included. As nearly every rose makes an exception to some rule or other, the selections should be only broadly interpreted. The lists of varieties are not in any particular order. Generally, the width to allow to each variety is approximately the same as its height, depending on how much height of wall or fence is available.

* Denotes roses described in Part 1, and † those described in Part 2; though shrubs, they are of lax growth and are equally at home with some support.

---

1. Graceful ramblers for arches, ropes, chains and 10-foot pillars; also for trees up to 18 feet. Grace is their great attribute: they should therefore be used so that this character can best be appreciated.

   All varieties in Chapter 6, "Old and New Garden Ramblers," except Félicité Perpétue, Francis E. Lester, Lykkefund, Patricia Macoun, Phyllis Bide, Rambling Rector, and Venusta Pendula.

   wichuraiana
   multiflora
   * Mme Plantier

   All the Large-flowered Ramblers in Chapter 9 except Albertine, Breeze Hill, City of York, and Gerbe Rose.

2. Roses for walls, fences, pillars, up to 8 feet. Less graceful, and shorter, growers that are none the less tractable.

Dream Girl
Laure Davoust
Spectabilis
† Hermosa, Climbing
* Zéphirine Drouhin and the more
    vigorous Bourbons
Phyllis Bide
Gerbe Rose

Breeze Hill
Allen's Fragrant Pillar
Paul's Single White
Star of Persia
† Gruss an Teplitz
Most of the "New" Climbers,
    Chapter 9

3. Sprawlers for ground-cover, hanging over low walls, and covering low hedges, logs, and stumps.

† Max Graf
† Paulii Rosea
† Macrantha and varieties, except
    Harry Maasz
† Schneelicht
  wichuraiana
Magic Carpet

† *polliniana*
Félicité Perpétue
* Mme Plantier
† Lady Curzon
Sanders' White
† Paulii

4. Shrubby sprawlers, more vigorous and bushy than in List 3, for use as graceful informal shrubs, for growing over hedgerows, large stumps, low fences, and in general rather wild conditions.

* Complicata
† Harry Maasz
† Daisy Hill
† Lady Curzon
  Rambling Rector
  The Garland
† *setigera*
† *soulieana*
  multiflora
Goldfinch

Blush Noisette
Félicité Perpétue
Francis E. Lester
Kew Rambler
Flora
Albertine
Maigold
Most varieties in Chapter 9,
    "The 'New' Climbers"

5. Roses needing the protection of a wall in Surrey.

Aimée Vibert
The Old Musk Rose (*Rosa moschata*)
bracteata and varieties
banksiae and varieties
laevigata
—Cooperi
anemoneflora
Anemone
gigantea
sempervirens
sinowilsonii
brunonii
—La Mortola
Céline Forestier
Lamarque
Rêve d'Or
William A. Richardson

Belle Portugaise
La Follette
Sénateur Amic
Fortune's Yellow
Lady Hillingdon, Climbing
Princesse de Nassau
Reine Marie-Henriette
Solfaterre
Mlle de Sombreuil
Souvenir de Léonie Viennot
Souvenir d'un Ami
† Cramoisi Supérieur
Mme de Sancy de Parabère
Devoniensis
Maréchal Niel
Bush Tea Roses in Chapter 6,
    "The Noisette and Tea Roses"

6. For densely covering arbours, unsightly sheds, etc.

Félicité Perpétue
Albéric Barbier
Francis E. Lester
Kew Rambler
François Juranville
New Dawn
Albertine
Many "New" Climbers in Chapter 9

May Queen
Wedding Day
Rambling Rector
† Lady Curzon
Lykkefund
mulliganii
Sanders' White

7. Excessively strong roses for training into trees, making shoots up to 30–40 feet.

brunonii
—La Mortola } for sheltered districts only
Paul's Himalayan Musk Rambler
filipes Kiftsgate
rubus
Belvedere
Brenda Colvin

8. Very vigorous, hardy roses for training into trees, making shoots 20–30 feet.

Polyantha Grandiflora
helenae
mulliganii
Wedding Day
Betty Sherriff
Bobbie James
Albéric Barbier
La Perle
Mlle Cécile Brunner, Climbing
François Juranville

New Dawn
Rose-Marie Viaud
René André
Silver Moon
Mme d'Arblay
Mlle Claire Jacquier
Lykkefund
Ayrshire Splendens
Treasure Trove

9. Hardy large-flowered climbers for house walls, rather stiff in growth and generally bare at the base, where a shrub or short-growing clematis will be an added asset.

All the Hybrid Tea-style Climbers in
    Chapter 9
Mermaid
Gloire de Dijon

Mme Alfred Carrière
Mons. Paul Lédé, Climbing
Tallest "New" Climbers in
    Chapter 9

10. Single-flowered ramblers and climbers.

All wild species in Chapter 8
Wedding Day
Kew Rambler
Hiawatha
Evangeline
Francis E. Lester
Jersey Beauty
laevigata
banksiae 'Lutescens'
——*normalis*

Silver Moon
Anemone
Sénateur Amic
Cupid
Soldier Boy
Dainty Bess, Climbing
Mermaid
Paul's Perpetual White
gigantea
Una

11. Roses without prickles (ramblers, climbers, and shrubs).

multiflora Simplex ⎤
—Cress and Danieli ⎥
canina Brog's ⎥ under-stocks
† de la Grifferaie ⎦
* Zéphirine Drouhin
* Kathleen Harrop
* *gallica* (wild species)
* Cosimo Ridolfi
* Duchesse de Buccleugh
* Antonia d'Ormois
  Boursault varieties
† Morletii
† Dupontii
† *blanda*
† *sericea denudata*
† —*polyphylla*
* Chloris

* Blush Hip
* Mme Legras de St Germain
* Mme Plantier
* Prince Charles
† Mrs John Laing
  Aimée Vibert
† *foliolosa*
† *pendulina*
  Princesse de Nassau
  Goldfinch
  Rose-Marie Viaud
  Violette
  banksiae
  Lykkefund
  Veilchenblau

12. Roses for north walls, except in very exposed areas. This is a preliminary list of roses that have been observed thriving and flowering reasonably well without sun: they would flower better with sun. Any hardy rose will provide a number of blooms on a shady wall, provided it is not overhung by trees.

Gloire de Dijon
Mermaid
† Conrad F. Meyer
† Nova Zembla
  Félicité Perpétue
  Paul's Scarlet
  Purity
  New Dawn

Mme Grégoire Staechelin
May Queen
Albéric Barbier
Souvenir de Claudius Denoyel
Mons. Paul Lédé, Climbing
Leverkusen
* *alba* Semi-plena
* —Maxima

13. Roses suitable for growing as weeping standards: this is a term to describe ramblers that are propagated by budding high up on a stem of wild rose, to weep down like a fountain or umbrella.

† Raubritter
  The Fairy
  Ballerina

Graceful varieties among the Old and New Garden Ramblers of Chapter 8, and the Large-flowered Ramblers of Chapter 9.

———— • ————

14. Purple- and mauve-coloured ramblers, climbers, etc. It is not always realized that this colour is available.

Rose-Marie Viaud
Veilchenblau
Bleu Magenta
Violette
Amadis

Russeliana
Aschermittwoch
* Zigeunerknabe ⎫
* William Lobb   ⎬ shrubby
* Tour de Malakoff ⎭

———— • ————

15. Shrub roses suitable for walls, fences, and pillars.

† Kassel
† Buff Beauty
† Moonlight
† Francesca
† Pax
† Scarlet Fire
† Gruss an Teplitz
† Harry Maasz

† Gloire de Ducher
† Hugh Dickson
† Souvenir du Dr Jamain
† Mlle Cécile Brunner, Climbing
† Rosenwunder
† Düsterlohe
* Complicata
† Constance Spry

Many of these approximate the growth of the "New" Climbers in Chapter 9, which are also suitable.

———— • ————

16. Old roses of lax growth, described in Part 1, suitable for training on walls, fences, and pillars.

Blush Hip
Tour de Malakoff
Jeanne de Montfort
William Lobb
Bourbon Queen
Mme Ernst Calvat

Mme Isaac Pereire
Kathleen Harrop
Zéphirine Drouhin
Mme Legras de St Germain
Mme Plantier
Blairii Number 2

THE DISPLAY OF CLIMBERS AND RAMBLERS

ALTHOUGH ROSES as a whole are flimsy plants—being seldom really dense and almost always deciduous—ramblers and climbers enter very importantly into the design of the garden. As with all good gardening, the intending planter's question should be "what rose would be best there?" rather than the more frequent "where can I put this variety?" The importance of the ramblers and climbers is that as a rule they need artificial support, and the support must necessarily fit in with the house, paths, or walls, and all the main features of the garden. Therefore the rule should be first to decide where an arch, pillar, arbour, or other erection would be an asset to the garden, next to decide upon what form would be most appropriate, and then to select the most suitable roses for it.

However, all this presupposes a formal garden. Seldom do artificial erections look comfortable in a natural planting of shrubs and plants, with paths of grass or gravel gently curving and accentuating the contours. In such gardens certain roses will display themselves naturally and superbly, and be a tremendous addition to the garden through the colour and fragrance they give, and their period of flowering will automatically prolong the display of flowering shrubs, which in the main flower earlier. I recall 'The Garland' foaming over shrubs at Munstead Wood; *Rosa multiflora* arching over the path at Nymans, Sussex; the trails of 'Daisy Hill' and 'Lady Curzon' and 'Complicata' leading from the shrubs into trees in various informal gardens; and the vigorous species in the Synstylae Section climbing into trees at Nymans, Knightshayes Court in Devon, and elsewhere; the old apple trees disporting 'Mme Plantier' at Sissinghurst Castle, Kent and 'Rose-Marie Viaud', 'Albéric Barbier' and others growing likewise in many other gardens. To my mind there is nothing so beautiful as a living support for all sprawling or scrambling species roses, whether they be called shrubs, climbers, or ramblers. The sports of Hybrid Teas and similar stalwart roses are unsuitable for such culture, not only because of their stiff growth, but because their sophisticated flowers need, I think, association with buildings to make them acceptable.

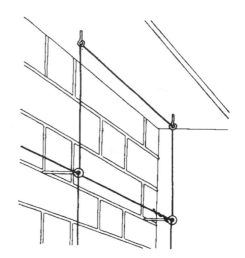

Figure I. Wires stretched through vine-eyes, 3 inches from brickwork.

As there is normally a house in a garden, it would be as well to consider the means of fixing roses to the walls before going round the garden to seek other opportunities to provide homes for them. The ideal method of securing climbers to house walls is to have "vine-eyes" built into the brickwork, projecting some four inches, ready for wiring later (Figure I). If the finish is brick, that is excellent but if the finish is to be stucco or stonedash or woodwork, which will need colour-washing or painting from time to time, difficulties at once present themselves. When the plants are thoroughly established and have reached full beauty, thickly intertwined, it may be necessary to take them down to apply a fresh coat to the wall surface. The only means of achieving this is to have the wire arranged in panels 6 feet or so wide, attached only at the eaves and at the base, so that they can be let down and bent outwards, complete with the plants, when required. To facilitate this, only pliant growers can be used, and they must be kept to their own strips of wire. But the whole job is so awkward that on such wall-finishes it is best to avoid climbing plants and grow a few shrubs; alternatively, to be severe so that when the evil day arrives we can cut the climbers down and let them grow up again. Sometimes this produces wonderful refreshment for the plants, but of course it will be two or three years at least before they are fully restored.

When wiring a building it is best to have perpendicular and horizontal wires securely fixed—the mesh may be 9 inches or I foot square for roses. Pig wire is very suitable for restricted spaces. The bare wire will not hurt the roses, and is nearly invisible when once the foliage arrives—in fact, against some walls it is unnoticeable at any time. Some people hammer nails into the wall, but this is not good for the wall, and neither is it as good or secure for the rose, because the nail must have a leather or stout webbing loop (Figure 2) to wrap round the stem of the plant, and in due course these give way. On no account should nails be hammered into stucco or stone-dash. On certain types of building, panels of trellis, preferably rectangular and not diamond-shaped, are appropriate and even decorative. They should be of seasoned wood (well steeped in a preservative non-toxic to plants) and about 1 inch by ½ inch securely fixed 4 inches from the wall, and securely joined at every crossing (Figure 3).

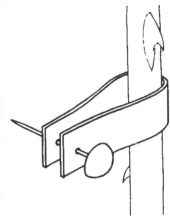

Figure 2. Large-headed nail and leather or plastic strap.

The other matter to consider at the outset of planting around the house is the position of drains, extensions of footings, and the projection of eaves. Here in Britain, one of the driest places in the garden can be the north or east wall, where the eaves project perhaps a foot and where no summer rains borne on south-west winds can fall. Footings are not usually a nuisance with modern buildings, but both these, drains, and manholes can ruin planting schemes around old houses. A paved path, too, can lead all water away from the narrow border along the house wall, especially if the paving is set in concrete—as it should be if permanence and ease of work are considered.

Figure 3. Metal bracket fixed to brickwork, to support wide-mesh wooden lattice.

Immediately adjoining the house is the first artificial extra we have to consider—the possible arch over the door. This must be designed in relation to the house (Figure 4) and the only rule left to planters is to choose a scented rose of graceful habit and without prickles; the colour must of course tone in with the paint on the door and windows. Sometimes a view will focus on to an insignificant door or window, which can be immeasurably enhanced by a surround of trellis, suitably designed—a *trompe l'oeil*—and gracefully enshrined in roses or other climbing plants (Figure 5).

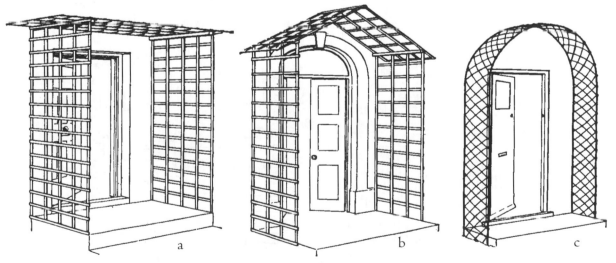

Figure 4. Various traditional arches for doorways: (a) and (b) wooden lattice, (c) galvanized wire.

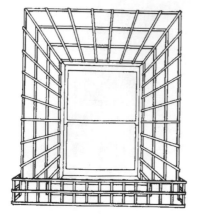

Figure 5. *Trompe l'oeil* of wooden lattice fixed flat on wall, which can support a climbing plant, to enhance a plain window.

Fences and walls surrounding the garden usually follow the boundaries, and provide support for a great variety of roses and other climbers. The ideal is to have wires or trellis as for the house walls; close-boarded fences should have a final rail added at the top, as roses can be very heavy, and if the boards project above the main top rail, as is usual, pieces of board often get broken in storms. These remarks refer to walls and solid fences, but in some places open fences (Figures 6, 7) may be chosen; they can look very well in thecountry if of cleft rail and posts; in built-up areas, posts and rails of prepared and painted wood (white or near white is really the only acceptable colour) can look very smart and also charming. It is an American idea, and an open fence of any of these materials hung informally with roses is a delightful method of defining an area without erecting too substantial and private a barrier. Quite unimposing, long-lasting, and effective is split chestnut paling. Near a period house with a Chinese interior, a Chippendale-style of fence-pattern might be chosen, in natural oak or painted, or a neat white fence of straight boards, spaced evenly apart. On sloping ground walls may be built to retain soil, and for these roses can be chosen to hang down. Open fences dividing one part of the garden from another are best made in the cleft style so that the rails are not all on one side of the posts, which gives a "front" and "back" appearance, and these interior fences must serve a definite purpose and be connected with the house or solid hedges or buildings. Transparent preservatives can be obtained for use when wood is preferred in its natural colour.country if of cleft rail and posts; in built-up areas, posts and rails of prepared and painted wood (white or near white is really the only acceptable colour) can look very smart and also charming. It is an American idea, and an open fence of any of these materials hung informally with roses is a delightful method of defining an area without erecting too substantial and private a barrier. Quite unimposing, long-lasting, and effective is split chestnut paling. Near a period house with a Chinese interior, a Chippendale-style of fence-pattern might be chosen, in natural oak

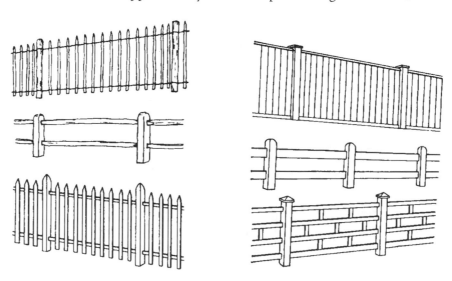

Figures 6, 7. Various fences of open wood-work, described in text.

or painted, or a neat white fence of straight boards, spaced evenly apart. On sloping ground walls may be built to retain soil, and for these roses can be chosen to hang down. Open fences dividing one part of the garden from another are best made in the cleft style so that the rails are not all on one side of the posts, which gives a "front" and "back" appearance, and these interior fences must serve a definite purpose and be connected with the house or solid hedges or buildings. Transparent preservatives can be obtained for use when wood is preferred in its natural colour.

Summerhouses and arbours can provide excellent positions for ramblers and climbers. The summerhouse can be quite a cheap plebeian affair if dense-growing ramblers are chosen, so that it becomes completely smothered— with close boarding inside to keep out the earwigs! Without boarding it would be an arbour, constructed of open poles and crossbars. An arbour can be a place to sit, and also can be used for passing through. At a junction of paths, for instance, two crossing arches can be made diagonally, each of two or three posts, and the whole top can be covered. Or if a path should change direction or alignment, a similar arbour can disguise it and turn its accident into an embellishment (Figure 8). These are all important features of a garden, to be given positions which govern other features such as arches, pergolas, pillars, and pyramids.

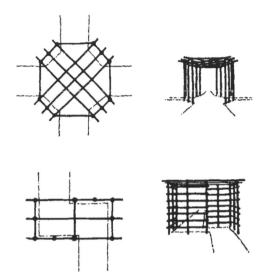

Figure 8. Elaborate arches or arbours at junction of paths, or to give reason to a twist in a path.

An arch arbitrarily placed along a path to provide a home for a couple of roses will always be a superfluous adornment, better removed; it should mark an entry or an exit, or have some such purpose. But a series of arches down a path is a different matter and can be very enjoyable, either separately spaced or connected in the form of a pergola. Even so, there should be a definite feature or view at each end to give a reason for such an important series of arches. Arches of single poles look rather insignificant, but two poles each side with crossbars and poles across the top complete also with crossbars, turn a wooden arch into a stronger unit both aesthetically and practically (Figure 9). An alternative is to erect metal pipes connected with wires and wire mesh, longer-lasting but less pleasant. If wood is used, trouble occurs usually just at ground level where rot sets in; the best preventative is to char the base or apply a preservative; either treatment should extend from the base to a height of six inches above ground level, the bark having been removed if natural wood is used. Every few years it is as well to remove a little soil and re-treat the length of wood from just below soil level to just above it. I find angle-irons, L-shaped in section, ideal for supporting weakened posts, when hammered in behind them. They are fairly inconspicu-

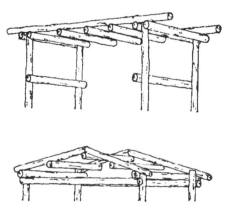

Figure 9. Detail of rustic arches.

ous. Another good idea is to sink wide pipes into the soil to take the size of wooden pole chosen, so that, when the wood rots, new posts can be inserted into the pipes without disturbing the climbing plants. If metal pipes are used for the entire uprights, they can be disguised by typing stout canes around them for the whole of their length (Figure 10). Curved metal arches supported on wooden pillars are very charming.

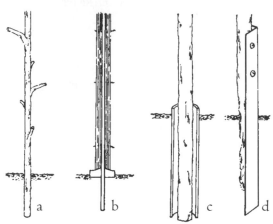

Figure 10. Example of different materials for posts to support roses as "pillars": (a) rustic post, (b) metal pipe covered with canes, (c) post inserted into drainpipe, (d) post that has rotted below ground being supported by an angle-iron.

Pergolas need big material if they are to be successful: nothing less than 6-inch-square timber, if they are to be of this material. Pillars of masonry are best, with heavy timber crossbars; the masonry can be rubble with rough plaster covering, rounded or square, with fairly straight branches laid across; brick to match the house, or brick tinted with a wash after building, with rough-hewn beams or beams out of old barns; or fancy-work of brick, stone, and tile with prepared wooden beams—each scheme is progressively more sophisticated. Occasionally the dignity of the house and the means of the owner may permit the use of Doric columns.

The minimum width for brick pillars is a brick and a half, or 14 inches square, except in very tiny gardens where one brick square might be permissible. The lowest three courses should be 2 inches wider all around to form a plinth, and a concrete capital, cast easily by any intelligent builder, should fit the top, with a hole for a dowel pin left in the centre to pass through the cross-beam, which should cross the path and project beyond the edge of each capital. In a pergola these first cross-beams should support the next which follow the length of the path, thus revealing the sky between them when we look down the pergola (Figure 11). If the first beams run down the length of the path, connecting the pillars at the sides of the path, and the next beams are all across the path, we get the effect of a wooden ceiling, which to me is heavy and unattractive (Figure 12). It is of course necessary, in erecting such a fine feature as this can be, to ensure that adequate foundations are made to support the masonry. Nothing is so irritating and disappointing as a post or pillar that is not perpendicular from all angles.

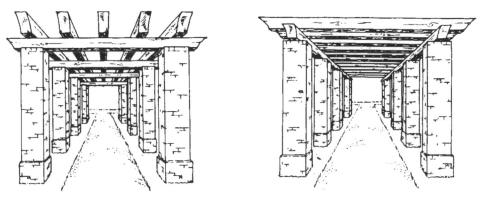

Figures 11, 12. Construction of pergolas: brick pillars supporting wooden beams.

Pillars on their own may be of wood, prepared and painted, or of larch with 9-inch side shoots retained, or of brick, or actual classical pillars of stone (Figure 13). The more beautiful they are, the less overwhelming should be the roses chosen. Isolated pillars to take pillar roses can be connected with a wooden beam—when I believe they become a "peristyle" if surrounding a court or alcove—or chains or ropes. Chains hang best, but thick rope about ¾-inch diameter makes a good substitute; only very pliant roses will achieve the graceful effect that is desired.

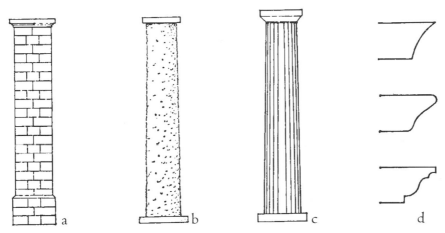

Figure 13. Pillars: (a) brick, (b) roughcast, (c) stone, (d) some alternative finishes for ends of cross-beams.

The width for any arch is dictated by the width of the path, and the minimum width for a path to take two people abreast (the only hospitable and pleasant way of walking around; how I have hated following an otherwise kind host because of his narrow paths!) is 6 feet between arches; 7 feet is preferable. Remembering that climbing plants will hang from the crossbars, 7 feet is also the minimum height. For the sake of proportion I should make the arch 8 feet minimum width, and thus qualify what I wrote earlier about its being an important garden feature.

Another way of displaying our roses is on pyramids. Newly-designed gardens are apt to appear rather flat for some years, and pyramid-shaped structures of wood can speedily be covered with roses to give height and substance along a formal walk within two or three years. In a long straight walk, such pyramids can be helpful in creating interest, or simpler structures can be made as tripods with three strong posts (Figures 14, 15).

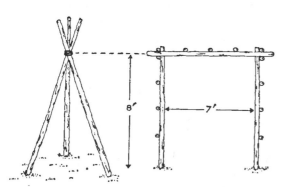

Figure 14. Tripod and simple arch of stout poles, showing proportions.

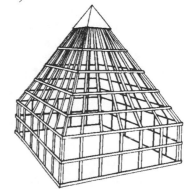

Figure 15. Pyramid of wooden lattice to add temporary height to a garden.

It will be seen that there is a great variety of material and erection to provide homes for our rambling and climbing roses, and I hope that these descriptions and drawings, and the lists in the preceding section, will provide answers to most questions that greet the beginner when selecting roses.

We have still to consider rose hedges. While these are usually composed of shrub roses, ramblers are also suitable, but they need initial support, either a post-and-rail fence, or just a couple of wires at about 2 feet and 4 feet from the ground on stout posts every 10 feet or so. (It is best to plant roses between the posts along any sort of fence; there is then less disturbance to the roots if new posts have to be put in later.) The roses of the lax-growing classes should be planted about 10 feet apart, or closer if a mingling of colours and shapes is required. There is no limit to the possibilities of ramblers for display in the garden; the contrasts of colours, shapes, and styles is almost infinite, and a very long display can be achieved if early and late flowering varieties are included.

It remains to consider companions for roses. Earlier in this book, and in my previous writings, I have said how I prefer roses mixed with other things; they are often desperately dull on their own. Even though they may be our favourite flower, their planting should not be carried to excess. No meal would be acceptable if given entirely to caviare, and no symphony would be enjoyed which was composed entirely for clarinets. To me the most interesting gardens are those where a wide selection of plant form and flower is used for effect through the entire year. If roses are planted to excess, the areas devoted to them will be dull for seven months of the year, and exhibit a fussiness for the remaining months, since their leaves are small and the effect of the flowers—whether large or small—is "spotty."

Rose beds—by which I mean the conventional geometrical designs prescribed in lawn or paving for the reception of Hybrid Teas and Floribundas—are dull areas for most of the year; especially as the general method of culture is to leave the soil bare beneath them, a custom evolved in days when "bedding" roses were too weak to stand competition from ground-covering plants. Arches and other supports for ramblers and climbers can be bare of blossom for very much longer. Of course the foliage of roses has its beauty, but I do not think we should tolerate it on its own as much as we do.

Companions in any walk of life are best if they provide contrast or complement. Considering colour first, if we want contrast it is best provided by blue, all other colours being found in roses, though mauve and purple are scarce among ramblers and climbers. There are many blue, mauve, and purple border plants, though few shrubs in these tones; some that come quickly to mind are buddlejas, lavenders, *Ceratostigma*, and *Caryopteris*; sages, hardy geraniums (rather too early-flowering), *Echinops*, eryngiums, and delphiniums; agapanthuses, *Stokesia*, and *Catananche*, with many clematises among climbers. I should seldom look for plants of similar colours to roses as companions for them unless the contrast in size, texture, and shape of blooms was sufficient, such as escallonias, fuchsias, and honeysuckles, or the larger blooms of hollyhocks and lilies.

As a rule roses are so delightsome in themselves, and are such universal favourites, that I consider their companions most valuable when they not only provide colour before the roses start to flower but also have good foliage as a contrast to the roses. Here again we can choose soft or strong characters. No background for roses in my opinion is so good as a first-class yew hedge. If you can bear your ramblers and climbers to hang over such a hedge you will have a picture that none can but praise. The velvety uniform dark green will show up all but the darkest of roses and enhance the purity of the clearest colours. Other hedges, through the evergreens to the deciduous, are less good. For the arches and pergolas some of the vines, providing large flat solid leaves, are the very best of contrasts; of greyish tinge in its greenery is 'Black Cluster', a hardy black grape, while the Claret Vine, *Vitis vinifera* 'Purpurea', is well known for its similar clusters of fruit borne amid foliage that from August onwards assumes an ever deeper wine-colour. *Vitis coignetiae* is the largest-leaved (but rampageous) and most brilliant in autumn; for smaller arches the 'Dutchman's pipe', *Aristolochia macrophylla*, can provide equal magnificence of greenery, without the autumn colour.

Roses are best displayed in growing trees when these have comparatively small leaves. Most of the big-leaved trees are too coarse, dark, and luxuriant. I like climbing roses appearing out of columnar cypresses; from ancient apples and pears, thorns and laburnums; the strongest foaming out of pines; but there are certain trees which may be considered too dignified to be the host for roses, and among these I would number the magnolias, trees of great majesty and character of line. There are many colour contrasts that come to mind, such as a purplish rambler in a silver weeping pear; a scarlet, white or yellow climber peering out from a coppery-leaved prunus; a brilliant yellow rose enhancing a golden holly or maple—or just the white scented trails of *Rosa mulliganii* hanging out of any greenery, wafting fragrance through the garden.

> . . . strength may wield the ponderous spade,
> May turn the clod, and wheel the compost home;
> But elegance, chief grace the garden shows,
> And most attractive, is the fair result
> Of thought, the creature of a polished mind.
>
> William Cowper, 1731–1800

PART 4

Practical Points

12

For True Gardeners

CULTIVATION

MUCH HAS been written and spoken about the preparation of the ground for roses, and their actual planting. I am convinced that good rose cultivation calls for a few fundamentals, the first of which is *initial* deep digging, providing undesirable subsoil is not brought to the surface. Unsatisfactory results are generally obtained when a hole of about a foot square is made in an established border, or in grass.

The ground where the roses are to go should be prepared and dug throughout, if possible; but where isolated plants are to be put in, the ground should be dug to a depth of 18 inches over an area 3 feet in diameter. The less cultivated the soil may be, the greater the area that should be prepared. (This is a counsel of perfection; I may say again that the Old Roses in particular are thrifty and give good results even in neglect.) The admixture of well-decayed manure or, failing this increasingly elusive commodity, a combination of bone-meal and hoof-and-horn together with some form of humus such as garden compost or leaf-mould, is helpful in poor soils, although roses are best left to fend for themselves in rich soils.

The next essential, after planting at the right depth, is firming of the soil. Provided the ground is not in a squelchy condition, the full force of the heel is needed to firm the soil round the roots. Roses should not be planted in heavy soil when it is in a wet and sticky condition, but it is impossible to buy roses or for nurserymen to deliver them just when conditions are perfect, at the onset of the autumn rains. They are better "healed in" and will thus wait safely for weeks, if necessary, for suitable planting weather.

The most fundamental rule of cultivation after planting is to maintain a good humus content in the soil by mulching, which also helps to keep down summer weeds, conserve moisture, and minimize labour. Well-rotted manure or garden compost, dead leaves, or lawn mowings can all be used. Lawn mowings can be spread over the ground as soon as cut, to the depth of 1 or 2 inches, and can be repeated again later in the season. I wrote fairly extensively about this in *Colour in the Winter Garden*,* and it works admirably on my light soil. In heavy, damp soils a growing mulch is probably much safer. Whether the mulch be of carpeting plants, or dead leaves, or lawn mowings, that is nature's way. She does not grow her shrubs all alone on bare earth, but always with a complement of lowly foliage or foliar "debris."

Roses are not particular in regard to soil, and all, apart from the few weak-growing varieties, may be expected to thrive anywhere. Although they will indeed grow on poor soils, and much beauty and enjoyment can thereby be obtained from them, it is only fair to add that

---

* Revised edition, 1994. Weidenfeld and Nicolson, U.K.; Sagapress, Inc. / Timber Press, Inc., U.S.

they are incomparably more prolific, richer in colour, and more sumptuously bedight in a good, well-dug medium loam: they are worthy of the best we can give them. In my opinion many of the old and other shrub roses prefer a lighter soil, so long as it is deep and well mulched.

There has been much written about growing roses on their own roots, and I would not deter anyone from doing so. It must be remembered, however, that such understocks as *Rosa canina* are very tough; their roots will stand being maimed and dried better than those of most shrubs; they are deep-questing and vigorous, and will thrive on a variety of soils. Roses produced in nurseries in the United Kingdom are usually budded on to a form of our English Brier, *R. canina froebellii* or 'Laxa', which is generally acknowledged to be the best understock for Britain today. Unfortunately, while not nearly so prone to suckering as the common Rugosa understock or *R. multiflora*, it is as yet raised from seed and occasional individuals occur that do produce suckers. Suckers are also produced by root-bruising at planting, or when forking in manure, etc.; unwanted suckers can also occur when the scion has been inserted too high on the rootstock, but this seldom happens in up-to-date nurseries.

When suckers from the rootstock have to be removed, it is best to uncover the root to see where they arise, and to pull them off, which generally ensures freedom from recurrence. I find an ordinary claw-headed hammer an excellent tool for the job; the sucker can be grasped near the base and pulled; the more it is pulled, the tighter it becomes clasped in the claw; the hand is well away from prickles; and with a tug the sucker comes out. It is no use cutting suckers off at ground level: this only acts like pruning, and two or three shoots will spring from the cut.

Many roses will root from cuttings, and it may be that many of the species are best grown like this. Unfortunately, own-root roses do not make such a uniform crop as those budded on an understock, and this can cause difficulties for the nurseryman. Gallicas and roses of Rugosa or China derivation root fairly readily, the Gallicas and Rugosas in particular speedily forming a thicket when grown on their own roots. This is not altogether desirable in a small garden, although it may be ideal where there is plenty of room, and for covering the ground; they will not run so fast in heavier soils. The Damasks, Albas, and Centifolias are not so ready to run about, and many of the Provence roses are by no means easy to strike from cuttings.

Black spot is a nuisance in some districts, in some seasons, sometimes; but not usually in large towns, where the sulphur in the air prevents its incidence. It can attack almost all roses, and there are different "strains" of the fungus blowing about the country during the summer, hence one can never be sure where infection is coming from. The spores take a fortnight to develop in the tissues of the leaves. Spraying with sulphur preparations is helpful; but spraying is a tiresome job and has to be done weekly to have any effect. Although the diseased leaves are unsightly, black spot does not very greatly affect strong-growing plants. I have known gardens where the disease has been successfully controlled by attention to cultivation: avoidance of strong nitrogenous manures, and the use of bone-meal and compost.

Unlike black spot, aphides (greenfly) and other pests rather like towns, with their fences and walls and poor soils; but there are many proprietary brands of insecticide available, for application systemically or directly.

The Old Roses in particular do not seem to approve of our climate in south-east England. I used to look at Redouté's drawings with amazement, wondering why he so exaggerated the length of stem, the luxuriance of the leaves, and the size of the flowers. A visit to Hidcote Manor, in Gloucestershire, speedily proved that the cooler climate and retentive soil in the Cotswolds produce far better flowers than we can obtain in sunny Surrey. Sample blooms which reach me for naming from the west and north are nearly always of better quality than my own, and are, of course, some weeks later. All this is rather surprising in a flower cradled in the Mediterranean region, a flower commemorating "Rhodes the isle whose very name means rose," but it once again goes to prove that coolness at the root will give rise to good growth, and a cool atmosphere ensures the gentle development of the flower. Here in the Woking area the temperature varies greatly from night to day, extremes being frequent, and a scorching heat not unusual. In very hot districts, therefore, I suggest a cool exposure for the Old Roses, so that their blooms may develop slowly and their beauties last as long as possible. They will not thrive under trees, although they will grow in such positions; they are essentially children of the sun and revel in full exposure. Shade from a wall is a different matter, and some of the best specimens of my acquaintance grow where their roots are shaded and their flowers are in full sun.

PRUNING

PRUNING IS A SUBJECT which has exercised rose-growers' minds very greatly for many years. A long chapter is given to it by William Paul in his first edition of *The Rose Garden* of 1848. The roses we have been considering in this book should be treated as flowering shrubs, rather than as roses of the same ilk as the bedding or exhibition roses of many manuals.

Broadly there is only one rule, which applies to all roses and other hard-wooded plants, and that is: *Prune immediately after flowering.* This has three further qualifications:

(g) If the rose flowers only once in the growing season, the pruning should then be done immediately after the flowers are over *removing from the base* all the oldest, weakest wood. If a display of berries or heps is expected, some shoots should be left; further pruning must be done in late winter after the heps have gone;

(h) If the rose goes on producing flowers through summer and autumn—i.e., is "recurrent," "remontant," "repeat-flowering," or "perpetual"—the pruning is left until late winter, when we *shorten side-shoots* and occasionally remove very old wood from the base;

(i) If subsequent heps or berries are expected from varieties in (b) then we do not remove spent flowers.

Armed with these basic principles, we can consider the various groups of roses.

The Old Roses

These do not need pruning during the first spring after planting, and many growers do not prune them afterwards, apart from removing old, spent wood. The habit of the plants when established is to produce strong, long shoots from near the base of the plant, which grow up in late summer. It is these shoots which form the foundation of the bush; and in the spring they send forth side-shoots up to a foot in length, which bear the best flowers. The following season these side-shoots break again, each bearing shorter flowering shoots, and this is repeated with waning strength every season until the branch dies. After three or four years it is best to remove one or two of the older branches from the base, encouraging fresh growth to carry on the life of the plant, and this is all the pruning that need be given. Sometimes a strong young shoot will spring from half-way up one of these old branches, and the old top twigs should then be removed to this point only. As these roses flower best on growth of the previous summer, this work should be carried out immediately after flowering. The Alba Roses need less pruning than the other groups, and old branches make a beautiful head of twigs which go on flowering well for many years. These pruning rules will produce what I would call well-furnished informal flowering shrubs.

If the roses are grown in formal beds, a little more pruning may be given. In addition to the occasional and methodical removal of whole or portions of branches, the flowering side-shoots should be shortened *in the winter.* By cutting these shoots back to about 2 or 3 inches, a more limited number of flowering shoots will again be produced, with a consequent better quality of bloom. In gardens where several plants of one variety are grown, it is useful to prune a plant or two quite severely every year; the result will be a few blooms of superlative quality late in the following season, and a great rejuvenation of the bushes for subsequent years.

The only other suggestion I have to make is that the long new shoots from the base may be shortened by about one-third to keep them within the bounds of the bush, and to prevent damage at flowering time. In windy seasons these long shoots, if left to their original length, will whip about and the flowers and leaves may become lacerated, beating against other prickly stems. This work may be done at any time during the winter or early spring.

Further details of pruning, relating to specific groups, are given in the introductory remarks to the various sections.

Species and Modern Shrub Roses

With very few exceptions, I think all our shrub roses give a better effect if not pruned at all than if they are constantly being snipped about. Let us leave out the Poly-poms and the Chinas and also the Hybrid Perpetuals for the moment, and consider the species and larger shrub roses. As with the Old Roses, a healthy species rose will throw up great stems every now and again, which gradually replace the old stems. Therefore remove every year, if possible, one or two really old stems, on which multitudes of small branches are growing. Usually they will be the darkest stems with the roughest bark and the most branching twigs. Their removal will allow the new stems more room; again like the Old Roses, the best flowers are produced on side-shoots from the big branches of the previous year. The more constantly a shrub is encouraged to throw up new basal shoots, by nourishing or pruning or both, the better the display will be.

The above remarks apply to all species and once-flowering hybrids; even colonizers like *Rosa pimpinellifolia* need thinning out sometimes. If the rose is not expected to give heps, the pruning can be done *immediately* after flowering, which will save the plant from feeding the unwanted branches during the summer, and it will probably throw up a new shoot at once. Rugosa roses may be clipped over every February if a dense, bushy effect is required; their response in bloom will be surprising.

The perpetual or recurrent-flowering roses owing affinity to the China Rose approach in style to the modern Bedding Roses. The Chinas themselves make much soft wood in late summer; every shoot bears a bloom, and the large basal shoots are crowned with a head of blooms. Obviously, nourishment is necessary for so much effort to be satisfactory, but too much nitrogenous feeding may cause the wood to be soft and to suffer in the frosts of autumn and winter. They will need a careful inspection in February, and all small wood should be spurred back. The occasional removal of an old branch is helpful, but the bushes build themselves up gradually and need to have a number of stems retained more or less permanently.

The Bourbon Roses, producing flowers as they do throughout the summer, need to be pruned almost entirely in the winter. After the first burst of bloom is over in July some of the smaller twiggy growth can be removed, but all other pruning can be safely left until the winter.

Hybrid Perpetuals are mostly very vigorous. Shoots arising from the base during the summer may achieve 6 to 7 feet in height, and may often bear a cluster of blooms at the top. If they were not so erect, they could quite well be considered as normal shrubs, but unfortunately most of them are rather lanky; it is useless to reduce those long shoots to about 3 feet in an attempt to keep the bushes to reasonable size. The way to achieve a glorious display is to bend the new shoots over and tie them to the bases of neighbouring plants; they will then bear flowers along their whole length. If grown on a fence, pillar or wall, these long shoots will flower only at the top in the following season if trained upright; by bending them or training them horizontally, more flowers will be obtained; or they may be shortened if absolutely necessary. Small twiggy wood should be spur-pruned in the normal way in February.

Poly-poms need hard pruning, removing all weak twiggy shoots and leaving the stronger wood slightly longer. Their main display is on the young wood of the current season, and the more there is of this, the better.

Hybrid Musks and the English Roses *can* be left unpruned, but pruning encourages the production of strong new shoots after midsummer, with a corresponding increase of late bloom. Both these and the Lambertianas need, therefore, occasional removal of big, old branches, and the shortening of shoots that have flowered; those that are not perpetual and do not produce heps can be pruned after flowering. Those which approach the species in their single flowers will need the same attention as the species roses.

Climbing and Rambling Roses

The Musk Roses and the Old and New Ramblers (Chapter 8) and the Large-flowered Ramblers (Chapter 9) may have their oldest and weakest wood removed after flowering, unless a display of heps is expected, in which case some shoots should be left; further pruning is then done in late winter when the heps have gone. The Musks and Large-flowered Ramblers really manage very well, after a little attention during the first two years or so, without regular pruning, but will benefit from a clean-out every five years thereafter; or, if you prefer, they may be left in a glorious tangle. The Old and New Ramblers benefit from regular and drastic pruning, except for those of *sempervirens* descent. The recurrent bloomers among the Large-flowered Ramblers must be treated circumspectly.

The Noisettes and Tea Roses (Chapter 6), and the Large-flowered Climbers of Hybrid Tea style and the "New" Climbers (Chapter 9) should be left unpruned until late winter, when side-shoots should be shortened and old wood may occasionally be removed from the base. February is usually a good month, but I do it whenever a mild day occurs from Christmas onwards.

The Banksian, Macartney, and Cherokee Roses and their forms and hybrids remain (Chapter 10). As indicated in the introductory remarks to that chapter, the Banksian roses require practically no pruning; *Rosa laevigata* and its varieties really need very little pruning, but that little should be done immediately after flowering; *R. bracteata* and its hybrids are perpetual-flowering shrubs, and an occasional thinning-out in late winter is all that is required.

It can be seen that among the Climbers and Ramblers, only the Garden Ramblers require any systematic attention; all the others, and even these, can be left to themselves if the taste of the owner prefers. By this I mean that, if we like free-growing tangles with rather less flower, we need not bother about pruning except once in a while to remove really spent old wood. However, if we are training ramblers on supports in a neatly-kept garden, pruning should be done regularly. Those ramblers which are given trees and hedgerows as supports are best left to themselves, after the initial attention of pruning away all the first few years' growth as soon as a mighty shoot arises once the plant is established.

The most frequent question about pruning roses is the treatment in the first spring of planting. If you are hard-hearted you may cut all the Musks, the Old and New Ramblers, and the Large-flowered Ramblers to 6 inches above the ground in the spring following planting; the others may be shortened to about 4 feet. But I generally leave the whole lot as they are until after their first flowering and then, when their roots are fully established, they can be treated properly, removing all weak growth.

The above pruning is sufficient to keep most roses in good flowering trim, provided the soil is maintained in a healthy condition. Pruning will not make a bush grow unless the soil has nutritive qualities, and on poor soils pruning must be gentle. On very rich soils pruning must again be sparingly done, or loss of bloom may result. The more highly bred the rose is, and by this I refer to the perpetual-flowering modern bedding roses, the more pruning is necessary to ensure the constant supply of bloom that is expected of them. The more you must prune to produce perfect blooms, the more you must feed; likewise, the more you feed, the more you must keep the plants within bounds. It is a vicious circle, but necessary with Hybrid Teas, Floribundas, and Poly-poms.

FRAGRANCE

> Because the breath of flowers is far sweeter in the air (whence it comes and goes, like the warbling of music), than in the hand, therefore nothing is more fit for delight, than to know what be the flowers and plants that do best perfume the air. Roses, damask and red, are fast flowers of their smells; so that you may walk by a whole row of them, and find nothing of their sweetness; yea though it be in a morning's dew. . . . That which, above all others, yields the sweetest smell in the air, is the violet, especially the white double violet, which comes twice a year. . . . Next to that is the musk-rose; then the strawberry leaves dying . . . then sweet-brier, then wallflowers . . . pinks, gilliflowers . . . the lime trees, honeysuckles. But those which perfume the air most delightfully . . . being trodden upon and crushed are . . . burnet, wild thyme, and water-mints; therefore, you are to set whole alleys of them, to have the pleasure when you walk or tread.

So FRANCIS BACON in his essay, "Of Gardens" (1625).

In 1673 Sir Robert Boyle told of walking in a garden with a friend who could not bear the smell of Damask roses in an alley where there were some Red Roses (*Rosa gallica*). Although the alley was wide and the bushes not very near, "he abruptly broke off the discourse we were engag'd in, to complain of the harm the Perfume did to his Head, and desired me to pass into a Walk that had no roses growing near it."

These two extracts are conflicting. No doubt some of us have a much more developed sense of smell than others, and I can detect a fragrance in the air from a group of Old Roses myself, although it does not approach the volume of the scent given off by the Musk Rose or Sweet Brier.

If we can accept as a fact that scent is the main cause of the popularity of the rose, it may be as well to trace the development of fragrance from the Old Roses onwards.

I do not think anyone will dispute the claim of the Old Roses, headed by *Rosa gallica*, to preeminence in fragrance among hybridized groups. Their only competitors are the Noisettes and their close relatives the Hybrid Musks, a few modern roses such as 'Whisky Mac' and 'Fragrant Cloud', and 'Perdita' and others of David Austin's breeding. The difference between these groups is one not only of a different scent, but also of its freedom on the air. But a bowl of Gallicas or Damasks or others of their type can hold their own indoors with members of any group.

Compared with them the China Roses are almost devoid of scent, and the Tea Rose is only delicately perfumed. It is evident that when these two new groups became fused with the old groups the volume of scent decreased in the new hybrids and became altered in quality. There were exceptions; most of the Bourbons which remain today are as fragrant as any of the Old Roses, but as in shape of bloom various seedlings approached the old or new styles, so no doubt the scent followed first one parent and then another.

Judging by the various writings of the nineteenth century I think we can say that most of the Hybrid Perpetuals were not as fragrant as the Old Roses. They were bred for size of bloom, for exhibition, and for the new colours and recurrent habit of flowering, and towards the close of the century became more and more plants which would produce large, brilliant blooms for the show bench under the care of expert head gardeners. Thus the old "Garden Roses," as they were called even then, became relegated to the less progressive gardens. But many of the old, richly coloured Hybrid Perpetuals did retain much of the Damask fragrance. As the Tea Roses brought their refining influence gradually into this group, giving rise to the Hybrid Teas, the scent gradually altered again, sharpening and yet thickening as the first few Pernetianas appeared. Today a bunch of Hybrid Teas of assorted colours picked at random will give a wonderful variety of scents. If selected varieties are picked, noted for their fragrance, I do not think anyone could be dissatisfied.

Unfortunately, the trend towards the fusion of Hybrid Teas and Floribundas is not likely to improve scent. There is little fragrance inherent in the descendants of the Poly-poms, and only gradually have a few Floribundas appeared which are really fragrant. This does not augur well for the immediate future.

What extremes we have been through can be visualized by recalling 'Paul Neyron' (1869), 'Frau Karl Druschki' (1906), and 'Covent Garden' (1919), all scentless but good roses otherwise. 'Reine des Violettes' (1860), 'Mme Abel Chatenay' (1895), and 'General MacArthur' (1905) are noted for their fragrance; in fact, to my senses at least, 'Mme Abel Chatenay' stands apart from all roses for its intense piercing fragrance.

The reason why these different species and groups of roses vary so much—not only in quantity but in quality of scent—is because scent varies as much as colour or any other factor in each individual. In an extremely complex group like the Hybrid Teas almost anything may be obtained from a pod of seed, with extremes of variation except where the parentage has been suitably controlled.

Rose scent itself is a highly complex oily substance composed mainly of geraniol, but also including up to a dozen other foreign or allied substances, all contributing in some way to the fragrance of each flower. Scent is produced mainly in the petals and is given forth when the growth of the flower and the atmospheric conditions are right. From this it will be seen why double roses have more volume of scent than singles, except for the Musk group of species, whose scent is apparently in the stamens rather than in the petals. We all know that scent is especially apparent in most flowers when the air is neither too cold nor too hot; in fact, what is normal for us is normal for plants of the same latitude. In extreme conditions, such as wilting, extra scent may be released, although I believe it is not yet known what causes the release. Tiny globules of oily, fragrant substances can readily be seen with the naked eye in the skin of an orange, and also in a leaf of Bog Myrtle or *Magnolia*, but a flower-petal being the flimsy thing it is, the scent-chambers are minute and cannot be seen without high magnification. Usually the best fragrance is obtained from a newly opened flower growing on a healthy, well-established plant on a windless day when growth is exuberant; since most fragrant plants inhabit the areas of the earth where humans thrive, rather than the tops of mountains where there is too much wind or deserts where it is too dry, we may expect fragrance to be at its best on a day when the air is warm and moist rather than dry, when the plant will be functioning well. It is not that the moist air conveys scent better than dry, but that the plant is giving it forth in greatest quantity.

We are at a disadvantage in discussing scent. So far as I am aware, there is nothing corresponding to the rainbow or spectrum to help us to measure and classify the sensations we experience in sniffing fragrance, and yet we depend upon it so much in our daily lives. Even our palate—which can distinguish only the four primary qualities, sour, salt, sweet, and bitter—depends upon the nose for all its finer assessment of flavours. (How useful it is, for instance, to be able to pinch one's nose during the taking of unpalatable medicine!) I find it very difficult to describe scents to anyone. We all have a different set of values and associations. If only one had been able to play with the principal scents in little bottles at school, sampling them and mixing them as one did water-colours, all might be different. As it is, we have a vocabulary arrived at only through association; while much the same may be true at least of colours, these are so obvious that their vocabulary has become part of one's general education. I am convinced that the development of one's powers of smelling can be an education; if one deliberately smells every flower and leaf, one soon acquires a sense of values, learning to distinguish groups of plants quite easily. While the smell of a crushed oak leaf or a bracken frond may be instantly detected, the multitudinous combinations of an involved group like hybrid roses may be a very different matter.

It is natural that we should acquire a standard for comparison of rose scents from the ancestral Old Roses which grew around the Mediterranean, some of which form such an important industry in Bulgaria. If the fragrance of these roses be called typical, then we have several species with other and widely different scents. Most noted and accepted is the fragrance of the Tea Rose. I have often been asked why they are called Tea Roses and whether they make tea from the leaves in China. This is not the answer. The flowers smell of a freshly opened packet of tea, preferably what is known as "slightly tarry," not the tarry Lapsang. This delicious odour can easily be detected in several Tea Hybrids, particularly 'Lady Hillingdon', and in 'Graham Thomas'.

The next most accepted term is "Musk," although the rose scent to which this generally refers is not really true musk but somehow became attached to the English Musk rose, which is thought to have been *Rosa arvensis*. And yet in some books this species is described as scentless; I always find it delicious. This Musk fragrance to me seems to merge imperceptibly through all sorts of fine fruity odours including lemon and orange and heavier ones to the Austrian Brier's peculiar odour. I am not sufficiently educated in musk to be able to appreciate where the one leaves off and the other begins. I have however made some attempt in this book to indicate the amount of variety and possible pleasure to be obtained from making even a cursory examination of rose scents.

'Polyantha Grandiflora' is orange to me; *Rosa bracteata* and 'Morning Stars' nearly pure lemon; 'Adam Messerich' raspberry and 'Vanity' sweet peas. 'Ayrshire Splendens', 'Belle Amour', 'Magenta', and 'Constance Spry' are redolent of myrrh, while the typical Rugosas, 'Souvenir de St Anne's' and 'Fritz Nobis', remind me of cloves; *R. wichuraiana* hybrids like 'La Perle' are as fresh as green apples, 'Gerbe Rose' as peonies. 'Lavender Lassie' smells exactly like lilac. There is an absorbing study in rose scents alone. Without doubt the most valuable rose scent is that of the *R. moschata* group, which carries for yards in the air; on warm days a planting of such as *R. mulliganii*, *R. multiflora*, and 'Polyantha Grandiflora' can be detected a hundred yards away. Their scent is as all-pervading as the philadelphuses which flower with them. In the narrow confines of modern gardens great species like these, and still greater ones like *R. brunonii*, cannot be given room, but this quality of floating fragrance is also fortunately in several Hybrid Musks, particularly 'Cornelia', 'Felicia', and 'Penelope'.

There is no doubt that scent in the garden air is a precious addition to our careful plantings for colour, flower and leaf, and form of growth. Yet I have never heard of gardens of scent except for the blind, as if it were an attribute not appreciated by those blessed with vision. I see no reason why scent should not act as a complement to the exploitation of the visual arts. There are many plants whose scent is carried on the air apart from these two great examples, the Musk Roses and the *Philadelphus* or Mock Orange. Early in the year we have the Winter Sweet, *Chimonanthus praecox*, *Berberis sargentii*, and sarcococcas; *Prunus mume* 'Benichidori', a Japanese apricot which anticipates a breath of hyacinths; wallflowers, heliotrope; stocks—both bedding strains and the Night Scented; pinks of all kinds and *Lilium candidum*; magnolias of the later-flowering species, especially *Magnolia grandiflora*, *M. obovata*, and the hybrids *M.* × *thompsonii* and *M.* × *wiesneri*; certain azaleas and rhododendrons; *Viburnum carlesii* and its near relatives and hybrids; *Humea elegans* and Tobacco Flowers, Laburnum, Lime or Linden, *Wisteria*, and many more. They are the very breath of the garden, its life and joy, and as the scent comes and goes on each varying eddy, so it varies too in intensity and quality. With these flowers that give so much there are some leaves to note, equally free of their scent: the Douglas Fir, Sweet Brier or *Rosa eglanteria*, *Hebe cupressoides*; Balsam Poplar in early spring, and in October the fallen leaves of *Cercidiphyllum japonicum*, which spread a subtle aroma of ripe strawberries. From the fields come wafts of beans, mustard, clover; the waste places give us elder and gorse.

Roses with fragrant foliage are not many, and none is so good and rich in quality as the Sweet Brier. *Rosa primula*, *R. setipoda*, the hybrid 'Wintoniensis', *R. multibracteata*, and *R. glutinosa* are the main other sorts, apart from the fragrance of the flower stalks and calyces of the Old Moss Roses; these all give off a little fragrance, but are especially delightful to handle and crush, when the scent is more forthcoming, as with lavender and thyme, pelargoniums, and most herbs.

The main difference between these two types of fragrance is that in the petals the scent is formed and released by natural growth as the flowers expand, from minute cells on the surface. In leaves like those of mint and thyme the scent is formed and stored in cells and glands; it is therefore released only when the containers are bruised or broken. All the distillations of rose fragrance are made from the floral parts, not the leaves, and it has been an enormous industry in the Old World. It is recorded that rose-water was made as early as the year A.D. 810. Professor Flückiger, in 1862, published notices and extracts from the Imperial Library in Paris giving details from a Persian source. One of the provinces of Persia had to pay an annual tribute of thirty thousand bottles of rose-water to Baghdad, and the industry exported a large quantity as far as Morocco and China. Certain districts gave especially fine fragrance and high prices were paid for the finest products. Rose-water was considered in ancient days to be the cure for almost every ill. It is still used in cosmetics and as a popular cure.

It is said that the presence of an oily substance floating on the surface of rose-water was first observed in Italy and Germany in the sixteenth and seventeenth centuries, and when this was separated from the water it commanded an infinitely higher price. Slightly later this substance was separated and extracted in Persia (Iran). This "attar," as it is called, gave rise to a greatly increased industry. Kaempfer mentioned that in 1684 the Persian distilleries were in a flourishing condition; the extract was even more valuable than gold and was the scent most appreciated and sought-after in various countries. I have not been able to trace what species of rose was used; authors sometimes state it was *Rosa moschata*. As, however, *R. damascena* was subsequently used in India and Bulgaria it seems more probable that it was this rose. The Bulgarian industry dates from the beginning of the eighteenth century, and prior to the Second World War Miss Lindsay introduced from the Caspian Provinces of Persia a Damask Rose which we now call 'Gloire de Guilan' and which she stated was used for the extraction of attar. From some forgotten source I was told also that another Damask, 'Ispahan', is similarly used in Turkey.

The district of Kazanlik has given its name to *Rosa damascena* 'Trigintipetala', which we grow in Britain, and this is undoubtedly the rose growing in great quantity in Bulgaria. Professor V. M. Staicov, of the Bulgarian State Agricultural Institute for Investigation of Medical and Aromatic Plants, was kind enough to send me pressed specimens and, later, propagating material of various roses in his fields. In addition to this particular Damask Rose, a form of *R. alba* almost identical to *R. alba* 'Semi-plena' is also grown. Both flower only once during the growing season.

A paper* on the distribution of the oil in the flower parts shows that in the Bulgarian clone of Damask Rose the oil is found in almost every part of the flower—petals, stamens, calyx, etc.—but that most of it (92 per cent) resides in the petals, which constitute 75 per cent of the weight of the flower. At daybreak the flowers start to open, developing a cup-formation; it is at this moment that they contain most oil, of which nearly 30 per cent is lost by twelve o'clock and 70 to 80 per cent by 4 p.m. Therefore, the harvesting has to be done from 5 a.m. to 9 to 10 a.m., and the gathered flowers complete with calyx are processed the same day, since after twenty-four hours almost 30 per cent of the oil is lost, due mainly to evaporation. The oil is today distilled by steam in large copper stills of about 250 to 500 gallons capacity.

The quantities are astronomical. About three tons of flowers (approximately 1,200,000 blooms) are required to produce rather less than 2¼ pounds of attar, and this amounts to the yield from four to five acres of Damask Rose plants. Five to six tons of *Rosa alba* are necessary to give the same quantity, but this rose is grown on a very limited scale in Bulgaria. Professor Staicov told me that the cultivation of these roses in Bulgaria was concentrated in a picturesque valley sheltered from the cold north winds by the Balkan Mountains, with the Sredna Gora on the south acting as a check to the dry, hot air penetrating from the Aegean Sea. The rivers Toundja and Strema and their numerous tributaries bring moisture and fertility. The climate is moderate and equable. The Damask Rose grows best on well-drained, sunny mountain slopes and hillsides, where the air is cool and damp, especially during the flowering period.

The Kazanlik valley has become world famous as the "Valley of Roses," and it must be a

---

* Staicov and Zolotowitch, 1957.

great experience to be there in June, when on crisp mornings the delicate fragrance is carried from the fields and distilleries over the whole valley, in which well over 7000 acres are devoted to this crop. This area is steadily increasing. In the old days the roses were grown in thick rows; the modern method is to cultivate them singly in the row, facilitating mechanical tillage and control of pests and diseases, and thereby greatly increasing the yield.

By the last week of May the harvest begins, continuing for about three weeks; it is sometimes curtailed by a hot, dry spell, but is prolonged in cool, damp weather, when the yield and quality of the oil are higher. I had read elsewhere that *Rosa alba* flowers slightly later and its flowers contain more stereoptene, which adds increased "oil of geranium," an adulteration frowned upon by specialists but useful for lower-grade samples; a little book published in 1894, *Rhodologia*, by J. C. Sawyer, FLS, gave a fairly full account of the industry in those days. Now, Professor Staicov has informed me, the Bulgarian State controls the whole of the production and guarantees absolute purity, and the attar is justly famous throughout the world, not only on its own, but as an ingredient of high-grade perfumes and cosmetics. Many of us are familiar with the scent of attar through the flavour of the pink-coloured Turkish delight, and I believe it is also used in marshmallow. But this gives only a tithe of the delight afforded by the pure liquid in a tiny phial which reached me from Kazanlik.

Turkey and other countries in the Mediterranean region and in the Middle East have also been contributors to supplies of attar. In Germany an industry was once concentrated near Leipzig, and the neighbourhood of Grasse in the south of France is still famous for its productions, but the attar, I understand, contains considerably more stereoptene.

Much the same procedure obtains in other countries and districts where this very special Damask Rose has been grown commercially for centuries. Michael Hayward, stationed at Taif, Saudi Arabia, has sent me an absorbing account of his visit to the rose fields of Al-Hada, from which I have his permission to give the following extracts.

> The garden was on a broad gentle slope and arranged into a geometrical grid of rose lines and irrigation channels. The beds were raised and the water gulleys took a precise zig-zag course down the hillside. The ditches were dry and baked, and I pondered at the enormous task of supplying sufficient water for thousands of rose bushes, and of maintaining the moisture on the well-drained slopes.
>
> The individual flower was indeed an interesting puzzle. The small, loosely semi-double blooms of the most exquisite warm pink and bright stamens of pure Arabian gold were held in large clusters. The tall, dense foliage was a dark matt green and rudely healthy, with not a trace of black spot, nor a pest or aphis to be seen. Surely a Damask flower, and I wondered if this was the 'Kazanlik' rose (a variety of *Rosa* × *damascena trigintipetala*) grown in vast quantities in Bulgaria for the production of attar, the oil extract much sought-after by the wealthy in world-wide markets.
>
> It was estimated that at the peak of the flowering period an established bush could be topped with up to two hundred blooms to be plucked every morning, and a mature bush would produce over three thousand blooms during the season. The season begins annually on 1 April, the beginning of the Arabian summer, and lasts for a complete month until the bushes have exhausted themselves. A weary bush would retire at twenty years and the stock would be replenished from plants grown on their own roots in polythene

containers kept under the dappled shade of a large apricot tree. The bushes are pruned back in late December during the cool, damp season and are then heavily manured with cow and goat dung. When the camel market comes to town the younger sons are sent with buckets to collect camel droppings, a highly-prized source of nutrients during the hectic flowering season.

The discovery of attar extraction from freshly picked rose blooms is shrouded in mystery and legend. One such fable heralds from India and centres upon a Mogul Emperor and a Princess who saw, while rowing on a stream of rose-water flowing through the Royal Gardens, the oily substance floating on the surface. Whether the invention can be attributed to the canals of India is open to speculation, but it is historical accuracy that specialized alchemists of Indian origin—working with the apothecaries of Mecca and Taif—became the undisputed masters in the production of one variety of attar obtained by the distillation of sandalwood-oil through petals of Al-Hada roses. With Al-Hada's reputation as a region of great fertility and rich heritage from time immemorial, this jewel of Arabia was no land of make-believe but a real testament to a timeless legacy.

It is plain that not only has the rose through its scent provided mankind with a precious distillation, but that the work necessary to extract tiny quantities of precious liquid has meant the employment of vast numbers of people, and the preservation for two hundred years, or more, of one vigorous type of Damask Rose, grown in the fields from division. This scent is, according to Dr Hurst, the product of the fusion of two roses, *Rosa gallica* and *R. phoenicea*. Through later hybridization with *R. moschata* and *R. chinensis*, the Bourbon and Hybrid Perpetual Roses were evolved, and not until towards the end of the nineteenth century was the "dark red rose" beloved by our parents an established fact. Its scent was strong only occasionally, and bore a resemblance to *R. damascena;* thus the Damask scent in dark red roses that one so often hears about is rather hypothetical.

I should find it difficult to say which rose scent I like best. To me, there are none that are objectionable. For pure sweetness and softness one cannot find anything to surpass the Old Roses, but the rich, fruity scents in the Hybrid Teas are also of special appeal, and their sharper and more exciting scents fit their angular shapes and vivid colours, I think, very appropriately. Those who wish to delve into the fascinations of scent in flowers should read *The Scent of Flowers and Leaves,* by F. A. Hampton (Dulau), a little book of absorbing interest.

In addition to the prowess of *Rosa damascena* in the matter of distillations, *R. gallica officinalis* has an equal claim to fame, as the particular rose that gave rise to another industry, that of the dried petals. From these, conserves were made in great variety, and an enormous industry arose at Provins, near Paris, which still flourishes. There was a similar though smaller industry devoted to this rose for commercial purposes at Mitcham, Surrey. The Hungarian commercial variant, *R. gallica* 'Conditorum', presumably was also used. *Rosa gallica* has the priceless character of retaining its scent particularly well after drying; possibly other roses may have this advantage, but they have not been exploited commercially. The Provins industry exported products all over the northern hemisphere in vast quantities. Because *R. gallica officinalis* was often called the Red Damask in old books, there is considerable confusion over these two. The petals were made into powder, syrup, jam, candy, cordial, wine, or just dried. Constance Spry used to make rose-petal jam from this species, as anyone who sampled the resulting rose-petal cake will well remember.

Vita Sackville-West sent me this amusing extract, from a letter of the future Louis XIII, aged four, to his father Henri IV, in 1605:

> Papa, all the apothecaries of Provins have come to me to beg me to ask you, very humbly, to give my company a different garrison-post, because my *gendarmes* like the *conserve de roses* and I am afraid they will eat it all and I shall have none left. I eat some every night when I go to bed. . . .

PART 5

From Other Pens

13

The Work of Dr C. C. Hurst

Yet, though thou fade,
From thy dead leaves let fragrance rise.

Edmund Waller

EACH OF MY previous historical references has, perforce, gone a little too far, with the result that the next has had to start chronologically earlier, and this will be no exception. I have mentioned how Dr Hurst had been conducting his research into the botanical and cytological evolution of the genus *Rosa* at Cambridge University Botanic Garden, from 1922 onwards, and in Chapter I, I recorded various writings on roses during the period between the two wars. With the very greatest respect and pleasure I now want to write my little appreciation of what Dr Hurst has done for us.

C. C. Hurst (1870–1947) had already been engaged for some years in pioneer work on Heredity when Mendel's papers were discovered in 1900, and from that time he took a leading part with Bateson, of the John Innes Horticultural Institution, in the foundation of the new science of Genetics. His experiments covered many plants and animals, including Man, and in 1909 he founded the Burbage Experiment Station for Genetics in Leicestershire.

Among many other things, he was working on the production of pedigree rose stocks, resulting in some highly satisfactory types. He also enthusiastically collected old-fashioned roses and rose species, together with the many books, old and new, which have been written on this very favourite genus.

Unhappily the First World War intervened. Hurst, one of the leaders in the Leicestershire Territorials, was in the forces for five years, and on his return he found it impossible to resuscitate the Experiment Station, which had lost its working staff and experimental horses to the war, the poultry, rabbits, etc., for food, and most of the plants from neglect, while the grants of money for the various projects had ceased to exist.

One of the few things left was the hardier part of his rose collection, which he took up again with renewed interest. Since most geneticists were now feeling that little more could be done without co-ordinating the study of hereditary characters with that of the genes and chromosomes, he went up to Trinity College, Cambridge, in 1922, to work on the cytology of *Rosa*.

This new approach elucidated many of the difficult points in this genus, especially with regard to classification. Hurst planned to write a monograph of *Rosa* from this new angle, and much material was collected, but the Second World War interrupted its publication. His war work as a member of the Royal Observer Corps brought on a severe illness from which he never fully recovered, and he died in 1947 with his work on *Rosa* still unfinished.

Fortunately his voluminous and careful notes were in the capable hands of his widow, and Mrs Hurst, who shared the burden of much of her husband's work, had a skill and knowledge that enabled her to co-ordinate these findings into a book rich in rose lore and scientific charts. Her book, *The Loom of Life* (The Humanist Library), appeared in 1964, and in subsequent years she edited all her husband's notes and presented them to Cambridge University. She was good enough, not only to furnish me with the above notes on her husband's life, but also to let me make full use of her library of Rose books, and added considerably to my own knowledge of roses from her deep fund of experience.

Dr Hurst did not, however, die without having some of his writings recorded, and, in collaboration with Mabel S. G. Breeze, produced his 'Notes on the Origin of the Moss Rose' in 1922. These were published in Part I of Vol. 47 of the *Journal* of the Royal Horticultural Society, and make absorbing reading. In 1941, in the March, July, and August numbers of the same *Journal*, a more exhaustive and comprehensive survey of roses appeared, entitled 'Notes on the Origin and Evolution of our Garden Roses'. These have been of the most inestimable value to me in classifying my collection, and I would like to feel that they are widely read and appreciated by all who grow roses. His style, at once pithy, lucid, and attractive, leads one on from one considered aspect to another, every paragraph well thought out and packed with historical detail. Since the *Journals* are not readily available to everyone, I approached Mrs Hurst for permission to have these invaluable notes republished, and to my delight she readily agreed.

It is, to me, a very happy thought that the work of Dr Hurst's most able brain is thus to be given increased publicity; his notes will do much to foster that wider interest in *Rosa* that is needed to appreciate the genus as a whole, from a horticultural point of view. Even in this century some new Moss Roses have been raised, and who knows but that some of the older types may be revived and given a further chance to share in the future races of garden roses? At least we may well feel glad that cytology arrived just in time for this great pioneer to unravel many of the mysteries woven in the Old Roses, before they became too confused or even extinct. His work was far in advance of all other rose genealogists, and it is surprising how few writers on the subject have availed themselves of the theories he put forward and the work which he carried out.

NOTES ON THE ORIGIN
AND EVOLUTION OF OUR GARDEN ROSES
by C. C. HURST, SC.D., PH.D. (CANTAB.), F.L.S.
(1941)

I. ANCIENT GARDEN ROSES
2000 B.C.—A.D. 1800

THE INTRODUCTION of the China Rose to England towards the end of the eighteenth century caused a complete revolution in the garden Roses of Europe, America, and the Near East. The effects of this introduction from the Far East first became evident in the Noisette and Bourbon hybrids which appeared in the early years of the nineteenth century, so that we may take A.D. 1800 as a natural line of division between ancient and modern garden Roses.

The ancient Roses, for the most part, flowered only once a year, in the early summer, while the modern Roses bloom continuously from early summer to late autumn. In a favourable climate like the Riviera they may flower all the year round, since they are potentially perpetual. Recent research shows that this habit of continuous flowering is due to the action of a Mendelian recessive gene introduced into our modern Roses by the China and Tea Roses, already cultivated in China for a thousand years or more. A similar mutation was observed by the writer in the Botanic Gardens at Cambridge a few years ago in a batch of wild seedlings of one of the Chinese Musk Roses, *R. Helenae* Rehd. and Wils., from seeds received by Mr Reginald Cory.

There was one ancient Rose which under favourable conditions of high culture and special pruning often produced a second crop of flowers in the autumn. This Rose was known in England as the Monthly Rose, in France as Quatre-Saisons, and in ancient Rome as *Rosa bifera*. It was, however, uncertain and sporadic in its second flowering, and was in no sense a continuous bloomer like the China Rose. In the days of summer-flowering Roses a few scattered blooms in the autumn were highly prized.

A. THE RED ROSE OF LANCASTER (*Rosa rubra* Blackw. 1757)[*]

The Red Rose is the foundation species from which most of our garden Roses have been evolved. The species, in its dwarf wild state, extends from France to Persia and has produced many natural hybrids with other species. The history of the garden Red Rose is lost in the night of time. According to Gravereaux it was the Rose of the Persian Magi, and the Median Fire Worshippers of the twelfth century B.C., who cultivated it for their religious ceremonies. According to their sacred writings of the ninth century B.C. (the Zend Avesta) this Rose was dedicated to an archangel. In the fourth and third centuries B.C. the Red Rose was apparently cultivated by the ancient Greeks and also at Miletus in Asia Minor, whence it was imported by the ancient Romans in the first century of our era. Pliny describes it as vivid red in colour with not more than twelve petals. In the sixth century it appears as the Rose of the *Codex Caesareus* at Constantinople, which has been identified by Gravereaux as the Dwarf Red Rose known as *R. pumila*. In the twelfth century the dark Red Rose was cultivated by the Arabs in Spain with the tradition that it was brought from Persia in the seventh century.

The Apothecary's Rose of Provins (R. gallica officinalis Thory)

In the thirteenth century the town of Provins, south-east of Paris, became the centre of a great industry which persisted for more than six centuries, although its greatest production

---

[*] Syn. *Rosa gallica* L., 1759 (*non* 1753). *Rosa gallica* L., 1753, was a species of the Caninae, near to *R. canina tomentella* (Léman), and it was not until 1759 that Linnaeus described the *R. gallica* of authors. In the meantime Mrs Elizabeth Blackwell had described and figured the species under the name of *Rosa rubra* (the Red Rose) in 1757.

[Mrs Blackwell's name *Rosa rubra* cannot be taken into consideration in matters of priority, as it is contrary to Art. 79 (4) of the 1952 Code of Botanical Nomenclature. Trew's edition of Mrs Blackwell's *Herbarium* does not consistently use Linnaean binomials, nor does it cite references to Linnaeus; *R. gallica* should therefore be adopted. GDR

"Red" as applied to the Old Roses is only a comparative term. All dark pink roses, before the arrival of Slater's Crimson China, were called red. GST]

was in the seventeenth century. This industry arose through the discovery that a certain variety of the Red Rose had the peculiar chemical property of preserving the delicate perfume of its petals even when dried and reduced to powder. The apothecaries of the period developed this discovery by making conserves and confections of Roses, in various forms, which gave rise to a great industry in the course of centuries. Documents show that in 1310 the town was able to offer presents of conserves and dried Roses to the Archbishop of Sens on his solemn entry, to Charles VII and Joan of Arc in 1429, to Henry II in 1556, to Louis XIV in 1650, 1668, 1678, and 1681, to the Queen of Louis XV in 1725, and to the Emperor Napoleon I in 1814. In 1600 the historian of Henry IV remarked that the main street of the town of Provins was peopled with apothecaries, who make the famous conserve of Provins Roses which is sent all over France. The Provins Roses were also much appreciated in India and England, and in 1860, 36,000 kilos of Provins Rose petals were sent to America. This peculiar scented variety of the Red Rose grown at Provins for more than six hundred years became known as the Apothecary's Rose and was beautifully figured by Redouté in 1817. There is a particularly good photograph of the Rose in Edward Bunyard's book *Old Garden Roses*, 1936, Plate 25, under the name of 'Red Gallica'. For more than three hundred years this Rose of Provins has been known in England as the Red Damask Rose, although, as Bunyard points out, it is botanically a *gallica* (*rubra*) and not a Damask. It was called a Damask because it was believed to have been brought originally from Damascus by a Crusader. The original plant, from which many thousands of bushes have been clonally propagated and grown at Provins and elsewhere, was said to have been brought to Provins from the Valley of Damascus by Thibaut Le Chansonnier on his return from one of the Crusades. Thibaut IV was King of Navarre and also Count of Champagne and Brie, which explains his interest in the town of Provins. Born in 1201, he was the author of sixty-six poems, and evidently fond of Roses since he sings of them in his verses. In *Le Roman de la Rose*, written about 1260 (later translated by Chaucer as *Romaunt of the Rose*), there is a reference to the Roses from the 'land of the Saracens', and it is probable that we are indebted to the Crusaders for the introduction from Eastern gardens of superior varieties of the Red, Musk, and Damask Roses.

Rosa Mundi

At some time in its history, the date of which is at present unknown, the ancient Rose of Provins gave rise by a bud-sport (somatic mutation) to the old-fashioned favourite striped Rose, *Rosa Mundi*, which occasionally reverts to its bud-parent. *Rosa Mundi* is often mentioned and figured by the old herbalists (Clusius in 1583, Besler in 1613, Caspar Bauhin in 1623), under various names, and there is a drawing of it by Robert in Paris at the Jardin des Plantes dated 1640. There is a popular tradition that this Rose is intimately associated with the Fair Rosamond of Henry II, and in the older writers the name of the Rose is often written as one word, *Rosamonde*. The Fair Rosamond seems to have died in 1176, so that perhaps an earlier Crusader found the striped form in a Syrian garden, and on his return presented it to her after giving it her name.

Both the ancient Rose of Provins and its bud-sport, *Rosa Mundi*, are tetraploid with twenty-eight chromosomes in their body-cells and fourteen in their male and female germ-cells.

Up to the seventeenth century only a few varieties of the Red Rose were cultivated in Europe; in 1629 Parkinson notes about a dozen; in the eighteenth century Dutch horticulturists, thanks to Van Eden and others, took up the breeding of the Red Rose on a large scale, and the dozen varieties of Parkinson soon became a thousand. Early in the nineteenth century, owing to the ardour and enthusiasm of the Empress Josephine, many of these were cultivated in France, England, and Italy, whereas hitherto their cultivation had been confined to Holland, Belgium, and Germany. Very few of these varieties of the Red Rose are now in cultivation, but owing to the courtesy and kindness of M. Gravereaux of La Belle Roseraie de L'Haÿ I have been able to examine the chromosomes of a large number of the old Roses which are preserved in his collection. It may be said that all the garden varieties of the Red Rose examined are tetraploid with twenty-eight chromosomes in the body-cells and fourteen in both the male and female germ-cells, while many of the hybrids are triploids.

B. THE DAMASK ROSE (*Rosa damascena* Blackw., 1757)

To the gardener the old Damask Roses are a very natural and charming group with their damask colouring, damasked pattern of the flowers and, above all, the damask fragrance of their perfume; he also likes to believe the old tradition of 1551 that they came originally from Damascus with the returning Crusaders.

The botanist is not so happy about the old Damask Roses, although he has always been willing to admit that they are a natural group and has usually given them the rank of a species; he realizes, however, that their characters are very near to those of *R. rubra* and that these are sufficient to prove the origin of the Damask from the Red Rose. At the same time he is aware that there are certain characters in the Damask Roses which are quite foreign to the Red Rose.

Analyses show that some of the Damask characters foreign to *R. rubra* are those of *R. phoenicia* Boiss., while the others are those of *R. moschata* Miller. It is evident therefore that the Damask Roses are all hybrids of *rubra*, but that some are hybrids of *phoenicia*, while others are hybrids of *moschata*.

Consequently the Damask Roses can be divided into two natural and distinct groups:

(1) × *R. damascena* (*rubra* × *phoenicia*). The Summer Damask Rose.
(2) × *R. bifera* (*rubra* × *moschata*). The Autumn Damask Rose.

(1) THE SUMMER DAMASK ROSE (× *R. damascena* Blackw.)

The York and Lancaster Rose

To this group belongs the old striped Damask, the York and Lancaster Rose, which has often been confused in our gardens with the striped Red Rose, *Rosa Mundi*. There should be no difficulty, however, in distinguishing these two striped Roses, since (apart altogether from the striking differences between them in habit, armature, leaves, and flowers) the pattern and colours of the striping are altogether different in the two Roses. In the *Rosa Mundi* the ground colour of the petals is pale rose-pink, irregularly but heavily striped and blotched all over with rosy-red. In the York and Lancaster the ground colour of the petals is white, irregularly but lightly marked or blotched with blush-pink or rose, the striping and blotching being only partial. This famous Rose was faithfully described by John Parkinson in 1629, and there is little doubt that it is the Rose mentioned by Shakespeare in *Henry VI*, in the scene of the plucking of red and white Roses in the Temple Garden. In Shakespeare's Sonnet XCIX we get an intimate picture of the York and Lancaster Rose which will appeal to the practical gardener.

> The Roses fearfully on thorns did stand,
> One blushing shame, another white despair;
> A third, nor red nor white, had stolen of both
> And to his robbery had annexed thy breath;
> But, for his theft, in pride of all his growth
> A vengeful canker eat him up to death.

These lines are of peculiar interest because they show that Shakespeare had more than a casual acquaintance with the York and Lancaster Rose; he must have had personal experience in growing the plant. My own experience is that this variety, in spite of its vigorous growth, has a poor constitution and does not last long without propagation and renewal.

The York and Lancaster Rose is a tetraploid with twenty-eight chromosomes in its body-cells and fourteen in its male and female germ-cells. The chromosomes show definite signs of hybridity, with irregular pairing and weakened affinity. In two cases whole sets of seven chromosomes acted independently of the others in somatic divisions. Such disturbances are likely to affect metabolism and weaken the plant's constitution. The young pollen-grains were not healthy, about one-half being degenerate. The embryo-sac formation was normal and healthy.

The Holy Rose

Another interesting but rather mysterious Rose, belonging to the first group of Summer Damask Roses, is the Holy Rose. Our knowledge of this Rose is somewhat scanty, yet it seems to go much farther back in history than any other garden Rose, and there are indications that it may have had a distant part to play in the evolution of our garden Roses. The little we know of its history is both curious and chequered. It was first found in Abyssinia, in the Christian Province of Tigre, where it had been planted in the courtyards of religious sanctuaries. It was described by Richard in 1848 in his *Flora of Abyssinia* under the name of *Rosa sancta*.* The Holy Rose forms a low erect bush, and is intermediate in its characters between the Red and the Phoenician Rose. Indeed, except for its single flowers with five or six petals, it would pass well for a dwarf Damask Rose. Since its *phoenicia* parent is not a cultivated plant, the Holy Rose is presumably a natural hybrid with its home in Asia Minor and Syria, where its two parents overlap, and the question arises how it came to be transported to Abyssinia. The story of St Frumentius may help to solve that problem. St Frumentius was born in Phoenicia about A.D. 300, and it is said that while on a voyage he was captured by Ethiopians, taken to Axum, the Abyssinian capital, and became the King's Secretary. He is said to have converted the Abyssinians to Christianity, and secured its introduction to that country. In 326 he was consecrated Bishop of Axum by Athanasius at Alexandria, and died in 360.

In view of the above facts it seems likely that the Holy Rose may have been introduced to Abyssinia from Phoenicia (Syria) by the Phoenician Apostle of Ethiopia, St Frumentius, in the fourth century A.D. This also may explain why the Rose was planted within the precincts of the Christian churches in his diocese, and thus preserved through the centuries.

---

* In view of the earlier and quite different *R. sancta* Andrews (1827), Rehder in 1922 amended *R. sancta* Richard (1848) to *R. Richardii*, and now both Richard's and Rehder's specific names become synonyms of × *R. damascena* Blackw.

The Rose of the Tombs

We next hear of the mysterious Holy Rose in the tombs of Egypt. The tomb in which it was found was in the cemetery of the town of Arsinoe of Fayoum in Upper Egypt, near to the Labyrinth Pyramid, and judging by other remains found alongside the Holy Rose it belonged to a period between the second and the fifth centuries A.D. The remains of this Rose were twined into garlands when found in the Egyptian tomb in 1888 by the eminent English archaeologist, Sir Flinders Petrie, who sent them to Kew Gardens for identification. Dr Oliver, having ascertained that they were Roses, forwarded them to Professor Crépin, Director of the Brussels Botanic Garden. Crépin reported that the nine Roses composing the garland were all of the same variety and were identical with *Rosa sancta* Richard, cultivated at the present day in the courtyards of religious edifices in Abyssinia. Crépin considered them to be a new form of *R. gallica* (*R. rubra*), but he did not think that they had ever been indigenous in Abyssinia or Egypt, but that they had been introduced from Italy, Greece, or Asia Minor. There may be some connection between the garlands of Abyssinian Holy Roses in the Egyptian tomb and St Frumentius of Abyssinia, but until further evidence is obtained it remains a mystery.

The Minoan Rose in Crete

Finally we arrive at the island of Crete, where Sir Arthur Evans, in the course of his remarkable excavations, unearthed a fresco-painting near the ancient palace of Cnossos that included a lifelike representation of a Rose, which I saw in 1926 and which seemed to me to bear a striking resemblance to the Holy Rose of Abyssinia, Egypt, and Asia Minor. It is hoped that further excavations will bring to light more of these Minoan Roses and add to our present scanty knowledge of them.

The central date of the great historic Minoan civilization of Crete may be put at about 2000 B.C. It apparently maintained close contact with Egypt, Phoenicia, and Greece, and there is no doubt that the beautiful Phoenician Roses would appeal to the high artistic sense of the Minoans. The selection of a single-flowered Rose by the Minoan artist for his fresco-painting does not necessarily mean that garden Roses were not cultivated by the Minoans; the double garden Roses of the time may have been too heavy for his artistic purpose.

So far as I have been able to trace, this Minoan fresco-painting is the earliest representation of a Rose in historical times.

(2) THE AUTUMN DAMASK ROSE ($\times$ *R. bifera* [Poiret])[*]

The Autumn Damask Roses are also very ancient and, like their parents *rubra* and *moschata*, have always been renowned for their fragrance and free-flowering qualities. We first hear of them in the island of Samos towards the tenth century B.C., where they are said to have flowered twice a year and were freely used in the cult of Aphrodite (or Venus), which was

---

[*] [Now generally recognized as *R. damascena* var. *semperflorens* (Loisel) Rowley. My rediscovery of the ancient Musk Rose, flowering from August onwards, is recorded in Chapter 8, "The Mystery of the Musk Rose," and sheds further light on the ancestry of the Autumn Damask Rose. GST]

later introduced to Greece and Rome, together with the Roses, which played a most important part in the ceremonies. There is little doubt that the Roses which Herodotus mentions
as growing in Macedonia in the gardens of Midas, each with sixty petals and surpassing all
other Roses in fragrance, were the Autumn Damask Roses × *R. bifera*, and not *R. centifolia*, as
we used to believe. As we shall see later, *R. centifolia*, as we know it, and as the eighteenth and
nineteenth centuries knew it, first arose in Holland in the eighteenth century of our era and
was therefore unknown to the ancient Greeks and Romans. Their Roses with a hundred petals, which naturally they called *Rosa centifolia*, were not our *centifolia*, but evidently our *bifera*
Damask Rose, which we know was cultivated by them at a later period at Paestum, Pompeii,
and other places. It is possible that Midas, who was King of Phrygia, may have brought the
Roses of Herodotus to Macedonia from his gardens in Asia Minor, and that afterwards they
were distributed in Greece and Italy. Many Roses of the same kind were grown in Egypt for
the Roman market, especially in the winter, as Martial tells us 'roses in winter bear the highest
price'. In the first century B.C. Virgil, in his Georgics, sings of the Roses of Paestum and of
their flowering twice a year, 'biferique Rosaria Paesti', which can only refer to our Autumn
Damask Rose. Frescoes of this Rose were found in the ruins of Pompeii, which was destroyed
in A.D. 79, and Pliny himself perished in the catastrophe through his eagerness to get a near
view of the great eruption of Vesuvius. In the tenth century, according to the Arab physician
Avicenna, the same Rose was cultivated on a large scale in Syria for making rose-water and
for medicines. In the twelfth century it appears with the Arabs in Spain, and Ibn-el-Awam
describes our Damask Rose with much detail, suggesting that it came from the East.

The Rose of Alexandria

In the sixteenth century, Nicolas Monardes, a Spanish physician, wrote a medical treatise
on the Roses of Persia or Alexandria, which he said the Italians, Gauls, Germans, and others
call Damascenae, because they believe them to have come from Damascus. His description
agrees with the Autumn Damask Rose, although he says nothing of its flowering twice a year.
There is, however, indirect evidence that these Spanish Damask Roses did flower twice a year,
for M. Lachaume, writing to the *Journal des Roses* in 1879 from Havannah, Cuba, states that
in almost every Spanish home in Cuba there is the antique Quatre-Saisons Rose, which in
Cuba is universally known as the Alexandria Rose. This Rose and its name have evidently
been handed down in Cuba from generation to generation from the time the Spanish colonists settled there in the sixteenth century. Other Spanish plants were also brought at the
same time, and have survived with the Rose as souvenirs of their native homes in Spain. From
M. Lachaume's detailed description of the Alexandria Rose, and his statement that it flowers
twice a year, there can be no doubt that it is our Autumn Damask Rose, and it is most likely
the same Rose as Monardes's Spanish Damascena of 1551, which he thought came from Persia or Alexandria, through the Arabs and the Moors.

In modern times the Autumn Damask Rose is still preferred to any other kind for the
commercial production of rose-water and attar of Roses as in the old days, and there are vast
plantations of this variety of Rose in Turkey, Bulgaria, Egypt, Persia, India, and Morocco. All
the varieties of Damask Roses so far examined, except one, prove to be tetraploid with
twenty-eight chromosomes in the body-cells and fourteen in the male and female germ-cells.
The exception is a seedling Damask Rose in Kew Gardens which proves to be a pentaploid
with thirty-five chromosomes in the body-cells, twenty-one in the female germ-cells, and

fourteen in the male. This interesting Rose was raised at Kew from seeds of a hip gathered from the Rose growing on Omar's grave at Naishapur.

> When Omar died, the Rose did weep
> Its petals on his tomb;
> He would be laid, where North winds keep
> The Rose in freshest bloom.
>
> Anna Hills, 1884

C. THE WHITE ROSE OF YORK (*Rosa alba* L.)

This familiar old garden Rose has persisted through the centuries, and has been in general cultivation from the times of the Greeks and Romans. In the thirteenth century it was rather neatly described by the Universal Doctor of the Schoolmen, Albertus Magnus, as 'the white garden rose which has often fifty or sixty petals, it is very bushy, and the branches are long and thin in a tree of which the trunk often attains the thickness of one's arm'. In 1307 Crescentius, the Italian agriculturist, recommends it for planting a hedge. The Italian painters of the fifteenth century were fond of this Rose, and portrayed the large 'Double White' and the 'Maiden's Blush' varieties (*alba maxima* and *alba regalis*), the flowers of which appear to be identical with those grown today.

In the Wars of the Roses the 'Double White' English Rose was traditionally adopted as a badge by the Yorkists. The old herbalists note and figure this Rose in the sixteenth century, and it usually appears first on their lists of Roses as 'most ancient and knowne Rose . . . King of all others' (Parkinson). In 1753 Linnaeus made it a species under the name of *R. alba*, and although it is obviously a garden plant most botanists have regarded it as a species until 1873, when Christ suggested that it was a hybrid between *gallica* (*R. rubra*) and *canina*, and Crépin, with others, have agreed with this interpretation.

An analysis of the characters of × *R. alba* L. shows the definite influence of *R. phoenicia* Boiss. in this hybrid, and I feel bound to conclude, therefore, that × *R. damascena*, rather than *R. rubra*, was one parent, and that a white-flowered, almost prickleless form of *R. canina* was the other. Further, from the chromosome number we can say definitely that *canina* was the female parent and not the male. × *R. alba* is a hexaploid with forty-two chromosomes; *R. canina* is a pentaploid with twenty-eight chromosomes in the female germ-cells and seven in the male; × *R. damascena* is a tetraploid with fourteen chromosomes in both male and female germ-cells. Consequently, if *R. canina* had been the male parent, × *R. alba* would have been a triploid with twenty-one chromosomes instead of a hexaploid with forty-two.

The only white-flowered *canina* with few prickles known to me is *R. c. Froebelii* Christ, which grows in Kurdistan, and possibly extends to the Crimea and the Caucasus. This is the form of Briar known in gardens as *R. laxa*, and formerly used as a stock for budding garden Roses. It has no connection whatever with the *R. laxa* of Retzius or of Lindley, nor, as Rehder suggests, with *R. coriifolia* Fries.

× *R. alba* has been reported as growing wild in the Crimea, and it may be that it originated there as a natural hybrid; it has also been reported from several places in Central Europe, but these may be garden escapes or otherwise of garden origin.

In the singles and semi-double forms of × *R. alba* which are fertile, the female germ-cells carry twenty-eight chromosomes, while the male germ-cells carry only fourteen. All the seedlings examined have forty-two chromosomes.

D. THE OLD CABBAGE ROSE (*Rosa centifolia* L.)

For many years most of us have believed that the Old Cabbage Rose of our great-grand-mothers was the most ancient Rose in the world. We all followed the old herbalists who agreed that *Rosa centifolia*, the Queen of Roses and the Queen of Flowers, was cultivated by the Greeks and Romans, noted by Herodotus, and named by Theophrastus and Pliny. We took it all in, and it seemed to us the most natural thing in the world for the classic Roses with a hundred petals and the most fragrant of perfumes to be our *Rosa centifolia*, especially as Theo-phrastus and Pliny called them by that name. Modern research has changed all that, and will not be denied. It appears now that our *R. centifolia* did not actually arrive until the eighteenth century, and is therefore the youngest of all our old Roses.

Thanks to the initial spade-work of the late Edward Bunyard we are now in a position to trace the origin, or rather the evolution, of the *R. centifolia* of Linnaeus, commonly known in England as the 'Provence' or 'Cabbage Rose'. Space will not allow full details here, and a brief summary must suffice.

Analysis shows that *R. centifolia* L. is not a wild species as many have supposed, nor is it a simple primary hybrid like the Damask Roses. It is a complex hybrid of four distinct wild species, *R. rubra*, *R. phoenicia*, *R. moschata*, and *R. canina*, and may therefore be presumed to have had a garden origin. Such a combination can, of course, be made in many different ways, and we have no knowledge of the actual steps taken. The quickest way to arrive at the combina-tion is no doubt the direct cross between × *R. bifera* (*rubra* × *moschata*) and × *R. alba* (*canina* × *damascena*), which would give the whole combination. Experience of plant breeding, however, leads one to suppose that, working under the usual system of trial and error, many steps were taken, both backwards and forwards, before the object was attained.

Evidence from many varied sources in literature and art shows that *R. centifolia* L. was grad-ually and slowly evolved from the end of the sixteenth century to the beginning of the eighteenth century, when it apparently reached the perfection of a florist's flower. Definitely we owe this superb Rose to the genius and industry of the Dutch breeders who first took the matter in hand about 1580, and persevered until they attained perfection about 1710.

Soon after that date the old Moss Rose appeared in Holland as a bud-sport of the per-fected type of × *R. centifolia*, which was, of course, completely sterile sexually, owing to the complete doubleness of the flowers. Afterwards at least sixty-two other bud-sports appeared, either from the original × *R. centifolia* or from its sports. These were much cultivated in the first half of the nineteenth century, and a few are still grown to this day. At Burbage I grew and studied about twenty of these bud mutations for many years, and during that time several of them reverted to the bud-parent × *R. centifolia* without any variation, so far as I could see, which suggests that these sports came from the stock of one seedling plant of × *R. centifolia*, existent about 1710.

The true type of × *R. centifolia*, i.e., the perfected form which produced the Moss Rose, is tetraploid with twenty-eight chromosomes in the body-cells and fourteen in the male and female germ-cells. Owing to doubleness the germ-cells do not mature and fail to reach the final stage. Only once did I succeed in getting a seed, and that failed to germinate.

Most of the bud-sports have the same number of chromosomes as their parent, but a few, like the Rose of the Painters, are triploid with twenty-one chromosomes in the body-cells and irregular numbers in the germ-cells which fail to mature.

From the above notes it will be seen that the most important of our ancient garden Roses have originated from four wild species of *Rosa*, namely the Red Rose (*R. rubra* Blackw.

1757),* the Phoenician Rose (*R. phoenicia* Boiss.), the Musk Rose (*R. moschata* Miller), and the Dog Rose (*R. canina* L.). This completes a brief survey of the ancient foundation Roses from which our Garden Roses, ancient and modern, have sprung. There are a few other ancient garden forms still in cultivation which have not been noted, such as the Double Cinnamon Rose, the Double Sweet Briar, the Double Sulphur Rose, and the Miniature forms, such as the Burgundy Rose, the Rose de Meaux, and others of that kind; these have not been noted because up to now they have not been directly concerned in the evolution of our modern Roses. They have had their day, but so far have not succeeded in establishing a dynasty. Included in this category are the less ancient forms of the eighteenth century, such as the Ayrshire Roses from *R. arvensis* Huds., the Evergreen Roses from *R. sempervirens* L., and the Burnet or Scots Roses from *R. spinosissima* L., 1762 (non 1753). Finally, there are the important Yellow and Copper Austrian Briars from *R. lutea* Miller which, though very ancient, did not come into the direct line of modern Roses until the dawn of the twentieth century. These will be noted in the next article on the origin and evolution of our modern Roses since A.D. 1800.

II. MODERN GARDEN ROSES

1800–1940

Great events oft from little causes spring, and it is a remarkable fact that the most important improvement of our garden Roses in the last century was due to the introduction from China of a minute Mendelian gene, so small that it is quite invisible to the naked eye. The chromosome thread on which this tiny Rose gene is borne is plainly seen under a high-powered lens of an ordinary microscope, but an electron microscope would be required to make out the outline of the gene itself.

A pair of these genes, one from the father and one from the mother, is present in every growing cell of our best modern Roses, whether they be exquisite Teas, shapely Hybrid Teas, gay-coloured Pernets, dazzling Poulsens, or lowly Poly-Poms. In normal conditions of growth these genes cause a continuous pushing of shoots, with every shoot a flowering shoot, so that our modern Roses tend to flower all the year round, unlike the ancient Roses which for the most part flowered naturally only once a year.

In Rose breeding, except for certain complications met with in annual autumn-flowering species, this gene for perennial flowering behaves as a simple Mendelian recessive to the dominant wild gene for annual flowering. It is evidently a mutation which still appears from time to time in a state of nature among the wild Roses of China just as it did a thousand or more years ago when the Chinese gardeners first discovered it. This mutation seems to be peculiar to China and to the genus *Rosa*, although it is not limited to one species since I have found it in several Chinese species of *Rosa*.

China is a country rich in Roses, both wild and cultivated; indeed with its wealth of species it is considered by some botanists to be the original home and cradle of the genus. It was not, however, from these magnificent wild species that our modern garden Roses have sprung. That is reserved for future centuries. It was the humble dwarf China Rose that had been cultivated in Chinese gardens for more than a thousand years and bore the precious gene for continuous flowering which, transferred by hybridization to our Western garden Roses early in the nineteenth century, changed them as by a magic wand.

---

* Syn. *R. gallica* L., 1759 (*non* 1753).

E. CHINA ROSES (Sect. *Indicae* Thory)

Since the introduction of the Poly-Poms in 1875 China Roses have become rather old-fashioned, but they are still grown and cultivated by those who appreciate the loveliness of translucent colours.

The earliest records of the China Rose are found in the Chinese screen paintings of the tenth century on which are portrayed Blush China Roses which appear to be identical with the Blush Tea-scented China introduced to England in 1809. The earliest trace of the introduction of the China Rose to Europe that I have been able to find is in the National Gallery, London, where there is a painting by the Florentine artist, Angelo Bronzino, dating from about 1529, which shews a smiling cupid with his hands full of Pink China Roses in the act of throwing them over Folly, who is embracing Venus (Bronzino, No. 651). The small rose-pink flowers with translucent petals, incurved stamens, reflexed sepals, and small firm ovate shining leaflet are precisely those of the Pink China, and we may safely conclude that this Rose was cultivated in Italy early in the sixteenth century. It may have been this China Rose which Montaigne saw in flower at the Jesuit Monastery at Ferrara when he visited Italy in November 1678, and was told that the Rose flowered all the year round.

Among the early botanical specimens in the British Museum there is a quaint little remnant of a Crimson China Rose neatly arranged in a paper vase in the Herbarium of Gronovius (1690–1760). It is labelled 'Chineesche Eglantier Roosen', and dated 1733.* It was on this specimen of Gronovius that Jacquin founded his figure of the Crimson China in 1768 under the name of *R. chinensis*. In 1750 Peter Osbeck, a pupil of Linnaeus, and a collector of specimens for the Linnean Herbarium, set sail for China and the East Indies. On his return to Sweden in 1752 he published a brief account of his travels in which he describes his discovery of *Rosa indica* in the gardens of the Custom House at Canton on 29th October 1751.

The China Roses of Linnaeus

The China Roses in the Herbarium of Linnaeus at the Linnean Society of London include three Crimson Chinas, one Pink China, one Blush Tea China, and one hybrid China, which is apparently a cross with *R. multiflora* Thunb. The most interesting and important specimen is the Blush Tea China (Sheet 38) which Linnaeus, in his own handwriting, indicates as his type specimen of *R. indica*. It is probable that this is the *R. indica* found by Peter Osbeck in 1751 in the Custom House garden at Canton.

The Pink China specimen (Sheet 37), according to Linnaeus, came from the Botanic Garden at Upsala, whither it had been brought from China, probably by Osbeck in 1752. It is the *R. sinica* of Murray in Linn. Syst. Veg. 1774, which according to the elder Aiton (1789) was cultivated by Philip Miller in 1759. This is an early date for the cultivation of the China Rose in England, but it seems hardly likely that Aiton was mistaken because in the early part of that year he was a pupil of Miller at Chelsea, and thus had an opportunity of knowing the plant at first hand. Miller was in close touch with Linnaeus at that time, and may well have received the Pink China direct from Upsala. In 1769 Sir John Hill, in his *Hortus Kewensis*, records the cultivation of *R. indica* L. in the gardens of the Princess Augusta at Kew House when Aiton was in charge.

---

* By some mischance the date of this specimen is given as 1704 by both Willmott (1911) and Bunyard (1936), and the latter refers to it as the Blush China, although it is definitely a Crimson China.

In the younger Martyn's French edition of Miller's *Dictionary* of 1785, it is stated that a Deep Red China Rose was cultivated in England at that time, but I have been unable to trace its origin. French authors agree that the China Rose came to France through England, but they give a bewildering array of dates of their introduction from China and India to England, ranging between 1710 and 1780, and so far I have been unable to confirm these from English sources. In 1781 the Pink China was introduced to Holland by the Dutch East India Company, and in her *Memoirs* the Baroness D'Oberkirch relates that she saw this Chinese Rose in the gardens at Haarlem in 1782, and at once recognized the flower which was so often delineated on Chinese screens and fans. None of these early introductions of the China Rose to Italy, Sweden, Holland, and England, however, seems to have played any part in the development of our modern Roses. That role was apparently reserved for four special English introductions of 1792, 1793, 1809, and 1824, each of which had a definite and permanent influence on the evolution of our garden Roses.

THE FOUR STUD CHINAS

(1) SLATER'S CRIMSON CHINA, 1792 (*Rosa chinensis* Jacq.)

The first of the four stud Chinas was Slater's Crimson China, which was imported from China by Gilbert Slater of Knot's Green, Leytonstone, about 1792. The original plant was figured by Curtis in *Bot. Mag.* in 1794 under the name of *R. semperflorens*, and there is a specimen of it in the British Museum from Kew Gardens. Slater's Crimson China must have been introduced to France soon afterwards, for in 1798 Cels, the Paris nurseryman, Thory, the French botanist, and Redouté, the famous artist, commenced their breeding experiments with it in or about that year.

Slater's Crimson China reached Austria, Germany, and Italy before the close of the eighteenth century, and early in the nineteenth century in Italy it became the parent of the Portland Rose,* and thus grandparent of the first Hybrid Perpetual 'Rose du Roi'. Slater's Crimson China is still in cultivation in old gardens, and there is an admirable modern figure of it in Willmott (1911) under the name of *R. chinensis semperflorens*. In its characters it is very near to Henry's Crimson China, collected in 1885 in the San-yu-tung Glen near Ichang in the Province of Hupeh, Central China, which is generally considered to be the wild species and original ancestor of the China Roses. Slater's Crimson China differs from the wild species in its dwarf habit, semi-double flowers, and perennial flowering, all of which are Mendelian characters, the genes for the first and last characters being closely linked in the same chromosome.

Like most of the cultivated Crimson Chinas Slater's form is a triploid with twenty-one chromosomes in the body-cells, fourteen in the female germ-cells, and seven in the male. Consequently the pollen is very defective, and on the average only one grain in seven is fertile. This 14 per cent fertility would no doubt be fatal to survival in a state of nature, but it is sufficient for the gardener and hybridist to raise new kinds of Roses. Some of the cultivated Crimson Chinas are, however, diploid with fourteen chromosomes in the body-cells and seven in the male and female germ-cells, having retained their wild simplicity. I found one of

---

* [It is now considered that the parents of the Portland Rose were *R. gallica* and *R. damascena* var. *semperflorens* and that they owe nothing to *R. chinensis*. GST]

these diploid Crimson Chinas in the Gravereaux collection at La Roseraie de l'Haÿ, near Paris. In spite of its air of culture it was a typical wild Crimson China with single cherry-red flowers, while in habit it was a graceful short climber. Its diploid chromosome behaviour was entirely regular and normal as in a species, with no signs of hybridity, consequently the pollen and embryo-sacs were regular and the plant was as fully fertile as a wild species.

(2) PARSONS'S PINK CHINA, 1793 (*R. chinensis* Jacq. × *R. gigantea* Collett)

Parsons's Pink China was first seen in his garden at Rickmansworth in 1793, according to Andrews (1805), and was said by the younger Aiton (1811) to have been introduced from China about 1789 by Sir Joseph Banks. In the Banksian Herbarium there are three specimens of the Pink China, two of which closely resemble Parsons's Pink China; one of these is marked 'China prope Canton, Lord Macartney', and the other 'Hort. Kew 1795 China'. Lindley, in 1820, based his *R. indica* on the Macartney specimen, crediting the collection of it to Sir George Staunton, who accompanied Lord Macartney's embassy to China in 1792. It is therefore possible that Parsons's Pink China was sent home by him to Sir Joseph Banks, who was at that time Director of Kew.

Soon after 1793 Colville secured a stock of Parsons's Pink China, and sent it out as the Pale China Rose, presumably to distinguish it from Slater's Crimson China of 1792. Parsons's Pink China soon arrived in France, for it was seen in the greenhouses of Dr Barbier in Paris in 1798, and Thory tells us that he and Redouté started to raise seedlings from it in that year.

About 1800 Parsons's Pink China appeared in North America, at Charleston in South Carolina, no doubt through the agency of the two brothers Louis and Philippe Noisette, who were nurserymen in Paris and Charleston respectively, and about 1802, in the hands of John Champneys of Charleston, Parsons's Pink China became a grandparent of the French Noisette Rose from which later on came our best Climbing Yellow Teas such as 'Maréchal Niel' and 'Gloire de Dijon'.

In 1805, at Colville's nursery in England, Parsons's Pink China gave rise to the Dwarf Pink China, a miniature Rose known in England as the Fairy Rose or *R. Lawranceana*. Louis Noisette imported this Rose to France and called it Bengale Pompon. It was largely planted at Lyon, and in 1868 became a grandparent of the first Poly-Poms and ancestor of the Poulsen Roses.

About 1810 Parsons's Pink China appeared in the French island of Bourbon (Réunion), where the colonists used it to form hedges, and towards 1815, by natural crossing with the Autumn Damask Rose, also used as a hedge plant, it became a grandparent of the French Bourbon Rose, and thus an ancestor of the Teas, Hybrid Perpetuals, and Hybrid Teas.

Parsons's Pink China is still in cultivation in country gardens, and there is an excellent figure of it in Redouté (1817) under the name of *R. indica vulgaris*. Analyses of its characters show the influence of the Wild Crimson China (*R. chinensis*) in sixteen of these, while the remaining twelve characters show the influence of another species, the Wild Tea Rose (*R. gigantea*). Parsons's Pink China may therefore be regarded as a hybrid between *chinensis* and *gigantea*. It is not, of course, an ordinary primary hybrid produced directly* between the two species, but rather

---

* Genetical confirmation of this is found in the appearance of true-breeding *gigantea* characters in the original crosses of Noisette and Bourbon with Blush and Yellow Chinas, giving rise to the race of Tea Roses (*R. gigantea* Collett).

a derivative hybrid derived after generations of crossings in Chinese gardens. Parsons's Pink China is a diploid with fourteen chromosomes in the body-cells and seven in both male and female germ-cells. Although a diploid, its chromosomes are not regular in their behaviour and weak pairings in the germ-cell divisions lead to defective pollen and embryo-sacs and consequent sterility. In this respect the Pink Chinas behave as hybrids rather than pure species. Among the newer varieties of the Pink China I have found several triploid forms with twenty-one chromosomes, which have no doubt arisen by a duplication of the chromosomes in a pollen or egg-cell, as in the case of the triploid Crimson Chinas.

(3) HUME'S BLUSH TEA-SCENTED CHINA, 1809

(*R. chinensis* Jacq. × *R. gigantea* Collett)

Hume's Blush China is said to have been imported in 1809 by Sir A. Hume, Bart., from the East Indies, at that time a comprehensive term which included China. It was figured by Andrews in 1810 under the name of *R. indica odorata* from a plant flowering in Colville's nursery. In the same year special arrangements were made by both the British and French Admiralties for the safe transit of plants of this new Tea-scented China to the Empress Josephine at Malmaison in spite of the fierce war that was raging between England and France at that time. In 1817 Redouté published a beautiful and accurate figure of the original plant under the name of *R. indica fragrans*, which shows it to be a China considerably modified by the influence of the Wild Tea Rose (*R. gigantea*), the bias in favour of that species being about 2 : 1. It was not, however, a true Tea Rose as some have supposed,* since it shows the influence of the Wild Crimson China (*R. chinensis*) in eleven of its characters out of the thirty-one examined, the remaining twenty characters showing the influence of the Wild Tea Rose (*R. gigantea*). Hume's Blush China must therefore be regarded as a derivative hybrid from *gigantea* and *chinensis*. Crossed with the Bourbon, Noisette, and Yellow China towards 1830 Hume's Blush China gave rise to typical Tea Roses. Living material of the Rose is no longer available,† but like its ancestral species it was most likely a diploid with fourteen chromosomes. Material of its ancestral species the Wild Tea Rose (*R. gigantea*) from both Cambridge and Burbage proved to be diploid.

(4) PARKS'S YELLOW TEA-SCENTED CHINA, 1824

(*R. chinensis* Jacq. × *R. gigantea* Collett)

The fourth and last of the Stud Chinas is Parks's Yellow China, which was brought from China by Parks for the R.H.S. in 1824. The following year it was imported to France by the enthusiastic Rose breeder Hardy, of the Royal Luxembourg Gardens, where its novel colour made it a general favourite. There is a good figure of the original in the 1835 edition of Redouté under the name of *R. indica sulphurea*, with a description by Pirolle. At first sight, with its large yellow flowers, thick tea-scented petals, and bright green leaves, Parks's Yellow China looks more like a Tea than a China, and reminds one rather of the yellow variety of *R. gigantea*

---

* It was on this assumption that Rehder in 1915 reduced *R. gigantea* Collett to a variety of *R. odorata* Sweet, a name given by Sweet in 1818 to Hume's Blush China.

† [Now rediscovered, 1992. GST]

discovered in Manipur by Sir George Watt in 1882. An analysis of its characters, however, shows the influence of ten China characters to twenty of the Wild Tea Rose, so that the plant must be regarded as a hybrid. Parks's Yellow China was the ancestor of many remarkable Roses; crossed with the Noisettes it produced the typical Yellow Teas which, crossed with the Pink Teas derived from Hume's Blush China and the Bourbon, gave rise to those exquisite shades of refined colouring peculiar to Teas in which the pink and yellow are indescribably mixed and blended. Through the Teas, Parks's Yellow China was the ancestor of many of the Hybrid Teas, Pernets, Poly-Poms, and Poulsen Roses. No living material of Parks's Yellow China has been available since 1882,* but there is little doubt that it was a diploid with fourteen chromosomes, since both ancestral species were diploid, and crossed with the diploid Noisettes its descendants proved to be diploid.

In concluding the account of the four Stud Chinas which have had such a powerful influence in moulding our modern garden Roses, it may be interesting to note that China Roses similar to the four Stud Chinas are still cultivated in Chinese gardens. In South-western China, in the province of Yunnan, some of them are largely used for hedges. The Wild Tea Rose (*R. gigantea*) also grows there naturally in ravines and on grassy hills, and in the same locality at the same elevation garden forms of the Crimson China (*R. chinensis*) are still cultivated there. The port of Yunnan is Canton, from which the four Stud Chinas are presumed to have come. It seems therefore fairly safe to conclude that the four Stud Chinas which revolutionized our old garden Roses originated in South-western China in the province of Yunnan, and probably not far from Mengtsze.

F. THE NOISETTE ROSE

Miller's White Musk × *Parsons's Pink China*
Rosa moschata Miller × (*R. chinensis* Jacq. × *R. gigantea* Collett)

The honour of the first introduction of the Chinese gene for perennial flowering to our western Roses belongs to an American citizen, John Champneys, a wealthy rice planter of Charleston in South Carolina, who was a great gardener. About 1802 he fertilized the old White Musk Rose of Miller with pollen of the new Pink China of Parsons, which he had recently received from France through the brothers Noisette of Charleston and Paris. The result was a handsome hybrid, which combined the climbing habit, large open clusters of flowers and odour of the Musk with the semi-double pink flowers of the China and the handsome foliage of both. Champneys called it *R. moschata hybrida*, but the Rose became such a great favourite in America that it came to be known as Champneys's Pink Cluster or the Champneys Rose. A few years afterwards Philippe Noisette, the French nurseryman at Charleston, sowed seeds of Champneys's hybrid and thus in the second generation raised the original French Noisette Rose, which he sent to his brother, Louis Noisette of Paris, in 1814, who distributed it in Europe in 1819. This Rose was figured by Redouté in 1821 under the name of *R. Noisettiana*, and quickly became a popular garden Rose. In the second generation Mendelian segregation took place, and the Noisette was less tall and more compact in growth than Champneys's Hybrid; the flowers were blush-white, borne in large dense clusters, equally fragrant, but above all they were produced continuously from June to the winter frosts.

---

* [Now rediscovered, 1990. GST]

Up to 1830 there was little variation in the Noisette race bred from seed except those with violet-crimson flowers which were hybridized with *multiflora* and *chinensis*, and those with lax flower clusters which were hybridized with *R. sempervirens* L. Among the latter was the old favourite 'Aimée Vibert', raised by Vibert in 1828, and still prominent in old gardens.

Towards 1830 attempts were made to create a Yellow Noisette by crossing the Blush Noisette with Parks's new Yellow China. This cross had far-reaching results since it gave rise not only to the Yellow Noisette, but also to the Yellow Tea Roses. In 1830 'Lamarque' and 'Jaune Desprez' appeared, and in 1833 Smith's Yellow, the last being a true dwarf Yellow Tea, although classed as a Noisette on account of its origin. The first two were yellowish Noisettes which, selfed, gave Yellow Climbing Teas: 'Céline Forestier' in 1842 and 'Cloth of Gold' (Chromatella) and 'Solfatare' in 1843. 'Cloth of Gold' was the parent of the famous 'Maréchal Niel'. Further breeding swamped the old Noisette characters, and transformed the Noisette into a Climbing Tea as seen in 'Gloire de Dijon' (1853), 'Maréchal Niel' (1864), 'Rêve d'Or' (1860), 'Bouquet d'Or' (1872), 'Caroline Kuester' (1872), 'William Allen Richardson' (1878), and 'Mme Alfred Carrière' (1879).

The original Blush Noisette proves to be a diploid with fourteen chromosomes, and all its early descendants, including the Yellow Teas, prove to be diploid except 'Gloire de Dijon', which is a tetraploid with twenty-eight chromosomes. Champneys's Hybrid must therefore have been a diploid as its parents were. Miller's Musk Rose is now very rare, but it is still in the Cambridge Botanic Garden where it was examined.

G. THE BOURBON ROSE

Pink Autumn Damask × *Parsons's Pink China*
(*R. rubra* Blackw. × *R. moschata* Miller) × (*R. chinensis* Jacq. × *R. gigantea* Collett)

The Bourbon Rose, like the Noisette and all other new races of Roses, appeared in the second generation of a cross in accordance with Mendel's Laws of Segregation and Fixity. The first generation of the Bourbon was a natural hybrid between the Pink Autumn Damask and Parsons's Pink China, found growing in a garden with its parents in the French island of Bourbon in 1817 by the Parisian botanist Bréon, who was in charge of the Botanic Garden at the time. It was a vigorous and decorative hybrid, intermediate in character between the Damask and China parents. Locally and in the adjacent island of Mauritius it was known as the 'Rose Edward'. In 1819 Bréon sent seeds of the new hybrid to his friend Jacques, the celebrated gardener of King Louis Philippe in Paris, and from these seeds Jacques raised the first French Bourbon Rose and called it 'Rosier de l'Île Bourbon'. The new Rose was distributed in France about 1823 and in England about 1825. It was figured by Redouté in 1824 under the curious name of *R. canina Burboniana*. This Rose of the second generation was a better garden Rose than its parent the 'Rose Edward', partly because of its more compact habit, but mainly by its abundant autumn flowering. Mendelian segregation had given it a double dose of the China gene for continuous flowering, and it was a beautiful semi-double Rose with brilliant rose-coloured flowers, and nearly evergreen foliage. From its Damask grandparent it inherited a delicious fragrance which was particularly marked in the late autumn months.

During its reign of about half a century from 1820 to 1870 the Bourbon Rose contributed much to the development of our garden Roses. Crossed with Hume's Blush China it helped to create our Pink Tea Roses, and it was the main source of the typical Hybrid Perpetuals which, after all, were only the Bourbon writ large. In 1825 the remarkable Bourbon 'Gloire des Rosomanes' appeared with its perennial scarlet-crimson flowers, and vigorous habit of growth, and became the chief ancestor of the scarlet and crimson Hybrid Perpetuals with their rich Damask fragrance. Although from the first the Bourbon was a distinct type of Rose with its stout prickly stems, vivid rose-coloured flowers with rounded imbricated petals and broad leathery leaves, various breaks occurred from time to time through segregation as well as through hybridization. Between 1834 and 1841 the China reversion 'Hermosa' appeared independently with four different breeders, and it is unlikely that all these were due to a China back-cross. In 1831, the Bourbon-Noisette 'Mme Desprez' appeared, adding purple to the rose colour which, in 1839, became a vivid crimson in 'Dr Rocques' (Crimson Globe). 'Mme Desprez' added to her laurels in 1842 by producing that wonderful Bourbon Rose 'Souvenir de la Malmaison', which in its turn produced the popular 'Gloire de Dijon'. In both cases the other parent was a Tea Rose, and as in the case of the Noisette repeated crossings with the Tea Roses towards the middle of the nineteenth century completely changed the character of the original Bourbon and improved it out of existence. Both the original Bourbon and 'Souvenir de la Malmaison' are triploids with twenty-one chromosomes, while 'Gloire de Dijon' is a tetraploid with twenty-eight.

H. THE TEA ROSE (*Rosa gigantea* Collett)*

Hume's Blush and Parks's Yellow Chinas × Bourbons and Noisettes

The first typical Pink Tea Rose, appropriately enough, was called 'Adam', and was raised by a florist of that name at Rheims in 1833. Its characters are intermediate between those of Hume's Blush China and the original Bourbon, and it is no doubt a hybrid between them.

The first typical Yellow Tea Rose was raised in England in the same year and was called Smith's Yellow; this was a cross made between the Blush Noisette and Parks's Yellow China in an attempt to raise a Yellow Noisette and was duly sent out as such. Later, Foster of Devonport back-crossed the Yellow China with Smith's Yellow, and raised in 1838 the beautiful Tea 'Devoniensis' with its thick creamy-white petals, pale straw-pink centre, and sweet fragrance. In 1839 appeared the remarkable Tea Rose 'Safrano', with the outside petals bright rose and the inner petals butter-yellow; it appears to have been raised from Parks's Yellow China crossed with Noisette 'Desprez'. 'Safrano' became the head of a special line of yellow and copper Teas, including 'Mme Falcot' (1858), 'Perle des Jardins' (1874), and many others. Various inter-crossings between the yellow Noisette-Teas and the pink Bourbon-Teas gave rise between 1840 and 1890 to the most exquisite Roses ever produced, but after that date they gradually lost their typical qualities by crossings with the new Hybrid Teas which they had helped to make, and today the typical Tea Rose has disappeared from general cultivation. All the typical Teas examined are diploid with fourteen chromosomes, except 'Gloire de Dijon', which is tetraploid. The later Tea 'Lady Hillingdon' (1910) is a triploid with twenty-one chromosomes, and is not a true Tea.

It is to be hoped that the old Tea will be revived, if only for crossing with the new Pernet and Poulsen Roses. We cannot afford to lose its valuable breeding qualities of colour, form, and fragrance.

---

* [In view of their hybrid origin, Tea Roses are now classed as *R. × odorata.* GST]

J. HYBRID CHINAS

Chinas, Noisettes, and Bourbons × French, Provence, Damask, and other Summer Roses

Early in the nineteenth century the term Hybrid China was used in a special sense to cover all hybrids between the perennial and the summer-flowering groups. At that time nearly all the Roses grown in gardens were summer-flowering, and of these the so-called French Rose (*R. rubra* Blackw.*) held pride of place, with more than a thousand varieties in all the colours of the period. When the ever-blooming China came and was considered sufficiently hardy to plant outside about 1810, it was only natural that hybrids began to appear, and in 1815 the first two Hybrid Chinas came to light. The first was raised in England by Brown of Slough from Hume's Blush China fertilized by a French Rose, and was known as Brown's 'Superb Blush'. The second was one of Descemet's 10,000 seedlings rescued by Vibert, when the allied armies marched on Paris, and was known as 'Zulmé', or 'Bengale Descemet'. Up to 1830 about forty varieties of Hybrid Chinas appeared in France and two in England. Towards 1830 four superior varieties were produced which are particularly interesting to us, since they became the actual parents of the large Hybrid Perpetuals. One of these was 'Malton', a China-French hybrid, while the other three were 'Brennus', 'Athalin', and 'Général Allard', which were Bourbon-French hybrids. In flowers and foliage these varieties combined almost all that was beautiful in Roses but, like all the Hybrid Chinas without exception, they failed in one important character. They flowered only once a year owing to the Mendelian dominance of the gene for summer-flowering over the recessive gene for continuous flowering. These four Hybrid Chinas were all tetraploid with twenty-eight chromosomes, while the original Hybrid China was triploid with twenty-one.

K. HYBRID PERPETUALS

Hybrid Chinas × Portlands, Bourbons, and Noisettes

The first Hybrid Perpetual was the famous 'Rose du Roi', raised in 1816 by Souchet in the garden of the king at Sèvres, St Cloud, Paris, from the original Portland Rose whose history is chequered and somewhat obscure. It is known to have been in Dupont's nursery in Paris in 1809, and that Dupont obtained it from England and named it after the Duchess of Portland, who probably found it or obtained it from Italy early in the century. In England it was known as the *Rosa Paestana* or 'Scarlet Four Seasons', and was said to have been brought from Italy from the neighbourhood of the classic Paestum. The Portland Rose was a bright red verging on scarlet, and if treated well and pruned in a certain way it flowered twice a year, in summer and autumn. It was generally regarded as a cross between the French Rose and the Autumn Damask. Judging from Redouté's accurate figure of 1817 it is evidently a China-Damask-French hybrid which may well have originated in Italy, where, owing to the favourable climate, the China Roses had been largely cultivated in the open ever since their introduction about 1798. From the colour and dwarf habit of the Portland it may be presumed that the China parent concerned was 'Slater's Crimson China'.†

---

* 1757. Syn. *R. gallica* L. 1759 (*non* 1753).

† [It is now considered that the parents of the Portland Rose were *R. gallica* and *R. damascena* var. *semperflorens* and that they owe nothing to *R. chinensis*. GST]

The 'Rose du Roi', with its charming crimson flowers, very double and very fragrant, and above all its continuous flowering throughout the season without special treatment and pruning, was certainly a great advance on its Portland parent, and it reigned supreme until the coming of the larger Hybrid Perpetuals in 1837, which displaced the smaller Portland and Bourbon Hybrid Perpetuals.

The fortunate raiser of these large-flowered Hybrid Perpetuals was Laffay, the well-known Rose breeder of Auteuil, who introduced the first typical Hybrid Perpetual 'Princesse Hélène' in 1837; he followed this up with 'Mme Laffay' and 'Duchess of Sutherland' in 1839, and finally crowned his success in 1842 with that famous 'Rose de la Reine', with its large, strangely cupped flowers of a beautiful lilac-rose and fragrant as a Cabbage Rose. From 1837 to 1843 Laffay produced eighteen Hybrid Perpetuals of merit, and it is understood that all these were raised from seeds of the Hybrid Chinas (mostly Bourbon-French) selfed, and crossed with Portlands and Bourbons. In this way pairs of the recessive genes for continuous flowering were brought together and the Hybrid Perpetuals created. This also explains why many of the earlier and some of the later Hybrid Perpetuals sent out were not truly perpetual. From 1840 other breeders joined in, and in 1851 a new type appeared in 'Victor Verdier' from a Bourbon-Tea cross. In 1852 'Jules Margottin' and the famous 'Général Jacqueminot' arrived, the former a Brennus perpetual (Hybrid China selfed) and the latter a descendant of the Bourbon 'Gloire des Rosomanes'. 'The General', with its brilliant scarlet-crimson flowers and damask fragrance, was a fertile tetraploid, and left a host of descendants of a similar type. From 1840 to 1890 the Hybrid Perpetual completely dominated the outside Rose garden until it was gradually replaced by the Hybrid Tea, which it helped to make. All the Hybrid Perpetuals examined are regular tetraploids with twenty-eight chromosomes, show traces of hybridity in their weak pairings, and are sterile to some degree.

L. HYBRID TEAS

Hybrid Perpetuals × Teas

The first Hybrid Tea was the favourite Rose 'La France', which was raised by Guillot in 1867 out of the Hybrid Perpetual 'Mme Victor Verdier' by the Tea 'Mme Bravy'. It was a worthy representative of its class with its silvery lilac-pink flowers of excellent shape and delicious fragrance. It combined the free-flowering habit, fine shape, and delicate colouring of the Tea with the hardiness and vigorous growth of the Hybrid Perpetual. In 1873 'Cheshunt Hybrid' and 'Captain Christy' appeared, but it was not until 1884 that the Hybrid Tea was recognized as a new group distinct from the Hybrid Perpetuals. Up to 1895, when 'Mme Abel Chatenay' and 'Mrs W. J. Grant' appeared, Hybrid Teas were mostly bred on the original lines, but afterwards they were not only bred *inter se*, but also back-crossed to the Hybrid Perpetual, giving 'Liberty', 'Richmond', and other red bedding and decorative Roses.

In 1905 the Hybrid Teas began to change their original characters owing to their hybridization with the new Pernet Rose which appeared in 1900. At first the influence of the Pernet Roses on the Hybrid Teas was slight, but gradually year by year the Pernet characters permeated the Hybrid Teas in geometrical progression, so that at the present time it is rare to see an original Hybrid Tea among the new Roses without a trace of the Pernet influence. These Roses are still called Hybrid Teas, but they have lost their original characters. The cause of this revolution is that for the first time in a century a new species, *R. lutea* Miller, has been incorporated with our garden Roses.

All the Hybrid Teas examined prove to be tetraploid with twenty-eight chromosomes.

M. THE PERNET ROSE[*]

Hybrid Perpetual × Austrian Briar (R. lutea Miller)[†]

The twentieth century, like the nineteenth, opened with the introduction of a new species to the garden Roses of the period. Last century it was *R. chinensis* from China, with its habit of continuous flowering, this century it is *R. lutea* from Persia, with its brilliant yellow flowers. Both species have revolutionized our garden Roses as no other species have done during the two centuries. *R. lutea* Miller is an ancient cultivated species grown by the Saracens in Syria, Tripoli, Tunis, and Egypt in the twelfth century, and in the same period cultivated by the Arabs and Moors in Spain, who had a tradition that it was brought from Persia in the seventh century. It is no doubt an oriental species, and has been reported in a wild state from the Crimea through Asia Minor and Persia to Turkestan, and even in the Punjab, Afghanistan, and Tibet. Some of these, however, may be garden escapes, since it has been found in several places in Europe growing apparently wild. It was figured by Gesner in 1542, Lobel in 1581, Dodonaeus in 1583, and exactly described by Dalechamps in 1587. Clusius found it in Austria towards 1583 and introduced it to the Netherlands and England, where it has been known ever since as the Austrian Briar. There were two forms of this, the Austrian Yellow and the Austrian Copper, both well-known garden plants. The Yellow is the ordinary *R. lutea*, while the Copper is a bicolor form with the petals of two distinct colours, bright nasturtium-red on the upper inner surface and shaded yellow on the lower outer surface, the general effect being a coppery-red. Cornuti in 1635 and Miller in 1768 gave this form specific rank under the name of *R. punicea*, and Jacquin in 1770 as *R. bicolor*. We now know that the Copper is simply a bud-sport of the Yellow, and that often the two colours may be found on the same bush. This explains why so many of our dazzling Pernet Roses, bred from the yellow, present this fantastic bicolor effect. The Pernet Roses originally came from the Persian Yellow Rose, which appears to be only a double form of *R. lutea*. It was brought from Persia by Sir Henry Willock in 1838.

After a thousand years of cultivation in gardens *R. lutea* had become notoriously sterile in both seeds and pollen, and it was no easy matter to incorporate the species with the partially sterile garden Roses. All the more credit is therefore due to the persistent and untiring efforts of that great Rose breeder Pernet-Ducher of Lyon, which were ultimately crowned with success. From 1883 to 1888 he patiently and persistently crossed thousands of Hybrid Perpetuals with pollen of Persian Yellow, following a fixed idea of his own. All these crosses failed except one with 'Antoine Ducher', which gave him a few seeds in 1888. 'Antoine Ducher', the grandmother of the Pernet Rose, was just an ordinary Hybrid Perpetual raised by Ducher in 1866 with large, full, shining rose-red flowers and a strong old rose fragrance.

Two hybrids were reared and the first flowered in 1891. This was interesting in its preponderance of the paternal *lutea* characters, but being completely sterile it took no part in the creation of the Pernet race, and was sent out as a Pillar Rose under the name of 'Rhodophile Gravereaux'. The other plant first flowered in 1893, but it was not until 1894 that it showed itself in its true colours. On the whole it was more like the mother Hybrid Perpetual in its habit of growth, large globular full flowers shaded with rose, and in its delicious old rose fragrance. On the other hand, it resembled the father *lutea* in its red-brown wood, prickles,

---

[*] The rules of nomenclature prevent the use of 'Pernetiana'.

[†] Since there is doubt about Hermann's older name *R. foetida* of 1762 I am using the next oldest name, which is Miller's *R. lutea* of 1768.

rounded leaflets, solitary flowers with bicolor petals which were orange-red within and golden-yellow without, and in its summer-flowering. This unnamed seedling was retained by Pernet as a breeder, and when mated with Hybrid Teas produced in the second generation the first Pernet Rose, 'Soleil d'Or', and many which followed it. As in the cases of the Noisette and the Bourbon the second generation was necessary to fix the continuous flowering in the race, in accordance with Mendel's Laws. 'Soleil d'Or' was first exhibited at Lyon in 1898, and was sent out in 1900 as a forerunner of the Pernet Roses of the twentieth century. After forty years' breeding the Pernet Roses have become thoroughly incorporated with the Hybrid Teas, and have revolutionized their colours and colour patterns. One of the chief contributions made by the Pernet Rose is the production of deep yellow Roses, much deeper and richer, but perhaps not so refined as the paler yellow of the Tea Rose. That was Pernet-Ducher's original aim in bringing in *lutea*, and his object has been achieved. No one, however, could have foreseen the myriads of new shades, tones, and patterns of colours which have been created in our garden Roses by the simple introduction of a yellow species. The peculiar glistening foliage and the numerous exaggerated prickles of the Pernet Roses are also rather unexpected in the product, constituting as they do new types of foliage and prickles which in a wild species we should probably regard as specific. Early in the century there was another side to the picture. Side by side with the good qualities of *lutea* introduced by the Pernets there were naturally some bad ones, such as bad constitution and winter die-back, liability to Black Spot, and consequent early loss of leaves, flat-topped and quartered flowers, lack of fragrance or presence of disagreeable odours, and complete sterility of seeds and pollen. Fortunately by careful breeding with the best Hybrid Teas and rigid selection these faults have largely disappeared in the latest Pernet-Hybrid Teas that are now being bred for the dual purpose of garden decoration and exhibition.

Since both *R. lutea* Persian Yellow and the Hybrid Perpetual 'Antoine Ducher' are tetraploids with twenty-eight chromosomes, it follows that Pernet-Ducher's two hybrids of the first generation are also tetraploid. 'Soleil d'Or' and the 'Lyon-Rose' have been examined and both found to be tetraploid with fourteen pairs. The chromosomes of both varieties show signs of hybridity, and the pollen is defective. The same may be said of *R. lutea* Austrian Yellow and its bud-sport Austrian Copper, in which I found only about 5 per cent of fertile pollen.

N. THE POLY-POMPON ROSE[*]

Japanese Multiflora × Dwarf Pink China
R. multiflora Thunb. × (*R. chinensis* Jacq. × *R. gigantea* Collett)

About 1860 Jean Sisley of Lyon received from his son in Japan seeds of the wild *R. multiflora* of Thunberg, a strong climbing Rose with single white flowers, which was quite different from the Chinese Multiflora of gardens, which had pink or crimson double flowers. Guillot, the famous Rose breeder of Lyon, planted some of these Japanese Multifloras in his nursery, and in 1868 saved seeds from them. The result was a medley of forms in the flowers, large and small; single, semi-double, and full; white, rose, and cream; but all were climbers and summer-flowering like the mother parent, and all closely resembled the Noisette Rose in their wood and foliage. One of these had large, tinged white flowers with two rows of petals and

---

[*] The rules of nomenclature prevent the use of 'Polyantha' or 'Floribunda'.

produced good seeds, which were sown in 1872, and thus produced in the second generation the first two Poly-Poms, 'Paquerette' and 'Mignonette'. Both varieties were dwarf Pompons a few inches high, while their fellows in the same batch of seedlings were tall climbers several feet high like their mother parent. Both were continuous in their flowering right through the season from May to December from their first year, while their tall fellows were summer-flowering in their second year. 'Paquerette' was a pure white, while 'Mignonette' was rosy-pink and white; both combined the characters of *multiflora* and the Dwarf Pink China, and it is evident that in 1868 the original Japanese Multifloras were naturally fertilized with Dwarf Pink Chinas, which at that time were commonly grown in the Lyon nurseries as specimens.

This Dwarf Pink China was known in the Lyon nurseries as Bengale Pompon, and was raised in England in 1805, where it was known as *R. Lawranceana* or the Fairy Rose. The first Poly-Pom, 'Paquerette', was exhibited at Lyon in 1873 and distributed in 1875. 'Mignonette' was not sent out until 1881, but it became the chief ancestor of most of our modern varieties through its remarkable offspring 'Gloire de Polyantha' (1887), and its line of 'Mme Norbert Levavasseur' (1903), 'Orleans Rose' (1909), 'Edith Cavell' (1917), and 'Coral Cluster' (1921).

In 1880 'Cécile Brunner' and 1883 'Perle d'Or' introduced the characters of the Tea Rose.* In 1903 the well-known Crimson Rambler became an ancestor of the Poly-Poms, and in 1911 'Dorothy Perkins' entered the list. In 1920 the Pernet Rose was introduced by 'Rayon d'Or', giving the Poly-pom 'Evaline'. One of the most popular Poly-Poms of today is 'Éblouissant' (1918), which is a pure China descended from a dwarf Crimson China, and is about the smallest of the Poly-poms. 'Yvonne Rabier' (1910), derived from the Japanese species *R. wichuraiana* with its pure white flowers and handsome glossy foliage, is still a popular variety. Most of the modern varieties, however, while retaining their dwarf habit and contin-uous flowering, produce their flowers in tight bunches of rosettes of the Crimson Rambler type.

All the Poly-Poms examined prove to be diploid with fourteen chromosomes. The original 'Paquerette' and its ancestral species *R. chinensis*, *R. gigantea*, and *R. multiflora* are all diploid.

The Pernet and *lutea* Poly-Poms have not been examined, but they may be expected to be triploids with twenty-one chromosomes.

O. THE POLUSEN ROSE†

Poly-Pom × Hybrid Tea

In 1924 a new and distinct group of garden Roses appeared from Denmark, and caused quite a sensation in British and American Rose circles. They were originated by the Danish Rose breeder Poulsen by crossing the Poly-Pom with a Hybrid Tea. He crossed the Poly-Pom 'Orleans Rose' with pollen of the Hybrid Tea 'Red Star' and raised therefrom two seedlings of similar type and habit of growth, but with very different flowers. Both were vigorous growers, producing large open clusters of flowers on long stems, which in 'Else Poulsen' were amaranth-pink with carmine reverse and semi-double, while those of 'Kirsten Poulsen' were

---

* These varieties are now classed with the Poulsen Roses owing to their taller habit of growth.

† The rules of nomenclature prevent the use of 'Polyantha' or 'Floribunda'. ['Floribunda' is now accepted as a group name for these large-flowered 'polyanthas'. GST]

bright cherry-scarlet and single. In 1928 'Greta Poulsen' appeared, with rich crimson-pink flowers, while in 1930 'D. T. Poulsen', with deep blood-red flowers which are not very lasting, proved rather a disappointment. In 1932 this was amply made up by the appearance of the remarkable 'Karen Poulsen', with dazzling scarlet single flowers which defy description. This Rose was raised by Poulsen out of 'Kirsten Poulsen' by pollen of 'Vesuvius'. In 1935 in 'Anne Poulsen' there came a development towards the Hybrid Tea which seems to be a move away from the typical Poulsen Rose. Its flowers are a lovely velvety crimson with a delightful fragrance, but the blooms are large and full, produced in small clusters, and the general habit is not so vigorous. A similar type appeared in 1939 in 'Poulsen's Copper' with flowers rosy-cerise on a copper base, large and double in small clusters, but the growth is vigorous. The latest Poulsen Roses to appear are 'Poulsen's Pink' and 'Poulsen's Yellow', which seem to be a similar type. The future will show if these are to displace the original type, and other breeders are now taking a hand on somewhat different lines. The chromosomes of the Poulsens have not been examined, but most should be triploids with twenty-one.

GENERAL

Space will not allow me to deal with the evolution and development of various minor groups of garden Roses, in which so many different species have been concerned in the nineteenth and twentieth centuries. Ayrshire Roses from *R. arvensis* Huds., Evergreen Roses from *R. sempervirens* L., Sweet Briars from *R. Eglanteria* Mill., Scotch Roses from *R. spinosissima* L., Banksian Roses from *R. Banksiae* Ait., Prairie Roses from *R. setigera* Michx., Musk Roses from *R. moschata* Miller, Rugosa Roses from *R. rugosa* Thunb., Macartney Roses from *R. bracteata* Wendl., Cherokee Roses from *R. laevigata* Michx., Microphylla Roses from *R. microphylla* Roxb., Multiflora Climbers from *R. multiflora* Thunb., Wichuraiana Climbers from *R. wichuraiana* Crép., and the old cultivated Roses of American species which, crossed with the China Rose, gave us the Old Boursault Roses which for more than a century have passed as hybrids of *R. alpina* L. All these interesting garden Roses must be left for future articles.

In conclusion, we find that the major groups of our garden Roses are descended from seven main species, namely: *R. rubra* Blackw., *R. phoenicia* Boiss., *R. moschata* Miller, *R. canina* L., *R. chinensis* Jacq., *R. gigantea* Collett, and *R. lutea* Miller. The specific characters of these species can still be traced in our garden Roses, and it is the happy combinations of these various characters that have given us the manifold beauties of the Rose.

Note on Diagram 1 (page 321)

The earliest stages in the evolution of garden roses have long excited speculation, which until recently had no more foundation than the fancied resemblances of long-cultivated garden roses to certain of the wild species. It was not until 1920, when cytology, the study of chromosomes, was first applied to the Rose, that these speculations could be tried and tested. Great credit is due to Dr C. C. Hurst (and no less to his widow, Mrs R. Hurst) for realizing the value of chromosome studies, and using them to supplement his great morphological and historical survey of Rose history. The article reprinted on pages 298–320 gives an outline of his findings, but it is only a summary of a much greater work which he unfortunately never lived to publish. However, further chromosome studies of garden roses by Ann Wylie, of Manchester University, fill in many of the missing details.

Hurst's work forms the basis of the two family trees shown in Diagrams 1 and 2. The former epitomizes his solution of the difficult problem of the early stages. It is but one of many possible solutions, and as such must still be regarded as pure speculation, but at least it is feasible in the light of existing knowledge of rose chronology and breeding behaviour.

All that it lacks is experimental proof—the re-synthesis of the ancestral hybrids from their wild parent species. To make and rear sufficient crosses to attempt this recapitulation of Rose history is an ambitious and lengthy, but not impossible, task.

GDR

First Stages in the Evolution
of Garden Roses in Europe
PRE–1800

by Gordon D. Rowley *after* Hurst, 1941 *and* MSS.

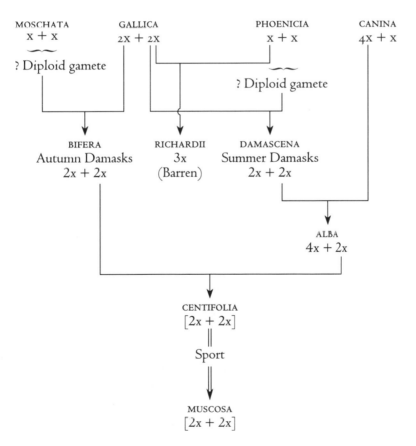

x = haploid chromosome number (n = 7)

Diagram I

Simplified Genealogy of the Main Groups of Garden Roses
by Gordon D. Rowley *after* Hurst, 1941

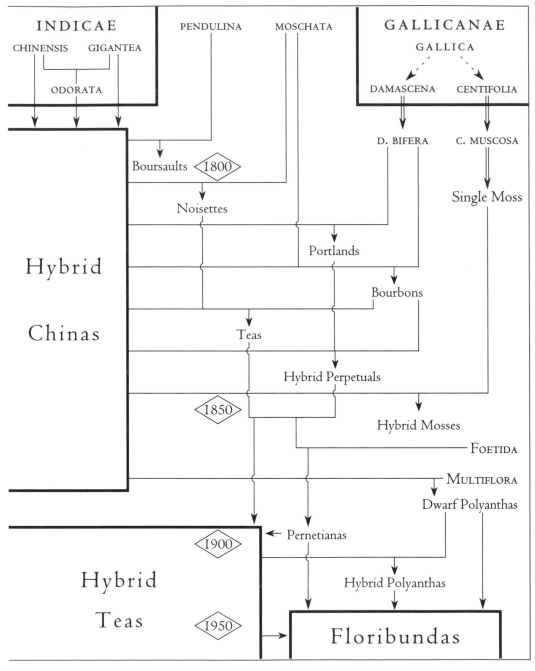

A single line indicates hybridization
A double line indicates sporting
A dotted line indicates possible relationship

Diagram 2

Notes on Diagram 2 (page 322)

Any attempt at a two-dimensional family tree of garden roses is bound to be an over-simplification of the facts. The impression it gives of new groups springing into being by the union of old, whilst true in a broad sense, requires a word of explanation. The first members of a new group, like the earliest Hybrid Teas, are usually very distinct from anything that has gone before, and were in fact selected by their raisers for combining the best features of widely dissimilar parents. Later introductions, however, include backcrosses and hybrids combining characters of three and more groups, so that even where their pedigrees are known their grouping under one name or another is barely possible.

True, the dominant groups in favour at any time over the past one hundred and fifty years show genetic continuity, from the Portlands and Hybrid Perpetuals, through the Hybrid Teas, to the modern Hybrid Polyanthas and Floribundas. But concurrently with these ran many smaller alliances, sometimes centering round other species such as *Rosa rugosa*, *R. pimpinellifolia*, or *R. eglanteria*.

The tendency in recent years has been to interbreed both major and minor groups, and blur the outlines of the older recognized types. Hence the modern dilemma over Floribundas, and the growing awareness that distinctions based on ancestry will largely have to be forsaken in favour of simple, artificial classifications based on habit, flower size and grouping, and so on.

The concept of a family "tree" does not, therefore, give an ideal picture of rose evolution in the garden and nursery. Rather we should visualize a delicate sponge—a network in which the branches diverge and reunite, sometimes coming to a dead end (through sterility or just neglect), sometimes picking up a new strand (as when a new species makes its debut).

Nor can our genealogy ever near completion while so many roses are of unrecorded parentage. Truly it has been said that "the fascination of pedigree-hunting no doubt lies in its inscrutable conundrums."

GDR, 1957

From chromosome counts taken since this figure was drawn, Gordon Rowley tells me that the Boursault roses are unlikely to have been derived from *Rosa pendulina*, but most probably from *R. blanda*.

GST, 1980

NOTES ON THE ORIGIN OF THE MOSS ROSE
by C. C. HURST, SC.D., PH.D. (CANTAB.), F.L.S., *and*
MABEL S. G. BREEZE, B.SC.

In 1908 experiments were undertaken at Burbage to investigate the genetics of certain variable species and garden hybrids of *Rosa* (Hurst, 1911).* These experiments were continued until the outbreak of war in 1914, when more urgent affairs demanded priority, and it was not until 1919 that it was possible to resume the experiments and to prepare a report on what had been done. Among the many interesting problems in the genetics of *Rosa*, the question of the Moss Rose presented itself as one of outstanding interest from many points of view. But before attacking the problem genetically it seemed necessary to trace as far as possible the history of the original Moss Rose, its direct descendants, and its parent species. The following notes represent the more important results of these researches.

---

* Names and dates in brackets refer to the bibliography at the end of this paper.

Characters peculiar to the Moss Rose

The original Moss Rose, *R. muscosa* of Miller (1768), appears to be identical in all its external characters with the old Cabbage Rose, *R. centifolia* (Linnaeus, 1753), except that it possesses the following additional characters: The stems, branches, petioles, stipules, pedicels, peduncles, and calyx-tubes are densely covered with irregular aciculi and glandular branched bristles, while the sepals are copiously compound and covered on the back and edges with multitudinous branched gland-edged mossy processes, which give off a resinous or balsamic odour when bruised. In other words, the Moss Rose differs from the Cabbage Rose in its multiplicity of glandular organs. It is important, however, to note that the difference is not simply that of presence or absence of glands, for the Cabbage Rose is glandular in parts, e.g., petioles, stipules, peduncles, and sepals. Nor is it a difference merely of many or few glands, nor even of more extended or less extended glandular areas. It is also a difference of compound or simple glands, and these are multitudinous partly on account of the extension and increased density of the glandular areas, but mainly through the multiplicate branching of the gland-bearing organs (cf. Blondel, 1889).

Whether the presence of these additional characters in the Moss Rose entitles it to specific rank, or whether it should be regarded as a variety of *R. centifolia* L., is a question concerning which systematists are divided. Miller, who appears to have been the first to describe the Moss Rose fully (1760), gives it specific rank under the name of *R. muscosa* (1768), which is accepted by the following: Du Roi (1772), Retzius (1779), Curtis (1793), Willdenow (1799), Aiton (1789) (1811), Lawrance (1799), Rössig (1802), Andrews (1805), Persoon (1807), Deleuze and Desfontaines (1809), Thory and Redouté (1817), and Prévost (1829); on the other hand, the following authorities regard the Moss Rose as a variety of *R. centifolia* L. (or its synonym *R. provincialis* Mill.): Linnaeus (1762), Dumont de Courset (1805), Smith (1815), Seringe (1818), Lindley (1820), Guimpel (1825), Rössig (1826), Crépin (1892), and Willmott (1912).

Some modern authors, e.g., Regel (1877), Dippel (1893), Köhne (1893), Bois (1896), Rehder (1902), and Schneider (1906), place both the Moss Rose and *R. centifolia* L. under *R. gallica* L.

Characters common to the Moss Rose and the Cabbage Rose

Whatever the systematic status of the Moss Rose may be, one thing is certain, all authorities agree that the old Moss Rose and the old Cabbage Rose are closely allied. Anyone who has seen the two growing side by side, and has carefully examined them, must acknowledge that they have many characters in common, which are quite distinct from any other species or sub-species. For example, both have very double globular flowers, which are red in the bud and rose-pink when open. Both have about a hundred short and broad petals, which are closely incurved and rolled inwards towards the centre, which is frequently quartered like a crown. Both yield the same distinctive fragrance from the petals, which is peculiar to *R. centifolia* L. and distinct from the fragrance of *R. gallica* L. (The resinous and balsamic odour from the mossy glands of the Moss Rose is naturally much more powerful than the odour from the same area in the Cabbage Rose, which is but faint.) Both have cernuous or nodding flowers, usually solitary or up to three only, unlike those of *R. damascena* Mill., which are usually erect and many, in corymbs or clusters. Both have the sepals spreading and persistent, not reflexed and deciduous as in *R. damascena* Mill. and *R. gallica* L. Both have a medium habit of growth, not so tall and prickly as *R. damascena* Mill., nor so dwarf and bushy as *R. gallica* L. Both have leaves softer to the touch than the more rigid and coriaceous leaves of *R. gallica* L. and the allied forms. Last, but not least in importance, both the old Moss Rose and the old Cabbage Rose are sterile, inasmuch as neither develops perfect fruits (which all the allied species do as a rule), and neither has been known to produce fertile seeds so far as we can ascertain. So far, all attempts to obtain seed from the old Moss Rose and the old Cabbage Rose at Burbage have failed, both outside and under glass, though miniature fruits were sometimes obtained containing no seeds.* In view of the fact that some apparently good pollen was found and that some of the styles appeared to be normal and not petaloid, the result is so far unexpected. From the genetic point of view the sterility of the old Moss Rose is a serious disadvantage, but this difficulty is not insuperable, as will be seen later. A full discussion of this important question of sterility must be deferred for a time, and for the present we simply record the fact.

History of the old Cabbage Rose (*R. centifolia* L.)†

The old Cabbage Rose has been freely cultivated in European fields and gardens for more than two thousand years. About 450 B.C. Herodotus observes that the Roses growing in Macedonia, near the gardens of Midas, have sixty petals, and are the most fragrant in the world. This is a very neat description of the Cabbage Rose, and at the same time a critical one, because it is difficult to conceive how such a description can be applied to any other known species of *Rosa*. A century later Theophrastus, the first historian of the Rose, mentions the Roses with a hundred petals, and calls them *Centifolia*. In the first century Pliny, who devotes a whole chapter to Roses, repeats the observations of Theophrastus, and adds that the *Rosa Centifolia* grows at Campania in Italy, and near Philippi, a city in Greece (Macedonia). He also states that these Centifolia Roses grow naturally on Mount Panfaeus close by, with a hundred leaves but small, and when transplanted into richer soil do thrive mightily, and prove to be much fairer than those growing on the mountain; all of which seems quite natural. From other classic authors we learn that vast numbers of Rose petals were used by the Greeks and Romans for their decorations and festivities, and it is reasonable to suppose that the Cabbage Rose with its hundred petals and delicious fragrance was cultivated for this purpose in the fields of Italy, Greece, and Macedonia. In these circumstances it does not necessarily follow that the Cabbage Rose is a true native of the south of Europe, as many of the early authorities conclude (Smith, 1815); on the other hand, it appears more probable, as Lindley (1820) believed, that the Cabbage Rose was introduced into Europe from Asia at a remote period. As a matter fact, early in the nineteenth century Bieberstein (1808) found the Cabbage Rose growing apparently wild on the eastern side of the Caucasus, on the borders of Armenia and Persia. Rau (1816) states that it is a native of northern Persia, and Boissier (1872) gives the habitat as eastern Caucasus, while according to Loureiro (1790) it is a native of China.

Notwithstanding these records we are inclined to believe that the Cabbage Rose has been cultivated in the fields and gardens of Asia from time immemorial, and that its native country

---

* In 1921 a few fruits matured under glass, and one contained a seed, the germination of which has not yet been tested.

† [NB. Readers will realize, on reading Dr Hurst's notes on page 306, that he subsequently revised some of these opinions on the origin of the Old Cabbage Rose. GDR]

can only be surmised. The fact of its sterility suggests an origin under cultivation, and it is worthy of note that *R. centifolia* L. does not 'stool' so freely as *R. gallica* L., nor does it root so well from cuttings and layers as *R. damascena* Mill., so that its chances of survival and increase in a wild state would be very small. The fact that the habitats given are on the borders of or in Persia is also significant, for Persia is a country which has been famous for its fragrant Roses from the earliest times. Flückiger (1862) refers to a Persian document in the National Library in Paris which states that in the year 810 the province of Farsistan was required to pay an annual tribute of 30,000 bottles of Rose-water to the Treasury of Baghdad. The most important cultivations of Roses for distilling Rose-water were near Shiraz, and are 'even to this day' (Flückiger, 1883). Lindley (1820) in commenting on the celebrated Roses of Shiraz, praised so enthusiastically by Kaempfer (1712), suggests that the Rose of Shiraz may be the Cabbage Rose (*R. centifolia* L.) or possibly *R. damascena* Mill. It was at Shiraz that one of the manuscripts of the *Rubáiyát* of Omar Khayyám was transcribed in 1460. The immortal Persian poet and philosopher, who flourished in the eleventh and twelfth centuries, was a passionate lover of the Rose—as well as of the Vine—and red, white, yellow, and flesh-coloured Roses are referred to in the *Rubáiyát*.

It is related by FitzGerald (1859) that one day in a garden Omar Khayyám said to one of his pupils, Khwajah Nizami of Samarcand, 'My tomb shall be in a spot where the North wind may scatter Roses over it', and it was so, for on his grave at Naishapur a Rose-tree was planted. In Willmott (1914) the late Dr J. G. Baker (whose botanical knowledge of Roses was unrivalled) relates how a hip of this Rose was brought home by Mr Simpson, the artist of the *Illustrated London News*, and sent to Kew by the late Mr Bernard Quaritch, from which seedlings were raised which proved to be *R. damascena* Mill., a species, as we have seen, that is allied to the Cabbage Rose, *R. centifolia* L., but distinct from it. All of which goes to confirm Lindley's conjecture, that the celebrated Rose of Shiraz may have been one of these species. The date of the introduction of the Cabbage Rose to England is unknown; it may have come during the Roman occupation of Britain with the 'English' Elm, or it may have come later through the monastery and convent gardens, in which, according to Amherst (1895), Roses were cultivated as far back as the eleventh century, in the reign of William Rufus. On the authority of Anselm it is related that the Red King, in order to see the twelve-year-old Matilda at the convent of Romsey, entered the convent on the pretext of looking at the roses in the garden.

The late Canon Ellacombe (1905) believed that the Cabbage Rose was certainly in cultivation in England in the fifteenth century and probably earlier. He identifies it with the 'Rose of Rone' of Chaucer, and with the 'Provincial Rose' of Shakespeare, and adds that the name of this Rose would be more properly written 'Provence or Provins'. It is a curious fact that at Burbage the old Cabbage Rose for eighty years at least has been more commonly called and known as the 'Red Province', which is the old name used by the English Herbalists, Gerard (1596), Parkinson (1629), and Salmon (1710). Apparently Miller (1733) was the first to change 'Province' to 'Provence', though he still retained *provincialis* for the Latin name. It may be that the old name for the Cabbage Rose, 'Red Province', has lingered on in remote country districts for centuries, like that archaic word of Chaucer, 'glede', which is still in common use at Burbage to signify the glowing embers in the fire. Baker in Willmott (1914) states that the first botanical figure of the Cabbage Rose (*R. centifolia* L.) is that of L'Obel (1581), who describes it under the name of *R. damascena maxima*. Gerard (1596) includes it in his catalogue of plants under the name of '*R. damascena flore multiplici*, the Great Holland Rose, commonly called the Province Rose'. In his Herbal of 1597, however, he describes and figures it under the name of 'R. Hollandica sive Batava, the Great Holland Rose or Great Province'. Clusius (1601) describes it under the name of R. centifolia batavica. Parkinson (1629) describes fully and figures what is undoubtedly the Cabbage Rose under the name of 'R. provincialis sive Hollandica Damascena, the Great Double Damaske Province or Holland Rose, that some call Centifolia Batavica incarnata'.

Ellacombe (1905) suggested that Parkinson's (1629) 'R. Anglica rubra, the English Red Rose', is the Cabbage Rose, but the description

> abideth low and shooteth forth many branches from the roote . . . with a
> greene barke thinner set with prickles . . . red or deepe crimson colour . . .
> with many more yellow threds in the middle, the sent . . . is not comparable
> to the excellencie of the damaske Rose, yet this Rose being well dryed and
> well kept, will hold both colour and sent longer than the damaske, bee it
> never so well kept

seems to correspond precisely with the characters of R. gallica L., the old French Rose, and not at all with R. centifolia L., the old Cabbage Rose.[*]

Ferrarius (1633), in Italy, describes the Cabbage Rose under the name of R. Batava centifolia. Chabraeus (1677), in Switzerland, describes and figures it under the name of R. centifolia rubella plena. In her monograph of the genus Rosa (1914), Miss Ellen Willmott draws attention to the interesting fact that the Cabbage Rose was a favourite subject with the old Dutch painters, especially Van Huysum (1682–1749), who excelled in portraying it. Liger (1708), in France, mentions it under the name of 'La Rose d'Hollande à cent feuilles, avec odeur'. Salmon (1710) describes and figures it as 'The Great Double Damask Province, or Holland Rose'. Finally, Linnaeus (1753), describes the Cabbage Rose under its accepted name of R. centifolia. Miller (1768), owing to a misunderstanding of Linnaeus's diagnoses of 1753 and 1762 (which it must be admitted were not very clear), describes the Cabbage Rose under the name of R. provincialis, the Provence Rose, and others followed him. Fortunately Lindley (1820) cleared the matter up, and since then the Cabbage Rose has been known correctly under the original name of Linnaeus, R. centifolia. In conclusion it may be useful to mention that the most accurate and lifelike coloured drawing of the old Cabbage Rose is to be found in Redouté (1817). Miss Willmott (1912) considers this to be the most beautiful of all his wonderful drawings of Roses, and we agree.

History of the Old Moss Rose

The Old Moss Rose is of recent origin compared with the Cabbage Rose. Its mossy flower-buds and stalks, and bristly stems and branches, together form such a striking variation that its appearance could hardly fail to be noticed by even the most casual observer. So far as we can trace, no mention of it is made by any of the ancient authors who were familiar

---

[*] It is interesting to compare Parkinson's remarks above, concerning the drying properties of the 'English Red Rose', with the statement of a modern practical chemist, Sawer (1894), who states that 'the flowers of R. gallica (which are used officinally) are but feebly odoriferous when freshly gathered; their perfume develops gradually in the process of desiccation, while that of the Damask Rose is almost destroyed by drying'. From this it appears that there is a real physiological and chemical difference between R. gallica L. and R. damascena Mill., apart from their morphological differences which to some modern systematists appear to be negligible.

with the Cabbage Rose, nor do any of the old herbalists appear to have noted it. If it had been in existence in their day, the balsamic odour of its mossy glands would surely have attracted them in their search for medicinal virtues and specifics. Gerard (1596) does not mention the Moss Rose in his Catalogue of Plants, but Dr Daydon Jackson (1876), in his edition of Gerard's Catalogue, suggests that Gerard's *R. holosericea*, the Velvet Rose, may be the Moss Rose (*R. muscosa* Mill.). This plant is described and figured by Gerard (1597), and the flowers and fruits are described as 'double with some yellow thrums in the midst of a deepe and black red colour resembling red crimson velvet . . . when the flowers be faded there followe red berries full of hard seeds'. This description does not appear to correspond at all with the old Moss Rose which has pink flowers when expanded, and is so double that the stamens and styles are seldom exposed, and finally being sterile rarely, if ever, sets either fruits or seeds. The figure (which is identical with that of L'Obel, 1581) shows no trace of the familiar and striking mossiness, while the flowers are 'semi-single' (two rows of petals), with stamens and styles fully exposed, and it is bearing rounded fruits. Parkinson (1629) also gives figures of both the single and the double Velvet Rose. In his description he states that they have 'very few or no thorns at all upon them . . . very often seven flowers on a stalk . . . yet for all the double rowe of leaves these roses stand but like single flowers . . . all of them of a smaller sent than the ordinary red Rose'. Salmon (1710), after repeating Parkinson's description of the Single and Double Velvet Rose, states that 'there is another Velvet Rose much more double than the last, consisting oftentimes of sixteen leaves or more in a Rose, and most of them of an equal bigness, of the colour of the first single Velvet Rose or something brisker, but all of them of a weaker smell than the Common Red Rose'. Lawrance (1799) and Andrews (1805) figure both the Single and Double Velvet Rose under the name of *R. centifolia*, but both appear to be forms of *R. gallica* L., the old French Rose. Thory (1817) refers *R. holosericea* to *R. gallica* L., quoting L'Obel's figure which is the same as Gerard's. Finally Lindley (1820) refers *R. holosericea* to *R. gallica* L.

In any case, judging by the descriptions quoted above, it seems clear that whatever Gerard's Velvet Rose (*R. holosericea*) may have been, it was not the Moss Rose (*R. muscosa* Mill.),*and we can find no evidence that the Moss Rose was known in England in 1596, to support the repeated statements in the books on garden Roses from Rivers (1840) to Pemberton (1920), that it was introduced in that year from Holland.

So far as we know, there is no mention of the Moss Rose in Chaucer, Shakespeare, or in any literature of that period. Parkinson (1629) describes in detail twenty-eight forms of Roses, but none corresponds in any way to the Moss Rose. Ferrarius (1633) in Italy, Chabraeus (1677) in Switzerland, Liger (1708) in France, and Salmon (1710) in England, give long lists, descriptions, and figures of various kinds of Roses, but there is no trace of the Moss Rose in any of them. There is, however, in Ducastel (1746), quoted by Paquet (1845) and Jamain and Forney (1873), a circumstantial account of the existence of the Moss Rose in the south of France, at Carcassonne, as far back as 1696, and this appears to be the earliest date mentioned for the existence of the Moss Rose. The account is that the Hundred-leaved Moss Rose was in cultivation in Cotentin, Messin, and La Manche in 1746, and that it was brought there by Fréard Ducastel, who had found it at Carcassonne, where it had been known for half a century.

The first botanical reference to the Moss Rose is apparently that of Boerhaave (1720) in his Index of Plants cultivated in the Physic Garden at Leyden, under the name *Rosa rubra plena spinosissima, pedunculo muscosa*. In 1724 the Moss Rose is said to have been in cultivation in Lon-

---

* Dr Jackson, to whom I submitted this opinion, concurs.

don, for Miller (1724) states that it is included in Robert Furber's Catalogue of Plants cultivated for sale at Kensington. Miller (1760) tells us that he first saw the Moss Rose 'in the
year 1727, in the garden of Dr Boerhaave near Leyden, who was so good as to give me one
of the plants'. On the whole we consider it safer to accept Miller's 1727 date.

Martyn (1807) refers to what is apparently the first figure of the Moss Rose in *Hort.-Angl.*,
a Catalogue of Trees, Shrubs, Plants, and Flowers cultivated for sale in the Gardens near London, 1730 (folio)
(66 n. 14, t. 18), in which it is called *Rosa provincialis spinosissima pedunculo muscoso*, and under the
same name it appears in Miller (1733) who adds 'or the Moss Provence Rose'.

The second illustration of the Moss Rose that we can trace is in that exquisite little book,
The Flower Garden Display'd by Furber (1732) under the name of 'Moss Provence Rose'. The
coloured drawing, though rather fantastic, is unmistakable. In the letterpress it is called the
'Moss Province Rose', and it is said to be 'like the Province Rose, and bears blossoms almost
as double as that, only somewhat redder; and all the stalks are covered with a green Down,
like Moss, which gives it its name'. The drawing is said to have been 'coloured from the life'.
Willmott (1912) mentions that there is a specimen of the Moss Rose in the British Museum
from the Chelsea Physic Gardens (Miller's) with the date 1735. About the year 1735 is the
period which Shailer (1852), quoted by Darwin (1893), gives as the first introduction of the
old Red Moss Rose into England. He states:

> It was sent over with some orange trees from the Italian States to Mr Wrench
> of the Broomhouse Nurseries, Fulham, in or about the year 1735. It re-
> mained in that family twenty years without being much noticed and circu-
> lated, until a nurseryman of the name of Grey of Fulham brought it into
> note.

In 1746, as we have already noted, the Moss Rose was in cultivation in France in four districts
of the south and west. Linnaeus (1753) does not mention the Moss Rose. Miller (1760)
published a coloured drawing of the Moss Rose, with an interesting description of the plant,
and following Boerhaave (1720) describes it as

> *Rosa rubra plena, spinosissima, pedunculo muscosa.* The most prickly double red Rose
> with a mossy footstalk, commonly called the Moss Provence Rose . . . . This
> sort sends out but few stalks from the root. These are covered with a dark
> brown bark, and closely armed with sharp thorns, the leaves are composed
> of five oblong oval lobes, which are hairy and sawed on their edges; the foot-
> stalks of the flowers are strong, standing erect, and are covered with a dark-
> green moss, as is also the Empalement of the Flowers. The flowers are the
> same shape and colour as the common Provence Rose, and have the like
> agreeable odour. It flowers in June or July, but is not succeeded by fruits.

Linnaeus (1762) adds *R. rubra plena spinosissima pedunculo muscoso* of Miller (1760) to *R. centifolia* as probably belonging to it. Martyn (1807) quotes Retzius's (1779) description of the
Moss Rose, which is worth requoting for its originality and acute observation:

> Stem very prickly and hispid; peduncles long, beset with curled strigae ter-
> minated by a resinous globule, as are also the whole calyxes: these strigae are
> often branched. Petioles less hispid and unarmed. Leaflets very large 3 or 5,
> smooth. The colour and smell of the clammy resinous glands are very much
> the same as in the Flowering Raspberry, or *Rubus odoratus*.

(It is, of course, the fragrant foliage of the *Rubus* to which Retzius refers and not the flowers.) De Grace (1784) mentions the Moss Rose in France.

It is said (Wright, 1911) that in 1785 the Moss Rose was sent from Caen Wood, Highgate, by Lord Mansfield to Mme de Genlis in France as a new introduction to that country. (Cf. Vibert's reference, page 330.) We have already seen that it was in cultivation in four districts in France in 1746, and at Carcassonne in the south of France as far back as about 1696.

Rössig (1802) gives under the name of *R. muscosa* the figure of a pink Moss Rose, less mossy than usual, and states that it is found on the Alps.

Brotero (1804) includes *R. muscosa* in his *Flora of Portugal*, while Rivers (1840) alludes to a traveller's report that the Moss Rose grew wild in the neighbourhood of Cintra, but considers that most likely the plants were of garden origin.

Andrews (1805) states of the Moss Rose (*R. muscosa provincialis*): 'There can be little, if any doubt, that this beautiful variety is the spontaneous effusion of Nature in this country, of which we ever shall regard it as indigenous, since we have never heard of any importations of this species, but frequent exportations.'

Thory (1817) appears to have taken this 'effusion' of Andrews quite seriously, and replies as follows:

> A cet égard, indépendamment de ce qu'une conclusion de cette espèce est inadmissible en histoire naturelle, nous ferons observer qu'il n'est pas rare de voir les Iconographes anglais considérer beaucoup de plantes comme indigènes au sol de leur pays, toutes les fois que le lieu dans lequel elles végètent naturellement leur est inconnu, circonstance qui doit faire rejecter toutes les assertions de ce genre.

Apparently Thory had not seen Ducastel.

Origin of the Moss Rose

We have reviewed the history of the Old Moss Rose and have traced it back to about the year 1696, when it was apparently in cultivation at Carcassonne, in the south of France, until it was found there by Ducastel, and introduced by him to the gardens of three districts in the north-west of France. We have seen that it was in cultivation in Holland in 1720, in England in 1727, and in Italy in 1735. Andrews (1805) states that

> . . . the origin of this beautiful Rose has ever been considered as enveloped in obscurity, but we have no hesitation in assigning it to the Province, to which it assimilates in every particular—with the addition of a rich luxuriant Moss, that gives it a decided superiority, and at the same time a specific distinction. . . . There can be little if any doubt that this beautiful variety is the spontaneous effusion of Nature in this country.

Rivers (1840) states: 'The Moss Rose or Mossy Provence Rose is most probably an accidental sport or seminal variety of the Common Provence Rose.'

Vibert (1844) of Angers, France, states, curiously enough, that the first Moss Rose, the Common Moss, was discovered in England. He quotes the statement of Mme de Genlis in her *Botanique Historique* that she brought the first plant of the Moss Rose to Paris from England a few years before the Revolution of 1789, but he seems sceptical about her further statement that in Germany, round Berlin, the Moss Rose grew as high as cherry-trees! Vibert proceeds to say that the Moss Rose is evidently a sport of Nature, a happy accident that Art has fixed, and that the date of introduction has not been preserved in a positive manner. He remarks that in France in 1810 only the Common Moss was known, and that the species *R. centifolia* has produced more sports or side-steps ('jeux ou écarts') than all the other species of *Rosa* put together.

Loiseleur-Deslongchamps (1844) also states that the Moss Rose originated in England, and that Miller is supposed to have been the first cultivator of it in 1724.

Paul (1848) states:

> The history of the Moss Rose is wrapped in obscurity. It was first introduced to England from Holland [in the 1888 edition he adds 'in 1596'] and it is generally believed that it was a sport from the Provence Rose: that it was not originated by seed, as most new varieties are, but by a branch of the Provence Rose sporting . . . flowers enveloped in Moss.
>
> Some tribes of plants are more disposed to sport than others; and the Provence and Moss Roses possess this peculiar property to a remarkable degree.

Finally Darwin (1893), who devoted considerable attention to the question of the origin of the Moss Rose, states: 'Its origin is unknown, but from analogy it probably arose from the Provence Rose (*R. centifolia*) by bud-variation.' After a careful survey of the facts available to him in 1868, Darwin concludes: 'That the original Moss Rose was the product of bud-variation is probable.' Many facts have come to light since the time of Darwin, which more fully confirm this conclusion.

Records show that on three distinct occasions the Moss Rose mutation has appeared among the Cabbage Roses. First, about 1696, the Old Moss Rose appeared, as we have seen, in the south of France. Second, in 1801, the Moss de Meaux appeared in the west of England as a bud-mutation on the Rose de Meaux (Hare, 1818). Third, about 1843, the Unique Moss appeared in France, as a bud-mutation on the Rose Unique (Vibert, 1844; Paul, 1848).

Both the mother parents probably originated as bud-variations of the Old Cabbage Rose, the Rose de Meaux about 1637 in France (Willmott, 1912), and the Rose Unique in 1775 in the east of England (Shailer, 1852).

A confirmation of this view is found in the fact that both the Rose de Meaux and the Rose Unique reverted by bud-variation to the Old Cabbage Rose (Andrews, 1810; Rivers, 1840).

Origin of the Rose Unique

The Rose Unique, or White Provence, is a white Cabbage Rose, which differs from the Old Pink Cabbage Rose in colour only. As a matter of fact it is not a true albino, but a tinged white with pink buds.

Usually the flower is pure white when expanded, but the five outer petals are tinged with colour, and occasionally the centre of the flower too. There is an excellent coloured drawing of this Rose in Redouté (1817) under the name of *R. centifolia mutabilis*, or Rosier Unique. Andrews (1805) also figures it under the name of *R. provincialis alba*, White Provence or Rose Unique. This Rose was apparently found in a garden in the eastern counties in 1775. Andrews (1805) states that its introduction in 1777 was entirely accidental, through the medium of the late Mr Greenwood, Nurseryman, a great admirer and collector of Roses, who, in an excursion which he usually made every summer, in passing the front garden of Mr Richmond, a baker near Needham in Suffolk, there perceived the present charming plant, where it had been placed by a carpenter who found it near a hedge on the contiguous premises of a Dutch merchant, whose old mansion he was repairing. Mr Greenwood, requesting a little cutting of it, received from Mr Richmond the whole plant; when Mr Greenwood, in return for a plant so valuable, presented him with an elegant silver cup with the Rose engraved upon it; and which in commemoration has furnished food for many a convivial hour. It is of dwarf growth, and remains in flower nearly six weeks longer than the other Province Roses, which renders it still the more estimable.

We wish it had been in our power to have accounted for its having been till so lately a stranger to us, and whence indigenous; but at present our information is entirely confined to the knowledge of its casual introduction, and until some further light is thrown upon the subject to elucidate its genealogy, we shall regard it as a native!

Another account is that of Rivers (1840), who states:

The Unique Provence is a genuine English Rose, which, I believe, was found by Mr Greenwood, then of the Kensington Nursery, in some cottage garden, growing among plants of the Common Cabbage Rose. This variety was at first much esteemed, and plants of it were sold at very high prices. Most probably this was not a seedling from the Old Cabbage Rose, as that is too double to bear seed in this country, but what is called by florists a sporting branch or sucker.

A final account is that given by Shailer (1852), and referred to by Darwin (1893). Shailer states:

The Rose Blanche Unique, or White Provins, was discovered by Mr Daniel Greenwood of Little Chelsea, Nurseryman. He was on a journey of business in the County of Norfolk in the month of July 1775, when, riding very leisurely along the road, he perceived a rose of great whiteness in the Mill; he alighted and on close inspection he discovered it to be a Provins Rose; he then sought an interview with the inmate of the Mill, who was an elderly female; he begged a flower, which was instantly given him; in return he gave her a guinea.

In cutting off the flower he cut three buds; he went to the first Inn, packed it up, and sent it direct to my father, at his Nursery, Little Chelsea, who was then his foreman, requesting him to bud it, which he did, and two of the buds grew: in the following autumn he went down to the same place, where for five guineas he brought the whole stock away; he then made an arrangement with my father to propagate it, allowing him 5s. per plant for three years; at the expiration of that time he sold it out at 21s. per plant, my father's share amounting to upwards of £300.

Mr Greenwood sent the old lady at the Mill a superb silver Tankard, etc., to the amount of £60.

Darwin (1893), referring to Shailer's version above, states: 'Many other instances could be added of Roses varying by buds. The White Provence Rose apparently originated in this way,' with which we agree. The statement that Greenwood paid a guinea for one flower and three workable buds distinctly suggests that only one small shoot of this new White Rose was available at the time, and that it was a bud-variation growing on a Common Pink Cabbage Rose as Rivers suggests. The 'stock' that Greenwood bought for five guineas in the autumn was no doubt the original plant from which he cut the sport (cf. Andrews' account), because from his two budded plants and the old 'stock' plant Shailer would, with ordinary good fortune, get his 1,200 plants in the three years stated.*

Origin of the Rose de Meaux

The Rose de Meaux is a miniature Cabbage Rose which differs from the Old Cabbage Rose only in the smaller size of all its parts. There is a good coloured drawing of the Rose in Redouté (1817) under the name of *Rosa Pomponia* or Rosier Pompon. This Rose is an old inhabitant of French gardens, but its precise origin is not known. Miss Willmott (1912) suggests with good reason that it may have come from the garden of Doménique Séguier, Bishop of Meaux (1637), who was a great cultivator of Roses in his day. In any case, wherever it arose, there can be little doubt that it originated from the Old Cabbage Rose and probably as a bud-variation.

Aiton (1789) mentions two 'Rose de Meaux' as varieties of *R. provincialis* Mill. (i.e., *R. centifolia* L.), viz. 'the Great Dwarf Rose', which is no doubt the Spong Rose (*R. provincialis hybrida*) of Andrews (1805), a half-dwarf; and the 'Small Dwarf Rose', which is clearly the 'Rose de Meaux'. Both these forms are figured by Miss Lawrance (1799) under tt. 31 and 50 respectively.

During a period of more than two thousand years only three Moss Roses have been recorded that were not derived from Moss Roses. Two of the three are definitely recorded as bud-variations of Cabbage Roses, viz. Moss de Meaux (1801) in England and Unique Moss (1843) in France. The third is the Old Moss Rose, whose origin is in question. Each of the two is identical with the particular form which produced it, except in the 'Moss' character, which is additional. Further, the 'Moss' character is apparently identical in the three Moss Roses. None has been recorded as a seed-variation, and all are sterile, like the forms which produced them.

Further, on at least seven occasions between 1805 and 1873 the Old Moss Rose has reproduced the Old Cabbage Rose by bud-variation or 'bud-reversion' (Andrews, 1805; Hare, 1818; Lindley, 1820; Shailer, 1822; Piper, 1842; Jamain, 1873; Darwin, 1893).

The conclusion, therefore, is irresistible that the original Moss Rose mutation arose as a bud-variation of the Old Cabbage Rose (*R. centifolia* L.).

We conclude, therefore, that the original Moss Rose first appeared at Carcassonne, in the south of France, about the year 1696, as a bud-mutation of the Old Cabbage Rose (*R. centifolia* L.).

The second 'Moss' mutation was the 'Moss de Meaux', which appeared in the west of England in 1801 as a bud-mutation of Rose de Meaux.

The third and last 'Moss' mutation was the 'Unique Moss', which appeared in France about 1843 as a bud-mutation of Rose Unique.

---

* [It
  & Hudson). Mr J. N. Harvey kindly sent me this correction. GST]

All other Moss Roses have been derived directly or indirectly from one of the three original mutations. As a matter of fact, between 1788 and 1832 no less than seventeen distinct
Moss Roses appeared as bud-variations of the Old Moss Rose in England and France. One
of these had single and fertile flowers (Shailer, 1852), and became the ancestor of many
hybrid Moss Roses raised in England and France between 1824 and 1860.

Further confirmation of the origin of the Moss Rose may be found in the interesting fact
that twelve of the distinct bud-variations of the Old Moss Rose which appeared between
1788 and 1832 have precise parallels in twelve bud-variations of the Old Cabbage Rose
which appeared between 1637 and 1813, the only difference between them being the presence and absence of 'Moss' respectively. This can only be due to their like factorial compo-
sition in all respects except in the presence or absence of the 'Moss' factor.

Presumably this implies a common origin, and here we seem to get a glimpse of the true
nature of related species and varieties, for these twelve bud-variations are indistinguishable in
kind from the seed-variations that normally arise among seedlings of related species and
varieties of *Rosa*.

Another noteworthy fact has become prominent in the course of this inquiry, and that is
the comparatively few bud-variations recorded in the fertile *R. gallica* L. and *R. damascena* Mill.
compared with the large numbers found in the sterile *R. centifolia* L.

Is it possible that there is a definite connection between sterility and bud-variation? Are
we to regard bud-variation as an alternative mode of expression of variation in the presence
of sterility?

The facts in *Rosa* certainly point in that direction. It is interesting to note that no other
species of *Rosa* presents the 'Moss' mutation but *R. centifolia* L. No trace of it is ever seen in
the closely allied species or sub-species *R. damascena* Mill.* or *R. gallica* L. The nearest ana-
logues to the mossiness of *R. centifolia* L. are the extreme hairy and glandular forms of *R. rubiginosa* L. (Sweet Briar) and *R. moschata Brunonii* (Musk Rose), which, however, are quite
distinct from *R. centifolia muscosa* Seringe, both in their structure and their glandular secretions.

Genetic Significance

In concluding this inquiry it may be of interest to add a few genetic notes on the probable
nature and significance of the three definite appearances of this 'specific' bud-mutation, after
more than two thousand years of intensive cultivation and vegetative propagation.

That the 'Moss' character in *Rosa* is a genuine bud-mutation, and not a fluctuating variation or bud-variant, is evident from its somatic persistence through many bud-generations,
and its germinal persistence through various seed-generations.

Rivers (1840) states that 'plants produced by the seed of the Moss Rose do not always
show Moss; perhaps not more than two plants out of three will be mossy, as I have often
proved'.

Again, Darwin (1893) states that 'Mr Rivers informs me that his seedlings from the old
Single Moss Rose almost always produce Moss Roses'.

We do not yet know definitely whether the 'Moss' character in *Rosa* is to be identified with
a single Mendelian factor or not, though all the evidence so far is in favour of its being a sim-

---

* [Its repeat-flowering relative, *R. damascena* var. *semperflorens*, produced a white-flowered mossy sport in 1835.
   See page 44. GST]

ple dominant. If it is, and Rivers's matings of the Single Moss Rose were, on the average, one-half selfings and one-half crossings with other Roses, as they probably were, judging by his methods, the Mendelian expectation, on the average, would be the actual ratio he obtained, viz. 2 Moss: 1 Plain. It is evident that 'Moss' is a dominant character, for if it were recessive no hybrid Moss Roses would have the 'Moss' character, and we know that some have. It is also clear that the Single Moss, a bud-variation from the Old Moss Rose, is a heterozygous dominant, for according to Rivers (1840) and Darwin (1893) it throws 'Plain' as well as 'Moss' Roses from seed in the proportion of about one in three.

We have already seen that the Old Moss Rose produced 'plain' (i.e., 'unmossed') Cabbage Roses. So that it is probable that the first mutation of the Moss Rose was itself a heterozygous dominant for 'Moss'.

In view of the important results recently reported by Morgan (1919) and his colleagues, in their experiments with *Drosophila*, which have led them to formulate the chromosome theory of heredity, it seems on this hypothesis that if the first mutation of the Moss Rose was a heterozygous dominant, the mutational change would take place in one of the chromosomes in a single locus. In accordance with the 'presence and absence' method, this mutational change in a single locus from m to M involves the presence of an additional factor M, which is dominant to the normal allelomorph m from which the factor M is absent.

This conception, however, does not necessarily imply the actual presence or absence of a structural gene as Morgan seems to infer, and in the present state of knowledge it seems safer and sounder to continue the use of the non-committal term 'factor' with its 'presence and absence', which need not necessarily involve any assumption as to the nature or constitution of either the factor or its allelomorph, though it does provide an indispensable symbolic method of denoting the difference between them.

On the other hand, the reversionary change by which the Moss Rose reproduced the Cabbage Rose by bud-variation involves the absence of the factor M in a single locus of one of the chromosomes, either by somatic segregation with a reduction division, or by a reverse mutational change in the locus concerned. In any case it is evident that in view of Morgan's discoveries bud-mutations take on a new importance, and the case of the Moss Rose is clearly one of considerable genetic significance; for in a simple way it seems to narrow down to a fine point the difficult and usually complex problem of the origin of a definite mutation, and may bring us within measurable distance of the possibility of tracing the origin to a certain cause.

For the present, however, we must be content to work and wait patiently for the genetic and cytological facts, which alone can offer even an approximate solution.

List of Authors Cited

Aiton, W. T. 1789. *Hortus Kewensis*, edn 1, ii, p. 207.

———. 1811. *Hortus Kewensis*, edn 2, iii, p. 264.

Amherst, The Hon. Alicia. 1895. *A History of Gardening in England*, pp. 6 and 7.

Andrews, H. C. 1805–10. *Roses: a Monograph of the Genus Rosa*, with coloured figures (unnumbered).

Baker, J. G. 1914. In Willmott, Ellen, *The Genus Rosa*, xxv (Hist. Intro., x and xi).

'Banbury'. 1845. In *Gard. Chron.*, p. 564 (16 Aug.). (Cor. 'Sports'.)

Bateson, W., and Saunders, E. R. 1902. *Rep. Evol. Com. Roy. Soc.*, i, pp. 159 and 160.

Bieberstein, F. G., Marschall von. 1808. *Flora Taurico-Caucasica*, i, p. 397.

Blondel, Dr. 1889. *Les Produits odorants des Rosiers*. Paris, 1889. (also in *Bull. Soc. Bot. de France*, Feb. 1889).

Boerhaave, Hermann. 1720. *Index Plantarum Hort. Acad. Lugd. Bot.*, ii, p. 252.

Bois, A. G. J. M. 1896. *Atl. Pl. Jard.*, t. 86.

Boissier, E. P. 1872. *Flora orientalis*, ii, p. 676.

Brotero, F. De A. 1804. *Flora Lusitanica*, p. 345.

Caspary, Prof. 1865. *Schrift. Phys. Oek. Ges. König* (3 Feb.) (also *Trans. Hort. Congress, Amsterdam*, 1865).

Chabraeus, D. 1677. *Omn. Stirp. Sci. Icon.*, p. 106 with fig.

Clusius, C. 1601. *Rariorum Plantarum Historia*, iii, p. 113.

Crépin, F. 1892. *Bull. Soc. Bot. Belg.*, xxxi, pt. 2, p. 73.

Curtis, W. 1793. *Bot. Mag.*, i, t. 69.

Darwin, C. 1893. *Var. Animals and Plants Dom.*, edn 2, i, pp. 404–6.

Deleuze. 1809. In Desfontaines, R. L., *Hist. arb. Desf.*, Paris. *La Monographie du genre Rosa*.

Dippel, L. 1893. *Hand. Laubholz*, iii, p. 566.

Ducastel, F. 1746. *L'École du Jardinier Fleuriste*.

Dumont de Courset, G. L. M. 1805. *Le Botaniste Cultivateur*, v, p. 478.

Du Roi, J. P. 1772. *Harbk. Baum.*, ii, p. 368.

Ellacombe, Canon H. N. 1905. 'Roses' in *Cornhill Magazine* (July), p. 27 (see also Hill, 1919).

Ferrarius, J. B. 1633. *De Florum Cultura*, lib. iv, p. 203.

Fitzgerald, E. 1859. *The Rubáiyát of Omar Khayyám*. (Intro. to 1904 edn, Methuen.)

Flückiger. 1862 *Notices et extraits des manuscrits de la Bibliothèque Impériale*, xix, p. 364.

———. 1883. *Pharmacognosie des Pflanzenreichs*, p. 159.

Furber, R. 1724. *Catalogue of Plants* in Miller, 1724.

———. 1730. In *Hort. Angl.* Catalogue of Plants, 66, n. 14, t. 18.

———. 1732. In *The Flower Garden Display'd* (June), pp. 49, 53.

Gerard, J. 1596–9. (Reprint 1876 by B. Daydon Jackson.) *Catalogue of Cultivated Plants*.

———. 1597. *Herball*, Roses, chap. i, f. 6; chap. ii, p. 1085, f. 3.

———. 1633 (and Johnson, T.), *Herball*, lib. 3, p. 1262, fig. 6; p. 1266, fig. 4.

Grâce, De. 1784. *Le bon Jardinier*.

Guimpel, F., Otto, F., and Hayne, F. G. 1825. *Abbild. Deutsch. Holzart*, i, p. 47, t. 39.

Hare, T. 1818. *Trans. Hort. Soc. Lond.*, ii, p. 242. (Read 3 Sept. 1816.)

Herodotus (*circa* 450 B.C.). *Hist.*, lib. viii, cap. 138.

Hill, A. W. 1919. 'Henry Nicholson Ellacombe: a Memoir.' *Roses*, pp. 292–308.

Hurst, C. C. 1911. *Rep. IVe Conf. Int. Gen.* Paris, 1911.

Jackson, B. Daydon. 1876. Reprinted. *Of Gerard's Cat. Plants Cult. 1596–1599*.

Jamain, H., and Forney, E. 1873. *Les Roses* (Paris), p. 57.

Kaempfer, E. 1712. *Amoenitatum exoticarum*.

Köhne, E. 1893. *Deutsche Dendrol.*, p. 282.

Lawrance, Mary. 1799. *A Collection of Roses from Nature*, tt. 2, 14, 51.

Liger, L. 1704. Edn 1. *Le Jardinier Fleuriste*.

———. 1708. New edn. *Le Jardinier Fleuriste*, 11, chap. vii, pp. 515–600.

Lindley, J. 1815. *Bot. Reg.*, p. 53 (see Smith, 1815).

———. *Rosarum Monographia*, pp. 64–7.

Linnaeus, C. 1753. *Species Plantarum, Rosa*, edn 1, i, p. 491.

———. 1762. *Species Plantarum, Rosa*, edn 2, i, p. 704.

L'Obel, M. De. 1581. *Kruydtboeck*, ii, p. 240 with fig. and p. 241.

Loiseleur-Deslongchamps, J. L. A. 1844. *La Rose* (Paris), pp. 263–6.

Loureiro, J. De. 1790. *Flora Cochinchinensis*.

Martyn, T. 1807. New edn, *Miller's Dictionary*, iii, *Rosa*, 14 and 22.

Miller, P. 1724, 1731, 1733. *Gardener's Dictionary, Rosa*.

———. 1760. *Icones, Rosa*, ii, p. 148, pl. ccxxi, fig. 1.

———. 1768. *Gardener's Dictionary*, edn VIII, ii, *Rosa*, 22.

Morgan, T. H. 1919. *The Physical Basis of Heredity*.

Paquet, V. 1845. In *Choix des Plus Belles Roses*, sub. t. 1.

Parkinson, J. 1629. *Paradisi in Sole, Paradisus Terrestris* (1904 reprint), pp. 412–14, 415, fig. 2; 416, 419, ff. 3 and 4.

Paul, W. 1848. *The Rose Garden*, edn 1, p. 32.

———. 1888. *The Rose Garden*, edn 9, p. 2.

Pemberton, Rev. J. H. 1920. *Roses*, p. 62.

Persoon, C. H. 1807. *Synopsis Plantarum*, ii, p. 49.

Piper. 1842. *Report Roy. Hort. Soc. Lond.* in *Gard. Chron.*, p. 422 (25 June).

Pliny, C. (*circa* A.D. 50). *Hist. Nat.*, lib. xxi, cap. 4.

Prévost, J. 1829. *Catalogue des Rosiers*, p. 64.

Rau, A. 1816. *Enum. Ros. Wirceburgum*, p. 109.

Redouté, P. J., and Thory, C. A. 1817. Edn 1, *Les Roses*, i, with tt. (folio).

———. 1821. Edn 1, *Les Roses*, ii, with tt. (folio).

———. 1824. Edn 1, *Les Roses*, iii, with tt. (folio).

———. 1835. Edn 3, *Les Roses*, i, ii, iii, with tt. (8vo.) (and Pirolle, M.).

Regel, E. A. 1877. (*Tent. Ros. Monogr.*, p. 70) in *Act. Hort. Petrop.* v, pt. 2, p. 354.

Rehder, A. 1902. In Bailey, L. H., *Cycl. Amer. Hort.*, iv, p. 1552.

Retzius, A. J. 1779. *Obs. Bot.*, i, p. 20, No. 58.

Rivers, T. 1840. *The Rose Amateur's Guide*, edn 2, pp. 1–19.

Rössig, C. G. 1802–20. *Die Rosen*, No. 6.

Salmon, W. 1710. *The English Herbal*, pp. 952 and 953.

Sawer, J. C. 1894. *Rhodologia*, p. 13.

Schneider, C. K. 1906. *Ill. Handbuch Laubholz*, i, p. 547.

Seringe, N. C. 1818. *Mus. Helv.*, ii, p. 19.

———. 1825. In De Candolle, *Prodromus*, ii, p. 619.

Shailer, H. (sen.). 1822. *Trans. Hort. Soc., Lond.*, iv, p. 137 (Exh., 15 June 1819).

——— (jun.). 1852. *Gard. Chron.*, p. 759 (27 Nov.).

Smith, Sir James Edward. 1915. In Rees's *Encyclopaedia* (see *Bot. Reg.*, 1815, p. 53).

Theophrastus, E. (*circa* 350 B.C.). *Hist. Plant.*, lib. vi, cap. 6.

Thory, C. A., and Redouté, P. J. 1817. Edn 1, *Les Roses*, i, with tt. (folio).

———. 1821. Edn 1, *Les Roses*, ii, with tt. (folio).

———. 1824. Edn 1, *Les Roses*, iii, with tt. (folio).

———. 1835. Edn 3, *Les Roses*, i, ii, iii, with tt. (8vo.) (and Pirolle, M.).

Vibert, J. P. 1844. In Loiseleur-Deslongchamps, *La Rose*, pp. 266–72.

Willdenow, C. L. 1799. *Species Plantarum*, ii, p. 1074.

Willmott, Ellen. 1912. *The Genus Rosa*, xviii, pp. 341 and 345, tt.

———, and Baker, J. G. 1914. *The Genus Rosa* (Hist. Intro.), xxv.

Wright, W. P. 1911–14. *Roses and Rose Gardens*, p. 37. 0

BUD-VARIATIONS OF THE OLD CABBAGE ROSE (*Rosa centifolia* L.)

by C. C. HURST, SC.D., PH.D., (CANTAB.), F.L.S.

The chart of the Cabbage and Moss Roses by C. C. Hurst places on record all the written evidence that he was able to discover of the periodic "sporting" of *Rosa centifolia.* It will be seen that several mutations occurred again and again, and reversions were also frequent. Several such occurrences have been observed in my collection.

NOTE. $B_1, B_2, \ldots B_5$ Successive generations by sporting (mutation).
          F_1, F_2 Successive generations by seeding (sexual reproduction).

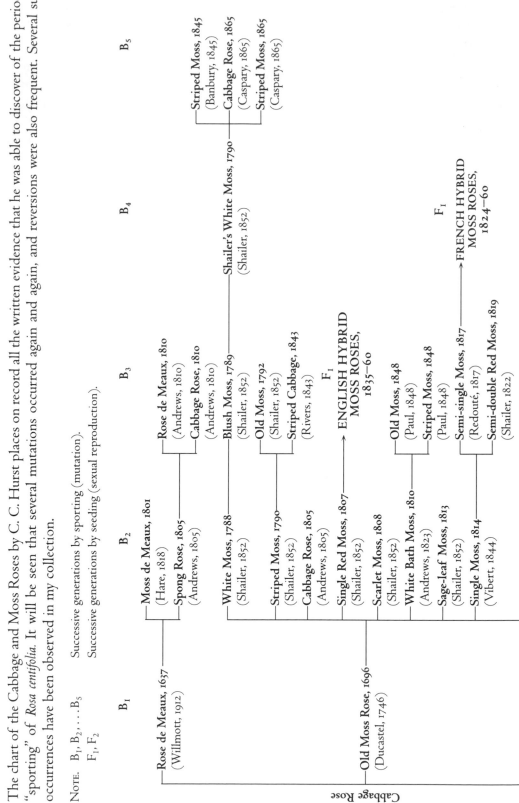

Cabbage Rose

Old Moss Rose, 1696
(Ducastel, 1746)

Cabbage Rose, 1816
(Hare, 1818)

Minor Moss, 1818
(Vibert, 1844)

Semi-double Moss, 1819
(Shailer, 1822)

Cabbage Rose, 1819
(Shailer, 1822)

Mottled Rose, 1819
(Shailer, 1822)

Cabbage Rose, 1820
(Lindley, 1820)

Tinwell Crimson Moss, 1820 —— Scarlet Cabbage, 1836
(Rivers, 1843)   (Rivers, 1843)

Deep Rose Moss, 1820
(Vibert, 1844)

Flesh Moss, 1822
(Vibert, 1844)

Striped Semi-double
Moss, 1824
(Vibert, 1844)

Striped Double Moss, 1826
(Vibert, 1844)

Proliferous Moss, 1828
(Vibert, 1844)

Zoe Moss, 1830
(Vibert, 1844)

Carnation Moss, 1832
(Vibert, 1844)

Cabbage Rose, 1842
(Piper, 1842)

Cabbage Rose, 1868
(Darwin, 1893)

Cabbage Rose, 1873
(Jamain, 1873)

B_3

Rose Unique, 1843
(Rivers, 1843)

Cabbage Rose, 1843
(Rivers, 1843)

F2

B_2

Unique Moss, 1843
(Vibert, 1844)

Striped Unique, 1843
(Rivers, 1843)

Perpetual Unique, 1920

Semi-double Cabbage Rose, 1796 ⟶ FRENCH PROVENCE AND
HYBRID PROVENCE ROSES,
1820–50

B_1

Rose Unique, 1775
(Shailer, 1852)

Blandford Rose, 1791
(Andrews, 1805)

Semi-double Cabbage, 1794 ⟶ Single Cabbage Rose, 1796

Carnation Rose, 1800
(Redouté, 1817)

Flesh Cabbage Rose, 1801
(Redouté, 1817)

Lettuce Rose, 1801
(Redouté, 1817)

Proliferous Rose, 1801
(Redouté, 1824)

Semi-double Provence, 1804
(Andrews, 1805)

Single Provence, 1805
(Andrews, 1805)

Celery Rose, 1805
(Redouté, 1835)

Blush Provence, 1805
(Andrews, 1805)

Leafy Rose, 1809
(Redouté, 1821)

Minor Cabbage, 1813
(Redouté, 1835)

Anemone Rose, 1815
(Redouté, 1835)

Crested Moss, 1826
(Jamain, 1873)

Cabbage Rose, 1843
(Rivers, 1843)

Cabbage Rose

14

Key to the Major Groups of Cultivated Roses

by GORDON D. ROWLEY

(Formerly Keeper, National Rose Species Collection, John Innes Institute) (1957)

THIS KEY IS designed to cover only the main groups of garden rose, in broad outline. It is well known that the system of classifying roses according to ancestry has many drawbacks, especially today when the lines of descent are complicated and interwoven. An artificial system of breakdown into classes based on habit, flower size and grouping, function, and general garden utility is badly needed to replace it, but has not been forthcoming. Hence the old categories are here retained. In addition to the main groups there are of course others—the side-branches of the rose family tree. There are the off-beat hybrids like 'Cantab', derived from *Rosa nutkana*, 'Cerise Bouquet' from *R. multibracteata*, and Kordes's Hybrid Pimpinellifolias. Other anomalies are roses bridging gaps between existing groups: 'Gloire des Rosomanes' (Bourbon × China), 'Cécile Brunner' (Tea × *R. multiflora*), and so on.

It is not practical to attempt to make a key for the identification of individual rose varieties. Apart from their enormous numbers, the very means of producing them by shuffling and reshuffling the same sets of genes in all possible combinations precludes a simple breakdown into groups. How, then, is one to name an old rose that has lost its label? Unlike the wild species, they cannot be re-collected in the type locality, or traced in a local flora. The only means is a search of the literature in the hopes of finding a description or plate to match: a task which has occupied Mr Thomas for many years now, with conspicuous success. It speaks much for his labours that the names of so many delightful old roses are back in circulation again after falling into neglect, or after the plants were thought to be extinct. It has been a pleasure to assist him botanically in his good work by drawing up the following key, and also by contributing the genealogies of hybrid *pimpinellifolias* and *eglanterias*, which I hope may add to the usefulness of the book.

A   Flowers quite single, with (4 to) 5 equal petals and numerous normal sta-   **WILD ROSES AND**
mens.*   **THEIR HYBRIDS**
(Species and varieties)

AA   Flowers full, double or semi-double, or at least with a few petaloid stami-   **GARDEN ROSES**
nodes or small accessory petals.   (Cultivars)

     B   Plants climbing or rambling, with long sprawling or arching shoots
tapering towards the tips (i.e. with leaves of progressively smaller size).

         C   Stipules with long, free tips, early deciduous. Flowers very small, I   **BANSKIANS**
(to I ½) inches in diameter

       CC   Stipules with short, free tips, not deciduous. Flowers larger, at least
above I inch diameter.

           D   Leaflets bright green, glossy, leathery and sub-evergreen.   **HYBRID WICHURAIANAS**

         DD   Leaflets dull green or flushed red, not (or scarcely) glossy, thin,
deciduous.

             E   Stipules fringed.   **CLIMBING POLYANTHAS**

           EE   Stipules not fringed, at most gland-edged.

               F   Plants almost or quite unarmed, with red, glaucous   **BOURSAULTS**
branches.

             FF   Plants prickly.

                 G   Strong climbers or arching shrubs with small to   **AYRSHIRES, NOISETTES**
medium blooms.   **AND TEAS**

               GG   Stiffly erect pillar roses or weakly climbing bushes   **CLIMBING H.T.S**
with large, exhibition-type blooms.

     BB   Plants not markedly climbing or rambling; leaves not diminishing
towards the apices of the shoots.

               H   Flowering season short, in early summer, with at   **OLD SHRUB ROSES**
best occasional blooms only in the autumn.

                 I   Tall shrubs with hooked prickles only.

                   J   Leaflets grey, scentless.   **ALBAS**

                 JJ   Leaflets green, sweet-brier scented.   **SWEET BRIERS**

               II   Medium to small shrubs with straight prickles
and/or bristles only.

                   K   Leaflets small, numerous, 7 to II   **SCOTCH ROSES**

                 KK   Leaflets large, few, 5 to 7.

                     L   Low shrubs with more or less doubly
toothed glandular leaves; flowers
dark pink, light crimson, purple or
murrey (rarely white).

                     M   Leaflets dark olive green, leathery,   **GALLICAS**
waxy; flowers held erect, mostly
crimson or purple.

                  MM   Leaflets light green, thin, rarely
slightly waxy; flowers nodding,
mostly pink.

---

* Except for 'Frühlingsmorgen', 'Mermaid', 'Nevada', and a few large-flowered backcrosses of garden roses
to species.

     For a key to the wild species of *Rosa*, see B. O. Mulligan in R.H.S. *Dictionary of Gardening*, iv, 1951,
1810–11.

N Buds covered in mossy resin-scented glands.	MOSSES
NN Buds not so.	CENTIFOLIAS
LL Medium, erect shrubs with simply toothed leaves, greyish, without glands; flowers white or pink; heps usually narrow and elongated.	DAMASKS

HH Flowering season long or with a marked resurgence in autumn.

O Dwarf shrublets 6 inches to 1½ feet.	POLY-POMS AND FAIRY ROSES
OO Medium bushes 2 to 5 feet.	
P Flowers large to very large, solitary or few per stem.	
Q Flowers flat or cupped, many-petalled, from short-conical or squat buds.	
R Flowers deeply set among the foliage on short stalks.	PORTLANDS
RR Flowers longer-stalked and held clear of the leaf canopy.	BOURBONS AND HYBRID PERPETUALS
QQ Flowers high-centered, few-petalled, from narrow, conical buds.	HYBRID TEAS
PP Flowers medium to small, numerous, borne in trusses.	HYBRID POLYANTHAS AND FLORIBUNDAS
OOO Large sprawling suckering shrubs.	
S Sparingly armed with scattered, conical often curved prickles.	HYBRID MUSKS AND ENGLISH ROSES
SS Densely armed with straight slender prickles.	HYBRID RUGOSAS

Origin of Kordes's Hybrid Rubiginosas

by Gordon D. Rowley (1960) *after* Wylie, 1955 (*redrawn and extended*)

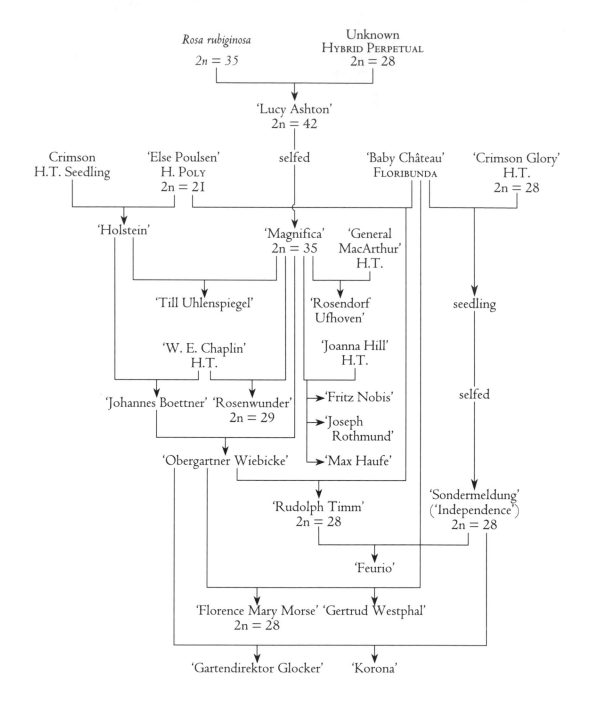

[For *rubiginosa* read *eglanteria*. GST, 1993.]

Modern Hybrid Spinosissimas
by Gordon D. Rowley

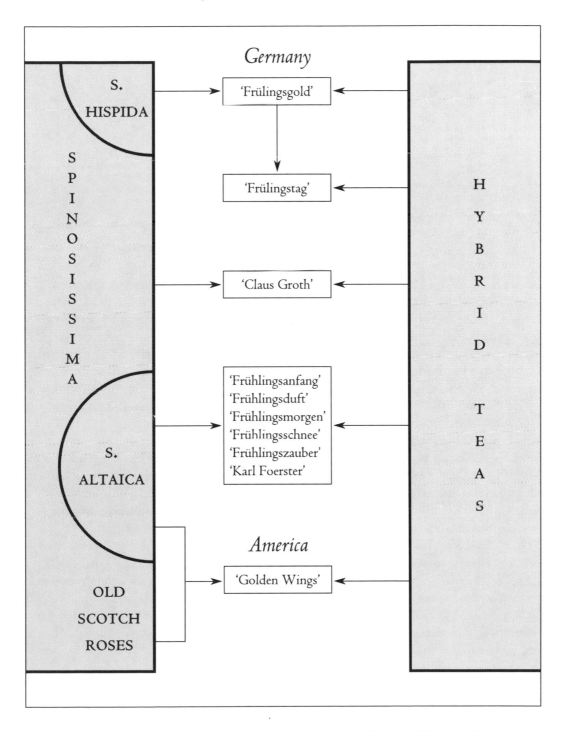

[For *spinosissima* read *pimpinellifolia*. For *altaica* read 'Grandiflora'. GST, 1993.]

15

The Botany of Climbing Roses
and the Derivation of Some Garden Climbers

by GORDON D. ROWLEY (1957)

Great families of yesterday we show,
And lords, whose parents were the Lord knows who.
Daniel Defoe, 1660–1731

A CLIMBING as distinct from bush habit is characteristic of one of the most natural and readily recognizable Sections of the Genus *Rosa*—the Synstylae. It also occurs in four other small Sections of one to two species each: the Indicae, Banksianae, Laevigatae, and Bracteatae. All these are diploids with fourteen chromosomes each, as are many of their garden progeny, and they have their centre of diversity in South-east Asia, the Synstylae extending thence along the southernmost limits of the genus to India, Arabia and North Africa, and Europe, with a single rather distinct species (*R. setigera*) native to the New World.

The characteristic habit, with a sharp distinction between long and short shoots, combines with other features to set the Synstylae apart from the remaining species of *Rosa*. The small, mostly white flowers are crowded into large flat or conical trusses. In the centre of each bloom the styles are tightly pressed together and exserted to stand up like the head of a pin, thus giving the name to the Section. They often persist on the fruit, which is a small globular red hep unlike the large flask- or urn-shaped heps of other Sections. The Indicae differ mainly in the reduction of the inflorescence to a few large flowers, and the remaining three climbing Sections stand rather isolated and have deciduous, almost free stipules.

Opinions differ widely on how many species comprise the Synstylae. Most authorities accept between one dozen and two, but Hurst went so far as to reduce them all to a single species. This extreme view finds support in the *Rosa moschata* complex, which extends in an apparently continuous belt from Europe (*R. moschata sens. str.*) to North-west Africa and Arabia (*R. abyssinica*), India (*R. brunonii*), Manchuria (*R. maximowicziana*) and to a peak of variation in Central China, where the magnificent *R. sinowilsonii* displays the upper size limit of the Section, with leaves often a foot long. In Huxley's terminology, *Rosa moschata* is a clone showing a gradient of characteristics throughout its distribution, although more field work is needed to ascertain whether clear discontinuities exist to justify recognition of several species. Meanwhile conservative botanists will tend to lump them all together, whereas horticulturists prefer to retain the names at least of those of garden merit. Just how much seedlings can vary I found out when Dr A. K. Janaki-Ammal sent me seed of wild Musk roses growing in parts of Nepal. The progeny ranged in foliage from glossy deep green to blue-grey and downy with

346

an attractive purple flush below. Flower and truss size also varied from plant to plant.

The change-over from bush to climbing habit in wild roses led to a corresponding change in habitat preference. Thus we find the climbers on the margins of woods and copses where the necessary support is to be found, rather than out in the open where the shrubby and thicket-forming types grow. They tolerate shade in the early years, but flowering is usually confined to branches that reach up above the undergrowth.

Wild hybrids between climbing and bush roses are relatively rare, but the cross appears in the ancestry of many groups of garden roses. It leads to a blurring of the sharp difference between the two habits and the occurrence of many intermediates. The genetics of climbing habit have not been fully worked out, and a somewhat complicated inheritance seems likely. On the other hand, there is no doubt that straight mutation often leads to a climbing sport arising from a bush rose, or the reverse change, and this mutation can be stabilized by vegetative propagation, even though it may affect only the surface tissues, the core remaining unaltered. Propagation by root cuttings of certain climbers has produced bush roses only because the new plant arises solely from the core tissue, not from the skin as in budding or normal grafting. As yet we have no certain method of inducing the change from bush to climber or *vice versa*, and experiments at the John Innes Institute give no support to the popular belief that hard pruning or propagation from lateral instead of long shoots can make a climber revert to a bush.

Hurst noticed that in *Rosa* perpetual flowering is associated with dwarf habit, arising by mutation from a climbing species (*R. chinensis, R. sempervirens, R. multiflora*) in which new shoots that would normally climb produce inflorescences instead. However, this is not inevitably so, as has been shown by the measure of success in selecting garden roses combining tall growth and long flowering season. Nor is repeat-flowering confined to descendants of climbing species: we have it to some extent in *R. rugosa* and *R. damascena.*

The following tables illustrate some of the ancestry of garden climbers and ramblers:

MULTIFLORA DERIVATIVES

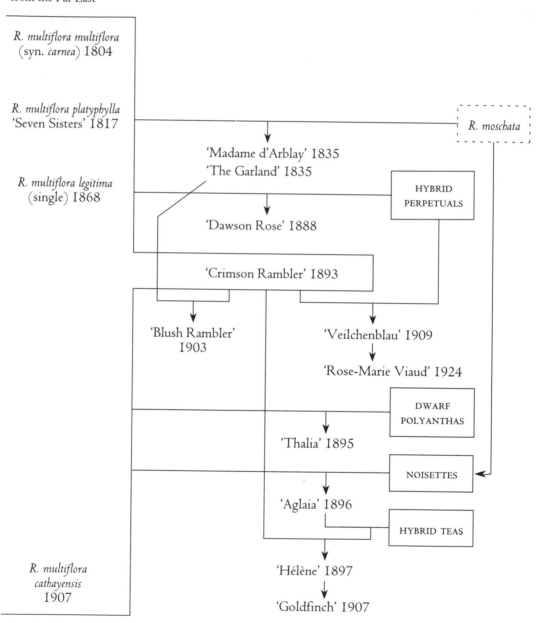

Rosa multiflora Thunb.

Ancestral varieties and early introductions from the Far East

R. multiflora multiflora (syn. *carnea*) 1804

R. multiflora platyphylla 'Seven Sisters' 1817

R. moschata

'Madame d'Arblay' 1835
'The Garland' 1835

R. multiflora legitima (single) 1868

HYBRID PERPETUALS

'Dawson Rose' 1888

'Crimson Rambler' 1893

'Blush Rambler' 1903

'Veilchenblau' 1909

'Rose-Marie Viaud' 1924

DWARF POLYANTHAS

'Thalia' 1895

NOISETTES

'Aglaia' 1896

HYBRID TEAS

R. multiflora cathayensis 1907

'Hélène' 1897

'Goldfinch' 1907

Broken lines indicate wild species.
Entire lines indicate cultivars.

LUCIAE (WICHURAIANA) DERIVATIVES

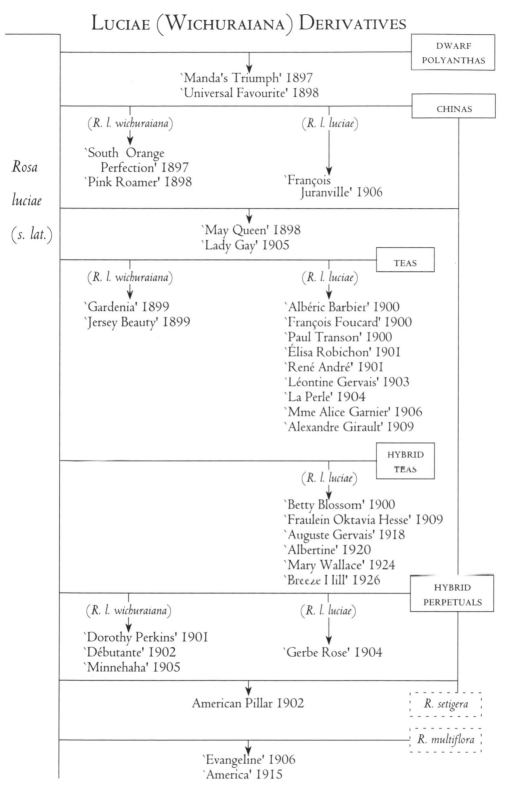

DWARF POLYANTHAS

`Manda's Triumph' 1897
`Universal Favourite' 1898

CHINAS

Rosa

luciae

(s. lat.)

(R. l. wichuraiana)

`South Orange
    Perfection' 1897
`Pink Roamer' 1898

(R. l. luciae)

`François
    Juranville' 1906

`May Queen' 1898
`Lady Gay' 1905

TEAS

(R. l. wichuraiana)

`Gardenia' 1899
`Jersey Beauty' 1899

(R. l. luciae)

`Albéric Barbier' 1900
`François Foucard' 1900
`Paul Transon' 1900
`Élisa Robichon' 1901
`René André' 1901
`Léontine Gervais' 1903
`La Perle' 1904
`Mme Alice Garnier' 1906
`Alexandre Girault' 1909

HYBRID TEAS

(R. l. luciae)

`Betty Blossom' 1900
`Fraulein Oktavia Hesse' 1909
`Auguste Gervais' 1918
`Albertine' 1920
`Mary Wallace' 1924
`Breeze Hill' 1926

HYBRID PERPETUALS

(R. l. wichuraiana)

`Dorothy Perkins' 1901
`Débutante' 1902
`Minnehaha' 1905

(R. l. luciae)

`Gerbe Rose' 1904

American Pillar 1902

R. setigera

R. multiflora

`Evangeline' 1906
`America' 1915

NOTE: *Rosa luciae* Franch. & Roche. is interpreted here in the broad sense as including both
R. luciae luciae and *R. luciae wichuraiana* (Syn. *R. wichuraiana* Crép.). Precise parentage is
indicated only where it is known or can be surmised with reasonable accuracy.

Later Luciae (Wichuraiana) Developments
towards perpetual-flowering pillar roses

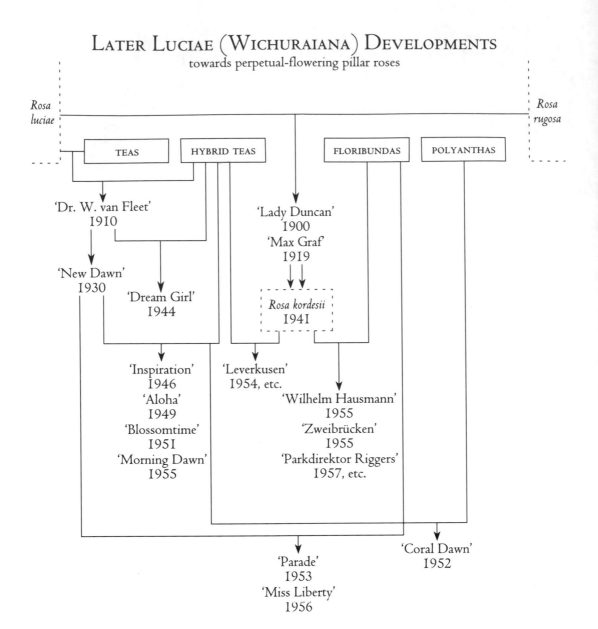

 Hardiness Zones

Rose	Hardiness Zones
Gallica Roses	4–9
Damask Roses	4–9
White Roses	4–9
Centifolia Roses	4–9
Moss Roses	4–9
Dog Rose and its relatives	5–8
Cinnamon Rose and its old world relatives	4–9
American Wild Roses	5–9
Wild Yellow Roses and related species	5–8
Wild Burnet Roses and their garden forms	5–9
Japanese or Rugosa Roses	3–9
Strange species and their hybrids	6–9
China Roses	7–9
Bourbon Roses	5–9
Hybrid Perpetual Roses	5–9
Poly-poms	4–9
Noisette and Tea Roses	7–9
Hybrid Musk Roses	5–9
Shrub Roses	4-9
New English Roses	5–9
Ramblers derived from the Musk or Synstylae Section of the genus *Rosa*	5–9
Old and new garden Ramblers	5–9
Large-flowered Ramblers	4–9
Large-flowered Climbers of Hybrid Tea style	5–9
"New" Climbers	4–9
Banskian Roses	7–9
The Macartney Rose, *Rosa bracteata*	6–9
The Cherokee Rose, *Rosa laevigata*	7–9

U.S. Hardiness Zones

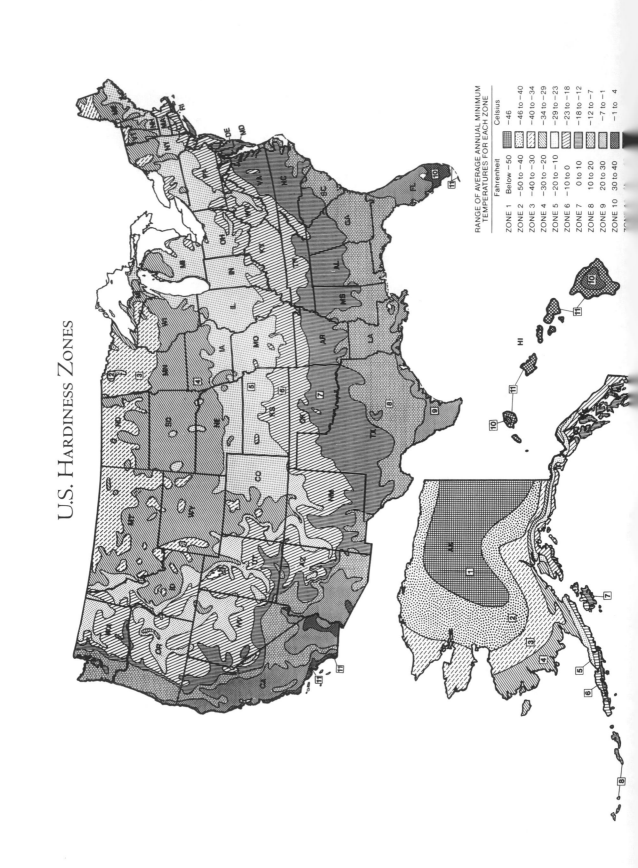

RANGE OF AVERAGE ANNUAL MINIMUM
TEMPERATURES FOR EACH ZONE

	Fahrenheit	Celsius
ZONE 1	Below −50	−46
ZONE 2	−50 to −40	−46 to −40
ZONE 3	−40 to −30	−40 to −34
ZONE 4	−30 to −20	−34 to −29
ZONE 5	−20 to −10	−29 to −23
ZONE 6	−10 to 0	−23 to −18
ZONE 7	0 to 10	−18 to −12
ZONE 8	10 to 20	−12 to −7
ZONE 9	20 to 30	−7 to −1
ZONE 10	30 to 40	−1 to 4

European Hardiness Zones

HARDINESS ZONE
TEMPERATURE RANGES

°F	ZONE	°C
below −50	1	below −45
−50 to −40	2	−45 to −40
−40 to −30	3	−40 to −34
−30 to −20	4	−34 to −29
−20 to −10	5	−29 to −23
−10 to 0	6	−23 to −7
0 to 10	7	−17 to −2
10 to 20	8	−12 to −7
20 to 30	9	−7 to −1
30 to 40	10	−1 to 5

 Bibliography

Addisonia, New York Botanical Garden, 1916 *et seq.*

Aiton, William, *Hortus Kewensis*, 1789

American *Rose Annual*, 1917 *et seq.*

Andrews, Henry C., *Roses*, 1805–28

Austin, David, *The Heritage of the Rose*, 1988

Bailey, L. H., *The Standard Cyclopedia of Horticulture*, 1927

Baird, Bessie Marie, *Roses for Southern Gardens*, 1948

Bauhin, Caspar, *Pinax*, 1671 edn

Beales, Peter, *Classic Roses*, 1985

Bean, W. J., *Trees and Shrubs Hardy in the British Isles*, 8th edn, 1980

Belgique Horticole, La, 1851–85

Berrisford, Judith, *Gardening on Lime*, 1963

Bois, E., and Trechslin, A.-M., *Roses*, 1962

Bonnet, E., et Barratte, G., *Catalogue raisonné des plantes vasculaires de la Tunisie*, 1896

Botanical Cabinet, Conrad Loddiges and Sons, Vols. 1–20, 1818–30

Botanical Magazine, The, 1787 *et seq.*

Botanical Register, The, 1815–47

Bowles, E. A., *My Garden in Summer*, 1914

Braam, A. E. van (artist C. H. B. Ker), *Icones plantarum sponte China*

Brougham, Henry Charles, 3rd Baron Brougham and Vaux, *List of Roses in Cultivation at Château Éléonore*, Cannes, 1898

Bunyard, Edward A., *Old Garden Roses*, 1936; also in *The New Flora and Silva*, Vol. 2

Carrière, E. A., *Production et Fixation des variétés dans les végétaux*, 1865

Choix des Plus Belles Roses, Paris, 1845–54

Cochet-Cochet et Mottet, S., *Les Rosiers*, Paris, 1896 *et seq.*

Crane, H. H., *Gardening on Clay*, 1963

Cranston, John, *Cultural Directions for the Rose*, 1875

Curtis, Henry, *Beauties of the Rose*, 1850–3

Darlington, Hayward Radcliffe, *Roses*, 1911

Desfontaines, Renato, *Flora Atlantica*, 1798

Dickerson, Brent C., *The Old Rose Advisor*, 1992

Drapiez, P. A. J., *Herbier de l'amateur de Fleurs*, 1828–35

Duhamel du Monceau, Henri Louis, *Traité des arbres et arbustes*, 1819

Dumont de Courset, G. L. M., *Le Botaniste Cultivateur*, 2nd edn, Vol. V, 1811

Duruz, Selwyn, *Flowering Shrubs*, 1952

Edwards, Gordon, *Roses for Enjoyment*, 1962

Ellacombe, Henry N., *In a Gloucestershire Garden*, 1895

————, *Plant Lore and Garden Craft of Shakespeare*, 1896

Floral Magazine, The, 1861–71 and 1872–81

Flore des Serres et des Jardins de l'Europe, 1845–67

Florist and Pomologist, The, 1862–84

Garden, The, founded by William Robinson, 1871 *et seq.*

Gardeners' Chronicle, 1841 *et seq.*

Gartenflora, 1852 *et seq.*

Garten-Zeitung, Berlin, 1882–5

Gault, S. Millar, and Synge, Patrick M., *The Dictionary of Roses in Colour*, 1971

Gerard, John, *The Herball*, 1597

Gibson, Michael, *The Book of the Rose*, 1980

Gore, Mrs, *The Rose Fancier's Manual*, 1838

Hariot, Paul, *Le Livre d'Or des Roses*, 1904

Harkness, Jack, *Roses*, 1978

Harvey, N. P., *The Rose in Britain*, 1951

Herrmann, Johannes, *Dissertatio inauguratis botanico medica de Rosa*, 1762

Hibberd, Shirley, *Garden Favourites*, 1858

Hillier and Sons, Winchester, England, *Rose Catalogue*

————, *Manual of Trees and Shrubs*, 3rd edn, 1973

Hoffmann, Julius, *The Amateur Gardener's Rose Book*, 1905

Hole, Dean S. Reynolds, *A Book about Roses*, 1870

Horticulteur Français, L', 1851–72

Hu, Hsen-Hsu, *Icones Plantarum Sinicarum*, 1929

Illustration Horticole, L', 1854–96

Illustrierte Rosengarten (M. Lebl, Editor), Stuttgart, 1875(?)–79

Iwasaki, Tsunemasa (edited by Ida Kuratavo), *Phonzo Soufo*, 1921

Jacquin, N. J. von, *Flora Austriaca*, 1773–8

————, *Plantarum rariorum horti Schönbrunnensis*, 1797–1804

Jäger, August, *Rosenlexicon*, 1960

Jahandiz, Émile, et Maire, Dr René, *Catalogue des Plantes du Maroc*, 1931

Jamain, Hippolyte, et Fourney, Eugène, *Les Roses*, 1893

Jardin Fleuriste, Le, 1851–4

Jekyll, Gertrude, and Mawley, Edward, *Roses for English Gardens*, 1902

Journal des Roses, 1877–1914

Keays, Mrs Frederick Love, *Old Roses*, 1935

Kingsley, Rose, *Roses and Rose Growing*, 1908

Komlosy, *Rosenalbum*, 1868–75

Krüssmann, Gerd, *Roses*, 1934

Lancaster, Roy, *Travels in China*, 1989

Lawrance, Mary, *A Collection of Roses from Nature*, 1799

Lazaro e Ibiza, *Compendio de la Flora Española*, 1921

Le Rougetel, Hazel, *A Heritage of Roses*, 1988

Leroy, André, *History of the Rose*, 1956

Lindley, John, *Rosarum monographia*, 1820

Lobel, Matthias de, *Plantarum seu stirpium icones*, Antwerp, 1581

Loudon, *Hortus Britannicus*, 1830

Lowe, Richard Thomas, *A Manual Flora of Madeira*, 1868

McFarland, J. Horace, *Modern Roses*, V, 1952

————, *Roses of the World in Colour*, 1937

Meehan's Monthly, 1891 *et seq.*

Meehan, Th., *Native Flowers and Ferns of the United States*, Vols. 1 and 2, 1897

Miller, Philip, *The Gardener's Dictionary*, 1768

Mollet, Claude, *Théâtre des plans et jardinages . . .* , 1663

Mulligan, B. O., in RHS *Dictionary of Gardening*, 1951

Nestel's Rosengarten, E. Schweizerbartsche Verlagshandlung, 1866–9

New Flora and Silva, Vols. 1–12, 1929 *et seq.*

Niedtner, Th., *Die Rose*, 1880

Park, Bertram, *Guide to Roses*, Collins, 1956

Parkinson, John, *Paradisi in Sole Paradisus Terrestris*, 1629

————, *Theatrum botanicum*, 1640

Parsons, Samuel B., *The Rose*, 1847

Paul, William, *The Rose Garden*, 1848, 1872 *et seq.*

Paxton's Magazine of Botany, 1834–49

Phillips, Roger, and Rix, Martyn, *Roses*, 1985

Plus Belles Roses au début du vingtième siècle, Les, Société Nationale d'Horticulture de France, 1912

Prince, William, *Manual of Roses*, 1846

Ray, John, *Historia plantarum*, Vol. II, 1688

Redouté, P. J., *Les Roses*, 1817–24

Reeves' Drawings of Chinese Plants (RHS Library), 1812–31, Vol. 2

Rehder, Alfred, *Manual of Cultivated Trees and Shrubs*, 1947

Revue de l'Horticulture, Belge et Étrangère, La, 1875–1915

Revue Horticole, La, 1846 *et seq.*

Rivers, Thomas, *Rose Amateur's Guide*, 1843 *et seq.*

Roessig, D., *Les Roses*, 1802–20

Rose Annual, The, National Rose Society of Great Britain, 1907 *et seq.*

Rosenzeitung (ed. C. P. Strassheim), Verein deutscher Rosenfreunde, 1886 1933

Roses et Rosiers, Paris, 187–?

Rowley, G. D., 'Some naming problems in *Rosa*', in *Bulletin van de Rijksplantentuin*, Brussels, 30 Septembre 1959

Royal Horticultural Society, *Journal*, 1856 *et seq.*

Sabine, Joseph, in *Transactions of the Horticultural Society*, 1822

Schlechtendahl, D. F. L. von, and Langethal, L. E., *Flora von Deutschland*, 1880–8, 5th edn

Shepherd, Roy E., *History of the Rose*, 1954

Siebold, Philipp Franz von, and Zuccarini, Joseph Gerhard, *Flora Japonica*, 1835–70

Simon, Léon, et Cochet, Pierre, *Nomenclature de tous les Roses*, 1906

Singer, Max, *Dictionnaire des Roses*, 1885

Singleton, Esther, *The Shakespeare Garden*, 1922

Smith, Tom, *Rose Catalogues*, Daisy Hill Nurseries

Société Nationale d'Horticulture de France, *Les Plus Belle Roses au début du vingtième siècle*, 1912

Sowerby, James, and Smith, Sir James Edward, *English Botany*, 1790–1814, etc.

Step, Edward, *Favourite Flowers*, 1896–7

Stevens, G. A., *Climbing Roses*, 1933

Strassheim, C. P., *Rosenzeitung*, Verein deutscher Rosenfreunde, 1886–1933

Sweet, Robert, *The British Flower Garden*, 1st and 2nd series, 7 vols., 1823–9 and 1831–8

Thomas, G. C., *The Practical Book of Outdoor Rose Growing*, 1920

Thomas, G. S., *The Manual of Shrub Roses*, 4th edn, 1964, Sunningdale Nurseries, Windlesham, Surrey

———, *The Old Shrub Roses*, revised edn, 1961

———, *Shrub Roses of Today*, 1962

———, *Climbing Roses, Old and New*, revised edn, 1983

———, *An English Rose Garden* (U.S. title: *The Art of Gardening with Roses*), 1991

Thomas, H. H., *The Rose Book*, 1913

Wallich, Nathaniel, *Plantae Asiaticae Rariores*, Vol. II, 1831

Willmott, Ellen, *The Genus Rosa*, 1910–14

Wilson, E. H., *If I were to make a garden*, 1931

Wilson, Helen Van Pelt, *Climbing Roses*, 1955

Wylie, A. P., in *Journal of the Royal Horticultural Society*, Vol. LXXIX, page 555 *et seq.*, December 1954

———, "The History of Garden Roses," in *Endeavour*, Vol. XIV, No. 56, October 1955

Young, Wing Commander N., in *The Rose Annual*, National Rose Society, 1962

Index